People Across Am~~erica love~~

A DINN~~ER A DAY~~

"I loved not having to think up what to fix every night, and my kids were wild about the desserts."

—Diana, medical transcriber, OH

"How wonderful to have everything laid out for me . . . a whole week's worth of delicious dinner suggestions at a glance . . . and with the Countdown, I didn't even have to think about what I was doing."

—Cindy, dental hygienist, WA

"How I wish I had this book when I was first married. I can't wait to get my hands on it now. . . . I'm going to be the first in line at my bookstore. . . . A DINNER A DAY should be the hottest gift item of the season."

—Mary Ellen, homemaker, MO

"My whole family has a great time with these recipes. . . . The kids even got with the program and wanted to help cook."

—Joanne, theater coordinator, WA

"Thanks to your innovative cookbook, my life will be so much easier . . . and, wonder of wonders, my twelve-year-old daughter is now interested in cooking."

—Carol, teacher, NY

"A DINNER A DAY should be on everyone's kitchen counter—open."

—Susan, attorney, MA

"This book is a steal at any price . . . great meals, easy fixing. . . . Each night is a whole new adventure, and my family is as excited about it as I am."

—Cynthia, bookkeeper, CA

more . . .

"I loved the shopping list! I went to the store once all week. How great! This is perfect for people who don't have time to agonize about what to make for dinner every night."

—Erin, sales clerk, WA

"I'm going to give A DINNER A DAY as a Christmas present to everyone I know—myself included."

—Joan, beautician, OR

"What a time-saver the shopping list was. . . . I don't know how you ever came up with so many great meals—one more delicious than the next—but I am sure glad you did."

—Sue, legal secretary, TX

"What a pleasure it is now to go into my kitchen . . . what wonderful meals you've created. I can't wait to have a whole year's worth to play with."

—Marion, homemaker, MN

"I work every day. I don't want to have to work hard when I get home. Thanks for turning my dinner hour into a joy instead of another job."

—Judy, interior decorator, GA

"I'm really picky when it comes to food . . . your recipes are terrific. . . . My son would never eat Brussels sprouts until I fixed your Sprouts & Onions. Now he can't get enough of them."

—Wendy, registered nurse, AL

A DINNER A DAY

Complete Meals in Minutes for Every Weeknight of the Year

SALLY SONDHEIM
AND
SUZANNAH SLOAN

WARNER BOOKS

A Time Warner Company

Copyright © 1996 by Suzannah Sloan and Sally Sondheim
All rights reserved.

Warner Books, Inc., 1271 Avenue of the Americas, New York, NY 10020

Visit our Web site at
http://pathfinder.com/twep

 A Time Warner Company

Printed in the United States of America

First Printing: November 1996

10   9   8   7

Library of Congress Cataloging-in-Publication Data
Sondheim, Sally.
   A dinner a day : complete meals in minutes for every weeknight of the year / Sally Sondheim and Suzannah Sloan.
     p. cm.
   Includes index.
   ISBN 0-446-67145-2
   1. Dinners and dining. 2. Menus. 3. Quick and easy cookery.
I. Sloan, Suzannah. II. Title.
TX737.S66 1996
642'.4—dc20   96-17523
                                       CIP

Text design by Stanley S. Drate / Folio Graphics Co., Inc.
Cover design by Mary Ann Smith
Cover photo by Mary Ellen Bartley

We dedicate this book to
Howard Schage,
William C. Newell
and
Hal Sparks
who valiantly swallowed our failures as well as our successes.

In an undertaking of this size, there are bound to be many people who had a hand in making it happen.

We would be less than nowhere without our cadre of home-cooking testers:

Diana, Bill, Harrison and Parker Browning
Cindy and Claudio Bucceri
Erin and Jeff Chandler
Mary-Ellen, John, Megan and Sarah Cooper
Joanne, Ed, Christina, Charles and
Robyn Ellis
Janice, Tom and Jennifer Guisness
Carol, Joe and Stephanie Harmon
Susan and Jay Hurley
Cathy, Wilson, Ceanna and Trevor Leake

Cynthia, Mark, David, Brian and Kimba Lee
Joan, Charles and Andrea McKenna
Sue, Steve and Adam Neely
Alice and Ed Poake
Marion and Richard Powell
Maureen, Tim, Ricky and Tanya Rieman
Judy, Ted and Rebecca Rosen
Denise, Joe and Justin Roulanaitis
Wendy, Peter, Scott and Susie Trask
Jane and Bill Zabinski

And we sincerely thank our very supportive group of tasters:

David Chall
Joanne Chase
Shawna Clark
John Hilden
Anna Johansen

Sue Klein
Pamela Teige
Helen Sturdy Townley
M'Lin Kendrick-Stafford

We are indebted to Gary Reese, Rick Nakata, Glenn Sigrist, Todd Kowalski and the entire staff of the Town & Country Market, Bainbridge Island, Washington, for their patience, their expertise, and their enthusiasm.

We also wish to thank Linda Stenn for her market research, Dick Friedrich for his encouragement, Nancy Warner Hopkins for her lifesaving suggestions, Myrna Black for her advice, Esther Newberg, our agent, who didn't let uncertainty stand in her way, and Liv Blumer, our editor and a kindred spirit, we think.

INTRODUCTION

WHAT'S IN A NAME?

Everything. *A Dinner A Day* means exactly what it says. And we say it to you every Monday through Friday for an entire year. From the very first page, you will see that this is unlike any other cookbook you have ever owned. At any price. Perhaps that's because it comes from an unlikely source; not two professional chefs, not two trained dietitians, not two culinary experts—but two working mothers. Two women from opposite sides of the country who came together, first as friends and then with a common focus: translating the love of good food into the monumental achievement of putting a delicious, nutritious meal on the family table, night after night, year after year.

Our first step was to put dinner in its proper perspective. Once we realized that preparing the evening fare need not be the focus of an entire day, but simply an enjoyable and creative hour, we were able to take all the worry out of planning and still retain the confidence that we could achieve great things.

We are both products of mothers who rotated half a dozen basic menus, week in and week out. Suzannah grew up knowing, if it were Tuesday, that meant meat loaf, and Sally knew, if it were Friday, that meant flounder. We were adults by the time we discovered that the sky wouldn't fall if we had pasta on Friday or chicken on Tuesday. Today, we are both champions of innovation and variety, as well as masters of stress-free, fuss-free cooking. And now you can be, too.

The question "What's for dinner?" no longer has to be perceived as a dire threat. From now on, it will be a loving gift.

Each of us raised three children while we held down a full-time job. Each of us spent years figuring out that our commitment to our careers did not have to shortchange our families. We learned that, even with limited time and resources, we could produce terrific dinners, five nights a week, in an hour or less, that would have our families licking their plates.

As our children grew up and began to emulate us, and as our friends begged for our secret, it occurred to us that, if we could share some of what we had learned the hard way, we might make things easier for others. Then once we found that over 70 percent of the families in this country prefer to home-cook on a regular basis, we knew exactly what to do: provide our fool-proof method to everyone who wants to put meals on the table that can make each evening memorable and have even the cook looking forward to dinner.

Our secret is simple: we have redesigned old-fashioned home cooking to fit perfectly into today's more fragmented lifestyle. In other words, the taste that used to take our grandmothers all day to prepare can now be produced by you in a matter of minutes.

Sometimes we think we must be clones, because so often we both have the same idea for the same recipe at the same moment. At other times, we solve a problem precisely because we are two different people who can come at it from totally distinct perspectives. Either way, one of our biggest joys in preparing this cookbook was our discovery of how willing most foods are to work with one another in helping us create new and exciting taste experiences.

Depending on where you live and your ethnic or cultural background, some of our foods and food combinations may seem unusual to you; okay, even weird. We admit to doing this on purpose. So often, we tend to rely on the few foods that are familiar to us, that are easy to prepare, and that we know our families will eat. Just like our mothers did. Without realizing it, we narrow our options and close the door on potentially wonderful discoveries. Think of all the foods that grow on this planet, and how lucky we are that they do. Then think how many of them you've never even tasted. So we have deliberately presented you with many different dishes, and we encourage you to try them. We don't believe you'll be disappointed.

Nowadays, both Sally and Suzannah live on picturesque Bainbridge Island in the middle of the Pacific Northwest's Puget Sound, where Sally spends her time out of the kitchen in her glorious garden, growing many of the fruits and vegetables we have incorporated into our recipes, while Suzannah spends her time away from the computer refining many of the irresistible combinations of foods that make *A Dinner A Day* so extraordinary.

The result is a totally new concept of "fast food": a treasure trove of complete, family-tested and perfected meals for every Monday through Friday, for an entire year, in which we have not repeated a single recipe!

Whether you are a single parent, the cooking half of a two-income family, or an overcommitted stay-at-home mom, *A Dinner A Day* will work for you. We have not merely created recipes for you to follow, we have created entire meals. Forget searching through half a dozen sections of a cookbook, or pulling out three or four different books in an effort to find an exciting entree, the right accompaniments, and then an appropriate dessert. It's no longer necessary. *A Dinner A Day* presents each meal to you in its entirety on two facing pages, and is composed of dishes that have been carefully designed to go perfectly with one another and allow you to maximize your time and enjoyment. With each meal comes a step-by-step Countdown to ensure that your dinner is on the table, start to finish, in 60 minutes or less. And we include a complete shopping list for every week of the year, day-coded for easy reference. In other words, we have provided you with all the things we wish had been available to us during all those years that we were stressing over what to fix for dinner for our families.

Because this cookbook encompasses an entire year, we have been able to take full advantage of the availability and cost-effectiveness of seasonal foods and the pleasures of seasonal cooking. In line with today's health-conscious attitudes, our menus emphasize poultry, pasta and seafood; we celebrate soups and salads; we make vegetarian magic; we provide low-fat alternatives that will not sacrifice taste; and we recommend exciting combinations of herbs and spices as options to seasoning with salt. And for those of you who just cannot resist, we offer desserts to satisfy every sweet tooth.

You can use this cookbook every single weeknight; you can use it two or three times a week; you can even use it once or twice a month—however you choose to use it, *A Dinner A Day* will quickly become as indispensable to your kitchen as a teakettle. It is the cookbook of the next century, prepared for the cooks of today and tomorrow in an easy-to-follow format that will allow even a beginner to achieve spectacular results. It's all in the name.

THE STARTING POINT

Your life is about to change. Everything you ever dreaded about providing dinner for your family is about to disappear. But before it does, take a moment or two to read through these few pages and see for yourself how effortlessly *A Dinner A Day* is going to redefine your relationship with your kitchen. You'll find that our surefire method makes the evening meal one less thing you have to worry about in your busy day, because we have already taken the anxiety out of both the planning and the preparation.

260 Complete Menus

First and foremost, this book presents 260 complete dinner menus, one for every weeknight of the year—without a single repetition. If you've ever had a son turn up his nose at a turnip, a spouse curl a lip at an artichoke, or a daughter stick out her tongue at Swiss chard, tell them not to worry; they won't have to eat that dish again for the rest of the year.

For a Family of Four

Despite the fact that both of us had a family of five, we decided that, in keeping with the national trend, we would create all of our menus for an average family of four. Most of our recipes can be adapted for less or more, according to the size and appetite of your family; however, you should keep in mind that altering the number of portions may also alter some of the cooking times.

Every Meal at a Glance

You'll find that we have not presented our recipes in specific categories, such as meat, poultry or pasta, but in complete dinner menus, which means you will not have to keep flipping back and forth to different pages for cooking instructions. The entire meal is laid out for you on two facing pages.

A Well-Balanced Year

In looking over the menus, you'll notice that not only does each dish fit perfectly into its meal, but each meal is carefully positioned within its week; each week is properly balanced within its month; each month complements its season and the seasons, in turn, round out the entire year.

Time-Tested Results

One more thing that makes *A Dinner A Day* unique is that, unlike other cookbooks, when we tell you that a meal can be prepared, start to finish, in 60 minutes or less, we mean everything having to do with that meal, including assembling all the required ingredients, gathering the necessary cooking equipment and peeling, grating, shredding and chopping basic foods. You will find a number of menus that require you to do some simple tasks in the morning, but even these have been accounted for in the total preparation time. All we have excluded is the time it will take you to get through your supermarket, and you will see that we've even taken the pain out of that.

Over the past two years, everyday cooks like you and like us, from all parts of the country, have been road-testing our menus on their families, and confirming our claims.

THE HEART OF THE MATTER

Jumping into *A Dinner A Day* because you've spotted a menu that looks good enough to try at the last minute might not be the most efficient way to use this cookbook. We suggest you follow the daily instructions, even if you are using a single menu.

Read Before You Shop

We recommend that you read through an entire week of menus before you head for the market. This will enable you to make whatever recipe adjustments are necessary. For example, if, in glancing through a particular week, you realize you need to alter food amounts, or you come across a dish or even an entire menu you feel may not be appropriate for your family because of personal tastes or food allergies, or you find menus listed for days on which you have made other plans, you may simply change or eliminate those items in the shopping list, using the handy day identification codes as your guide.

Look Before You Cook

Get in the habit of looking over each individual menu carefully before beginning to cook. We often list simple instructions to be done in the morning. Also, when you are using fish that has been frozen, we advise you to place it in the refrigerator to thaw the night before you are going to use it.

Assemble Your Weapons

You will note that we ask you to assemble your ingredients and cooking equipment prior to beginning preparation, because we have incorporated this assembly in the 60-minute time frame. If you do not have the space to assemble all the required items, we suggest that you familiarize yourself with what you will need, and its location in your kitchen, so that you can reach it all quickly.

If You Change Courses

If, for any reason, you choose to *eliminate* a dish from a menu, be careful to adjust your ingredients and equipment accordingly, as well as the relevant steps in the Countdown. If you choose to *substitute* a dish in a menu, be careful to exchange the necessary ingredients and equipment and adapt the Countdown.

MARKET RESEARCH

In our efforts to simplify the dinner process and eliminate the hassle, we consider the ritual of purchasing the food every bit as important as the ritual of preparing it.

An Innovation in Shopping

A marvelous innovation with *A Dinner A Day* is the Weekly Shopping List. In it, we have included all the food ingredients necessary for the preparation of each dinner in the week, compiled in one convenient and comprehensive list, and organized into general sections that should correspond to the placement of products in the majority of markets across the country.

Catch That Code

Each item on the shopping list is followed by a letter or letters indicating the day of the week on which that particular item will be used. This helpful identification code will simplify any menu adjustments you might find necessary to make.

Taking Stock of Staples

We have identified a significant number of nonperishable refrigerated and nonrefrigerated ingredients, which we have used throughout this book, as staple items. These are items that can and should be kept on hand at all times. We strongly suggest that, each week, you take stock of your staples before you shop. Nothing is more frustrating than starting to prepare a meal and discovering you either lack, or lack enough of, a necessary ingredient. As a reminder, each Weekly Shopping List suggests that you check the staples to be used during the upcoming week prior to making your weekly purchases.

Sizing up Ingredients

To facilitate your shopping, we have designated ingredients in two ways. When we call for using an entire product, we list the item by its size and amount (for example, 1 medium can [14½ ounces] cut-up tomatoes). However, when we call for using part of a can or jar or bottle or package, we list the item only by the amount the recipe requires (for example, ½ cup sweet pickles).

Variations on a Theme

Although we list cans, jars and bottles in specific sizes and amounts (for example, a large jar [28 ounces] pasta sauce), different manufacturers of a similar item may offer differing amounts (for example, a large jar [30 ounces] pasta sauce). Purchase whatever is available in your market because any minor differences in amounts will not significantly alter a recipe.

Grate Cheese of Choice

Many of our recipes call for cheese. In some cases, we call for purchasing cheese that is already shredded because some cheeses, such as cheddar and mozzarella, come packaged that way and, although usually more expensive, it saves time. You are, however, free to buy block cheese and grate it yourself. On other occasions, we simply call for an amount of cheese, such as Gruyère and Gouda which do not come grated, and instruct you to grate it.

Whatever You Like

In many instances, you will notice that we do not identify specific varieties of food. For example, because it makes little difference to the recipe, we frequently leave the cut of a lamb or pork chop up to the buyer, to select according to cost, availability and preference. For the same reasons, we have for the most part chosen not to specify the type of lettuce that should be used in making salads. Similarly, if we don't specify a type of melon or pear, we mean whatever is available in your particular market at the time we call for it. The same is true for other items such as apples, onions and tomatoes. We're easy.

IN OTHER WORDS

Product availability varies considerably across the country, and you may find it necessary to make occasional substitutions. Wherever possible, we have provided suggestions that will minimize the effect of a substitution in a particular recipe.

Fishing Around

As you will see, we fix a lot of fish in this cookbook. It's best, of course, to purchase fresh fish when it's called for in a recipe, but that may not always be possible.

• Several kinds of seafood, such as sole, halibut, salmon, cod, shrimp and scallops, may be available, already frozen, in your freezer department.

• Your fishmonger may agree to provide you with frozen fish that he would ordinarily thaw before selling.

• You can purchase fish that has not been previously frozen and freeze it, but please do not buy fish that has been frozen and thawed and then try to refreeze it.

• Clams must be purchased fresh and cannot be frozen. If you cannot obtain fresh clams, you can use canned whole clams instead.

• When freezing fresh fish, wrap it carefully to keep it from drying out or losing its flavor, as well as to protect other items you may have in your freezer.

• In rare instances, you can substitute canned fish for fresh, but the result will not be the same.

While fish is generally available across the country, not all varieties may be found in your particular area. You can substitute:

Grouper or cod for bass
Flounder for cod
Sole for flounder
Grouper, cod or red snapper for halibut
Red snapper, orange roughy or cod for perch
Halibut, orange roughy or cod for red snapper
Red snapper or orange roughy for salmon
Flounder for sole
Any sole for Dover sole, lemon sole or petrale sole
Shark, tuna or marlin for swordfish
Sole, cod or red snapper for orange roughy

Pasta Preferences

Some varieties of pasta are available in both dried and fresh packages. In our recipes, the only significant difference between the two is the cooking time, with fresh pasta taking approximately half the time of dried pasta to cook. The choice is up to you.

Throughout this cookbook, we call for various types of pasta. Pasta generally comes in three basic types: ribbon (such as fettuccine and lasagna), tubular (such as spaghetti and macaroni) and stuffed (such as tortellini and ravioli). Within each category, you can substitute as appropriate.

Either/Or

One of the best things about creating a cookbook for an entire year is the ability to make full use of the fresh seasonal fruits and vegetables that are finding their way into more and more markets across the country. Even so, there may be some products that your market does not carry. Please feel free to substitute such things as a small cantaloupe for a papaya and spinach or beet greens for Swiss chard. If fresh artichokes are not available or cost-effective, substitute a vegetable of your choice.

If any of the fresh vegetables we call for are not available in your area, you are free to substitute frozen vegetables (such as sugar snap peas and wax beans), prepared according to package directions and incorporated into the remainder of the recipe.

We call for a variety of fresh berries in our menus. If you find any of these are not available or cost-effective, you can use frozen and adjust your instructions.

The Stuff of Life

A host of different breads pop up in our menus because we believe bread doesn't have to be boring. However, if sourdough bread is not available in your area, feel free to substitute any white loaf. If peasant bread is not available, substitute a hearty rye or whole wheat or pumpernickel loaf. If crumpets are unavailable, substitute English or Australian muffins. If Boboli bread is unavailable, substitute pan bread or English or Australian muffins.

You will note that we do not call for a bread in every meal. However, if bread is a regular part of your family's dinner, go ahead and put it on the table. We won't object.

We frequently call for angel food loaf cakes in our desserts. If the loaf variety is unavailable in your area, you can substitute part of an angel food ring cake.

Tis the Seasoning

It is always a pure delight to use fresh herbs in cooking because they so enhance the flavor and aroma of foods. However, we hesitate to ask you to buy a quantity of a fresh herb when only a small amount is required. Therefore, you are free to substitute dried herbs wherever you wish, generally on a ratio of three parts fresh to one part dried.

We use one herb, parsley, throughout this book because it does wonderful things for food, is relatively inexpensive, is available all year long and can be found in every market in the country. We recommend you buy it fresh and use it liberally.

Garlic is another flavor enhancer we use almost to excess. It's such a wonderful and healthful substitute for salt seasoning, we could not resist. You are of course free to omit the garlic as you choose, but be warned that the dish will not be as flavorful.

You will note that a recipe may occasionally call for a seasoning salt, but that we rarely add salt and pepper to our dishes. That's because we prefer to season our foods with herbs and spices. However, most of our recipes do call for seasoning to taste, so you are free to include whatever additional seasoning your family prefers. Play with the dishes. Adapt them to your particular taste. Experiment. Have fun. You can rarely go very wrong. That's one of the joys of using this cookbook.

The Thick and the Thin of It

We make no pretensions about *A Dinner A Day* being a low-fat or low-calorie cookbook. It is instead a cookbook for the way most Americans prefer to eat. However, if we expect people to use our menus for an entire year, we must naturally be concerned about things like cholesterol and weight control. Wherever possible, we offer low-fat alternatives to milks, creams, cheeses, oils and mayonnaise, and you are always free to substitute a low-fat margarine for butter. There are also low-fat editions of cream soups now available in many market areas.

We have tended to exempt desserts from dietary concerns on the assumption that if your family is dieting you will either omit dessert or substitute fresh fruit. However, there are now many low-fat pound cakes and cookies on the market, as well as low-fat and fat-free ice creams and frozen yogurts, that will allow you to enjoy our desserts without feeling guilty.

In our desserts, we frequently call for whipped cream as a garnish. Since a dollop usually does it, we use the prepared kind in a can. However, you are free to substitute a nondairy whipped topping for the whipped cream, or omit it altogether.

In other words, you may take our dishes the way they are or you may adapt them quite easily to suit you and your family.

Frozen Fundamentals

In devising our desserts, we have selected specific flavors of ice cream and frozen yogurt that may not be available in your area. In that case, you can choose a similar flavor or any flavor that you feel will complement the remaining ingredients.

We occasionally call for frozen berries. If any of the ones we specify are not in your freezer section, substitute one that is.

Alcoholic Alternatives

You cannot help but note that we frequently use alcohol in our cooking. Wines and spirits add wonderful flavor to foods, produce pleasing aromas and are not harmful when used in moderation. When cooked, the alcoholic content evaporates, leaving only the essence behind. If for any reason you do not wish to cook with alcohol, we have offered substitutes. Where we have used noncooked liqueurs in desserts, we have suggested syrups or extracts. There is now a full range of nonalcoholic Italian syrups available in many market areas. While using alcohol in your cooking will always enhance the result, it is entirely optional.

TOOLS OF THE TRADE

Kitchens vary so greatly in size and layout, and cooks differ so greatly in style, that it would be next to impossible for us to suggest a single list of equipment that is suitable for every home. Instead, we will talk briefly about the equipment that we used in creating the recipes for this cookbook, and then leave it up to you.

Toys in the Kitchen

There are a few small appliances that we couldn't function without.

• An electric hand mixer is an indispensable device that always makes mixing, beating and blending chores, such as we call for in puddings and cakes, seem easy.

• We use a slow cooker for a number of our meals. It's a great gadget for busy people because it lets you dump everything into it and then leave it to do its thing while you're busy doing your thing. A number of slow cookers, from the Crock Pot to the Nesco, are now on the market at relatively low cost. If you're planning to purchase one, be sure it holds at least five quarts.

• Another small appliance we wouldn't be without is a wok and the special utensils that go with it. Talk about fast and healthful cooking—with a wok, it doesn't get any better. There are stove-top as well as electric versions, in carbon steel as well as nonstick. It's your choice. Of course, if you don't see a wok in your future, a large skillet will work almost as well.

• There are always things you just can't prepare properly without a blender. From desserts to butters to sauces to soups, it's a miracle worker.

• We make a lot of terrific soups and stews in this cookbook. This means we frequently call for a Dutch oven, which is a wide, two-handled pot, 6 to 8 quarts in size.

• As you get into our recipes, you may wonder why we use a double boiler to fix many of our rice dishes. The answer is simple: with a double boiler, you put the ingredients in the top, bring water to a boil in the bottom, then leave it alone, and you end up with perfect results every time. A 2- to 3- quart double boiler is the right size for our purposes. An alternative to the double boiler is, of course, the electric rice cooker, which also delivers fuss-free rice, but we like the double boiler for its versatility in helping to make other dishes as well.

• If you have a full-blown steamer appliance for steaming vegetables, by all means use it. If not, you might want to consider the inexpensive, stainless-steel, fan-style vegetable steamer insert that works perfectly in a 2-quart saucepan, or a bamboo steamer that is used with a skillet. Either will handle all the steaming jobs we call for.

Pot Pourri

Every kitchen has its supply of basic pots and pans. We use them all, and probably more.

• We call for skillets in small, medium and large sizes. On occasion, we even call for two large skillets at the same time. Small skillets are 7 to 8 inches in diameter, while medium skillets are 9 to 10 inches in diameter and large skillets usually run 11 to 12 inches in diameter. There are some even larger; it's up to you. Regardless of size, you should have tight-fitting lids for all your skillets. But if you don't, aluminum foil can sometimes come to the rescue.

- As with the skillets, we use small, medium and large saucepans. A lot. Small saucepans run from 1 to $1^1/_2$ quarts in size; medium saucepans generally hold 2 to 3 quarts; and large saucepans can take up to 5 quarts. We also use a 6 to 8-quart stockpot for cooking pasta. As with the skillets, all your saucepans should have tight-fitting lids.

- We do our share of baking in this cookbook, from biscuits to puddings, from fish to fowl, and from casseroles to cakes. As a result, we use baking pans, baking dishes, cookie sheets, muffin tins, and casseroles of all sizes. You're safest with ovenproof baking pans and dishes that are 8x8, 9x9, 7x11, 9x13 and 10x14 inches in dimension, and casseroles that hold from 1 to $2^1/_2$ quarts. We've also been known to use a broiler-proof pan, a flame-proof casserole and a roasting pan.

- We mix a lot, beat a lot and blend a lot. You can never have too many bowls in your kitchen. Sets of bowls generally come in 3 nested sizes. We use them all and then some. Two sets are even better, unless you like to clean up as you cook.

- We drain pasta and large vegetables in a colander, and use strainers for small vegetables and berries. These are items that almost every kitchen has, and you should use what you have.

Sleight of Hand

Our favorite section of the kitchen is the drawer where live all the wonderful little tools you simply couldn't cook without. First on the list is knives. There is not enough we can say about having a good set of knives. They are worth their weight in steel. In this book, we use five basic knives.

- A chef's knife, the heavy, wedge-shaped chopping knife, that comes in 6-, 8- and 10-inch blade lengths.

- A utility knife, with a $4^1/_2$- to 6-inch blade, that is perfect for almost every small mincing, slicing and dicing job.

- A paring knife, with a blade that's $2^1/_2$ to $3^1/_2$ inches long, that we use for miscellaneous odd jobs, such as hulling strawberries.

- A slicing knife, which has a long, thin blade of 6 to 8 inches and is wonderful for producing thin slices of tomatoes, onions, potatoes, apples, and so on.

- A serrated bread knife, which generally has an 8-inch blade and which will cut all the breads and cakes you can serve.

It's a smart idea to keep a good knife sharpener around and to sharpen your knives every time you use them. It doesn't take long, and you'll appreciate the results.

After the knives, we like the assortment of cooking utensils that every kitchen manages to accumulate.

• You can never have too many cooking spoons; large spoons, slotted spoons, wooden spoons and ladles all get used. Not to mention a cooking fork for piercing potatoes, fluffing rice and flaking fish.

• Spatulas get used a lot—solid ones, slotted ones, long ones—for turning delicate foods such as fish.

• We'd never be without tongs to turn cooking foods such as chicken pieces and chops.

• A spreader is a necessity for frosting cakes, saucing meat and fish, and buttering breads, among many other things.

• A general scraper (we use the hard rubber kind) is essential for scraping out blenders and bowls.

• We use three different kinds of graters in our cookbook: one for citrus, one for cheese and one for vegetables.

• We make very good use of a vegetable peeler. We've even been known to grate with it.

• A vegetable brush comes in very handy for potatoes and clams and other diverse uses.

• A kitchen can't be called a real kitchen without a complete set of both dry and liquid measures. Unless you're great at guessing, you'll use them in every recipe.

• And then there's always that group of miscellaneous stuff that works hard to keep the food coming but never gets much praise. At the top of that list is the whisk, without which our salad dressings and sauces just wouldn't be the same.

• There just isn't any substitute for a sifter in combining baking ingredients and dusting cakes with confectioners' sugar and cocoa.

• The pastry brush is an invaluable little tool for glazing meats and breads. The bulb baster is the only tool we know that keeps cooking foods juicy and efficiently degreases a pan. And there's the apple corer, which we use in a number of our apple dishes.

• We periodically call for a pastry board, but don't go out and buy one; any wooden or plastic chopping surface will do just fine. Biscuit cutters come in various sizes, but so do glasses, and they work, too.

• There aren't any utensils that can do what a melon-baller does, so we use one. We frequently use a mallet for such chores as pounding meats to a desired thickness and crushing nuts for a dessert. And, speaking of dessert, where would we be in this world without an ice cream scoop?

Microwaveless in America

Somewhere along the way, you're bound to notice that we have not called for what is rapidly becoming a kitchen basic—the microwave oven. This was no oversight. We have deliberately chosen not to use microwave recipes because there are still many homes that don't have one. And we were able to produce all of our meals in an hour or less without it. However, if you do own a microwave, you are free to adapt as many of our recipes as you like, and save even more time than we allow. It's no secret that the microwave works miracles with vegetables and fish.

TIME IS OF THE ESSENCE

It's not enough for us to tell you that you can fix a whole dinner in 60 minutes or less, just because we say it's so. If you're not a super-well-organized cook, chances are the vegetables will get cold while you're waiting for the meat. Trying to prepare a meal that consists of several different dishes, each with its own set of instructions, isn't always easy. So we aren't just going to tell you that you can get that meal on the table; we're going to show you exactly how.

We call it the *Countdown*, and it's a chronology of cooking steps, incorporating every dish in the dinner, that will take you from pantry to table smoothly and with the confidence of knowing that it will all be ready when you are. Just as we've taken the stress out of choosing the meal, and the hassle out of shopping for the ingredients, we've now taken all the planning out of the preparation because, at the end of a long day, that should be the last thing for you to have to worry about.

With the entire menu in full view, following the Countdown is easy. And it's all included in the 60 minutes, from the moment you walk into the kitchen to the moment you sit down at the table. In fact, we've done everything for you but the dishes.

THE KITCHEN SINK

There are a number of miscellaneous thoughts we had while creating *A Dinner A Day* that we felt were important enough to warrant discussion, although we couldn't seem to find the right niche for them. Hence, the kitchen sink.

• Because there can be such a great difference between the way gas stoves and electric stoves operate, not to mention between different types of electric burners, we've opted not to include specific cooking levels in our recipes. As a general rule, we set the burner to high for boil, to medium for cook, and to low for simmer. We'll let you decide what variations are appropriate for your equipment.

• As you will see, we have created, from scratch, all the salad dressings that appear in this book. We did this primarily because homemade dressings are less costly than bottled dressings, they are quick and easy to produce, they taste better and we can control the ingredients. We have designed no two salads alike, and we prepare only as much dressing as we will use.

• Many of our recipes call for grated fresh orange or lemon peel. There is a dried kind available, but we far prefer fresh. We suggest that, when oranges and lemons are plentiful and cost-effective, you take a few moments to grate the peels, placing them in individual, resealable plastic bags and freezing them for future use. If properly sealed, they will keep in your freezer indefinitely.

• Unless you are particularly fond of squeezing fresh lemons and limes all the time, try keeping bottles of juice in the refrigerator. In most of our recipes, you will find that there is no significant difference between the fresh and the bottled.

• We call for several kinds of ginger in this cookbook: fresh, candied (or crystallized) and ground. Candied and ground ginger come in jars and will keep on your shelf for a year. Fresh ginger can be sealed in a plastic bag and kept frozen indefinitely. While frozen, ginger can be both grated and sliced.

Well, that's it. We've done our job. Now you can do yours.

A DINNER A DAY

JANUARY
WEEK ONE

Monday

LIP-SMACKIN' CHICKEN
BROCCOLI SUNRISE
MELTING MOMENTS

Tuesday

LINGUINI MARINARA
SALAD MILANO
ITALIAN BREADSTICKS
GONDOLA PEARS

Wednesday

HAM STEAK DIJON
GLAZED SWEET POTATOES
CORN DIABLO
TAP-TAP-TAPIOCA PUDDING

Thursday

SIMPLY STROGANOFF
FLUFFY STEAMED WHITE RICE
CARROT-SPROUT SALAD
CINNAMON APPLES

Friday

JUST FOR THE HALIBUT
PRAISE THE POTATOES
SPUNKY SPINACH
ORANGE CARAMEL

CHECK STAPLES

- ☐ Butter
- ☐ Flour
- ☐ Cornstarch
- ☐ Granulated sugar
- ☐ Dark brown sugar
- ☐ Long-grain white rice
- ☐ Regular or light vegetable oil
- ☐ Regular or light olive oil
- ☐ Red wine vinegar
- ☐ White wine vinegar
- ☐ Apple cider vinegar
- ☐ Lemon juice
- ☐ Lime juice
- ☐ Worcestershire sauce
- ☐ Tabasco sauce
- ☐ Soy sauce
- ☐ Kitchen Bouquet
- ☐ Dijon mustard
- ☐ Regular or low-fat mayonnaise
- ☐ Honey
- ☐ Dark raisins
- ☐ Grated Parmesan cheese
- ☐ Whole allspice
- ☐ Dried basil
- ☐ Bay leaves
- ☐ Ground cinnamon
- ☐ Ground ginger
- ☐ Italian seasoning
- ☐ Dry mustard
- ☐ Ground nutmeg
- ☐ Dried oregano
- ☐ Paprika
- ☐ Pepper
- ☐ Salt
- ☐ Vanilla extract

SHOPPING NOTE

● If you are shopping once a week and cannot arrange to purchase fresh halibut on the day you plan to use it, you can purchase *not previously frozen* halibut and freeze it, placing it in the refrigerator to thaw the night before you are ready to use it. Or you can purchase *still frozen* halibut and keep it frozen until the night before you are ready to use it.

MEAT & POULTRY

2 lean cooked ham steaks
($^3/_4$ pound each) (W)
$1^1/_4$ pounds lean sirloin
steak (Th)
4 chicken breast halves (M)

FISH

4 halibut steaks ($1^1/_4$ pounds)
(F)

FRESH PRODUCE

Vegetables

12 small new red potatoes (M)
12 small new white potatoes (F)
$1^1/_4$ pounds broccoli (M)
1 pound spinach (F)
8 medium mushrooms (Th)
3 medium carrots (Th)
3 medium onions—2 (M), 1 (Th)
1 small red onion (T)
2 medium shallots (F)
8 scallions (green onions)—
    2 (W), 3 (Th), 3 (F)
1 head garlic (M, T)
1 bunch parsley (T, Th, F)
1 very small bunch dill (F)
$^1/_2$ pound bean sprouts (Th)
1 medium head lettuce (T)
$^1/_2$ pound tomatoes (F)
1 medium cucumber (T)

Fruit

4 large pears (T)
4 large baking apples (Th)
1 medium orange (M)
4 large oranges (F)

CANS, JARS & BOTTLES

Soup

1 can ($10^3/_4$ ounces) chicken
    broth (M)
1 can ($14^1/_2$ ounces) vegetable
    broth (F)

Vegetables

1 large can (28 ounces) whole
    Italian tomatoes with
    basil (T)
1 can (11 ounces) whole kernel
    corn (W)
1 can (17 ounces) plain sweet
    potatoes (W)

Fruit

1 small can (8 ounces) sliced
    pineapple (W)

Condiments

1 small jar (2 ounces) diced
    pimientos (W)
1 small can ($3^1/_2$ ounces) pitted
    black olives (T)

PACKAGED GOODS

Pasta, Rice & Grains

16 ounces linguini (T)

Baked Goods

4 frankfurter buns (T)

Nuts & Seeds

$^1/_2$ cup pecan pieces (M)

Dessert & Baking Needs

$^1/_2$ cup graham cracker
    crumbs (T)

4 tablespoons instant
    tapioca (W)
3 tablespoons strawberry
    gelatin (Th)

WINES & SPIRITS

1 cup dry white wine (or
    nonalcoholic white wine or
    vegetable broth)—
    $^1/_2$ cup (T), $^1/_2$ cup (F)
2 tablespoons dry sherry
    (or beef broth) (Th)
1 tablespoon creme de menthe
    liqueur (or nonalcoholic
    Italian creme de menthe
    syrup) (M)

REFRIGERATED PRODUCTS

Dairy

2 cups half-and-half (W)
$^1/_2$ cup whipping cream (F)
2 cups regular or low-fat sour
    cream (Th)
2 eggs (W)

Cheese

1 small package (3 ounces)
    cream cheese (T)

Juice

$^1/_4$ cup orange juice (M)

FROZEN GOODS

Fruit

1 package (12 ounces)
    sweetened raspberries (M)

Desserts

1 pint vanilla ice cream (M)

MONDAY

Lip-Smackin' Chicken

2 medium onions
4 chicken breast halves
2 tablespoons Kitchen Bouquet
2 tablespoons butter
12 small new red potatoes
1 clove garlic
1 bay leaf
3 whole allspice
3 tablespoons flour
1 can (10³/₄ ounces) chicken broth
Seasoning to taste

Broccoli Sunrise

1¹/₄ pounds broccoli
1 medium orange
1 tablespoon butter
1 tablespoon flour
Seasoning to taste
¹/₄ cup orange juice

Melting Moments

1 package (12 ounces) frozen sweetened
   raspberries
1 tablespoon creme de menthe liqueur (or
   nonalcoholic Italian creme de menthe
   syrup)
1 pint vanilla ice cream
¹/₂ cup pecan pieces

EQUIPMENT

Large roasting pan	Vegetable brush
Medium saucepan	Citrus grater
Small saucepan	Whisk
Colander	Pastry brush
Assorted kitchen knives	Ice cream scoop
Measuring cups and spoons	Aluminum foil
Assorted cooking utensils	

COUNTDOWN

1 Assemble the ingredients and equipment
2 Do Step 1 of the *Lip-Smackin' Chicken*
3 Do Step 1 of the *Melting Moments*
4 Do Steps 2–3 of the *Lip-Smackin' Chicken*
5 Do Steps 1–3 of the *Broccoli Sunrise*
6 Do Step 4 of the *Lip-Smackin' Chicken*
7 Do Step 4 of the *Broccoli Sunrise*
8 Do Steps 5–6 of the *Lip-Smackin' Chicken*
9 Do Step 5 of the *Broccoli Sunrise*
10 Do Step 7 of the *Lip-Smackin' Chicken*
11 Do Step 2 of the *Melting Moments*

Lip-Smackin' Chicken

1 Preheat the oven to 400°F.

2 Peel and slice the onions. Place them in an ungreased roasting pan. Place the chicken, skin side up, over the onions. Brush the chicken skins with Kitchen Bouquet. Season to taste. Dot the chicken with butter.

3 Scrub and quarter the potatoes. Peel and chop the garlic. Place the potatoes and the garlic around the chicken. Add the bay leaf and the allspice. Cover the pan with aluminum foil, and roast for 15 minutes.

4 Uncover the roasting pan. Baste the chicken and the potatoes, and continue roasting until the potatoes are tender and the chicken is golden, 15 to 20 minutes.

5 Remove the chicken, the potatoes and the onions from the pan and keep them warm.

6 Pour off all but 3 tablespoons of the drippings. Heat a burner and place the roasting pan over it. Add the flour and whisk until the mixture is golden, about 3 minutes. Add the broth, and continue cooking and stirring until the sauce is smooth. Season to taste, and then let the sauce simmer for another 4 minutes.

7 Return the chicken to the pan and coat the pieces with the gravy. Serve the chicken with the potatoes and onions, and pass the remaining gravy.

Broccoli Sunrise

1 Bring water to a boil in a medium saucepan.

2 Trim the broccoli and cut it into bite-size florets.

3 Grate 1 tablespoon of peel from the orange, then peel the orange, section it, and cut the sections in half.

4 Cook the broccoli in boiling water until it is crisp-tender, about 5 minutes.

5 Drain the broccoli. Melt the butter in the same saucepan. Add the flour and season to taste. Whisk the mixture until it is well blended. Add the orange juice and whisk until the sauce is smooth. Add the orange peel. Return the broccoli to the saucepan, tossing the florets until they are well coated. Add the orange sections and toss for 20 seconds more.

Melting Moments

1 Set the package of frozen berries out to thaw.

2 Combine the thawed berries and the creme de menthe in a small saucepan and heat through. Drizzle the mixture over scoops of vanilla ice cream and top each serving with pecan pieces.

TUESDAY

Linguini Marinara

¹/₄ cup regular or light olive oil
1 tablespoon fresh parsley (when chopped)
2 cloves garlic
1 large can (28 ounces) whole Italian tomatoes with basil
1 teaspoon dried oregano
¹/₂ teaspoon dried basil
Seasoning to taste
16 ounces linguini
¹/₂ cup dry white wine (or nonalcoholic white wine or vegetable broth)

Salad Milano

1 medium head lettuce
1 medium cucumber
1 small red onion
1 small can (3¹/₂ ounces) pitted black olives
1 clove garlic
1 tablespoon fresh parsley (when chopped)
2 tablespoons apple cider vinegar
2 tablespoons regular or light olive oil
1 teaspoon Dijon mustard
Seasoning to taste

Italian Breadsticks

3 tablespoons butter
4 frankfurter buns
¹/₄ cup grated Parmesan cheese
³/₄ teaspoon Italian seasoning

Gondola Pears

1 small package (3 ounces) cream cheese
4 large pears
2 tablespoons lemon juice
¹/₂ cup graham cracker crumbs
¹/₄ cup honey

EQUIPMENT

Blender	Assorted kitchen knives
Stockpot	Measuring cups and
Large covered skillet	spoons
Cookie sheet	Assorted cooking
Large bowl	utensils
2 small bowls	Vegetable peeler
Shallow bowl	Pastry brush
Colander	Whisk

COUNTDOWN

1 Assemble the ingredients and equipment
2 Do Step 1 of the *Italian Breadsticks*
3 Do Steps 1–5 of the *Linguini Marinara*
4 Do Steps 1–2 of the *Gondola Pears*
5 Do Steps 2–4 of the *Italian Breadsticks*
6 Do Step 1 of the *Salad Milano*
7 Do Steps 6–7 of the *Linguini Marinara*
8 Do Steps 2–3 of the *Salad Milano*
9 Do Step 8 of the *Linguini Marinara*
10 Do Steps 3–4 of the *Gondola Pears*

Linguini Marinara

1 Heat the oil in a large skillet.

2 Chop the parsley. Peel and halve the garlic and sauté it in the oil until golden.

3 Chop the tomatoes in the blender. *Do not puree.*

4 Add the tomatoes to the skillet and return it to the heat. Add the oregano and the basil and season to taste. Bring the mixture to a boil, then reduce the heat and simmer, covered, for 30 minutes.

5 Bring water to a boil in a stockpot.

6 Cook the linguini in the stockpot until it is almost tender, 3 to 4 minutes if you are using fresh pasta and 7 to 8 minutes if you are using dried pasta.

7 Add the wine and the parsley to the sauce, correct the seasoning, and let the sauce simmer for another 5 minutes.

8 Drain the linguini. Remove the garlic from the sauce and spoon the sauce over the linguini.

Salad Milano

1 Wash and dry the lettuce and tear it into bite-size pieces. Peel and slice the cucumber. Peel and slice the red onion. Drain the olives. Combine all the ingredients in a large bowl.

2 Peel and mince the garlic. Chop the parsley. Whisk the garlic and the parsley with the vinegar, the oil and the mustard until well blended. Season to taste.

3 Toss the salad with the dressing.

Italian Breadsticks

1 Preheat the oven to 350°F.

2 Melt the butter. Split the frankfurter buns, and slice the halves lengthwise into 3 strips each. Place the strips on an ungreased cookie sheet, cut sides up, and brush them with the melted butter.

3 In a small bowl, mix the Parmesan cheese with the Italian seasoning and spread the mixture on the bread strips.

4 Bake the bread until it is toasted and crisp, 8 to 10 minutes.

Gondola Pears

1 Set the cream cheese out to soften.

2 Core the pears and cut them in half. Place 2 pear halves on each dessert plate, and sprinkle them with lemon juice to keep them from browning. Refrigerate until you are ready to use.

3 Place the graham cracker crumbs in a shallow bowl. Cut the cream cheese into eighths. Roll the cheese into balls and then roll the balls in the cracker crumbs.

4 Place the coated cream cheese balls in the center of each pear half. Drizzle honey over each serving.

WEDNESDAY

Ham Steak Dijon

2 lean cooked ham steaks (³/₄ pound each)
2 tablespoons Dijon mustard
2 tablespoons dark brown sugar
¹/₂ teaspoon ground nutmeg
1 small can (8 ounces) sliced pineapple

Glazed Sweet Potatoes

2 tablespoons dark brown sugar
1 teaspoon cornstarch
¹/₄ teaspoon ground ginger
¹/₄ teaspoon salt
¹/₂ cup reserved pineapple juice
1 can (17 ounces) plain sweet potatoes

Corn Diablo

2 scallions (green onions)
1 can (11 ounces) whole kernel corn
1 small jar (2 ounces) diced pimiento
¹/₈ teaspoon paprika
Seasoning to taste

Tap-Tap-Tapioca Pudding

¹/₃ cup + 2 tablespoons sugar
4 tablespoons instant tapioca
2 cups half-and-half
2 eggs
2 teaspoons vanilla extract

EQUIPMENT

Electric hand mixer	Assorted kitchen knives
2 medium saucepans	Measuring cups and
Small saucepan	spoons
Medium bowl	Assorted cooking
2 small bowls	utensils
Strainer	Whisk

COUNTDOWN

1 Assemble the ingredients and equipment
2 Do Step 1 of the *Ham Steak Dijon*
3 Do Steps 1–4 of the *Tap-Tap-Tapioca Pudding*
4 Do Steps 2–3 of the *Ham Steak Dijon*
5 Do Step 1 of the *Glazed Sweet Potatoes*
6 Do Step 4 of the *Ham Steak Dijon*
7 Do Steps 1–2 of the *Corn Diablo*
8 Do Step 2 of the *Glazed Sweet Potatoes*
9 Do Step 5 of the *Ham Steak Dijon*

Ham Steak Dijon

1 Preheat the broiler.

2 Pat the ham steaks dry with paper towels. Place them on a broiler tray.

3 In a small bowl, combine the mustard, the brown sugar and the nutmeg. Spread the mixture over the ham steaks. Broil the steaks, 3 or 4 inches from the heat, until the mustard mixture begins to bubble, about 4 minutes.

4 Drain the pineapple, reserving $1/2$ cup of the juice for the potatoes. Lay the pineapple slices over the ham steaks in a single layer, 2 slices per steak. Broil the steaks until the pineapple begins to brown, 3 to 4 minutes.

5 Cut the ham steaks in half before serving.

Glazed Sweet Potatoes

1 Combine the brown sugar, the cornstarch, the ginger, and the salt in a medium saucepan. Add the reserved pineapple juice and cook, whisking until the mixture is bubbly. Reduce the heat and simmer for 2 minutes more.

2 Drain the sweet potatoes and stir them into the sugar mixture. Simmer until the potatoes are heated through.

Corn Diablo

1 Trim and slice the scallions. Drain the corn.

2 Combine the scallions, the corn, the undrained pimientos and the paprika in a small saucepan. Season to taste and simmer until heated through.

Tap-Tap-Tapioca Pudding

1 Combine $1/3$ cup of the sugar, the tapioca and the half-and-half in a medium saucepan.

2 Separate the eggs. In a medium bowl, beat the egg whites until they form peaks, 4 to 5 minutes. Gradually add the remaining sugar and beat until the mixture is stiff, 1 to 2 minutes.

3 Add the egg yolks to the saucepan and beat them into the half-and-half mixture. Slowly bring the mixture to a rolling boil, then remove the saucepan from the heat. Add the vanilla and blend well.

4 In a slow stream, pour the tapioca mixture into the egg whites and fold together. Set the pudding aside at room temperature until you are ready to serve, at least 10 minutes. It will thicken as it cools.

THURSDAY

Simply Stroganoff

1 medium onion
8 medium mushrooms
3 scallions (green onions)
1 tablespoon fresh parsley (when chopped)
1¼ pounds lean sirloin steak
¼ cup regular or light vegetable oil
2 tablespoons dry sherry (or beef broth)
2 tablespoons flour
½ teaspoon dried basil
½ teaspoon ground nutmeg
2 cups regular or low-fat sour cream
Seasoning to taste

Fluffy Steamed White Rice

1 cup long-grain white rice
2 cups water

Carrot-Sprout Salad

2 tablespoons regular or low-fat mayonnaise
1 teaspoon white wine vinegar
1 teaspoon soy sauce
½ teaspoon sugar
Seasoning to taste
3 medium carrots
½ pound fresh bean sprouts

Cinnamon Apples

4 large baking apples
½ cup boiling water
3 tablespoons strawberry gelatin
¼ cup dark raisins
3 tablespoons dark brown sugar
2 teaspoons vanilla extract
2 teaspoons ground cinnamon

EQUIPMENT

Large covered skillet	Assorted cooking
Small skillet	utensils
Double boiler	Vegetable peeler
9x9-inch glass baking	Vegetable grater
dish	Apple corer
Large bowl	Whisk
Assorted kitchen knives	
Measuring cups and	
spoons	

COUNTDOWN

1 Assemble the ingredients and equipment
2 Do Step 1 of the *Fluffy Steamed White Rice*
3 Do Steps 1–4 of the *Cinnamon Apples*
4 Do Steps 1–2 of the *Carrot-Sprout Salad*
5 Do Steps 1–2 of the *Simply Stroganoff*
6 Do Step 2 of the *Fluffy Steamed White Rice*
7 Do Step 3 of the *Simply Stroganoff*

Simply Stroganoff

1 Peel and slice the onion. Wash, pat dry, trim and slice the mushrooms. Trim and chop the scallions. Chop the parsley. Slice the beef into thin strips across the grain.

2 Heat the oil in a large skillet. Add the onion slices and sauté until they are translucent, about 5 minutes. Add the meat, the sherry, the flour, the basil and the nutmeg and cook for 2 minutes. Add the mushrooms and cook for another 2 minutes. The meat should be very light pink inside. Fold in the sour cream, season to taste and heat through. Add the scallions, cover the skillet and remove it from the heat.

3 Sprinkle the stroganoff with the parsley.

Fluffy Steamed White Rice

1 Place the rice and the water in the top of a double boiler. Bring water in the bottom of the double boiler to a boil. Reduce the heat, cover and simmer until all the liquid is absorbed and the rice is tender, 30 to 40 minutes.

2 Fluff the rice before serving.

Carrot-Sprout Salad

1 In a large bowl, whisk together the mayonnaise, the vinegar, the soy sauce and the sugar. Season to taste.

2 Peel and grate the carrots. Add them to the bowl. Add the bean sprouts. Toss the carrots and the sprouts with the dressing and refrigerate until you are ready to serve.

Cinnamon Apples

1 Preheat the oven to 375°F.

2 Wash and core the apples, being careful not to cut through the bottoms. Prick through the skin several times with the tip of a sharp knife.

3 Bring $1/2$ cup of water to a boil in a small skillet. Add the gelatin and stir until it is dissolved.

4 Place the apples in a 9x9-inch glass baking dish. Put the raisins and the brown sugar in the apple cavities. Pour the gelatin mixture over the raisins, allowing it to drizzle down the sides. Top the apples with the vanilla and the cinnamon and bake for 20 minutes.

FRIDAY

Just for the Halibut

4 halibut steaks (1¹/₄ pounds)
1¹/₂ tablespoons regular or light olive oil
Seasoning to taste

SALSA:
¹/₂ pound fresh tomatoes
3 scallions (green onions)
2 tablespoons fresh dill (when chopped)
2 tablespoons fresh parsley (when chopped)
1 teaspoon red wine vinegar
2 teaspoons lime juice
¹/₄ teaspoon Tabasco sauce

Praise the Potatoes

12 small new white potatoes
2 tablespoons fresh parsley (when chopped)
1 can (14¹/₂ ounces) vegetable broth
¹/₂ cup dry white wine (or nonalcoholic white
    wine or additional vegetable broth)
2 tablespoons dry mustard
Seasoning to taste

Spunky Spinach

1 pound fresh spinach
2 medium shallots
4 tablespoons butter
¹/₂ teaspoon Worcestershire sauce
Seasoning to taste

Orange Caramel

4 large oranges
¹/₂ cup dark brown sugar
¹/₂ cup whipping cream
1 teaspoon vanilla extract
2 teaspoons butter

EQUIPMENT

2 large covered skillets	Assorted cooking
Medium saucepan	utensils
Small saucepan	Whisk
Assorted kitchen knives	Vegetable brush
Measuring cups and	Pastry brush
spoons	

COUNTDOWN

1 Assemble the ingredients and equipment
2 Do Step 1 of *Just for the Halibut*
3 Do Steps 1–2 of *Praise the Potatoes*
4 Do Step 1 of the *Spunky Spinach*
5 Do Steps 2–3 of *Just for the Halibut*
6 Do Step 1 of the *Orange Caramel*
7 Do Step 3 of *Praise the Potatoes*
8 Do Step 4 of *Just for the Halibut*
9 Do Step 2 of the *Spunky Spinach*
10 Do Step 5 of *Just for the Halibut*
11 Do Step 2 of the *Orange Caramel*

Just for the Halibut

1 Preheat the broiler.

2 Wipe the halibut steaks with damp paper towels. Lightly brush both sides of the steaks with the oil, and season to taste.

3 Chop the tomatoes. Trim and chop the scallions. Chop the dill. Chop the parsley. Combine the tomatoes, the scallions, the dill and the parsley in a small saucepan with the vinegar, the lime juice and the Tabasco sauce. Simmer the salsa until it is hot.

4 Broil the halibut steaks on one side for 4 to 5 minutes, depending on thickness. Turn the steaks and broil 2 to 3 minutes more.

5 Serve the halibut topped with the salsa.

Praise the Potatoes

1 Scrub and quarter the potatoes, but do not peel them. Chop the parsley.

2 In a large skillet, combine the broth, the wine and the mustard. Bring the mixture to a boil. Add the potatoes, cover the skillet, reduce the heat and cook for 25 minutes.

3 Remove the cover from the skillet and simmer the potatoes, uncovered, until the broth is reduced by half, about 10 minutes. Season to taste and sprinkle with the parsley.

Spunky Spinach

1 Rinse, dry and stem the spinach. Peel and chop the shallots.

2 Melt the butter in a large skillet. Add the shallots and toss them lightly for 1 minute. Add the spinach and the Worcestershire sauce and toss to combine thoroughly. Cover the skillet, reduce the heat and steam the spinach until it is crisp-tender, 1 to 2 minutes. Season to taste.

Orange Caramel

1 Peel and slice the oranges. Place them on individual dessert plates and refrigerate until you are ready to use.

2 Combine the brown sugar and the cream in a medium saucepan. Heat the mixture to boiling, whisking constantly. Reduce the heat and simmer, uncovered, until the sauce is slightly thickened, about 5 minutes. Remove the saucepan from the heat, whisk in the vanilla and the butter, and spoon the sauce over the orange slices.

JANUARY
WEEK TWO

WEEK AT A GLANCE

Monday

LEAVE ME ALONE STEW
EASY TO PLEASE SALAD
SOURDOUGH (OR ITALIAN) BREAD
CHERRY TORTE

Tuesday

FOO KING FLOUNDER
MOST EXCELLENT NOODLES
CHINA SLAW
IMPERIAL PINEAPPLE

Wednesday

GRANNY'S SAUSAGE & BEAN SOUP
MOUTHWATERING SALAD
PEASANT (OR OTHER HEARTY) BREAD
PUDDING PARFAIT

Thursday

PROVINCIAL POULET
FRENCH GREEN SALAD
BISCUITS SUR LA TABLE
OOH LA LA CHOCOLATE

Friday

CLAM-UP CAPELLINI
ZANY ZUCCHINI
GARLIC BREAD
NEAPOLITAN DELIGHT

CHECK STAPLES

- ☐ Butter
- ☐ Cornstarch
- ☐ Bisquick
- ☐ Granulated sugar
- ☐ Dark brown sugar
- ☐ Sweetened cocoa
- ☐ Marshmallow topping
- ☐ Regular or light vegetable oil
- ☐ Regular or light olive oil
- ☐ Sesame oil
- ☐ Red wine vinegar
- ☐ White wine vinegar
- ☐ Rice vinegar
- ☐ Lemon juice
- ☐ Worcestershire sauce
- ☐ Soy sauce
- ☐ Dijon mustard
- ☐ Regular or low-fat mayonnaise
- ☐ Honey
- ☐ Golden raisins
- ☐ Dried basil
- ☐ Bay leaves
- ☐ Cayenne pepper
- ☐ Dried snipped chives
- ☐ Whole cloves
- ☐ Italian seasoning
- ☐ Dry mustard
- ☐ Dried oregano
- ☐ Red pepper flakes
- ☐ Sesame seeds
- ☐ Dried tarragon
- ☐ Pepper
- ☐ Salt

SHOPPING NOTES

- If you are shopping once a week and cannot arrange to purchase fresh flounder on the day you plan to use it, you can purchase *not previously frozen* flounder and freeze it, placing it in the refrigerator to thaw the night before you are ready to use it. Or you can purchase *still frozen* flounder and keep it frozen until the night before you are ready to use it.
- If you are shopping once a week and cannot arrange to purchase fresh clams on the day you plan to use them, you can substitute 3 cans (10 ounces each) whole clams.

MEAT & POULTRY

2 pounds lean beef stew cubes (M)

3/4 pound regular, light or turkey Polish kielbasa sausage (W)

1 1/2 pounds boneless, skinless chicken breast (Th)

FISH

1 1/4 pounds flounder fillets (T)

48 hard-shelled clams (F)

FRESH PRODUCE

Vegetables

2 large baking potatoes (M)
2 medium zucchini (F)
2 medium carrots (M)
4 stalks celery—2 (M), 2 (Th)
1 large onion (M)
2 medium onions—1 (W), 1 (Th)
1 small onion (F)
1 small red onion (W)
5 scallions (green onions)— 2 (Th), 3 (F)
1 head garlic (M, T, W, F)
1 bunch parsley (M, F)
1 very small bunch dill (W)
1 medium head green cabbage (Th)
1 very small (or half) head green cabbage (T)
1 very small (or half) head red cabbage (T)
2 medium heads lettuce— 1 (W), 1 (Th)
1 medium cucumber (Th)
4 radishes (Th)

Fruit

1 large green apple (M)
2 medium bananas (M)
1/2 pound seedless red grapes (M)
1 pound fresh (or net weight canned) pineapple chunks (T)
1 medium orange (T)
1 pink grapefruit (M)

CANS, JARS & BOTTLES

Soup

1 can (14 1/2 ounces) beef broth—3/4 cup (M), 1 cup (W)

Vegetables

2 medium cans (14 1/2 ounces each) cut-up tomatoes— 1 (M), 1 (Th)
1 medium can (14 1/2 ounces) stewed tomatoes (W)
1 medium can (16 ounces) tomato puree (W)
1 medium can (15 ounces) tomato sauce (Th)
1 can (15 ounces) white beans (W)

Condiments

4 maraschino cherries for garnish (F)

Spreads

1 jar (12 ounces) cherry preserves (M)

Dessert Needs

1 can (21 ounces) cherry pie filling (M)

PACKAGED GOODS

Pasta, Rice & Grains

8 ounces multicolored pasta spirals (T)
16 ounces capellini (angel hair pasta) (F)
1 cup quick-cooking rice (Th)

Baked Goods

1 loaf sourdough or Italian bread (M)
1 loaf peasant (or other hearty) bread (W)
1 small loaf French bread (F)
1 chocolate loaf cake (Th)

Nuts & Seeds

1/2 cup sliced almonds (T)

Dessert & Baking Needs

1 small package (3.4 ounces) instant vanilla pudding mix (W)
1 small package (3.4 ounces) instant butterscotch pudding mix (W)
1/2 cup flaked coconut (M)
4 Hershey's Kisses for garnish (Th)

WINES & SPIRITS

1 tablespoon dry white wine (or nonalcoholic white wine or rice vinegar) (T)
1 cup + 2 tablespoons dry white wine (or nonalcoholic white wine or vegetable broth) (F)
3 tablespoons Kirsch liqueur (or nonalcoholic Italian cherry syrup) (M)
2 teaspoons Amaretto liqueur (or nonalcoholic Italian almond syrup) (T)

REFRIGERATED PRODUCTS

Dairy

1 quart whole milk (W)
2/3 cup buttermilk (Th)
1 cup whipping cream (M)
Whipped cream for garnish (W)
6 tablespoons regular or light sour cream—3 tablespoons (M), 3 tablespoons (T)

FROZEN GOODS

Vegetables

1 package (9 ounces) cut green beans (M)
1 package (9 ounces) chopped spinach (W)

Desserts

1 pound cake (M)
1 pint almond frozen yogurt (T)
1 pint chocolate frozen yogurt (Th)
1 pint chocolate ice cream (F)
1 pint vanilla ice cream (F)
1 pint strawberry ice cream (F)

MONDAY

Leave Me Alone Stew

1 large onion
4 whole cloves
2 large baking potatoes
2 medium carrots
2 stalks celery
2 cloves garlic
2 tablespoons parsley (when chopped)
2 pounds lean beef stew cubes
1 bay leaf
1 teaspoon Worcestershire sauce
3/4 cup beef broth
1 medium can (14 1/2 ounces) cut-up tomatoes
Seasoning to taste
1 package (9 ounces) frozen cut green beans
Cornstarch

Easy to Please Salad

1/2 pound seedless red grapes
1 large green apple
1 pink grapefruit
2 medium bananas
3 tablespoons lemon juice
3 tablespoons regular or light sour cream
1/2 cup flaked coconut

Sourdough (or Italian) Bread

Cherry Torte

1 frozen pound cake
1 jar (12 ounces) cherry preserves
3 tablespoons Kirsch liqueur (or nonalcoholic Italian cherry syrup)
1 can (21 ounces) cherry pie filling
1 cup whipping cream
2 tablespoons sugar

EQUIPMENT

Slow cooker
Electric hand mixer
Large bowl
Medium bowl
2 small bowls
Assorted kitchen knives

Measuring cups and spoons
Assorted cooking utensils
Vegetable peeler

COUNTDOWN

IN THE MORNING:
  Do Steps 1–4 of the *Leave Me Alone Stew*
BEFORE DINNER:
  1 Assemble the remaining ingredients and equipment
  2 Do Steps 1–3 of the *Cherry Torte*
  3 Do Steps 1–2 of the *Easy to Please Salad*
  4 Do Step 5 of the *Leave Me Alone Stew*
  5 Do Step 4 of the *Cherry Torte*

Leave Me Alone Stew

1 Peel and quarter the onion and stud the quarters with the cloves. Peel and cube the potatoes. Peel and slice the carrots. Trim and slice the celery. Peel and chop the garlic. Chop the parsley.

2 Combine the onion, the potatoes, the carrots, the celery, the garlic and the parsley in a slow cooker. Add the beef cubes and the bay leaf.

3 In a small bowl, combine the Worcestershire sauce with the beef broth and the tomatoes. Season the mixture to taste and pour it over the meat. Add the frozen beans, stirring to blend.

4 Set the slow cooker to cook on the low setting for 10 to 12 hours or on the high setting for 5 to 6 hours, depending on your schedule.

5 Before serving, you can thicken the stew with increments of 1 tablespoon cornstarch dissolved in 2 tablespoons cold water. Use chunks of fresh bread to sop up the stew.

Easy to Please Salad

1 Wash and separate the grapes. Core and chop the apple. Peel and section the grapefruit. Peel and slice the bananas.

2 In a large bowl, combine the lemon juice and the sour cream with the coconut. Add the fruit and toss it lightly with the dressing.

Cherry Torte

1 Set the pound cake out to thaw slightly, about 10 minutes. In a small bowl, combine the cherry preserves with 2 tablespoons of the Kirsch.

2 Cut the cake horizontally into 3 layers. Spread the bottom layer with half of the preserve mixture. Place the second layer on top and spread it with the remaining preserve mixture. Place the third layer on top and spread it with the cherry pie filling.

3 In a medium bowl, beat the cream, the sugar and the remaining Kirsch until stiff peaks form. Frost the sides of the torte generously with half the whipped cream mixture. Refrigerate the torte and the remaining whipped cream until you are ready to serve.

4 Slice the torte and pass the remaining whipped cream.

TUESDAY

Foo King Flounder

1 1/4 pounds flounder fillets
Seasoning to taste
2 tablespoons soy sauce
1 tablespoon honey
1 tablespoon dry mustard
1 tablespoon dry white wine (or nonalcoholic
    white wine or rice vinegar)
1 clove garlic
2 teaspoons sesame oil

Most Excellent Noodles

8 ounces multicolored pasta spirals
3 tablespoons butter
1/4 cup sesame seeds

China Slaw

2 tablespoons regular or low-fat mayonnaise
3 tablespoons regular or light sour cream
2 tablespoons rice vinegar
1 teaspoon lemon juice
Seasoning to taste
1 very small (or half) head green cabbage
1 very small (or half) head red cabbage
1 medium orange

Imperial Pineapple

1 pound fresh (or net weight canned)
    pineapple chunks
2 teaspoons Amaretto liqueur (or nonalcoholic
    Italian almond syrup)
1 pint almond (or similar) frozen yogurt
1/2 cup sliced almonds

EQUIPMENT

Large covered skillet	Assorted kitchen knives
Large saucepan	Measuring cups and
9x13-inch glass baking	spoons
dish	Assorted cooking
Cookie sheet	utensils
Large bowl	Vegetable grater
Medium bowl	Whisk
Small bowl	Ice cream scoop
Colander	

COUNTDOWN

1 Assemble the ingredients and equipment
2 Do Steps 1–2 of the *Most Excellent Noodles*
3 Do Steps 1–3 of the *China Slaw*
4 Do Step 1 of the *Imperial Pineapple*
5 Do Step 3 of the *Most Excellent Noodles*
6 Do Steps 1–2 of the *Foo King Flounder*
7 Do Step 4 of the *Most Excellent Noodles*
8 Do Steps 3–5 of the *Foo King Flounder*
9 Do Step 5 of the *Most Excellent Noodles*
10 Do Step 4 of the *China Slaw*
11 Do Step 2 of the *Imperial Pineapple*

Foo King Flounder

1 Wash the flounder fillets, pat them dry with paper towels and season them to taste.

2 Combine the soy sauce, the honey, the dry mustard and the wine in a 9x13-inch glass baking dish. Place the fish in the dish, coat the fillets with the marinade, and let them stand.

3 Peel and mince the garlic. Heat the sesame oil in a large skillet. Add the garlic and sauté it for 2 minutes.

4 Arrange the fish in the skillet in a single layer, reserving the marinade. Cook until the fish flakes easily with a fork, 2 to 3 minutes on each side.

5 Pour the reserved marinade over the fish and cook for 1 minute. Then cover the skillet and remove it from the heat until you are ready to serve.

Most Excellent Noodles

1 Preheat the oven to 350°F.

2 Bring water to a boil in a large saucepan.

3 Cook the pasta in the boiling water until it is almost tender, 7 to 9 minutes.

4 Drain the pasta and spread it out on a cookie sheet. Dot the pasta with the butter and bake for 10 minutes, turning once or twice, being careful not to let it burn.

5 Sprinkle the sesame seeds over the pasta and bake for 5 minutes more.

China Slaw

1 In a large bowl, whisk together the mayonnaise, the sour cream, the vinegar and the lemon juice. Season to taste.

2 Grate the cabbage into the bowl. Toss the cabbage with the dressing, cover the bowl and refrigerate until you are ready to use.

3 Peel and section the orange and refrigerate until you are ready to use.

4 Just before serving, toss the slaw with the orange sections.

Imperial Pineapple

1 Place the pineapple in a medium bowl. Toss it with the Amaretto and then refrigerate until you are ready to use.

2 Place scoops of frozen yogurt in individual dessert dishes. Top the yogurt with the pineapple mixture and sprinkle each serving with sliced almonds.

WEDNESDAY

Granny's Sausage & Bean Soup

1 package (9 ounces) frozen chopped spinach
3/4 pound regular, light or turkey Polish kielbasa sausage
1 medium onion
2 cloves garlic
2 tablespoons fresh dill (when chopped)
1 can (15 ounces) white beans
1 medium can (14 1/2 ounces) stewed tomatoes
1 medium can (16 ounces) tomato puree
1 cup water
1 cup beef broth
1/8 teaspoon cayenne pepper
Seasoning to taste

Mouthwatering Salad

1 medium head lettuce
1 small red onion
1 clove garlic
1 1/2 teaspoons Dijon mustard
1 teaspoon regular or low-fat mayonnaise
3 tablespoons regular or light olive oil
2 tablespoons red wine vinegar
1/4 teaspoon dried basil
1/2 teaspoon dried tarragon
Seasoning to taste

Peasant (or Other Hearty) Bread

Pudding Parfait

1 quart whole milk
1 small package (3.4 ounces) instant vanilla pudding mix
1 small package (3.4 ounces) instant butterscotch pudding mix
Whipped cream for garnish

EQUIPMENT

Electric hand mixer	Assorted kitchen knives
Dutch oven	Measuring cups and
Large bowl	spoons
3 medium bowls	Assorted cooking
Small bowl	utensils
Strainer	Whisk

COUNTDOWN

1 Assemble the ingredients and equipment
2 Do Step 1 of *Granny's Sausage & Bean Soup*
3 Do Steps 1–2 of the *Pudding Parfait*
4 Do Steps 2–4 of *Granny's Sausage & Bean Soup*
5 Do Steps 1–2 of the *Mouthwatering Salad*

Granny's Sausage & Bean Soup

1 Place the package of spinach in a medium bowl of warm water to partially thaw.

2 Chop the sausage. Peel and chop the onion. Peel and mince the garlic. Chop the dill.

3 Cook the sausage and the onion in a Dutch oven, stirring, until both are lightly browned, about 10 minutes. Drain off any excess fat.

4 Drain and rinse the beans and add them to the Dutch oven. Stir in the garlic, the stewed tomatoes, the tomato puree, the spinach, the water, the broth, the dill and the cayenne pepper. Season to taste. Bring the mixture to a boil, stirring occasionally. Then reduce the heat and simmer, uncovered, for 15 minutes. Serve the soup with chunks of fresh bread.

Mouthwatering Salad

1 Wash and dry the lettuce and tear it into bite-size pieces. Peel and slice the red onion. Place both ingredients in a large bowl.

2 Mince the garlic. In a small bowl, combine the mustard and the mayonnaise. Add the oil in a very thin stream, beating constantly with a whisk. The dressing should remain thick. Beat in the vinegar. The dressing should be thinner but still creamy. Add the basil and the tarragon and season to taste. Whisk the garlic into the dressing and drizzle the dressing over the lettuce and the onion.

Pudding Parfait

1 Pour 2 cups of the milk into a medium bowl. Add the vanilla pudding mix and beat with an electric hand mixer until well blended, 1 to 2 minutes. In a second bowl, repeat the process with the remaining milk and the butterscotch pudding mix.

2 Spoon a layer of vanilla pudding into the bottom of 4 parfait glasses. Add a layer of butterscotch pudding, then repeat. Top each serving with a dollop of whipped cream and refrigerate for at least 20 minutes.

THURSDAY

Provincial Poulet

1¹/₂ pounds boneless, skinless chicken breast
1 medium onion
1 medium head green cabbage
1 tablespoon regular or light vegetable oil
¹/₄ cup white wine vinegar
3 tablespoons dark brown sugar
1 medium can (15 ounces) tomato sauce
1 medium can (14¹/₂ ounces) cut-up tomatoes
1 cup quick-cooking rice
¹/₄ cup golden raisins
Seasoning to taste

French Green Salad

1 medium head lettuce
2 stalks celery
1 medium cucumber
2 scallions (green onions)
4 radishes
3 tablespoons regular or light vegetable oil
2 tablespoons white wine vinegar
1 tablespoon sugar
1 teaspoon Dijon mustard
Seasoning to taste

Biscuits sur la Table

2¹/₄ cups Bisquick
1 tablespoon dried snipped chives
1 tablespoon Italian seasoning
²/₃ cup buttermilk

Ooh La La Chocolate

1 chocolate loaf cake
1 pint chocolate frozen yogurt
2 tablespoons sweetened cocoa
4 Hershey's Kisses for garnish

EQUIPMENT

Large covered skillet
Large bowl
Medium bowl
Small bowl
Cookie sheet
Assorted kitchen knives
Measuring cups and
  spoons

Assorted cooking
  utensils
Vegetable grater
Whisk
Ice cream scoop
Sifters

COUNTDOWN

1 Assemble the ingredients and equipment
2 Do Step 1 of the *Biscuits sur la Table*
3 Do Steps 1–2 of the *French Green Salad*
4 Do Steps 1–3 of the *Provincial Poulet*
5 Do Steps 2–3 of the *Biscuits sur la Table*
6 Do Step 3 of the *French Green Salad*
7 Do Steps 1–2 of the *Ooh La La Chocolate*

Provincial Poulet

1 Cut the chicken into thin strips. Peel and chop the onion. Grate the cabbage.

2 Heat the oil in a large skillet. Add the chicken and the onion and cook, stirring, until the chicken turns white, 4 to 6 minutes.

3 Add the vinegar, the brown sugar, the tomato sauce, the tomatoes with their juice, the cabbage, the rice and the raisins. Season to taste. Bring the mixture to a boil, stirring. Then reduce the heat, cover the skillet and simmer until the cabbage and the rice are tender, about 20 minutes.

French Green Salad

1 Wash and dry the lettuce and tear it into bite-size pieces. Trim and slice the celery. Peel and slice the cucumber. Trim and slice the scallions. Trim and slice the radishes. Combine the ingredients in a large bowl.

2 In a small bowl, whisk together the oil, the vinegar, the sugar and the mustard until well blended. Season to taste.

3 Toss the salad with the dressing.

Biscuits sur la Table

1 Preheat the oven to 450°F.

2 In a medium bowl, combine the Bisquick, the chives and the Italian seasoning. Add the buttermilk and fold it in gently until the liquid is absorbed. Drop the mixture by tablespoon onto an ungreased cookie sheet.

3 Bake the biscuits until golden brown, 8 to 10 minutes.

Ooh La La Chocolate

1 Cut the cake into 8 slices and place 2 slices on each dessert plate.

2 Place scoops of frozen yogurt over the slices. Sprinkle the yogurt with the cocoa. Top each serving with a Hershey's Kiss.

FRIDAY

Clam-up Capellini

1 small onion
3 cloves garlic
2 tablespoons fresh parsley (when chopped)
2 tablespoons butter
48 hard-shelled clams (or 3 cans [10 ounces each] whole clams)
2 tablespoons regular or light olive oil
1 cup dry white wine (or nonalcoholic white wine or vegetable broth)
$1/4$ teaspoon red pepper flakes
1 teaspoon dried oregano
Seasoning to taste
16 ounces capellini (angel hair pasta)

Zany Zucchini

2 medium zucchini
3 scallions (green onions)
1 teaspoon regular or light olive oil
2 tablespoons dry white wine (or nonalcoholic white wine or vegetable broth)
Seasoning to taste

Garlic Bread

2 cloves garlic
3 tablespoons softened butter
1 small loaf French bread

Neapolitan Delight

1 pint chocolate ice cream
1 pint vanilla ice cream
1 pint strawberry ice cream
1 cup marshmallow topping
4 maraschino cherries for garnish

EQUIPMENT

Stockpot	Measuring cups and
Large covered	spoons
saucepan	Assorted cooking
Medium skillet	utensils
Small skillet	Vegetable brush
Small bowl	Ice cream scoop
Colander	Aluminum foil
Assorted kitchen knives	

COUNTDOWN

1 Assemble the ingredients and equipment
2 Do Steps 1–2 of the *Garlic Bread*
3 Do Step 1 of the *Clam-up Capellini*
4 Do Step 1 of the *Zany Zucchini*
5 Do Steps 2–5 of the *Clam-up Capellini*
6 Do Step 2 of the *Zany Zucchini*
7 Do Steps 6–7 of the *Clam-up Capellini*
8 Do Steps 1–2 of the *Neapolitan Delight*

Clam-up Capellini

1 Bring water to a boil in a stockpot.

2 Peel and mince the onion. Peel and mince the garlic. Chop the parsley.

3 Melt the butter in a small skillet. Sauté the onion and the garlic until both are soft, 3 to 4 minutes.

4 Scrub the fresh clams, discarding any open shells that do not close when tapped. In a large saucepan, heat the olive oil, the wine, the red pepper flakes and the oregano. Season to taste. Add the clams, turning to coat well. Cover the saucepan and cook until the clams open, 4 to 5 minutes. Discard any clams that do not open. (If you are using canned clams, combine them, undrained, with the other ingredients and heat through.)

5 Cook the capellini in the stockpot until it is almost tender, 2 to 3 minutes if you are using fresh pasta and 4 to 5 minutes if you are using dried pasta.

6 Add the onion, the garlic and the parsley to the clams. Stir to combine.

7 Drain the pasta. Toss with the clam sauce.

Zany Zucchini

1 Scrub the zucchini and cut it into $1/4$-inch rounds. Trim and chop the scallions.

2 Heat the oil in a medium skillet. Sauté the zucchini and the scallions for 3 minutes. Add the wine, season to taste, cover the skillet, remove it from the heat and let the zucchini steam for 2 minutes.

Garlic Bread

1 Preheat the oven to 325°F.

2 Peel and mash the garlic. In a small bowl, combine the garlic with the softened butter. Slice the French loaf in half lengthwise. Spread the garlic butter on the cut sides of the bread. Reassemble the loaf and wrap it in aluminum foil. Heat the bread in the oven until you are ready to serve, at least 15 minutes.

Neapolitan Delight

1 Place a small scoop each of chocolate, vanilla and strawberry ice cream in individual dessert bowls.

2 Top each serving with a generous amount of marshmallow topping and a maraschino cherry.

JANUARY
WEEK THREE

WEEK AT A GLANCE

Monday

LAMB ON THE LAM
POSSE PASTA
STAND-OFF SALAD
WHIPPED COCOA CAKE

Tuesday

BRANDY CHICKEN
BETTER BRUSSELS SPROUTS
SMALL SALAD
CITRUS PUDDING

Wednesday

CORNY CHOWDER
TERRIFIC TUNA SALAD
ROSEMARY'S BREAD
COCONUT DREAMS

Thursday

SPAGHETTI SAUSAGE SURPRISE
TICKLED PINK SALAD
COOL CUSTARD

Friday

BLESS MY SOLE
HEAVENLY RICE
PARADISE PLUMS

CHECK STAPLES

- ☐ Butter
- ☐ Flour
- ☐ Cornstarch
- ☐ Granulated sugar
- ☐ Dark brown sugar
- ☐ Sweetened cocoa
- ☐ Long-grain white rice
- ☐ Regular or light vegetable oil
- ☐ Regular or light olive oil
- ☐ Red wine vinegar
- ☐ White wine vinegar
- ☐ Lemon juice
- ☐ Grated fresh lemon peel
- ☐ Worcestershire sauce
- ☐ Kitchen Bouquet
- ☐ Dijon mustard
- ☐ Regular or low-fat mayonnaise
- ☐ Grated Parmesan cheese
- ☐ Seasoned bread crumbs
- ☐ Ground allspice
- ☐ Dried basil
- ☐ Celery seeds
- ☐ Ground cinnamon
- ☐ Dried marjoram
- ☐ Dry mustard
- ☐ Ground nutmeg
- ☐ Onion powder
- ☐ Paprika
- ☐ Dried rosemary
- ☐ Dried tarragon
- ☐ Pepper
- ☐ Salt
- ☐ Vanilla extract

SHOPPING NOTE

● If you are shopping once a week and cannot arrange to purchase fresh sole on the day you plan to use it, you can purchase *not previously frozen* sole and freeze it, placing it in the refrigerator to thaw the night before you are ready to use it. Or you can purchase *still frozen* sole and keep it frozen until the night before you are ready to use it.

MEAT & POULTRY

4 large lean lamb chops
($3/4$-inch thick) (M)
1 pound sweet Italian pork or
turkey sausage (Th)
3 pounds chicken thighs (T)

FISH

4 sole fillets ($1^1/4$ pounds) (F)

FRESH PRODUCE

Vegetables

1 pound Brussels sprouts (T)
1 pound zucchini (Th)
4 large mushrooms (Th)
1 stalk celery (M)
3 small onions—1 (T), 1 (Th), 1 (F)
2 small red onions—1 (T), 1 (W)
5 scallions (green onions)—
4 (W), 1 (F)
1 head garlic (M-F)
1 bunch parsley (W, Th, F)
3 medium heads lettuce—
1 (T), 1 (W), 1 (Th)
$1^3/4$ pounds tomatoes—
$1/2$ pound (W), $1^1/4$ pounds
(Th)
1 medium red bell pepper (W)
1 small bunch radishes (W)

Fruit

1 large tart green apple (M)
1 large pear (M)
1 large melon (M)
3 medium bananas (W)
$1/2$ pound seedless red grapes (M)
1 medium orange (M)
1 large pink grapefruit (Th)

CANS, JARS & BOTTLES

Soup

1 can ($10^3/4$ ounces) chicken
broth—$1/4$ cup (T), 1 cup (W)
1 can ($14^1/2$ ounces) vegetable
broth (F)

1 can ($10^3/4$ ounces) cream of
potato soup (W)

Vegetables

1 can ($14^1/2$ ounces) stewed
tomatoes—1 cup (M), $3/4$ cup
(Th)
1 can (15 ounces) cream-style
corn (W)
1 can (11 ounces) whole kernel
corn (W)

Fish

1 large can (12 ounces) solid
white tuna (W)
1 can (2 ounces) flat anchovy
fillets (W)
1 can ($4^1/4$ ounces) small
cooked shrimp (F)

Oriental Products

1 can (8 ounces) sliced water
chestnuts (T)

Fruit

1 can (11 ounces) mandarin
oranges (T)
1 large can (30 ounces) purple
plums in heavy syrup (F)

Condiments

2 tablespoons capers (W)
1 small jar (2 ounces) diced
pimiento (M)

PACKAGED GOODS

Pasta, Rice & Grains

12 ounces rotini (M)
16 ounces spaghetti (Th)

Baked Goods

1 small loaf French bread (W)

Nuts & Seeds

$1/2$ cup sliced almonds (M)

Dessert & Baking Needs

1 small package (3.4 ounces)
instant lemon pudding
mix (T)
$1^1/2$ cups flaked coconut (W)

WINES & SPIRITS

$1/4$ cup dry white wine (or
nonalcoholic white wine or
chicken broth) (T)
$1/2$ cup dry white wine (or
nonalcoholic white wine or
clam juice) (F)
3 tablespoons dry red wine (or
nonalcoholic red wine or
beef broth) (Th)
$1/4$ cup brandy (or chicken
broth) (T)

REFRIGERATED PRODUCTS

Dairy

$3^3/4$ cups whole milk—$1^1/4$ cups
(T), $2^1/2$ cups (Th)
2 cups regular or low-fat
milk (W)
$3/4$ cup whipping cream—
$1/2$ cup (M), $1/4$ cup (T)
$1^1/4$ cups regular or light sour
cream—$3/4$ cup (T),
$1/2$ cup (W)
5 eggs   2 (W), 3 (Th)

Deli

4 slices bacon (W)

FROZEN GOODS

Vegetables

1 package (9 ounces) chopped
asparagus (M)
1 package (9 ounces) green
beans (W)
1 package (9 ounces) peas and
carrots (F)

Desserts

1 pound cake (M)

MONDAY

Lamb on the Lam

1 package (9 ounces) frozen chopped
    asparagus
4 large lean lamb chops ($^3/_4$-inch thick)
1 tablespoon Kitchen Bouquet
Seasoning to taste
1 stalk celery
1 tablespoon butter
1 cup stewed tomatoes*
$^1/_2$ teaspoon dried rosemary
2 teaspoons cornstarch
1 tablespoon water
$^1/_4$ cup grated Parmesan cheese

Posse Pasta

1 clove garlic
1 small jar (2 ounces) diced pimiento
12 ounces rotini
3 tablespoons regular or light olive oil
$1^1/_2$ teaspoons paprika

Stand-off Salad

2 tablespoons sugar
2 tablespoons lemon juice
1 tablespoon water
$^1/_4$ teaspoon celery seeds
$^1/_4$ teaspoon dry mustard
$^1/_3$ cup regular or light vegetable oil
Seasoning to taste
1 large melon
1 large tart green apple
1 large pear
$^1/_2$ pound seedless red grapes
1 medium orange

*Reserve the balance of the can for use on Thursday.

Whipped Cocoa Cake

1 frozen pound cake
$^1/_2$ cup whipping cream
$^1/_2$ cup sweetened cocoa
$^1/_2$ cup sliced almonds

EQUIPMENT

Electric hand mixer	Assorted kitchen knives
Large saucepan	Measuring cups and
Medium saucepan	spoons
Large bowl	Assorted cooking
2 medium bowls	utensils
2 small bowls	Whisk
Colander	Pastry brush

COUNTDOWN

1 Assemble the ingredients and equipment
2 Do Step 1 of the *Whipped Cocoa Cake*
3 Do Step 1 of the *Lamb on the Lam*
4 Do Step 1 of the *Posse Pasta*
5 Do Steps 2–3 of the *Whipped Cocoa Cake*
6 Do Steps 1–2 of the *Stand-off Salad*
7 Do Step 2 of the *Posse Pasta*
8 Do Steps 2–5 of the *Lamb on the Lam*
9 Do Step 3 of the *Posse Pasta*
10 Do Step 6 of the *Lamb on the Lam*
11 Do Step 3 of the *Stand-off Salad*
12 Do Step 7 of the *Lamb on the Lam*

Lamb on the Lam

1 Preheat the broiler. Set the package of asparagus in a medium bowl of hot water to thaw.

2 Lightly brush the lamb chops with Kitchen Bouquet and place them on the rack of a broiler pan. Season to taste. Broil the chops, 3 or 4 inches from the heat, turning once, until they reach the desired doneness (5 to 7 minutes total time for rare).

3 Trim and slice the celery on the bias into 1/2-inch pieces.

4 Melt the butter in a medium saucepan and cook the celery until it is tender but not brown, about 5 minutes.

5 Stir in the undrained tomatoes and the rosemary. Season to taste. Bring the mixture to a boil. Stir in the asparagus, return the mixture to a boil, then reduce the heat and simmer for 5 minutes.

6 In a small bowl, dissolve the cornstarch in the water and stir it into the tomato mixture. Cook and stir until the sauce is thick and begins to bubble. Then cook, stirring, for 2 minutes more.

7 Spoon the sauce over the lamb chops. Sprinkle the tops with Parmesan cheese.

Posse Pasta

1 Bring water to a boil in a large saucepan. Peel and mince the garlic. Drain the pimientos.

2 Cook the pasta in the boiling water until it is almost tender, 8 to 10 minutes.

3 Drain the pasta. Heat the oil in the same saucepan. Sauté the garlic until it is golden, about 2 minutes. Return the pasta and add the pimiento and the paprika. Toss to combine.

Stand-off Salad

1 In a small bowl, combine the sugar, the lemon juice, the water, the celery seeds and the dry mustard. Whisk until the sugar dissolves. Gradually add the vegetable oil, whisking until the mixture is thick. Season to taste. Cover the bowl and refrigerate until you are ready to use.

2 Chunk the fresh fruit into 1/2-inch cubes. Place the fruit in a large bowl and refrigerate until you are ready to serve.

3 Top the fruit with the dressing, tossing lightly to coat.

Whipped Cocoa Cake

1 Set the pound cake out to partially thaw, about 15 minutes.

2 In a medium bowl, whip the cream and the cocoa until stiff peaks form.

3 Cut the cake into 8 slices. Spoon the whipped cream over the slices, and top them with the sliced almonds. Refrigerate until you are ready to serve.

TUESDAY

Brandy Chicken

1 small onion
1 clove garlic
3 tablespoons butter
3 pounds chicken thighs
Seasoning to taste
3 tablespoons flour
$1/4$ cup dry white wine (or nonalcoholic white
   wine or additional chicken broth)
$1/4$ cup chicken broth*
$1/4$ cup brandy (or additional chicken broth)
$1/4$ cup whipping cream
2 teaspoons dried tarragon
$1/2$ teaspoon Dijon mustard
$1/8$ teaspoon paprika
$1/4$ teaspoon ground nutmeg

Better Brussels Sprouts

1 pound Brussels sprouts
1 can (8 ounces) sliced water chestnuts
1 tablespoon butter
$1/8$ teaspoon ground allspice
Seasoning to taste

Small Salad

1 medium head lettuce
1 small red onion
3 teaspoons regular or light olive oil
2 teaspoons red wine vinegar
$1/4$ teaspoon dried tarragon
Seasoning to taste

Citrus Pudding

$1^1/4$ cups whole milk
1 small package (3.4 ounces) instant lemon
   pudding mix
$3/4$ cup regular or light sour cream
1 can (11 ounces) mandarin oranges

EQUIPMENT

Electric hand mixer	Assorted kitchen knives
Large ovenproof skillet	Measuring cups and
Large saucepan	spoons
Small saucepan	Assorted cooking
Medium bowl	utensils
2 small bowls	Whisk

COUNTDOWN

1 Assemble the ingredients and equipment
2 Do Steps 1–4 of the *Brandy Chicken*
3 Do Steps 1–3 of the *Better Brussels Sprouts*
4 Do Steps 1–2 of the *Citrus Pudding*
5 Do Steps 1–2 of the *Small Salad*
6 Do Step 4 of the *Better Brussels Sprouts*
7 Do Steps 5–6 of the *Brandy Chicken*
8 Do Step 5 of the *Better Brussels Sprouts*
9 Do Step 3 of the *Small Salad*
10 Do Step 7 of the *Brandy Chicken*

*Reserve the balance of the can for use on Wednesday.

Brandy Chicken

1 Preheat the oven to 425°F. Peel and thinly slice the onion. Peel and mince the garlic.

2 Melt the butter in a large ovenproof skillet. Sauté the onion and the garlic until both are soft, about 5 minutes.

3 Coat each chicken thigh by turning it in the melted butter. Season to taste.

4 Arrange the thighs in the skillet and bake them, occasionally basting with the drippings, until they are done, about 30 minutes.

5 Remove the chicken thighs and keep them warm.

6 Add the flour to the pan drippings and cook until well blended. Add the wine, the broth and the brandy. Bring the mixture to a boil and cook, stirring, until the alcohol is burned off and the liquid begins to reduce, about 5 minutes.

7 In a small bowl, combine the cream, the tarragon, the mustard, the paprika and the nutmeg. Add the mixture to the skillet and cook, stirring occasionally, until the sauce is thickened. Return the chicken to the skillet and coat each piece with the sauce.

Better Brussels Sprouts

1 Bring water to a boil in a large saucepan.

2 Wash, trim and stem the Brussels sprouts. If they are large, cut them in half before cooking.

3 Simmer the sprouts in the boiling water until they are crisp-tender, 8 to 10 minutes.

4 Drain the sprouts well. Drain the water chestnuts.

5 Melt the butter in the saucepan. Mix in the allspice. Season to taste. Add the Brussels sprouts and the water chestnuts to the saucepan and toss them in the butter to coat and heat through.

Small Salad

1 Wash and dry the lettuce, tear it into bite-size pieces and divide it among individual salad plates. Peel and thinly slice the red onion and arrange the slices on the lettuce.

2 In a small bowl, whisk together the oil, the vinegar and the tarragon. Season to taste.

3 Drizzle the dressing over the salad.

Citrus Pudding

1 In a medium bowl, combine the milk and the pudding mix. Beat until the mixture is well blended, about 2 minutes. Fold in the sour cream.

2 Drain the mandarin oranges, reserving 4 sections. Fold the remainder into the pudding mixture. Divide the pudding among 4 dessert dishes and top each serving with a reserved orange section. Refrigerate for at least 20 minutes.

WEDNESDAY

Corny Chowder

4 slices bacon
4 scallions (green onions)
1 can (10³/₄ ounces) cream of potato soup
1 can (15 ounces) cream-style corn
1 can (11 ounces) whole kernel corn
1 cup chicken broth reserved from Tuesday
2 cups whole or low-fat milk
2 teaspoons Worcestershire sauce
¹/₂ teaspoon celery seeds
Seasoning to taste
¹/₄ teaspoon paprika

Terrific Tuna Salad

2 eggs
1 large can (12 ounces) solid white tuna
1 can (2 ounces) flat anchovy fillets
1 clove garlic
1 tablespoon fresh parsley (when chopped)
2 tablespoons capers
¹/₃ cup regular or light olive oil
¹/₄ cup white wine vinegar
Seasoning to taste
1 package (9 ounces) frozen green beans
1 medium head lettuce
1 small red onion
1 medium red bell pepper
1 small bunch radishes
¹/₂ pound fresh tomatoes

Rosemary's Bread

1 tablespoon fresh parsley (when chopped)
1 small loaf French bread
2 tablespoons butter
¹/₂ teaspoon dried rosemary
¹/₂ teaspoon onion powder

Coconut Dreams

2 tablespoons lemon juice
¹/₂ cup regular or light sour cream
1¹/₂ cups flaked coconut
3 medium bananas

EQUIPMENT

Large saucepan	Assorted kitchen knives
2 small saucepans	Measuring cups and
Small skillet	spoons
Large bowl	Assorted cooking
Medium bowl	utensils
3 shallow bowls	Aluminum foil

COUNTDOWN

1 Assemble the ingredients and equipment
2 Do Step 1 of the *Rosemary's Bread*
3 Do Step 1 of the *Terrific Tuna Salad*
4 Do Steps 1–3 of the *Corny Chowder*
5 Do Step 2 of the *Terrific Tuna Salad*
6 Do Step 2 of the *Rosemary's Bread*
7 Do Step 3 of the *Terrific Tuna Salad*
8 Do Step 3 of the *Rosemary's Bread*
9 Do Steps 4–6 of the *Terrific Tuna Salad*
10 Do Steps 1–2 of the *Coconut Dreams*
11 Do Steps 7–8 of the *Terrific Tuna Salad*
12 Do Step 4 of the *Corny Chowder*

Corny Chowder

1 Dice the bacon. Sauté it in a small skillet until it is crisp and drain on a paper towel.

2 Trim and slice the scallions.

3 In a large saucepan, combine the cream of potato soup, the cream-style corn, the undrained whole kernel corn, the broth, the milk, the Worcestershire sauce, the scallions and the celery seeds. Season to taste. Bring the mixture to a boil, then reduce the heat and simmer for 10 minutes.

4 Just before serving the soup, stir in the bacon pieces and sprinkle with the paprika.

Terrific Tuna Salad

1 Cover the eggs with water in a small saucepan and bring it to a boil. Hard-cook the eggs, 10 to 12 minutes.

2 Drain and flake the tuna. Chop the anchovies. Peel and mince the garlic. Chop the parsley.

3 Combine the tuna, the anchovies, the capers, the garlic and the parsley in a medium bowl. Add the olive oil and the vinegar. Season to taste. Combine the ingredients and let the mixture stand for 15 minutes.

4 Remove the hard-cooked eggs from the saucepan and chill them in the freezer for 10 minutes. Cook the green beans in the egg water according to package directions.

5 Wash, dry and shred the lettuce. Peel and thinly slice the red onion. Seed and slice the bell pepper. Trim and slice the radishes. Chop the tomatoes. Combine the ingredients in a large bowl.

6 Drain the beans and let them chill in the refrigerator until you are ready to use.

7 Slice the hard-cooked eggs.

8 Toss the beans and one sliced egg with the salad. Top the salad with the tuna mixture and toss lightly. Garnish the salad with the second sliced egg.

Rosemary's Bread

1 Preheat the oven to 350°F.

2 Chop the parsley. Slice the French bread in half and set it on a sheet of aluminum foil, cut sides up.

3 In a small saucepan, melt the butter and mix in the rosemary, the onion powder and the parsley. Brush the cut sides of the bread with the butter mixture, and bake until the bread is hot and crispy, about 10 minutes.

Coconut Dreams

1 Place the lemon juice in one shallow bowl. Place the sour cream in a second shallow bowl. Place the coconut in a third shallow bowl.

2 Peel the bananas and cut them into 1/2-inch chunks. Dip the banana chunks in the lemon juice, then dip them in the sour cream, then roll them in the coconut. Leave the bananas in the coconut bowl and refrigerate until you are ready to serve.

THURSDAY

Spaghetti Sausage Surprise

1 small onion
1 clove garlic
1 tablespoon fresh parsley (when chopped)
1¼ pounds fresh tomatoes
⅓ cup regular or light olive oil
2 tablespoons butter
¾ cup stewed tomatoes reserved from Monday
¼ teaspoon dried marjoram
¼ teaspoon dried basil
Seasoning to taste
1 pound fresh zucchini
4 large mushrooms
1 pound sweet Italian pork or turkey sausage
¼ cup regular or light vegetable oil
¼ teaspoon ground nutmeg
3 tablespoons dry red wine (or nonalcoholic
    red wine or beef broth)
1 pound spaghetti
¼ cup grated Parmesan cheese

Tickled Pink Salad

1 medium head lettuce
1 large pink grapefruit
3 tablespoons regular or low-fat mayonnaise
1 teaspoon lemon juice
1 teaspoon Dijon mustard
1 teaspoon dark brown sugar
Seasoning to taste

Cool Custard

2½ cups whole milk
3 eggs
½ cup sugar
1 teaspoon vanilla extract
¼ teaspoon salt
2 tablespoons ground cinnamon

EQUIPMENT

Stockpot	Colander
Large covered skillet	Assorted kitchen knives
Medium saucepan	Measuring cups and
Small saucepan	spoons
1½-quart casserole	Assorted cooking
9x13-inch baking pan	utensils
Large bowl	Whisk
Small bowl	

COUNTDOWN

1 Assemble the ingredients and equipment
2 Do Step 1 of the *Cool Custard*
3 Do Steps 1–2 of the *Spaghetti Sausage Surprise*
4 Do Steps 2–3 of the *Cool Custard*
5 Do Steps 1–2 of the *Tickled Pink Salad*
6 Do Steps 3–8 of the *Spaghetti Sausage Surprise*
7 Do Step 3 of the *Tickled Pink Salad*
8 Do Step 9 of the *Spaghetti Sausage Surprise*

Spaghetti Sausage Surprise

1 Peel and dice the onion. Peel and mince the garlic. Chop the parsley. Chop the tomatoes.

2 Heat half of the olive oil in a medium saucepan. Add the butter to the oil, add the onion, the garlic and the parsley and sauté for 5 minutes. Add the chopped tomatoes and the stewed tomatoes to the saucepan and mix well. Add the marjoram and the basil. Season to taste. Reduce the heat and simmer the mixture, stirring occasionally, for 25 minutes.

3 Bring water to a boil in a stockpot.

4 Slice the zucchini into $1/8$-inch rounds. Rinse, pat dry, trim and slice the mushrooms. Remove the sausage meat from its casings.

5 Heat the vegetable oil in a large skillet and sauté the zucchini until golden brown, about 4 minutes. Drain the zucchini on a paper towel and wipe out the skillet.

6 Heat the remaining olive oil in the skillet and sauté the sausage meat until it browns, stirring to crumble it into small pieces. Add the mushrooms and the nutmeg. Season to taste. Mix gently. Add the wine and cook until the alcohol evaporates, about 5 minutes.

7 Cook the spaghetti in the stockpot until it is almost tender, 3 to 4 minutes if you are using fresh pasta and 6 to 7 minutes if you are using dried pasta.

8 Add the tomato mixture to the skillet and blend well. Cover the skillet, reduce the heat and simmer the sauce for 4 minutes. Add the zucchini and simmer for 1 minute more.

9 Drain the pasta, return it to the stockpot, toss it with the sauce and sprinkle with the Parmesan cheese.

Tickled Pink Salad

1 Wash and dry the lettuce and tear it into bite-size pieces. Peel and section the grapefruit. Arrange the grapefruit over the lettuce on individual salad plates.

2 In a small bowl, whisk together the mayonnaise, the lemon juice, the mustard and the brown sugar. Season to taste.

3 Spoon the dressing over the lettuce and the grapefruit.

Cool Custard

1 Preheat the oven to 350°F.

2 Scald the milk in a small saucepan until tiny bubbles form around the edge. In a large bowl, combine the eggs, the sugar, the vanilla and the salt. Whisk until the mixture is well blended. Slowly add the milk and mix well. Pour the mixture into a $1\frac{1}{2}$-quart casserole and sprinkle it with the cinnamon.

3 Place 1 inch of hot water in a 9x13-inch baking pan. Stand the casserole carefully in the water. Bake the custard until a knife comes out cleanly when inserted in its center, 35 to 40 minutes.

FRIDAY

Bless My Sole

1 small onion
2 cloves garlic
4 sole fillets (1¼ pounds)
Seasoning to taste
3 tablespoons butter
1 can (4¼ ounces) small cooked shrimp
4 teaspoons seasoned bread crumbs
1 tablespoon lemon juice
½ cup dry white wine (or nonalcoholic white
    wine or clam juice)
1 tablespoon flour

Heavenly Rice

1 package (9 ounces) frozen peas and carrots
1 scallion (green onion)
2 tablespoons fresh parsley (when chopped)
1 cup long-grain white rice
1 can (14½ ounces) vegetable broth
½ cup water

Paradise Plums

1 large can (30 ounces) purple plums in heavy
    syrup
2 tablespoons cornstarch
½ teaspoon salt
½ teaspoon ground cinnamon
⅛ teaspoon ground allspice
2 tablespoons lemon juice
1 tablespoon butter
1 tablespoon grated fresh lemon peel

EQUIPMENT

9x9-inch glass baking   Assorted kitchen knives
  dish   Measuring cups and
Medium covered   spoons
  saucepan   Assorted cooking
2 small saucepans   utensils
Small bowl   Whisk
Strainer

COUNTDOWN

1 Assemble the ingredients and equipment
2 Do Steps 1–2 of the *Heavenly Rice*
3 Do Steps 1–5 of the *Bless My Sole*
4 Do Steps 1–2 of the *Paradise Plums*
5 Do Steps 6–7 of the *Bless My Sole*
6 Do Step 3 of the *Heavenly Rice*
7 Do Step 3 of the *Paradise Plums*

Bless My Sole

1 Preheat the oven to 350°F. Grease a 9x9-inch glass baking dish.

2 Peel and mince the onion, reserving 2 tablespoons for the sauce. Peel and mince the garlic, reserving 1 clove for the sauce. Rinse the fish fillets and pat them dry with paper towels. Season to taste.

3 Melt 1 tablespoon of the butter in a small saucepan. Drain the shrimp and add them to the butter. Add the remaining onion, the remaining garlic and the bread crumbs.

4 Place one-fourth of the mixture at the wide end of each fillet. Roll up the fillets and place them in the baking dish, seam side down.

5 In a small bowl, combine the lemon juice, the wine, the reserved onion and the reserved garlic. Pour the mixture over the fillets. Bake until the fish is just opaque, but still moist, 20 to 25 minutes.

6 Remove the fish and keep it warm. Reserve the cooking juices.

7 Melt the remaining butter in the saucepan. Whisk in the flour and cook until the mixture is bubbly. Gradually stir in the reserved cooking juices and whisk until the mixture is thickened. Spoon the sauce over the fish.

Heavenly Rice

1 Set the package of frozen vegetables out to thaw. Trim and chop the scallion. Chop the parsley.

2 Bring the rice, the broth and the water to a boil in a medium saucepan. Add the scallion and the parsley. Cover the saucepan, reduce the heat and simmer the rice for 15 minutes. Add the vegetables, stir to combine, re-cover the pan and simmer for another 10 minutes.

3 Fluff the rice before serving

Paradise Plums

1 Drain the plums, reserving the syrup.

2 In a small saucepan, combine the cornstarch, the salt, the cinnamon, the allspice and the reserved plum syrup. Cook, stirring, until the mixture thickens and bubbles, about 3 minutes. Add the lemon juice and the butter, and stir until well blended. Heat the mixture through and then cover the pan and remove it from the burner.

3 Divide the plums among individual dessert dishes. Drizzle each serving with the warm sauce and sprinkle with the lemon peel.

JANUARY
WEEK FOUR

WEEK AT A GLANCE

Monday

PORK KABOB-BOBS
FLUFFY STEAMED WHITE RICE
SUFFERIN' SUCCOTASH
APPLE CRISPIES

Tuesday

KISS MY BASS
AND THE BEET GOES ON
A PEELING SALAD
APRICOT AFTERTHOUGHT

Wednesday

TOUCHDOWN CHICKEN
GOALPOSTS
SUPER BOWL SALAD
PUNTIN' PUDDIN'

Thursday

SUNDOWNER SOUP
A PEAR TO REMEMBER
BEYOND BISCUITS
CHOCO-ROO

Friday

PUFFED-UP PASTA SHELLS
BRAGGADOCIO SALAD
PEACH SPARKLERS

CHECK STAPLES

- ☐ Butter
- ☐ Flour
- ☐ Cornstarch
- ☐ Granulated sugar
- ☐ Dark brown sugar
- ☐ Confectioners' sugar
- ☐ Long-grain white rice
- ☐ Regular or light vegetable oil
- ☐ Regular or light olive oil
- ☐ Sesame oil
- ☐ White wine vinegar
- ☐ Apple cider vinegar
- ☐ Rice vinegar
- ☐ Lemon juice
- ☐ Grated fresh lemon peel
- ☐ Grated fresh orange peel
- ☐ Soy sauce
- ☐ Dijon mustard
- ☐ Honey
- ☐ Dark raisins
- ☐ Grated Parmesan cheese
- ☐ Dried basil
- ☐ Ground cinnamon
- ☐ Curry powder
- ☐ Ground ginger
- ☐ Dried mint
- ☐ Ground nutmeg
- ☐ Italian seasoning
- ☐ Paprika
- ☐ Poppy seeds
- ☐ Seasoning salt
- ☐ Sesame seeds
- ☐ Dried thyme
- ☐ Pepper
- ☐ Salt
- ☐ Vanilla extract

SHOPPING NOTE

● If you are shopping once a week and cannot arrange to purchase fresh sole on the day you plan to use it, you can purchase *not previously frozen* sole and freeze it, placing it in the refrigerator to thaw the night before you are ready to use it. Or you can purchase *still frozen* sole and keep it frozen until the night before you are ready to use it.

MEAT & POULTRY

1¼ pounds lean boneless pork loin (M)
1 pound lean ground beef (Th)
4 boneless, skinless chicken breast halves (W)

FISH

1¼ pounds bass fillets (T)

FRESH PRODUCE

Vegetables

1 medium zucchini (W)
1 pound spinach (F)
1 medium bunch Swiss chard (or spinach) (Th)
1 pound mushrooms— ½ pound (T), ½ pound (F)
7 medium carrots—2 (W), 5 (Th)
3 stalks celery (Th)
1 large onion (M)
2 medium onions—1 (T), 1 (Th)
2 small onions—1 (M), 1 (T)
1 small red onion (W)
5 scallions (green onions)— 5 (T), 3 (F)
1 head garlic (M, T, W, F)
1 bunch parsley (T, F)
1 large head lettuce (W, Th)
1 medium head lettuce (T)
1 ripe avocado (W)
1 large tomato (F)
2 medium cucumbers— 1 (T), 1 (F)
1 large green bell pepper (M)
1 large red bell pepper (M)

Fruit

4 large red apples (M)
1 large green apple (T)
2 large pears (Th)
1 pound fresh (or net weight canned) pineapple chunks (M)
1 large orange (W)

CANS, JARS & BOTTLES

Soup

1 can (10¾ ounces) beef consommé (W)
1 can (14½ ounces) beef broth (Th)

Vegetables

1 medium can (15 ounces) julienne beets (T)
1 large can (28 ounces) crushed tomatoes with puree (Th)
1 medium can (15 ounces) tomato sauce (F)

Oriental Products

1 can (8 ounces) whole water chestnuts (M)

Fruit

1 large can (29 ounces) sliced peaches (F)

Spreads

1 jar (12 ounces) apricot preserves (T)

PACKAGED GOODS

Pasta, Rice & Grains

1 package (12 ounces) jumbo pasta shells (F)
¾ cup quick-cooking oatmeal (M)

Baked Goods

1 angel food loaf cake (T)
1 package (3 ounces) ladyfingers (or angel food cake) (Th)

Fruits

8 large dried apricots (T)

Nuts & Seeds

½ cup walnut pieces (Th)
½ cup sliced almonds (F)

Dessert & Baking Needs

1 ounce (1 square) unsweetened chocolate (Th)

WINES & SPIRITS

¼ cup dry sherry (or beef broth) (Th)

REFRIGERATED PRODUCTS

Dairy

2 cups whole milk (Th)
2 cups half-and-half (W)
Whipped cream for garnish (M, Th)
¾ cup regular or light sour cream—¼ cup (M), ⅓ cup (W), 2 tablespoons (Th)
6 eggs—2 (W), 1 (Th), 3 (F)

Cheese

1 small container (15 ounces) regular or fat-free ricotta cheese (F)
¼ pound Gruyère cheese (T)
¾ cup shredded regular or low-fat mozzarella cheese (F)

Juice

½ cup + 1 tablespoon orange juice—½ cup (T), 1 tablespoon (W)

Deli

3 slices prosciutto ham (optional) (F)
1 large package (8) large refrigerator buttermilk biscuits (Th)

FROZEN GOODS

Vegetables

1 package (9 ounces) baby lima beans (M)
1 package (9 ounces) whole kernel corn (M)

Desserts

1 pint vanilla frozen yogurt (F)

MONDAY

Pork Kabob-Bobs

2 cloves garlic
1/4 cup rice vinegar
2 teaspoons honey
2 tablespoons soy sauce
2 teaspoons ground ginger
1 teaspoon sesame oil
1 teaspoon Dijon mustard
Seasoning to taste
1 1/4 pounds lean boneless pork loin
1 large green bell pepper
1 large red bell pepper
1 large onion
1 can (8 ounces) whole water chestnuts
1 pound fresh (or net weight canned)
   pineapple chunks
1 tablespoon flour

Fluffy Steamed White Rice

2 cups long-grain white rice*
4 1/4 cups water

Sufferin' Succotash

1 package (9 ounces) frozen baby lima beans
1 package (9 ounces) frozen whole kernel corn
1 small onion
2 tablespoons butter
1/4 cup regular or light sour cream
1 teaspoon curry powder
1 tablespoon grated fresh lemon peel

*Making extra rice tonight provides cooked rice for the dessert on Wednesday.

Apple Crispies

4 large red apples
3/4 cup quick-cooking oatmeal
1/2 cup flour
3/4 cup dark brown sugar
1 teaspoon ground cinnamon
2 teaspoons vanilla extract
8 tablespoons softened butter
Whipped cream for garnish

EQUIPMENT

Double boiler	Measuring cups and
Medium covered	spoons
saucepan	Assorted cooking
Small saucepan	utensils
9x9-inch glass baking	8 skewers
dish	Apple corer
Large bowl	Vegetable peeler
Medium bowl	Whisk
Assorted kitchen knives	Pastry blender

COUNTDOWN

IN THE MORNING:
   1 Do Step 1 of the *Pork Kabob-Bobs*
   2 Do Step 1 of the *Sufferin' Succotash*
BEFORE DINNER:
   1 Assemble the remaining ingredients and equipment
   2 Do Steps 1–2 of the *Apple Crispies*
   3 Do Step 1 of the *Fluffy Steamed White Rice*
   4 Do Step 2 of the *Pork Kabob-Bobs*
   5 Do Step 3 of the *Apple Crispies*
   6 Do Step 3 of the *Pork Kabob-Bobs*
   7 Do Steps 2–3 of the *Sufferin' Succotash*
   8 Do Step 2 of the *Fluffy Steamed White Rice*
   9 Do Step 4 of the *Pork Kabob-Bobs*
   10 Do Step 4 of the *Apple Crispies*

Pork Kabob-Bobs

1 Peel and mince the garlic, and combine it in a large bowl with the vinegar, the honey, the soy sauce, the ginger, the sesame oil and the mustard. Season to taste. Cut the pork into 1½-inch cubes and add them to the bowl, coating each cube with the marinade. Cover the bowl and refrigerate it.

2 Seed the bell peppers and cut each of them into 8 wedges. Peel the onion and cut it into 8 wedges. Drain the water chestnuts.

3 Preheat the broiler. Remove the pork from the marinade, reserving the liquid. Skewer the pork cubes alternately with the vegetables and the pineapple. Set the skewers on a broiler rack and broil, 3 or 4 inches from the heat, turning until each side is cooked and the meat is no longer pink in the middle, 10 to 15 minutes.

4 Mix the flour with 2 tablespoons of the reserved marinade. Heat the remaining marinade in a small saucepan. Add the flour mixture to the saucepan and whisk until the sauce begins to thicken. Spoon the sauce over the kabobs.

Fluffy Steamed White Rice

1 Combine the rice and the water in the top of a double boiler. Bring water to a boil in the bottom of the double boiler, reduce the heat, cover and simmer until all the liquid is absorbed and the rice is tender, 30 to 40 minutes.

2 Reserve 1¾ cups of the cooked rice. Fluff the remainder of the rice and use it as a bed for the kabobs.

Sufferin' Succotash

1 Set the lima beans and the corn in the refrigerator to thaw.

2 Peel and chop the onion.

3 Melt the butter in a medium saucepan. Add the onion and sauté until it is soft, about 5 minutes. Reduce the heat, add the thawed vegetables, the sour cream, the curry powder and the lemon peel. Cover the saucepan and simmer until the vegetables are heated through, about 5 minutes.

Apple Crispies

1 Preheat the oven to 350°F. Grease a 9x9-inch glass baking dish.

2 Peel, core and slice the apples, and place them in the dish.

3 In a medium bowl, combine the oatmeal, the flour, the brown sugar, the cinnamon and the vanilla. Cut the softened butter into small pieces and blend them into the oatmeal mixture until well mixed. Spread the mixture over the apple slices and bake until the crisp is lightly browned and the apple slices are tender, 30 to 35 minutes.

4 Top the crisp with dollops of whipped cream.

TUESDAY

MENU

Kiss My Bass

1¼ pounds bass fillets
1 tablespoon fresh parsley (when chopped)
½ pound mushrooms
1 medium onion
¼ pound Gruyère cheese
3 tablespoons butter
Seasoning to taste
½ teaspoon paprika

And the Beet Goes On

1 small onion
1 large green apple
2 tablespoons butter
1 medium can (15 ounces) julienne beets
⅛ teaspoon ground cinnamon
1 tablespoon apple cider vinegar
Seasoning to taste

A Peeling Salad

1 medium head lettuce
2 scallions (green onions)
1 medium cucumber
1 clove garlic
1 teaspoon grated fresh lemon peel
1 teaspoon grated fresh orange peel
3 tablespoons regular or light vegetable oil
2 tablespoons rice vinegar
½ teaspoon Dijon mustard
Seasoning to taste
1 tablespoon sesame seeds

Apricot Afterthought

8 large dried apricots
½ cup orange juice
2 tablespoons softened butter
1 cup confectioners' sugar
1 angel food loaf cake
1 jar (12 ounces) apricot preserves

EQUIPMENT

Large skillet	Assorted cooking
Medium skillet	utensils
9x9-inch glass baking	Cheese grater
dish	Apple corer
Large bowl	Vegetable peeler
2 small bowls	Whisk
Assorted kitchen knives	Spreader
Measuring cups and	
spoons	

COUNTDOWN

IN THE MORNING:
  Do Step 1 of the *Apricot Afterthought*
BEFORE DINNER:
  1 Assemble the remaining ingredients and equipment
  2 Do Steps 1–5 of the *Kiss My Bass*
  3 Do Steps 2–3 of the *Apricot Afterthought*
  4 Do Step 1 of *And the Beet Goes On*
  5 Do Step 1 of *A Peeling Salad*
  6 Do Step 2 of *And the Beet Goes On*
  7 Do Steps 2–3 of *A Peeling Salad*
  8 Do Step 6 of the *Kiss My Bass*

Kiss My Bass

1 Preheat the oven to 400°F.

2 Rinse the fish fillets and pat them dry with paper towels. Chop the parsley. Wash, pat dry, trim and slice the mushrooms. Peel and slice the onion. Grate the cheese.

3 Melt the butter in a large skillet. Sauté the onion and the mushrooms for 5 minutes.

4 Grease a 9x9-inch glass baking dish. Cover the bottom of the dish with half of the onion-mushroom mixture. Sprinkle on half of the grated cheese.

5 Fold the fish fillets in half and place them on top of the cheese. Cover the fish with the remaining onion-mushroom mixture. Season to taste. Top with the remaining cheese and the paprika. Bake for 20 minutes.

6 When the fish flakes easily with a fork, remove the dish and turn the oven up to broil. Broil the fish 3 inches from the heat until the cheese bubbles, about 1 minute. Sprinkle with the parsley.

And the Beet Goes On

1 Peel and mince the onion. Peel, core and slice the apple. Melt the butter in a medium skillet. Sauté the onion and the apple until they are soft, 5 to 6 minutes.

2 Drain the beets and add them to the skillet. Add the cinnamon and the vinegar. Season to taste and simmer for 5 minutes more.

A Peeling Salad

1 Wash and dry the lettuce and tear it into bite-size pieces. Trim and chop the scallions. Peel and slice the cucumber. Combine the lettuce, the scallions and the cucumber in a large bowl.

2 Peel and mince the garlic. In a small bowl, whisk the garlic with the grated lemon and orange peels, the oil, the vinegar and the mustard. Season to taste.

3 Toss the salad with the dressing and sprinkle with the sesame seeds.

Apricot Afterthought

1 Cut the apricots in half. Place them in a small bowl, cover them with the orange juice and refrigerate them until you are ready to use.

2 Combine the softened butter with the confectioners' sugar in a small bowl. Drain the apricots, reserving the orange juice. Add the juice to the butter mixture, a little at a time, until it is the consistency of spreadable frosting.

3 Slice the cake in half lengthwise. Spread the bottom layer with half of the frosting mixture, and top with the preserves. Place the top layer of cake over the bottom layer and spread it with the remaining frosting. Top the cake with the apricot halves, arranged with the cut sides down. Refrigerate until you are ready to serve.

WEDNESDAY

Touchdown Chicken

4 boneless, skinless chicken breast halves
2 tablespoons flour
Seasoning to taste
1 clove garlic
2 tablespoons butter
1 can (10³/₄ ounces) beef consommé
¹/₃ cup regular or light sour cream
2 tablespoons grated Parmesan cheese

Goalposts

2 medium carrots
1 tablespoon butter
1 medium zucchini
¹/₄ cup water
¹/₄ teaspoon dried basil
Seasoning to taste

Super Bowl Salad

1 large head lettuce*
1 small red onion
1 large orange
1 ripe avocado
1 tablespoon orange juice
1 clove garlic
3 tablespoons regular or light olive oil
2 tablespoons white wine vinegar
2 teaspoons sugar
1 teaspoon Dijon mustard

Puntin' Puddin'

2 cups half-and-half
2 eggs
¹/₂ cup sugar
2 teaspoons vanilla extract
1³/₄ cups cooked rice reserved from Monday
¹/₂ cup dark raisins (optional)
2 teaspoons ground cinnamon

EQUIPMENT

Large covered skillet	Assorted kitchen knives
Medium covered skillet	Measuring cups and
Small saucepan	spoons
9x13-inch broiler-proof	Assorted cooking
pan	utensils
9x13-inch baking pan	Vegetable peeler
1-quart casserole	Vegetable brush
Large bowl	Whisk
Small bowl	

COUNTDOWN

1 Assemble the ingredients and equipment
2 Do Steps 1–4 of the *Puntin' Puddin'*
3 Do Steps 1–2 of the *Super Bowl Salad*
4 Do Steps 1–2 of the *Touchdown Chicken*
5 Do Steps 1–2 of the *Goalposts*
6 Do Step 3 of the *Super Bowl Salad*
7 Do Steps 3–4 of the *Touchdown Chicken*

---

*Reserve 4 large lettuce leaves for use on Thursday.

Touchdown Chicken

1 Wipe the chicken with damp paper towels. Dust the pieces with flour and season them to taste.

2 Peel and mince the garlic. In a large skillet, melt the butter and sauté the garlic for 1 minute. Add the chicken and sauté until the pieces are golden brown on each side, about 15 minutes. Add the consommé, cover the skillet, reduce the heat and simmer for 30 minutes.

3 Add the sour cream to the chicken and mix well. Season to taste. When heated through, remove the chicken to a 9x13-inch broiler-proof pan. Cook and stir the sauce until it thickens, about 5 minutes.

4 Heat the broiler. Pour the sauce over the chicken, sprinkle with the cheese and broil until the sauce bubbles and the cheese melts, 1 to 2 minutes.

Goalposts

1 Peel and julienne the carrots. Melt the butter in a medium skillet and add the carrots. Cover and cook for 5 minutes.

2 Scrub and julienne the zucchini. Add the zucchini to the carrots. Add the water, reduce the heat, cover the skillet and steam the vegetables for 3 minutes. Remove the skillet from the heat and drain any remaining liquid. Stir in the basil and season to taste. Cover the skillet and keep warm until you are ready to serve.

Super Bowl Salad

1 Remove 4 large leaves from the head of lettuce. Wash, dry and shred the remaining lettuce. Peel and slice the red onion. Peel and section the orange. Arrange the lettuce, the onion slices and the orange sections on individual salad plates. Peel and slice the avocado. Sprinkle the slices with orange juice to keep them from browning.

2 Peel and mince the garlic. Whisk the garlic in a small bowl with the olive oil, the vinegar, the sugar and the mustard until well blended.

3 Arrange the avocado slices over the lettuce, onion and orange. Drizzle the salad with the dressing.

Puntin' Puddin'

1 Preheat the oven to 350°F.

2 Scald the half-and-half in a small saucepan until tiny bubbles form around the edge. Remove the saucepan from the heat and let it stand.

3 Beat the eggs in a 1-quart casserole. Add the sugar, the vanilla, the cooked rice and the raisins, if desired. Mix the ingredients well. Slowly blend in the half-and-half. Sprinkle the cinnamon on top. Place 1 inch of water in a 9x13-inch baking pan. Set the casserole carefully in the baking pan.

4 Bake the pudding until the top is firm and lightly browned, 35 to 40 minutes.

THURSDAY

Sundowner Soup

1 medium onion
1 pound lean ground beef
3 stalks celery
5 medium carrots
1 medium bunch Swiss chard (or spinach)
1 large can (28 ounces) crushed tomatoes with
    puree
1 can (14^1/$_2$ ounces) beef broth
^{1}/$_4$ cup dry sherry (or additional beef broth)
2 cups water
^{1}/$_3$ cup long-grain white rice
1 teaspoon dried basil
1 teaspoon dried thyme
1 tablespoon seasoning salt
Seasoning to taste

A Pear to Remember

2 large pears
2 tablespoons lemon juice
4 lettuce leaves reserved from Wednesday
^{1}/$_2$ cup walnut pieces
2 tablespoons honey
2 tablespoons regular or light sour cream
^{1}/$_4$ teaspoon dried mint

Beyond Biscuits

1 egg
1 tablespoon poppy seeds
1 large package (8) large refrigerator
    buttermilk biscuits

Choco-Roo

^{2}/$_3$ cup sugar
3 tablespoons cornstarch
^{1}/$_8$ teaspoon salt
2 cups whole milk
1 square (1 ounce) unsweetened chocolate
1 teaspoon vanilla extract
1 package (3 ounces) ladyfingers (or angel
    food cake)
Whipped cream for garnish

EQUIPMENT

Dutch oven
Medium saucepan
Cookie sheet
2 medium bowls
Small bowl
Shallow bowl
Assorted kitchen knives

Measuring cups and
    spoons
Assorted cooking
    utensils
Pastry brush
Whisk

COUNTDOWN

1 Assemble the ingredients and equipment
2 Do Steps 1–2 of the *Choco-Roo*
3 Do Steps 1–5 of the *Sundowner Soup*
4 Do Steps 1–3 of *Beyond Biscuits*
5 Do Steps 1–2 of *A Pear to Remember*
6 Do Step 6 of the *Sundowner Soup*
7 Do Steps 3–4 of *A Pear to Remember*
8 Do Step 3 of the *Choco-Roo*

Sundowner Soup

1 Peel and chop the onion.

2 Cook the beef and the onion in a Dutch oven, stirring occasionally, until the beef is browned and the onion is limp, 5 to 7 minutes.

3 Trim and chop the celery. Peel and slice the carrots. Rinse, trim and chop the Swiss chard.

4 Drain off any fat from the Dutch oven. Stir in the celery and the carrots and cook for 3 minutes.

5 Mix in the tomatoes, the broth, the sherry, the water, half of the Swiss chard, the rice, the basil, the thyme and the seasoning salt. Season to taste. Bring the mixture to a boil. Reduce the heat, cover the Dutch oven and simmer the soup for 15 minutes.

6 Stir the remaining Swiss chard into the Dutch oven and season the soup to taste. Cover the Dutch oven again and cook for 5 minutes more.

A Pear to Remember

1 Peel, core and halve the pears, and place them in a medium bowl. Sprinkle them with the lemon juice to keep them from browning.

2 Wash and dry the lettuce leaves and place them on individual salad plates.

3 Drain the pears and place them on the lettuce, reserving the lemon juice. Fill the pear cavities with the walnut pieces.

4 Add the honey, the sour cream and the mint to the reserved lemon juice and blend well. Drizzle the dressing over the pears.

Beyond Biscuits

1 Preheat the oven to 375°F.

2 Beat the egg in a small bowl. Place the poppy seeds in a shallow bowl.

3 Split the biscuits from the package. Brush the tops of the biscuits with the beaten egg and then dip them in the poppy seeds. Place the biscuits on an ungreased cookie sheet and bake until they are golden, 12 to 14 minutes.

Choco-Roo

1 Combine the sugar, the cornstarch and the salt in a medium saucepan. Gradually add the milk. Add the chocolate. Cook, stirring constantly, until the mixture begins to bubble. Add the vanilla and cook for 1 minute more.

2 Split the ladyfingers in half lengthwise and line a medium bowl with them. Pour the chocolate mixture over the ladyfingers. Cover the bowl and let it stand until you are ready to serve.

3 Top the dessert with dollops of whipped cream.

FRIDAY

Puffed-up Pasta Shells

3 slices prosciutto (optional)
2 teaspoons fresh parsley (when chopped)
1 egg
3/4 cup shredded regular or low-fat
    mozzarella cheese
1 container (15 ounces) regular or fat-free
    ricotta cheese
1/4 cup grated Parmesan cheese
2 tablespoons Italian seasoning
Seasoning to taste
1 package (12 ounces) jumbo pasta shells
1 medium can (15 ounces) tomato sauce

Braggadocio Salad

2 eggs
1 pound fresh spinach
3 scallions (green onions)
1 clove garlic
1/2 pound mushrooms
1 large fresh tomato
1 medium cucumber
1/4 cup regular or light vegetable oil
3 tablespoons apple cider vinegar
1/2 teaspoon ground nutmeg
1/2 teaspoon honey
Seasoning to taste

Peach Sparklers

1 pint vanilla frozen yogurt
1 large can (29 ounces) sliced peaches
1/2 cup sliced almonds

EQUIPMENT

Stockpot	Assorted kitchen knives
Large skillet	Measuring cups and
9x13-inch glass baking	spoons
dish	Assorted cooking
Small saucepan	utensils
Large bowl	Ice cream scoop
Colander	

COUNTDOWN

1 Assemble the ingredients and equipment
2 Do Steps 1–5 of the *Puffed-up Pasta Shells*
3 Do Steps 1–6 of the *Braggadocio Salad*
4 Do Steps 1–2 of the *Peach Sparklers*

Puffed-up Pasta Shells

1 Preheat the oven to 350°F. Bring water to a boil in a stockpot.

2 Chop the prosciutto and the parsley. Beat the egg. In a large bowl, mix the 3 cheeses together. Stir in the egg and the prosciutto. Add the parsley and the Italian seasoning. Season to taste. Gently combine the ingredients.

3 Cook the pasta shells in the boiling water until they are just tender, stirring occasionally, 9 to 10 minutes. Drain the shells well and rinse them under cold water until they are cool enough to handle.

4 Fill the shells with the cheese mixture.

5 Spread just enough of the tomato sauce to cover the bottom of a 9x13-inch glass baking dish. Arrange the stuffed shells on the sauce in a single layer. Cover the shells with the remaining sauce. Bake the pasta for 30 minutes.

Braggadocio Salad

1 Cover the eggs with water in a small saucepan. Bring the water to a boil and hard-cook the eggs, 10 to 12 minutes.

2 Wash, dry and chop the spinach. Trim and chop the scallions. Peel and mince the garlic. Wash, pat dry and slice the mushrooms. Chop the tomato. Peel and chop the cucumber.

3 Drain the eggs and place them in the freezer to chill for 15 minutes.

4 In a large skillet, heat the oil and sauté the scallions, the garlic and the mushrooms until the scallions and the garlic are soft and the mushrooms are lightly browned, 4 to 5 minutes.

5 Add the spinach, the tomato, the cucumber, the vinegar, the nutmeg and the honey. Season to taste. Cook and stir the mixture until the spinach is heated through, shiny and slightly wilted, barely 2 minutes.

6 Peel and chop the eggs and sprinkle them over the spinach.

Peach Sparklers

1 Place scoops of frozen yogurt in individual dessert dishes.

2 Spoon the sliced peaches and their syrup over the yogurt and top each serving with sliced almonds.

JANUARY
WEEK FIVE

WEEK AT A GLANCE

Monday

SIMMERING PAELLA
SAFFRON RICE
CARAWAY SALAD
TART TORTE

Tuesday

SAGEBRUSH PORK
SIDESADDLE POTATOES
BRONCO BEETS
TRAIL PUDDING

Wednesday

WINTER GARDEN LINGUINI
FROSTY SALAD
CRUSTY CHIVE ROLLS
THIRSTY PEARS & ORANGES

Thursday

CHICKEN & GRAPES
AMIABLE POTATOES
SUBTLE SALAD
LEMON SNAP

Friday

HANG-ON HALIBUT
RESCUED RICE
CARROT-LEEK COVER-UP
CHEERY CHERRIES

CHECK STAPLES

☐ Butter
☐ Flour
☐ Granulated sugar
☐ Dark brown sugar
☐ Confectioners' sugar
☐ Marshmallow topping
☐ Italian praline syrup
☐ Long-grain white rice
☐ Regular or light vegetable oil
☐ Regular or light olive oil
☐ Red wine vinegar
☐ Lemon juice
☐ Grated fresh lemon peel
☐ Grated fresh orange peel
☐ Worcestershire sauce
☐ Dijon mustard
☐ Regular or low-fat mayonnaise
☐ Grated Parmesan cheese
☐ Chicken bouillon cubes
☐ Dried basil
☐ Bay leaves
☐ Caraway seeds
☐ Cayenne pepper
☐ Chili powder
☐ Ground ginger
☐ Italian seasoning
☐ Dry mustard
☐ Ground nutmeg
☐ Instant minced onion
☐ Paprika
☐ Saffron threads
☐ Dried sage
☐ Dried tarragon
☐ Pepper
☐ Salt
☐ Vanilla extract

SHOPPING NOTES

● Purchase fresh chicken and freeze it. You will use it frozen.

● If you are shopping once a week and cannot arrange to purchase fresh clams on the day you plan to use them, you can substitute 1 can (10 ounces) whole clams.

● If you are shopping once a week and cannot arrange to purchase fresh halibut on the day you plan to use it, you can purchase *not previously frozen* halibut and freeze it, placing it in the refrigerator to thaw the night before you are ready to use it. Or you can purchase *still frozen* halibut and keep it frozen until the night before you are ready to use it.

MEAT & POULTRY

$1/2$ pound lean cooked ham steak (M)

8 lean boneless pork chops ($1^{1}/4$ pounds) (T)

2 pounds chicken thighs and drumsticks (M)

3 pounds chicken quarters (Th)

FISH

12 small steamer clams (M)

4 halibut steaks ($1^{1}/4$ pounds) (F)

FRESH PRODUCE

Vegetables

3 large sweet potatoes (T)

$1^{1}/2$ pounds small new red potatoes (Th)

1 medium bunch broccoli (W)

1 small head cauliflower (W)

8 medium carrots—2 (M), 6 (F)

1 large onion (M)

1 small onion (F)

2 small red onions—1 (W), 1 (Th)

2 medium leeks (F)

2 scallions (green onions) (W)

1 head garlic (M, W, Th, F)

1 bunch parsley (Th, F)

1 bunch chives (W, Th, F)

3 medium heads lettuce— 1 (M), 1 (W), 1 (Th)

$1/2$ pound tomatoes (Th)

1 medium cucumber (W)

1 small dried chili pepper (W)

Fruit

2 large very ripe pears (W)

1 large banana (M)

$1/2$ pound seedless green grapes (Th)

1 pint strawberries (M)

2 small oranges (W)

1 small lemon (F)

CANS, JARS & BOTTLES

Soup

1 can ($14^{1}/2$ ounces) chicken broth (Th)

1 can ($14^{1}/2$ ounces) vegetable broth (F)

Vegetables

1 medium can ($14^{1}/2$ ounces) stewed tomatoes (M)

1 large can (28 ounces) cut-up tomatoes (W)

1 medium can (15 ounces) sliced beets (T)

Fruit

1 small can (8 ounces) crushed pineapple (T)

1 small can ($8^{3}/4$ ounces) pitted dark cherries in syrup (F)

Juice

1 cup apple cider (T)

$1/2$ cup white grape juice (Th)

PACKAGED GOODS

Pasta, Rice & Grains

16 ounces linguini (W)

Baked Goods

4 crusty dinner rolls (W)

4 slices stale bread (F)

Nuts & Seeds

$1/2$ cup pine nuts (T)

Dessert & Baking Needs

1 small package (3.4 ounces) instant coconut cream pudding mix (T)

1 box (10 ounces) shortbread cookies (W)

1 small box (7 ounces) ginger snaps (Th)

WINES & SPIRITS

3 tablespoons dry white wine (or nonalcoholic white wine or chicken broth) (Th)

2 tablespoons dry white wine (or nonalcoholic white wine or clam juice) (F)

$1/2$ cup dry sherry (or nonalcoholic red wine or vegetable broth) (W)

REFRIGERATED PRODUCTS

Dairy

$1^{1}/4$ cups whole milk (T)

1 cup buttermilk (F)

$3/4$ cup + 2 tablespoons regular or light sour cream— 2 tablespoons (M), $3/4$ cup (T)

Cheese

1 cup regular or low-fat small-curd cottage cheese (M)

FROZEN GOODS

Fish

$1/2$ pound cooked prawns (M)

Vegetables

1 package (9 ounces) green peas (M)

Desserts

1 pound cake (M)

1 pint lemon frozen yogurt (Th)

1 pint cherry swirl ice cream (F)

MONDAY

Simmering Paella

2 medium carrots
1 large onion
$1/2$ pound lean cooked ham steak
1 bay leaf
2 pounds frozen chicken thighs and
    drumsticks
2 cloves garlic
1 medium can ($14^1/2$ ounces) stewed tomatoes
2 chicken bouillon cubes
1 teaspoon chili powder
Seasoning to taste
$1/2$ pound frozen cooked prawns
12 small steamer clams (or 1 can [10 ounces]
    whole clams)
1 package (9 ounces) frozen green peas

Saffron Rice

1 cup long-grain white rice
$1/2$ teaspoon saffron threads
1 teaspoon instant minced onion
$2^1/4$ cups water
Seasoning to taste

Caraway Salad

1 medium head lettuce
2 cloves garlic
$1^1/2$ teaspoons lemon juice
3 tablespoons regular or light olive oil
2 tablespoons regular or light sour cream
1 teaspoon caraway seeds
$1/4$ teaspoon dry mustard
Seasoning to taste

Tart Torte

1 frozen pound cake
1 large banana
1 tablespoon lemon juice
1 pint fresh strawberries
1 cup regular or low-fat small-curd cottage
    cheese
$1/3$ cup confectioners' sugar
2 teaspoons vanilla extract

EQUIPMENT

Electric hand mixer	Measuring cups and
Slow cooker	spoons
Double boiler	Assorted cooking
Large bowl	utensils
Medium bowl	Whisk
2 small bowls	Vegetable peeler
Assorted kitchen knives	Vegetable brush

COUNTDOWN

IN THE MORNING:
  1 Do Step 1 of the *Tart Torte*
  2 Do Steps 1–3 of the *Simmering Paella*
BEFORE DINNER:
  1 Assemble the remaining ingredients and
     equipment
  2 Do Step 1 of the *Saffron Rice*
  3 Do Steps 1–2 of the *Caraway Salad*
  4 Do Step 4 of the *Simmering Paella*
  5 Do Steps 2–5 of the *Tart Torte*
  6 Do Step 3 of the *Caraway Salad*
  7 Do Step 2 of the *Saffron Rice*
  8 Do Step 5 of the *Simmering Paella*

Simmering Paella

1 Peel the carrots and cut them into $1/2$-inch-thick slices. Peel and coarsely chop the onion. Cube the ham. Place the carrots, the onion and the ham in a slow cooker. Add the bay leaf and the frozen chicken.

2 Peel and mince the garlic. In a medium bowl, combine the garlic with the undrained tomatoes, the bouillon cubes and the chili powder. Season to taste. Add the mixture to the slow cooker.

3 Cover the slow cooker and cook on the low setting for 8 to 10 hours or on the high setting for 4 to 5 hours, depending on your schedule.

4 Remove the prawns from the freezer. Scrub the fresh clams, discarding any open ones that do not close when tapped. Add the frozen prawns, the clams (fresh or canned), and the frozen peas to the slow cooker. Cook on the high setting for 20 minutes more.

5 Before serving, remove the bay leaf from the paella and discard any fresh clams that have not opened.

Saffron Rice

1 Combine the rice, the saffron threads, the instant minced onion and the water in the top of a double boiler. Season to taste. Bring water to a boil in the bottom of the double boiler, cover, reduce the heat and cook until the liquid is absorbed and the rice is tender, 30 to 40 minutes.

2 Fluff the rice before serving.

Caraway Salad

1 Wash and dry the lettuce, tear it into bite-size pieces and place it in a large bowl. Refrigerate until you are ready to use.

2 Peel and mince the garlic. In a small bowl, whisk together the garlic, the lemon juice, the olive oil, the sour cream, the caraway seeds and the dry mustard. Season to taste.

3 Toss the lettuce with the dressing.

Tart Torte

1 Set the pound cake out to thaw.

2 Peel and slice the banana. Sprinkle the slices with lemon juice to keep them from browning. Slice the strawberries. Slice the pound cake into 3 horizontal layers.

3 In a small bowl, beat together the cottage cheese, the confectioners' sugar and the vanilla.

4 Reserve several banana slices for garnish and lay the rest over the bottom layer of the cake. Spread one-third of the cheese mixture over the bananas. Set aside several berry slices for garnish, and top the cheese layer with half of the remaining berries.

5 Add the middle layer of cake. Spread with half of the remaining cheese mixture and all of the remaining berries. Add the top layer of cake. Frost the top of the cake with the remaining cheese mixture. Garnish with the reserved banana slices and berries. Let the cake stand until you are ready to serve.

TUESDAY

Sagebrush Pork

1 tablespoon regular or light vegetable oil
8 lean boneless pork chops (1¹/₄ pounds)
1 teaspoon dried sage
¹/₂ tablespoon Dijon mustard
1 cup apple cider
1 tablespoon dark brown sugar
Seasoning to taste

Sidesaddle Potatoes

3 large sweet potatoes
3 tablespoons butter
¹/₂ teaspoon ground nutmeg
Seasoning to taste

Bronco Beets

1 medium can (15 ounces) sliced beets
1 tablespoon butter
1 tablespoon lemon juice
¹/₂ teaspoon Worcestershire sauce
¹/₄ teaspoon cayenne pepper
Seasoning to taste

Trail Pudding

1 small can (8 ounces) crushed pineapple
1 small package (3.4 ounces) instant coconut
cream pudding mix
1¹/₄ cups whole milk
³/₄ cup regular or light sour cream
¹/₂ cup pine nuts

EQUIPMENT

Electric hand mixer	Measuring cups and
Large skillet	spoons
Medium covered skillet	Assorted cooking
9x13-inch baking pan	utensils
Medium bowl	Vegetable brush
Assorted kitchen knives	Pastry brush

COUNTDOWN

1 Assemble the ingredients and equipment
2 Do Steps 1–2 of the *Trail Pudding*
3 Do Steps 1–3 of the *Sidesaddle Potatoes*
4 Do Step 1 of the *Sagebrush Pork*
5 Do Steps 1–2 of the *Bronco Beets*
6 Do Steps 2–4 of the *Sagebrush Pork*

Sagebrush Pork

1 Heat the oil in a large skillet. Sauté the pork chops, quickly searing each side. Reduce the heat. Sprinkle the chops with the sage and cook until they are tender, turning them occasionally, about 10 minutes.

2 Remove the pork chops and keep them warm.

3 Add the mustard, the cider and the brown sugar to the skillet. Season to taste. Bring the mixture to a boil and cook until it has reduced by half, about 5 minutes.

4 Return the pork chops to the skillet and coat them with the sauce.

Sidesaddle Potatoes

1 Preheat the oven to 425°F.

2 Scrub the potatoes and cut them into eighths. Arrange them skin side down in a 9x13-inch baking pan.

3 Melt the butter and brush the potatoes with it. Sprinkle with the nutmeg, season to taste and bake until the potatoes are tender, 20 to 25 minutes.

Bronco Beets

1 Drain the beets.

2 Melt the butter in a medium skillet. Add the beets, the lemon juice, the Worcestershire sauce and the cayenne pepper. Season to taste. Sauté the beets until they are heated through, 3 to 4 minutes. Remove the skillet from the heat and cover to keep warm until you are ready to serve.

Trail Pudding

1 Drain the pineapple.

2 In a medium bowl, combine the pudding mix, the milk and the sour cream until the mixture is well blended. Fold in the pineapple and the pine nuts. Spoon the pudding into individual dessert dishes and refrigerate for at least 20 minutes.

WEDNESDAY

Winter Garden Linguini

2 cloves garlic
1 small dried chili pepper
6 tablespoons regular or light olive oil
1 large can (28 ounces) cut-up tomatoes
1 teaspoon dried basil
3 bay leaves
Seasoning to taste
1 medium bunch broccoli
1 small head cauliflower
$^1/_2$ cup dry sherry (or nonalcoholic red wine or
    vegetable broth)
16 ounces linguini
Grated Parmesan cheese

Frosty Salad

1 medium head lettuce
2 scallions (green onions)
1 small red onion
1 medium cucumber
1 clove garlic
1 teaspoon Dijon mustard
$^1/_2$ tablespoon regular or low-fat mayonnaise
2 tablespoons regular or light olive oil
1 tablespoon red wine vinegar
$^1/_8$ teaspoon dried basil
$^1/_4$ teaspoon dried tarragon
Seasoning to taste

Crusty Chive Rolls

2 tablespoons fresh chives (when chopped)
4 crusty dinner rolls
2 tablespoons olive oil
1 teaspoon Italian seasoning

Thirsty Pears & Oranges

2 large very ripe pears
2 small oranges
2 tablespoons butter
2 teaspoons dark brown sugar
2 tablespoons Italian praline syrup
1 box (10 ounces) shortbread cookies

EQUIPMENT

Stockpot	Assorted kitchen knives
Large covered skillet	Measuring cups and
Medium skillet	spoons
Large saucepan	Assorted cooking
Cookie sheet	utensils
Large bowl	Pastry brush
Small bowl	Apple corer
Colander	Whisk

COUNTDOWN

1 Assemble the ingredients and equipment
2 Do Step 1 of the *Crusty Chive Rolls*
3 Do Steps 1–6 of the *Winter Garden Linguini*
4 Do Steps 1–2 of the *Frosty Salad*
5 Do Step 7 of the *Winter Garden Linguini*
6 Do Step 1 of the *Thirsty Pears & Oranges*
7 Do Step 2 of the *Crusty Chive Rolls*
8 Do Step 8 of the *Winter Garden Linguini*
9 Do Step 3 of the *Crusty Chive Rolls*
10 Do Step 3 of the *Frosty Salad*
11 Do Step 9 of the *Winter Garden Linguini*
12 Do Steps 2–3 of the *Thirsty Pears & Oranges*

Winter Garden Linguini

1 Peel and finely mince the garlic. Mince the chili pepper. Heat the oil in a large skillet and sauté the garlic and the chili pepper until the garlic is golden brown, 3 to 5 minutes.

2 Add the tomatoes to the skillet. Add the basil and the bay leaves. Season to taste. Stir the mixture well, cover the skillet and cook for 20 minutes.

3 Bring water to a boil in a large saucepan.

4 Cut the broccoli and the cauliflower into bite-size florets, and cook them in the boiling water for 5 minutes.

5 Bring water to a boil in a stockpot.

6 Drain the broccoli and the cauliflower and add them with the sherry to the skillet. Simmer, uncovered, for 5 minutes.

7 Remove the skillet from the heat and remove the bay leaves. Then cover the skillet and let it stand.

8 Cook the linguini in the boiling water until it is almost tender, 2 to 3 minutes if you are using fresh pasta and 6 to 7 minutes if you are using dried pasta.

9 Drain the pasta and return it to the stockpot. Toss the pasta with the sauce, and top it with the Parmesan cheese.

Frosty Salad

1 Wash and dry the lettuce and tear it into bite-size pieces. Trim and chop the scallions. Peel and slice the red onion. Peel and slice the cucumber. Combine the ingredients in a large bowl and refrigerate until you are ready to use.

2 Mince the garlic. In a small bowl, whisk together the mustard and the mayonnaise. Slowly add the oil, whisking constantly. Whisk in the vinegar. Add the garlic, the basil and the tarragon, and whisk until the mixture is well blended. Season to taste.

3 Toss the salad with the dressing.

Crusty Chive Rolls

1 Preheat the broiler.

2 Chop the chives. Split the dinner rolls in half and place the split sides down on an ungreased cookie sheet. Broil the rolls until they are golden, 1 to 2 minutes.

3 Turn the rolls over, brush them with the oil and sprinkle them with the snipped chives and the Italian seasoning. Return them to the broiler and continue broiling until they are lightly golden, 1 to 2 minutes. Be careful not to let them burn.

Thirsty Pears & Oranges

1 Cut the pears in half, then core and slice them. Peel and section the oranges. Set both aside.

2 Melt the butter in a medium skillet. Add the pears and cook them, stirring occasionally, until they soften, 3 to 4 minutes.

3 Stir in the brown sugar and cook until the sugar begins to caramelize, about 2 minutes. Pour in the praline syrup, stir, and cook until hot, 1 to 2 minutes. Add the orange sections and toss them gently with the pears until they are heated through. Serve the fruit with the shortbread cookies.

THURSDAY

Chicken & Grapes

3 pounds chicken quarters
Seasoning to taste
8 cloves garlic
$^1/_2$ pound seedless green grapes
3 tablespoons butter
3 tablespoons dry white wine (or nonalcoholic
    white wine or chicken broth)
$^1/_2$ cup white grape juice
$^3/_4$ cup chicken broth
1 tablespoon flour

Amiable Potatoes

$1^1/_2$ pounds small new red potatoes
1 cup chicken broth
1 tablespoon fresh parsley (when chopped)
1 tablespoon fresh chives (when chopped)
3 tablespoons butter
Seasoning to taste

Subtle Salad

1 tablespoon fresh parsley (when minced)
1 medium head lettuce
1 small red onion
$^1/_2$ pound fresh tomatoes
1 tablespoon lemon juice
1 tablespoon red wine vinegar
Seasoning to taste
3 tablespoons regular or light olive oil

Lemon Snap

1 small box (7 ounces) ginger snaps
1 pint lemon frozen yogurt
Marshmallow topping for garnish
1 tablespoon grated fresh lemon peel for
    garnish

EQUIPMENT

2 large covered skillets	Assorted cooking
Large bowl	utensils
Small bowl	Vegetable brush
Assorted kitchen knives	Whisk
Measuring cups and	Ice cream scoop
spoons	

COUNTDOWN

1 Assemble the ingredients and equipment
2 Do Steps 1–2 of the *Amiable Potatoes*
3 Do Step 1 of the *Subtle Salad*
4 Do Step 3 of the *Amiable Potatoes*
5 Do Steps 1–2 of the *Chicken & Grapes*
6 Do Step 2 of the *Subtle Salad*
7 Do Step 3 of the *Chicken & Grapes*
8 Do Step 1 of the *Lemon Snap*
9 Do Steps 4–8 of the *Chicken & Grapes*
10 Do Step 4 of the *Amiable Potatoes*
11 Do Step 3 of the *Subtle Salad*
12 Do Step 2 of the *Lemon Snap*

Chicken & Grapes

1 Season the chicken to taste. Trim, but do not peel, the garlic. Rinse and separate the grapes.

2 Melt 2 tablespoons of the butter in a large skillet. Add the garlic and the chicken, skin side down. Lightly brown the chicken on both sides, then cover the skillet, reduce the heat and cook for 10 minutes.

3 Discard any fat from the skillet. Turn the chicken quarters, add the wine, cover the skillet and simmer for another 10 minutes.

4 Uncover the skillet and add 3 tablespoons of the grape juice. Recover the skillet and allow the chicken to absorb the aroma and the flavor of the grape juice. Cook for 7 minutes more.

5 Remove the chicken breasts and keep them warm.

6 Add ½ cup of the broth to the skillet. Continue to cook the garlic and the hind-quarters, uncovered, until the chicken is done, about 5 minutes more. (About ¼ cup of syrupy juice should remain in the skillet.) Return the chicken breasts to the skillet. Turn the chicken quarters in the syrup to glaze them. Discard the garlic.

7 Remove the chicken from the skillet and keep it warm.

8 Combine the remaining butter and the flour until well blended. Add the mixture to the skillet. Increase the heat and stir to thicken. Add the remaining broth, the remaining grape juice and the grapes to the skillet. Swirl gently to combine. Season to taste. Return the chicken to the skillet and coat the quarters with the sauce.

Amiable Potatoes

1 Scrub the potatoes, but do not peel them. Arrange them in a single layer in a large skillet. Add the broth and bring it to a boil. Cover the skillet and cook the potatoes until about half of the liquid has evaporated, 4 to 5 minutes.

2 Chop the parsley. Chop the chives.

3 Reduce the heat under the skillet, add the butter, and simmer the potatoes, uncovered, until they are tender, 20 to 25 minutes.

4 Sprinkle the potatoes with the parsley and the chives and season to taste. Remove the skillet from the heat and cover to keep warm until you are ready to serve.

Subtle Salad

1 Mince the parsley.

2 Wash and dry the lettuce and tear it into bite-size pieces. Peel and slice the red onion. Chop the tomatoes. Combine the ingredients in a large bowl and refrigerate until you are ready to use.

3 In a small bowl, combine the parsley with the lemon juice and the vinegar. Season to taste. Whisk in the oil until well blended.

4 Toss the salad with the dressing.

Lemon Snap

1 Crumble the ginger snaps. Place half the crumbs in the bottom of individual dessert dishes.

2 Add scoops of frozen yogurt to the dessert dishes. Top the yogurt with the remaining ginger snap crumbs. Add a dollop of marshmallow topping and sprinkle with the grated lemon peel.

FRIDAY

Hang-on Halibut

4 slices stale bread
1 cup buttermilk
Seasoning to taste
4 halibut steaks (1¼ pounds)
1 small onion
1 cup regular or low-fat mayonnaise
2 tablespoons dry white wine (or nonalcoholic
   white wine or clam juice)
½ teaspoon paprika
1 small lemon as garnish

Rescued Rice

1 can (14½ ounces) vegetable broth
2 tablespoons water
1 clove garlic
2 tablespoons fresh chives (when chopped)
½ cup fresh parsley (when chopped)
2 tablespoons regular or light vegetable oil
1 cup long-grain white rice
1 bay leaf

Carrot-Leek Cover-up

6 medium carrots
2 medium leeks
6 tablespoons butter
2 tablespoons water
1 teaspoon ground ginger
2 teaspoons sugar
Seasoning to taste

Cheery Cherries

1 small can (8¾ ounces) pitted dark cherries
   in syrup
2 tablespoons grated fresh orange peel
2 tablespoons confectioners' sugar
1 pint cherry swirl ice cream

EQUIPMENT

Blender	Assorted kitchen knives
9x13-inch glass baking dish	Measuring cups and spoons
2 medium covered saucepans	Assorted cooking utensils
2 small saucepans	Vegetable peeler
Small bowl	Ice cream scoop
Shallow bowl	Aluminum foil

COUNTDOWN

IN THE MORNING:
   Do Step 1 of the *Hang-on Halibut*
BEFORE DINNER:
   1 Assemble the remaining ingredients and
      equipment
   2 Do Step 2 of the *Hang-on Halibut*
   3 Do Step 1 of the *Carrot-Leek Cover-up*
   4 Do Steps 3–5 of the *Hang-on Halibut*
   5 Do Steps 1–5 of the *Rescued Rice*
   6 Do Steps 6–7 of the *Hang-on Halibut*
   7 Do Steps 2–3 of the *Carrot-Leek Cover-up*
   8 Do Step 8 of the *Hang-on Halibut*
   9 Do Step 6 of the *Rescued Rice*
   10 Do Steps 1–2 of the *Cheery Cherries*

Hang-on Halibut

1 Set the bread slices out to dry.

2 Place the buttermilk in a shallow bowl. Season to taste. Add the fish, turning to coat the steaks, and marinate for 30 minutes.

3 Preheat the oven to 425°F. Grease a 9x13-inch glass baking dish.

4 Process the stale bread in a blender. It should yield about 1 cup of bread crumbs.

5 Peel and chop the onion.

6 Drain the halibut on paper towels. Wipe out the shallow bowl. Place the bread crumbs in the bowl. Dip both sides of the fish steaks in the crumbs and arrange them side by side in the baking dish.

7 Combine the mayonnaise, the wine and the onion in a small bowl, and spread the mixture evenly over the fish. Cover the fish with a thin layer of bread crumbs and sprinkle the paprika on top. Bake until the fish flakes easily when tested with a fork, 10 to 12 minutes.

8 Cut the lemon into 4 wedges and use as garnish for the fish.

Rescued Rice

1 Bring the vegetable broth and the water to a boil in a small saucepan.

2 Peel and mince the garlic. Chop the chives. Chop the parsley.

3 Heat the oil in a medium saucepan. Add the garlic and sauté for 2 minutes.

4 Add the rice, the chives, the parsley and the bay leaf to the garlic. Cook, stirring, for 2 minutes.

5 Add the boiling broth to the rice mixture. Cover the saucepan, reduce the heat and simmer until all the liquid is absorbed and the rice is tender, 20 to 25 minutes.

6 Fluff the rice. Discard the bay leaf.

Carrot-Leek Cover-up

1 Peel the carrots and cut them into thin strips. Trim the leeks and remove the outer green leaves. Slice them lengthwise and wash them well to remove any grit. Cut them into thin strips.

2 Melt the butter in a medium saucepan. Add the cold water, the ginger and the sugar. Season to taste and heat, stirring, until the sugar is dissolved.

3 Add the carrots and the leeks and stir to mix. Lay a sheet of aluminum foil tightly down on the vegetables. Then cover the saucepan and cook until the vegetables are crisp-tender, 5 to 7 minutes. Shake the pan occasionally to prevent the vegetables from sticking.

Cheery Cherries

1 Drain and chop the cherries, reserving $1/4$ cup of the syrup. Combine the cherries and the reserved syrup in a small saucepan with the orange peel and the confectioners' sugar. Heat until the mixture is slightly thickened, about 2 minutes.

2 Place scoops of ice cream in individual dessert bowls, and top the ice cream with the cherries and sauce.

FEBRUARY
WEEK ONE

WEEK AT A GLANCE

Monday

FIRESIDE SOUP
FAMILIAR SALAD
BAKIN' BISCUITS
SPICY APPLE SLICES

Tuesday

PORK CHOPS PIZZAZZ
HOT POTATO SALAD
TOASTY BOBOLI
WINTER FRUIT TOSS-UP

Wednesday

CHICKEN 'N' CHOKES
NECESSARY NOODLES
COMPLEMENTARY CORN
ICE CREAM WEDNESDAE

Thursday

OH MY COD
RED RICE HOUSTON
HEY DILLY-DILLY
HOT CHOCOLATE BANANAS

Friday

RAVE REVIEW RAVIOLI
CRITICALLY ACCLAIMED SALAD
BUTTERSCOTCH APPLAUSE

CHECK STAPLES

- [ ] Butter
- [ ] Flour
- [ ] Bisquick
- [ ] Granulated sugar
- [ ] Dark brown sugar
- [ ] Marshmallow topping
- [ ] Italian praline syrup
- [ ] Long-grain white rice
- [ ] Regular or light vegetable oil
- [ ] Regular or light olive oil
- [ ] Red wine vinegar
- [ ] Apple cider vinegar
- [ ] Rice vinegar
- [ ] Lemon juice
- [ ] Lime juice
- [ ] Worcestershire sauce
- [ ] Tabasco sauce

- [ ] Dijon mustard
- [ ] Grated Parmesan cheese
- [ ] Seasoned bread crumbs
- [ ] Ground allspice
- [ ] Dried basil
- [ ] Bay leaves
- [ ] Chili powder
- [ ] Dried cilantro
- [ ] Ground cinnamon
- [ ] Dried dill
- [ ] Garlic powder
- [ ] Dried marjoram
- [ ] Ground nutmeg
- [ ] Instant minced onion
- [ ] Dried oregano
- [ ] Paprika
- [ ] Sesame seeds
- [ ] Dried thyme
- [ ] Pepper
- [ ] Salt

SHOPPING NOTE

● If you are shopping once a week and cannot arrange to purchase fresh cod on the day you plan to use it, you can purchase *not previously frozen* cod and freeze it, placing it in the refrigerator to thaw the night before you are ready to use it. Or you can purchase *still frozen* cod and keep it frozen until the night before you are ready to use it.

MEAT & POULTRY
$1/2$ pound lean cooked ham
  steak (M)
4 lean loin pork chops ($3/4$-inch
  thick) (T)
4 boneless, skinless chicken
  breast halves (W)

FISH
$1^1/4$ pounds cod fillets (Th)

FRESH PRODUCE
Vegetables
3 medium baking potatoes (T)
1 pound spinach (F)
6 medium mushrooms (F)
3 medium carrots—2 (M), 1 (F)
4 stalks celery—2 (M), 2 (T)
2 medium onions—1 (M), 1 (Th)
3 small onions—1 (T), 1 (Th),
  1 (F)
4 scallions (green onions)—
  2 (Th), 2 (F)
1 head garlic (M–F)
1 bunch parsley (M, Th)
2 medium heads lettuce—1 (M),
  1 (Th)
1 pound tomatoes—$1/2$ pound
  (M), $1/2$ pound (Th)
2 medium cucumbers—
  1 (M), 1 (Th)
1 small green bell pepper (T)
1 bunch radishes (M, Th)

Fruit
4 large tart green apples (M)
1 large pear (T)
2 small melons (T)
4 large bananas (Th)
$1/2$ pound seedless red grapes (T)
2 medium lemons (W)

CANS, JARS & BOTTLES
Soup
2 cans ($10^3/4$ ounces each)
  vegetable soup (M)
1 can ($10^3/4$ ounces) chicken
  broth (W)

1 can ($10^3/4$ ounces) beef
  broth (Th)

Vegetables
1 cup tomato juice (Th)
1 small can (6 ounces) tomato
  paste (T, F)
1 medium can ($14^1/2$ ounces)
  cut-up tomatoes (F)
1 can (11 ounces) whole kernel
  corn (W)
1 can (15 ounces) white
  beans (M)
1 small can (4 ounces) chopped
  mushrooms (T)
1 can ($8^1/2$ ounces) quartered
  artichoke hearts (W)

Fish
1 can ($4^1/4$ ounces) baby
  shrimp (F)

Fruit
1 small can (8 ounces) crushed
  pineapple (W)

Condiments
1 tablespoon capers (W)

PACKAGED GOODS
Pasta, Rice & Grains
8 ounces small shell
  macaroni (M)
8 ounces medium egg
  noodles (W)
1 cup Grape-nuts cereal (F)

Baked Goods
1 cup croutons (F)
2 small (8-inch) Boboli breads
  (or 4 English or Australian
  muffins) (T)

Fruit
12 pitted prunes (T)

Nuts & Seeds
$1/2$ cup peanut halves (W)

Dessert & Baking Needs
1 small package (3.4 ounces)
  instant butterscotch
  pudding mix (F)
$1/2$ cup semisweet chocolate
  chips (Th)
$1/2$ cup butterscotch chips (F)

WINES & SPIRITS
1 tablespoon dry white wine (or
  nonalcoholic white wine or
  clam juice) (Th)
2 tablespoons dry vermouth (or
  nonalcoholic white wine or
  chicken broth) (W)

REFRIGERATED PRODUCTS
Dairy
2 cups whole milk (F)
2 tablespoons whole or low-fat
  milk (Th)
$2/3$ cup buttermilk (M)
Whipped cream for garnish (M)
$1/2$ cup regular or low-fat plain
  yogurt (Th)
1 egg (F)

Cheese
4 thin slices regular or low-fat
  mozzarella cheese (T)

Juice
1 cup orange juice (T)

Deli
10 slices bacon—4 slices (T),
  6 slices (Th)
1 pound cheese ravioli (F)

FROZEN GOODS
Vegetables
1 package (20 ounces) frozen
  carrots, cauliflower and
  broccoli (T)

Desserts
1 pint butter brickle (or other)
  ice cream (W)

MONDAY

Fireside Soup

$^1/_2$ pound lean cooked ham steak
1 medium onion
2 stalks celery
2 medium carrots
1 clove garlic
2 tablespoons regular or light vegetable oil
2 cans (10$^3/_4$ ounces each) vegetable soup
1 quart water
1 can (15 ounces) white beans
$^1/_2$ teaspoon dried thyme
1 bay leaf
8 ounces small shell macaroni
Seasoning to taste

Familiar Salad

1 medium head lettuce
$^1/_2$ pound fresh tomatoes
1 medium cucumber
$^1/_2$ bunch radishes*
2 tablespoons fresh parsley (when chopped)
2 tablespoons red wine vinegar
3 tablespoons regular or light olive oil
1 teaspoon Dijon mustard
Seasoning to taste

Bakin' Biscuits

$^2/_3$ cup buttermilk
1 teaspoon instant minced onion
2$^1/_4$ cups Bisquick
$^1/_2$ teaspoon sesame seeds

Spicy Apple Slices

4 large tart green apples
2 tablespoons lemon juice
$^2/_3$ cup dark brown sugar
1 teaspoon ground cinnamon
1 teaspoon ground allspice
4 tablespoons butter
Whipped cream for garnish

EQUIPMENT

Dutch oven	Assorted cooking
Large covered skillet	utensils
Cookie sheet	Apple corer
3 large bowls	Vegetable peeler
Small bowl	Whisk
Assorted kitchen knives	
Measuring cups and	
spoons	

COUNTDOWN

1 Assemble the ingredients and equipment
2 Do Step 1 of the *Bakin' Biscuits*
3 Do Steps 1–3 of the *Fireside Soup*
4 Do Step 2 of the *Bakin' Biscuits*
5 Do Steps 1–2 of the *Familiar Salad*
6 Do Step 4 of the *Fireside Soup*
7 Do Step 3 of the *Bakin' Biscuits*
8 Do Step 1 of the *Spicy Apple Slices*
9 Do Step 5 of the *Fireside Soup*
10 Do Step 3 of the *Familiar Salad*
11 Do Steps 2–3 of the *Spicy Apple Slices*

---

* Reserve the remaining radishes for use on Thursday.

Fireside Soup

1 Dice the ham. Peel and chop the onion. Trim and chop the celery. Peel and chop the carrots. Peel and mince the garlic.

2 Heat the oil in a Dutch oven and sauté the onion, the celery, the carrots and the garlic until they are soft, about 5 minutes. Add the ham and sauté until it is lightly browned, about 5 minutes.

3 Stir in the soup, the water, the undrained beans, the thyme and the bay leaf. Heat the mixture to boiling. Reduce the heat, cover the Dutch oven, and simmer for 15 minutes.

4 Stir in the pasta. Continue cooking until the pasta is tender, 10 to 12 minutes.

5 Discard the bay leaf. Season the soup to taste.

Familiar Salad

1 Wash and dry the lettuce and tear it into bite-size pieces. Chop the tomatoes. Peel and slice the cucumber. Trim and slice the radishes. Place the ingredients in a large bowl and refrigerate until you are ready to use.

2 Chop the parsley. In a small bowl, whisk the parsley, the vinegar, the oil and the mustard until well blended. Season to taste.

3 Toss the salad with the dressing.

Bakin' Biscuits

1 Preheat the oven to 450°F.

2 In a large bowl, combine the buttermilk and the minced onion. Let the mixture stand for 5 minutes.

3 Combine the Bisquick and the sesame seeds with the buttermilk mixture and blend until a dough forms. Mix the dough for 30 seconds. Drop the dough by spoonfuls onto an ungreased cookie sheet and bake until the biscuits are golden brown, 8 to 10 minutes.

Spicy Apple Slices

1 Peel, core and slice the apples. Place them in a large bowl and sprinkle them with the lemon juice to keep them from browning.

2 Toss the apples with the brown sugar, the cinnamon and the allspice, being sure to coat the apples well. Melt the butter in a large skillet. Add the apple rings, cover the skillet and cook until they are almost soft, 2 to 3 minutes. Uncover the skillet and sauté the apples in the sauce until they are lightly browned, 3 to 5 minutes.

3 Divide the apples among individual dessert dishes and top each serving with a dollop of whipped cream.

TUESDAY

Pork Chops Pizzazz

4 thin slices regular or low-fat mozzarella
 cheese
1 small green bell pepper
1 small can (4 ounces) chopped mushrooms
4 lean loin pork chops ($^3/_4$-inch thick)
Seasoning to taste
$^1/_2$ small can (6 ounces) tomato paste*
1 tablespoon apple cider vinegar
$^1/_2$ teaspoon instant minced onion
$^1/_2$ teaspoon garlic powder
1 teaspoon chili powder
$^1/_2$ teaspoon dark brown sugar

Hot Potato Salad

1 small onion
2 stalks celery
3 medium baking potatoes
4 slices bacon
1 package (20 ounces) frozen carrots,
 cauliflower and broccoli
1 tablespoon flour
$^1/_4$ cup apple cider vinegar
$^1/_2$ cup water
2 tablespoons sugar
Seasoning to taste

Toasty Boboli

2 small (8-inch) Boboli breads (or 4 English
 or Australian muffins)
1 clove garlic
3 tablespoons softened butter

*Reserve the balance of the can for use on Friday.

Winter Fruit Toss-up

12 pitted prunes
1 cup orange juice
2 small melons
1 large pear
$^1/_2$ pound seedless red grapes
$^1/_2$ teaspoon ground nutmeg
2 tablespoons Italian praline syrup

EQUIPMENT

Large covered skillet	Measuring cups and
Large covered	spoons
saucepan	Assorted cooking
Small saucepan	utensils
Cookie sheet	Whisk
Medium bowl	Vegetable peeler
Small bowl	Pastry brush
Strainer	Melon-baller
Assorted kitchen knives	

COUNTDOWN

IN THE MORNING:
 Do Step 1 of the *Winter Fruit Toss-up*
BEFORE DINNER:
 1 Assemble the remaining ingredients and
  equipment
 2 Do Step 1 of the *Pork Chops Pizzazz*
 3 Do Step 2 of the *Winter Fruit Toss-up*
 4 Do Steps 1–2 of the *Hot Potato Salad*
 5 Do Steps 2–3 of the *Pork Chops Pizzazz*
 6 Do Steps 3–6 of the *Hot Potato Salad*
 7 Do Steps 1–2 of the *Toasty Boboli*
 8 Do Steps 4–5 of the *Pork Chops Pizzazz*
 9 Do Step 3 of the *Toasty Boboli*
 10 Do Steps 3–4 of the *Winter Fruit Toss-up*

Pork Chop Pizzazz

1 Preheat the broiler.

2 Halve the cheese slices diagonally. Seed and chop the bell pepper. Drain the mushrooms.

3 Trim any excess fat from the pork chops and place them on a rack in an unheated broiler pan. Season them to taste. Broil the chops, 3 or 4 inches from the heat, turning once, until they are almost cooked through, about 10 minutes total.

4 Combine the tomato paste with the vinegar, the onion, the garlic powder, the chili powder and the brown sugar. Brush the chops with the mixture. Top each chop with 2 cheese triangles and a portion of the chopped bell pepper and the mushrooms.

5 Broil the chops, 3 or 4 inches from the heat, just until the cheese melts, 1 to 2 minutes.

Hot Potato Salad

1 Bring water to a boil in a large saucepan.

2 Peel and chop the onion. Trim and chop the celery. Peel the potatoes and cut them into ½-inch cubes. Dice the bacon.

3 Cook the potatoes with the frozen vegetables in the boiling water until they are just tender, about 10 minutes.

4 Sauté the bacon in a large skillet until it is crisp, about 5 minutes. Drain the bacon on a paper towel.

5 Remove all but 1 tablespoon of the drippings from the skillet. Add the onion and the celery, and sauté them until they are soft, about 5 minutes. Whisk the flour into the skillet. Gradually add the vinegar and the water, whisking until the mixture is smooth. Add the sugar and cook until the sauce is hot and slightly thickened. Season to taste.

6 Drain the potatoes and the vegetables, and return them to the saucepan. Add the bacon. Toss the mixture with the hot sauce. Cover the saucepan to keep warm until you are ready to serve.

Toasty Boboli

1 Cut each Boboli in half. Peel and mince the garlic.

2 Blend the garlic in a small bowl with the softened butter and spread the mixture over the bread.

3 Place the bread on an ungreased cookie sheet and place the sheet in the broiler to toast, 1 to 2 minutes.

Winter Fruit Toss-up

1 Place the prunes in a small saucepan. Cover them with the orange juice and refrigerate them.

2 Halve and seed the melons. Using a melon-baller, scoop out the melon, leaving the shells intact. Place the melon balls in a medium bowl. Rinse and separate the grapes and add them to the melon balls. Chill the melon balls and the grapes in the refrigerator until you are ready to serve.

3 Core and chunk the pear and add it to the melon balls and the grapes. Spoon the mixture into the melon shells.

4 Stir the nutmeg into the prune mixture. Add the praline syrup. Heat until the mixture is just warm and then pour the sauce over the fruit.

WEDNESDAY

Chicken 'n' Chokes

1 clove garlic
1 can (8¹/₂ ounces) quartered artichoke hearts
2 medium lemons
¹/₄ cup flour
Seasoning to taste
4 boneless, skinless chicken breast halves
2 tablespoons butter
1 tablespoon regular or light vegetable oil
1 can (10³/₄ ounces) chicken broth
2 tablespoons dry vermouth (or nonalcoholic
*   white wine or additional chicken broth)*
¹/₄ teaspoon dried marjoram
1 bay leaf
1 tablespoon capers

Necessary Noodles

8 ounces medium egg noodles
1¹/₂ tablespoons butter
1 teaspoon dried cilantro
Seasoning to taste

Complementary Corn

1 can (11 ounces) whole kernel corn
2 tablespoons butter
2 tablespoons lime juice
1 teaspoon paprika
Seasoning to taste

Ice Cream Wednesdae

1 small can (8 ounces) crushed pineapple
1 pint butter brickle (or other) ice cream
Marshmallow topping for garnish
¹/₂ cup peanut halves for garnish

EQUIPMENT

Large covered skillet	Assorted kitchen knives
Large saucepan	Measuring cups and
Medium covered	spoons
saucepan	Assorted cooking
Shallow bowl	utensils
Colander	Ice cream scoop

COUNTDOWN

1 Assemble the ingredients and equipment
2 Do Step 1 of the *Necessary Noodles*
3 Do Steps 1–4 of the *Chicken 'n' Chokes*
4 Do Step 2 of the *Necessary Noodles*
5 Do Steps 1–2 of the *Complementary Corn*
6 Do Step 3 of the *Necessary Noodles*
7 Do Step 5 of the *Chicken 'n' Chokes*
8 Do Steps 1–2 of the *Ice Cream Wednesdae*

Chicken 'n' Chokes

1 Peel and mince the garlic. Drain the artichoke hearts. Cut each lemon into 4 slices.

2 Place the flour in a shallow bowl and season it to taste. Dredge the chicken breasts in the seasoned flour to coat, shaking off any excess.

3 In a large skillet, melt the butter with the oil. Add the chicken and cook until it is lightly browned, about 4 minutes per side. Remove the chicken and keep it warm.

4 Add the garlic to the skillet and sauté it for 1 minute. Add the broth, the vermouth, the marjoram and the bay leaf. Bring the mixture to a boil, stirring. Return the chicken to the skillet, add the artichoke hearts, the capers and 4 of the lemon slices. Season to taste. Reduce the heat, cover the skillet and simmer until the liquid begins to thicken and the flavors are blended, 10 to 15 minutes.

5 Discard the bay leaf and the lemon slices from the skillet. Arrange the chicken and artichokes over the noodles. Cover with the sauce and garnish with the remaining lemon slices.

Necessary Noodles

1 Bring water to a boil in a large saucepan.

2 Cook the noodles in boiling water until they are almost tender, 3 to 5 minutes.

3 Drain the noodles, return them to the saucepan and toss them with the butter and the cilantro. Season to taste.

Complementary Corn

1 Bring the undrained corn to a boil in a medium saucepan. Reduce the heat and simmer for 2 minutes.

2 Drain the corn and return it to the saucepan. Add the butter, the lime juice and the paprika. Season to taste. Toss the mixture and cook until it is heated through.

Ice Cream Wednesdae

1 Drain the pineapple. Place scoops of ice cream in individual dessert dishes.

2 Top the ice cream with the crushed pineapple and a dollop of marshmallow topping, and sprinkle with the peanuts.

THURSDAY

Oh My Cod

1 1/4 pounds cod fillets
1 tablespoon lemon juice
Seasoning to taste
1 medium onion
1 clove garlic
6 slices bacon
2 tablespoons fresh parsley (when chopped)
2 tablespoons butter
2 tablespoons regular or light olive oil
1 tablespoon Worcestershire sauce
1 tablespoon dry white wine (or nonalcoholic
     white wine or clam juice)
1/3 cup seasoned bread crumbs

Red Rice Houston

1 small onion
3 tablespoons fresh parsley (when chopped)
2 tablespoons butter
1 cup long-grain white rice
1 can (10 3/4 ounces) beef broth
1 cup tomato juice
1/8 teaspoon Tabasco sauce

Hey Dilly-Dilly

1 medium head lettuce
1 medium cucumber
2 scallions (green onions)
1/2 bunch radishes reserved from Monday
1/2 pound fresh tomatoes
1/2 cup regular or low-fat plain yogurt
1 tablespoon rice vinegar
2 teaspoons dried dill
Seasoning to taste

Hot Chocolate Bananas

1/2 cup semisweet chocolate chips
2 tablespoons whole or low-fat milk
2 tablespoons butter
4 large bananas
1/2 teaspoon ground cinnamon

EQUIPMENT

Large covered skillet	2 small bowls
Medium skillet	Assorted kitchen knives
Small skillet	Measuring cups and
Double boiler	spoons
Small saucepan	Assorted cooking
9x13-inch glass baking	utensils
dish	Vegetable peeler
Large bowl	

COUNTDOWN

1 Assemble the ingredients and equipment
2 Do Step 1 of *Oh My Cod*
3 Do Steps 1–3 of the *Red Rice Houston*
4 Do Steps 2–4 of *Oh My Cod*
5 Do Step 1 of the *Hot Chocolate Bananas*
6 Do Steps 1–2 of the *Hey Dilly-Dilly*
7 Do Steps 5–6 of *Oh My Cod*
8 Do Step 3 of the *Hey Dilly-Dilly*
9 Do Step 4 of the *Red Rice Houston*
10 Do Steps 2–3 of the *Hot Chocolate Bananas*

Oh My Cod

1 Preheat the oven to 350°F. Grease a 9x13-inch glass baking dish.

2 Wipe the cod fillets with damp paper towels and place them in the dish in a single layer. Sprinkle the fish with lemon juice and season to taste.

3 Peel and chop the onion. Peel and mince the garlic. Dice the bacon. Chop the parsley.

4 Melt the butter in a medium skillet and sauté the onion and the garlic until the onion is translucent, about 5 minutes. Spoon the mixture over the fillets. Wipe out the skillet. Sauté the bacon until it is crisp and drain it on a paper towel.

5 In a small bowl, combine the parsley, the bacon, the oil, the Worcestershire sauce, the wine and the bread crumbs, and spoon the mixture over the fillets.

6 Bake just until the fish flakes easily with a fork, 10 to 12 minutes.

Red Rice Houston

1 Peel and mince the onion. Chop the parsley.

2 Melt the butter in a small skillet and sauté the onion until it is soft, about 3 minutes.

3 Combine the onion and the parsley with the rice, the broth, the juice and the Tabasco sauce in the top of a double boiler. Bring water to a boil in the bottom of the double boiler, reduce the heat, cover and simmer until all the liquid is absorbed and the rice is tender, 30 to 40 minutes.

4 Fluff the rice before serving.

Hey Dilly-Dilly

1 Wash and dry the lettuce and tear it into bite-size pieces. Peel and slice the cucumber. Trim and chop the scallions. Trim and slice the radishes. Chop the tomatoes. Combine the ingredients in a large bowl.

2 In a small bowl, whisk together the yogurt, the vinegar and the dill. Season to taste.

3 Toss the salad with the dressing.

Hot Chocolate Bananas

1 In a small saucepan, melt the chocolate chips in the milk, whisking until smooth. Let the mixture cool.

2 Melt the butter in a large skillet. Peel the bananas and cut them in half lengthwise, then cut the halves across. Place the flat sides down in the hot butter and sprinkle them with cinnamon. Sauté them for 2 minutes and then turn them over. Cover the skillet and cook the bananas for 2 minutes more.

3 Spoon the melted chocolate evenly onto individual dessert plates. Arrange the bananas on top of the chocolate.

FRIDAY

Rave Review Ravioli

1 pound fresh cheese ravioli
1 small onion
1 clove garlic
1 tablespoon regular or light olive oil
$^1/_2$ small can (6 ounces) tomato paste reserved
    from Tuesday
1 medium can (14$^1/_2$ ounces) cut-up tomatoes
$^1/_2$ teaspoon dried basil
$^1/_2$ teaspoon dried oregano
Seasoning to taste
$^1/_2$ cup grated Parmesan cheese

Critically Acclaimed Salad

1 egg
1 clove garlic
3 tablespoons regular or light olive oil
2 tablespoons lemon juice
1$^1/_2$ teaspoons Dijon mustard
Seasoning to taste
1 pound fresh spinach
1 medium carrot
2 scallions (green onions)
6 medium mushrooms
1 can (4$^1/_4$ ounces) baby shrimp
1 cup croutons

Butterscotch Applause

1 small package (3.4 ounces) instant
    butterscotch pudding mix
2 cups whole milk
1 cup Grape-nuts cereal
$^1/_2$ cup butterscotch chips

EQUIPMENT

Electric hand mixer	Small bowl
Stockpot	Assorted kitchen knives
Large covered	Measuring cups and
saucepan	spoons
Small saucepan	Assorted cooking
Colander	utensils
Large bowl	Whisk
Medium bowl	Vegetable peeler

COUNTDOWN

1 Assemble the ingredients and equipment
2 Do Step 1 of the *Critically Acclaimed Salad*
3 Do Step 1 of the *Rave Review Ravioli*
4 Do Step 1 of the *Butterscotch Applause*
5 Do Step 2 of the *Rave Review Ravioli*
6 Do Steps 2–4 of the *Critically Acclaimed Salad*
7 Do Steps 3–4 of the *Rave Review Ravioli*
8 Do Steps 5–6 of the *Critically Acclaimed Salad*
9 Do Step 5 of the *Rave Review Ravioli*
10 Do Step 2 of the *Butterscotch Applause*

Rave Review Ravioli

1 Bring water to a boil in a stockpot.

2 Cook the ravioli in the boiling water until it is almost tender, about 10 minutes.

3 Peel and chop the onion. Peel and mince the garlic. Heat the oil in a large saucepan. Sauté the onion and the garlic until they are soft, about 5 minutes.

4 Add the tomato paste, the canned tomatoes, the basil and the oregano. Season to taste. Bring the mixture to a boil, cover the saucepan and remove it from the heat.

5 Drain the ravioli. Top it with the sauce and sprinkle with the grated Parmesan cheese.

Critically Acclaimed Salad

1 Cover the egg with water in a small saucepan. Bring the water to a boil and hard-cook the egg, 10 to 12 minutes.

2 Drain the egg and chill it in the freezer for 10 minutes.

3 Peel and mince the garlic. In a small bowl, whisk together the garlic, the oil, the lemon juice and the mustard until well blended. Season to taste.

4 Wash, dry and stem the spinach and tear it into bite-size pieces. Peel and grate the carrot. Trim and slice the scallions. Wash, pat dry and slice the mushrooms. Drain the shrimp. Combine the ingredients in a large bowl.

5 Peel and chop the hard-cooked egg and add it to the spinach mixture.

6 Toss the salad with the dressing and top with the croutons.

Butterscotch Applause

1 In a medium bowl, beat the pudding mix and the milk until well blended. Fold in half of the Grape-nuts. Pour the mixture into individual dishes and refrigerate for at least 20 minutes.

2 Sprinkle the pudding with the remaining cereal and the butterscotch chips.

FEBRUARY
WEEK TWO

WEEK AT A GLANCE

Monday

ANTI-DEPRESSION DINNER
HAS BEANS
PROVIDENT PEARS
HARD TIMES CAKE

Tuesday

HONEST ABE CHICKEN
STOVEPIPE POTATOES
GETTYSBURG BROCCOLI
EMANCIPATION PIE

Wednesday

BEEF BRISKET BARBEQUE
GREAT MASHERS
BEANS & BELLS
A SAUCE OF A DIFFERENT COLOR

Thursday

STRAW & GRASS PASTA
CALICO SALAD
DELICIOUS BISCUITS
CHOCOLATE CALORIES

Friday

HEART & SOLE
UNFORGETTABLE RICE
SWEETHEART SALAD
SECRET PUDDING

CHECK STAPLES

☐ Butter
☐ Vegetable shortening
☐ Flour
☐ Baking soda
☐ Bisquick
☐ Granuated sugar
☐ Dark brown sugar
☐ Confectioners' sugar
☐ Unsweetened cocoa
☐ Long-grain white rice
☐ Regular or light vegetable oil
☐ Regular or light olive oil
☐ White wine vinegar
☐ Balsamic vinegar
☐ Apple cider vinegar
☐ Lemon juice
☐ Grated fresh lemon peel
☐ Worcestershire sauce

☐ Dijon mustard
☐ Ketchup
☐ Honey
☐ Dark raisins
☐ Candied ginger
☐ Grated Parmesan cheese
☐ Beef bouillon cubes
☐ Cayenne pepper
☐ Chili powder
☐ Ground cinnamon
☐ Dry mustard
☐ Ground nutmeg
☐ Instant minced onion
☐ Paprika
☐ Dried sage
☐ Seasoning salt
☐ Sesame seeds
☐ Dried tarragon
☐ Pepper
☐ Salt
☐ Vanilla extract

SHOPPING NOTE

● If you are shopping once a week and cannot arrange to purchase fresh sole on the day you plan to use it, you can purchase *not previously frozen* sole and freeze it, placing it in the refrigerator to thaw the night before you are ready to use it. Or you can purchase *still frozen* sole and keep it frozen until the night before you are ready to use it.

MEAT & POULTRY

$2^1/_2$ pounds lean fresh beef
    brisket (W)
3 pounds chicken pieces (T)

FISH

$1^1/_4$ pounds lemon sole
    fillets (F)

FRESH PRODUCE

Vegetables

4 medium sweet potatoes or
    yams (T)
2 pounds baking potatoes (W)
1 medium bunch broccoli (T)
4 medium mushrooms (F)
2 medium carrots (F)
1 small carrot (Th)
2 large onions—1 (M), 1 (T)
1 medium onion (W)
2 small red onions—1 (T), 1 (Th)
1 small leek (F)
3 scallions (green onions) (F)
1 head garlic (M, W, Th, F)
1 bunch parsley (M, W, Th, F)
1 bunch chives (W, Th)
1 small head green cabbage (M)
2 medium heads lettuce—1 (Th),
    1 (F)
1 ripe avocado (F)
$^1/_2$ pound tomatoes (F)
1 medium cucumber (Th)
2 small red bell peppers (W)
1 small yellow bell pepper (Th)

Fruit

5 medium stalks rhubarb (or 16
    ounces frozen or canned) (W)
1 large orange (W)

CANS, JARS & BOTTLES

Soup

1 can ($10^3/_4$ ounces) onion
    soup (F)

Vegetables

1 medium can ($14^1/_2$ ounces)
    cut-up tomatoes (M)

Fruit

1 large can (29 ounces) pear
    halves (M)

Dessert Needs

1 can (16 ounces) chocolate
    frosting (Th)

PACKAGED GOODS

Pasta, Rice & Grains

12 ounces wide egg
    noodles (M)
8 ounces medium egg
    noodles (Th)
8 ounces medium spinach
    noodles (Th)

Nuts & Seeds

2 tablespoons sliced
    almonds (F)

Dessert & Baking Needs

1 prepared 9-inch shortbread
    pie shell (T)
1 small package (3.4 ounces)
    instant lemon pudding
    mix (T)
1 envelope unflavored
    gelatin (F)

WINES & SPIRITS

2 tablespoons dry vermouth (or
    nonalcoholic white wine or
    clam juice) (F)

REFRIGERATED PRODUCTS

Dairy

2 cups whole milk (T)
1 cup whole or low-fat milk—
    $^1/_2$ cup (W), $^1/_2$ cup (F)
1 cup buttermilk—$^2/_3$ cup (Th),
    $^1/_2$ cup (F)
$^1/_2$ cup half-and-half (M)
2 cups regular or light sour
    cream (Th)
1 container (8 ounces) regular
    or low-fat cherry yogurt (F)
1 egg (Th)

Deli

2 slices bacon (T)
4 thin slices prosciutto ham (Th)

FROZEN GOODS

Vegetables

1 package (9 ounces) baby lima
    beans (M)
1 package (9 ounces) green
    beans (W)
1 package (9 ounces) green
    peas (Th)

Desserts

1 small container (8 ounces)
    frozen whipped topping (T)
1 pint vanilla frozen yogurt (W)

MONDAY

Anti-Depression Dinner

1 small head green cabbage
1 large onion
2 tablespoons butter
12 ounces wide egg noodles
1 medium can (14^1/$_2$ ounces) cut-up tomatoes
1 tablespoon seasoning salt
Seasoning to taste
^{1}/$_2$ cup half-and-half

Has Beans

1 package (9 ounces) frozen baby lima beans
4 cloves garlic
1 tablespoon fresh parsley (when chopped)
3 tablespoons butter
^{1}/$_4$ teaspoon dried sage
Seasoning to taste

Provident Pears

1 large can (29 ounces) pear halves
1 tablespoon candied ginger pieces
1 tablespoon lemon juice
2 tablespoons dark brown sugar
^{1}/$_2$ teaspoon ground cinnamon

Hard Times Cake

1 cup granulated sugar
1 cup water
1 cup dark raisins
^{1}/$_2$ cup vegetable shortening
2 cups flour
^{1}/$_2$ teaspoon ground nutmeg
1 teaspoon ground cinnamon
1 teaspoon baking soda dissolved in 1
    teaspoon warm water
2 tablespoons confectioners' sugar

EQUIPMENT

2 large covered skillets	Colander
Large saucepan	Assorted kitchen knives
Medium covered saucepan	Measuring cups and spoons
2 small saucepans	Assorted cooking utensils
8x8-inch baking pan	Vegetable grater
Large bowl	
Small bowl	

COUNTDOWN

1 Assemble the ingredients and equipment
2 Do Steps 1–4 of the *Hard Times Cake*
3 Do Steps 1–3 of the *Provident Pears*
4 Do Steps 1–3 of the *Anti-Depression Dinner*
5 Do Steps 1–3 of the *Has Beans*
6 Do Steps 4–7 of the *Anti-Depression Dinner*
7 Do Step 4 of the *Provident Pears*
8 Do Step 5 of the *Hard Times Cake*

Anti-Depression Dinner

1 Bring water to a boil in a large saucepan.

2 Grate the cabbage. Peel and slice the onion.

3 Melt the butter in a large skillet. Sauté the onion until it is soft, about 5 minutes. Add the cabbage and sauté until the cabbage is wilted, 5 to 7 minutes.

4 Cook the noodles in the boiling water until they are almost tender, 3 to 5 minutes.

5 Add the tomatoes and their juice and the seasoning salt to the skillet. Mix the ingredients to combine. Season to taste.

6 Add the half-and-half to the cabbage mixture and stir to blend and heat.

7 Drain the noodles and add them to the cabbage mixture, tossing to combine. Cover the skillet, remove it from the heat and keep warm.

Has Beans

1 Bring a small amount of water to a boil in a medium saucepan and cook the beans according to package directions.

2 Peel and mince the garlic. Chop the parsley.

3 Melt the butter in a large skillet. Sauté the garlic until it is golden, 2 to 3 minutes. Drain the beans and add them to the skillet and sauté until they are warmed through. Add the sage and the parsley and toss to combine. Season to taste. Cover to keep warm.

Provident Pears

1 Drain the pears, reserving the syrup in a small bowl.

2 Chop the candied ginger.

3 In a small saucepan, combine the lemon juice, the chopped ginger, the brown sugar, and $1/4$ cup of reserved pear syrup. Bring the mixture to a boil and cook until the sugar is dissolved and the ginger is softened, about 5 minutes.

4 Place the pears in individual dessert dishes. Pour the sauce over the pears and sprinkle with the cinnamon.

Hard Times Cake

1 Preheat the oven to 350°F. Grease and flour an 8x8-inch baking pan.

2 Combine the granulated sugar, the water, the raisins and the shortening in a small saucepan and boil the mixture for 3 minutes. Remove the saucepan from the heat and let it cool slightly.

3 Combine the flour, the nutmeg and the cinnamon in a large bowl. Add the sugar mixture and combine. Add the baking soda mixture to the sugar mixture and blend well.

4 Pour the batter into the baking pan and bake until the cake is lightly browned on top, about 35 minutes.

5 Dust the warm cake with the confectioners' sugar.

TUESDAY

Honest Abe Chicken

3 pounds chicken pieces
4 tablespoons butter
1 1/2 cups Bisquick
Seasoning to taste
1 large onion

Stovepipe Potatoes

4 medium sweet potatoes or yams
3 tablespoons butter
2 tablespoons honey

Gettysburg Broccoli

2 slices bacon
1 medium bunch broccoli
1 small red onion
2 tablespoons lemon juice
1/2 teaspoon seasoning salt

Emancipation Pie

1 small package (3.4 ounces) instant lemon
pudding mix
2 cups whole milk
1 prepared 9-inch shortbread pie shell
1 tablespoon lemon juice
1 small container (8 ounces) frozen whipped
topping
2 tablespoons grated fresh lemon peel

EQUIPMENT

Electric hand mixer	Assorted kitchen knives
Large skillet	Measuring cups and
10x14-inch baking pan	spoons
Medium saucepan	Assorted cooking
Medium bowl	utensils
Shallow bowl	Vegetable brush
Steamer insert	Aluminum foil
Strainer	

COUNTDOWN

1 Assemble the ingredients and equipment
2 Do Step 1 of the *Stovepipe Potatoes*
3 Do Step 1 of the *Emancipation Pie*
4 Do Steps 2–3 of the *Stovepipe Potatoes*
5 Do Steps 1–5 of the *Honest Abe Chicken*
6 Do Steps 1–4 of the *Gettysburg Broccoli*
7 Do Step 2 of the *Emancipation Pie*
8 Do Step 6 of the *Honest Abe Chicken*
9 Do Step 5 of the *Gettysburg Broccoli*
10 Do Step 4 of the *Stovepipe Potatoes*

Honest Abe Chicken

1 Wipe the chicken with damp paper towels.

2 Melt half the butter in a 10x14-inch baking pan.

3 Place the Bisquick in a shallow bowl. Season it to taste. Roll the chicken pieces in the mixture to coat. Place the chicken in the pan over the melted butter. Dot the chicken with the remaining butter.

4 Peel and quarter the onion and arrange it around the chicken.

5 Reduce the oven temperature to 350°F. Place the chicken in the oven, between the baking potatoes, and bake for 20 minutes.

6 Turn the chicken and continue baking until the pieces are lightly browned, about 20 minutes.

Stovepipe Potatoes

1 Preheat the oven to 400°F.

2 Scrub the potatoes. Pierce each several times with a fork or the tip of a sharp knife.

3 Wrap the potatoes separately in aluminum foil and place them along both sides of the oven to bake, about 50 minutes.

4 Cut the potatoes in half. Dot the halves with the butter, and drizzle them with the honey.

Gettysburg Broccoli

1 Bring 1 inch of water to a boil in a medium saucepan.

2 Dice the bacon and sauté it in a large skillet until crisp.

3 Trim and cut the broccoli into bite-size florets. Peel and chop the onion.

4 Drain the bacon on a paper towel, reserving the drippings. Add the onion to the skillet and sauté until it is limp, about 5 minutes.

5 Place the steamer in the saucepan. Place the broccoli in the steamer. Cover the saucepan and steam the broccoli until it is crisp-tender, 2 to 3 minutes. Drain the broccoli and add it to the skillet. Add the lemon juice, the seasoning salt and the bacon. Toss to combine. Remove the skillet from the heat and cover to keep warm until you are ready to serve.

Emancipation Pie

1 In a medium bowl, combine the pudding mix and the milk and beat until the mixture is well blended. Pour the pudding into the prepared pie shell and refrigerate for at least 10 minutes.

2 Fold the lemon juice into the whipped topping. Spread the mixture over the pie and sprinkle it with the grated lemon peel. Refrigerate for at least 20 minutes.

WEDNESDAY

Beef Brisket Barbecue

2 cloves garlic
1 medium onion
2^1/$_2$ pounds fresh lean beef brisket
^{3}/$_4$ cup water
^{1}/$_4$ cup Worcestershire sauce
1 tablespoon apple cider vinegar
1 beef bouillon cube
^{1}/$_2$ teaspoon dry mustard
^{1}/$_2$ teaspoon chili powder
^{1}/$_4$ teaspoon cayenne pepper
Seasoning to taste
^{1}/$_2$ cup ketchup
2 tablespoons dark brown sugar
2 tablespoons butter

Great Mashers

2 teaspoons fresh parsley (when chopped)
2 teaspoons fresh chives (when chopped)
2 pounds baking potatoes
^{1}/$_2$ cup whole or low-fat milk
3 tablespoons butter
Seasoning to taste
^{1}/$_2$ teaspoon paprika

Beans & Bells

2 small red bell peppers
1 package (9 ounces) frozen green beans
1 teaspoon instant minced onion
1 tablespoon butter
1 tablespoon sesame seeds
Seasoning to taste

A Sauce of a Different Color

5 medium stalks fresh rhubarb (or 16 ounces
    frozen or canned)
1 large orange
^{3}/$_4$ cup sugar
1^1/$_2$ cups water
1 pint vanilla frozen yogurt

EQUIPMENT

Electric hand mixer	Assorted kitchen knives
Slow cooker	Measuring cups and
Large covered	spoons
saucepan	Assorted cooking
2 medium saucepans	utensils
Small saucepan	Vegetable peeler
Small bowl	Citrus grater
Strainer	Ice cream scoop

COUNTDOWN

IN THE MORNING:
  Do Steps 1–4 of the *Beef Brisket Barbecue*
BEFORE DINNER:
  1 Assemble the remaining ingredients and equipment
  2 Do Steps 1–2 of the *Great Mashers*
  3 Do Step 1 of *A Sauce of a Different Color*
  4 Do Steps 1–2 of the *Beans & Bells*
  5 Do Step 2 of *A Sauce of a Different Color*
  6 Do Step 3 of the *Great Mashers*
  7 Do Steps 3–5 of the *Beans & Bells*
  8 Do Step 5 of the *Beef Brisket Barbecue*
  9 Do Step 4 of the *Great Mashers*
  10 Do Step 3 of *A Sauce of a Different Color*

Beef Brisket Barbecue

1 Peel and mince the garlic. Peel and slice the onion. Trim the fat from the brisket.

2 In a small bowl, combine the water, the Worcestershire sauce, the vinegar, the bouillon cube, the mustard, the chili powder, the cayenne pepper and the garlic. Season the mixture to taste and reserve $1/2$ cup in the refrigerator for the sauce.

3 Place the brisket in a slow cooker and cover it with the remaining mixture

4 Cook the brisket on the low setting for 8 to 10 hours or on the high setting for 5 to 6 hours, depending on your schedule.

5 Remove the brisket from the cooker, reserving the cooking liquid. Slice the meat against the grain. Combine the cooking liquid, the reserved sauce, the ketchup, the brown sugar and the butter in a small saucepan. Heat the mixture thoroughly and serve it over the meat and potatoes.

Great Mashers

1 Bring water to a boil in a large saucepan.

2 Chop the parsley. Chop the chives. Peel and cube the potatoes. Boil the potatoes until they are tender, 10 to 15 minutes.

3 Drain the potatoes and return them to the saucepan. Reduce the heat and shake the saucepan gently over the burner until they dry. Beat in the milk in small amounts until the potatoes are smooth and fluffy, adding more milk, if necessary. Add the butter, season to taste and beat vigorously until the potatoes are light and fluffy. Cover to keep warm.

4 Sprinkle the potatoes with the paprika, the parsley and the chives.

Beans & Bells

1 Bring half an inch of water to a boil in a medium saucepan.

2 Seed and coarsely chop the bell peppers.

3 Cook the beans, the peppers and the instant minced onion in the boiling water until the vegetables are crisp-tender, about 3 minutes.

4 Drain the beans and peppers. Melt the butter in the same saucepan. Sauté the sesame seeds until they are golden, 2 to 3 minutes.

5 Return the vegetables to the saucepan and toss with the sesame seed mixture. Season to taste. Cover to keep warm.

A Sauce of a Different Color

1 Cut the rhubarb into $1/2$-inch pieces. Grate the peel from the orange. Juice the orange. Place the rhubarb, the sugar, the juice and the water in a medium saucepan. Cook until the rhubarb is tender, 5 to 10 minutes. Adjust the sugar to taste. (Make sure some liquid remains in the bottom of the saucepan so that the rhubarb does not burn, adding water if necessary.)

2 Remove the saucepan from the heat, cover and let it stand.

3 Place scoops of frozen yogurt in individual dessert bowls. Top with the orange-rhubarb sauce and sprinkle with the grated orange peel.

THURSDAY

Straw & Grass Pasta

1 package (9 ounces) frozen green peas
8 ounces medium egg noodles
8 ounces medium spinach noodles
4 thin slices prosciutto ham
2 tablespoons regular or light olive oil
1 cup regular or low-fat sour cream
Seasoning to taste
$^1/_4$ cup grated Parmesan cheese

Calico Salad

1 medium head lettuce
1 medium cucumber
1 small red onion
1 small carrot
1 small yellow bell pepper
1 clove garlic
3 tablespoons regular or light olive oil
2 tablespoons white wine vinegar
$^1/_2$ teaspoon dried tarragon
$^1/_2$ teaspoon sugar
$^1/_2$ teaspoon Dijon mustard
Seasoning to taste

Delicious Biscuits

2 tablespoons butter
2 tablespoons fresh parsley (when chopped)
2 tablespoons fresh chives (when chopped)
$2^1/_4$ cups Bisquick
$^2/_3$ cup buttermilk

Chocolate Calories

1 cup flour
1 cup sugar
1 cup regular or light sour cream
1 egg
1 teaspoon baking soda
3 tablespoons unsweetened cocoa
1 teaspoon vanilla extract
1 can (16 ounces) chocolate frosting

EQUIPMENT

Electric hand mixer	Assorted kitchen knives
Stockpot	Measuring cups and
Medium skillet	spoons
8x8-inch baking pan	Assorted cooking
9-inch pie plate	utensils
2 large bowls	Pastry board
Medium bowl	Vegetable peeler
Small bowl	Biscuit cutter
Colander	Whisk

COUNTDOWN

1 Assemble the ingredients and equipment
2 Do Steps 1–2 of the *Chocolate Calories*
3 Do Step 1 of the *Straw & Grass Pasta*
4 Do Steps 1–2 of the *Calico Salad*
5 Do Steps 1–3 of the *Delicious Biscuits*
6 Do Steps 2–5 of the *Straw & Grass Pasta*
7 Do Step 3 of the *Calico Salad*
8 Do Step 3 of the *Chocolate Calories*

Straw & Grass Pasta

1 Bring water to a boil in a stockpot. Set the package of peas out to thaw.

2 Cook the noodles in the boiling water until they are almost tender, 3 to 5 minutes.

3 Dice the prosciutto. Heat 1 tablespoon of the oil in a medium skillet and sauté the prosciutto for 2 minutes.

4 Drain the noodles, return them to the stockpot and toss them with the remaining oil. Cover to keep warm.

5 Stir the peas and the sour cream into the skillet. Heat the mixture through and season to taste. Pour the sauce over the noodles and toss to coat. Sprinkle with the Parmesan cheese.

Calico Salad

1 Wash and dry the lettuce and tear it into bite-size pieces. Peel and chop the cucumber. Peel and thinly slice the red onion. Peel and thinly slice the carrot. Seed and chop the bell pepper. Combine the ingredients in a large bowl and refrigerate until you are ready to use.

2 Peel and mince the garlic. In a small bowl, whisk together the garlic, the oil, the vinegar, the tarragon, the sugar and the mustard until well blended. Season to taste.

3 Toss the salad with the dressing.

Delicious Biscuits

1 Preheat the oven to 450°F. Flour a pastry board.

2 Melt the butter. Place half of the melted butter in a 9-inch pie plate.

3 Chop the parsley. Chop the chives. In a medium bowl, combine the Bisquick with the buttermilk, the remaining melted butter, the parsley and the chives. Turn the dough out onto the pastry board, kneading 9 or 10 times before patting it out to a $1/2$-inch thickness. Cut the dough with a floured biscuit cutter. Place the biscuits in the pie plate and bake until they are golden brown, 8 to 10 minutes.

Chocolate Calories

1 Preheat the oven to 350°F. Grease an 8x8-inch baking pan.

2 In a large bowl, beat the flour, the sugar, the sour cream, the egg, the baking soda, the cocoa and the vanilla until the mixture is thoroughly blended. Pour the batter into the pan and bake until a toothpick stuck in the center comes out clean, about 30 minutes. Let the cake cool.

3 Spread the cooled cake with the frosting.

FRIDAY

Heart & Sole

1 clove garlic
2 tablespoons fresh parsley (when chopped)
1¼ pounds lemon sole fillets
1 teaspoon lemon juice
Seasoning to taste
4 tablespoons butter
1 small leek
2 medium carrots
2 tablespoons dry vermouth (or nonalcoholic
    white wine or clam juice)
⅓ cup buttermilk

Unforgettable Rice

2 tablespoons fresh parsley (when chopped)
1 cup long-grain white rice
1 can (10¾ ounces) onion soup
1 cup water

Sweetheart Salad

1 medium head lettuce
3 scallions (green onions)
½ pound fresh tomatoes
4 medium mushrooms
1 ripe avocado
2 tablespoons balsamic vinegar
3 tablespoons regular or light vegetable oil
1 teaspoon honey
Seasoning to taste

Secret Pudding

¼ cup sugar
1 envelope unflavored gelatin
½ cup whole or low-fat milk
6 ice cubes
1 container (8 ounces) regular or low-fat
    cherry yogurt
2 tablespoons sliced almonds

EQUIPMENT

Blender	Assorted kitchen knives
Large skillet	Measuring cups and
Double boiler	spoons
2 medium saucepans	Assorted cooking
Small saucepan	utensils
Large bowl	Vegetable peeler
2 small bowls	Whisk
Strainer	

COUNTDOWN

1 Assemble the ingredients and equipment
2 Do Step 1 of the *Heart & Sole*
3 Do Step 1 of the *Unforgettable Rice*
4 Do Steps 1–3 of the *Secret Pudding*
5 Do Steps 1–2 of the *Sweetheart Salad*
6 Do Steps 2–4 of the *Heart & Sole*
7 Do Step 2 of the *Unforgettable Rice*
8 Do Step 3 of the *Sweetheart Salad*
9 Do Steps 5–6 of the *Heart & Sole*
10 Do Step 4 of the *Secret Pudding*

Heart & Sole

1 Peel and mince the garlic. Chop the parsley.

2 Sprinkle the sole fillets with the lemon juice. Season them to taste.

3 Melt the butter in a large skillet. Add the garlic and cook for 1 minute. Add the fish to the garlic. Cook the fish, turning once, until it is opaque, 6 to 8 minutes.

4 Trim, thoroughly wash and julienne the leek. Peel and julienne the carrots. Bring a small amount of water to a boil in a medium saucepan. Cook the carrots until they are crisp-tender, about 4 minutes, adding the leek after the first 2 minutes and returning the water to a boil.

5 Drain the vegetables. Carefully remove the fish from the skillet, arrange it on a platter with the vegetables and keep them warm.

6 Increase the heat under the skillet. Add the vermouth to the fish juices. Cook for 1 minute. Add the buttermilk and cook, whisking, until the sauce is smooth. Season the sauce to taste and pour it over the fish and vegetables. Sprinkle with the parsley.

Unforgettable Rice

1 Chop the parsley. Combine the parsley, the rice, the soup and the water in the top of a double boiler. Bring water in the bottom of the double boiler to a boil. Reduce the heat, cover and simmer until all the liquid is absorbed and the rice is tender, 30 to 40 minutes.

2 Fluff the rice before serving.

Sweetheart Salad

1 Wash and dry the lettuce and tear it into bite-size pieces. Trim and chop the scallions. Chop the tomatoes. Wash, pat dry and slice the mushrooms. Peel, pit and chunk the avocado. Combine the ingredients in a large bowl.

2 In a small bowl, whisk together the vinegar, the oil and the honey. Season to taste.

3 Toss the salad with the dressing.

Secret Pudding

1 In a small bowl, mix the sugar and the gelatin.

2 In a small saucepan, scald the milk. Pour the milk into a blender. Add the sugar-gelatin mixture, cover and process until the gelatin and the sugar are dissolved, about 2 minutes.

3 With the blender running, add the ice, 1 cube at a time, through the hole in the lid, until the mixture is smooth. Add the yogurt and process until the mixture is well blended. Pour the pudding into individual dishes and refrigerate for at least 20 minutes.

4 Top the pudding with the sliced almonds.

FEBRUARY
WEEK THREE

WEEK AT A GLANCE

Monday

WASHINGTON WHITE FISH
PRESIDENTIAL PEAS & POTATOES
MONUMENTAL SLAW
CHERRIES BY GEORGE

Tuesday

SPEEDY MANICOTTI
NAPOLI SALAD
MOUNT VESUVIUS

Wednesday

CANDY APPLE PORK CHOPS
YUMMY RED CABBAGE
GINGER SNAP PUDDING

Thursday

THE ONLY GAME IN TOWN
SCRUMPTIOUS SQUASH
NUT 'N' HONEY SALAD
FALLEN ANGEL CAKE

Friday

CHOW DOWN TUNA CASSEROLE
A DIFFERENT BEET SALAD
FRIENDLY PEARSUASION

CHECK STAPLES

☐ Butter
☐ Granulated sugar
☐ Dark brown sugar
☐ Corn syrup
☐ Sweetened cocoa
☐ Regular or light vegetable oil
☐ Regular or light olive oil
☐ Red wine vinegar
☐ White wine vinegar
☐ Apple cider vinegar
☐ Lemon juice
☐ Worcestershire sauce
☐ Soy sauce
☐ Kitchen Bouquet

☐ Dijon mustard
☐ Regular or low-fat mayonnaise
☐ Honey
☐ Grated Parmesan cheese
☐ Beef bouillon cubes
☐ Whole allspice
☐ Bay leaves
☐ Dried dill
☐ Ground ginger
☐ Italian seasoning
☐ Ground nutmeg
☐ Dried thyme
☐ Pepper
☐ Salt

SHOPPING NOTE

● If you are shopping once a week and cannot arrange to purchase fresh white fish on the day you plan to use it, you can purchase *not previously frozen* fish and freeze it, placing it in the refrigerator to thaw the night before you are ready to use it. Or you can purchase *still frozen* fish and keep it frozen until the night before you are ready to use it.

MEAT & POULTRY
4 lean pork chops
($^3/_4$-inch thick) (W)
2 whole Cornish game hens (Th)

FISH
$1^1/_4$ pounds boneless, skinless
white fish fillets (M)

FRESH PRODUCE
Vegetables
12 small new red potatoes (M)
2 medium zucchini (Th)
2 medium crookneck
squash (Th)
2 medium carrots—1 (M), 1 (Th)
6 stalks celery—3 (Th), 3 (F)
1 medium onion (Th)
3 small onions—1 (M), 1 (Th),
1 (F)
1 medium red onion (W)
7 scallions (green onions)—
1 (M), 3 (T), 3 (F)
1 head garlic (T, Th)
1 bunch parsley (M, W)
1 bunch chives (M, T)
1 very small (or half) head
green cabbage (M)
1 pound red cabbage (W)
3 medium heads lettuce—1 (T),
1 (Th), 1 (F)
$^1/_2$ pound tomatoes (T)
2 medium cucumbers—1 (T),
1 (F)

Fruit
1 large green apple (W)
4 small red apples (Th)
2 large pears (F)
2 small cantaloupes (M)
1 small pink grapefruit (F)

CANS, JARS & BOTTLES
Soup
1 can ($10^3/_4$ ounces) cream of
mushroom soup (F)

Vegetables
1 medium can (15 ounces)
sliced beets (F)

1 large jar (28 ounces) pasta
sauce (T)

Fish
1 can (6 ounces) solid white
tuna (F)

Oriental Foods
1 can (8 ounces) sliced water
chestnuts (F)
1 large can ($8^1/_2$ ounces) chow
mein noodles (F)

Fruit
1 small can ($8^3/_4$ ounces) pitted
dark cherries in syrup (M)

Juice
$1^1/_4$ cups apple cider (W)

Spreads
$^1/_2$ cup apricot preserves (Th)

Dessert Needs
1 jar ($11^3/_4$ ounces) strawberry
topping (T)

PACKAGED GOODS
Pasta, Rice & Grains
1 box (8 ounces) manicotti
tubes (T)

Baked Goods
$1^1/_2$ cups cornbread
stuffing (Th)
1 angel food loaf cake (Th)

Nuts & Seeds
$^1/_2$ cup pecan pieces (Th)
$^1/_2$ cup unsalted cashew
pieces (F)

Dessert & Baking Needs
1 small package (3.4 ounces)
instant banana cream
pudding mix (W)
12 chocolate wafers (T)
1 small box (7 ounces) ginger
snap cookies (W)

1 package (12 ounces)
semisweet chocolate
chips (Th)

WINES & SPIRITS
$^1/_4$ cup dry white wine (or
nonalcoholic white wine or
chicken broth) (W)
$^1/_4$ cup dry red wine (or
nonalcoholic red wine or
vegetable broth) (W)
3 tablespoons Kirsch liqueur (or
nonalcoholic Italian cherry
syrup) (M)

REFRIGERATED PRODUCTS
Dairy
2 cups whole milk (W)
$^1/_4$ cup whole or low-fat milk (F)
Whipped cream for garnish (M)
$^1/_4$ cup regular or low-fat plain
yogurt (M)
1 egg (T)

Cheese
1 small container (15 ounces)
regular or fat-free ricotta
cheese (T)
$^1/_2$ pound sliced regular or low-
fat mozzarella cheese (T)
1 small package (3 ounces)
cream cheese (Th)

Deli
8 slices dry salami (T)

FROZEN GOODS
Vegetables
1 package (9 ounces) green
peas (M)
1 package (12 ounces) spinach
soufflé (T)

Desserts
1 quart French vanilla ice
cream (T)
1 pint vanilla frozen yogurt (F)

MONDAY

Washington White Fish

1¼ pounds boneless, skinless white fish fillets
2 tablespoons lemon juice
1 scallion (green onion)
2 tablespoons softened butter
¼ cup grated Parmesan cheese
1½ tablespoons regular or low-fat
    mayonnaise
⅛ teaspoon Worcestershire sauce
Seasoning to taste

Presidential Peas & Potatoes

12 small new red potatoes
1 teaspoon fresh parsley (when chopped)
1 tablespoon fresh chives (when chopped)
1 package (9 ounces) frozen green peas
2 tablespoons butter
Seasoning to taste

Monumental Slaw

2 tablespoons regular or low-fat mayonnaise
¼ cup regular or low-fat plain yogurt
1 tablespoon lemon juice
1 teaspoon dried dill
Seasoning to taste
1 small (or half) head green cabbage
1 small onion
1 medium carrot

Cherries by George

1 small can (8¾ ounces) pitted dark cherries
    in syrup
3 tablespoons Kirsch liqueur (or nonalcoholic
    Italian cherry syrup)
2 small cantaloupes
Whipped cream for garnish

EQUIPMENT

Large saucepan	Assorted cooking
Medium covered	utensils
saucepan	Vegetable peeler
9x13-inch broiler-proof	Vegetable brush
pan	Vegetable grater
Large bowl	Pastry brush
Small bowl	Whisk
Assorted kitchen knives	
Measuring cups and	
spoons	

COUNTDOWN

1 Assemble the ingredients and equipment
2 Do Steps 1–2 of the *Monumental Slaw*
3 Do Steps 1–2 of the *Washington White Fish*
4 Do Steps 1–2 of the *Presidential Peas & Potatoes*
5 Do Step 1 of the *Cherries by George*
6 Do Step 3 of the *Presidential Peas & Potatoes*
7 Do Steps 3–4 of the *Washington White Fish*
8 Do Step 4 of the *Presidential Peas & Potatoes*
9 Do Step 5 of the *Washington White Fish*
10 Do Step 2 of the *Cherries by George*

Washington White Fish

1 Preheat the broiler.

2 Pat the fish fillets with damp paper towels. Grease a 9x13-inch broiler-proof pan and arrange the fish in it in a single layer. Brush the fish with the lemon juice.

3 Trim and chop the scallions. In a small bowl, combine the scallions with the softened butter, the Parmesan cheese, the mayonnaise and the Worcestershire sauce. Season to taste.

4 Place the fish in the broiler, 3 or 4 inches from the heat, and broil for 4 minutes.

5 Carefully turn the fish. Spread it evenly with the mayonnaise-cheese mixture, then return it to the broiler and continue broiling until the fish is golden and flakes easily with a fork, 2 to 3 minutes.

Presidential Peas & Potatoes

1 Bring water to a boil in a large saucepan. Scrub the potatoes, but do not peel them. Cook the potatoes in the boiling water until they are firm but tender, 10 to 15 minutes.

2 Chop the parsley and the chives.

3 Bring $1/2$ inch water to a boil in a medium saucepan. Cook the peas a scant 3 minutes.

4 Drain the potatoes and the peas. Place both in the potato saucepan and toss them with the butter, the parsley and the chives. Season to taste. Cover the saucepan until you are ready to serve.

Monumental Slaw

1 In a large bowl, whisk together the mayonnaise, the yogurt, the lemon juice and the dill until well blended. Season to taste.

2 Grate the cabbage. Peel and grate the onion. Peel and grate the carrot. Add the ingredients to the bowl. Toss the cabbage mixture with the dressing and refrigerate until you are ready to serve.

Cherries by George

1 Drain the cherries and toss them with the Kirsch.

2 Halve the cantaloupes and remove the seeds. Place the halves on individual dessert dishes. Place the cherries in the melon cavities and top each serving with a dollop of whipped cream.

TUESDAY

Speedy Manicotti

1 package (12 ounces) frozen spinach soufflé
1 small container (15 ounces) regular or fat-
    free ricotta cheese
1 egg
3 tablespoons fresh chives (when chopped)
2 tablespoons Italian seasoning
Seasoning to taste
1 box (8 ounces) manicotti tubes
1 large jar (28 ounces) pasta sauce
$1/2$ pound sliced regular or low-fat mozzarella
    cheese

Napoli Salad

1 medium head lettuce
1 medium cucumber
3 scallions (green onions)
$1/2$ pound fresh tomatoes
8 slices dry salami
1 clove garlic
3 tablespoons regular or light olive oil
2 tablespoons red wine vinegar
$1/2$ teaspoon Worcestershire sauce
$1/2$ teaspoon Dijon mustard
Seasoning to taste

Mount Vesuvius

12 chocolate wafers
1 quart French vanilla ice cream
1 jar ($11^3/4$ ounces) strawberry topping

EQUIPMENT

Stockpot	Measuring cups and
9x13-inch glass baking	spoons
dish	Assorted cooking
Large bowl	utensils
Medium bowl	Vegetable peeler
Small bowl	Whisk
Colander	Ice cream scoop
Assorted kitchen knives	Aluminum foil

COUNTDOWN

IN THE MORNING:
  Do Step 1 of the *Speedy Manicotti*
BEFORE DINNER:
  1 Assemble the remaining ingredients and
    equipment
  2 Do Steps 2–5 of the *Speedy Manicotti*
  3 Do Step 1 of the *Mount Vesuvius*
  4 Do Steps 6–7 of the *Speedy Manicotti*
  5 Do Steps 1–2 of the *Napoli Salad*
  6 Do Step 8 of the *Speedy Manicotti*
  7 Do Step 3 of the *Napoli Salad*
  8 Do Step 2 of the *Mount Vesuvius*

Speedy Manicotti

1 Set the spinach soufflé in the refrigerator to thaw.

2 Preheat the oven to 350°F.

3 Bring water to a boil in a stockpot.

4 Combine the thawed spinach soufflé, the ricotta cheese and the egg in a medium bowl. Chop the chives and add them to the mixture. Blend in the Italian seasoning and season to taste.

5 Cook the manicotti tubes in the boiling water until they are almost tender, 10 to 12 minutes.

6 Drain the manicotti tubes and run them under cold water until they are cool enough to handle.

7 Spoon half the pasta sauce into the bottom of a 9x13-inch glass baking dish. Fill the manicotti tubes with the spinach mixture. (You should have about 1 cup left over.) Lay the tubes over the pasta sauce in the dish in a single layer. Spoon the rest of the sauce over the pasta, spread the remaining spinach mixture over the sauce and top the whole thing with the sliced mozzarella cheese. Cover the dish with aluminum foil and bake for 35 minutes.

8 Remove the foil from the manicotti and continue cooking until the cheese bubbles, 5 to 10 minutes more.

Napoli Salad

1 Wash and dry the lettuce and tear it into bite-size pieces. Peel and slice the cucumber. Trim and chop the scallions. Chop the tomatoes. Chop the salami. Combine the ingredients in a large bowl.

2 Peel and mince the garlic. In a small bowl, whisk together the garlic, the olive oil, the vinegar, the Worcestershire sauce and the mustard until well blended. Season to taste.

3 Toss the salad lightly with the dressing.

Mount Vesuvius

1 Crumble the chocolate wafers.

2 Mound 2 scoops of ice cream in each dessert bowl. With a wooden spoon handle, make a center hole in the ice cream. Fill the hole halfway with crumbled wafers. Then sprinkle more wafer crumbs around the base of the ice cream. Fill the remainder of the hole with the strawberry topping until it spills over the sides, then sprinkle with the remaining wafer crumbs.

WEDNESDAY

Candy Apple Pork Chops

2 tablespoons butter
2 tablespoons regular or light vegetable oil
4 lean pork chops ($^3/_4$-inch thick)
Seasoning to taste
$^1/_4$ cup dry white wine (or nonalcoholic white
     wine or chicken broth)
$1^1/_4$ cups apple cider
1 large green apple
1 teaspoon lemon juice

Yummy Red Cabbage

4 tablespoons butter
1 medium red onion
$^1/_3$ cup fresh parsley (when chopped)
1 pound red cabbage
$^1/_4$ cup dry red wine (or nonalcoholic red wine
     or vegetable broth)
$^1/_4$ cup red wine vinegar
2 tablespoons apple cider vinegar
$^1/_4$ teaspoon ground nutmeg
1 tablespoon honey
Seasoning to taste

Ginger Snap Pudding

1 small package (3.4 ounces) instant banana
     cream pudding mix
2 cups whole milk
$^1/_4$ teaspoon ground ginger
1 small box (7 ounces) ginger snap cookies

EQUIPMENT

Electric hand mixer	Measuring cups and
Large skillet	spoons
Large covered	Assorted cooking
saucepan	utensils
2 medium bowls	Vegetable peeler
Small bowl	Vegetable grater
Strainer	Apple corer
Assorted kitchen knives	Whisk

COUNTDOWN

1 Assemble the ingredients and equipment
2 Do Steps 1–3 of the *Yummy Red Cabbage*
3 Do Steps 1–2 of the *Ginger Snap Pudding*
4 Do Steps 1–6 of the *Candy Apple Pork Chops*
5 Do Step 4 of the *Yummy Red Cabbage*
6 Do Step 7 of the *Candy Apple Pork Chops*
7 Do Step 3 of the *Ginger Snap Pudding*

Candy Apple Pork Chops

1 Melt 1 tablespoon of butter with the oil in a large skillet. Season the pork chops and brown them, 4 to 6 minutes per side. Remove the chops from the skillet.

2 Pour off any excess fat and deglaze the skillet with the wine, scraping any bits off the bottom with a spatula and stirring well. Add 1 cup of the apple cider and bring it to a boil, whisking constantly, until the liquid is reduced to 1 cup, about 5 minutes.

3 Cut the apple in half, and peel, core and cut them into very thin slices. Place them in a medium bowl and sprinkle them with lemon juice to keep them from browning.

4 Return the chops to the skillet. Reduce the heat and simmer until the chops are tender, 15 to 20 minutes, turning from time to time.

5 Remove the chops and keep them warm. Strain the skillet juices into a small bowl and reserve. Add the remaining cider and butter to the skillet and cook until the butter is melted. Place the apple slices in the skillet in a single layer. Cook the apples, turning carefully to coat. Continue cooking until the cider is reduced to a glaze and the apple slices are caramelized, but still holding their shape, about 10 minutes. Spoon the apple slices over the pork chops.

6 Wipe out the skillet. Return the reserved juices to the skillet and reduce them to the consistency of light syrup.

7 Serve the sauce with the pork and apples.

Yummy Red Cabbage

1 Melt the butter in a large saucepan. Peel and chop the onion. Chop the parsley. Sauté the onion in the butter until it is translucent, about 5 minutes.

2 Peel off and discard the tough outer leaves of the cabbage. Then grate it directly into the saucepan with the onion.

3 Combine the wine, both vinegars, the nutmeg and the honey, and add the dressing to the onion-cabbage mixture. Season to taste. Toss to coat the cabbage and onion. Then cover and cook until the cabbage is either crisp (about 20 minutes) or soft (about 30 minutes), depending on personal taste. Stir occasionally.

4 Toss the parsley with the cabbage.

Ginger Snap Pudding

1 Combine the pudding mix, the milk and the ginger in a medium bowl and beat until well blended. Spoon the pudding into individual dishes and refrigerate for at least 20 minutes.

2 Crumble the ginger snaps.

3 Sprinkle the crumbled ginger snaps over the pudding.

THURSDAY

The Only Game in Town

2 whole Cornish game hens
Seasoning to taste
2 tablespoons Kitchen Bouquet
3 tablespoons butter
1 stalk celery
1 medium onion
2 lettuce leaves*
1 medium carrot
1 clove garlic
1 beef bouillon cube
3 whole allspice
1 bay leaf
1 cup water
$1/2$ cup apricot preserves

CORNBREAD STUFFING:
4 tablespoons butter
2 stalks celery
1 small onion
$1^1/2$ cups cornbread stuffing mix
Seasoning to taste

Scrumptious Squash

2 medium zucchini
2 medium crookneck squash
1 clove garlic
1 tablespoon regular or light olive oil
1 teaspoon dried thyme
Seasoning to taste
$1/4$ cup water

Nut 'n' Honey Salad

4 small red apples
1 medium head lettuce

*Steal 2 leaves of lettuce from the salad.

1 small package (3 ounces) cream cheese
$1/2$ cup pecan pieces
3 tablespoons white wine vinegar
2 tablespoons regular or light vegetable oil
1 tablespoon honey
Seasoning to taste

Fallen Angel Cake

1 package (12 ounces) semisweet chocolate chips
4 tablespoons butter
3 tablespoons corn syrup
1 angel food loaf cake
$2/3$ cup sweetened cocoa

EQUIPMENT

Large covered skillet
Double boiler
9x13-inch baking pan
Large bowl
Small bowl
Assorted kitchen knives
Measuring cups and spoons
Assorted cooking utensils
Pastry brush
Apple corer
Whisk

COUNTDOWN

1 Assemble the ingredients and equipment
2 Do Step 1 of *The Only Game in Town*
3 Do Step 1 of the *Fallen Angel Cake*
4 Do Steps 2–4 of *The Only Game in Town*
5 Do Step 2 of the *Fallen Angel Cake*
6 Do Step 1 of the *Scrumptious Squash*
7 Do Steps 1–2 of the *Nut 'n' Honey Salad*
8 Do Step 5 of *The Only Game in Town*
9 Do Step 3 of the *Fallen Angel Cake*
10 Do Steps 2–3 of the *Scrumptious Squash*
11 Do Step 6 of *The Only Game in Town*
12 Do Step 3 of the *Nut 'n' Honey Salad*

The Only Game in Town

1 Preheat the oven to 400°F.

2 Rinse and pat dry the game hens. Season the inside and outside of the birds to taste and lightly brush the skins with the Kitchen Bouquet.

3 Melt 4 tablespoons of the butter. Trim and finely chop 1 stalk of celery. Trim and finely chop the small onion. In a large bowl, combine the cornbread stuffing mix with the celery and the onion. Add the melted butter and mix well. Season to taste.

4 Stuff the game hens with the cornbread mixture, packing tightly. Place 2 lettuce leaves on the bottom of the baking pan. Lay the birds, breast side down, on the lettuce. Halve the medium onion. Trim and cut the remaining celery stalk in half. Scrub and cut the carrot in half. Peel and halve the garlic. Surround the hens with the vegetables, the bouillon cube, the spices and the water. Melt 3 tablespoons of butter and drizzle half of it over the birds, and top with half of the apricot preserves. Bake until the hens are browned, about 20 minutes.

5 Turn the hens breast side up. Drizzle them with the remaining butter and top with the remaining apricot preserves. Cook until the breasts are golden brown, about 20 minutes.

6 To serve, cut the game hens in half lengthwise.

Scrumptious Squash

1 Scrub and trim the zucchini and the squash and slice them into $1/4$-inch rounds. Peel and chop the garlic.

2 In a large skillet, heat the oil and sauté the garlic for 1 minute. Add the zucchini, the squash rounds and the thyme, and sauté them for 3 minutes. Season to taste.

3 Add the water to the skillet, bring it to a boil, then cover and remove it from the heat.

Nut 'n' Honey Salad

1 Core and slice the apples. Wash and dry the lettuce and place 1 leaf on each salad plate. Tear the remaining leaves into bite-size pieces and distribute on the plates. Top the lettuce with the apple slices. Top the apples with dollops of cream cheese. Top the cream cheese with the pecan pieces.

2 In a small bowl, whisk the vinegar, the vegetable oil and the honey until well blended. Season to taste.

3 Drizzle the dressing over the salad.

Fallen Angel Cake

1 Bring water to a boil in the bottom of a double boiler. Combine the chocolate chips, the butter and the corn syrup in the top of the double boiler. Cover, reduce the heat and cook, stirring occasionally, until the chocolate is melted.

2 Remove the chocolate mixture from the heat and allow it to cool slightly.

3 Slice the cake lengthwise into 2 layers. Spread the bottom layer with a third of the chocolate mixture. Cover with the top cake layer. Spread the remaining mixture over the top and sides of the cake. Dust the top with the cocoa, and refrigerate until you are ready to serve.

FRIDAY

Chow Down Tuna Casserole

1 large can (8$^1/_2$ ounces) chow mein noodles
1 can (6 ounces) solid white tuna
3 scallions (green onions)
3 stalks celery
1 can (8 ounces) sliced water chestnuts
1 can (10$^3/_4$ ounces) cream of mushroom soup
$^1/_4$ cup whole or low-fat milk
2 tablespoons soy sauce
Seasoning to taste
$^1/_2$ cup unsalted cashew pieces

A Different Beet Salad

1 medium can (15 ounces) sliced beets
1 medium cucumber
1 small onion
1 medium head lettuce
3 tablespoons regular or light olive oil
1 tablespoon lemon juice
$^1/_2$ teaspoon Worcestershire sauce
$^1/_2$ teaspoon Dijon mustard
$^1/_2$ teaspoon honey
Seasoning to taste

Friendly Pearsuasion

1 small pink grapefruit
2 large pears
1 tablespoon lemon juice
2 tablespoons butter
2 tablespoons dark brown sugar
1 pint vanilla frozen yogurt

EQUIPMENT

Medium skillet	Assorted cooking
1$^1/_2$-quart casserole	utensils
Medium bowl	Vegetable peeler
Small bowl	Citrus grater
Strainer	Whisk
Assorted kitchen knives	Ice cream scoop
Measuring cups and spoons	

COUNTDOWN

1 Assemble the ingredients and equipment
2 Do Step 1 of the *Chow Down Tuna Casserole*
3 Do Steps 1–2 of the *Friendly Pearsuasion*
4 Do Steps 2–5 of the *Chow Down Tuna Casserole*
5 Do Steps 1–3 of *A Different Beet Salad*
6 Do Steps 3–4 of the *Friendly Pearsuasion*

Chow Down Tuna Casserole

1 Preheat the oven to 350°F.

2 Grease a 1¹/₂-quart casserole. Place half of the chow mein noodles in the bottom of the casserole. Drain and flake the tuna and layer it over the noodles.

3. Trim and chop the scallions. Trim and chop the celery. Drain the water chestnuts. Layer the scallions, the celery and the water chestnuts over the tuna.

4 In a small bowl, blend the mushroom soup with the milk and the soy sauce. Season to taste. Pour the mixture over the tuna and vegetables, and top with the remaining chow mein noodles. Sprinkle the cashew pieces over the noodles.

5 Bake the casserole until it is heated through and bubbly, about 30 minutes.

A Different Beet Salad

1 Drain the beets. Peel and slice the cucumber. Peel and thinly slice the onion. Wash and dry the lettuce and place the leaves on individual salad plates. Arrange the cucumbers, the beets and the onion over the lettuce.

2 In a small bowl, whisk together the olive oil, the lemon juice, the Worcestershire sauce, the Dijon mustard and the honey. Season to taste.

3 Drizzle the dressing over the salad.

Friendly Pearsuasion

1 Peel and section the grapefruit.

2 Core and thinly slice the pears and sprinkle them with the lemon juice to keep them from browning.

3 Melt the butter in a medium skillet. Add the pear slices and the brown sugar, and sauté until the pears are slightly softened, 2 to 3 minutes, adding the reserved grapefruit sections for the final minute.

4 Distribute the pear mixture among individual dessert dishes. Top with a scoop of frozen yogurt.

FEBRUARY
WEEK FOUR

Monday

EMBRACEABLE EWE
FLUFFY STEAMED WHITE RICE
EVERBEANS
PEACH DIVINE

Tuesday

INCREDIBLE EDIBLE CHICKEN
FRIVOLOUS CARROTS
HELLO DILLY
LAZY SALLY CAKE

Wednesday

KISS-ME-NOT PASTA
FICKLE ASPARAGUS
TOMATO TEASERS
STRAWBERRY TEMPTATION

Thursday

CLEVER COD CASSEROLE
GOLDEN BROCCOLI
HOT BACON SALAD
BANANA PUDDING BANANA

Friday

POPEYE'S FRITTATA
GALLEY TOSS
CRUNCHY ICE CREAM PARFAIT

CHECK STAPLES

- ☐ Butter
- ☐ Flour
- ☐ Baking powder
- ☐ Cornstarch
- ☐ Granulated sugar
- ☐ Dark brown sugar
- ☐ Long-grain white rice
- ☐ Regular or light vegetable oil
- ☐ Regular or light olive oil
- ☐ White wine vinegar
- ☐ Balsamic vinegar
- ☐ Distilled white vinegar
- ☐ Lemon juice
- ☐ Grated fresh lemon peel
- ☐ Soy sauce
- ☐ Dijon mustard
- ☐ Regular or low-fat mayonnaise
- ☐ Seasoned bread crumbs
- ☐ Ground allspice
- ☐ Ground cinnamon
- ☐ Cream of tartar
- ☐ Ground nutmeg
- ☐ Paprika
- ☐ Dried savory
- ☐ Pepper
- ☐ Salt
- ☐ Vanilla extract

SHOPPING NOTE

● If you are shopping once a week and cannot arrange to purchase fresh cod on the day you plan to use it, you can purchase *not previously frozen* cod and freeze it, placing it in the refrigerator to thaw the night before you are ready to use it. Or you can purchase *still frozen* cod and keep it frozen until the night before you are ready to use it.

MEAT & POULTRY

4 lean lamb chops (³/₄-inch thick) (M)
4 boneless, skinless chicken breast halves (T)

FISH

1¹/₄ pounds cod fillets (Th)

FRESH PRODUCE

Vegetables

1 pound new red potatoes (F)
1 pound green beans (M)
1¹/₂ pounds asparagus (W)
1 medium bunch broccoli (Th)
12 Chinese snow peas (Th)
³/₄ pound spinach (F)
¹/₄ pound mushrooms (F)
1 pound carrots (T)
1 small carrot (Th)
1 medium onion (F)
2 small onions—1 (T), 1 (Th)
1 medium shallot (W)
8 scallions (green onions)—
    4 (T), 4 (Th)
1 head garlic (W, Th)
1 bunch parsley (T, W, Th)
1 small bunch dill (T, W)
1 very small (or half) head red cabbage (Th)
1 medium head lettuce (T)
4 firm large tomatoes (W)
1 pound tomatoes (F)
1 small green bell pepper (Th)

Fruit

1 medium red apple (T)
1 pound tart green apples (F)
2 medium bananas (Th)

1 pint strawberries (W)
1 large orange (M)

CANS, JARS & BOTTLES

Soup

1 can (10³/₄ ounces) chicken broth (M)

Vegetables

1 jar (6¹/₂ ounces) marinated artichoke hearts (F)

Fruit

1 large can (29 ounces) sliced peaches (M)
1 large can (20 ounces) crushed pineapple (T)

Condiments

4 maraschino cherries for garnish (F)

PACKAGED GOODS

Pasta, Rice & Grains

16 ounces spaghetti (W)

Nuts & Seeds

2 tablespoons sliced almonds (M)
1 cup pecan pieces (T)

Dessert & Baking Needs

1 box yellow cake mix (T)
4 prepared shortcake dessert cups (W)
16 Oreo cookies (F)
1 small package (3.4 ounces) instant banana cream pudding mix (Th)
1 cup flaked coconut (T)

WINES & SPIRITS

2 tablespoons dry white wine (or nonalcoholic white wine or clam juice) (Th)
2 tablespoons marsala wine (or nonalcoholic red wine + 1 tablespoon sugar) (W)
2 tablespoons dry sherry (or nonalcoholic red wine or chicken broth) (T)

REFRIGERATED PRODUCTS

Dairy

2 cups whole milk (Th)
1 cup whole or low-fat milk (F)
Whipped cream for garnish (M, F)
¹/₂ cup regular or light sour cream (T)
3 eggs—3 (W, Th), 3 (F)

Cheese

³/₄ cup shredded regular or low-fat mozzarella cheese (W)
1 pound shredded regular or low-fat Monterey Jack cheese (F)

Juice

¹/₄ cup orange juice (M)

Deli

6 slices bacon (Th)

FROZEN GOODS

Desserts

1 quart vanilla fudge ice cream (F)

MONDAY

Embraceable Ewe

4 lean lamb chops (³/₄-inch thick)
2 tablespoons regular or light vegetable oil
1 can (10³/₄ ounces) chicken broth
2 tablespoons soy sauce
1 tablespoon distilled white vinegar
1 large orange
¹/₄ cup orange juice
2 tablespoons dark brown sugar
2 tablespoons cornstarch
1 teaspoon ground nutmeg
Seasoning to taste

Fluffy Steamed White Rice

1 cup long-grain white rice
2 cups water

Everbeans

1 pound fresh green beans
2 tablespoons sliced almonds
1 tablespoon butter
1 teaspoon lemon juice
Seasoning to taste

Peach Divine

1 large can (29 ounces) sliced peaches
³/₄ cup sugar
1¹/₄ cups flour
¹/₄ teaspoon salt
¹/₂ teaspoon ground cinnamon
4 tablespoons softened butter
1 teaspoon vanilla extract
Whipped cream for garnish

EQUIPMENT

Small skillet	Assorted kitchen knives
Medium covered	Measuring cups and
saucepan	spoons
Small saucepan	Assorted cooking
Double boiler	utensils
9-inch pie plate	Pastry blender
2 small bowls	Whisk

COUNTDOWN

1 Assemble the ingredients and equipment
2 Do Step 1 of the *Peach Divine*
3 Do Step 1 of the *Fluffy Steamed White Rice*
4 Do Steps 2–3 of the *Peach Divine*
5 Do Steps 1–2 of the *Everbeans*
6 Do Steps 1–4 of the *Embraceable Ewe*
7 Do Steps 3–4 of the *Everbeans*
8 Do Steps 5–6 of the *Embraceable Ewe*
9 Do Step 2 of the *Fluffy Steamed White Rice*
10 Do Step 4 of the *Peach Divine*

Embraceable Ewe

1 Preheat the broiler.

2 Broil the lamb chops until they are browned on both sides (a total of 8 to 10 minutes for medium-rare).

3 Heat the oil in a small skillet. Stir in the broth, the soy sauce and the vinegar. Bring the mixture to a boil and cook until it is reduced by half, about 10 minutes.

4 Peel and section the orange. In a small bowl, combine the orange juice, the brown sugar, the cornstarch and the nutmeg. Whisk the mixture until it is smooth.

5 Remove the chops and keep them warm.

6 Stir the cornstarch mixture into the skillet. Bring the sauce to a boil. Add the orange sections and heat through. Season to taste. Pour the sauce over the lamb chops.

Fluffy Steamed White Rice

1 Place the rice and the water in the top of a double boiler. Bring water in the bottom of the double boiler to a boil. Reduce the heat, cover and simmer until all the liquid is absorbed and the rice is tender, 30 to 40 minutes.

2 Fluff the rice before serving.

Everbeans

1 Bring water to a boil in a medium saucepan.

2 Trim and string the beans and cook them in the boiling water until they are crisp-tender, 8 to 10 minutes.

3 Melt the butter in a small saucepan. Sauté the sliced almonds in the butter until they are golden, about 5 minutes. Remove the almonds from the heat and add the lemon juice.

4 Drain the beans and toss them with the sauce. Season to taste. Cover to keep warm until you are ready to serve.

Peach Divine

1 Preheat the oven to 350°F.

2 Grease the bottom of a 9-inch pie plate.

3 Drain the peaches and place them in the pie plate. In a small bowl, combine the sugar, the flour, the salt and the cinnamon. Fold in the softened butter and the vanilla, and spread the mixture over the peaches. Bake for 30 minutes.

4 Top each serving with a dollop of whipped cream.

TUESDAY

Incredible Edible Chicken

4 boneless, skinless chicken breast halves
1 small onion
2 tablespoons fresh parsley (when chopped)
$^1/_4$ cup flour
$^1/_4$ teaspoon paprika
Seasoning to taste
2 tablespoons regular or light vegetable oil
$^1/_2$ cup regular or light sour cream
$^1/_4$ cup regular or low-fat mayonnaise
2 tablespoons dry sherry (or nonalcoholic red
    wine or chicken broth)
2 tablespoons water

Frivolous Carrots

1 pound carrots
1 medium red apple
2 tablespoons dark brown sugar
2 tablespoons butter
1 tablespoon lemon juice

Hello Dilly

1 medium head lettuce
4 scallions (green onions)
3 tablespoons fresh parsley (when chopped)
3 tablespoons fresh dill (when chopped)
2 tablespoons white wine vinegar
$^1/_2$ tablespoon Dijon mustard
$^1/_4$ teaspoon sugar
3 tablespoons regular or light olive oil
Seasoning to taste

Lazy Sally Cake

1 large can (20 ounces) crushed pineapple
1 box yellow cake mix
1 cup flaked coconut
1 cup pecan pieces
$^1/_4$ cup dark brown sugar
3 tablespoons butter

EQUIPMENT

Large skillet	Assorted cooking
Medium covered	utensils
saucepan	Vegetable peeler
9x13-inch glass baking	Apple corer
dish	Whisk
Large bowl	Plastic bag
2 small bowls	Mallet
Assorted kitchen knives	Waxed paper
Measuring cups and	
spoons	

COUNTDOWN

1 Assemble the ingredients and equipment
2 Do Steps 1–3 of the *Lazy Sally Cake*
3 Do Steps 1–2 of the *Incredible Edible Chicken*
4 Do Step 1 of the *Hello Dilly*
5 Do Steps 1–2 of the *Frivolous Carrots*
6 Do Steps 3–4 of the *Incredible Edible Chicken*
7 Do Step 3 of the *Frivolous Carrots*
8 Do Step 2 of the *Hello Dilly*
9 Do Step 4 of the *Frivolous Carrots*
10 Do Steps 5–6 of the *Incredible Edible Chicken*
11 Do Step 3 of the *Hello Dilly*

Incredible Edible Chicken

1 Place the chicken breasts between 2 pieces of waxed paper and pound out from the center with a mallet to flatten them into a uniform 1/2-inch thickness.

2 Peel and chop the onion. Chop the parsley.

3 Combine the flour and the paprika in a plastic bag. Season to taste. Place the chicken breasts in the plastic bag and coat them evenly.

4 Heat the oil in a large skillet. Sauté the chicken and the onion, turning once, until the breasts are cooked through and are lightly browned on both sides, about 10 minutes.

5 Remove the chicken from the skillet and keep it warm.

6 Wipe out the skillet. Combine the sour cream, the mayonnaise, the sherry and the water in the skillet and whisk until smooth. Heat the mixture but do not let it boil. Pour the sauce over the chicken and sprinkle with the parsley.

Frivolous Carrots

1 Bring water to a boil in a medium saucepan.

2 Peel and thinly slice the carrots. Core and slice the apple.

3 Cook the carrots in the boiling water for 10 minutes.

4 Drain the carrots and return them to the saucepan. Add the sliced apple, the brown sugar, the butter and the lemon juice. Mix the ingredients well. Then cover the saucepan and cook the mixture until the apple slices are tender, about 5 minutes.

Hello Dilly

1 Wash and dry the lettuce and tear it into bite-size pieces. Trim and slice the scallions. Combine the lettuce and the scallions in a large bowl. Chop the parsley. Chop the dill.

2 In a small bowl, whisk together the vinegar, the mustard and the sugar. Add the oil, the parsley and the dill and whisk until the mixture is well blended. Season to taste.

3 Toss the salad with the dressing.

Lazy Sally Cake

1 Preheat the oven to 350°F.

2 Grease a 9x13-inch glass baking dish. Spread the undrained pineapple in the dish. Cover the pineapple evenly with the yellow cake mix.

3 In a small bowl, combine the coconut, the nuts and the brown sugar, and spread the mixture over the cake mix. Cut the butter into small pieces and dot the top of the cake with them. Bake until the cake is set, 40 to 45 minutes.

WEDNESDAY

Kiss-Me-Not Pasta

1 cup fresh parsley (when chopped)
2 tablespoons fresh dill (when chopped)
6 cloves garlic
16 ounces spaghetti
4 tablespoons butter
4 tablespoons regular or light olive oil
Seasoning to taste

Fickle Asparagus

1¹/₂ pounds fresh asparagus
1 medium shallot
2 tablespoons butter
Seasoning to taste

Tomato Teasers

4 firm large fresh tomatoes
3 tablespoons regular or light olive oil
Seasoning to taste
¹/₂ cup seasoned bread crumbs
³/₄ cup shredded regular or low-fat
*   mozzarella cheese*

Strawberry Temptation

1 pint fresh strawberries
3 egg yolks*
¹/₄ cup sugar
2 tablespoons marsala wine (or 2 tablespoons
*   nonalcoholic red wine + 1 tablespoon*
*   sugar)*
4 prepared shortcake dessert cups

*Reserve the egg whites for use on Thursday.

EQUIPMENT

Electric hand mixer	Measuring cups and
Stockpot	spoons
Large covered skillet	Assorted cooking
Double boiler	utensils
Small saucepan	Whisk
Small bowl	Pastry brush
Colander	Aluminum foil
Assorted kitchen knives	

COUNTDOWN

1 Assemble the ingredients and equipment
2 Do Step 1 of the *Strawberry Temptation*
3 Do Steps 1–2 of the *Kiss-Me-Not Pasta*
4 Do Step 1 of the *Fickle Asparagus*
5 Do Steps 1–2 of the *Tomato Teasers*
6 Do Steps 3–4 of the *Kiss-Me-Not Pasta*
7 Do Step 2 of the *Fickle Asparagus*
8 Do Steps 3–5 of the *Tomato Teasers*
9 Do Step 5 of the *Kiss-Me-Not Pasta*
10 Do Steps 2–3 of the *Strawberry Temptation*

Kiss-Me-Not Pasta

1 Bring water to a boil in a stockpot.

2 Chop the parsley. Chop the dill. Mince the garlic.

3 Cook the pasta until it is almost tender, 2 to 3 minutes if you are using fresh pasta and 7 to 8 minutes if you are using dried pasta.

4 Melt the butter with the oil in a small saucepan. Sauté the garlic until it is golden brown, about 5 minutes. Mix in the parsley and the dill, season to taste and heat the mixture through.

5 Drain the pasta and return it to the stockpot. Toss the pasta with the sauce.

Fickle Asparagus

1 Trim the asparagus and slice it diagonally into 2-inch pieces. Peel and chop the shallot.

2 Melt the butter in a large skillet. Add the shallot and the asparagus. Season to taste and sauté until the asparagus is just tender, 3 to 7 minutes, depending on thickness. Remove the skillet from the heat and cover to keep warm until you are ready to serve.

Tomato Teasers

1 Preheat the broiler.

2 Cut the tomatoes in half. Brush the cut halves with 1 tablespoon of the oil and season to taste.

3 Place a sheet of aluminum foil over the broiler tray. Place the tomatoes on the foil and broil them, 3 or 4 inches from the heat, for 2 minutes.

4 In a small bowl, combine the remaining oil with the bread crumbs. Spoon the mixture over the tomatoes and sprinkle with the cheese.

5 Return the tomatoes to the broiler and cook until bubbly, 1 to 2 minutes.

Strawberry Temptation

1 Wash, dry, trim and slice the strawberries.

2 Bring water to a boil in the bottom of a double boiler. Using an electric hand mixer, beat the egg yolks, the sugar and the wine in the top of the double boiler until the mixture is foamy and very thick, 5 to 7 minutes. Be careful not to overcook or the mixture will curdle.

3 Fill the dessert cups with the strawberries and pour the egg yolk mixture on top.

THURSDAY

Clever Cod Casserole

1 small green bell pepper
1 small carrot
1 small onion
1 tablespoon fresh parsley (when chopped)
$1^1/_4$ pounds cod fillets
2 tablespoons dry white wine (or nonalcoholic white wine or clam juice)
$^1/_2$ teaspoon dried savory
Seasoning to taste
2 tablespoons butter

Golden Broccoli

1 medium bunch broccoli
12 fresh Chinese snow peas
3 cloves garlic
3 tablespoons regular or light olive oil
3 tablespoons lemon juice
Seasoning to taste
1 tablespoon grated fresh lemon peel

Hot Bacon Salad

6 slices bacon
1 very small (or half) head red cabbage
4 scallions (green onions)
2 tablespoons balsamic vinegar
$1^1/_2$ tablespoons sugar
Seasoning to taste

Banana Pudding Banana

1 small package (3.4 ounces) instant banana cream pudding mix
2 cups whole milk
3 egg whites reserved from Wednesday
2 tablespoons sugar
$^1/_8$ teaspoon cream of tartar
2 medium bananas
$^1/_4$ teaspoon ground cinnamon
$^1/_8$ teaspoon ground nutmeg

EQUIPMENT

Electric hand mixer	Assorted kitchen knives
2 small skillets	Measuring cups and
Large saucepan	spoons
7x11-inch glass baking dish	Assorted cooking utensils
Large bowl	Vegetable grater
Medium bowl	Vegetable peeler
Small bowl	Aluminum foil

COUNTDOWN

1 Assemble the ingredients and equipment
2 Do Steps 1–2 of the *Banana Pudding Banana*
3 Do Steps 1–4 of the *Clever Cod Casserole*
4 Do Step 1 of the *Golden Broccoli*
5 Do Steps 1–4 of the *Hot Bacon Salad*
6 Do Steps 2–5 of the *Golden Broccoli*
7 Do Step 3 of the *Banana Pudding Banana*

Clever Cod Casserole

1 Preheat the oven to 450°F.

2 Seed and chop the bell pepper. Peel and thinly slice the carrot. Peel and chop the onion. Chop the parsley.

3 Grease a 7x11-inch glass baking dish and arrange the cod fillets in it in a single layer. Sprinkle the onion over the fish.

4 Combine the bell pepper, the carrot, the parsley, the wine and the savory. Season to taste. Spoon the mixture over the fish. Dot the fish with the butter and bake, loosely covered with aluminum foil, until the fish flakes easily when tested with a fork, 10 to 15 minutes.

Golden Broccoli

1 Bring water to a boil in a large saucepan.

2 Cut the broccoli into bite-size florets. Trim and string the snow peas. Peel and mince the garlic.

3 Cook the broccoli in the boiling water until it is crisp-tender, about 5 minutes, adding the snow peas for the final 30 seconds.

4 Drain the vegetables and return them to the saucepan.

5 Heat the oil in a small skillet. Sauté the garlic until it is golden, about 2 minutes. Add the lemon juice. Season to taste. Toss the sauce with the broccoli and sprinkle with the lemon peel.

Hot Bacon Salad

1 Dice the bacon and sauté it in a small skillet until crisp, about 5 minutes, draining it on a paper towel and reserving the drippings.

2 Coarsely grate the cabbage into a large bowl.

3 Trim and chop the scallions. Add the scallions, the vinegar and the sugar to the bacon drippings in the skillet and mix well. Season to taste. Return the bacon and cook until the mixture is heated through.

4 Toss the cabbage with the hot bacon mixture.

Banana Pudding Banana

1 In a medium bowl, beat the pudding mix and the milk until well blended. Refrigerate for at least 20 minutes.

2 In a small bowl, whip the egg whites until they are frothy. Gradually add the sugar and the cream of tartar and beat until the mixture is stiff. Refrigerate until you are ready to use.

3 Peel and slice the bananas. Layer the bananas and the pudding into individual parfait glasses, reserving several banana slices for garnish. Top the pudding with the whipped egg whites and the reserved bananas. Sprinkle each serving with cinnamon and nutmeg.

FRIDAY

Popeye's Frittata

3/4 pound spinach
1/4 pound mushrooms
1 jar (6 1/2 ounces) marinated artichoke hearts
4 tablespoons butter
3 eggs
1 cup flour
1 teaspoon baking powder
1 cup whole or low-fat milk
Seasoning to taste
1 pound shredded regular or low-fat Monterey
  Jack cheese
1 pound fresh tomatoes

Galley Toss

1 pound new red potatoes
2 tablespoons butter
1 medium onion
1 pound tart green apples
1 tablespoon dark brown sugar
1 teaspoon ground allspice
Seasoning to taste

Crunchy Ice Cream Parfait

16 Oreo cookies
1 quart vanilla fudge ice cream
Whipped cream for garnish
4 maraschino cherries for garnish

EQUIPMENT

Large covered skillet
7x11-inch glass baking
  dish
Large bowl
Assorted kitchen knives
Measuring cups and
  spoons

Assorted cooking
  utensils
Vegetable brush
Apple corer
Ice cream scoop

COUNTDOWN

1 Assemble the ingredients and equipment
2 Do Steps 1–4 of *Popeye's Frittata*
3 Do Steps 1–4 of the *Galley Toss*
4 Do Step 5 of *Popeye's Frittata*
5 Do Step 5 of the *Galley Toss*
6 Do Steps 1–2 of the *Crunchy Ice Cream Parfait*

Popeye's Frittata

1 Preheat the oven to 350°F.

2 Wash, dry and stem the spinach and tear it into bite-size pieces. Wash, pat dry, trim and slice the mushrooms. Drain and chop the artichoke hearts.

3 Melt the butter in a 7x11-inch glass baking dish.

4 Beat the eggs in a large bowl. Mix the flour, the baking powder and the milk into the eggs. Season to taste. Add the mushrooms, the spinach, the artichokes and three-fourths of the cheese, and combine. Pour the mixture into the baking dish over the melted butter and bake for 20 minutes.

5 Slice the tomatoes and place them over the top of the frittata. Sprinkle with the remaining cheese, and bake until the frittata is golden brown, about 20 minutes more. Let the frittata cool slightly before serving.

Galley Toss

1 Scrub the potatoes, but do not peel. Slice them into $1/8$-inch rounds.

2 Melt the butter in a large skillet. Add the potatoes and sauté them until they are golden, 8 to 12 minutes.

3 Peel and thinly slice the onion. Core and halve the unpeeled apples and cut them into $1/4$-inch slices.

4 Add the apples, the onion and more butter, if necessary, to the skillet. Stir to coat the ingredients. Then sauté until the potatoes and apples are barely tender, about 7 minutes. Do not overcook.

5 Add the brown sugar and the allspice, and stir to combine. Season to taste. Turn off the heat and cover the skillet to keep warm until you are ready to serve.

Crunchy Ice Cream Parfait

1 Chunk the Oreo cookies.

2 Alternate layers of fudge ice cream and Oreo cookie chunks in parfait glasses. Top each serving with a dollop of whipped cream and a maraschino cherry.

MARCH
WEEK ONE

WEEK AT A GLANCE

Monday

VELVET CHICKEN
LEMON SILK PILAF
GREEN SATIN SALAD
BLUEBERRY BROCADE

Tuesday

PERFECT PERCH
IDEAL POTATOES
CORNY SNOW PEAS
CHERRY DELIGHT

Wednesday

EASY ON THE CHILI
LIGHTLY-LIGHTLY SALAD
MUNCHIN' MUFFINS
GINGER-CRUNCH PEACHES

Thursday

MARDI GRAS MACARONI
FRENCH QUARTER SALAD
CARNIVAL PUDDING

Friday

SOMETHING'S FISHY HERE
IT'S ALL RICE WITH ME
FAR OUT SALAD
BUTTERSCOTCH FUN

CHECK STAPLES

- □ Butter
- □ Flour
- □ Cornstarch
- □ Cornmeal
- □ Baking powder
- □ Bisquick
- □ Granulated sugar
- □ Multicolored sprinkles
- □ Chocolate sprinkles
- □ Long-grain white rice
- □ Regular or light vegetable oil
- □ Regular or light olive oil
- □ Walnut oil
- □ Red wine vinegar
- □ White wine vinegar
- □ Lemon juice
- □ Grated fresh lemon peel
- □ Dijon mustard
- □ Candied ginger
- □ Grated Parmesan cheese
- □ Plain bread crumbs
- □ Dried basil
- □ Bay leaves
- □ Chili powder
- □ Ground cinnamon
- □ Ground cumin
- □ Dried dill
- □ Dried oregano
- □ Dried tarragon
- □ Pepper
- □ Salt

SHOPPING NOTES

- ● If you are shopping once a week and cannot arrange to purchase fresh seafood on the day you plan to use it, you can purchase *not previously frozen* seafood and freeze it, placing it in the refrigerator to thaw the night before you are ready to use it. Or you can purchase *still frozen* seafood and keep it frozen until the night before you are ready to use it.
- ● If you cannot arrange to purchase fresh clams on the day you plan to use them, you may substitute 1 can (10 ounces) of whole clams.

SHOPPING LIST

MEAT & POULTRY

1 pound bulk pork or turkey sausage (W)
3 pounds chicken pieces (M)

FISH

1¼ pounds skinless perch fillets (T)
1½ pounds firm fish fillets, such as cod (F)
12 medium clams in shells (F)
½ pound medium shrimp, shelled and deveined (F)

FRESH PRODUCE

Vegetables

1¼ pounds small new red potatoes (T)
1 small bunch broccoli (Th)
1 medium zucchini (Th)
¾ pound Chinese snow peas (T)
¼ pound spinach (M)
6 large mushrooms (M)
1 large carrot (Th)
1 stalk celery (M)
2 medium onions—1 (W), 1 (F)
2 small onions—1 (M), 1 (F)
2 medium shallots—1 (T), 1 (F)
3 scallions (green onions)—1 (T), 2 (Th)
1 head garlic (W, Th, F)
1 bunch parsley (M, T)
1 bunch chives (M, Th)
2 medium heads lettuce—1 (M), 1 (Th)
1 small head lettuce (F)
1 package (16 ounces) mixed salad greens (W)
1 bunch watercress (F)
2 ripe avocados (F)
½ pound tomatoes (Th)
1 medium cucumber (W)
2 large green bell peppers (W)
1 medium green bell pepper (F)

Fruit

½ pint strawberries (Th)
2 pink grapefruit (F)

CANS, JARS & BOTTLES

Soup

1 can (14½ ounces) chicken broth (M)
2 cans (14½ ounces each) vegetable broth (F)
1 can (10¾ ounces) vegetable soup (W)
1 can (10¾ ounces) bean and bacon soup (W)
1 can (10¾ ounces) cheddar cheese soup (Th)

Vegetables

2 medium cans (14½ ounces each) cut-up tomatoes—1 (Th), 1 (F)
1 small can (6 ounces) tomato paste (F)
1 can (11 ounces) whole kernel corn (T)

Fruit

1 small can (8¾ ounces) pitted dark cherries in syrup (T)
1 large can (29 ounces) sliced peaches (W)
1 small can (8 ounces) pineapple chunks (Th)
1 can (11 ounces) mandarin oranges (Th)

Juice

1 small can (6 ounces) pineapple juice (M)
2 tablespoons tomato juice (Th)

Condiments

1 small jar (2 ounces) diced pimiento (T)

Dessert Needs

½ cup butterscotch topping (F)

PACKAGED GOODS

Pasta, Rice & Grains

8 ounces elbow macaroni (Th)

Nuts & Seeds

1 cup pecan pieces (M)
½ cup sliced almonds (F)

Dessert & Baking Needs

1 box yellow cake mix (M)
1 small package (3.4 ounces) instant vanilla pudding mix (Th)
4 prepared shortcake dessert cups (F)

WINES & SPIRITS

2 teaspoons dry white wine (or nonalcoholic white wine or chicken broth) (M)
½ cup dry white wine (or nonalcoholic white wine or clam juice) (T)

REFRIGERATED PRODUCTS

Dairy

2 cups whole milk (Th)
1 cup whole or low-fat milk (W)
½ cup buttermilk (T)
¼ cup half-and-half (M)
Whipped cream for garnish (M)
6 eggs—2 (M, T), 1 (T), 3 (W)

Cheese

½ pound shredded regular or low-fat Monterey Jack cheese (Th)

FROZEN GOODS

Vegetables

1 package (20 ounces) mixed vegetables (W)

Fruit

2 pounds blueberries (M)

Desserts

1 pint cherry vanilla ice cream (T)
1 pint vanilla ice cream (F)

MONDAY

Velvet Chicken

1 small onion
3 pounds chicken pieces
1 stalk celery with leaves
1 large parsley sprig

PARSLEY BUTTER SAUCE:
1/4 cup fresh parsley (when chopped)
4 tablespoons butter
1 tablespoon flour
2 teaspoons dry white wine (or nonalcoholic
    white wine or chicken broth)
Seasoning to taste

Lemon Silk Pilaf

2 tablespoons butter
1 cup long-grain white rice
1 can (14 1/2 ounces) chicken broth
2 tablespoons water
Seasoning to taste
2 tablespoons fresh parsley (when chopped)
2 teaspoons fresh chives (when chopped)
2 tablespoons grated Parmesan cheese

LEMON-CREAM SAUCE:
1 tablespoon lemon juice
1 teaspoon grated fresh lemon peel
2 egg yolks*
1/4 cup half-and-half

Green Satin Salad

1/4 pound fresh spinach
1 medium head lettuce
6 large mushrooms
2 tablespoons lemon juice

*Reserve the egg whites for use on Tuesday.

1 tablespoon Dijon mustard
1 tablespoon sugar
1 teaspoon dried dill
3 tablespoons regular or light olive oil
Seasoning to taste

Blueberry Brocade

2 pounds frozen blueberries
7 tablespoons butter
1 small can (6 ounces) pineapple juice
1 box yellow cake mix
1 cup pecan pieces
Whipped cream for garnish

EQUIPMENT

Dutch oven	Assorted kitchen knives
Large covered	Measuring cups and
saucepan	spoons
2 small saucepans	Assorted cooking
9x13-inch baking pan	utensils
2 large bowls	Whisk
2 small bowls	

COUNTDOWN

1 Assemble the ingredients and equipment
2 Do Step 1 of the *Blueberry Brocade*
3 Do Step 1 of the *Velvet Chicken*
4 Do Step 1 of the *Lemon Silk Pilaf*
5 Do Step 2 of the *Blueberry Brocade*
6 Do Steps 1–3 of the *Green Satin Salad*
7 Do Step 2 of the *Lemon Silk Pilaf*
8 Do Step 2 of the *Velvet Chicken*
9 Do Steps 3–4 of the *Lemon Silk Pilaf*
10 Do Steps 3–4 of the *Velvet Chicken*
11 Do Step 4 of the *Green Satin Salad*
12 Do Step 3 of the *Blueberry Brocade*

Velvet Chicken

1 Quarter the unpeeled onion and place it in a Dutch oven with the chicken pieces, the celery stalk and the parsley sprig. Season to taste. Cover the chicken with cold water and bring it to a boil. Reduce the heat, cover and simmer until the chicken is tender, about 45 minutes.

2 Chop the parsley.

3 Melt the butter in a small saucepan. Add the flour and whisk to combine. Stir in the wine and the parsley. Season to taste. Cook the sauce just long enough for the alcohol to evaporate, about 3 minutes.

4 Top the chicken with the parsley butter sauce.

Lemon Silk Pilaf

1 Melt the butter in a large saucepan. Add the rice and cook until it turns opaque, about 2 minutes. Add the broth and the water. Season to taste. Bring the mixture to a boil, reduce the heat, cover and simmer until all the liquid is absorbed and the rice is tender, 20 to 25 minutes.

2 Chop the parsley and the chives.

3 Combine the lemon juice, the lemon peel, the egg yolks and the half-and-half in a small saucepan. Whisk until the mixture is heated and well blended.

4 Fold the lemon–cream sauce gently into the rice, and sprinkle with the Parmesan cheese, the parsley and the chives.

Green Satin Salad

1 Rinse, dry and stem the spinach. Wash, dry and shred the lettuce. Wash, pat dry and slice the mushrooms.

2 In the bottom of a large bowl, whisk together the lemon juice, the mustard, the sugar, the dill and the oil until thick. Season to taste.

3 Add the sliced mushrooms and toss to coat. Add the spinach and the lettuce and then refrigerate until you are ready to use.

4 Toss the salad before serving.

Blueberry Brocade

1 Preheat the oven to 350°F. Set the package of blueberries in a large bowl of warm water to thaw.

2 Melt the butter. Combine the thawed blueberries and the pineapple juice. Spread the mixture in the bottom of a 9x13-inch baking pan. Sprinkle the cake mix over the blueberries and drizzle the melted butter over the cake mix. Top with the chopped nuts and bake until lightly browned, 45 to 50 minutes.

3 Top with dollops of whipped cream.

TUESDAY

Perfect Perch

1 scallion (green onion)
1 tablespoon fresh parsley (when chopped)
1¼ pounds skinless perch fillets
3 tablespoons lemon juice
1 egg yolk
4 tablespoons softened butter
½ teaspoon dried tarragon
½ cup dry white wine (or nonalcoholic white
    wine or clam juice)
½ cup buttermilk
Seasoning to taste
½ cup plain bread crumbs

Ideal Potatoes

1¼ pounds small new red potatoes
1 small jar (2 ounces) diced pimiento
1 tablespoon butter
Seasoning to taste

Corny Snow Peas

1 medium shallot
¾ pound Chinese snow peas
1 can (11 ounces) whole kernel corn
2 tablespoons butter
1 teaspoon Dijon mustard
¼ teaspoon dried basil
Seasoning to taste

Cherry Delight

1 small can (8¾ ounces) pitted dark cherries
    in syrup
1 teaspoon cornstarch
3 egg whites (2 reserved from Monday)
1½ tablespoons sugar
1 pint cherry vanilla ice cream

EQUIPMENT

Blender	Small bowl
Electric hand mixer	Assorted kitchen knives
Large skillet	Measuring cups and
Medium covered	spoons
saucepan	Assorted cooking
2 small saucepans	utensils
7x11-inch glass baking	Vegetable peeler
dish	Ice cream scoop

COUNTDOWN

1 Assemble the ingredients and equipment
2 Do Steps 1–5 of the *Perfect Perch*
3 Do Step 1 of the *Ideal Potatoes*
4 Do Steps 6–7 of the *Perfect Perch*
5 Do Step 1 of the *Corny Snow Peas*
6 Do Step 2 of the *Ideal Potatoes*
7 Do Step 2 of the *Corny Snow Peas*
8 Do Steps 1–4 of the *Cherry Delight*

Perfect Perch

1 Preheat the oven to 350°F.

2 Trim and chop the scallion. Chop the parsley.

3 Wipe the fish fillets with damp paper towels and arrange them in a single layer in a 7x11-inch glass baking dish. Sprinkle the fish with the lemon juice and let stand.

4 Drop the egg yolk into a blender. Add the butter and process until the mixture is smooth. Add the scallion, the parsley and the tarragon and blend well. Scrape the mixture into a small bowl.

5 Combine the wine and the buttermilk in a small saucepan. Bring the mixture to a boil, stirring constantly, and cook for 1 minute. Season to taste.

6 Fold each fish fillet in thirds, as if folding a letter, and return, seam side down, to the baking dish. Spread the herb butter evenly over the fillets. Pour the buttermilk mixture carefully around the fish and sprinkle with the bread crumbs.

7 Bake until the bread crumbs are golden brown and the fish flakes easily with a fork, 15 to 20 minutes.

Ideal Potatoes

1 Scrub and quarter the potatoes. Drain the pimientos. In a medium saucepan, cover the potatoes with cold water. Cover the saucepan and bring the water to a boil. Reduce the heat and cook until the potatoes are tender, 10 to 15 minutes.

2 Drain the potatoes and return them to the saucepan. Add the butter and toss to combine. Season to taste and toss with the pimiento. Cover to keep warm until you are ready to serve.

Corny Snow Peas

1 Peel and chop the shallot. Trim and string the snow peas. Drain the corn.

2. Melt the butter in a large skillet. Add the shallot and sauté for 2 minutes. Add the snow peas and the corn and sauté for 2 minutes. Add the mustard and the basil, and season to taste.

Cherry Delight

1 Drain the cherries, reserving $1/4$ cup of the liquid.

2. Mix the reserved cherry liquid with the cornstarch and heat the mixture in a small saucepan until it thickens, about 2 minutes.

3. Beat the egg whites with the sugar until stiff peaks form.

4. Top scoops of ice cream with the egg white mixture and the drained cherries, and drizzle with the hot sauce.

WEDNESDAY

Easy on the Chili

1 package (20 ounces) frozen mixed vegetables
1 medium onion
2 large green bell peppers
2 cloves garlic
1 pound bulk pork or turkey sausage
1 can (10³/₄ ounces) vegetable soup
1 can (10³/₄ ounces) bean and bacon soup
1¹/₄ cups water
3 tablespoons chili powder
2 tablespoons ground cumin
1 tablespoon white wine vinegar
Seasoning to taste

Lightly-Lightly Salad

1 package (16 ounces) mixed salad greens
1 medium cucumber
1 clove garlic
3 tablespoons regular or light olive oil
2 tablespoons white wine vinegar
¹/₄ teaspoon sugar
¹/₈ teaspoon dried oregano
Seasoning to taste

Munchin' Muffins

1 cup flour
1 cup cornmeal
2 tablespoons sugar
4 teaspoons baking powder
¹/₂ teaspoon salt
1 cup whole or low-fat milk
2 eggs
¹/₄ cup regular or light vegetable oil

Ginger-Crunch Peaches

1 large can (29 ounces) sliced peaches
2 tablespoons candied ginger
2 tablespoons water
³/₄ cup sugar
1 egg
1¹/₄ cups Bisquick
¹/₂ teaspoon ground cinnamon
4 tablespoons butter

EQUIPMENT

Dutch oven	Assorted kitchen knives
Large bowl	Measuring cups and
3 medium bowls	spoons
3 small bowls	Assorted cooking
8x8-inch glass baking	utensils
dish	Whisk
12-cup muffin tin	

COUNTDOWN

1 Assemble the ingredients and equipment
2 Do Step 1 of *Easy on the Chili*
3 Do Steps 1–4 of the *Ginger-Crunch Peaches*
4 Do Steps 2–4 of *Easy on the Chili*
5 Do Steps 1–4 of the *Munchin' Muffins*
6 Do Steps 1–2 of the *Lightly-Lightly Salad*

Easy on the Chili

1 Set the package of frozen vegetables in a medium bowl of warm water to thaw.

2 Peel and chop the onion. Seed and chop 1 bell pepper. Seed and thinly slice the second bell pepper, reserving it for garnish. Peel and mince the garlic.

3 In a Dutch oven, sauté the sausage, the onion, the chopped pepper and the garlic until the meat is browned and the vegetables are tender, about 10 minutes.

4 Remove any fat from the Dutch oven. Stir in both soups, the vegetables, the water, the chili powder, the cumin and the vinegar. Season to taste. Bring the mixture to a boil, reduce the heat and simmer, uncovered, stirring occasionally, for 30 minutes.

Lightly-Lightly Salad

1 Rinse and dry the salad greens and place them in a large bowl. Peel and chop the cucumber. Toss the cucumber with the greens.

2 Peel and mince the garlic. In a small bowl, whisk the garlic with the oil, the vinegar, the sugar and the oregano. Season to taste and blend well. Toss the salad with the dressing.

Munchin' Muffins

1 Preheat the oven to 425°F. Grease a 12-cup muffin tin.

2 Combine the flour, the cornmeal, the sugar, the baking powder and the salt in a medium bowl.

3 In a small bowl, blend the milk, the eggs and the oil. Make a well in the center of the dry ingredients and add the liquid ingredients all at once, stirring gently to mix.

4 Fill the muffin cups two-thirds full and bake until the muffins are golden on top, about 15 minutes.

Ginger-Crunch Peaches

1 Preheat the oven to 400°F.

2 Drain the peaches. Cut the ginger into small pieces.

3 Place the peaches in an 8x8-inch glass baking dish. Sprinkle the water, 1/4 cup of the sugar and the ginger pieces over the peaches.

4 Beat the egg in a small bowl with a fork. In a medium bowl, mix the Bisquick with the remaining sugar and the cinnamon. Pour the egg slowly into the dry mixture, stirring constantly, until the mixture is crumbly. Spread the mixture evenly over the fruit. Dot with the butter and bake until the crust is golden brown, about 25 minutes.

THURSDAY

Mardi Gras Macaroni

2 tablespoons fresh chives (when chopped)
8 ounces elbow macaroni
1 can (10³/₄ ounces) cheddar cheese soup
1 medium can (14¹/₂ ounces) cut-up tomatoes
1 teaspoon Dijon mustard
Seasoning to taste
¹/₂ pound shredded regular or low-fat
    Monterey Jack cheese
¹/₂ pound fresh tomatoes

French Quarter Salad

1 small bunch broccoli
1 medium zucchini
1 large carrot
2 scallions (green onions)
1 medium head lettuce
1 clove garlic
2 tablespoons tomato juice
1 tablespoon red wine vinegar
1 tablespoon lemon juice
1 teaspoon regular or light olive oil
1 teaspoon Dijon mustard
¹/₈ teaspoon Tabasco sauce
Seasoning to taste

EQUIPMENT

Electric hand mixer	Measuring cups and
Large saucepan	spoons
Medium saucepan	Assorted cooking
2-quart casserole	utensils
Large bowl	Vegetable grater
Medium bowl	Vegetable brush
Small bowl	Vegetable peeler
Colander	Whisk
Assorted kitchen knives	

Carnival Pudding

1 small package (3.4 ounces) instant vanilla
    pudding mix
2 cups whole milk
¹/₂ pint fresh strawberries
1 can (11 ounces) mandarin oranges
1 small can (8 ounces) pineapple chunks
Multicolored sprinkles

COUNTDOWN

1 Assemble the ingredients and equipment
2 Do Steps 1–2 of the *Mardi Gras Macaroni*
3 Do Steps 1–3 of the *Carnival Pudding*
4 Do Step 3 of the *Mardi Gras Macaroni*
5 Do Steps 1–2 of the *French Quarter Salad*
6 Do Steps 4–5 of the *Mardi Gras Macaroni*
7 Do Steps 3–4 of the *French Quarter Salad*
8 Do Step 6 of the *Mardi Gras Macaroni*
9 Do Step 5 of the *French Quarter Salad*

Mardi Gras Macaroni

1 Preheat the oven to 425°F.

2 Bring water to a boil in a large saucepan. Chop the chives.

3 Cook the pasta in the boiling water until it is almost tender, 9 to 11 minutes.

4 In a 2-quart casserole, stir together the soup, the canned tomatoes and the mustard. Season to taste.

5 Drain the pasta and add it to the casserole. Top the mixture with three-fourths of the shredded cheese. Place the casserole in the oven, reduce the temperature to 400°F and bake until the macaroni is hot and bubbly, about 25 minutes.

6 Slice the tomatoes. Top the casserole with the tomato slices. Sprinkle with the remaining cheese and continue baking until the cheese melts, about 5 minutes. Sprinkle with the chives.

French Quarter Salad

1 Bring 1 inch of water to a boil in a medium saucepan.

2 Cut the broccoli into bite-size florets, and blanch them in the boiling water for 1 minute. Drain and rinse under cold water, and place them in a large bowl.

3 Scrub and grate the zucchini. Peel and grate the carrot. Trim and slice the scallions. Add the ingredients to the broccoli. Wash and dry the lettuce and place the leaves on individual plates.

4 Peel and mince the garlic. In a small bowl, combine the garlic with the tomato juice, the vinegar, the lemon juice, the oil, the mustard and the Tabasco sauce. Season to taste and whisk until the mixture is well blended.

5 Toss the vegetables with the dressing, and spoon the mixture over the lettuce.

Carnival Pudding

1 Combine the pudding mix and the milk in a medium bowl and beat until well blended.

2 Stem and slice the strawberries. Drain the oranges. Drain the pineapple.

3 Layer half of the pudding into individual parfait glasses. Add a layer of berries, then a layer of pineapple, then a layer of oranges. Add the remaining pudding, top with the sprinkles and refrigerate for at least 20 minutes.

FRIDAY

Something's Fishy Here

1 medium onion
3 cloves garlic
1 medium green bell pepper
1/4 cup regular or light vegetable oil
1 medium can (14 1/2 ounces) cut-up tomatoes
2 cans (14 1/2 ounces each) vegetable broth
1 small can (6 ounces) tomato paste
1 bay leaf
1 teaspoon dried basil
1 1/2 pounds firm fish fillets, such as cod
1/2 pound medium shrimp, shelled and deveined
12 medium clams in shells (or 1 can [10 ounces] whole clams)
Seasoning to taste

It's All Rice with Me

2 cups water
1 small onion
2 tablespoons butter
1/2 cup sliced almonds
1 cup long-grain white rice
1 teaspoon salt

Far Out Salad

2 pink grapefruit
2 ripe avocados
1 large bunch watercress
1 small head lettuce
1 medium shallot
2 tablespoons white wine vinegar
1/2 teaspoon dried tarragon
Seasoning to taste
3 tablespoons walnut oil

Butterscotch Fun

4 prepared shortcake dessert cups
1 pint vanilla ice cream
1/2 cup butterscotch topping
Chocolate sprinkles

EQUIPMENT

Dutch oven	Measuring cups and
1 1/2-quart burner-proof	spoons
covered casserole	Assorted cooking
Large bowl	utensils
Medium bowl	Whisk
Small bowl	Vegetable brush
Assorted kitchen knives	Ice cream scoop

COUNTDOWN

1 Assemble the ingredients and equipment
2 Do Step 1 of *It's All Rice with Me*
3 Do Steps 1–3 of *Something's Fishy Here*
4 Do Steps 2–5 of *It's All Rice with Me*
5 Do Steps 4–5 of *Something's Fishy Here*
6 Do Steps 1–5 of the *Far Out Salad*
7 Do Step 6 of *It's All Rice with Me*
8 Do Step 6 of *Something's Fishy Here*
9 Do Steps 1–2 of the *Butterscotch Fun*

Something's Fishy Here

1 Peel and chop the onion. Peel and mince the garlic. Seed and chop the bell pepper.

2 Heat the oil in a Dutch oven. Sauté the onion, the garlic and the bell pepper until the onion is translucent and the pepper is tender, about 10 minutes.

3 Add the undrained tomatoes. Stir in the broth, the tomato paste, the bay leaf and the basil. Bring the mixture to a rolling boil and cook, uncovered, for 15 minutes.

4 Cut the fish fillets into 1-inch pieces. Rinse the shrimp. Scrub the clams, discarding any open ones that do not close when tapped.

5 Add the fish, the clams (fresh or canned) and the shrimp to the Dutch oven. Season to taste. Cover and simmer until the fish flakes easily with a fork, the shrimp are pink, and the clams shells are opened, about 5 minutes.

6 Discard the bay leaf and any unopened clams.

It's All Rice with Me

1 Preheat the oven to 375°F.

2 Bring the water to a boil.

3 Peel and finely chop the onion.

4 Melt the butter in a 1½-quart casserole. Add the onions and the almonds and sauté, stirring, until the onion is translucent and the almonds are lightly browned, 5 to 7 minutes.

5 Add the rice and stir until it is coated with the butter. Pour in the boiling water and the

salt, stir and bake, covered, until the rice has absorbed all the water and is tender but still firm, 20 to 25 minutes.

6 Fluff the rice before serving.

Far Out Salad

1 Peel and section the grapefruit over a medium bowl, reserving all the juice. Peel, pit and slice the avocados and add them to the grapefruit, tossing very gently to coat them with the juice.

2 Wash, dry and stem the watercress. Wash and dry the lettuce and tear it into bite-size pieces. Place both ingredients in a large bowl.

3 Peel and finely chop the shallot. In a small bowl, combine the shallot with the vinegar and the tarragon, and season to taste. Add 1 tablespoon of the reserved grapefruit juice. In a slow, steady stream, add the walnut oil, whisking vigorously until the mixture is well blended.

4 Add half of the dressing to the watercress and lettuce, tossing until the greens are lightly coated.

5 Place the greens on individual plates. Alternate avocado slices and grapefruit sections on top of the greens and drizzle with the remaining dressing.

Butterscotch Fun

1 Place the dessert cups on individual plates.

2 Fill the cups with scoops of vanilla ice cream, and top with the butterscotch sauce and the chocolate sprinkles.

MARCH
WEEK TWO

Monday

UNDERSTATED LIVER FETTUCCINE
WAX ELOQUENT
WELL-SPOKEN SALAD
FINE FRUIT

Tuesday

PORK CHOPS DELISH-IOSO
ONION RICE PILAF
FORTY CARROTS
LUSCIOUS LEMON PIE

Wednesday

CHICKEN PAPRIKA
CRAZY FRIES
MARMALADE BEETS
SWEET NOTHING

Thursday

BOSTON CLAM CHOWDER
AVOCADOS QUINCY
BACK BAY BISCUITS
ALEXANDER GRAHAM BROWNIES

Friday

BUTTONS 'N' BOWS
TECHNICOLOR TOSS
FRIED FRENCH BREAD
CAKE OF THE ANGELS

CHECK STAPLES

- ☐ Butter
- ☐ Flour
- ☐ Granulated sugar
- ☐ Dark brown sugar
- ☐ Confectioners' sugar
- ☐ Sweetened cocoa
- ☐ Long-grain white rice
- ☐ Regular or light vegetable oil
- ☐ Regular or light olive oil
- ☐ Red wine vinegar
- ☐ Apple cider vinegar
- ☐ Lemon juice
- ☐ Grated fresh lemon peel
- ☐ Worcestershire sauce
- ☐ Tabasco sauce
- ☐ Dijon mustard
- ☐ Regular or low-fat mayonnaise
- ☐ Honey
- ☐ Plain bread crumbs
- ☐ Beef bouillon cubes
- ☐ Cayenne pepper
- ☐ Celery seeds
- ☐ Cream of tartar
- ☐ Dried basil
- ☐ Dried dill
- ☐ Garlic powder
- ☐ Italian seasoning
- ☐ Dry mustard
- ☐ Dried oregano
- ☐ Paprika
- ☐ Dried rosemary
- ☐ Dried sage
- ☐ Seasoning salt
- ☐ Dried thyme
- ☐ Pepper
- ☐ Salt
- ☐ Vanilla extract

MEAT & POULTRY

4 lean center-cut pork chops ($^3/_4$-inch thick) (T)
$^1/_2$ pound chicken livers (M)
$2^1/_2$ pounds chicken breasts (W)

FRESH PRODUCE

Vegetables

1 pound small new white potatoes (W)
5 medium baking potatoes (Th)
1 pound golden wax beans (or frozen) (M)
1 medium carrot (M)
1 pound baby carrots (T)
7 stalks celery—2 (M), 5 (Th)
1 large onion (Th)
1 medium onion (W)
4 small onions—1 (M), 2 (T), 1 (F)
2 small red onions—1 (M), 1 (F)
1 head garlic (M, F)
1 bunch parsley (W)
2 medium heads lettuce—1 (M), 1 (F)
2 ripe avocados (Th)
1 pound tomatoes—$^1/_2$ pound (Th), $^1/_2$ pound (F)
1 medium cucumber (M)
1 small red bell pepper (F)
1 small yellow bell pepper (F)

Fruit

1 pound seedless green grapes (M)
2 medium oranges (M)
$^1/_2$ pound fresh (or net weight canned) pineapple chunks (F)

CANS, JARS & BOTTLES

Soup

1 can ($14^1/_2$ ounces) vegetable broth (T)

Vegetables

1 medium can ($14^1/_2$ ounces) cut-up tomatoes (M)
1 medium can ($14^1/_2$ ounces) stewed tomatoes (T)
2 cans (4 ounces each) button mushrooms (F)
1 medium can (15 ounces) cubed beets (W)

Fish

2 cans ($6^1/_2$ ounces each) minced clams (Th)

Juice

1 bottle (8 ounces) clam juice (Th)

Spreads

1 tablespoon orange marmalade (W)

Dessert Needs

2 cans (14 ounces each) regular or low-fat sweetened condensed milk—1 (T), 1 (Th)

PACKAGED GOODS

Pasta, Rice & Grains

12 ounces fettuccine (M)
12 ounces pasta bows (F)

Baked Goods

1 small loaf French bread (F)
1 angel food loaf cake (W, F)

Nuts & Seeds

2 tablespoons chopped walnuts (M)

Dessert & Baking Needs

1 prepared 9-inch shortbread pie shell (T)

2 cups graham cracker crumbs (Th)
1 small (6 ounces) package semisweet chocolate chips (Th)

WINES & SPIRITS

3 tablespoons dry sherry (or nonalcoholic red wine or chicken broth) (M)
2 tablespoons dry sherry (or nonalcoholic red wine or clam juice) (Th)
1 tablespoon brandy (optional) (Th)

REFRIGERATED PRODUCTS

Dairy

1 cup whole or low-fat milk (T)
1 quart + 1 cup half-and-half—1 quart (Th), 1 cup (F)
1 cup regular or low-fat plain yogurt (M)
7 eggs —1 (M), 3 (T), 3 (F)

Juice

$^1/_4$ cup orange juice (W)

Deli

7 slices bacon—3 (M), 4 (Th)
1 package (7.05 ounces) small refrigerator biscuits (Th)

FROZEN GOODS

Desserts

1 small container (8 ounces) frozen whipped topping (W)

MONDAY

Understated Liver Fettuccine

3 slices bacon
1 small onion
$1/2$ pound fresh chicken livers
2 tablespoons butter
1 medium can ($14^1/2$ ounces) cut-up tomatoes
3 tablespoons dry sherry (or nonalcoholic red
    wine or chicken broth)
$1/2$ teaspoon dried sage
Seasoning to taste
12 ounces fettuccine
1 tablespoon regular or light vegetable oil

Wax Eloquent

1 pound wax beans (fresh or frozen)
2 tablespoons butter
$1/2$ teaspoon dried rosemary
$1/2$ teaspoon dried thyme
Seasoning to taste

Well-Spoken Salad

1 egg
1 medium head lettuce
2 stalks celery
1 medium carrot
1 small red onion
1 medium cucumber
1 clove garlic
3 tablespoons regular or light olive oil
2 tablespoons red wine vinegar
$1/2$ teaspoon sugar
$1/4$ teaspoon celery seeds
$1/4$ teaspoon dry mustard
$1/8$ teaspoon cayenne pepper
$1/8$ teaspoon Tabasco sauce
Seasoning to taste

Fine Fruit

2 medium oranges
1 pound seedless green grapes
1 cup regular or low-fat plain yogurt
2 tablespoons dark brown sugar
2 tablespoons chopped walnuts

EQUIPMENT

Stockpot	Colander
Medium skillet	Assorted kitchen knives
Medium covered saucepan	Measuring cups and spoons
Small saucepan	Assorted cooking utensils
Large bowl	Whisk
Medium bowl	Vegetable peeler
Small bowl	

COUNTDOWN

1 Assemble the ingredients and equipment
2 Do Step 1 of the *Well-Spoken Salad*
3 Do Step 1 of the *Understated Liver Fettuccine*
4 Do Steps 2–3 of the *Well-Spoken Salad*
5 Do Steps 2–4 of the *Understated Liver Fettuccine*
6 Do Step 1 of the *Wax Eloquent*
7 Do Step 4 of the *Well-Spoken Salad*
8 Do Steps 1–2 of the *Fine Fruit*
9 Do Step 5 of the *Understated Liver Fettuccine*
10 Do Steps 2–3 of the *Wax Eloquent*
11 Do Steps 5–6 of the *Well-Spoken Salad*
12 Do Steps 6–8 of the *Understated Liver Fettuccine*

Understated Liver Fettucine

1 Bring water to a boil in a stockpot.

2 Dice the bacon. In a medium skillet, sauté the bacon until it is crisp, about 5 minutes.

3 Peel and chop the onion. Rinse the chicken livers, pat them dry with a paper towel and cut them into $1/2$-inch pieces.

4 Drain the bacon on a paper towel. Discard all but 2 tablespoons of the drippings from the skillet. Melt the butter with the drippings, add the onion and sauté until it is golden, about 10 minutes.

5 Add the chicken livers and sauté, stirring, until they are just cooked, about 2 minutes. Remove the livers and reserve. Add the tomatoes, the sherry and the sage to the skillet. Season to taste. Cook, stirring occasionally, until the sauce begins to thicken, about 10 minutes.

6 Cook the pasta in the boiling water until it is almost tender, 2 to 3 minutes if you are using fresh pasta and 6 to 7 minutes if you are using dried pasta.

7 Drain the pasta, return it to the stockpot and toss it with the oil.

8 Return the bacon and the livers to the skillet, cook just long enough to heat through and toss the sauce with the pasta.

Wax Eloquent

1 Bring water to a boil in a medium saucepan.

2 Trim and string the wax beans and cook them until they are crisp-tender, 4 to 5 minutes.

3 Drain the beans, return them to the saucepan and toss them with the butter, the rosemary and the thyme. Season to taste. Cover to keep warm until you are ready to serve.

Well-Spoken Salad

1 Cover the egg with water in a small saucepan. Bring the water to a boil and hard-cook the egg, 10 to 12 minutes.

2 Wash and dry the lettuce and tear it into bite-size pieces. Trim and slice the celery. Peel and chop the carrot. Peel and slice the red onion. Peel and slice the cucumber. Combine the ingredients in a large bowl.

3 Peel and mince the garlic. In a small bowl, whisk together the garlic, the oil, the vinegar, the sugar, the celery seeds, the dry mustard, the cayenne pepper and the Tabasco sauce. Season to taste.

4 Remove the egg from the saucepan and chill in the freezer for 10 minutes.

5 Peel and chop the egg. Add it to the salad.

6 Toss the salad with the dressing.

Fine Fruit

1 Peel and section the oranges. Wash, dry and separate the grapes. Place both in a medium bowl.

2 Sread the fruit evenly with a layer of yogurt and sprinkle with the brown sugar and the walnuts. Refrigerate until you are ready to serve.

TUESDAY

Pork Chops Delish-ioso

4 lean pork chops (³/₄-inch thick)
Seasoning to taste
2 tablespoons regular or light vegetable oil
1 small onion
2 tablespoons flour
1 tablespoon dry mustard
¹/₄ teaspoon dried oregano
1 beef bouillon cube
1 cup whole or low-fat milk
1 medium can (14¹/₂ ounces) stewed tomatoes
2 tablespoons apple cider vinegar

Onion Rice Pilaf

1 small onion
2 tablespoons butter
1 cup long-grain white rice
1 can (14¹/₂ ounces) vegetable broth
¹/₄ cup water

Forty Carrots

1 pound baby carrots
2 tablespoons butter
1 teaspoon dark brown sugar
Seasoning to taste

Luscious Lemon Pie

3 eggs
1 can (14 ounces) regular or low-fat
    sweetened condensed milk
¹/₂ cup lemon juice
1 teaspoon grated fresh lemon peel
1 prepared 9-inch shortbread pie shell
¹/₂ teaspoon cream of tartar
¹/₃ cup sugar

EQUIPMENT

Electric hand mixer	Small bowl
Large skillet	Strainer
Medium skillet	Assorted kitchen knives
Medium covered	Measuring cups and
saucepan	spoons
Double boiler	Assorted cooking
Steamer insert	utensils
Medium bowl	Whisk

COUNTDOWN

1 Assemble the ingredients and equipment
2 Do Step 1 of the *Luscious Lemon Pie*
3 Do Steps 1–3 of the *Onion Rice Pilaf*
4 Do Steps 1–2 of the *Pork Chops Delish-ioso*
5 Do Step 1 of the *Forty Carrots*
6 Do Steps 2–5 of the *Luscious Lemon Pie*
7 Do Step 3 of the *Pork Chops Delish-ioso*
8 Do Step 2 of the *Forty Carrots*
9 Do Step 4 of the *Pork Chops Delish-ioso*
10 Do Step 3 of the *Forty Carrots*
11 Do Step 4 of the *Onion Rice Pilaf*
12 Do Step 5 of the *Pork Chops Delish-ioso*

Pork Chops Delish-ioso

1 Season the pork chops to taste.

2 Heat the oil in a large skillet. Cook the chops, turning once, until they are browned on the outside, but still moist on the inside, 20 to 25 minutes.

3 Peel and chop the onion.

4 Remove the chops and keep them warm. Drain the skillet, reserving 1 tablespoon of the drippings. Add the onion and sauté until it is soft, about 5 minutes. Whisk in the flour, the dry mustard and the oregano. Add the bouillon cube and the milk. Cook and whisk until the bouillon cube is dissolved and the sauce begins to thicken and bubble. Then cook and whisk 1 minute more. Stir in the undrained tomatoes and the vinegar. Cook until the mixture is heated through.

5 Return the pork to the skillet and coat the chops with the sauce.

Onion Rice Pilaf

1 Bring water to a boil in the bottom of a double boiler.

2 Peel and chop the onion.

3 In a medium skillet, melt the butter and sauté the onion and the rice until they are lightly browned, about 5 minutes. Transfer the mixture to the top of the double boiler. Add the broth and the water, reduce the heat, cover and simmer until all the liquid is absorbed and the rice is tender, 30 to 40 minutes.

4 Fluff the rice before serving.

Forty Carrots

1 Bring water to a boil in a medium saucepan.

2 Trim the baby carrots, if necessary. Place them in a steamer insert, place the steamer insert in the saucepan and steam the carrots until they are crisp-tender, 10 to 15 minutes.

3 Drain the carrots. Melt the butter and the brown sugar in the saucepan. Return the carrots to the saucepan and toss to coat. Season to taste. Cover to keep warm until you are ready to serve.

Luscious Lemon Pie

1 Preheat the oven to 375°F.

2 Separate the eggs. In a medium bowl, beat the egg yolks. Whisk in the milk, the lemon juice and the lemon peel. Pour the mixture into the pie shell.

3 In a small bowl, beat the egg whites with the cream of tartar until they are foamy. Gradually add the sugar and continue beating until the whites are stiff and glossy.

4 Spread the mixture on top of the pie, sealing around the edge of the crust.

5 Bake the pie until the peaks turn golden brown, about 10 minutes.

WEDNESDAY

Chicken Paprika

Seasoning to taste
2¹/₂ pounds chicken breasts
4 tablespoons softened butter
1 teaspoon Dijon mustard
1 teaspoon red wine vinegar
1 tablespoon paprika
³/₄ cup plain bread crumbs

Crazy Fries

1 pound small new white potatoes
1 medium onion
1 tablespoon fresh parsley (when chopped)
2 tablespoons regular or light vegetable oil
1 tablespoon seasoning salt
Seasoning to taste

Marmalade Beets

1 medium can (15 ounces) cubed beets
2 tablespoons butter
1 tablespoon orange marmalade
¹/₄ cup orange juice
Seasoning to taste

Sweet Nothing

1 small container (8 ounces) frozen whipped
    topping
¹/₄ cup sweetened cocoa
¹/₂ angel food loaf cake*
¹/₄ cup confectioners' sugar

*Reserve the balance of the cake for use on Friday.

EQUIPMENT

Large covered skillet	Assorted cooking
Medium saucepan	utensils
9x13-inch baking pan	Sifter
Small bowl	Whisk
Assorted kitchen knives	Pastry brush
Measuring cups and	
spoons	

COUNTDOWN

1 Assemble the ingredients and equipment
2 Do Step 1 of the *Sweet Nothing*
3 Do Steps 1–2 of the *Chicken Paprika*
4 Do Step 1 of the *Crazy Fries*
5 Do Steps 3–4 of the *Chicken Paprika*
6 Do Step 2 of the *Crazy Fries*
7 Do Steps 1–2 of the *Marmalade Beets*
8 Do Step 3 of the *Crazy Fries*
9 Do Step 2 of the *Sweet Nothing*

Chicken Paprika

1 Preheat the broiler.

2 Season the chicken to taste and broil, 5 inches from the heat, until the skin is browned, 5 to 7 minutes per side. Remove the chicken from the broiler and turn the oven temperature to 375°F.

3 In a small bowl, whisk together the butter, the mustard, the vinegar and the paprika. Season to taste.

4 Place the chicken, skin side up, in a 9x13-inch baking pan. Brush with the seasoned butter and sprinkle with the bread crumbs. Bake until the coating is crisp and the chicken is tender, 15 to 20 minutes.

Crazy Fries

1 Scrub, but do not peel, the potatoes and cut them into ³/₄-inch cubes. Peel and chop the onion. Chop the parsley.

2 In a large skillet, heat the oil and sauté the potatoes and the onion until they are lightly browned, about 5 minutes. Add the seasoning salt. Reduce the heat, cover the skillet and cook, stirring occasionally, until the potatoes are cooked through but not burned, about 15 minutes.

3 Season to taste. Toss the potatoes with the parsley.

Marmalade Beets

1 Drain the beets.

2 Melt the butter in a medium saucepan. Add the beets, the marmalade and the orange juice and combine. Season to taste. Heat thoroughly.

Sweet Nothing

1 Set the whipped topping out to thaw.

2 Slice the loaf cake in half horizontally. Fold the cocoa into the thawed whipped topping. Spread the bottom layer with half of the topping. Replace the top layer and spread it with the remaining topping. Dust the top of the cake with the confectioners' sugar.

THURSDAY

Boston Clam Chowder

4 slices bacon
5 stalks celery
1 large onion
2 tablespoons butter
5 medium baking potatoes
2 cans (6$^1/_2$ ounces each) minced clams
1 cup clam juice
2 tablespoons dry sherry (or nonalcoholic
    white wine or additional clam juice)
4 cups half-and-half
Seasoning to taste
$^1/_4$ cup flour

Avocados Quincy

2 ripe avocados
1 tablespoon lemon juice
$^1/_2$ pound fresh tomatoes
2 teaspoons dried basil
$^1/_4$ cup regular or light olive oil
2 tablespoons red wine vinegar
$^1/_8$ teaspoon Worcestershire sauce
$^1/_4$ teaspoon sugar
Seasoning to taste

Back Bay Biscuits

1 package (7.05 ounces) small refrigerator
    biscuits
1$^1/_2$ tablespoons Dijon mustard
1 tablespoon dried dill

Alexander Graham Brownies

2 cups graham cracker crumbs
1 can (14 ounces) regular or low-fat
    sweetened condensed milk
1 small package (6 ounces) semisweet
    chocolate chips
1 tablespoon brandy (optional)
1$^1/_2$ teaspoons vanilla extract
$^1/_4$ teaspoon salt

EQUIPMENT

Dutch oven	Assorted kitchen knives
Medium skillet	Measuring cups and
Small saucepan	spoons
9x9-inch baking pan	Assorted cooking
Cookie sheet	utensils
Medium bowl	Vegetable peeler
Small bowl	Whisk

COUNTDOWN

1 Assemble the ingredients and equipment
2 Do Steps 1–3 of the *Alexander Graham Brownies*
3 Do Steps 1–2 of the *Boston Clam Chowder*
4 Do Step 1 of the *Avocados Quincy*
5 Do Steps 1–2 of the *Back Bay Biscuits*
6 Do Steps 3–4 of the *Boston Clam Chowder*
7 Do Step 2 of the *Avocados Quincy*
8 Do Step 3 of the *Back Bay Biscuits*
9 Do Step 5 of the *Boston Clam Chowder*
10 Do Step 4 of the *Alexander Graham Brownies*

Boston Clam Chowder

1 Chop the bacon and cook it in a medium skillet until it is crisp, about 5 minutes. Trim and chop the celery. Peel and chop the onion. Drain the bacon on a paper towel. Remove all but 1 tablespoon of the drippings from the skillet, add 1 tablespoon of the butter and sauté the celery and the onion until they are soft, about 6 minutes.

2 Bring water to a boil in a Dutch oven. Peel the potatoes and cut them into $1/2$ inch cubes and boil them until they are tender, about 10 minutes.

3 Drain the potatoes and return them to the Dutch oven. Add the undrained clams, the clam juice, the celery and onion mixture, the remaining butter, the sherry, and 2 cups of the half-and-half. Season to taste. Heat the mixture through, but do not let it boil.

4 In a small bowl, whisk together the flour and the remaining half-and-half and add it to the Dutch oven, blending to thicken the chowder. Cover and barely simmer the chowder until you are ready to serve.

5 Crumble the bacon and sprinkle it over the chowder.

Avocados Quincy

1 Peel, halve and pit the avocados. Arrange them on individual plates and sprinkle them with the lemon juice to keep them from browning.

2 Chop the tomatoes. In a small saucepan, combine the tomatoes, the basil, the oil, the vinegar, the Worcestershire sauce and the sugar. Season to taste. Bring the mixture to a rolling boil and drizzle it over the avocados.

Back Bay Biscuits

1 Preheat the oven to 375°F.

2 Arrange the biscuits on an ungreased cookie sheet, and bake until they are lightly browned, about 10 minutes.

3 Remove the biscuits from the oven and turn on the broiler. Split the biscuits in half, spread the cut sides lightly with the mustard and then sprinkle with the dill. Place the biscuits 3 or 4 inches from the heat, and broil until the mustard is bubbly but not brown, 1 to 2 minutes.

Alexander Graham Brownies

1 Preheat the oven to 350°F. Grease a 9x9-inch baking pan.

2 In a medium bowl, combine the graham cracker crumbs, the condensed milk, the chocolate chips, the brandy, the vanilla and the salt. Spread the mixture evenly in the baking pan.

3 Bake the brownies until the top starts to brown and crust, 20 to 25 minutes.

4 Let the brownies cool and then cut them into squares.

FRIDAY

MENU

Buttons 'n' Bows

$^1/_2$ pound fresh tomatoes
1 small onion
2 cans (4 ounces each) button mushrooms
12 ounces pasta bows
1 tablespoon regular or light vegetable oil
2 tablespoons dried dill
1 tablespoon Italian seasoning
Seasoning to taste
$^1/_2$ cup regular or low-fat mayonnaise
1 cup half-and-half

Technicolor Toss

1 medium head lettuce
1 small red bell pepper
1 small yellow bell pepper
1 small red onion
1 clove garlic
2 tablespoons red wine vinegar
3 tablespoons regular or light olive oil
$^1/_2$ teaspoon honey
1 teaspoon Dijon mustard
Seasoning to taste

Fried French Bread

2 tablespoons butter
1 teaspoon garlic powder
1 small loaf French bread

Cake of the Angels

$^1/_2$ cup sugar
$^1/_4$ cup water
3 eggs
1 teaspoon vanilla extract
$^1/_2$ angel food loaf cake reserved from
    Wednesday
$^1/_2$ pound fresh (or net weight canned)
    pineapple chunks

EQUIPMENT

Electric hand mixer	2 small bowls
Large skillet	Colander
Large saucepan	Strainer
Medium saucepan	Assorted kitchen knives
Small covered	Measuring cups and
saucepan	spoons
9x9-inch baking pan	Assorted cooking
Large bowl	utensils
Medium bowl	Whisk

COUNTDOWN

1 Assemble the ingredients and equipment
2 Do Steps 1–3 of the *Cake of the Angels*
3 Do Steps 1–2 of the *Buttons 'n' Bows*
4 Do Steps 1–2 of the *Technicolor Toss*
5 Do Steps 3–4 of the *Buttons 'n' Bows*
6 Do Steps 1–2 of the *Fried French Bread*
7 Do Step 5 of the *Buttons 'n' Bows*
8 Do Step 3 of the *Technicolor Toss*
9 Do Steps 4–5 of the *Cake of the Angels*

Buttons 'n' Bows

1 Bring water to a boil in a large saucepan.

2 Peel and chop the tomatoes. Peel and chop the onion. Drain the mushrooms.

3 Cook the pasta in the boiling water until it is almost tender, 7 to 9 minutes.

4 Heat the oil in a medium saucepan and sauté the onion until it is limp, about 5 minutes. Add the tomatoes, the dill and the Italian seasoning. Season to taste. Fold the mushrooms into the tomato mixture. Add the mayonnaise and the half-and-half, and blend well. Season to taste. Heat the mixture thoroughly, but do not let it boil.

5 Drain the pasta, return it to the saucepan and toss it with the sauce. Cover and keep warm until you are ready to serve.

Technicolor Toss

1 Wash and dry the lettuce and tear it into bite-size pieces. Seed the bell peppers and cut them into thin strips. Peel and thinly slice the onion and separate it into rings. Combine the ingredients in a large bowl.

2 Peel and mince the garlic. In a small bowl, whisk together the garlic, the vinegar, the oil, the honey and the mustard. Season to taste.

3 Toss the salad with the dressing.

Fried French Bread

1 Melt the butter in a large skillet. Add the garlic powder.

2 Cut the bread into ½-inch slices and sauté the slices in the butter and garlic powder until they are golden, turning once, 2 to 3 minutes per side.

Cake of the Angels

1 In a small saucepan, combine 6 tablespoons of the sugar with the water. Bring the mixture to a boil and cook just until the sugar dissolves, about 1 minute. Remove the saucepan from heat.

2 Separate the eggs. Beat the yolks in a small bowl. Pour the sugar mixture into the beaten yolks in a thin stream. Return the mixture to the saucepan and simmer, whisking, until it is thickened, about 15 minutes.

3 Strain the sauce, then stir in the vanilla and let it cool.

4 Preheat the broiler. Whip the egg whites and the remaining sugar in a medium bowl until stiff peaks form.

5 Cut the cake into 4 slices and place them in a 9x9-inch baking pan. Spoon the pineapple chunks over the cake slices, drizzle the sauce over the pineapple, top with the egg white mixture and broil until the meringue turns lightly golden, about 1 minute.

MARCH
WEEK THREE

WEEK AT A GLANCE

Monday

CORNED BEEF BRISKET
NEW ENGLAND VEGETABLES
SHAMROCK PARFAIT

Tuesday

TANG KEW CHICKEN
SHANGHAIED RICE
ORIENTAL SALAD
YUM-YUM PUDDING

Wednesday

UNPRETENTIOUS PASTA
SALAD CRUNCH
THE LOAF BOAT
CHOCO-CHERRY CAKE

Thursday

RED LENTIL SOUP
ASPARA-BEAN SALAD
DILLICIOUS MUFFINS
BANANA MUENSTER

Friday

ROLY-POLY FLOUNDER
POTATO TUMBLES
CONFETTI SLAW
NOT-QUITE-PEARS HÉLÈNE

CHECK STAPLES

- ☐ Butter
- ☐ Flour
- ☐ Baking powder
- ☐ Cornstarch
- ☐ Granulated sugar
- ☐ Dark brown sugar
- ☐ Confectioners' sugar
- ☐ Multicolored sprinkles
- ☐ Chocolate syrup
- ☐ Italian hazelnut syrup
- ☐ Long-grain white rice
- ☐ Regular or light vegetable oil
- ☐ Regular or light olive oil
- ☐ Sesame oil
- ☐ Walnut oil
- ☐ Red wine vinegar
- ☐ Balsamic vinegar
- ☐ Lemon juice
- ☐ Grated fresh orange peel
- ☐ Fresh ginger
- ☐ Soy sauce
- ☐ Dijon mustard
- ☐ Regular or low-fat mayonnaise
- ☐ Honey
- ☐ Grated Parmesan cheese
- ☐ Bay leaves
- ☐ Caraway seeds
- ☐ Dried chervil
- ☐ Dried chives
- ☐ Ground cinnamon
- ☐ Whole cloves
- ☐ Dried dill
- ☐ Garlic powder
- ☐ Ground nutmeg
- ☐ Onion powder
- ☐ Sesame seeds
- ☐ Pepper
- ☐ Salt
- ☐ Vanilla extract

SHOPPING NOTE

● If you are shopping once a week and cannot arrange to purchase fresh flounder on the day you plan to use it, you can purchase *not previously frozen* flounder and freeze it, placing it in the refrigerator to thaw the night before you are ready to use it. Or you can purchase *still frozen* flounder and keep it frozen until the night before you are ready to use it.

MEAT & POULTRY

1 lean corned beef brisket (3 to 4 pounds) (M)
1¼ pounds boneless chicken breasts (T)

FISH

1¼ pounds flounder fillets (F)

FRESH PRODUCE

Vegetables

4 large baking potatoes (M)
1 pound small new red potatoes (F)
1 medium bunch broccoli (T)
¾ pound asparagus (Th)
½ pound green beans (Th)
¾ pound mushrooms— ½ pound (T), ¼ pound (F)
9 medium carrots—6 (M), 2 (Th), 1 (F)
2 stalks celery—2 (Th), 1 (F)
1 large onion (W)
3 medium onions—2 (M), 1 (Th)
1 small onion (T)
1 medium shallot (Th)
11 scallions (green onions)— 2 (T), 3 (W), 6 (F)
1 head garlic (T, W, Th)
1 bunch parsley (T, W, Th, F)
¼ pound bean sprouts (T)
1 large head green cabbage (M)
1 very small (or half) head green cabbage (F)
1 very small (or half) head red cabbage (F)
1 medium head Napa cabbage (T)
1 medium head lettuce (W)
1 large tomato (Th)
1 medium tomato (F)

Fruit

2 large pears (F)

4 medium bananas (Th)
2 small limes (M)

CANS, JARS & BOTTLES

Soup

1 can (14½ ounces) oriental broth (T)
3 cans (10¾ ounces each) beef broth (Th)
1 can (10¾ ounces) cream of shrimp soup (F)

Vegetables

1 medium can (14½ ounces) cut-up tomatoes (W)

Oriental Foods

1 can (5 ounces) sliced bamboo shoots (T)
1 can (11 ounces) lychees in syrup (T)

Fruit

1 small can (8 ounces) pineapple chunks (T)

Dessert Needs

1 can (21 ounces) cherry pie filling (W)
2 drops green food coloring (optional) (M)

PACKAGED GOODS

Pasta, Rice & Grains

16 ounces spaghetti (W)
3 cups red lentils (Th)

Baked Goods

1 small loaf French bread (W)
1 cup croutons (W)

Nuts & Seeds

¼ cup pecan pieces (F)

Dessert & Baking Needs

1 small package (3.4 ounces) instant vanilla pudding mix (T)
4 almond cookies (T)
1 package chocolate cake mix (W)

WINES & SPIRITS

3 tablespoons dry red wine (or nonalcoholic red wine or tomato juice) (Th)
3 tablespoons dry sherry (or nonalcoholic red wine or chicken broth) (T)
¼ cup dry sherry (or nonalcoholic red wine or clam juice) (F)
1 teaspoon Amaretto liqueur (or nonalcoholic Italian almond syrup) (T)

REFRIGERATED PRODUCTS

Dairy

1¼ cups whole milk (T)
1 cup whole or low-fat milk (Th)
1 cup whipping cream (M)
¾ cup regular or light sour cream (T)
3 eggs—1 (M), 1 (W), 1 (Th)

Cheese

8 slices Muenster cheese (Th)
1 cup shredded regular or low-fat Swiss cheese (F)

Deli

6 slices bacon (W)

FROZEN GOODS

Desserts

1 pint vanilla ice cream (F)

MONDAY

Corned Beef Brisket

2 medium onions
1 bay leaf
3 teaspoons grated fresh orange peel
6 whole cloves
1 1/2 cups water
1 lean corned beef brisket (3 to 4 pounds)

GLAZE:
1/4 cup Dijon mustard
2 tablespoons dark brown sugar
1 tablespoon honey
Seasoning to taste

New England Vegetables

4 large baking potatoes
6 medium carrots
1 large head green cabbage
Seasoning to taste

Shamrock Parfait

2 small limes
1 cup granulated sugar
2 tablespoons cornstarch
1/2 teaspoon ground nutmeg
1/8 teaspoon salt
1 cup water
1 egg
2 drops green food coloring (optional)
1 cup whipping cream
2 tablespoons confectioners' sugar
1 teaspoon vanilla extract
Multicolored sprinkles

EQUIPMENT

Slow cooker	Colander
Electric hand mixer	Assorted kitchen knives
Large covered saucepan	Measuring cups and spoons
Medium covered saucepan	Assorted cooking utensils
9x13-inch baking pan	Whisk
Medium bowl	Vegetable peeler
2 small bowls	

COUNTDOWN

IN THE MORNING:
  Do Step 1 of the *Corned Beef Brisket*
BEFORE DINNER:
  1 Assemble the remaining ingredients and equipment
  2 Do Step 2 of the *Corned Beef Brisket*
  3 Do Steps 1–4 of the *Shamrock Parfait*
  4 Do Step 1 of the *New England Vegetables*
  5 Do Step 3 of the *Corned Beef Brisket*
  6 Do Step 2 of the *New England Vegetables*
  7 Do Steps 4–5 of the *Corned Beef Brisket*
  8 Do Step 3 of the *New England Vegetables*
  9 Do Step 5 of the *Shamrock Parfait*

Corned Beef Brisket

1 Peel and slice the onions. Combine the onions with the bay leaf, the orange peel, the cloves and the water in a slow cooker. Add the corned beef, fat side up. Cover and cook on the low setting for 8 to 10 hours or on the high setting for 5 to 6 hours, depending on your schedule.

2 Preheat the oven to 375°F.

3 Remove the beef from the cooking liquid to a 9x13-inch baking pan, fat side up, reserving the cooking liquid for the New England Vegetables.

4 In a small bowl, whisk together the mustard, the brown sugar and the honey until smooth. Season to taste. Spread the mixture over the fat side of the corned beef. Bake, basting occasionally with the glaze, for 20 minutes

5 Remove the brisket from the oven and slice it across the grain.

New England Vegetables

1 Peel the potatoes and cut them into sixths. Peel and cut the carrots into 1-inch chunks. Cut the cabbage into wedges. Place the ingredients in a large saucepan. Season to taste.

2 Pour the reserved brisket liquid over the vegetables. Add water to cover if necessary. Bring the liquid to a boil, then reduce the heat, cover the saucepan and cook the vegetables until they are tender, about 20 minutes.

3 Drain the vegetables before serving.

Shamrock Parfait

1 Grate 1 teaspoon of lime peel. Juice the limes to $1/4$ cup.

2 Combine the granulated sugar, the cornstarch, the nutmeg, the salt and the water in a medium saucepan. Bring to a boil and cook until the mixture is thickened, 5 to 7 minutes. Add the lime juice and cook 1 minute more.

3 In a small bowl, whisk the egg with 2 tablespoons of the hot liquid until blended and add it to the saucepan. Cook for 2 minutes and then remove the saucepan from the heat. Add the lime peel and the food coloring, if desired. Cover the saucepan and let the mixture cool in the refrigerator until you are ready to serve.

4 In a medium bowl, whip the cream until it is thick. Fold in the confectioners' sugar and the vanilla. Refrigerate the mixture until you are ready to use.

5 Fold the whipped cream mixture into the lime mixture. Spoon it into individual serving dishes and top with the multicolored sprinkles.

TUESDAY

Tang Kew Chicken

1¼ pounds boneless, skinless chicken breasts
1 medium bunch broccoli
½ pound mushrooms
2 scallions (green onions)
1 tablespoon fresh ginger (when grated)
2 tablespoons regular or light vegetable oil
1 teaspoon sesame oil
3 tablespoons soy sauce
3 tablespoons dry sherry (or nonalcoholic red
    wine or chicken broth)
Seasoning to taste
1 teaspoon cornstarch dissolved in 2
    tablespoons cold water

Shanghaied Rice

2 tablespoons fresh parsley (when chopped)
1 small onion
1 clove garlic
1 tablespoon sesame oil
1 cup long-grain white rice
1 can (14½ ounces) oriental broth
¼ cup water
1 tablespoon soy sauce

Oriental Salad

1 medium head Napa cabbage
1 can (5 ounces) sliced bamboo shoots
1 small can (8 ounces) pineapple chunks
¼ pound fresh bean sprouts
2 tablespoons soy sauce
2 tablespoons regular or light vegetable oil
1 tablespoon sesame seeds
Seasoning to taste

Yum-Yum Pudding

1 small package (3.4 ounces) instant vanilla
    pudding mix
1¼ cups whole milk
¾ cup regular or light sour cream
1 teaspoon Amaretto liqueur (or nonalcoholic
    Italian almond syrup)
1 can (11 ounces) lychees in syrup
4 almond cookies

EQUIPMENT

Electric hand mixer	Assorted kitchen knives
Wok and wok utensils	Measuring cups and
Medium skillet	spoons
Double boiler	Assorted cooking
Large bowl	utensils
Medium bowl	Citrus grater
Small bowl	

COUNTDOWN

1 Assemble the ingredients and equipment
2 Do Steps 1–2 of the *Shanghaied Rice*
3 Do Step 1 of the *Yum-Yum Pudding*
4 Do Steps 1–2 of the *Oriental Salad*
5 Do Steps 1–3 of the *Tang Kew Chicken*
6 Do Step 3 of the *Shanghaied Rice*
7 Do Step 3 of the *Oriental Salad*
8 Do Step 2 of the *Yum-Yum Pudding*

Tang Kew Chicken

1 Cut the chicken into 1-inch strips. Cut the broccoli into bite-size florets. Wash, pat dry and slice the mushrooms. Trim and chop the scallions. With a citrus grater, grate the ginger.

2 Heat both oils in a wok. Add the chicken and stir-fry until it is opaque, about 2 minutes.

3 Add the broccoli to the wok and stir-fry for 1 minute. Add the mushrooms, the scallions, the ginger, the soy sauce and the sherry, and stir-fry for 2 minutes. Season to taste. Add the cornstarch mixture and stir-fry until the food is heated through and the sauce has thickened, 1 to 2 minutes.

Shanghaied Rice

1 Chop the parsley. Peel and chop the onion. Peel and mince the garlic.

2 In a medium skillet, heat the sesame oil and sauté the onion and the garlic until the onion is translucent and the garlic is golden, about 6 minutes. Turn the mixture into the top of a double boiler. Add the rice, the broth, the water and the soy sauce. Bring water to a boil in the bottom of the double boiler, reduce the heat, cover and simmer until all the liquid is absorbed and the rice is tender, 30 to 40 minutes.

3 Fluff the rice and sprinkle it with the parsley.

Oriental Salad

1 Trim and chop the cabbage. Drain the bamboo shoots. Drain the pineapple, reserving 2 tablespoons of the juice. Combine the ingredients in a large bowl. Add the bean sprouts and toss lightly.

2 In a small bowl, whisk together the reserved pineapple juice, the soy sauce, the oil and the sesame seeds. Season to taste.

3 Toss the salad with the dressing.

Yum-Yum Pudding

1 Combine the pudding mix and the milk in a medium bowl and beat until well blended. Blend in the sour cream and the Amaretto. Spoon the pudding into individual dessert dishes and refrigerate for at least 20 minutes.

2 Spoon the lychees and their syrup over the pudding, and serve with the almond cookies.

WEDNESDAY

Unpretentious Pasta

6 slices bacon
1 large onion
3 tablespoons fresh parsley (when chopped)
1 clove garlic
4 tablespoons regular or light olive oil
1 large can (28 ounces) cut-up tomatoes
16 ounces spaghetti
Seasoning to taste
1/2 cup grated Parmesan cheese

Salad Crunch

1 medium head lettuce
3 scallions (green onions)
1 clove garlic
2 tablespoons regular or light olive oil
1 tablespoon walnut oil
1 tablespoon red wine vinegar
1 teaspoon Dijon mustard
1 tablespoon lemon juice
1/4 teaspoon sugar
Seasoning to taste
1 cup croutons

The Loaf Boat

1 small loaf French bread
2 tablespoons softened butter
1 teaspoon onion powder
1 teaspoon garlic powder
1/4 cup grated Parmesan cheese

Choco-Cherry Cake

1 egg
1 package chocolate cake mix
1 can (21 ounces) cherry pie filling
1 tablespoon Italian hazelnut syrup

EQUIPMENT

Electric hand mixer	Assorted kitchen knives
Stockpot	Measuring cups and
Large skillet	spoons
9x13-inch baking pan	Assorted cooking
2 large bowls	utensils
Small bowl	Whisk
Colander	Aluminum foil

COUNTDOWN

1 Assemble the ingredients and equipment
2 Do Steps 1–3 of the *Choco-Cherry Cake*
3 Do Steps 1–4 of the *Unpretentious Pasta*
4 Do Steps 1–2 of the *Salad Crunch*
5 Do Step 5 of the *Unpretentious Pasta*
6 Do Steps 1–3 of *The Loaf Boat*
7 Do Steps 6–7 of the *Unpretentious Pasta*
8 Do Step 3 of the *Salad Crunch*

Unpretentious Pasta

1 Bring water to a boil in a stockpot.

2 Dice the bacon and sauté it in a large skillet until it is almost crisp, 3 to 4 minutes.

3 Peel and chop the onion. Chop the parsley. Peel and mince the garlic.

4 Drain all but 1 tablespoon of the drippings from the skillet. Add the oil and heat. Add the onion and sauté until it is translucent, about 5 minutes. Add the garlic and sauté for 1 minute. Add the tomatoes and cook until the sauce is reduced and thickened, about 10 minutes.

5 Cook the pasta in the boiling water until it is almost tender, 3 to 4 minutes if you are using fresh pasta and 6 to 7 minutes if you are using dried pasta.

6 Drain the pasta and return it to the stockpot.

7 Season the sauce to taste and toss it with the pasta and the parsley. Sprinkle with the Parmesan cheese.

Salad Crunch

1 Wash and dry the lettuce, tear it into bite-size pieces and place it in a large bowl. Trim and chop the scallions and combine them with the lettuce.

2 Peel and mince the garlic. In a small bowl, whisk together the garlic, both oils, the vinegar, the mustard, the lemon juice and the sugar. Season to taste.

3 Toss the salad with the dressing and top with the croutons.

The Loaf Boat

1 Preheat the broiler.

2 Slice the bread in half lengthwise. Spread the cut sides with the softened butter. Place the bread on a sheet of aluminum foil.

3 Sprinkle the cut sides of the bread with the onion powder, the garlic powder and the cheese, and place it on the broiler rack, 3 or 4 inches from the heat. Broil until the cheese begins to bubble, 2 to 3 minutes.

Choco-Cherry Cake

1 Preheat the oven to 350°F. Grease and flour a 9x13-inch baking pan.

2 Beat the egg in a large bowl. Add the cake mix and beat until well blended. Fold in the cherry filling and the hazelnut syrup. Mix well.

3 Pour the batter into the pan and bake until the top of the cake is firm, 20 to 25 minutes.

THURSDAY

Red Lentil Soup

2 cloves garlic
1 medium onion
2 medium carrots
2 stalks celery
1 large fresh tomato
3 cups red lentils
3 cups water
3 cans (10³/₄ ounces each) beef broth
2 tablespoons red wine vinegar
2 tablespoons lemon juice
1 bay leaf
3 tablespoons dark brown sugar
3 tablespoons dry red wine (or nonalcoholic
    red wine or tomato juice)
Seasoning to taste
2 tablespoons fresh parsley (when chopped)

Aspara-Bean Salad

³/₄ pound fresh asparagus
¹/₂ pound fresh green beans
1 medium shallot
3 tablespoons regular or light olive oil
2 tablespoons red wine vinegar
1 teaspoon Dijon mustard
1 teaspoon lemon juice
1 tablespoon dried chives
Seasoning to taste

Dillicious Muffins

2 cups flour
¹/₄ cup sugar
1 tablespoon baking powder
¹/₂ teaspoon salt
1 teaspoon caraway seeds
1 tablespoon dried dill
1 egg
1 cup whole or low-fat milk
¹/₄ cup vegetable oil

Banana Muenster

8 slices Muenster cheese
4 medium bananas
2 teaspoons ground cinnamon
1 tablespoon sugar

EQUIPMENT

Slow cooker	Assorted kitchen knives
Electric hand mixer	Measuring cups and
Medium saucepan	spoons
9x13-inch baking pan	Assorted cooking
12-cup muffin tin	utensils
2 large bowls	Whisk
Small bowl	Vegetable peeler

COUNTDOWN

IN THE MORNING:
  Do Steps 1–2 of the *Red Lentil Soup*
BEFORE DINNER:
  1 Assemble the remaining ingredients and
     equipment
  2 Do Steps 1–5 of the *Dillicious Muffins*
  3 Do Steps 1–5 of the *Aspara-Bean Salad*
  4 Do Steps 3–4 of the *Red Lentil Soup*
  5 Do Steps 1–3 of the *Banana Muenster*

Red Lentil Soup

1 Peel and chop the garlic. Peel and chop the onion. Peel and chop the carrots. Trim and chop the celery. Chop the tomato.

2 Combine the lentils, the water, the broth, the garlic, the onion, the carrots, the celery, the tomato, the vinegar, the lemon juice, the bay leaf and the brown sugar in a slow cooker. Cook on the low setting for 8 to 10 hours or on the high setting for 4 to 5 hours, depending on your schedule.

3 Add the wine and cook on the high setting for 5 minutes more. Season to taste.

4 Chop the parsley and sprinkle it over the soup as garnish.

Aspara-Bean Salad

1 Bring water to a boil in a medium saucepan.

2 Trim the asparagus and cut it into 1½-inch pieces. Trim and string the green beans and cut them into 1-inch pieces. Peel and chop the shallot.

3 Cook the asparagus and the beans in the boiling water until they are crisp-tender, about 5 minutes.

4 In a large bowl, whisk the oil, the vinegar, the mustard, the lemon juice and the chives until well blended. Season to taste.

5 Drain the vegetables, add them to the dressing and toss to combine.

Dillicious Muffins

1 Preheat the oven to 425°F. Grease a 12-cup muffin tin.

2 Combine the flour, the sugar, the baking powder and the salt in a large bowl. Add the caraway seeds and the dill.

3 Beat the egg in a small bowl. Add the milk and the oil and combine.

4 Make a well in the center of the dry ingredients and add the liquid ingredients all at once. Fold the mixture carefully until the dry ingredients are absorbed.

5 Fill the cups two-thirds full and bake until the muffins are golden, 20 to 25 minutes.

Banana Muenster

1 Preheat the oven to 400°F. Grease a 9x13-inch baking pan.

2 Cut the cheese slices in half. Peel and slice the bananas in half lengthwise and then cut them once again into quarters. Sprinkle the bananas with the cinnamon and the sugar. Cover each quarter with a half slice of cheese.

3 Place the bananas in the baking pan and bake them until the cheese is melted and begins to bubble, about 10 minutes.

FRIDAY

Roly-Poly Flounder

1 medium tomato
1 stalk celery
$^1/_4$ pound mushrooms
3 scallions (green onions)
1 can (10$^3/_4$ ounces) cream of shrimp soup
Seasoning to taste
1$^1/_4$ pounds flounder fillets
$^1/_4$ cup dry sherry (or nonalcoholic red wine or
    clam juice)
1 cup shredded regular or low-fat Swiss cheese

Potato Tumbles

1 pound small new red potatoes
$^1/_4$ cup fresh parsley (when chopped)
3 tablespoons butter
1 tablespoon Dijon mustard
$^1/_4$ teaspoon dried chervil
Seasoning to taste

Confetti Slaw

$^1/_2$ cup regular or low-fat mayonnaise
2 tablespoons balsamic vinegar
1 teaspoon sugar
1 teaspoon caraway seeds
Seasoning to taste
1 very small (or half) head green cabbage
1 very small (or half) head red cabbage
3 scallions (green onions)
1 medium carrot

Not-Quite-Pears Hélène

2 large pears
1 tablespoon lemon juice
1 pint vanilla ice cream
Chocolate syrup
$^1/_4$ cup pecan pieces

EQUIPMENT

2 medium saucepans	Assorted cooking
7x11-inch glass baking	utensils
dish	Whisk
Large bowl	Vegetable grater
2 medium bowls	Vegetable peeler
Strainer	Ice cream scoop
Assorted kitchen knives	
Measuring cups and	
spoons	

COUNTDOWN

1 Assemble the ingredients and equipment
2 Do Steps 1–4 of the *Roly-Poly Flounder*
3 Do Steps 1–2 of the *Potato Tumbles*
4 Do Steps 1–2 of the *Confetti Slaw*
5 Do Step 1 of the *Not-Quite-Pears Hélène*
6 Do Step 3 of the *Potato Tumbles*
7 Do Steps 5–6 of the *Roly-Poly Flounder*
8 Do Step 2 of the *Not-Quite-Pears Hélène*

Roly-Poly Flounder

1 Preheat the oven to 350°F.

2 Peel and chop the tomato. Trim and chop the celery. Wash, pat dry and chop the mushrooms. Trim and chop the scallions.

3 In a medium bowl, combine the tomato, the celery, the mushrooms and the scallions with ¼ cup of the soup. Season to taste. Place 3 tablespoons of the mixture in the center of each flounder fillet and roll it up, securing it with toothpicks to keep it closed.

4 Place the fish rolls, seam side down, in a 7x11-inch glass baking dish and bake until the fish flakes easily with a fork, 20 to 25 minutes.

5 In a medium saucepan, combine the remaining soup and the sherry. Heat thoroughly.

6 Discard any liquid in the baking dish. Pour the sauce over the fish rolls and sprinkle with the cheese. Continue baking until the cheese is melted, 3 to 4 minutes.

Potato Tumbles

1 Bring water to a boil in a medium saucepan.

2 Scrub the potatoes and cut them in quarters. Chop the parsley. Cook the potatoes in the boiling water until they are tender, 10 to 15 minutes.

3 Drain the potatoes. Melt the butter in the saucepan. Stir in the mustard, the parsley and the chervil. Return the potatoes to the saucepan and toss to coat them. Season to taste.

Confetti Slaw

1 In a large bowl, whisk together the mayonnaise, the vinegar, the sugar and the caraway seeds until well blended. Season to taste.

2 Grate the cabbage. Trim and thinly slice the scallions. Peel and grate the carrot. Add the cabbage, the scallions and the carrot to the mayonnaise mixture and toss until thoroughly coated. Refrigerate until you are ready to serve.

Not-Quite-Pears Hélène

1 Peel, core and halve the pears. Place them in a medium bowl and sprinkle them with lemon juice to keep them from browning. Cover the bowl and refrigerate until you are ready to use.

2 Place the pear halves, cut sides up, in individual serving dishes. Top with scoops of ice cream. Drizzle the ice cream with chocolate syrup and sprinkle with the pecans.

MARCH

WEEK FOUR

CHECK STAPLES

- ☐ Butter
- ☐ Flour
- ☐ Cornstarch
- ☐ Granulated sugar
- ☐ Dark brown sugar
- ☐ Confectioners' sugar
- ☐ Chocolate sprinkles
- ☐ Brown rice
- ☐ Regular or light vegetable oil
- ☐ Regular or light olive oil
- ☐ Red wine vinegar
- ☐ White wine vinegar
- ☐ Lemon juice
- ☐ Lime juice
- ☐ Grated fresh lemon peel
- ☐ Grated fresh orange peel
- ☐ Worcestershire sauce
- ☐ Tabasco sauce
- ☐ Dijon mustard
- ☐ Grated Parmesan cheese
- ☐ Plain bread crumbs
- ☐ Chicken bouillon cubes
- ☐ Ground cinnamon
- ☐ Ground cloves
- ☐ Curry powder
- ☐ Garlic powder
- ☐ Dry mustard
- ☐ Ground nutmeg
- ☐ Onion powder
- ☐ Paprika
- ☐ Poppy seeds
- ☐ Dried rosemary
- ☐ Dried thyme
- ☐ Pepper
- ☐ Salt

SHOPPING NOTE

• If you are shopping once a week and cannot arrange to purchase fresh seafood on the day you plan to use it, you can purchase *not previously frozen* seafood and freeze it, placing it in the refrigerator to thaw the night before you are ready to use it. Or you can purchase *still frozen* seafood and keep it frozen until the night before you are ready to use it.

MEAT & POULTRY

4 boneless, skinless chicken
  breast halves (W)

FISH

4 halibut steaks (1$^1/_4$
  pounds) (Th)
8 ounces scallops (F)

FRESH PRODUCE

Vegetables

1 large eggplant (T)
1 pound green beans (T)
1 pound spinach (M)
$^1/_2$ pound mushrooms (T)
1 large bunch celery (W, F)
2 medium onions—1 (T), 1 (W)
3 small onions—1 (M), 1 (W),
  1 (Th)
1 medium red onion (M)
1 medium shallot (F)
7 scallions (green onions)—
  3 (M), 4 (F)
1 head garlic (M, T, F)
1 bunch parsley (M, Th, F)
2 medium heads lettuce—1 (M),
  1 (F)
4 medium tomatoes (T)
2 medium cucumbers—1 (M),
  1 (F)
1 large green bell pepper (F)
1 small red bell pepper (F)

Fruit

2 small red apples (W)
1 medium banana (T)
$^1/_4$ pound seedless green
  grapes (T)
8 large strawberries (T)
1 small lemon (W)

CANS, JARS & BOTTLES

Soup

1 can (14$^1/_2$ ounces) vegetable
  broth (W)
1 can (10$^3/_4$ ounces) beef
  broth (Th)

Vegetables

1 medium can (14$^1/_2$ ounces)
  cut-up tomatoes (W)
1 can (11 ounces) whole kernel
  corn (F)

Fish

1 can (6.05 ounces) boneless,
  skinless red salmon (M)

Juice

$^1/_4$ cup clam juice (M)
$^1/_4$ cup tomato juice (F)

Condiments

1 small jar (2 ounces) diced
  pimiento (W)

Dessert Needs

1 can (20 ounces) apple pie
  filling (F)
1 jar (12$^1/_4$ ounces) caramel
  topping (F)

PACKAGED GOODS

Pasta, Rice & Grains

12 ounces linguini (M)
8 ounces orzo (W)
8 ounces penne (F)

Baked Goods

4 French rolls (F)

Nuts & Seeds

$^1/_3$ cup pecan pieces (W)
$^1/_2$ cup sliced almonds (Th)

Dessert & Baking Needs

1 prepared 9-inch chocolate pie
  shell (Th)
1 envelope unflavored
  gelatin (T)
1 small package (3.9 ounces)
  instant chocolate fudge
  pudding mix (Th)
$^1/_3$ cup semisweet chocolate
  chips (W)
$^1/_3$ cup mini-marshmallows (W)

WINES & SPIRITS

$^1/_4$ cup dry white wine (or
  nonalcoholic white wine or
  clam juice) (M)
$^1/_4$ cup dry white wine (or
  nonalcoholic white wine or
  vegetable broth) (T)
$^1/_4$ cup Kahlua liqueur (or
  nonalcoholic Italian coffee
  syrup) (Th)

REFRIGERATED PRODUCTS

Dairy

1 cup whole milk (Th)
1$^1/_2$ cups whole or low fat
  milk—1 cup (M), $^1/_2$ cup (T)
Whipped cream for garnish (T)
3 eggs—2 (M), 1 (T)

Cheese

8 ounces regular or low-fat
  small-curd cottage
  cheese (T)

Juice

2 tablespoons orange juice (M)

Deli

3 slices bacon (M)

FROZEN GOODS

Vegetables

1 package (9 ounces) artichoke
  hearts (M)
1 package (20 ounces) crinkle-
  cut carrots (Th)
1 package (9 ounces) Brussels
  sprouts (Th)

Juice

1 can (12 ounces) frozen apple
  juice concentrate (T, Th)

Desserts

1 pint butter pecan ice
  cream (W)
1 container (8 ounces) frozen
  whipped topping (Th)
1 pound cake (F)

MONDAY

Hooked on Linguini

1 small onion
2 cloves garlic
2 tablespoons fresh parsley (when chopped)
12 ounces linguini
2 tablespoons regular or light olive oil
1 teaspoon grated fresh lemon peel
2 tablespoons lemon juice
1/4 cup clam juice
1/4 cup dry white wine (or nonalcoholic white
    wine or additional clam juice)
Seasoning to taste
1 can (6.05 ounces) boneless, skinless red
    salmon
1/2 cup grated Parmesan cheese

Hot Greens

3 slices bacon
1 clove garlic
3 scallions (green onions)
1 package (9 ounces) frozen artichoke hearts
1 pound fresh spinach
1/8 teaspoon Tabasco sauce
Seasoning to taste

Red Onion Vinaigrette

1 medium head lettuce
1 medium red onion
1 medium cucumber
2 tablespoons white wine vinegar
1 teaspoon Dijon mustard
3 tablespoons regular or light olive oil
1/8 teaspoon Worcestershire sauce
Seasoning to taste

Orange Pudding Cake

2 eggs
2 tablespoons softened butter
1/4 cup granulated sugar
2 tablespoons orange juice
1 tablespoon grated fresh orange peel
2 tablespoons flour
1 cup whole or low-fat milk
1/4 cup confectioners' sugar

EQUIPMENT

Electric hand mixer	Strainer
Stockpot	Assorted kitchen knives
Large skillet	Measuring cups and
Medium covered skillet	spoons
Medium saucepan	Assorted cooking
9x9-inch baking pan	utensils
Large bowl	Vegetable peeler
Medium bowl	Whisk
2 small bowls	Sifter
Colander	

COUNTDOWN

1 Assemble the ingredients and equipment
2 Do Steps 1–4 of the *Orange Pudding Cake*
3 Do Steps 1–2 of the *Hooked on Linguini*
4 Do Steps 1–2 of the *Red Onion Vinaigrette*
5 Do Steps 1–3 of the *Hot Greens*
6 Do Steps 3–5 of the *Hooked on Linguini*
7 Do Steps 4–6 of the *Hot Greens*
8 Do Step 6 of the *Hooked on Linguini*
9 Do Step 3 of the *Red Onion Vinaigrette*
10 Do Step 5 of the *Orange Pudding Cake*

Hooked on Linguini

1 Bring water to a boil in a stockpot.

2 Peel and chop the onion. Peel and mince the garlic. Chop the parsley.

3 Cook the pasta in the boiling water until it is almost tender, 2 to 3 minutes if you are using fresh pasta and 6 to 7 minutes if you are using dried pasta.

4 Heat the oil in a medium skillet. Sauté the onion until it is translucent, about 5 minutes. Add the remaining garlic and sauté for 1 minute more. Stir in the lemon peel, the lemon juice, the clam juice, the wine and the parsley. Season to taste. Bring the mixture to a boil, reduce the heat and simmer for 2 minutes.

5 Drain and flake the salmon and add it to the skillet. Do not stir. Cover the skillet and remove it from the heat.

6 Drain the pasta and return it to the stockpot. Toss it with the sauce and sprinkle with the Parmesan cheese. Cover to keep warm until you are ready to serve.

Hot Greens

1 Bring water to a boil in a medium saucepan.

2 Chop the bacon and sauté it in a large skillet until it is crisp, about 5 minutes.

3 Peel and mince the garlic. Trim and chop the scallions. Drain the bacon on a paper towel, reserving the drippings.

4 Cook the artichokes in the boiling water until they are crisp-tender, about 5 minutes. Rinse, dry and chop the spinach. Add the spinach to the artichokes for the last 2 minutes of cooking.

5 Sauté the garlic and the scallions in the bacon drippings for 3 minutes. Stir in the Tabasco sauce. Season to taste.

6 Drain the vegetables well and add them to the skillet. Return the bacon to the skillet and toss.

Red Onion Vinaigrette

1 Wash and dry the lettuce and tear it into bite-size pieces. Distribute it among individual salad plates. Peel and thinly slice the red onion. Peel and thinly slice the cucumber. Arrange the onion and the cucumber over the lettuce.

2 In a small bowl, whisk together the vinegar, the mustard, the oil and the Worcestershire sauce. Season to taste.

3 Drizzle the dressing over the salad.

Orange Pudding Cake

1 Preheat the oven to 375°F. Grease a 9x9-inch baking pan.

2 Separate the eggs, placing the yolks in a large bowl and the whites in a medium bowl.

3 Cream the butter in a small bowl. Add the sugar to the butter and beat well. Beat the egg yolks until they are thick and lemon colored. Add the butter mixture to the beaten yolks. Beat in the juice and the orange peel. Fold in the flour and stir in the milk.

4 Beat the egg whites until they are stiff. Fold them into the orange mixture. Pour the batter into the baking pan and bake for 35 minutes. Let the cake cool for several minutes, and then refrigerate until you are ready to serve.

5 Dust the cake with the confectioners' sugar.

TUESDAY

Meatless Moussaka

1 large eggplant
$^1/_4$ cup regular or light olive oil
1 medium onion
1 clove garlic
4 medium tomatoes
2 tablespoons butter
1 cup regular or low-fat small-curd cottage
　　cheese
1 egg
$^1/_2$ cup grated Parmesan cheese
2 tablespoons flour
$^1/_4$ teaspoon curry powder
$^1/_4$ cup plain bread crumbs
$^1/_4$ cup dry white wine (or nonalcoholic white
　　wine or vegetable broth)
$^1/_2$ cup whole or low-fat milk
$^1/_4$ teaspoon ground cinnamon
$^1/_8$ teaspoon ground nutmeg
Seasoning to taste

Athenian Beans

1 pound fresh green beans
$^1/_2$ pound mushrooms
2 tablespoons butter
1 teaspoon Dijon mustard
$1^1/_2$ tablespoons lemon juice
Seasoning to taste

Fruit of the Gods

1 envelope unflavored gelatin
$^3/_4$ cup cold water
$^3/_4$ cup frozen apple juice concentrate*
3 ice cubes
8 large fresh strawberries
1 medium banana
$^1/_4$ pound seedless green grapes
Whipped cream for garnish

EQUIPMENT

Large skillet	Small bowl
Medium skillet	Assorted kitchen knives
Medium covered saucepan	Measuring cups and spoons
Small saucepan	Assorted cooking utensils
9x9-inch glass baking dish	Whisk
Cookie sheet	Aluminum foil
Large bowl	

COUNTDOWN

1 Assemble the ingredients and equipment
2 Do Steps 1–8 of the *Meatless Moussaka*
3 Do Steps 1–2 of the *Fruit of the Gods*
4 Do Steps 1–3 of the *Athenian Beans*
5 Do Step 9 of the *Meatless Moussaka*
6 Do Steps 4–5 of the *Athenian Beans*
7 Do Step 3 of the *Fruit of the Gods*

---

*Reserve the balance of the can for use on Thursday.

Meatless Moussaka

1 Preheat the broiler. Grease a 9x9-inch glass baking dish.

2 Trim and cut the eggplant into $1/4$-inch slices. Brush the slices with the oil and place them on an ungreased cookie sheet. Broil the eggplant, 3 or 4 inches from the heat, until browned, 3 to 4 minutes per side.

3 Peel and slice the onion. Peel and mince the garlic. Slice the tomatoes.

4 Remove the eggplant from the broiler and set the oven temperature to 375°F.

5 Melt 1 tablespoon of the butter in a large skillet and sauté the onion until it is limp, about 5 minutes.

6 In a large bowl, combine the cottage cheese, the egg, 2 tablespoons of the Parmesan cheese, 1 tablespoon of the flour and the curry powder. Add the onion to the cheese mixture. Stir in the garlic and the bread crumbs.

7 Melt the remaining butter in the skillet. Whisk in the remaining flour and cook for 1 minute. Whisk in the wine and bring the mixture to a boil. Add the milk, the cinnamon and the nutmeg, return to a boil and whisk until the sauce is thick and smooth, 2 to 3 minutes. Season to taste. Stir in 2 more tablespoons of the Parmesan cheese and remove the skillet from the heat.

8 Place a third of the tomato slices in the bottom of the baking dish. Add a third of the eggplant slices. Add a third of the onion mixture. Add another third of the tomato slices. Top with another third of the eggplant slices. Spread the cottage cheese mixture over the eggplant. Top the mixture with the remaining eggplant. Cover everything evenly with the sauce. Top the sauce with the remaining tomato slices. Cover the baking pan lightly with aluminum foil and bake for 15 minutes.

9 Remove the foil, sprinkle the remaining Parmesan cheese evenly over the top, and bake until the moussaka is bubbly and golden brown, 10 to 15 minutes more.

Athenian Beans

1 Rinse and string the green beans. Wash, pat dry and slice the mushrooms.

2 Bring water to a boil in a medium saucepan.

3 Melt the butter in a medium skillet. Add the mushrooms and sauté until browned, 8 to 10 minutes.

4 Cook the beans until they are crisp-tender, about 5 minutes.

5 Drain the beans and return them to the saucepan. Add the mushrooms. Blend the mustard with the lemon juice. Add the mixture to the vegetables and toss to combine. Season to taste. Cover to keep warm until you are ready to serve.

Fruit of the Gods

1 In a small saucepan, soften the gelatin in the cold water. Add the juice concentrate and bring the mixture to a boil, stirring. Cook until the gelatin is completely dissolved, 3 to 4 minutes. Add the ice cubes and stir until the mixture is smooth and slightly thickened, about 2 minutes.

2 Hull and slice the strawberries. Peel and slice the banana. Separate and slice the grapes. Divide half of the gelatin mixture among individual dessert dishes. Add the fruit. Spoon the remaining gelatin mixture over the top of the fruit and place it in the refrigerator for at least 30 minutes.

3 Top the gelatin with dollops of whipped cream.

WEDNESDAY

Charleston Chicken

4 boneless, skinless chicken breast halves
2 teaspoons regular or light vegetable oil
1 small lemon
1 medium onion
1 medium can (14^1/$_2$ ounces) cut-up tomatoes
1 teaspoon dark brown sugar
^{1}/$_4$ teaspoon dried thyme
^{1}/$_4$ teaspoon garlic powder
^{1}/$_4$ teaspoon Worcestershire sauce
Seasoning to taste
2 small red apples
^{1}/$_2$ teaspoon cornstarch dissolved in 1
    tablespoon cold water

Orzo Sashay

8 ounces orzo
1 small onion
2 tablespoons butter

Celery Stalkings

1 can (14^1/$_2$ ounces) vegetable broth
1 large bunch celery*
1 small jar (2 ounces) diced pimiento
Seasoning to taste

Wild & Crazy Ice Cream

1 pint butter pecan ice cream
^{1}/$_3$ cup pecan pieces
^{1}/$_3$ cup semisweet chocolate chips
^{1}/$_3$ cup mini-marshmallows

*Reserve 1 stalk of celery for use on Friday.

EQUIPMENT

Large covered skillet	Assorted cooking
Medium skillet	utensils
Large saucepan	Apple corer
Medium saucepan	Waxed paper
Medium bowl	Mallet
Strainer	Whisk
Assorted kitchen knives	Ice cream scoop
Measuring cups and	
spoons	

COUNTDOWN

1 Assemble the ingredients and equipment
2 Do Step 1 of the *Orzo Sashay*
3 Do Steps 1–4 of the *Charleston Chicken*
4 Do Step 2 of the *Orzo Sashay*
5 Do Steps 5–6 of the *Charleston Chicken*
6 Do Steps 1–2 of the *Celery Stalkings*
7 Do Step 3 of the *Orzo Sashay*
8 Do Step 3 of the *Celery Stalkings*
9 Do Step 7 of the *Charleston Chicken*
10 Do Steps 1–2 of the *Wild & Crazy Ice Cream*

Charleston Chicken

1 Place the chicken breasts between 2 sheets of waxed paper and pound them with a mallet to a $\frac{1}{2}$-inch thickness.

2 Heat the oil in a large skillet. Add the chicken and cook until the breasts are lightly browned, 4 to 5 minutes per side.

3 Thinly slice the lemon. Peel and slice the onion. Scatter the onion over the chicken.

4 In a medium bowl, combine the tomatoes, the brown sugar, the thyme, the garlic powder and the Worcestershire sauce. Season to taste. Pour the mixture over the chicken. Top the breasts with the lemon slices and bring the liquid to a boil. Cover the skillet, reduce the heat and simmer for 10 minutes.

5 Core and thinly slice the apples.

6 Add the apples to the chicken and cook until the chicken is tender, about 10 minutes more.

7 Remove the chicken and apples, and keep them warm. Whisk the cornstarch mixture into the skillet. Bring the mixture to a boil and cook, whisking, until it thickens, about 3 minutes. Spoon the sauce over the chicken and apples.

Orzo Sashay

1 Bring water to a boil in a large saucepan.

2 Cook the orzo in the boiling water until it is almost tender, 8 to 10 minutes.

3 Peel and chop the onion. Drain the orzo. Melt the butter in a medium skillet. Sauté the onion until it is soft, about 5 minutes. Add the orzo to the skillet and sauté until the orzo turns lightly golden, about 5 minutes.

Celery Stalkings

1 Bring the broth to a boil in a medium saucepan.

2 Trim and slice the celery. Add the celery to the broth and cook until it is crisp-tender, 7 to 9 minutes.

3 Drain the celery and return it to the saucepan. Toss it with the undrained pimientos. Season to taste.

Wild & Crazy Ice Cream

1 Place scoops of ice cream in individual dessert dishes.

2 Sprinkle each serving with one-fourth of the pecan pieces, the chocolate chips and the mini-marshmallows.

THURSDAY

Happy Halibut

3 tablespoons butter
1/2 teaspoon grated fresh lemon peel
1/4 cup lemon juice
1/8 teaspoon Tabasco sauce
Seasoning to taste
4 halibut steaks (1 1/4 pounds)
1/2 cup sliced almonds
1 tablespoon fresh parsley (when chopped)

Brown Bag Rice

1 small onion
2 tablespoons fresh parsley (when chopped)
2 teaspoons regular or light vegetable oil
1 teaspoon dried rosemary
1/2 cup brown rice
1 can (10 3/4 ounces) beef broth
1 tablespoon water
Seasoning to taste

Crinkled Carrots & Sprouts

1 package (20 ounces) frozen crinkle-cut
    carrots
1 package (9 ounces) frozen Brussels sprouts
3/4 cup frozen apple juice concentrate reserved
    from Tuesday
1 1/2 teaspoons cornstarch
1 chicken bouillon cube
1/8 teaspoon ground cloves
1 tablespoon butter
1 teaspoon lemon juice
Seasoning to taste

Quick Kahlua Pie

1 cup whole milk
1/4 cup Kahlua liqueur (or nonalcoholic
    Italian coffee syrup)
1 small package (3.9 ounces) instant
    chocolate fudge pudding mix
1 container (8 ounces) frozen whipped topping
1 1/2 teaspoons grated fresh orange peel
1 prepared 9-inch chocolate pie shell
Chocolate sprinkles

EQUIPMENT

Electric hand mixer	Measuring cups and
2 medium covered	spoons
saucepans	Assorted cooking
Small saucepan	utensils
Medium bowl	Pastry brush
Strainer	Whisk
Assorted kitchen knives	

COUNTDOWN

1 Assemble the ingredients and equipment
2 Do Step 1 of the *Happy Halibut*
3 Do Steps 1–2 of the *Quick Kahlua Pie*
4 Do Steps 1–2 of the *Brown Bag Rice*
5 Do Steps 2–3 of the *Happy Halibut*
6 Do Step 1 of the *Crinkled Carrots & Sprouts*
7 Do Step 4 of the *Happy Halibut*
8 Do Steps 2–3 of the *Crinkled Carrots & Sprouts*
9 Do Step 5 of the *Happy Halibut*
10 Do Step 3 of the *Brown Bag Rice*

Happy Halibut

1 Preheat the broiler.

2 Melt the butter in a small saucepan. Stir in the lemon peel, the lemon juice and the Tabasco sauce. Season to taste.

3 Place the fish on an unheated rack in a broiler pan. Brush the steaks with some of the lemon-butter mixture and broil them, 4 or 5 inches from the heat, for 10 minutes.

4 Brush the fish with more of the lemon butter, then carefully turn the steaks and brush the second side. Return to broiling until the fish flakes easily with a fork, about 10 minutes. Top the steaks with the almonds for the final 2 minutes of broiling.

5 Chop the parsley. Combine the parsley with the remaining lemon butter and drizzle it over the fish.

Brown Bag Rice

1 Peel and finely chop the onion. Chop the parsley. Heat the oil in a medium saucepan. Add the onion, the parsley and the rosemary and sauté the mixture for 5 minutes. Add the rice and sauté for 2 minutes more.

2 Add the broth and the water and season to taste. Cover the saucepan, reduce the heat and simmer until all the liquid is absorbed and the rice is tender, 20 to 25 minutes.

3 Fluff the rice before serving.

Crinkled Carrots & Sprouts

1 Bring water to a boil in a medium saucepan and cook the frozen carrots and Brussels sprouts until they are crisp-tender, 7 to 9 minutes.

2 Drain the vegetables. In the saucepan, whisk together the apple juice concentrate, the cornstarch, the bouillon cube and the cloves. Cook, whisking, until the mixture is thickened and bubbly, about 5 minutes. Then cook, stirring, for 2 minutes more.

3 Stir in the butter and the lemon juice. Return the carrots and the Brussels sprouts to the saucepan, and stir until the vegetables are reheated and well coated. Season to taste. Cover to keep warm until you are ready to serve.

Quick Kahlua Pie

1 In a medium bowl, combine the milk, the Kahlua, and the pudding mix. Beat until the mixture is well blended, 1 to 2 minutes. Fold in 1 cup of the whipped topping and the orange peel, and spread the mixture evenly in the pie crust.

2 Top the pie with the remaining whipped topping and the chocolate sprinkles. Refrigerate for at least 20 minutes.

FRIDAY

Penne for Your Thoughts

1 scallion (green onion)
1 large green bell pepper*
1 small red bell pepper
1 clove garlic
2 tablespoons fresh parsley (when chopped)
$1/2$ pound scallops
8 ounces penne (or other tubular pasta)
1 tablespoon regular or light olive oil
1 can (11 ounces) whole kernel corn
2 tablespoons lime juice
Seasoning to taste

Totally Green Salad

1 medium head lettuce
1 medium cucumber
1 stalk celery reserved from Wednesday
3 scallions (green onions)
1 medium shallot
1 tablespoon fresh parsley (when chopped)
2 tablespoons diced green pepper from the
    penne recipe
$1/4$ cup tomato juice
1 tablespoon regular or light olive oil
1 tablespoon red wine vinegar
$1/2$ teaspoon paprika
$1/8$ teaspoon dry mustard
Seasoning to taste

Poppycocks

2 tablespoons softened butter
1 teaspoon onion powder
1 tablespoon poppy seeds
4 French rolls

*Reserve 2 tablespoons of the green bell pepper for the
Totally Green Salad.

Frozen Hot Cake

1 frozen pound cake
1 can (20 ounces) apple pie filling
1 jar ($12^{1}/_{4}$ ounces) caramel topping

EQUIPMENT

Blender	Small bowl
Medium skillet	Colander
Large covered	Assorted kitchen knives
saucepan	Measuring cups and
Medium saucepan	spoons
Small saucepan	Assorted cooking
Cookie sheet	utensils
Large bowl	Vegetable peeler

COUNTDOWN

1 Assemble the ingredients and equipment
2 Do Step 1 of the *Poppycocks*
3 Do Step 1 of the *Frozen Hot Cake*
4 Do Steps 1–2 of the *Penne for Your Thoughts*
5 Do Steps 1–2 of the *Totally Green Salad*
6 Do Step 2 of the *Poppycocks*
7 Do Steps 3–5 of the *Penne for Your Thoughts*
8 Do Step 3 of the *Poppycocks*
9 Do Step 3 of the *Totally Green Salad*
10 Do Steps 2–4 of the *Frozen Hot Cake*

Penne for Your Thoughts

1 Bring water to a boil in a large saucepan.

2 Trim and thinly slice the scallion. Trim, seed and dice the bell peppers. Peel and mince the garlic. Chop the parsley. If you are using sea scallops, cut them in quarters.

3 Cook the pasta in the boiling water until it is almost tender, 7 to 9 minutes.

4 Heat the oil in a medium skillet. Add the scallion and the peppers, and sauté until they are tender, 3 to 4 minutes. Add the scallops and the undrained corn, and sauté for 3 minutes. Remove the skillet from the heat, stir in the garlic, the lime juice and the parsley. Season to taste.

5 Drain the pasta, return it to the saucepan and toss it with the sauce. Cover to keep warm until you are ready to serve.

Totally Green Salad

1 Wash and dry the lettuce and tear it into bite-size pieces. Peel and slice the cucumber. Trim and slice the celery. Trim and slice the scallions. Combine the ingredients in a large bowl.

2 Peel and chop the shallot. Chop the parsley. Place the shallot, the parsley and the green pepper in a blender and process together with the tomato juice, the oil, the vinegar, the paprika and the dry mustard until the mixture is smooth. Season to taste.

3 Toss the salad with the dressing.

Poppycocks

1 Preheat the broiler.

2 In a small bowl, combine the softened butter, the onion powder and the poppy seeds.

3 Slice the rolls in half horizontally. Spread the cut sides with the butter mixture. Place the rolls on an ungreased cookie sheet and broil them, 3 or 4 inches from the heat, until they are lightly toasted, 1 to 2 minutes.

Frozen Hot Cake

1 Set the pound cake out to partially thaw.

2 Cut the cake into 8 slices.

3 In a medium saucepan, heat the apple pie filling until it is warmed through, about 3 minutes.

4 In a small saucepan, heat the caramel topping until it is bubbly, about 3 minutes. Spread the warm apple mixture over 4 of the cake slices. Add the second slice, and top the cake with the hot caramel topping.

APRIL
WEEK ONE

WEEK AT A GLANCE

Monday

SWEET & SOUR CHICKEN
SINGAPORE RICE
CHOP-CHOP SALAD
PAPAYA JUNKS

Tuesday

VEGETABLE LASAGNA
HERB'S SALAD
BASIL BREAD STICKUPS
FOOL'S CAKE

Wednesday

UPPITY PORK
SNIPPY POTATOES
OUTRAGEOUS ASPARAGUS
LEMON–BERRY PLEASURE

Thursday

CHICKEN ALPHABET SOUP
BEET IT SALAD
BUDDY BREAD
BANANA SCRAMBLE

Friday

SNAP IT UP
TAME WILD RICE
CUCUMBER-ONION SALAD
RAZZLEBERRY SHORTCAKE

CHECK STAPLES

- ☐ Butter
- ☐ Flour
- ☐ Cornstarch
- ☐ Baking soda
- ☐ Cornmeal
- ☐ Granulated sugar
- ☐ Dark brown sugar
- ☐ Unsweetened cocoa
- ☐ Long-grain white rice
- ☐ Regular or light vegetable oil
- ☐ Regular or light olive oil
- ☐ Sesame oil
- ☐ Red wine vinegar
- ☐ Apple cider vinegar
- ☐ Raspberry vinegar
- ☐ Rice vinegar
- ☐ Lemon juice
- ☐ Grated fresh orange peel
- ☐ Fresh ginger
- ☐ Worcestershire sauce
- ☐ Soy sauce
- ☐ Dijon mustard
- ☐ Honey
- ☐ Grated Parmesan cheese
- ☐ Ground allspice
- ☐ Dried basil
- ☐ Bay leaves
- ☐ Ground cinnamon
- ☐ Ground ginger
- ☐ Instant minced onion
- ☐ Poppy seeds
- ☐ Dried sage
- ☐ Seasoning salt
- ☐ Dried tarragon
- ☐ Dried thyme
- ☐ Pepper
- ☐ Salt

SHOPPING NOTE

● If you are shopping once a week and cannot arrange to purchase fresh snapper on the day you plan to use it, you can purchase *not previously frozen* snapper and freeze it, placing it in the refrigerator to thaw the night before you are ready to use it. Or you can purchase *still frozen* snapper and keep it frozen until the night before you are ready to use it.

MEAT & POULTRY

1¼ pounds lean boneless pork loin (W)

2 whole boneless, skinless chicken breasts (M)

1¼ pounds boneless, skinless chicken breasts (Th)

FISH

1¼ pounds red snapper fillets (F)

FRESH PRODUCE

Vegetables

12 small new white potatoes (W)

1 medium zucchini (T)

1½ pounds asparagus (W)

4 medium carrots—3 (Th), 1 (F)

5 stalks celery—1 (M), 4 (Th)

1 large onion (Th)

2 medium onions—1 (M), 1 (T)

1 medium red onion (F)

4 medium shallots—2 (W), 2 (F)

9 scallions (green onions)— 2 (M), 3 (T), 2 (Th), 2 (F)

1 head garlic (T, Th)

1 bunch parsley (T, W)

1 bunch chives (W)

1 very small (or half) head green cabbage (M)

3 medium heads lettuce—1 (T), 1 (Th), 1 (F)

1 large firm tomato (M)

½ pound tomatoes (T)

3 medium cucumbers—1 (T), 2 (F)

1 medium green bell pepper (M)

Fruit

2 ripe papayas (or 2 small cantaloupes) (M)

2 medium bananas (Th)

1 small white grapefruit (Th)

2 medium oranges (F)

CANS, JARS & BOTTLES

Soup

1 can (14½ ounces) oriental broth (M)

1 can (14½ ounces) vegetable broth (W)

2 cans (14½ ounces each) chicken broth (Th)

Vegetables

1 medium can (15 ounces) tomato sauce (T)

1 medium can (15¼ ounces) creamed corn (Th)

1 medium can (15 ounces) sliced beets (Th)

Oriental Products

1 can (8 ounces) sliced water chestnuts (M)

1 can (5 ounces) sliced bamboo shoots (M)

Fruit

1 small can (8 ounces) pineapple chunks (M)

PACKAGED GOODS

Pasta, Rice & Grains

8 ounces lasagna noodles (T)

8 ounces alphabet pasta (Th)

½ cup wild rice (F)

Baked Goods

1 small package (3 ounces) Italian breadsticks (T)

Nuts & Seeds

¼ cup chopped walnuts (F)

Dessert & Baking Needs

1 small package (3.4 ounces) instant lemon pudding mix (W)

WINES & SPIRITS

¼ cup dry white wine (or nonalcoholic white wine or clam juice) (F)

½ cup dry vermouth (or nonalcoholic white wine or chicken broth) (W)

3 tablespoons dry sherry (or nonalcoholic white wine or chicken broth) (Th)

1 tablespoon rum (or nonalcoholic Italian praline syrup) (Th)

2 tablespoons Kirsch liqueur (or nonalcoholic Italian cherry syrup) (F)

REFRIGERATED PRODUCTS

Dairy

1¼ cups whole milk (W)

1 cup buttermilk (Th)

¾ cup regular or light sour cream (W)

¼ cup regular or low-fat plain yogurt (Th)

5 eggs— 3 (M, T), 2 (Th)

Cheese

¾ cup regular or low-fat small-curd cottage cheese (T)

1 cup shredded regular or low-fat mozzarella cheese (T)

2 ounces bleu cheese (F)

Juice

1⅓ cups orange juice (W)

FROZEN GOODS

Vegetables

1 package (9 ounces) chopped broccoli (T)

Fruit

1 package (16 ounces) blueberries (W)

1 package (16 ounces) sweetened raspberries (F)

Desserts

1 pound cake (F)

1 pint vanilla ice cream (M)

1 medium container (12 ounces) frozen whipped topping (F)

MONDAY

Sweet & Sour Chicken

2 whole boneless, skinless chicken breasts
1 medium green bell pepper
1 medium onion
1 stalk celery
1 large firm tomato
1 can (8 ounces) sliced water chestnuts
1 can (5 ounces) sliced bamboo shoots
1 small can (8 ounces) pineapple chunks
1 tablespoon cornstarch
3 tablespoons regular or light vegetable oil
2 tablespoons soy sauce
Seasoning to taste

Singapore Rice

2 scallions (green onions)
1 cup long-grain white rice
1 can (14^1/$_2$ ounces) oriental broth
^{1}/$_4$ cup water
1 tablespoon lemon juice
1 tablespoon soy sauce

Chop-Chop Salad

3 tablespoons soy sauce
1 teaspoon sesame oil
2 teaspoons rice vinegar
^{1}/$_2$ teaspoon sugar
Seasoning to taste
1 very small (or half) head green cabbage
1 teaspoon fresh ginger (when grated)

Papaya Junks

2 ripe papayas (or 2 small cantaloupes)
1 tablespoon lemon juice
3 eggs*
3 tablespoons granulated sugar
1 pint vanilla ice cream
1 tablespoon dark brown sugar

EQUIPMENT

Electric hand mixer	Measuring cups and
Wok and wok utensils	spoons
Double boiler	Assorted cooking
9x9-inch glass baking	utensils
dish	Citrus grater
Large bowl	Whisk
Medium bowl	Pastry brush
2 small bowls	Ice cream scoop
Assorted kitchen knives	

COUNTDOWN

1 Assemble the ingredients and equipment
2 Do Step 1 of the *Singapore Rice*
3 Do Steps 1–2 of the *Chop-Chop Salad*
4 Do Steps 1–2 of the *Papaya Junks*
5 Do Steps 1–4 of the *Sweet & Sour Chicken*
6 Do Step 2 of the *Singapore Rice*
7 Do Steps 3–5 of the *Papaya Junks*

---

*Reserve 2 of the egg yolks for use on Tuesday.

Sweet & Sour Chicken

1 Cut the chicken breasts into ¹/₂-inch strips. Seed the bell pepper and cut it into ¹/₂-inch strips. Peel and chunk the onion. Trim and slice the celery. Chunk the tomato. Drain the water chestnuts. Drain the bamboo shoots. Drain the pineapple, reserving 2 tablespoons of the juice.

2 In a small bowl, whisk the cornstarch with the reserved pineapple juice.

3 Heat the oil in a wok.

4 Stir-fry the chicken in the hot oil for 2 minutes. Add the bell pepper and the onion, and stir-fry for 1 minute. Add the water chestnuts and the bamboo shoots, and stir-fry for 1 minute. Add the tomato, the pineapple and the soy sauce, and stir-fry for 1 minute. Season to taste. Make a well in the center of the wok and add the cornstarch mixture. Stir-fry until all the ingredients are coated and the sauce is thickened, 1 to 2 minutes.

Singapore Rice

1 Trim and chop the scallions. Place the scallions, the rice, the broth, the water, the lemon juice and the soy sauce in the top of a double boiler. Bring water in the bottom to a boil, cover, reduce the heat and simmer until all the liquid is absorbed and the rice is tender, 30 to 40 minutes.

2. Fluff the rice before serving.

Chop-Chop Salad

1 In a large bowl, whisk together the soy sauce, the sesame oil, the vinegar and the sugar. Season to taste.

2 Trim and chop the cabbage. Grate the ginger. Add both to the soy mixture and toss to combine. Cover and refrigerate until you are ready to use.

Papaya Junks

1 Cut the papayas in half lengthwise and discard the seeds. Place the papaya halves cut side up in a 9x9-inch glass baking dish, and drizzle with the lemon juice. Refrigerate until you are ready to use.

2 In a medium bowl, beat the egg whites until frothy. Gradually add the granulated sugar and continue to beat until the whites are stiff and glossy, but not dry.

3 Preheat the oven to 450°F.

4 Place scoops of ice cream in each papaya half. Spread with the egg white mixture, sealing the edges so that the ice cream is protected.

5 Beat the remaining egg yolk in a small bowl. With a pastry brush, coat the egg white mixture lightly with the beaten yolk. Sprinkle with the brown sugar, and bake until the meringue is lightly browned, 3 to 5 minutes.

TUESDAY

Vegetable Lasagna

1 package (9 ounces) frozen chopped broccoli
1 medium zucchini
1 medium onion
1 clove garlic
1 tablespoon fresh parsley (when chopped)
3/4 cup regular or low-fat small-curd cottage
    cheese
8 ounces lasagna noodles
1 1/2 teaspoons regular or light olive oil
2 egg yolks reserved from Monday
2 tablespoons grated Parmesan cheese
Seasoning to taste
1 medium can (15 ounces) tomato sauce
1 cup shredded regular or low-fat mozzarella
    cheese

Herb's Salad

1 medium head lettuce
3 scallions (green onions)
1/2 pound fresh tomatoes
1 medium cucumber
1 clove garlic
3 tablespoons regular or light vegetable oil
2 tablespoons red wine vinegar
1/2 teaspoon sugar
1/2 teaspoon dried tarragon
Seasoning to taste

Basil Bread Stickups

3 tablespoons regular or light olive oil
1 teaspoon instant minced onion
2 teaspoons dried basil
1/4 teaspoon pepper
1 package (3 ounces) Italian breadsticks

Fool's Cake

3 cups flour
2 cups sugar
1/4 cup + 2 tablespoons unsweetened cocoa
1 teaspoon salt
3/4 cup regular or light vegetable oil
2 tablespoons apple cider vinegar
2 cups cold water

EQUIPMENT

Stockpot	Colander
Large skillet	Assorted kitchen knives
9x13-inch baking pan	Measuring cups and
9x9-inch glass baking	spoons
dish	Assorted cooking
Large bowl	utensils
Medium bowl	Whisk
2 small bowls	Vegetable peeler

COUNTDOWN

1 Assemble the ingredients and equipment
2 Do Step 1 of the *Fool's Cake*
3 Do Steps 1–2 of the *Vegetable Lasagna*
4 Do Steps 2–4 of the *Fool's Cake*
5 Do Steps 3–8 of the *Vegetable Lasagna*
6 Do Steps 1–2 of *Herb's Salad*
7 Do Steps 1–2 of the *Basil Bread Stickups*
8 Do Step 3 of *Herb's Salad*

Vegetable Lasagna

1 Set the package of broccoli in a medium bowl of warm water to thaw.

2 Bring water to a boil in a stockpot.

3 Trim and thinly slice the zucchini. Peel and chop the onion. Peel and mince the garlic. Chop the parsley. Drain the excess liquid from the cottage cheese.

4 Cook the lasagna in the boiling water until it is tender but still chewy, 8 to 10 minutes.

5 Preheat the oven to 375°F. Drain the broccoli.

6 Heat the oil in a large skillet. Add the onion and cook until it is soft but not brown, 3 to 5 minutes. Add the zucchini and the garlic, and cook 1 minute more. Remove the skillet from the heat. Add the broccoli, the egg yolks, the cottage cheese, the Parmesan cheese and the parsley. Season to taste, and mix until the filling is well blended.

7 Drain the pasta. Spread 2 tablespoons of the tomato sauce on the bottom of a 9x9-inch glass baking dish. Arrange a single layer of lasagna noodles over the sauce. Spread half of the vegetable filling over the noodles. Spoon a third of the remaining tomato sauce over the filling. Make another layer with half of the remaining noodles, all of the remaining filling and half of the remaining tomato sauce. Top with the remaining noodles and sauce. Sprinkle the mozzarella evenly over the top.

8 Place the lasagna in the oven with the cake and bake, uncovered, until it is hot and bubbly, about 40 minutes.

Herb's Salad

1 Wash and dry the lettuce and tear it into bite-size pieces. Trim and slice the scallions. Chop the tomatoes. Peel and slice the cucumber. Combine the ingredients in a large bowl.

2 Peel and mince the garlic. In a small bowl, whisk together the garlic, the oil, the vinegar, the sugar and the tarragon. Season to taste.

3 Toss the salad with the dressing.

Basil Bread Stickups

1 In a small bowl, combine the oil and the instant minced onion, and let the mixture stand for 5 minutes.

2 Stir the basil and the pepper into the oil mixture, and use it as a dipping sauce for the breadsticks.

Fool's Cake

1 Preheat the oven to 375°F. Grease a 9x13-inch baking pan.

2 Add the flour, the sugar, the cocoa and the salt to the pan and mix well with a fork.

3 Make 3 wells in the dry ingredients. Put half of the oil into the first well and half into the third well. Pour the vinegar into the second well.

4 Pour the cold water over all, stirring well, and bake for 30 minutes. Remove it from the oven when it is lightly browned and firm to the touch.

WEDNESDAY

Uppity Pork

1¹/₄ pounds lean boneless pork loin
3 tablespoons flour
Seasoning to taste
3 tablespoons butter
¹/₂ cup dry vermouth (or nonalcoholic white
    wine or chicken broth)
¹/₂ teaspoon dried tarragon
2 teaspoons seasoning salt

Snippy Potatoes

12 small new white potatoes
1 can (14¹/₂ ounces) vegetable broth
2 teaspoons fresh chives (when chopped)
1 tablespoon fresh parsley (when chopped)
2 tablespoons butter
Seasoning to taste

Outrageous Asparagus

1¹/₂ pounds fresh asparagus
2 medium shallots
4 tablespoons butter
1¹/₄ teaspoons Dijon mustard
1¹/₃ cups orange juice
Seasoning to taste

Lemon-Berry Pleasure

1 package (16 ounces) frozen blueberries
1 small package (3.4 ounces) instant lemon
    pudding mix
1¹/₄ cups whole milk
³/₄ cup regular or light sour cream

EQUIPMENT

Electric hand mixer	Measuring cups and
2 large covered skillets	spoons
Medium covered	Assorted cooking
saucepan	utensils
Small saucepan	Vegetable brush
Medium bowl	Whisk
Assorted kitchen knives	

COUNTDOWN

1 Assemble the ingredients and equipment
2 Do Step 1 of the *Snippy Potatoes*
3 Do Steps 1–2 of the *Lemon-Berry Pleasure*
4 Do Steps 1–4 of the *Uppity Pork*
5 Do Steps 1–4 of the *Outrageous Asparagus*
6 Do Step 2 of the *Snippy Potatoes*
7 Do Steps 5–6 of the *Outrageous Asparagus*

RECIPES

Uppity Pork

1 Cut the pork loin into 8 slices. Flour and season the slices to taste. Reserve the seasoned flour.

2 Melt 1 tablespoon of the butter in a large skillet, and sauté the meat until it is brown on the outside but still moist on the inside, 3 to 5 minutes per side.

3 Remove the pork and keep it warm.

4 Melt the remaining butter in the skillet. Add the reserved flour and whisk until the mixture is smooth. Add the vermouth, the tarragon and the seasoning salt. Return the pork slices to the skillet and coat them with the sauce. Cover, remove from the heat and keep warm.

Snippy Potatoes

1 Scrub and quarter the potatoes. Place them in a medium saucepan with the broth. Bring the broth to a boil and cook until the potatoes are tender, 15 to 20 minutes.

2 Chop the chives. Chop the parsley. Drain the potatoes. Melt the butter in the saucepan. Add the chives and the parsley. Return the potatoes and toss them with the butter until they are coated and hot. Season to taste. Cover to keep warm.

Outrageous Asparagus

1 Bring $1\frac{1}{2}$ inches of water to a boil in a large skillet.

2 Rinse the asparagus and remove the tough ends. Peel and mince the shallots.

3 Melt 1 tablespoon of the butter in a small saucepan. Add the shallots and sauté until they are soft, 1 to 2 minutes. Add the mustard and the orange juice and bring the mixture to a boil. Then cook until the sauce is reduced to $\frac{2}{3}$ cup, about 5 minutes.

4 Cook the asparagus in the boiling water until it is crisp-tender, 3 to 8 minutes, depending on the thickness.

5 Add the remaining butter to the saucepan and whisk until it is well blended. Season to taste.

6 Drain the asparagus and top it with the sauce.

Lemon-Berry Pleasure

1 Rinse the blueberries in warm water to thaw.

2 Place the pudding mix and the milk in a medium bowl, and beat until well blended, 1 to 2 minutes. Add the sour cream and blend. Fold in half of the blueberries. Spoon the mixture into individual dessert dishes and top with the remaining berries. Refrigerate for at least 20 minutes.

THURSDAY

Chicken Alphabet Soup

1¼ pounds boneless, skinless chicken breasts
1 large onion
3 medium carrots
4 stalks celery
1 medium head lettuce
1 clove garlic
1½ tablespoons regular or light vegetable oil
2 cans (14½ ounces each) chicken broth
2 cups water
1 teaspoon ground allspice
1 bay leaf
8 ounces alphabet pasta
Seasoning to taste
3 tablespoons dry sherry (or nonalcoholic
    white wine or additional chicken broth)

Beet It Salad

1 medium can (15 ounces) sliced beets
1 small white grapefruit
2 scallions (green onions)
2 teaspoons grated fresh orange peel
⅛ teaspoon ground ginger
¼ cup regular or low-fat plain yogurt
1 tablespoon honey
2 teaspoons lemon juice
1 teaspoon poppy seeds

Buddy Bread

1 cup flour
1 cup cornmeal
½ teaspoon baking soda
½ teaspoon salt
1 cup buttermilk
1 medium can (15¼ ounces) creamed corn
2 eggs
⅓ cup regular or light vegetable oil

Banana Scramble

2 medium bananas
1 tablespoon butter
2 teaspoons lemon juice
1 tablespoon dark brown sugar
¼ teaspoon ground cinnamon
1 tablespoon rum (or nonalcoholic Italian
    praline syrup that will not ignite)

EQUIPMENT

Dutch oven	Assorted kitchen knives
Medium skillet	Measuring cups and
Small saucepan	spoons
9x9-inch baking pan	Assorted cooking
Large bowl	utensils
2 small bowls	Whisk
Strainer	Vegetable peeler

COUNTDOWN

1 Assemble the ingredients and equipment
2 Do Steps 1–3 of the *Buddy Bread*
3 Do Steps 1–4 of the *Chicken Alphabet Soup*
4 Do Steps 1–3 of the *Beet It Salad*
5 Do Step 5 of the *Chicken Alphabet Soup*
6 Do Step 4 of the *Beet It Salad*
7 Do Steps 1–2 of the *Banana Scramble*

Chicken Alphabet Soup

1 Cut the chicken breasts into bite-size pieces. Peel and chop the onion. Peel and chop the carrots. Trim and chop the celery. Wash, dry and shred the lettuce. Peel and mince the garlic.

2 Heat the oil in a Dutch oven until hot. Add the chicken and cook, stirring, until it turns white, 4 to 5 minutes. Remove and reserve.

3 Add the onion, the carrots, the celery and the garlic to the Dutch oven. Cook, stirring occasionally, until the onion is soft and the vegetables are crisp-tender, 5 to 7 minutes.

4 Stir the broth, the water, the allspice, the bay leaf, the alphabet pasta and the lettuce into the Dutch oven. Season to taste. Bring the soup to a boil, then reduce the heat. Return the chicken to the Dutch oven and simmer until the pasta and the carrots are tender, 15 to 20 minutes.

5 Before serving, remove the bay leaf and stir in the sherry.

Beet It Salad

1 Drain the beets. Peel and section the grapefruit. Trim and slice the scallions.

2 Arrange the beet slices on individual salad plates. Top the beets with the grapefruit sections.

3 In a small bowl, whisk together the orange peel, the ginger, the yogurt, the honey, the lemon juice and the poppy seeds.

4 Drizzle the dressing over the beets and grapefruit, and sprinkle with the scallions.

Buddy Bread

1 Preheat the oven to 350°F. Grease a 9x9-inch baking pan.

2 In a large bowl, blend the flour, the cornmeal, the baking soda and the salt. Add the buttermilk, the corn, the eggs and the oil. Mix thoroughly. Pour the mixture into the baking pan.

3 Bake until the bread is firm, 35 to 40 minutes.

Banana Scramble

1 Peel the bananas and cut them in half lengthwise. Melt the butter in a medium skillet. Add the bananas to the skillet, cut side down, and cook until they are warmed through and lightly browned on the bottom, about 2 minutes. Sprinkle the bananas evenly with the lemon juice, the brown sugar and the cinnamon.

2 Heat the rum in a small saucepan. When it is hot, ignite it and pour it over the bananas.

FRIDAY

Snap It Up

$^1/_4$ cup chopped walnuts
2 medium shallots
1 medium carrot
2 medium oranges
$1^1/_4$ pounds red snapper fillets
2 tablespoons flour
1 tablespoon seasoning salt
$^1/_4$ cup dry white wine (or nonalcoholic white
    wine or clam juice)
1 teaspoon dried thyme
Seasoning to taste
2 ounces bleu cheese

Tame Wild Rice

2 scallions (green onions)
$^1/_2$ cup wild rice
$^1/_2$ cup long-grain white rice
$2^1/_4$ cups water
4 tablespoons butter
1 teaspoon dried sage
Seasoning to taste

Cucumber-Onion Salad

2 medium cucumbers
1 medium red onion
1 medium head lettuce
3 tablespoons regular or light vegetable oil
2 tablespoons raspberry vinegar
$^1/_2$ teaspoon sugar
$^1/_8$ teaspoon Worcestershire sauce
Seasoning to taste

Razzleberry Shortcake

1 frozen pound cake
1 package (16 ounces) frozen sweetened
    raspberries
1 medium container (12 ounces) frozen
    whipped topping
2 tablespoons Kirsch liqueur (or nonalcoholic
    Italian cherry syrup)

EQUIPMENT

Large covered skillet	Measuring cups and
Double boiler	spoons
Small saucepan	Assorted cooking
Cookie sheet	utensils
Large bowl	Whisk
Small bowl	Citrus juicer
Shallow bowl	Citrus grater
Strainer	Vegetable peeler
Assorted kitchen knives	

COUNTDOWN

IN THE MORNING:
  Do Step 1 of the *Razzleberry Shortcake*
BEFORE DINNER:
  1 Assemble the remaining ingredients and
     equipment
  2 Do Step 1 of the *Snap It Up*
  3 Do Step 1 of the *Tame Wild Rice*
  4 Do Steps 1–2 of the *Cucumber-Onion Salad*
  5 Do Steps 2–7 of the *Snap It Up*
  6 Do Step 2 of the *Tame Wild Rice*
  7 Do Step 8 of the *Snap It Up*
  8 Do Step 3 of the *Cucumber-Onion Salad*
  9 Do Steps 2–4 of the *Razzleberry Shortcake*

Snap It Up

1 Preheat the broiler.

2 Spread the chopped walnuts on an ungreased cookie sheet. Toast the nuts 3 inches from the heat until they are brown, about 2 minutes. Remove the nuts and reserve.

3 Peel and chop the shallots. Peel and grate the carrot. Grate 2 tablespoons of orange peel and then juice the oranges.

4 Rinse the fish and pat it dry. Combine the flour with the seasoning salt in a shallow bowl and lightly dredge the fish in the mixture.

5 In a large skillet, combine the wine, the shallots, the carrot, the thyme, the orange juice and the orange peel and bring the mixture to a boil. Season to taste. Carefully add the fish, cover the skillet, reduce the heat and simmer until the fish is white and flakes easily when tested with a fork, 5 to 6 minutes.

6 Remove the fish from the skillet and cover to keep warm.

7 Increase the heat under the skillet and cook until the sauce is thick and reduced by half, 3 to 5 minutes.

8 Top each fillet with the toasted walnuts, the cheese and a spoonful of sauce.

Tame Wild Rice

1 Trim and chop the scallions. Combine them with the rice and the water in the top of a double boiler. Bring water in the bottom of the double boiler to a boil, cover and simmer until the liquid is absorbed and the rice is tender, 30 to 40 minutes.

2 Melt the butter in a small saucepan. Stir in the sage. Season to taste. Toss the mixture with the rice.

Cucumber-Onion Salad

1 Peel and slice the cucumbers. Peel and thinly slice the onion. Wash and dry the lettuce and tear it into bite-size pieces. Combine the ingredients in a large bowl.

2 In a small bowl, whisk together the oil, the vinegar, the sugar and the Worcestershire sauce. Season to taste.

3 Toss the salad with the dressing.

Razzleberry Shortcake

1 Set the pound cake out to thaw. Refrigerate the raspberries and the frozen topping.

2 Reserve 4 whole raspberries. Drain the remaining berries.

3 Fold the Kirsch into the whipped topping.

4 Cut the thawed cake into 12 vertical slices. Spread half the raspberries on 4 slices. Cover with a third of the whipped topping mixture. Add a second slice of cake and spread it with the remaining raspberries and another third of the whipped topping. Add the top slice of cake and spread it with the remaining whipped topping. Garnish with the reserved whole berries.

APRIL
WEEK TWO

Monday

ZIPPY TOMATO CONSOMMÉ
PASTA VERDE
HOLD-THE-GARLIC BREAD
ICE CREAM S'MORES

Tuesday

SEATTLE STEW
SWEET APPLE SAUCE
OPEN SESAMES
FORGET-ME-NUT CAKE

Wednesday

CHICKEN LITTLE
ASPIRING ASPARAGUS
DILLIGHTFUL SALAD
ORANGE JUBILATION

Thursday

ANGELS & EGGS
PEPPERED ZUCCHINI
BREAD ITALIANO
PEACHES 'N' CREAM 'N' COOKIES

Friday

BUSTER CRAB BISQUE
POCKETS FULL OF LOVE
BLUSHING PEARS

CHECK STAPLES

- ☐ Butter
- ☐ Flour
- ☐ Baking powder
- ☐ Baking soda
- ☐ Granulated sugar
- ☐ Dark brown sugar
- ☐ Confectioners' sugar
- ☐ Unsweetened cocoa
- ☐ Long-grain white rice
- ☐ Regular or light vegetable oil
- ☐ Regular or light olive oil
- ☐ Walnut oil
- ☐ Red wine vinegar
- ☐ White wine vinegar
- ☐ Lemon juice
- ☐ Grated fresh lemon peel
- ☐ Worcestershire sauce
- ☐ Tabasco sauce
- ☐ Dijon mustard
- ☐ Regular or low-fat mayonnaise
- ☐ Honey
- ☐ Ketchup
- ☐ Sweet pickle relish
- ☐ Grated Parmesan cheese
- ☐ Dried basil
- ☐ Bay leaves
- ☐ Cayenne pepper
- ☐ Celery seeds
- ☐ Ground cinnamon
- ☐ Curry powder
- ☐ Dried dill
- ☐ Garlic powder
- ☐ Italian seasoning
- ☐ Dried marjoram
- ☐ Ground nutmeg
- ☐ Dried oregano
- ☐ Sesame seeds
- ☐ Dried thyme
- ☐ Pepper
- ☐ Salt
- ☐ Vanilla extract

SHOPPING NOTE

● If you are shopping once a week and cannot arrange to purchase the cooked crabmeat on the day you plan to use it, you can purchase *not previously frozen* crabmeat and freeze it, placing it in the refrigerator to thaw the night before you are ready to use it. Or you can purchase *still frozen* crabmeat and keep it frozen until the night before you are ready to use it. You can also purchase imitation crabmeat; however, canned crabmeat will significantly alter the recipe.

MEAT & FISH

1 pound regular or light pork or turkey Polish kielbasa sausage (T)
3 pounds chicken pieces (W)

FISH

1 pound cooked crabmeat (F)

FRESH PRODUCE

Vegetables

1 small bunch broccoli (M)
$1^1/_2$ pounds asparagus (W)
$^3/_4$ pound zucchini (Th)
1 small parsnip (T)
$^1/_4$ pound mushrooms (M)
4 medium carrots—2 (T), 2 (F)
4 stalks celery—2 (M), 2 (T)
1 large onion (F)
1 medium onion (T)
1 small onion (M)
1 small sweet onion (W)
7 scallions (green onions)—
    1 (W), 2 (Th), 4 (F)
1 head garlic (M, W, Th, F)
1 bunch parsley (Th, F)
1 medium head red cabbage (T)
1 medium head lettuce (W)
1 small head lettuce (F)
1 ripe avocado (F)
$1^1/_2$ pounds tomatoes—
    $^1/_2$ pound (M), $^1/_2$ pound (Th),
    $^1/_2$ pound (F)
1 large yellow bell pepper (Th)
1 small red bell pepper (T)
1 small white radish (W)

Fruit

6 tart green apples (T)
4 large pears (F)
$^1/_4$ pound seedless red grapes (W)
2 medium bananas (W)
2 large oranges (W)
1 small lemon (M)

CANS, JARS & BOTTLES

Soup

1 can ($14^1/_2$ ounces) vegetable broth (M)
1 can ($14^1/_2$ ounces) chicken broth (W)
1 can ($10^3/_4$ ounces) cream of celery soup (W)

Vegetables

1 can (11 ounces) whole kernel corn (T)

Fruit

1 large can (29 ounces) peach halves (Th)

Juice

3 cups tomato juice (M)
1 quart cranberry-raspberry juice (F)

Dessert Needs

1 jar ($12^1/_4$ ounces) chocolate fudge topping (M)

PACKAGED GOODS

Pasta, Rice & Grains

8 ounces small shell pasta (M)
16 ounces angel hair pasta (capellini) (Th)

Baked Goods

1 loaf Italian bread (M, Th)
1 package crumpets (or English or Australian muffins) (T)
4 small pita breads (F)
1 cup croutons (W)

Soup

1 package (1.8 ounces) dried leek soup mix (W)

Nuts & Seeds

$^1/_2$ cup chopped walnuts (T)

Dessert & Baking Needs

8 whole graham crackers (M)
1 package (10 ounces) sugar cookies (Th)

WINES & SPIRITS

2 tablespoons dry sherry (or nonalcoholic white wine or clam juice) (F)
2 tablespoons Grand Marnier liqueur (or nonalcoholic Italian orange syrup) (W)

REFRIGERATOR PRODUCTS

Dairy

2 cups low-fat milk (T)
$4^3/_4$ cups half-and-half—
    $^3/_4$ cup (M), 4 cups (F)
Whipped cream for garnish (F)
1 cup regular or light sour cream (Th)
3 eggs (Th)

Cheese

$^1/_2$ cup shredded regular or low-fat mozzarella cheese (Th)
2 cups shredded regular or low-fat Monterey Jack cheese (F)

FROZEN GOODS

Vegetables

1 package (9 ounces) cut green beans (T)

Desserts

1 pint vanilla ice cream (M)

MONDAY

Zippy Tomato Consommé

1 small lemon
1 small onion
3 cups tomato juice
1 can (14^1/$_2$ ounces) vegetable broth
2 tablespoons lemon juice
2 stalks celery
1 bay leaf
2 teaspoons Worcestershire sauce
^{1}/$_2$ teaspoon sugar
1^1/$_4$ teaspoons dried thyme
^{1}/$_2$ teaspoon Tabasco sauce
Seasoning to taste

Pasta Verde

1 small bunch broccoli
^{1}/$_4$ pound mushrooms
1 clove garlic
^{1}/$_2$ pound fresh tomatoes
8 ounces small shell pasta
4 tablespoons butter
2 tablespoons flour
^{3}/$_4$ cup half-and-half
1 tablespoon lemon juice
Seasoning to taste
^{1}/$_2$ cup grated Parmesan cheese

Hold-the-Garlic Bread

^{1}/$_2$ loaf Italian bread*
2 tablespoons regular or light olive oil
1 teaspoon dried oregano
1 teaspoon dried basil

*Reserve the remainder of the bread for use on Thursday.

Ice Cream S'Mores

8 whole graham crackers
1 pint vanilla ice cream
1 jar (12^1/$_4$ ounces) chocolate fudge sauce

EQUIPMENT

Large skillet	Measuring cups and
Large saucepan	spoons
2 medium saucepans	Assorted cooking
Cookie sheet	utensils
Colander	Pastry brush
Strainer	Ice cream scoop
Assorted kitchen knives	

COUNTDOWN

1 Assemble the ingredients and equipment
2 Do Step 1 of the *Hold-the-Garlic Bread*
3 Do Steps 1–3 of the *Pasta Verde*
4 Do Steps 1–2 of the *Zippy Tomato Consommé*
5 Do Step 4 of the *Pasta Verde*
6 Do Step 2 of the *Hold-the-Garlic Bread*
7 Do Steps 5–6 of the *Pasta Verde*
8 Do Step 3 of the *Zippy Tomato Consommé*
9 Do Steps 1–2 of the *Ice Cream S'Mores*

Zippy Tomato Consommé

1 Grate ½ teaspoon lemon peel, then slice and reserve the lemon. Peel and quarter the onion.

2 Combine the tomato juice, the broth, the lemon juice, the celery, the onion, the bay leaf, the Worcestershire sauce, the sugar, the lemon peel, the thyme and the Tabasco sauce in a medium saucepan. Season to taste. Bring the mixture to a boil. Reduce the heat and simmer until just before you are ready to serve, at least 15 minutes.

3 Strain the soup, discarding the vegetables and the bay leaf. Garnish with the lemon slices.

Pasta Verde

1 Bring water to a boil in a medium saucepan. Trim and cut the broccoli into bite-size florets. Cook the broccoli until it is crisp-tender, about 5 minutes.

2 Bring water to a boil in a large saucepan.

3 Wash, pat dry and slice the mushrooms. Peel and mince the garlic. Chop the tomatoes. Drain the broccoli.

4 Cook the pasta until it is almost tender, about 7 minutes.

5 Melt the butter in a large skillet. Sauté the mushrooms and the garlic for 2 minutes. Add the flour, blend, and then gradually add the half-and-half and whisk until well blended. Add the broccoli and the lemon juice, and cook until hot, about 2 minutes. Add the tomatoes and toss. Season to taste. Add the Parmesan cheese and toss again.

6 Drain the pasta and return it to the saucepan. Toss the pasta with the sauce.

Hold-the-Garlic Bread

1 Preheat the broiler.

2 Slice the bread and place it on an ungreased cookie sheet. Brush the bread with the olive oil and sprinkle it with the oregano and the basil. Broil until the bread is lightly toasted, about 2 minutes.

Ice Cream S'Mores

1 Place a graham cracker on each dessert dish.

2 Top the cracker with scoops of ice cream. Drizzle the ice cream with the fudge sauce and top with a second graham cracker.

TUESDAY

Seattle Stew

1 package (9 ounces) frozen cut green beans
1 pound regular or light pork or turkey Polish
    kielbasa sausage
1 medium head red cabbage
1 medium onion
1 small red bell pepper
1 small parsnip
2 medium carrots
2 stalks celery
1 can (11 ounces) whole kernel corn
$1/4$ cup red wine vinegar
$1/8$ teaspoon cayenne pepper
Seasoning to taste

Sweet Apple Sauce

$1^1/2$ cups water
6 tart green apples
$1/2$ cup dark brown sugar
2 teaspoons vanilla extract
1 teaspoon ground cinnamon

Open Sesames

1 package crumpets (or English or Australian
    muffins)
2 tablespoons softened butter
$1/2$ teaspoon garlic powder
1 teaspoon sesame seeds

Forget-Me-Nut Cake

3 cups flour
1 cup sugar
$1/2$ cup unsweetened cocoa
2 teaspoons baking powder
2 teaspoons baking soda
2 cups low-fat milk
1 cup regular or low-fat mayonnaise
1 teaspoon vanilla extract
$1/2$ cup chopped walnuts

EQUIPMENT

Large covered skillet	Measuring cups and
Medium covered	spoons
saucepan	Assorted cooking
9x13-inch baking pan	utensils
Cookie sheet	Vegetable peeler
Medium bowl	Vegetable grater
Small bowl	Apple corer
Assorted kitchen knives	Ice cream scoop

COUNTDOWN

1 Assemble the ingredients and equipment
2 Do Steps 1–2 of the *Forget-Me-Nut Cake*
3 Do Step 1 of the *Seattle Stew*
4 Do Step 1 of the *Sweet Apple Sauce*
5 Do Steps 2–3 of the *Seattle Stew*
6 Do Step 2 of the *Sweet Apple Sauce*
7 Do Step 4 of the *Seattle Stew*
8 Do Steps 1–3 of the *Open Sesames*
9 Do Step 5 of the *Seattle Stew*

Seattle Stew

1 Run the green beans under warm water to thaw. Thinly slice the kielbasa. Grate the cabbage. Peel and chop the onion. Seed and chop the bell pepper. Peel and chunk the parsnip. Peel and slice the carrots. Trim and slice the celery.

2 Heat a large skillet until hot. Add the sausage and cook, stirring occasionally, until it is browned, 6 to 8 minutes. Remove the sausage and reserve it.

3 Drain off all but 1 tablespoon of the drippings from the skillet. Add the cabbage and the onion, and cook, stirring often, until soft, 6 to 8 minutes.

4 Add the parsnip, the carrots and the celery to the skillet and sauté until slightly softened, 5 to 6 minutes. Add the bell pepper and sauté 3 minutes more. Stir in the undrained corn, the thawed beans, the vinegar and the cayenne pepper. Heat to boiling, then reduce the heat and cook until the cabbage is tender, 4 to 5 minutes more. Season to taste.

5 Return the sausage to the skillet and mix it with the vegetables. Cover the skillet and heat through.

Sweet Apple Sauce

1 Bring water to a boil in a medium saucepan. Peel, core and quarter the apples. Add them to the saucepan and cook until they are soft, about 15 minutes, adding more water if necessary to keep them from burning.

2 Add the brown sugar, the vanilla and the cinnamon to the apples. Mix well. Cover the saucepan and remove it from the heat.

Open Sesames

1 Preheat the broiler. Place the crumpets on an ungreased cookie sheet.

2 In a small bowl, combine the softened butter and the garlic powder. Spread the mixture over the crumpets. Sprinkle with the sesame seeds.

3 Broil 3 to 4 inches from heat until the crumpets are lightly toasted, 2 to 3 minutes.

Forget-Me-Nut Cake

1 Preheat the oven to 350°F.

2 In a medium bowl, combine the flour with the sugar, the cocoa, the baking powder and the baking soda. Add the milk and the mayonnaise, and mix well. Fold in the vanilla. Pour the batter into a 9x13-inch baking pan, sprinkle with the nuts and bake until a toothpick inserted in the cake comes out clean, about 30 minutes.

WEDNESDAY

Chicken Little

2 cloves garlic
1 package (1.8 ounces) dried leek soup mix
1 cup long-grain white rice
1 can (14^1/$_2$ ounces) chicken broth
3 pounds chicken pieces
Seasoning to taste
1 can (10^3/$_4$ ounces) cream of celery soup

Aspiring Asparagus

1^1/$_2$ pounds fresh asparagus
1 scallion (green onion)
2 tablespoons butter
2 tablespoons lemon juice
1 tablespoon celery seeds
1 teaspoon walnut oil
Seasoning to taste

Dillightful Salad

1 medium head lettuce
1 small sweet onion
1 small white radish
4 tablespoons regular or light vegetable oil
3 tablespoons white wine vinegar
^{1}/$_2$ teaspoon sugar
1 teaspoon dried dill
^{1}/$_8$ teaspoon curry powder
Seasoning to taste
1 cup croutons

Orange Jubilation

2 large oranges
^{1}/$_2$ pound seedless red grapes
2 medium bananas
2 tablespoons Grand Marnier liqueur (or
    nonalcoholic Italian orange syrup)
1 teaspoon honey
^{1}/$_4$ cup confectioners' sugar

EQUIPMENT

Large covered skillet	Measuring cups and
1^1/$_2$-quart casserole	spoons
Large bowl	Assorted cooking
Medium bowl	utensils
Small bowl	Sifter
Assorted kitchen knives	Whisk

COUNTDOWN

1 Assemble the ingredients and equipment
2 Do Steps 1–3 of the *Chicken Little*
3 Do Steps 1–3 of the *Orange Jubilation*
4 Do Steps 1–2 of the *Dillightful Salad*
5 Do Steps 1–4 of the *Aspiring Asparagus*
6 Do Step 3 of the *Dillightful Salad*

Chicken Little

1 Preheat the oven to 375°F.

2 Peel and halve the garlic. Spread the leek soup mix on the bottom of a 1½-quart casserole. Add the rice and the chicken broth. Add the chicken and the garlic. Season to taste. Top with the cream of celery soup. Do not stir.

3 Bake for 45 minutes. Remove the garlic before serving.

Aspiring Asparagus

1 Trim the tough ends off the asparagus and slice diagonally into bite-size pieces. Trim and thinly slice the scallion.

2 Bring ½-inch of water to a boil in a large skillet. Steam the asparagus, covered, until it is crisp-tender, 3 to 8 minutes depending on thickness.

3 Drain the asparagus. Wipe out the skillet.

4 Melt the butter in the skillet. Sauté the scallion for 1 minute. Stir in the lemon juice, the celery seeds and the walnut oil. Season to taste. Return the asparagus to the skillet and toss to coat. Cover the skillet to keep warm.

Dillightful Salad

1 Wash and dry the lettuce and tear it into bite-size pieces. Peel and chop the onion. Peel and slice the radish. Combine the ingredients in a large bowl.

2 In a small bowl, whisk together the oil, the vinegar, the sugar, the dill and the curry powder. Season to taste.

3 Toss the salad with the dressing. Top with croutons.

Orange Jubilation

1 Peel and section the oranges. Rinse, separate and halve the grapes. Peel and slice the bananas. Place the fruit in a medium bowl.

2 Toss the fruit together with the Grand Marnier and the honey, and dust with the powdered sugar.

3 Refrigerate until you are ready to serve.

THURSDAY

Angels & Eggs

1 clove garlic
1/4 cup fresh parsley (when chopped)
3 eggs
1 teaspoon Italian seasoning
Seasoning to taste
4 tablespoons butter
16 ounces angel hair pasta (capellini)
1/2 cup grated Parmesan cheese

Peppered Zucchini

1 large yellow bell pepper
3/4 pound zucchini
2 tablespoons regular or light olive oil
1/2 teaspoon dried marjoram
1 teaspoon Dijon mustard
1 1/2 tablespoons lemon juice
Seasoning to taste

Bread Italiano

1 clove garlic
2 scallions (green onions)
1/2 pound fresh tomatoes
2 tablespoons regular or light olive oil
1/2 loaf Italian bread reserved from Monday
1/2 cup shredded regular or low-fat
    mozzarella cheese

Peaches 'n' Cream 'n' Cookies

1 large can (29 ounces) peach halves
1/4 teaspoon ground nutmeg
1 cup regular or light sour cream
1/4 cup firmly packed dark brown sugar
1 package (10 ounces) sugar cookies

EQUIPMENT

Stockpot	Assorted kitchen knives
Large covered skillet	Measuring cups and
Small skillet	spoons
Cookie sheet	Assorted cooking
9-inch pie plate	utensils
Medium bowl	Whisk
Small bowl	Aluminum foil
Colander	

COUNTDOWN

1 Assemble the ingredients and equipment
2 Do Step 1 of the *Angels & Eggs*
3 Do Steps 1–2 of the *Peaches 'n' Cream 'n' Cookies*
4 Do Steps 1–3 of the *Peppered Zucchini*
5 Do Steps 2–4 of the *Angels & Eggs*
6 Do Steps 1–3 of the *Bread Italiano*
7 Do Steps 5–7 of the *Angels & Eggs*
8 Do Step 3 of the *Peaches 'n' Cream 'n' Cookies*

Angels & Eggs

1 Bring water to a boil in a stockpot.

2 Peel and mince the garlic. Chop the parsley.

3 Whisk the eggs in a medium bowl, blend in the Italian seasoning and season to taste.

4 Melt the butter in a small skillet and sauté the garlic until soft, about 5 minutes.

5 Cook the pasta in the boiling water until it is almost tender, about 2 minutes if you are using fresh pasta and about 4 minutes if you are using dried pasta.

6 Add the eggs to the garlic butter and barely simmer, stirring constantly, for 30 seconds. Fold in the parsley and remove from the heat.

7 Drain the pasta and return it to the stockpot. Toss the pasta with the sauce and sprinkle with the Parmesan cheese. Cover to keep warm.

Peppered Zucchini

1 Seed the bell pepper and cut it into strips. Wash the zucchini and cut it lengthwise into 1/2-inch slices. Then cut the slices into 1/2-inch strips.

2 Heat the oil in a large skillet. Stir in the marjoram. Add the pepper strips and sauté them for 2 minutes. Add the zucchini and sauté until both vegetables are crisp-tender, 2 to 3 minutes.

3 Add the mustard and the lemon juice to the skillet, season to taste and stir to blend. Cover to keep warm.

Bread Italiano

1 Preheat the oven to 400°F. Line a cookie sheet with aluminum foil.

2 Peel and mince the garlic. Trim and thinly slice the scallions. Chop the tomatoes. In a small bowl, combine the garlic and the oil, and season to taste.

3 Slice the bread horizontally. Place the bread cut sides up on the aluminum foil. Drizzle the garlic mixture over the bread, and sprinkle with the scallions and the tomatoes. Top with the cheese, and bake until the cheese melts, 5 to 7 minutes.

Peaches 'n' Cream 'n' Cookies

1 Preheat the broiler.

2 Drain the peaches, and place them cut side down in a pie plate. Sprinkle them with the nutmeg, and spread with the sour cream. Top the sour cream with the brown sugar, and broil until the sugar bubbles, 3 to 5 minutes. Remove the peaches and let them cool until you are ready to serve.

3 Serve the sugar cookies with the peaches.

FRIDAY

Buster Crab Bisque

2 cloves garlic
1 large onion
2 tablespoons fresh parsley (when chopped)
3 teaspoons butter
1 pound cooked crabmeat
Seasoning to taste
1 quart half-and-half
2 tablespoons dry sherry (or nonalcoholic
    white wine or clam juice)
3 teaspoons lemon juice
3 tablespoons flour

Pockets Full of Love

1 small head lettuce
2 medium carrots
4 scallions (green onions)
$1/2$ pound fresh tomatoes
1 ripe avocado
$1/4$ cup regular or low-fat mayonnaise
3 tablespoons ketchup
1 tablespoon sweet pickle relish
4 small pita breads
2 cups shredded regular or low-fat Monterey
    Jack cheese

Blushing Pears

4 large pears
$1/2$ cup sugar
1 quart cranberry-raspberry juice
1 tablespoon ground cinnamon
$1^1/2$ teaspoons vanilla extract
Whipped cream for garnish

EQUIPMENT

2 large covered saucepans	Assorted cooking utensils
10x14-inch baking pan	Vegetable grater
Large bowl	Vegetable peeler
Small bowl	Whisk
Assorted kitchen knives	
Measuring cups and spoons	

COUNTDOWN

1 Assemble the ingredients and equipment
2 Do Steps 1–3 of the *Pockets Full of Love*
3 Do Steps 1–2 of the *Buster Crab Bisque*
4 Do Step 1 of the *Blushing Pears*
5 Do Step 3 of the *Buster Crab Bisque*
6 Do Step 2 of the *Blushing Pears*
7 Do Step 4 of the *Buster Crab Bisque*
8 Do Step 4 of the *Pockets Full of Love*
9 Do Steps 3–4 of the *Blushing Pears*

Buster Crab Bisque

1 Peel and mince the garlic. Peel and chop the onion. Chop the parsley.

2 Melt the butter in a large saucepan, and sauté the garlic and the onion until the onion is soft, about 6 minutes.

3 Flake the crabmeat and add it to the saucepan, mixing gently to combine. Season to taste. Cook for 1 minute. Reduce the heat, stir in all but 3 tablespoons of the half-and-half, cover the saucepan and simmer for 10 minutes. Do not let boil.

4 Stir the sherry and the lemon juice into the saucepan. Combine the flour and the reserved half-and-half, and stir it into the bisque, whisking to thicken. Cover the saucepan and barely simmer the bisque until you are ready to serve. Sprinkle with the parsley.

Pockets Full of Love

1 Preheat the oven to 325°F.

2 Wash, dry and shred the lettuce. Peel and grate the carrots. Trim and chop the scallions. Chop the tomatoes. Peel, pit and chop the avocado. Combine the ingredients in a large bowl.

3 In a small bowl, whisk together the mayonnaise, the ketchup and the relish.

4 Cut the pita breads in half. Spread the mayonnaise mixture on the insides of the pockets. Stuff the pockets with the vegetable mixture, packing gently. Top with the cheese. Place the stuffed pita breads in a 10x14-inch baking pan, and bake until they are warmed through, about 10 minutes.

Blushing Pears

1 Peel, core and halve the pears. Combine the sugar with the cranberry-raspberry juice in a large saucepan, and cook until the sugar is dissolved. Add the cinnamon and the vanilla, and bring the mixture to a boil. Carefully add the pear halves, reduce the heat and simmer the pears until they can be easily pierced with the tip of a sharp knife, about 15 minutes.

2 Carefully remove the pears from the liquid and keep them warm. Continue cooking until the pear liquid is reduced to about 1 cup.

3 Turn the heat off under the pear liquid and cover the saucepan to keep warm until you are ready to serve.

4 Pour a small amount of the pear liquid into individual serving dishes. Add the pears and top them with dollops of whipped cream.

APRIL

WEEK THREE

Monday

EGG FLOWER SOUP
CANTON STIR-FRY
FLUFFY STEAMED WHITE RICE
AUSPICIOUS PINEAPPLE

Tuesday

PEPPER STEAK
SWEET POTATO POLKA
DOCTORED PEAS & PEARLS
APPLE-MALLOW TOSS

Wednesday

TUSCAN BEAN SOUP
ALPINE SALAD
YODEL BREAD
ALMOND SOUFFLÉ

Thursday

FEAR OF FRYING
POTATO CLOUDS
COUNTRY GRAVY
THREE PEAS IN A POD
RUMMY PEACHES

Friday

PANGO PANGO PASTA
SOUTH SEA SALAD
INCREDIBLE COCONUT PIE

CHECK STAPLES

- ☐ Butter
- ☐ Flour
- ☐ Cornstarch
- ☐ Bisquick
- ☐ Granulated sugar
- ☐ Dark brown sugar
- ☐ Italian praline syrup
- ☐ Long-grain white rice
- ☐ Regular or light vegetable oil
- ☐ Regular or light olive oil
- ☐ Sesame oil
- ☐ White wine vinegar
- ☐ Lemon juice
- ☐ Fresh ginger
- ☐ Worcestershire sauce
- ☐ Soy sauce
- ☐ Kitchen Bouquet
- ☐ Dijon mustard
- ☐ Ketchup
- ☐ Grated Parmesan cheese
- ☐ Beef bouillon cubes
- ☐ Dried basil
- ☐ Cream of tartar
- ☐ Curry powder
- ☐ Dried dill
- ☐ Ground nutmeg
- ☐ Whole black peppercorns
- ☐ Salad seasoning
- ☐ Dried tarragon
- ☐ Pepper
- ☐ Salt
- ☐ Rum extract
- ☐ Vanilla extract

SHOPPING NOTE

● If you are shopping once a week and cannot arrange to purchase fresh scallops on the day you plan to use them, you may purchase *not previously frozen* scallops and freeze them, placing them in the refrigerator to thaw the night before you are ready to use them. Or you may purchase *still frozen* scallops and keep them frozen until the night before you are ready to use them.

MEAT & POULTRY

4 lean beef tenderloins (1¼ pounds) (T)
1 whole boneless, skinless chicken breast (M)
3 pounds chicken pieces (Th)

FISH

¾ pound scallops (F)

FRESH PRODUCE

Vegetables

4 medium sweet potatoes (T)
6 medium baking potatoes (Th)
1 small bunch broccoli (M)
½ pound green beans (F)
1 pound unshelled green peas (Th)
½ pound sugar snap peas (Th)
¾ pound Chinese snow peas—½ pound (M), ¼ pound (Th)
¾ pound spinach (W)
4 large mushrooms (M)
¼ pound mushrooms (W)
6 medium carrots—3 (M), 3 (W)
5 stalks celery—2 (M), 1 (T), 2 (W)
¼ pound bean sprouts (M)
2 medium onions—1 (M), 1 (W)
1 medium red onion (F)
1 small red onion (W)
9 scallions (green onions)— 2 (M), 3 (Th), 4 (F)
1 head garlic (T, W)
1 bunch parsley (W, F)
2 medium heads lettuce—1 (W), 1 (F)
1 small bunch watercress (W)
1 ripe avocado (F)
½ pound tomatoes (F)
1 small cucumber (W)
1 large red bell pepper (M)

Fruit

2 large green apples (T)

1 small cantaloupe (T)
1 large pineapple (M)
½ pound seedless red grapes (T)
1 pink grapefruit (F)

CANS, JARS & BOTTLES

Soup

1 can (10¾ ounces) chicken broth (Th)
2 cans (14½ ounces each) chicken broth (M)
1 can (14½ ounces) oriental broth (M)
1 can (14½ ounces) vegetable broth (W)

Vegetables

1 large can (28 ounces) cut-up tomatoes (W)
1 can (15 ounces) white beans (W)

Fruit

1 large can (29 ounces) sliced peaches (Th)

Spreads

¼ cup orange marmalade (T)

Baking Needs

1 can (14 ounces) regular or low-fat evaporated milk (F)

PACKAGED GOODS

Pasta, Rice & Grains

12 ounces rotini (F)
8 ounces elbow macaroni (W)

Baked Goods

1 pound unsliced sourdough loaf (W)

Nuts & Seeds

¼ cup pecan pieces (T)

Dessert & Baking Needs

1 cup mini-marshmallows (T)
1 cup flaked coconut (F)

WINES & SPIRITS

½ cup dry red wine (or nonalcoholic red wine or ¼ cup red wine vinegar + ¼ cup steak sauce) (T)
1 teaspoon dry sherry (or nonalcoholic white wine or soy sauce) (M)
¼ cup dry sherry (or nonalcoholic red wine or beef broth) (W)
2 tablespoons Amaretto liqueur (or nonalcoholic Italian almond syrup) (W)

REFRIGERATED PRODUCTS

Dairy

1 quart whole or low-fat milk—¾ cup (W), 1¼ cups (Th), 2 cups (F)
¾ cup buttermilk (Th)
¼ cup regular or light sour cream (M)
9 eggs—2 (M), 3 (W), 4 (F)

Cheese

6 slices regular or low-fat Swiss cheese (W)

Juices

3 tablespoons orange juice (W)

FROZEN GOODS

Vegetables

1 package (9 ounces) peas & pearl onions (T)

Desserts

1 pint peach frozen yogurt (Th)

MONDAY

Egg Flower Soup

2 scallions (green onions)
2 cans (14½ ounces each) chicken broth
¾ cup oriental broth
2 slices fresh unpeeled ginger
2 eggs
1 teaspoon dry sherry (or nonalcoholic white
    wine or soy sauce)
Seasoning to taste

Canton Stir-Fry

1 whole boneless, skinless chicken breast
1 small bunch fresh broccoli
1 large red bell pepper
3 medium carrots
1 medium onion
2 stalks celery
4 large mushrooms
½ pound fresh Chinese snow peas
6 tablespoons regular or light vegetable oil
¼ pound fresh bean sprouts
1 cup oriental broth
1 teaspoon soy sauce
1½ teaspoons sugar
Seasoning to taste
2 tablespoons cornstarch dissolved in 2
    tablespoons cold water
1 tablespoon sesame oil

Fluffy Steamed White Rice

1 cup long-grain white rice
2 cups water

Auspicious Pineapple

1 large pineapple
¼ cup regular or light sour cream
¼ cup dark brown sugar

EQUIPMENT

Wok and wok utensils	Measuring cups and
Double boiler	spoons
Medium covered	Assorted cooking
saucepan	utensils
9x13-inch baking pan	Vegetable peeler
Small bowl	Whisk
Assorted kitchen knives	Aluminum foil

COUNTDOWN

1 Assemble the ingredients and equipment
2 Do Step 1 of the *Fluffy Steamed White Rice*
3 Do Steps 1–2 of the *Auspicious Pineapple*
4 Do Step 1 of the *Canton Stir-Fry*
5 Do Steps 1–4 of the *Egg Flower Soup*
6 Do Steps 2–5 of the *Canton Stir-Fry*
7 Do Step 2 of the *Fluffy Steamed White Rice*
8 Do Step 5 of the *Egg Flower Soup*
9 Do Step 3 of the *Auspicious Pineapple*

Egg Flower Soup

1 Trim and thinly slice the scallions, reserving half for garnish.

2 In a medium saucepan, combine the remaining scallion with the broth and the ginger and bring the broth to a boil.

3 In a small bowl, beat the eggs and the sherry together.

4 When the broth is boiling, remove the ginger and pour a thin, steady stream of the egg mixture into the broth, stirring constantly. Remove the saucepan from the heat, season to taste and cover to keep warm.

5 Sprinkle the reserved scallion over the soup.

Canton Stir-Fry

1 Cut the chicken into thin strips. Trim and cut the broccoli into bite-size pieces. Seed the bell pepper and cut it into strips. Peel and thinly slice the carrots. Peel and slice the onion, and then cut the slices in half. Trim and slice the celery. Wash, pat dry and slice the mushrooms. Trim and string the snow peas.

2 Heat the oil in the wok until it is hot.

3 Add the chicken, the broccoli, the carrots, the onion and the celery, and stir-fry for 2 minutes. Add the bell pepper and stir-fry for 1 minute. Add the mushrooms, the snow peas and the bean sprouts, and stir-fry for 1 minute.

4 Make a well in the center of the wok and add the broth, the soy sauce and the sugar.

Season to taste. Stir-fry for 2 minutes more.

5 Again, make a well in the center of the wok and add the cornstarch mixture and the sesame oil. Toss the mixture for 30 seconds, until the chicken and the vegetables are well coated and the sauce has thickened.

Fluffy Steamed White Rice

1 Place the rice and the water in the top of a double boiler. Bring water in the bottom of the double boiler to a boil. Reduce the heat, cover and simmer until all the liquid is absorbed and the rice is tender, 30 to 40 minutes.

2 Fluff the rice before serving.

Auspicious Pineapple

1 Skin and core the pineapple, removing all the brown spurs, and slice it into 1-inch-thick rounds.

2 Line a 9x13-inch baking pan with aluminum foil. Place the pineapple slices on the foil. Spread them with the sour cream and sprinkle them with the brown sugar.

3 Preheat the broiler. Broil the pineapple 3 or 4 inches from the heat until the brown sugar caramelizes, about 5 minutes.

TUESDAY

Pepper Steak

2 cloves garlic
$1/2$ cup whole black peppercorns
$1/2$ cup dry red wine (or nonalcoholic red wine
     or $1/4$ cup red wine vinegar + $1/4$ cup steak
     sauce)
1 teaspoon Worcestershire sauce
1 beef bouillon cube
$1/4$ cup water
Seasoning to taste
4 lean beef tenderloins ($1 1/4$ pounds)
1 tablespoon flour

Sweet Potato Polka

4 medium sweet potatoes
2 tablespoons butter
2 tablespoons dark brown sugar

Doctored Peas & Pearls

1 stalk celery
1 tablespoon butter
1 leaf lettuce*
1 package (9 ounces) frozen peas & pearl
     onions
$1/4$ cup water
$3/4$ teaspoon ground nutmeg
Seasoning to taste

Apple-mallow Toss

2 large green apples
1 small cantaloupe
$1/2$ pound seedless red grapes

*Steal the lettuce leaf from the salad on Wednesday.

2 tablespoons lemon juice
$1/4$ cup orange marmalade
2 tablespoons Italian praline syrup
$1/4$ cup pecan pieces
1 cup mini-marshmallows

EQUIPMENT

Large covered skillet	Assorted kitchen knives
Large saucepan	Measuring cups and
Medium covered	spoons
saucepan	Assorted cooking
Small saucepan	utensils
7x11-inch glass baking	Whisk
dish	Vegetable peeler
Large bowl	Plastic bag
Small bowl	Mallet
Strainer	

COUNTDOWN

1 Assemble the ingredients and equipment
2 Do Step 1 of the *Sweet Potato Polka*
3 Do Steps 1–3 of the *Pepper Steak*
4 Do Step 2 of the *Sweet Potato Polka*
5 Do Step 1 of the *Apple-mallow Toss*
6 Do Step 4 of the *Pepper Steak*
7 Do Step 3 of the *Sweet Potato Polka*
8 Do Step 1 of the *Doctored Peas & Pearls*
9 Do Step 5 of the *Pepper Steak*
10 Do Step 2 of the *Doctored Peas & Pearls*
11 Do Step 4 of the *Sweet Potato Polka*
12 Do Step 6 of the *Pepper Steak*
13 Do Step 3 of the *Doctored Peas & Pearls*
14 Do Step 2 of the *Apple-mallow Toss*

Pepper Steak

1 Peel and chop the garlic. Crush the peppercorns in a plastic bag with a mallet.

2 Combine the red wine, the Worcestershire sauce, the bouillon cube and the water in a small bowl. Season to taste.

3 Place the tenderloins in a 7x11-inch glass baking dish, and press the garlic and the peppercorns into them. Cover the meat with the marinade. Cover the dish and let it stand for 30 minutes.

4 Preheat the broiler.

5 Broil the tenderloins according to taste, reserving the marinade.

6 Strain the marinade into a small saucepan to remove the peppercorns, and bring to a boil. Whisk in the flour to thicken the sauce, and drizzle it over the beef.

Sweet Potato Polka

1 Bring water to a boil in a large saucepan.

2 Peel and quarter the potatoes, and cook them in the boiling water until they are almost tender, 10 to 12 minutes.

3 Drain the potatoes and run them under cold water to cool. Then cut them into $1/4$-inch slices.

4 In a large skillet, melt the butter and sauté the potatoes until they are lightly browned, about 5 minutes. Sprinkle the potatoes with the brown sugar and toss them several times to coat. Reduce the heat and simmer the potatoes until the sugar is dissolved, 2 to 3 minutes. Remove the skillet from the heat and cover to keep warm.

Doctored Peas & Pearls

1 Trim and chop the celery. Melt the butter in a medium saucepan. Sauté the celery until it is soft, 3 to 4 minutes.

2 Add the lettuce leaf to the saucepan. Add the frozen peas and pearl onions, the water and the nutmeg. Season to taste. Cover the saucepan and simmer until the peas and onions are heated through, about 5 minutes.

3 Remove the lettuce leaf. Cover to keep warm.

Apple-mallow Toss

1 Core and chop the apples. Remove the rind from the melon and cut the flesh into chunks. Wash and separate the grapes. Combine the fruit in a large bowl, sprinkle it with lemon juice, and refrigerate until you are ready to use.

2 Heat the marmalade and the praline syrup in a small saucepan, whisking until smooth. Distribute the fruit among individual dessert dishes. Drizzle the sauce over the fruit and top with the pecan pieces and the mini-marshmallows.

WEDNESDAY

Tuscan Bean Soup

1 medium onion
4 cloves garlic
2 stalks celery
3 medium carrots
2 tablespoons fresh parsley (when chopped)
$3/4$ pound fresh spinach
1 can (15 ounces) white beans
1 tablespoon regular or light olive oil
1 can ($14^1/2$ ounces) vegetable broth
1 large can (28 ounces) cut-up tomatoes
8 ounces elbow macaroni
2 teaspoons dried basil
$1/4$ cup dry sherry (or nonalcoholic red wine or beef broth)
Seasoning to taste

Alpine Salad

1 medium head lettuce
1 small bunch watercress
1 small cucumber
1 small red onion
$1/4$ pound mushrooms
3 tablespoons orange juice
1 tablespoon regular or light olive oil
$1/2$ teaspoon salad seasoning
$1/4$ teaspoon dried dill
Seasoning to taste

Yodel Bread

4 tablespoons softened butter
$1/2$ teaspoon dried tarragon
1 pound unsliced sourdough bread loaf
6 slices regular or low-fat Swiss cheese

Almond Soufflé

$3/4$ cup whole or low-fat milk
$1^1/2$ tablespoons sugar
3 eggs
$1/8$ teaspoon cream of tartar
2 tablespoons Amaretto liqueur (or nonalcoholic Italian almond syrup)
2 tablespoons confectioners' sugar

EQUIPMENT

Electric hand mixer	Assorted kitchen knives
Dutch oven	Measuring cups and
Medium saucepan	spoons
1-quart casserole or	Assorted cooking
soufflé dish	utensils
2 large bowls	Whisk
Medium bowl	Vegetable peeler
2 small bowls	Aluminum foil
Strainer	Sifter

COUNTDOWN

1 Assemble the ingredients and equipment
2 Do Steps 1–3 of the *Yodel Bread*
3 Do Steps 1–2 of the *Tuscan Bean Soup*
4 Do Steps 1–2 of the *Alpine Salad*
5 Do Step 3 of the *Tuscan Bean Soup*
6 Do Step 4 of the *Yodel Bread*
7 Do Steps 1–4 of the *Almond Soufflé*
8 Do Step 3 of the *Alpine Salad*
9 Do Step 5 of the *Almond Soufflé*

Tuscan Bean Soup

1 Peel and chop the onion. Peel and mince the garlic. Trim and chop the celery. Peel and slice the carrots. Chop the parsley. Stem and chop the spinach. Drain and rinse the beans.

2 Heat the oil in a Dutch oven. Add the onion, the garlic, the celery and the carrots, and sauté until the onion is softened, 6 to 8 minutes.

3 Add the broth, the undrained tomatoes, the macaroni, the parsley, the basil, the beans and the spinach to the Dutch oven. Add the sherry. Season to taste. Bring the soup to a boil, reduce the heat and simmer until the macaroni is tender, 15 to 20 minutes.

Alpine Salad

1 Wash and dry the lettuce and tear it into bite-size pieces. Wash, dry and stem the watercress. Peel and slice the cucumber. Peel and thinly slice the red onion. Wash, pat dry, trim and slice the mushrooms. Combine the ingredients in a large bowl.

2 In a small bowl, whisk together the orange juice, the oil, the salad seasoning and the dill. Season to taste.

3 Toss the salad with the dressing.

Yodel Bread

1 Preheat the oven to 450°F.

2 In a small bowl, combine the softened butter and the tarragon. Slice the bread into 10 to 12 slices, cutting to—but not through—the bottom crust. Spread the cut surface of each slice with a portion of the butter mixture.

3 Cut the cheese slices into triangles and place a triangle between each slice of the bread. Wrap the loaf in aluminum foil.

4 Bake the bread until it is heated through, about 15 minutes.

Almond Soufflé

1 Combine the milk and the sugar in a medium saucepan, scald the mixture and then remove it from the heat.

2 Separate the eggs. Beat the eggs whites and the cream of tartar in a large bowl until stiff, about 3 minutes.

3 Beat the yolks in a medium bowl. Gradually stir the warm milk mixture into the beaten yolks.

4 Fold the Amaretto into the egg yolk mixture, and then fold the egg yolk mixture into the egg white mixture.

5 Preheat the oven to 350°F. Just before sitting down to eat, pour the mixture into a 1-quart casserole or soufflé dish and bake for 15 minutes. Dust with confectioners' sugar.

THURSDAY

Fear of Frying

2 cups regular or light vegetable oil
1 cup Bisquick
1 cup flour
Seasoning to taste
$^3/_4$ cup buttermilk
3 pounds chicken pieces

Potato Clouds

6 medium baking potatoes
2 scallions (green onions)
2 tablespoons butter
$^1/_4$ cup whole or low-fat milk
Seasoning to taste

Country Gravy

$^1/_4$ cup flour
1 cup whole or low-fat milk
1 can (10$^3/_4$ ounces) chicken broth
1 tablespoon Kitchen Bouquet
Seasoning to taste

Three Peas in a Pod

$^1/_2$ pound fresh sugar snap peas
$^1/_4$ pound fresh Chinese snow peas
1 pound unshelled green peas
1 scallion (green onion)
2 tablespoons butter
$^1/_2$ teaspoon sugar
Seasoning to taste

Rummy Peaches

1 large can (29 ounces) sliced peaches
3 tablespoons dark brown sugar
3 teaspoons lemon juice
1 tablespoon rum extract
1 pint peach frozen yogurt

EQUIPMENT

Electric hand mixer	Measuring cups and
2 large covered skillets	spoons
Large covered	Assorted cooking
saucepan	utensils
Medium saucepan	Whisk
9x13-inch baking pan	Vegetable peeler
2 shallow bowls	Ice cream scoop
Assorted kitchen knives	

COUNTDOWN

1 Assemble the ingredients and equipment
2 Do Steps 1–6 of the *Fear of Frying*
3 Do Step 1 of the *Potato Clouds*
4 Do Step 1 of *Three Peas in a Pod*
5 Do Step 7 of the *Fear of Frying*
6 Do Steps 1–2 of the *Country Gravy*
7 Do Step 2 of the *Potato Clouds*
8 Do Step 2 of *Three Peas in a Pod*
9 Do Steps 1–3 of the *Rummy Peaches*

Fear of Frying

1 Heat the oil in a large skillet to approximately $1/2$-inch deep. Do not let it get hot enough to smoke.

2 Combine the Bisquick and the flour in a shallow bowl. Season to taste. Put the buttermilk in another shallow bowl.

3 Dredge the chicken pieces in the flour, then dip them in the buttermilk, coat them well and dip them back in the flour.

4 Cook the chicken in the oil, turning to brown on all sides, 15 to 20 minutes.

5 Cover the skillet and cook for 10 minutes more.

6 Preheat the oven to 325°F.

7 Remove the chicken from the skillet and drain the pieces well on paper towels. Line a 9x13-inch baking pan with fresh paper towels. Arrange the chicken in a single layer in the baking pan and bake until the skins are crisp, about 15 minutes.

Potato Clouds

1 Peel and cube the potatoes. Trim the scallions. Place both in a large saucepan and cover them with water. Bring the water to a boil and cook until the potatoes are soft, 10 to 12 minutes.

2 Drain the potatoes. Discard the scallions. Add the butter and the milk, and beat until the potatoes are whipped. Season to taste. Cover to keep warm.

Country Gravy

1 Discard all but 2 tablespoons of the drippings from the chicken skillet. Add the flour and whisk, scraping up the brown bits from the bottom of the skillet, until the mixture is bubbly. Cook for 1 minute more.

2 Gradually add the milk, the broth and the Kitchen Bouquet. Cook, stirring constantly, until the sauce thickens. Season to taste.

Three Peas in a Pod

1 Trim and string the sugar snap peas and the snow peas. Shell the green peas. Trim and chop the scallion.

2 Melt the butter in a large skillet. Add the sugar and sauté the sugar snap peas and the scallion for 1 minute. Add the snow peas and the green peas, and sauté until they are crisp-tender, 2 to 3 minutes. Season to taste. Cover to keep warm.

Rummy Peaches

1 Drain the peaches, reserving the syrup in a medium saucepan.

2 Add the brown sugar and the lemon juice to the reserved syrup. Cook and stir until the sugar is dissolved and the sauce is hot, 2 to 3 minutes. Stir in the rum extract.

3 Spoon the peaches over scoops of frozen yogurt. Top with the hot rum sauce.

FRIDAY

Pango Pango Pasta

12 ounces rotini
$^1/_2$ pound fresh green beans
4 scallions (green onions)
2 tablespoons fresh parsley (when chopped)
$^1/_2$ pound fresh tomatoes
$^3/_4$ pound scallops
1 tablespoon regular or light vegetable oil
1 can (14 ounces) regular or low-fat
    evaporated milk
1 tablespoon curry powder
3 tablespoons flour
$1^1/_2$ tablespoons lemon juice
Seasoning to taste
$^1/_4$ cup grated Parmesan cheese

South Sea Salad

1 medium head lettuce
1 medium red onion
1 ripe avocado
1 pink grapefruit
3 tablespoons regular or light olive oil
2 tablespoons white wine vinegar
1 teaspoon Dijon mustard
$^1/_2$ teaspoon Worcestershire sauce
$^1/_2$ tablespoon ketchup
Seasoning to taste

Incredible Coconut Pie

2 cups whole or low-fat milk
$^3/_4$ cup sugar
$^1/_2$ cup Bisquick
4 eggs
4 tablespoons butter
2 teaspoons vanilla extract
1 cup flaked coconut

EQUIPMENT

Blender	Assorted kitchen knives
Stockpot	Measuring cups and
Large saucepan	spoons
Medium saucepan	Assorted cooking
9-inch pie plate	utensils
2 small bowls	Whisk
Colander	

COUNTDOWN

1 Assemble the ingredients and equipment
2 Do Steps 1–2 of the *Incredible Coconut Pie*
3 Do Step 1 of the *Pango Pango Pasta*
4 Do Steps 1–2 of the *South Sea Salad*
5 Do Steps 2–5 of the *Pango Pango Pasta*
6 Do Step 3 of the *Incredible Coconut Pie*
7 Do Step 3 of the *South Sea Salad*
8 Do Step 6 of the *Pango Pango Pasta*

Pango Pango Pasta

1 Bring water to a boil in a stockpot. Also bring water to a boil in a medium saucepan.

2 Cook the pasta in the stockpot until it is almost tender, about 10 minutes. Trim and string the green beans and cut them into 1-inch pieces. Cook them in the saucepan until they are crisp-tender, about 5 minutes.

3 Trim and chop the scallions, reserving 1 for garnish. Chop the parsley. Chop the tomatoes. If you are using sea scallops, cut them in half.

4 Drain the beans. Drain the pasta, return it to the stockpot and toss it with the oil.

5 In a large saucepan, combine 1 cup of the evaporated milk, the curry powder and the scallions and bring almost to a boil. In a small bowl, combine the remaining milk with the flour. Whisk the flour mixture into the sauce. Cook, stirring gently, until the sauce thickens, 8 to 10 minutes.

6 Stir in the lemon juice, the scallops, the tomatoes and the beans. Cook for 2 minutes more. Season to taste and toss with the pasta. Sprinkle with the reserved scallion, the parsley and the Parmesan cheese.

South Sea Salad

1 Wash and dry the lettuce and tear it into bite-size pieces. Peel and slice the red onion. Peel, pit and slice the avocado. Peel and section the grapefruit, reserving any juice in a small bowl. Distribute the lettuce among individual plates. Arrange the avocado and the grapefruit over the lettuce, and refrigerate until you are ready to use.

2 Whisk together the reserved grapefruit juice, the oil, the vinegar, the mustard, the Worcestershire sauce and the ketchup until well blended. Season to taste.

3 Drizzle the dressing over the salad.

Incredible Coconut Pie

1 Preheat the oven to 350°F. Grease a 9-inch pie plate.

2 Combine the milk, the sugar, the Bisquick, the eggs, the butter and the vanilla in a blender. Cover and process on low for 3 minutes. Fold in the coconut. Pour the mixture into the pie plate and let it stand until you are ready to bake.

3 Bake the pie for 40 minutes.

APRIL
WEEK FOUR

Monday

PEASANT PASTA
HAYSEED SALAD
COUNTRY BREAD
DOUBLE BUTTERSCOTCH PUDDING

Tuesday

ADAGIO CHICKEN
GARLICKY POTATOES
ELEGANT EGGPLANT
MELON-CHOLY BABY

Wednesday

SALMON TOPPER
BED OF SPINACH
CUCUMBER NUMBER
BAGELS, OF COURSE
APRIL SHOWERS

Thursday

PORK TERIYAKI
NUTTY RICE PILAF
PEPPERED LEEKS
SUN CHASERS

Friday

GREEN NOODLE CASSEROLE
KIND OF CORNY
HOT TOMATOES
SHADOW CAKE

CHECK STAPLES

- ☐ Butter
- ☐ Flour
- ☐ Granulated sugar
- ☐ Dark brown sugar
- ☐ Confectioners' sugar
- ☐ Multicolored sprinkles
- ☐ Long-grain white rice
- ☐ Regular or light vegetable oil
- ☐ Regular or light olive oil
- ☐ Red wine vinegar
- ☐ Balsamic vinegar
- ☐ Lemon juice
- ☐ Lime juice
- ☐ Grated fresh lemon peel
- ☐ Worcestershire sauce
- ☐ Soy sauce
- ☐ Dijon mustard
- ☐ Regular or low-fat mayonnaise
- ☐ Grated Parmesan cheese
- ☐ Seasoned bread crumbs
- ☐ Bay leaves
- ☐ Ground cinnamon
- ☐ Dried dill
- ☐ Ground ginger
- ☐ Paprika
- ☐ Dried rosemary
- ☐ Sesame seeds
- ☐ Pepper
- ☐ Salt
- ☐ Almond extract
- ☐ Vanilla extract

SHOPPING NOTES

● If you are shopping once a week and cannot arrange to purchase fresh salmon on the day you plan to use it, you can purchase *not previously frozen* salmon and freeze it, placing it in the refrigerator to thaw the night before you are ready to use it. Or you can purchase *still frozen* salmon and keep it frozen until the night before you are ready to use it.

● If you are shopping once a week and cannot arrange to purchase the cooked crabmeat on the day you plan to use it, you can purchase *not previously frozen* crabmeat and freeze it, placing it in the refrigerator to thaw the night before you are ready to use it. Or you can purchase *still frozen* crabmeat and keep it frozen until the night before you are ready to use it. You can also purchase imitation crabmeat; however, canned crabmeat will significantly alter the recipe.

SHOPPING LIST

MEAT & POULTRY

$^1/_2$ pound lean cooked ham
    steak (M)

1$^1/_4$ pounds lean boneless pork
    loin (Th)

4 boneless, skinless chicken
    breast halves (T)

FISH

4 salmon steaks (1$^1/_2$ pounds)
    (W)

1 pound cooked crabmeat (F)

FRESH PRODUCE

Vegetables

4 medium red potatoes (T)

5 Japanese eggplant (T)

1$^1/_2$ pounds spinach (W)

1 large onion (W)

1 medium onion (T)

1 small onion (Th)

1 small sweet onion (M)

3 large leeks (Th)

9 scallions (green onions)—
    4 (T), 5 (F)

1 head garlic (M–F)

1 bunch parsley (T, F)

1 bunch chives (M, W, F)

1 medium head lettuce (M)

$^1/_2$ pound tomatoes (M)

1 pint cherry tomatoes (F)

4 medium cucumbers (W)

1 small yellow bell pepper (Th)

1 small red bell pepper (F)

Fruit

1 medium cantaloupe (T)

1 small honeydew melon (T)

1 medium lemon (T)

3 medium oranges (Th)

CANS, JARS & BOTTLES

Soup

1 can (14$^1/_2$ ounces) chicken
    broth (Th)

Vegetables

1 can (11 ounces) whole kernel
    corn (F)

Condiments

1 small can (3$^1/_2$ ounces) pitted
    black olives (M)

3 tablespoons capers (T)

Spreads

2 tablespoons orange
    marmalade (T)

PACKAGED GOODS

Pasta, Rice & Grains

12 ounces fusilli (M)

8 ounces green (spinach)
    noodles (F)

Baked Goods

1 small loaf unsliced whole
    wheat bread (M)

4 bagels (W)

1 angel food loaf cake (F)

Nuts & Seeds

$^1/_4$ cup sunflower seeds (M)

$^1/_4$ cup unsalted cashew nut
    pieces (Th)

Dessert & Baking Needs

1 small package (3.4 ounces)
    instant butterscotch
    pudding mix (M)

$^1/_2$ cup butterscotch chips (M)

1 square (1 ounce) semisweet
    baking chocolate (F)

$^1/_2$ cup mini-marshmallows (M)

12 ginger snaps (T)

4 large oatmeal cookies (W)

WINES & SPIRITS

$^1/_2$ cup dry white wine (or
    nonalcoholic white wine or
    vegetable broth) (M)

$^1/_4$ cup dry sherry (or non-
    alcoholic white wine or
    chicken broth) (T)

2 tablespoons dry sherry (or
    nonalcoholic red wine or
    beef broth) (Th)

REFRIGERATED PRODUCTS

Dairy

2 cups whole milk (M)

$^3/_4$ cup whole or low-fat
    milk—11 tablespoons (M),
    1 tablespoon (W)

1$^1/_2$ cups regular or light sour
    cream—$^1/_2$ cup (T), 1 cup (F)

Cheese

1 large package (8 ounces)
    regular or light cream
    cheese (M)

$^3/_4$ cup shredded regular or low-
    fat cheddar cheese (F)

Juice

1 tablespoon orange juice (Th)

FROZEN GOODS

Vegetables

1 package (20 ounces) broccoli,
    carrots & cauliflower (M)

Desserts

1 pint maple nut (or similar) ice
    cream (W)

1 pint vanilla frozen yogurt (Th)

MONDAY

Peasant Pasta

1 large package (8 ounces) regular or light
    cream cheese
1 package (20 ounces) frozen broccoli,
    carrots & cauliflower
12 ounces fusilli
1 tablespoon regular or light vegetable oil
$^1/_2$ pound lean cooked ham steak
$^2/_3$ cup whole or low-fat milk
$^1/_2$ cup dry white wine (or nonalcoholic white
    wine or vegetable broth)
2 tablespoons Dijon mustard
Seasoning to taste
$^1/_4$ cup grated Parmesan cheese

Hayseed Salad

1 medium head lettuce
1 small sweet onion
$^1/_2$ pound fresh tomatoes
3 tablespoons regular or light olive oil
2 tablespoons red wine vinegar
$^1/_8$ teaspoon Worcestershire sauce
Seasoning to taste
$^1/_4$ cup sunflower seeds

Country Bread

2 cloves garlic
1 tablespoon fresh chives (when chopped)
1 small can (3$^1/_2$ ounces) pitted black olives
$^1/_4$ cup regular or light olive oil
Seasoning to taste
1 small unsliced loaf whole wheat bread

Double Butterscotch Pudding

1 small package (3.4 ounces) instant
    butterscotch pudding mix
2 cups whole milk
$^1/_2$ cup butterscotch chips
$^1/_2$ cup mini-marshmallows

EQUIPMENT

Electric hand mixer	Assorted kitchen knives
Blender	Measuring cups and
Large saucepan	spoons
Large bowl	Assorted cooking
Medium bowl	utensils
Small bowl	Whisk
Colander	Aluminum foil

COUNTDOWN

1 Assemble the ingredients and equipment
2 Do Step 1 of the *Peasant Pasta*
3 Do Step 1 of the *Double Butterscotch
   Pudding*
4 Do Steps 1–3 of the *Country Bread*
5 Do Step 2 of the *Peasant Pasta*
6 Do Steps 1–2 of the *Hayseed Salad*
7 Do Steps 3–6 of the *Peasant Pasta*
8 Do Step 3 of the *Hayseed Salad*
9 Do Step 7 of the *Peasant Pasta*
10 Do Step 2 of the *Double Butterscotch
   Pudding*

Peasant Pasta

1 Set the cream cheese out to soften and the frozen vegetables out to thaw. Bring water to a boil in a large saucepan.

2 Cook the fusilli in the boiling water until it is almost tender, about 10 minutes.

3 Drain the pasta well in a colander and toss it with the oil.

4 Chop the ham into 1/4-inch cubes.

5 Add the cream cheese and the milk to the saucepan. Cook, stirring constantly, until the cream cheese is melted and well blended with the milk. Add the wine and return the pasta and toss to coat.

6 Reduce the heat. Stir in the mustard, the ham and the vegetables, and season to taste. Cook, stirring occasionally, until the vegetables are hot and crisp-tender, 5 to 7 minutes.

7 Sprinkle the pasta with Parmesan cheese.

Hayseed Salad

1 Wash and dry the lettuce and tear it into bite-size pieces. Peel and slice the sweet onion. Chop the tomatoes. Combine the ingredients in a large bowl and refrigerate until you are ready to use.

2 In a small bowl, whisk together the oil, the vinegar and the Worcestershire sauce. Season to taste.

3 Toss the salad with the dressing and sprinkle with the sunflower seeds.

Country Bread

1 Preheat the oven to 375°F.

2 Peel and mash the garlic. Chop the chives. Drain the olives. Combine the ingredients in a blender with the olive oil, season to taste and process until pureed.

3 Cut the bread into vertical slices without cutting through the bottom crust. Spread the olive paste between the slices. Wrap the bread in aluminum foil and heat until you are ready to serve, about 30 minutes.

Double Butterscotch Pudding

1 In a medium bowl, beat together the pudding mix and the milk until well blended. Pour the mixture into individual serving dishes, and refrigerate for at least 20 minutes.

2 Top the pudding with the butterscotch chips and the mini-marshmallows.

TUESDAY

Adagio Chicken

4 boneless, skinless chicken breast halves
$1/2$ cup flour
$1/8$ teaspoon paprika
Seasoning to taste
4 tablespoons butter
1 tablespoon regular or light olive oil
1 medium lemon
$1/4$ cup fresh parsley (when chopped)
$1/4$ cup dry sherry (or nonalcoholic white wine
  or chicken broth)
3 tablespoons lemon juice
3 tablespoons capers

Garlicky Potatoes

1 tablespoon butter
1 tablespoon regular or light olive oil
4 medium red potatoes
1 medium onion
3 cloves garlic
Seasoning to taste

Elegant Eggplant

5 Japanese eggplant
1 tablespoon salt
4 scallions (green onions)
4 tablespoons regular or light vegetable oil
Seasoning to taste

Melon-choly Baby

1 medium cantaloupe
1 small honeydew melon
$1/2$ cup regular or light sour cream
2 tablespoons orange marmalade
12 ginger snaps

EQUIPMENT

Large covered skillet	Assorted cooking
Large skillet	utensils
9x13-inch glass baking	Meat mallet
dish	Waxed paper
Small bowl	Plastic bag
Colander	Vegetable brush
Assorted kitchen knives	
Measuring cups and	
spoons	

COUNTDOWN

1 Assemble the ingredients and equipment
2 Do Step 1 of the *Garlicky Potatoes*
3 Do Step 1 of the *Elegant Eggplant*
4 Do Steps 2–4 of the *Garlicky Potatoes*
5 Do Steps 1–3 of the *Melon-choly Baby*
6 Do Steps 1–3 of the *Adagio Chicken*
7 Do Step 2 of the *Elegant Eggplant*
8 Do Step 4 of the *Adagio Chicken*
9 Do Step 3 of the *Elegant Eggplant*
10 Do Step 4 of the *Melon-choly Baby*

Adagio Chicken

1 Place the chicken breasts between sheets of waxed paper and pound them with a mallet to a $1/4$-inch thickness.

2 Combine the flour and the paprika in a plastic bag. Season to taste. Add the chicken and shake the bag to coat the pieces well.

3 Melt the butter with the oil in a large skillet. Sauté until the chicken breasts are opaque, 2 to 3 minutes per side. Do not overcook. Remove the chicken from the skillet.

4 Slice the lemon. Chop the parsley. Drain off all but 2 tablespoons of the pan drippings. Stir in the sherry and the lemon juice. Bring the mixture to a boil, then reduce the heat. Return the chicken to the skillet, add the lemon slices and cook until the liquid is reduced and slightly thickened, about 5 minutes. Add the capers and gently mix them in. Season to taste. Remove the skillet from the heat, sprinkle with the parsley and cover to keep warm.

Garlicky Potatoes

1 Preheat the oven to 475°F.

2 Place the butter and the oil in a 9x13-inch glass baking dish and set it in the oven until the butter is melted.

3 Scrub the potatoes and cut them into sixths. Peel and cut the onion into eighths. Peel and halve the garlic.

4 Place the potatoes, the onion and the garlic in the baking dish with the butter and oil. Stir to coat well. Bake, turning occasionally, until the potatoes are golden brown and fork-tender, about 20 minutes. Season to taste.

Elegant Eggplant

1 Slice each eggplant lengthwise into $2^{1}/_{2}$ x $^{1}/_{2}$-inch pieces. Put the pieces in a colander and sprinkle them with the salt. Let them stand for 20 minutes. Trim and slice the scallions.

2 Rinse the eggplant pieces and pat them dry with paper towels.

3 Heat the oil in a large skillet and sauté the eggplant and the scallions until the eggplant pieces are lightly browned, 3 to 5 minutes. Season to taste.

Melon-choly Baby

1 Cut the melons in half, and then seed and slice them. Cut around the edges to remove the rind. Alternate the slices of melon on individual dessert plates, and refrigerate until you are ready to use.

2 Combine the sour cream and the marmalade in a small bowl. Refrigerate until you are ready to use.

3 Crumble the ginger snaps.

4 Top the melon slices with the sour cream mixture, and sprinkle with the crumbled ginger snaps.

WEDNESDAY

Salmon Topper

4 salmon steaks (1 1/2 pounds)
Seasoning to taste
1 teaspoon dried dill
1 tablespoon soy sauce
1 tablespoon butter

Bed of Spinach

1 1/2 pounds fresh spinach
1 large onion
1 clove garlic
3 tablespoons butter
Seasoning to taste

Cucumber Number

1/4 teaspoon dried rosemary
1/4 cup balsamic vinegar
1/4 cup regular or light olive oil
2 tablespoons Dijon mustard
1/8 teaspoon sugar
4 medium cucumbers
3 tablespoons fresh chives (when chopped)
Seasoning to taste

Bagels, of Course

2 tablespoons butter
4 bagels
1/4 cup sesame seeds

April Showers

1 tablespoon whole or low-fat milk
1/4 teaspoon vanilla extract
3 tablespoons confectioners' sugar
1 pint maple nut (or similar) ice cream
4 large oatmeal cookies
Multicolored sprinkles

EQUIPMENT

Large covered saucepan	Measuring cups and spoons
9x13-inch glass baking dish	Assorted cooking utensils
Cookie sheet	Whisk
Medium bowl	Vegetable peeler
2 small bowls	Pastry brush
Assorted kitchen knives	Ice cream scoop

COUNTDOWN

1 Assemble the ingredients and equipment
2 Do Step 1 of the *Salmon Topper*
3 Do Steps 1–3 of the *Cucumber Number*
4 Do Step 1 of the *April Showers*
5 Do Steps 1–2 of the *Bed of Spinach*
6 Do Step 1 of the *Bagels, of Course*
7 Do Steps 2–3 of the *Salmon Topper*
8 Do Step 2 of the *Bagels, of Course*
9 Do Steps 3–4 of the *Bed of Spinach*
10 Do Step 4 of the *Salmon Topper*
11 Do Step 2 of the *April Showers*

Salmon Topper

1 Preheat the broiler. Grease a 9x13-inch glass baking dish.

2 Rinse and pat dry the salmon and place it in the dish. Season to taste. Sprinkle the fish with half of the dill and half of the soy sauce, and broil 4 inches from the heat for 5 minutes.

3 Turn the salmon. Season to taste. Sprinkle with the remaining dill and the remaining soy sauce. Dot with the butter, and continue broiling until the fish flakes easily with a fork, 3 to 5 minutes.

4 Place the salmon steaks on portions of spinach to serve.

Bed of Spinach

1 Rinse, stem and chop the spinach. Peel and chop the onion. Peel and mince the garlic.

2 Melt the butter in a large saucepan. Add the onion and the garlic and sauté until the onion is very soft but not brown, about 10 minutes.

3 Stir in the spinach. Cover the saucepan and cook until the spinach is wilted, 2 to 4 minutes.

4 Uncover the saucepan and cook until all the liquid has evaporated, stirring occasionally. Remove the saucepan from the heat. Season to taste. Cover to keep warm.

Cucumber Number

1 In a medium bowl, whisk together the rosemary, the vinegar, the oil, the mustard and the sugar.

2 Peel and slice the cucumbers. Chop the chives. Add them both to the medium bowl.

3 Toss the dressing with the cucumbers and chives, season to taste and refrigerate until ready to serve.

Bagels, of Course

1 Melt the butter. Cut the bagels into very thin slices and place them on an ungreased cookie sheet. Brush the slices with the melted butter, and sprinkle with sesame seeds.

2 Preheat the broiler. Place the cookie sheet under the broiler and broil until the bagel slices are lightly toasted, 1 to 2 minutes.

April Showers

1 Whisk the milk, the vanilla and the confectioners' sugar in a small bowl until a glaze forms.

2 Place scoops of ice cream over each cookie in individual dessert dishes. Drizzle the sugar glaze over the ice cream and top with the sprinkles.

THURSDAY

Pork Teriyaki

1¹/₄ pounds lean boneless pork loin
2 cloves garlic
¹/₄ cup soy sauce
2 tablespoons dry sherry (or nonalcoholic red
    wine or beef broth)
¹/₂ teaspoon dark brown sugar
¹/₂ teaspoon ground ginger
Seasoning to taste

Nutty Rice Pilaf

¹/₄ cup unsalted cashew nut pieces
1 small onion
4 tablespoons butter
¹/₄ cup regular or light vegetable oil
1 cup long-grain white rice
1 can (14¹/₂ ounces) chicken broth
¹/₄ cup water
¹/₄ teaspoon grated fresh lemon peel
1 bay leaf

Peppered Leeks

3 large leeks
1 small yellow bell pepper
2 cloves garlic
4 tablespoons regular or light olive oil
2 tablespoons lemon juice
Seasoning to taste

Sun Chasers

3 medium oranges
2 tablespoons almond extract
2 tablespoons sugar
1 tablespoon orange juice
1 pint vanilla frozen yogurt

EQUIPMENT

Large skillet	Assorted cooking
Medium covered	utensils
saucepan	8 metal kabob skewers
Large bowl	Pastry brush
Medium bowl	Whisk
Small bowl	Ice cream scoop
Assorted kitchen knives	
Measuring cups and	
spoons	

COUNTDOWN

1 Assemble the ingredients and equipment
2 Do Steps 1–2 of the *Pork Teriyaki*
3 Do Steps 1–3 of the *Nutty Rice Pilaf*
4 Do Step 1 of the *Peppered Leeks*
5 Do Steps 3–4 of the *Pork Teriyaki*
6 Do Step 1 of the *Sun Chasers*
7 Do Step 2 of the *Peppered Leeks*
8 Do Step 4 of the *Nutty Rice Pilaf*
9 Do Steps 2–3 of the *Sun Chasers*

Pork Teriyaki

1 Remove any excess fat from the pork and cut the meat into 1½-inch cubes. Peel and mince the garlic.

2 Combine the garlic, the soy sauce, the sherry, the brown sugar and the ginger in a large bowl. Season to taste. Add the pork and toss the cubes to coat. Let the pork marinate at room temperature for 20 to 30 minutes.

3 Preheat the broiler.

4 Thread the pork cubes onto kabob skewers. Set the skewers 4 or 5 inches from the heat and broil, turning and basting several times with the marinade, until the pork is well browned outside but still moist inside, 10 to 12 minutes.

Nutty Rice Pilaf

1 Chop the nuts.

2 Peel and chop the onion. Melt the butter with the oil in a medium saucepan and sauté the onion until limp but not brown, about 6 minutes.

3 Mix in the rice. Stir in the broth and the water, and bring the mixture to a boil. Add the lemon peel, the bay leaf and the nuts. Cover the saucepan tightly and simmer until all the liquid is absorbed and the rice is tender, about 25 minutes.

4 Remove the bay leaf and fluff the rice before serving.

Peppered Leeks

1 Thoroughly wash the leeks. Remove the tough green ends and cut the remainder into thin strips. Seed the bell pepper and cut it into thin strips. Peel and mince the garlic.

2 Heat the oil in a large skillet. Add the garlic and sauté it for 2 minutes. Add the leeks and the bell pepper and sauté them for 2 minutes. Toss the leeks and the peppers with the lemon juice. Season to taste.

Sun Chasers

1 Peel and section the oranges. Cut each section in half and place them in a medium bowl. Toss the orange sections with the almond extract, and then refrigerate until you are ready to use.

2 Whisk the sugar and the orange juice in a small bowl until a glaze forms.

3 Place scoops of frozen yogurt in individual dessert dishes. Spoon the oranges on top, and drizzle the glaze over the oranges.

FRIDAY

Green Noodle Casserole

1 pound cooked crabmeat
5 scallions (green onions)
1 clove garlic
1 small red bell pepper
8 ounces green (spinach) noodles
$^1/_2$ cup regular or low-fat mayonnaise
1 cup regular or light sour cream
$^1/_4$ teaspoon Worcestershire sauce
Seasoning to taste
$^3/_4$ cup shredded regular or low-fat cheddar
    cheese

Kind of Corny

1 can (11 ounces) whole kernel corn
2 tablespoons fresh chives (when chopped)
1 tablespoon butter
1 tablespoon lime juice
Seasoning to taste

Hot Tomatoes

1 pint fresh cherry tomatoes
1 clove garlic
3 tablespoons fresh parsley (when chopped)
2 tablespoons regular or light olive oil
Seasoning to taste
$1^1/_2$ cups seasoned bread crumbs

Shadow Cake

1 square (1 ounce) semisweet baking chocolate
2 teaspoons butter
1 teaspoon vanilla extract
1 angel food loaf cake

EQUIPMENT

Large skillet	Colander
Large saucepan	Assorted kitchen knives
Medium covered	Measuring cups and
saucepan	spoons
Small saucepan	Assorted cooking
2-quart casserole	utensils
Small bowl	Whisk

COUNTDOWN

1 Assemble the ingredients and equipment
2 Do Steps 1–6 of the *Green Noodle Casserole*
3 Do Steps 1–2 of the *Shadow Cake*
4 Do Step 1 of *Kind of Corny*
5 Do Steps 1–2 of the *Hot Tomatoes*
6 Do Step 2 of *Kind of Corny*
7 Do Step 3 of the *Hot Tomatoes*

Green Noodle Casserole

1 Preheat the oven to 350°F. Grease a 2-quart casserole.

2 Bring water to a boil in a large saucepan.

3 Flake the crabmeat. Trim and chop the scallions. Peel and mince the garlic. Seed and dice the bell pepper.

4 Cook the noodles until they are almost tender, 4 to 6 minutes.

5 In a small bowl, whisk together the mayonnaise, the sour cream and the Worcestershire sauce. Season to taste.

6 Drain the noodles and place them in the bottom of the casserole. Place the crabmeat, the scallions and the bell pepper over the noodles. Pour the mayonnaise mixture over the crabmeat. Top with the cheese and bake for 30 minutes.

Kind of Corny

1 Drain the corn. Chop the chives.

2 Melt the butter in a medium saucepan. Sauté the corn for 3 minutes. Toss the corn with the chives and the lime juice. Season to taste. Remove the saucepan from the heat and cover it to keep warm until you are ready to serve.

Hot Tomatoes

1 Wash and stem the tomatoes. Peel and mince the garlic. Chop the parsley.

2 Heat the oil in a large skillet. Add the garlic and sauté for 1 minute. Add the tomatoes and the parsley. Season to taste. Sauté the tomatoes until they are slightly softened, 3 to 5 minutes.

3 Add the bread crumbs and simmer until the mixture is heated through, about 2 minutes.

Shadow Cake

1 Melt the chocolate with the butter in a small saucepan.

2 Blend in the vanilla and drizzle the mixture slowly over the angel food cake, allowing it to drip down the sides. Reserve the cake until you are ready to serve.

MAY

WEEK ONE

WEEK AT A GLANCE

Monday

ROYAL CHICKEN
RICE PRINCESS
DUCHESS SALAD
ICE CASTLES

Tuesday

MANHATTAN CLAM CHOWDER
SKYLINE SALAD
VILLAGE BREAD
PLAZA RING

Wednesday

BEEF IT UP
SPRING ASPARAGUS
SPICY APRICOT COMPOTE

Thursday

FUSILLI FLORENTINE
SWEET CARROT SALAD
SOUR MUFFINS
COCONUT PUDDING SUPREME

Friday

TUNA RICE DELIGHT
PALM-OLIVE SALAD
MARSHMALLOW MOOSE

CHECK STAPLES

- ☐ Butter
- ☐ Flour
- ☐ Cornstarch
- ☐ Bisquick
- ☐ Granulated sugar
- ☐ Dark brown sugar
- ☐ Confectioners' sugar
- ☐ Sweetened cocoa
- ☐ Chocolate sprinkles
- ☐ Long-grain white rice
- ☐ Regular or light vegetable oil
- ☐ Regular or light olive oil
- ☐ White wine vinegar
- ☐ Red wine vinegar
- ☐ Balsamic vinegar
- ☐ Raspberry vinegar
- ☐ Lemon juice
- ☐ Grated fresh lemon peel
- ☐ Dijon mustard
- ☐ Honey
- ☐ Chunk-style peanut butter
- ☐ Dark raisins
- ☐ Beef bouillon cubes
- ☐ Ground allspice
- ☐ Dried basil
- ☐ Ground cinnamon
- ☐ Ground cloves
- ☐ Curry powder
- ☐ Dried dill
- ☐ Garlic powder
- ☐ Ground ginger
- ☐ Dried marjoram
- ☐ Ground nutmeg
- ☐ Instant minced onion
- ☐ Onion powder
- ☐ Paprika
- ☐ Seasoning salt
- ☐ Dried savory
- ☐ Dried thyme
- ☐ Pepper
- ☐ Salt
- ☐ Vanilla extract

SHOPPING NOTE

● If you are shopping once a week and cannot arrange to purchase fresh clams on the day you plan to use them, you can substitute 3 cans (10 ounces each) of whole clams and omit cooking instructions.

MEAT & POULTRY
4 lean beef tenderloins (1½ pounds) (W)
1¼ pounds boneless, skinless chicken breasts (M)

FISH
3 dozen steamer clams (T)

FRESH PRODUCE
Vegetables
2 large baking potatoes (T)
1 small bunch broccoli (T)
1 small head cauliflower (T)
1½ pounds asparagus (W)
¾ pound spinach (Th)
1 pound mushrooms (W)
8 medium carrots—2 (M), 6 (Th)
4 stalks celery—2 (M), 2 (T)
3 medium onions—1 (M), 1 (T), 1 (Th)
1 large shallot (Th)
10 scallions (green onions)— 2 (T), 5 (W), 3 (F)
1 head garlic (T, W, Th)
1 bunch parsley (M, T, Th)
2 medium heads lettuce— 1 (M, T), 1 (F)
1 small head lettuce (Th)
1 pound tomatoes—½ pound (T), ½ pound (F)
1 medium cucumber (F)
1 medium green bell pepper (W)
1 small red bell pepper (W)

Fruit
1 large cantaloupe (M)
1 large banana (Th)
2 medium bananas (M)
4 kiwifruit (M)
1 pint strawberries (M)

CANS, JARS & BOTTLES
Soups
1 can (14½ ounces) chicken broth (M)
1 can (14½ ounces) vegetable broth (T, W)
1 can (10¾ ounces) cream of mushroom soup (F)

Vegetables
1 large can (28 ounces) cut-up tomatoes (T)
1 small can (6 ounces) tomato paste (T)
1 can (8½ ounces) artichoke hearts (W)
1 can (14½ ounces) hearts of palm (F)

Fish
1 can (6 ounces) solid white tuna (F)

Mexican Products
¼ cup diced green chilies (optional) (F)

Fruit
1 medium can (15¼ ounces) crushed pineapple in juice (W)

Condiments
1 small jar (2 ounces) diced pimientos (M)
3 tablespoons capers (Th)
1 small jar (3 ounces) pimiento-stuffed green olives (F)

PACKAGED GOODS
Pasta, Rice & Grains
12 ounces fusilli (corkscrew pasta) (Th)
1¼ cups Rice Krispies cereal (M)
1 package (11 ounces) potato chips (F)

Baked Goods
1 loaf French bread (T)
4 slices white bread (W)

Fruit
¼ pound dried apricots (W)

Nuts & Seeds
½ cup chopped walnuts (Th)

Dessert & Baking Needs
1 package (3 ounces) cherry-flavored gelatin (T)

1 small package (3.4 ounces) instant coconut cream pudding mix (Th)
½ cup semisweet chocolate chips (M)
¼ cup flaked coconut (Th)
48 large marshmallows (F)

WINES & SPIRITS
1 cup dry red wine (or nonalcoholic red wine or clam juice) (T)
1 tablespoon dry sherry (or nonalcoholic red wine or omit) (M)
⅓ cup dry sherry (or nonalcoholic red wine or beef broth) (W)

REFRIGERATED PRODUCTS
Dairy
1¼ cups whole milk (Th)
½ cup whole or low-fat milk (F)
1 cup half-and-half (M)
1 cup whipping cream (F)
1¼ cups regular or light sour cream (Th)
3 eggs—1 (M), 2 (Th)

Cheese
1 small package (3 ounces) cream cheese (T)
¾ cup regular or low-fat small-curd cottage cheese (F)

Deli
½ pound bacon (T)

FROZEN GOODS
Vegetables
2 packages (9 ounces each) green peas—1 (M), 1 (F)

Fruit
1 package (16 ounces) pitted cherries (T)

Desserts
1 pint vanilla ice cream (M)

MONDAY

Royal Chicken

1 package (9 ounces) frozen green peas
2 stalks celery
2 medium carrots
1 medium onion
1¼ pounds boneless, skinless chicken breasts
1 small jar (2 ounces) diced pimientos
4 tablespoons butter
3 tablespoons flour
¼ teaspoon ground nutmeg
Seasoning to taste
1 can (14½ ounces) chicken broth
1 cup half-and-half
1 egg
1 tablespoon lemon juice
1 tablespoon dry sherry (or nonalcoholic red
   wine or omit)

Rice Princess

2 tablespoons fresh parsley (when chopped)
1 cup long-grain white rice
2 cups water
2 teaspoons instant minced onion
1 teaspoon garlic powder

Duchess Salad

½ medium head lettuce*
1 large cantaloupe
4 kiwifruit
1 pint fresh strawberries
3 tablespoons regular or light vegetable oil
2 tablespoons raspberry vinegar
2 teaspoons honey

*Reserve the remainder of the lettuce for use on Tuesday.

⅛ teaspoon ground ginger
Seasoning to taste
2 medium bananas

Ice Castles

½ cup semisweet chocolate chips
¼ cup chunk-style peanut butter
1¼ cups Rice Krispies cereal
1 pint vanilla ice cream

EQUIPMENT

Large skillet	Assorted kitchen knives
Large saucepan	Measuring cups and
Small saucepan	spoons
Double boiler	Assorted cooking
4 freezer-safe custard	utensils
cups	Vegetable peeler
Medium bowl	Melon-baller
2 small bowls	Whisk
Strainer	Ice cream scoop

COUNTDOWN

1 Assemble the ingredients and equipment
2 Do Step 1 of the *Rice Princess*
3 Do Steps 1–2 of the *Ice Castles*
4 Do Step 1 of the *Royal Chicken*
5 Do Steps 1–2 of the *Duchess Salad*
6 Do Steps 2–8 of the *Royal Chicken*
7 Do Step 3 of the *Duchess Salad*
8 Do Step 2 of the *Rice Princess*
9 Do Step 3 of the *Ice Castles*

Royal Chicken

1 Bring water to a boil in a large saucepan. Set the package of peas out to thaw.

2 Trim and slice the celery. Peel and slice the carrots. Peel and chop the onion. Cut the chicken breasts into strips. Drain the pimientos. Cook the carrots and the celery in the boiling water for 3 minutes. Add the chicken and cook until it is white throughout, about 4 minutes. Add the thawed peas and cook for 1 minute more.

3 Melt the butter in a large skillet. Add the onion and sauté until soft, about 5 minutes.

4 Drain the chicken and the vegetables. Remove the onion from the skillet with a slotted spoon and add it to the chicken and vegetables.

5 Add the flour and the nutmeg to the skillet. Season to taste. Whisk, without browning, for 1 minute.

6 In a medium bowl, combine the broth with the half-and-half. Gradually whisk the mixture into the skillet, bring it to a boil and whisk until the sauce is smooth and thickened, 3 to 5 minutes.

7 Lightly beat the egg. Whisk 1 cup of the sauce into the beaten egg. Stir the mixture back into the skillet until it is well blended.

8 Add the chicken and the vegetables to the skillet and stir in the lemon juice, the sherry and the pimientos. Season to taste and cook until the mixture is heated through, about 3 minutes.

Rice Princess

1 Mince the parsley. Place the parsley, the rice, the water, the onion and the garlic powder in the top of a double boiler. Bring water to a boil in the bottom of the double boiler, reduce the heat, cover and simmer until all the liquid is absorbed and the rice is tender, 30 to 40 minutes.

2 Fluff the rice before serving.

Duchess Salad

1 Wash and dry the lettuce and arrange the leaves on individual salad plates. Halve and seed the melon, and scoop it into balls. Peel and slice the kiwi. Hull and halve the strawberries. Arrange the fruit over the lettuce and refrigerate until you are ready to serve.

2 In a small bowl, whisk together the oil, the vinegar, the honey and the ginger. Season to taste.

3 Peel and slice the bananas. Arrange them over the salad and drizzle the salad with the dressing.

Ice Castles

1 Grease 4 freezer-safe custard cups.

2 In a small saucepan, cook the chocolate chips with the peanut butter until melted. Remove the saucepan from the heat and fold in the Rice Krispies. Press the mixture into the bottom and sides of the custard cups and place the cups in the freezer for at least 15 minutes.

3 Remove the custard cups from the freezer. Dip the bottoms in hot water for several seconds and carefully remove each chocolate shell. Fill the shells with scoops of ice cream.

TUESDAY

Manhattan Clam Chowder

3 dozen fresh steamer clams (or 3 cans [10
    ounces each] whole clams)
1 cup dry red wine (or nonalcoholic red wine
    or clam juice)
1 cup water
1 cup vegetable broth*
$1/2$ pound bacon
1 medium onion
2 stalks celery
1 large can (28 ounces) cut-up tomatoes
2 large baking potatoes
2 tablespoons fresh parsley (when chopped)
$1/2$ teaspoon dried thyme
1 small can (6 ounces) tomato paste
Seasoning to taste

Skyline Salad

$1/2$ pound fresh tomatoes
2 scallions (green onions)
1 small bunch broccoli
1 small head cauliflower
1 clove garlic
2 teaspoons lemon juice
1 tablespoon white wine vinegar
3 tablespoons regular or light olive oil
Seasoning to taste
$1/2$ medium head lettuce reserved from
    Monday

Village Bread

1 loaf French bread
4 tablespoons softened butter
2 teaspoons dried dill
Seasoning to taste

*Reserve the balance of the can for use on Wednesday.

Plaza Ring

1 cup boiling water
1 package (3 ounces) cherry-flavored gelatin
1 small package (3 ounces) cream cheese
1 package (16 ounces) frozen pitted cherries

EQUIPMENT

Blender	Assorted kitchen knives
Dutch oven	Measuring cups and
Large covered	spoons
saucepan	Assorted cooking
Medium saucepan	utensils
$3^1/2$-cup ring mold	Whisk
Large bowl	Vegetable brush
2 small bowls	Vegetable peeler
Colander	
Fine strainer or	
cheesecloth	

COUNTDOWN

1 Assemble the ingredients and equipment
2 Do Steps 1–2 of the *Plaza Ring*
3 Do Steps 1–5 of the *Manhattan Clam
    Chowder*
4 Do Steps 1–5 of the *Skyline Salad*
5 Do Steps 1–3 of the *Village Bread*
6 Do Step 6 of the *Manhattan Clam Chowder*
7 Do Step 3 of the *Plaza Ring*

Manhattan Clam Chowder

1 Scrub the clams, discarding any that are open and do not close when tapped. In a large saucepan, combine the clams with the wine, the water and the broth. Bring the liquid to a boil, cover the saucepan, reduce the heat and simmer until the clams open, about 10 minutes.

2 Chop the bacon. Peel and chop the onion. Trim and chop the celery. Drain the tomatoes. Peel and chop the potatoes. Chop the parsley.

3 Let the clams cool in their liquid slightly, discarding any that did not open. Remove the clams from the shells, holding them over a large bowl as you work to catch the juices. Chop the clams. Strain the cooking liquid through a fine strainer or cheesecloth into the bowl and reserve. (If you are using canned clams, drain and reserve the liquid.)

4 In a Dutch oven, sauté the bacon until the fat is rendered, 2 to 3 minutes. Add the onion and the celery and cook, stirring occasionally, until both are softened, about 5 minutes. Add the thyme, the tomatoes and the tomato paste. Pour in the reserved clam juice and bring the mixture to a boil. Reduce the heat and simmer for 20 minutes.

5 Place the potatoes in the large saucepan with cold water to cover. Bring the water to a boil, reduce the heat and cook until the potatoes are tender, 15 to 20 minutes.

6 Drain the potatoes well and add them to the Dutch oven. Stir in the clams. Heat the chowder through, but do not boil. Season to taste. Stir in the parsley.

Skyline Salad

1 Quarter the tomatoes. Peel and slice the scallions. Place both in a large bowl.

2 Bring 1 inch of water to a boil in a medium saucepan. Trim and cut the broccoli into bite-size florets. Trim and cut the cauliflower into bite-size florets. Blanch them both in the boiling water for 1 minute. Drain the broccoli and the cauliflower, rinse them in cold water and add them to the tomatoes and scallions.

3 Peel and mince the garlic. In a small bowl, combine the garlic with the lemon juice, the vinegar and the oil. Season to taste.

4 Wash and dry the lettuce and arrange the leaves on individual plates.

5 Toss the vegetables with the dressing and spoon the mixture over the lettuce.

Village Bread

1 Preheat the broiler.

2 Cut the French bread in half lengthwise. In a small bowl, blend the softened butter with the dill. Season to taste. Spread the mixture evenly over the cut sides of the bread.

3 Place the bread under the broiler and broil until it is lightly toasted, 2 to 3 minutes.

Plaza Ring

1 Bring 1 cup of water to a boil. Combine the boiling water with the gelatin in a blender. Cover and process until the gelatin is dissolved, 15 to 30 seconds. Cut up the cream cheese and add it to the blender. Add the frozen cherries. Cover again and process until the mixture is smooth, 30 to 45 seconds.

2 Turn the mixture into a $3^1/2$-cup ring mold and chill it in the freezer for 30 minutes.

3 Unmold the cherry ring by placing the bottom of the mold in hot water for 30 seconds.

WEDNESDAY

Beef It Up

5 scallions (green onions)
1 pound mushrooms
1 medium green bell pepper
1 small red bell pepper
1 can (8¹/₂ ounces) artichoke hearts
4 slices white bread
2 tablespoons butter
1 tablespoon regular or light olive oil
4 lean beef tenderloins (1¹/₂ pounds)
¹/₃ cup dry sherry (or nonalcoholic red wine or
    beef broth)
¹/₄ cup vegetable broth reserved from Tuesday
1 beef bouillon cube
¹/₂ teaspoon seasoning salt
2 tablespoons flour dissolved in 2 tablespoons
    cold water
Seasoning to taste

Spring Asparagus

1¹/₂ pounds fresh asparagus
2 cloves garlic
2 teaspoons butter
¹/₂ cup vegetable broth reserved from Tuesday
¹/₂ teaspoon dried marjoram
¹/₂ teaspoon dried savory
1 teaspoon lemon juice
Seasoning to taste

Spicy Apricot Compote

¹/₄ pound dried apricots
1 tablespoon sugar
1 teaspoon cornstarch
¹/₄ teaspoon ground cinnamon
¹/₄ teaspoon ground ginger
¹/₄ teaspoon ground allspice
1 medium can (15¹/₄ ounces) crushed
    pineapple in juice
2 tablespoons dark raisins
¹/₂ cup water

EQUIPMENT

Large covered skillet	Measuring cups and
Large skillet	spoons
Small saucepan	Assorted cooking
Assorted kitchen knives	utensils

COUNTDOWN

1 Assemble the ingredients and equipment
2 Do Steps 1–3 of the *Spicy Apricot Compote*
3 Do Steps 1–2 of *Beef It Up*
4 Do Steps 1–2 of the *Spring Asparagus*
5 Do Steps 3–4 of *Beef It Up*
6 Do Steps 3–4 of the *Spring Asparagus*
7 Do Steps 5–6 of *Beef It Up*

Beef It Up

1 Trim and chop the scallions. Wash, pat dry and slice the mushrooms. Seed the bell peppers and cut them into thin strips. Drain and quarter the artichokes. Toast the bread slices, then remove the crusts and cut the toast to the shape of the fillets.

2 In a large skillet, melt 1 tablespoon of the butter with the oil. Add the beef tenderloins and cook, turning once, until they are browned outside and almost cooked to taste inside (3 to 4 minutes per side for medium-rare).

3 Remove the beef and keep it warm. (It will continue to cook.) Discard any fat from the skillet.

4 Melt the remaining butter in the skillet. Add the scallions and sauté until they are limp, 2 to 3 minutes. Add the mushrooms and the peppers, and sauté until the peppers are crisp-tender, 3 to 4 minutes.

5 Stir in the sherry, the broth, the bouillon cube and the seasoning salt, and heat the mixture to boiling. Blend in the flour mixture. Add the artichokes. Season to taste. Return the sauce to a boil, stirring occasionally, and cook until it thickens, 3 to 4 minutes.

6 Place each beef fillet on a bread slice and top it with a spoonful of the sauce.

Spring Asparagus

1 Bring a small amount of water to a boil in a large covered skillet.

2 Remove the tough ends from the asparagus. Peel and mince the garlic. Steam the asparagus in the boiling water, covered, until it is crisp-tender, 3 to 8 minutes, depending on thickness.

3 Drain the asparagus.

4 Melt the butter in the skillet. Sauté the garlic for 2 minutes. Add the broth, the marjoram, the savory and the lemon juice. Bring the mixture to a boil and cook for 1 minute. Return the asparagus to the skillet and cook until it is heated through, 1 to 2 minutes. Season to taste. Cover to keep warm.

Spicy Apricot Compote

1 Chop the apricots.

2 In a small saucepan, combine the sugar, the cornstarch, the cinnamon, the ginger and the allspice. Stir in the apricots, the undrained pineapple, the raisins and the water. Cook and stir until the mixture is thickened and bubbly, 3 to 4 minutes. Cook and stir for 2 minutes more.

3 Pour the mixture into individual dessert dishes and refrigerate for at least 15 minutes.

THURSDAY

Fusilli Florentine

1 medium onion
2 cloves garlic
3/4 pound fresh spinach
1 1/2 tablespoons fresh parsley (when chopped)
12 ounces fusilli (corkscrew pasta)
1 1/2 tablespoons regular or light olive oil
3/4 teaspoon dried basil
1/4 teaspoon ground nutmeg
Seasoning to taste
1/2 cup chopped walnuts

Sweet Carrot Salad

2 teaspoons grated fresh lemon peel
1/4 teaspoon curry powder
3 tablespoons regular or light olive oil
2 tablespoons balsamic vinegar
1 tablespoon dark brown sugar
Seasoning to taste
6 medium carrots
1 large shallot
3 tablespoons fresh parsley (when chopped)
1 small head lettuce

Sour Muffins

2 eggs
1/2 cup regular or light sour cream
1 1/2 cups Bisquick
1/4 teaspoon onion powder
3 tablespoons capers

Coconut Pudding Supreme

1 small package (3.4 ounces) instant coconut
    cream pudding mix
1/2 teaspoon ground cinnamon
1/2 teaspoon ground cloves
1 1/4 cups whole milk
3/4 cup regular or light sour cream
1 large banana
1/4 cup flaked coconut

EQUIPMENT

Electric hand mixer	Measuring cups and
Large skillet	spoons
Large saucepan	Assorted cooking
12-cup muffin tin	utensils
Large bowl	Whisk
2 medium bowls	Vegetable grater
Colander	Vegetable peeler
Assorted kitchen knives	

COUNTDOWN

1 Assemble the ingredients and equipment
2 Do Steps 1–2 of the *Coconut Pudding Supreme*
3 Do Step 1 of the *Sour Muffins*
4 Do Step 1 of the *Fusilli Florentine*
5 Do Steps 1–3 of the *Sweet Carrot Salad*
6 Do Step 2 of the *Sour Muffins*
7 Do Step 2 of the *Fusilli Florentine*
8 Do Step 3 of the *Sour Muffins*
9 Do Steps 3–5 of the *Fusilli Florentine*
10 Do Step 3 of the *Coconut Pudding Supreme*

Fusilli Florentine

1 Bring water to a boil in a large saucepan.

2 Peel and chop the onion. Peel and mince the garlic. Rinse, dry and chop the spinach. Chop the parsley.

3 Cook the fusilli in the boiling water until it is almost tender, about 10 minutes.

4 Heat the oil in a large skillet. Add the onion and the garlic, and cook until they are soft but not brown, about 5 minutes. Add the spinach, the parsley, the basil and the nutmeg. Season to taste. Cook, stirring occasionally, for 3 minutes.

5 Drain the pasta and return it to the saucepan. Toss the pasta with the sauce and sprinkle with the nuts.

Sweet Carrot Salad

1 In a medium bowl, whisk together the lemon peel, the curry powder, the oil, the vinegar and the brown sugar. Season to taste.

2 Peel and grate the carrots. Peel and mince the shallot. Chop the parsley. Add the ingredients to the dressing and toss to combine.

3 Wash and dry the lettuce. Arrange the leaves on individual plates, top them with the carrot mixture and refrigerate until you are ready to serve.

Sour Muffins

1 Preheat the oven to 400°F. Grease a 12-cup muffin tin.

2 Lightly beat the eggs in a large bowl. Blend in the sour cream. Stir in the Bisquick and the onion powder. Fold in the capers.

3 Fill the muffin cups two-thirds full. Bake until the muffins are golden, about 15 minutes.

Coconut Pudding Supreme

1 In a medium bowl, beat the pudding mix, the cinnamon, the cloves, the milk and the sour cream until well blended.

2 Spoon the mixture into individual dessert dishes and refrigerate for at least 20 minutes.

3 Peel and slice the banana. Arrange the slices over the pudding and sprinkle with the coconut.

FRIDAY

Tuna Rice Delight

1 package (9 ounces) frozen green peas
1 can (6 ounces) solid white tuna
3 scallions (green onions)
1 cup long-grain white rice
1 can (10³/₄ ounces) cream of mushroom soup
¹/₂ cup whole or low-fat milk
³/₄ cup regular or low-fat small-curd cottage
     cheese
¹/₄ cup canned diced green chilies (optional)
Seasoning to taste
1 package (11 ounces) potato chips

Palm-Olive Salad

1 medium head lettuce
¹/₂ pound fresh tomatoes
1 medium cucumber
1 can (14¹/₂ ounces) hearts of palm
1 small jar (3 ounces) pimiento-stuffed green
     olives
3 tablespoons regular or light olive oil
2 tablespoons red wine vinegar
¹/₂ teaspoon paprika
¹/₂ teaspoon Dijon mustard
Seasoning to taste

Marshmallow Moose

4 tablespoons sweetened cocoa
1¹/₂ cups water
48 large marshmallows
1 cup whipping cream
1 teaspoon vanilla extract
1 tablespoon confectioners' sugar
Chocolate sprinkles

EQUIPMENT

Electric hand mixer	Assorted kitchen knives
Medium saucepan	Measuring cups and
2-quart covered	spoons
casserole	Assorted cooking
Large bowl	utensils
Medium bowl	Whisk
Small bowl	Vegetable peeler

COUNTDOWN

1 Assemble the ingredients and equipment
2 Do Steps 1–4 of the *Tuna Rice Delight*
3 Do Steps 1–3 of the *Marshmallow Moose*
4 Do Steps 1–2 of the *Palm-Olive Salad*
5 Do Step 5 of the *Tuna Rice Delight*
6 Do Step 3 of the *Palm-Olive Salad*
7 Do Step 4 of the *Marshmallow Moose*

Tuna Rice Delight

1 Preheat the oven to 400°F. Set the package of frozen peas out to thaw.

2 Drain and flake the tuna. Trim and chop the scallions.

3 In a 2-quart covered casserole, combine the rice, the soup, the milk, the tuna, the cottage cheese, the scallions and the chilies. Season to taste and blend until well mixed.

4 Cover the casserole and bake for 25 minutes.

5 Remove the cover from the casserole and stir in the thawed peas. Crush the potato chips and sprinkle them over the top. Bake, uncovered, until the rice is tender, about 15 minutes more.

Palm-Olive Salad

1 Wash and dry the lettuce and tear it into bite-size pieces. Chop the tomatoes. Peel and slice the cucumber. Drain and slice the hearts of palm. Drain the olives. Combine the ingredients in a large bowl and refrigerate until you are ready to use.

2 In a small bowl, whisk together the oil, the vinegar, the paprika and the mustard. Season to taste.

3 Toss the salad with the dressing.

Marshmallow Moose

1 Heat the cocoa with the water in a medium saucepan. Add the marshmallows and stir until they are melted.

2 Remove the saucepan from the heat and refrigerate for at least 15 minutes.

3 In a medium bowl, whip the cream until it is thick. Fold in the vanilla and the confectioners' sugar and beat until it is stiff. Refrigerate for at least 15 minutes.

4 To serve, fold the whipped cream into the marshmallow mixture and spoon it into individual dessert dishes. Top with the sprinkles.

MAY
WEEK TWO

WEEK AT A GLANCE

Monday

JAMBALAYA
RIVERBOAT SALAD
BISCUIT BLUES
ICE CREAM SURPRISE CAKE

Tuesday

HONEY OF A LAMB CHOP
POTATO CHIPPERS
BRONZED BEANS
PEAK & VALLEY PUDDING

Wednesday

BARNYARD CHOWDER
GREEN & WHITE SALAD
ROLLED BISCUITS
POPULAR PIE

Thursday

PIZZA PASTA
CUCUMBER SOLO
ANCHOVY BREAD
HONEYDEW STING

Friday

TRY ME WHITE FISH
SWEET GEORGIA BROWNS
PRACTICAL PEAS & CARROTS
MAY TIME TORTE

CHECK STAPLES

- ☐ Butter
- ☐ Vegetable shortening
- ☐ Flour
- ☐ Bisquick
- ☐ Baking powder
- ☐ Granulated sugar
- ☐ Dark brown sugar
- ☐ Confectioners' sugar
- ☐ Unsweetened cocoa
- ☐ Chocolate syrup
- ☐ Long-grain white rice
- ☐ Regular or light olive oil
- ☐ Apple cider vinegar
- ☐ Rice vinegar
- ☐ Lemon juice
- ☐ Grated fresh orange peel
- ☐ Worcestershire sauce
- ☐ Tabasco sauce
- ☐ Dijon mustard
- ☐ Honey
- ☐ Grated Parmesan cheese
- ☐ Plain bread crumbs
- ☐ Dried basil
- ☐ Cayenne pepper
- ☐ Chili powder
- ☐ Italian seasoning
- ☐ Dried marjoram
- ☐ Onion powder
- ☐ Paprika
- ☐ Dried rosemary
- ☐ Dried sage
- ☐ Dried thyme
- ☐ Pepper
- ☐ Salt
- ☐ Vanilla extract

SHOPPING NOTE

● If you are shopping once a week and cannot arrange to purchase fresh seafood on the day you will use it, you can purchase *not previously frozen* seafood and freeze it, placing it in the refrigerator to thaw the night before you are ready to use it. Or you can purchase *still frozen* seafood and keep it frozen until the night before you are ready to use it.

SHOPPING LIST

MEAT & POULTRY
$1/4$ pound lean cooked ham steak (M)
4 lean lamb chops ($3/4$-inch thick) (T)
1 pound boneless, skinless chicken breasts (W)

FISH
$3/4$ pound medium shrimp, shelled and deveined (M)
$1 1/4$ pounds white fish fillets (F)

FRESH PRODUCE
Vegetables
1 pound medium baking potatoes (T)
3 medium baking potatoes (W)
1 pound sweet potatoes (F)
1 pound green beans (T)
1 medium zucchini (Th)
$1/4$ pound Chinese snow peas (W)
4 large mushrooms (W)
4 medium carrots—3 (W), 1 (Th)
1 pound baby carrots (F)
7 stalks celery—3 (M), 3 (W), 1 (Th)
3 medium onions—2 (M), 1 (W)
1 small onion (Th)
5 scallions (green onions)— 3 (T), 2 (W)
1 head garlic (M-F)
1 bunch parsley (M, W, Th, F)
2 medium heads lettuce—1 (W), 1 (Th)
1 small head lettuce (M)
3 medium cucumbers (Th)
2 medium green bell peppers (M)
1 small green bell pepper (Th)
1 small jicama (or turnip) (W)

Fruit
1 tart green apple (M)
1 large honeydew melon (Th)
2 medium bananas (M)
1 small white grapefruit (Th)
4 medium oranges—3 (M), 1 (F)

CANS, JARS & BOTTLES
Soup
1 can ($10^3/4$ ounces) beef broth (M)
2 cans ($10^3/4$ ounces each) chicken broth (W)
1 can ($14^1/2$ ounces) chicken broth (W)

Vegetables
1 large can (28 ounces) cut-up tomatoes (M)
1 medium can ($14^1/2$ ounces) crushed tomatoes (Th)
1 small can (8 ounces) tomato sauce (Th)

Fish
1 tube (1.58 ounces) anchovy paste (Th)

Fruit
1 medium can ($15^1/4$ ounces) pineapple chunks (M)

Juice
1 cup grapefruit juice (Th)
1 bottle (8 ounces) clam juice (F)

Condiments
4 maraschino cherries for garnish (Th)

Spreads
1 jar (10 ounces) orange marmalade (F)

Dessert Needs
1 can (16 ounces) vanilla frosting (F)

PACKAGED GOODS
Pasta, Rice & Grains
16 ounces small shell pasta (Th)
$1/2$ cup blue (or yellow) cornmeal (M)
$1/2$ cup Grape-nuts cereal (M)
24 Ritz crackers (W)

Baked Goods
1 small French baguette (Th)
1 angel food loaf cake (M)

Nuts & Seeds
$1/2$ cup sliced almonds (T)
16 whole almonds (T)
1 cup pecan pieces (W)

Dessert & Baking Needs
1 small package (3.4 ounces) instant vanilla pudding mix (T)

WINES & SPIRITS
$1/4$ cup dry sherry (or nonalcoholic white wine or vegetable broth) (W)
1 tablespoon Kirsch liqueur (or nonalcoholic Italian cherry syrup) (Th)

REFRIGERATED PRODUCTS
Dairy
2 cups whole milk (T)
$2 1/2$ cups whole or low-fat milk—$3/4$ cup (M), $2/3$ cup (W), 1 cup (F)
$1 1/2$ cups half-and-half (W)
1 cup whipping cream (W)
$1/2$ cup regular or light sour cream (M)
5 eggs (W)

Cheese
1 cup shredded regular or low-fat mozzarella cheese (Th)

FROZEN GOODS
Vegetables
1 package (9 ounces) green peas (F)

Desserts
1 pound cake (F)
1 quart rocky road (or similar) ice cream (M)
1 pint lemon frozen yogurt (Th)

MONDAY

Jambalaya

2 medium onions
2 medium green bell peppers
3 stalks celery
$1/4$ pound lean cooked ham steak
2 cloves garlic
3 tablespoons fresh parsley (when chopped)
$3/4$ pound medium shrimp, shelled and
    deveined
3 tablespoons butter
$1^1/4$ cups long-grain white rice
1 can ($10^3/4$ ounces) beef broth
1 large can (28 ounces) cut-up tomatoes
$1/2$ teaspoon Tabasco sauce
1 teaspoon dried basil
$1/2$ teaspoon dried thyme
$1/4$ teaspoon cayenne pepper
$1/2$ teaspoon chili powder
Seasoning to taste

Riverboat Salad

1 medium can ($15^1/4$ ounces) pineapple chunks
$1/2$ cup regular or light sour cream
1 teaspoon grated fresh orange peel
$1/2$ cup Grape-nuts cereal
3 medium oranges
1 tart green apple
2 medium bananas
1 small head lettuce

Biscuit Blues

$1^1/2$ cups flour
$1/2$ cup blue (or yellow) cornmeal
1 tablespoon sugar
3 teaspoons baking powder
1 teaspoon salt
$1/2$ cup vegetable shortening
$3/4$ cup whole or low-fat milk

Ice Cream Surprise Cake

1 quart rocky road (or similar) ice cream
1 angel food loaf cake
Chocolate syrup for garnish

EQUIPMENT

Dutch oven
Cookie sheet
2 large bowls
Assorted kitchen knives
Measuring cups and
  spoons
Assorted cooking
  utensils

Pastry board
Pastry blender
Whisk
Biscuit cutter
Ice cream scoop

COUNTDOWN

1 Assemble the ingredients and equipment
2 Do Step 1 of the *Ice Cream Surprise Cake*
3 Do Steps 1–3 of the *Jambalaya*
4 Do Step 1 of the *Biscuit Blues*
5 Do Steps 1–3 of the *Riverboat Salad*
6 Do Steps 2–3 of the *Biscuit Blues*
7 Do Step 2 of the *Ice Cream Surprise Cake*
8 Do Step 4 of the *Jambalaya*
9 Do Step 4 of the *Biscuit Blues*
10 Do Step 4 of the *Riverboat Salad*
11 Do Step 3 of the *Ice Cream Surprise Cake*

Jambalaya

1 Peel and chop the onions. Seed and chop the bell peppers. Trim and chop the celery. Cube the ham. Peel and mash the garlic. Chop the parsley. Rinse the shrimp.

2 Melt the butter in a Dutch oven. Add the onions, the bell peppers, the celery, the ham and the garlic. Cook, stirring occasionally, until the vegetables are soft, about 5 minutes.

3 Add the rice and cook, stirring often, for 3 minutes. Stir in the broth, the undrained tomatoes, the Tabasco sauce, 2 tablespoons of the parsley, the basil, the thyme, the cayenne pepper and the chili powder. Season to taste. Bring the mixture to a boil, reduce the heat, cover and simmer for 25 minutes.

4 Stir the shrimp into the Dutch oven and cook until they are pink, the rice is tender and all the liquid is absorbed, about 10 minutes. Garnish with the remaining parsley.

Riverboat Salad

1 Drain the pineapple, reserving 1 tablespoon of the juice.

2 In a large bowl, whisk together the reserved pineapple juice, the sour cream, the orange peel and the Grape-nuts.

3 Peel and section the oranges. Core and dice the apple. Slice the bananas. Add the ingredients to the sour cream mixture. Add the pineapple and fold the fruit and the dressing together. Refrigerate until you are ready to use.

4 Wash and dry the lettuce and arrange the leaves on individual salad plates. Top the lettuce with the fruit mixture.

Biscuit Blues

1 Preheat the oven to 450°F. Flour a pastry board.

2 In a large bowl, combine the flour, the cornmeal, the sugar, the baking powder and the salt. Add the shortening and cut it in with a pastry blender until the mixture resembles fine crumbs. Add just enough milk for the dough to form a ball.

3 Turn the dough out onto the pastry board and gently roll it in the flour to coat. Knead the dough lightly 10 to 12 times and pat it into a $1/2$-inch thickness.

4 Cut the dough with a floured biscuit cutter and place the biscuits on an ungreased cookie sheet. Bake until the biscuits are golden brown, 10 to 12 minutes.

Ice Cream Surprise Cake

1 Set the ice cream out to soften.

2 Cut a $1/2$-inch slice from the top of the cake. Scoop out the cake, leaving a $1/2$-inch shell all around. Pack the ice cream into the shell, replace the top of the cake and chill in the freezer for at least 20 minutes.

3 Slice the cake and drizzle it with chocolate syrup.

TUESDAY

Honey of a Lamb Chop

1½ tablespoons honey
1½ tablespoons Dijon mustard
1 clove garlic
1 teaspoon dried rosemary
Seasoning to taste
4 lean lamb chops (¾ inch thick)

Potato Chippers

1 pound medium baking potatoes
½ teaspoon paprika
1 teaspoon onion powder
Seasoning to taste
2 tablespoons water

Bronzed Beans

3 scallions (green onions)
1 pound fresh green beans
2 tablespoons butter
½ teaspoon dark brown sugar
Seasoning to taste

Peak & Valley Pudding

1 small package (3.4 ounces) instant vanilla
    pudding mix
2 cups whole milk
½ cup sliced almonds
16 whole almonds

EQUIPMENT

Electric hand mixer	Assorted kitchen knives
Medium saucepan	Measuring cups and
9x9-inch glass baking	spoons
dish	Assorted cooking
Large cookie sheet	utensils
Medium bowl	Whisk
Small bowl	Vegetable peeler
Strainer	

COUNTDOWN

1 Assemble the ingredients and equipment
2 Do Steps 1–2 of the *Peak & Valley Pudding*
3 Do Steps 1–3 of the *Honey of a Lamb Chop*
4 Do Steps 1–2 of the *Potato Chippers*
5 Do Steps 1–3 of the *Bronzed Beans*
6 Do Steps 4–5 of the *Honey of a Lamb Chop*
7 Do Step 3 of the *Potato Chippers*
8 Do Step 4 of the *Bronzed Beans*

Honey of a Lamb Chop

1 Combine the honey and the mustard in a small bowl. Peel and mash the garlic and add it to the bowl. Add the rosemary and season to taste. Blend well.

2 Place the lamb chops in a 9x9-inch glass baking dish. Spread the honey-mustard mixture over both sides of the chops and let them stand for 15 minutes.

3 Preheat the broiler.

4 Set the chops on a broiler rack, 3 or 4 inches from the heat, and broil, turning once, until they are browned on the outside and cooked to taste on the inside (5 to 7 minutes total for rare).

5 Remove the chops from the broiler and cover to keep warm.

Potato Chippers

1 Preheat the broiler.

2 Peel and thinly slice the potatoes, and arrange them in a single layer on a large cookie sheet. Sprinkle the slices with the paprika and the onion powder, and season them to taste. Sprinkle the potatoes with the water.

3 Set the potatoes 3 or 4 inches from the heat and broil, turning once, until they are brown and crisp, 3 to 4 minutes per side.

Bronzed Beans

1 Bring 1 inch of water to a boil in a medium saucepan.

2 Trim and chop the scallions. Trim and string the green beans.

3 Cook the beans until they are crisp-tender, 5 to 6 minutes.

4 Drain the beans well. Melt the butter in the saucepan. Sauté the scallions for 2 minutes. Add the brown sugar and the beans and toss gently until the beans are coated and heated through. Season to taste.

Peak & Valley Pudding

1 In a medium bowl, beat the pudding mix and the milk together until well blended. Pour half of the mixture into individual dessert dishes. Layer with the sliced almonds. Top with the remaining pudding.

2 Stick the whole almonds upright into the pudding and refrigerate for at least 20 minutes.

WEDNESDAY

Barnyard Chowder

2 eggs
3 medium baking potatoes
3 medium carrots
3 stalks celery
1 medium onion
3 tablespoons fresh parsley (when chopped)
1 pound boneless, skinless chicken breasts
1 can (14$^1/_2$ ounces) chicken broth
2 cans (10$^3/_4$ ounces each) chicken broth
1 teaspoon dried marjoram
Seasoning to taste
1$^1/_2$ cups half-and-half
3 egg yolks
$^1/_4$ cup flour
$^1/_4$ cup dry sherry (or nonalcoholic white wine
   or vegetable broth)

Green & White Salad

$^1/_4$ pound fresh Chinese snow peas
4 medium mushrooms
2 scallions (green onions)
1 small jicama (or turnip)
1 medium head lettuce
1 clove garlic
3 tablespoons regular or light olive oil
2 tablespoons rice vinegar
1 teaspoon Dijon mustard
Seasoning to taste

Rolled Biscuits

2 tablespoons butter
2$^1/_4$ cups Bisquick
1 teaspoon dried sage
$^2/_3$ cup whole or low-fat milk

Popular Pie

24 Ritz crackers
3 egg whites
1 cup granulated sugar
1 teaspoon vanilla extract
1 cup pecan pieces
1 cup whipping cream
3 tablespoons unsweetened cocoa
2 tablespoons confectioners' sugar

EQUIPMENT

Electric hand mixer	Assorted kitchen knives
Dutch oven	Measuring cups and
Medium saucepan	spoons
Small saucepan	Assorted cooking
9-inch pie plate	utensils
Cookie sheet	Pastry board
Large bowl	Whisk
3 medium bowls	Vegetable peeler
2 small bowls	Biscuit cutter

COUNTDOWN

1 Assemble the ingredients and equipment
2 Do Steps 1–3 of the *Popular Pie*
3 Do Steps 1–7 of the *Barnyard Chowder*
4 Do Steps 1–3 of the *Green & White Salad*
5 Do Steps 1–3 of the *Rolled Biscuits*
6 Do Step 8 of the *Barnyard Chowder*
7 Do Step 4 of the *Green & White Salad*
8 Do Step 4 of the *Popular Pie*

Barnyard Chowder

1 Cover 2 eggs with water in a small saucepan. Bring the water to a boil and hard-cook the eggs, 10 to 12 minutes.

2 Bring water to a boil in a medium saucepan.

3 Peel and dice the potatoes. Peel and slice the carrots. Trim and chop the celery. Peel and chop the onion. Chop the parsley.

4 Cut the chicken breasts into strips and cook in the boiling water until opaque throughout, 5 to 6 minutes.

5 Drain the eggs and run them under cold water until they are cool enough to handle, then peel them.

6 Bring the broth to a boil in a Dutch oven. Add the potatoes, the carrots, the celery, the onion and the marjoram. Season to taste. Cook until the vegetables are tender, about 10 minutes.

7 Drain and chop the chicken. Chop the hard-cooked eggs.

8 Scald the half-and-half in the egg saucepan. Whisk in the egg yolks. Gradually whisk in ½ cup of the hot broth and stir the mixture back into the soup. Combine the flour and the sherry, and whisk the mixture into the soup, cooking, but not boiling, until the soup begins to thicken. Add the chicken and the chopped eggs, cover and simmer until the soup is heated through. Sprinkle with the parsley.

Green & White Salad

1 Bring a small amount of water to a boil in a medium saucepan. Trim and string the snow peas, and blanch them in the boiling water for 1 minute. Drain the snow peas and plunge them into cold water. Blot them dry on paper towels.

2 Wash, pat dry, trim and slice the mushrooms. Trim and slice the scallions. Peel and chop the jicama. Combine the ingredients in a medium bowl with the snow peas.

3 Wash and dry the lettuce and place the leaves on individual salad plates.

4 Peel and mince the garlic. In a small bowl, whisk together the garlic, the oil, the vinegar and the mustard. Season to taste. Toss the vegetables with the dressing and spoon it over the lettuce.

Rolled Biscuits

1 Preheat the oven to 450°F.

2 Melt the butter and combine it with the Bisquick, the sage and the milk in a large bowl until a soft dough forms. Mix the dough with a fork until well blended. Dust a pastry board with Bisquick and turn the dough out onto the surface. Knead the dough until it is smooth, 5 or 6 times, then pat it out into a ½-inch thickness. Cut the dough with a biscuit cutter that has been coated with Bisquick and place the biscuits on an ungreased cookie sheet.

3 Bake the biscuits until they are golden brown, 8 to 10 minutes.

Popular Pie

1 Preheat the oven to 350°F. Grease a 9-inch pie plate.

2 Crush the Ritz crackers.

3 In a medium bowl, beat the egg whites until they are stiff. Slowly add the granulated sugar and the vanilla, and beat until the mixture is very stiff and glossy. Fold in the crushed crackers and the pecans, pour the mixture into the pie dish and bake for 30 minutes. Remove the pie and let it cool.

4 In a medium bowl, whip the cream until stiff peaks form. Fold in the cocoa and the confectioners' sugar. Spread the mixture over the cooled pie.

THURSDAY

Pizza Pasta

2 cloves garlic
1 small green bell pepper
1 stalk celery
1 small onion
1 medium zucchini
1 medium carrot
16 ounces small shell pasta
1 tablespoon Italian seasoning
$^1/_2$ teaspoon cayenne pepper
$^1/_8$ teaspoon Worcestershire sauce
1 small can (8 ounces) tomato sauce
$^1/_4$ cup grated Parmesan cheese
Seasoning to taste
1 medium can (14$^1/_2$ ounces) crushed
    tomatoes
1 cup shredded regular or low-fat mozzarella
    cheese

Cucumber Solo

1 medium head lettuce
3 medium cucumbers
1 tablespoon fresh parsley (when chopped)
1 clove garlic
2 tablespoons apple cider vinegar
2 tablespoons regular or light olive oil
1 teaspoon Dijon mustard
$^1/_8$ teaspoon Worcestershire sauce
Seasoning to taste

Anchovy Bread

2 tablespoons regular or light olive oil
1 small French bread baguette
1 tube (1.58 ounces) anchovy paste

Honeydew Sting

1 large honeydew melon
1 small white grapefruit
1 cup grapefruit juice
1 tablespoon Kirsch liqueur (or nonalcoholic
    Italian cherry syrup)
1 pint lemon frozen yogurt
4 maraschino cherries for garnish

EQUIPMENT

Stockpot	Assorted cooking
Large skillet	utensils
9x13-inch glass baking	Whisk
dish	Vegetable peeler
Large bowl	Vegetable brush
2 small bowls	Melon-baller
Colander	Ice cream scoop
Assorted kitchen knives	
Measuring cups and	
spoons	

COUNTDOWN

1 Assemble the ingredients and equipment
2 Do Steps 1–3 of the *Pizza Pasta*
3 Do Step 1 of the *Cucumber Solo*
4 Do Steps 4–5 of the *Pizza Pasta*
5 Do Steps 1–2 of the *Honeydew Sting*
6 Do Steps 1–2 of the *Anchovy Bread*
7 Do Step 2 of the *Cucumber Solo*
8 Do Step 3 of the *Anchovy Bread*
9 Do Step 3 of the *Honeydew Sting*

Pizza Pasta

1 Preheat the oven to 400°F. Grease a 9x13-inch glass baking dish. Bring water to a boil in a stockpot.

2 Peel and mince the garlic. Seed and chop the bell pepper. Trim and chop the celery. Peel and chop the onion. Wash and slice the zucchini. Peel and thinly slice the carrot.

3 Cook the pasta in the boiling water until it is slightly underdone, 5 to 6 minutes.

4 Drain the pasta, return it to the stockpot and toss it with the Italian seasoning, the cayenne pepper, the Worcestershire sauce, the garlic, the tomato sauce and the Parmesan cheese. Season to taste and turn the mixture into the baking dish.

5 Pour the crushed tomatoes over the pasta, spread the vegetables over the tomatoes, sprinkle with the mozzarella and bake for 30 minutes.

Cucumber Solo

1 Wash and dry the lettuce and tear it into bite-size pieces. Peel and slice the cucumbers. Combine the ingredients in a large bowl and refrigerate until you are ready to serve.

2 Chop the parsley. Peel and mince the garlic. In a small bowl, whisk together the parsley, the garlic, the vinegar, the oil, the mustard and the Worcestershire sauce. Season to taste and toss with the salad.

Anchovy Bread

1 Heat the oil in a large skillet.

2 Slice the baguette and sauté the slices in the oil until they are toasted on both sides, 8 to 10 minutes.

3 Spread the toasted slices lightly with the anchovy paste.

Honeydew Sting

1 Halve and seed the melon and scoop out the balls. Peel and section the grapefruit. Distribute the fruit among individual sherbet glasses.

2 In a small bowl, combine the grapefruit juice with the Kirsch, spoon it over the fruit and refrigerate until you are ready to use.

3 Top the fruit with a scoop of frozen yogurt and garnish with a maraschino cherry.

FRIDAY

MENU

Try Me White Fish

1¹/₄ pounds white fish fillets
1 clove garlic
1 tablespoon fresh parsley (when chopped)
2 tablespoons butter
2 tablespoons flour
1 bottle (8 ounces) clam juice
1 cup whole or low-fat milk
Seasoning to taste
2 tablespoons regular or light olive oil
1 cup plain bread crumbs

Sweet Georgia Browns

1 pound sweet potatoes
3 tablespoons butter
3 tablespoons sugar

Practical Peas & Carrots

1 pound fresh baby carrots
1 package (9 ounces) frozen green peas
1 tablespoon butter
Seasoning to taste
1 teaspoon lemon juice

May Time Torte

1 frozen pound cake
1 medium orange
1 jar (10 ounces) orange marmalade
1 can (16 ounces) vanilla frosting

EQUIPMENT

2 medium saucepans	Measuring cups and
Small saucepan	spoons
7x11-inch glass baking	Assorted cooking
dish	utensils
Small bowl	Whisk
Strainer	Vegetable brush
Assorted kitchen knives	

COUNTDOWN

1 Assemble the ingredients and equipment
2 Do Step 1 of the *May Time Torte*
3 Do Step 1 of the *Try Me White Fish*
4 Do Step 1 of the *Practical Peas & Carrots*
5 Do Steps 2–5 of the *Try Me White Fish*
6 Do Step 2 of the *Practical Peas & Carrots*
7 Do Steps 1–2 of the *Sweet Georgia Browns*
8 Do Step 2 of the *May Time Torte*
9 Do Step 6 of the *Try Me White Fish*
10 Do Step 3 of the *Practical Peas & Carrots*
11 Do Steps 3–4 of the *Sweet Georgia Browns*

Try Me White Fish

1 Preheat the oven to 425°F. Grease a 7x11-inch glass baking dish.

2 Wash, pat dry, and cut the fish fillets into 2-inch cubes.

3 Peel and mince the garlic. Chop the parsley.

4 Melt the butter in a small saucepan. Whisk in the flour and cook until the mixture is lemon colored, about 2 minutes. Whisk in the clam juice and the milk and bring the mixture to a boil. Continue whisking until the sauce is smooth and thick, 1 to 2 minutes. Reduce the heat and simmer for 3 minutes more. Season to taste.

5 Place the fish in a single layer in the baking dish. Pour the sauce over the fish.

6 In a small bowl, combine the oil, the bread crumbs, the garlic and the parsley. Spread the mixture over the sauce and bake until the fish is bubbly and light brown, 10 to 12 minutes.

Sweet Georgia Browns

1 Bring water to a boil in a medium saucepan.

2 Peel and quarter the potatoes and cook them in the boiling water until they are tender, about 15 minutes.

3 Drain the potatoes and run them under cold water until they are cool enough to handle. Slice the potatoes.

4 Melt the butter and the sugar in the saucepan, stirring until the sugar is dissolved and the mixture begins to caramelize, 5 to 7 minutes. Return the potato slices to the saucepan and sauté them until they are well glazed and heated through.

Practical Peas & Carrots

1 Bring water to a boil in a medium saucepan.

2 Scrub and trim the carrots, and cook them in the boiling water until they are crisp-tender, about 15 minutes.

3 Add the peas to the carrots and continue cooking until the peas are hot, 3 to 4 minutes. Drain the vegetables. Melt the butter in the saucepan. Return the vegetables and toss them in the butter to coat. Season to taste, add the lemon juice and toss again.

May Time Torte

1 Set the pound cake out to partially thaw.

2 Slice the orange and cut around the edges of each slice to remove the rind. Cut the cake into 4 horizontal layers. Spread the bottom layer with half of the marmalade. Add the second layer and spread it with one-third of the frosting. Add the third layer and spread it with the remaining marmalade. Add the top layer and spread it with the remaining frosting, swirling it down the sides of the cake. Top the cake with the orange slices.

MAY
WEEK THREE

WEEK AT A GLANCE

Monday

THREE-PEPPER PORK
FRUITY RICE
GO FOR CHOKES
RANCH PUDDING

Tuesday

MEXICALI CASSEROLE
RE-REFRIED BEANS
FIESTA FRUIT

Wednesday

HOT-TO-TROT TURKEY
SESAME POTATOES
MY FAVORITE SNAP PEAS
CRANBERRY CAKE

Thursday

LAZY LASAGNA
PISA SALAD
BOB-BOB-BOBOLI
TUTTI-FRUITTI BAKED CAKE

Friday

SHRIMP & SCALLOP AU GRATIN
SOURPUSS NOODLES
ASPARAGUS CRUNCH
MOCHA-NOLI

CHECK STAPLES

☐ Butter
☐ Flour
☐ Baking soda
☐ Bisquick
☐ Granulated sugar
☐ Dark brown sugar
☐ Confectioners' sugar
☐ Sweetened cocoa
☐ Long-grain white rice
☐ Regular or light vegetable oil
☐ Regular or light olive oil
☐ Red wine vinegar
☐ Balsamic vinegar
☐ Lemon juice
☐ Tabasco sauce
☐ Dijon mustard

☐ Dark raisins
☐ Grated Parmesan cheese
☐ Plain bread crumbs
☐ Instant or brewed coffee
☐ Chicken bouillon cubes
☐ Dried basil
☐ Bay leaves
☐ Ground cinnamon
☐ Whole cloves
☐ Garlic powder
☐ Dried oregano
☐ Dried sage
☐ Sesame seeds
☐ Pepper
☐ Salt
☐ Vanilla extract

SHOPPING NOTE

● If you are shopping once a week and cannot arrange to purchase fresh shellfish on the day you plan to use it, you can purchase *not previously frozen* shellfish and freeze it, placing it in the refrigerator to thaw the night before you are ready to use it. Or you can purchase *still frozen* shellfish and keep it frozen until the night before you are ready to use it.

MEAT & POULTRY

1 1/4 pounds lean boneless pork loin (M)

1 pound lean ground beef (Th)

1 1/2 pounds boneless turkey breast (W)

FISH

1/2 pound medium shrimp, shelled and deveined (F)

1/2 pound scallops (F)

FRESH PRODUCE

Vegetables

1 1/4 pounds small new red potatoes (W)

1 1/2 pounds asparagus (F)

4 medium artichokes (M)

3/4 pound sugar snap peas (W)

5 small mushrooms (W)

1 medium onion (Th)

2 small onions—1 (M), 1 (T)

12 scallions (green onions)—
2 (T), 5 (W), 3 (Th), 2 (T)

1 head garlic (Th, F)

1 bunch parsley (Th, F)

1 medium head lettuce (Th)

1 small head lettuce (T)

2 ripe avocados (T)

1 pound tomatoes—1/2 pound (T), 1/2 pound (Th)

1 medium cucumber (Th)

1 small green bell pepper (M)

1 small red bell pepper (M)

1 small yellow bell pepper (M)

Fruit

1 medium green apple (M)

1 medium pear (T)

1 medium banana (T)

1/2 pound seedless green grapes (T)

2 kiwifruit (W)

1 pint strawberries (T)

1 small lemon (M)

CANS, JARS & BOTTLES

Soup

1 can (14 1/2 ounces) vegetable broth (W)

Vegetables

1 can (14 1/2 ounces) herb-flavored tomato sauce (Th)

3 ounces sun-dried tomatoes (Th)

1 can (11 ounces) whole kernel corn (T)

1 jar (6 1/2 ounces) marinated artichoke hearts (Th)

Mexican Foods

2 cans (16 ounces each) vegetarian refried beans (T)

1 can (4.05 ounces) diced green chilies (T)

1 jar (16 ounces) salsa (T)

Fruit

1 medium can (15 1/4 ounces) pineapple chunks (T)

1 small can (8 3/4 ounces) fruit cocktail (Th)

Condiments

1 small jar (3 ounces) pimiento-stuffed green olives (Th)

Spreads

1 small can (8 ounces) whole cranberry sauce (M, W)

PACKAGED GOODS

Pasta, Rice & Grains

8 ounces medium egg noodles (Th)

8 ounces fine egg noodles (F)

1 package (11 ounces) tortilla chips (T)

Baked Goods

2 small Boboli breads (or English or Australian muffins) (Th)

4 cannoli shells (F)

Nuts & Seeds

1/2 cup sliced almonds (M)

1/2 cup pecan pieces (Th)

1/2 cup chopped walnuts (F)

Dessert & Baking Needs

1/2 cup semisweet chocolate chips (F)

WINES & SPIRITS

1/4 cup dry vermouth (or nonalcoholic white wine or chicken broth) (W)

6 tablespoons dry sherry (or nonalcoholic red wine or vegetable broth) (F)

REFRIGERATED PRODUCTS

Dairy

1 1/4 cups whole or low-fat milk—1/2 cup (M), 3/4 cup (T)

2 1/4 cups regular or light sour cream—2 cups (T), 1/4 cup (F)

3/4 cup regular or low-fat plain yogurt (W)

4 eggs—2 (T), 2 (Th)

Cheese

1 cup regular or low-fat small-curd cottage cheese (Th)

1 1/2 cups shredded regular or low-fat cheddar cheese (T)

1 1/2 cups shredded regular or low-fat Monterey Jack cheese (T)

Juice

1 tablespoon orange juice (M)

Deli

2 slices bacon (T)

FROZEN GOODS

Desserts

1 pound cake (W)

2 small containers (8 ounces each) frozen whipped topping—1 (W), 1 (F)

MONDAY

Three-Pepper Pork

1 small onion
1 small green bell pepper
1 small red bell pepper
1 small yellow bell pepper
1$^1/_4$ pounds lean boneless pork loin
Seasoning to taste
1 tablespoon regular or light olive oil
1 chicken bouillon cube dissolved in $^1/_2$ cup hot
   water
1 tablespoon balsamic vinegar
$^1/_2$ teaspoon dried sage

Fruity Rice

1 medium green apple
1 cup long-grain white rice
2 cups water
1 tablespoon orange juice
$^1/_4$ cup whole cranberry sauce*
1 tablespoon butter
$^1/_8$ teaspoon salt
$^1/_8$ teaspoon ground cinnamon

Go for Chokes

4 medium artichokes
1 small lemon
1 bay leaf
2 whole cloves
4 tablespoons butter
$^1/_4$ teaspoon garlic powder
$^1/_2$ teaspoon lemon juice

Ranch Pudding

2 tablespoons butter
2$^1/_2$ cups water
2 cups firmly packed dark brown sugar
$^1/_2$ cup whole or low-fat milk
1$^1/_2$ cups Bisquick
1 cup dark raisins
$^1/_2$ cup sliced almonds
1 teaspoon vanilla extract

EQUIPMENT

Dutch oven
Large covered skillet
Medium covered
   saucepan
Medium saucepan
Small saucepan
8x8-inch glass baking
   dish

Vegetable steamer
Medium bowl
Assorted kitchen knives
Measuring cups and
   spoons
Assorted cooking
   utensils

COUNTDOWN

1 Assemble the ingredients and equipment
2 Do Steps 1–2 of the *Ranch Pudding*
3 Do Steps 1–2 of the *Fruity Rice*
4 Do Steps 1–3 of the *Go for Chokes*
5 Do Steps 1–4 of the *Three-Pepper Pork*
6 Do Step 3 of the *Fruity Rice*
7 Do Steps 4–5 of the *Go for Chokes*

---

*Reserve the balance of the can for use on Wednesday.

Three-Pepper Pork

1 Peel and thinly slice the onion. Trim, seed and cut the bell peppers into thin strips.

2 Cut the pork into 8 slices and season to taste. Heat the oil in a large skillet and cook the pork slices, turning once, until lightly browned, 3 to 5 minutes per side. Reduce the heat, cover and cook until the pork is white throughout but still moist, about 5 minutes. Remove the chops and keep them warm.

3 Add the onion to the skillet and cook, stirring occasionally, until it is softened but not brown, about 5 minutes. Add the bell peppers and cook, tossing, until they are just softened but retain their bright color, 2 to 3 minutes.

4 Add the bouillon mixture, the balsamic vinegar and the sage to the skillet and simmer for 2 minutes. Season to taste. Return the pork to the skillet and cook, turning, until it is heated through, 1 to 2 minutes.

Fruity Rice

1 Peel, core and chop the apple.

2 In a medium covered saucepan, combine the rice and the water. Bring the mixture to a boil, stir in the apple, the orange juice, the cranberry sauce, the butter, the salt and the cinnamon. Reduce the heat, cover and simmer until all the liquid is absorbed and the rice is tender, about 25 minutes.

3 Fluff the rice before serving.

Go for Chokes

1 Bring 2 inches of water to a boil in a Dutch oven.

2 Trim the artichoke stems and remove the thorny tips on the leaves. Remove any loose bottom leaves. Slice the lemon.

3 Place the vegetable steamer in the Dutch oven. Add the artichokes, the lemon slices, the bay leaf and the cloves. Cover, reduce the heat and steam the artichokes until the leaves pull off easily, about 30 minutes, checking occasionally to make sure the water does not boil away.

4 Melt the butter in a small saucepan. Blend in the garlic powder and the lemon juice.

5 Drain the artichokes and pass the melted garlic butter for dipping.

Ranch Pudding

1 Preheat the oven to 350°F.

2 In a medium saucepan, blend the butter, the water and 1 cup of the brown sugar. Bring the mixture to a boil and cook for 5 minutes. Pour the mixture into an 8x8-inch glass baking dish. In a medium bowl, combine the remaining brown sugar, the milk, the Bisquick, the raisins, the nuts and the vanilla. Spoon the batter on top of the sugar mixture. (It will sink into the liquid and spread out as it bakes.) Bake for 45 minutes. Serve warm.

TUESDAY

Mexicali Casserole

$^1/_2$ pound fresh tomatoes
2 scallions (green onions)
1 small can (4.05 ounces) diced green chilies
1 can (11 ounces) whole kernel corn
$^3/_4$ cup whole or low-fat milk
2 eggs
$^1/_3$ cup flour
$1^1/_2$ cups shredded regular or low-fat cheddar
    cheese
$1^1/_2$ cups shredded regular or low-fat
    Monterey Jack cheese
Seasoning to taste
2 ripe avocados
2 cups regular or light sour cream
$^1/_4$ teaspoon Tabasco sauce
2 tablespoons lemon juice
1 small head lettuce
1 package (11 ounces) tortilla chips
1 jar (16 ounces) salsa

Re-Refried Beans

2 slices bacon
1 small onion
2 cans (16 ounces each) vegetarian refried
    beans
Seasoning to taste

Fiesta Fruit

1 pint fresh strawberries
1 medium pear
$^1/_2$ pound seedless green grapes
1 medium banana
1 medium can ($15^1/_4$ ounces) pineapple chunks
    in juice
$^1/_4$ teaspoon sugar
$^1/_8$ teaspoon ground cinnamon

EQUIPMENT

Large skillet	Measuring cups and
1½-quart casserole	spoons
Large bowl	Assorted cooking
Medium bowl	utensils
Assorted kitchen knives	Whisk

COUNTDOWN

1 Assemble the ingredients and equipment
2 Do Steps 1–6 of the *Mexicali Casserole*
3 Do Steps 1–2 of the *Fiesta Fruit*
4 Do Steps 1–4 of the *Re-Refried Beans*
5 Do Step 7 of the *Mexicali Casserole*

Mexicali Casserole

1 Preheat the oven to 375°F.

2 Chop the tomatoes. Trim and chop the scallions. Drain the chilies. Drain the corn.

3 In a 1½-quart casserole, whisk together the milk, the eggs and the flour until smooth. Add the tomatoes, the scallions, the chilies, the corn and the cheeses and mix well. Season to taste.

4 Bake the casserole until the center is set, 40 to 45 minutes.

5 Halve, pit and scoop out the avocados. In a medium bowl, mix the avocados with ½ cup of the sour cream, the Tabasco sauce and the lemon juice until well blended. Season to taste.

6 Wash, dry and shred the lettuce.

7 Serve the casserole with the tortilla chips and bowls of salsa, guacamole and shredded lettuce. Pass the remaining sour cream.

Re-Refried Beans

1 Chop the bacon. Peel and chop the onion.

2 Sauté the bacon in a large skillet until it is crisp, about 5 minutes, and then drain it on a paper towel, reserving 2 tablespoons of the drippings.

3 Sauté the onion in the bacon drippings until golden, about 10 minutes.

4 Add the beans to the skillet and sauté them for 5 minutes. Return the bacon and cook until the mixture is heated through. Season to taste.

Fiesta Fruit

1 Hull and halve the strawberries. Core and chunk the pear. Wash, separate and halve the grapes. Peel and slice the banana.

2 In a large bowl, combine the undrained pineapple with the rest of the fruit. Add the sugar and the cinnamon, and toss lightly to blend. Cover and refrigerate until you are ready to serve.

WEDNESDAY

Hot-to-Trot Turkey

$1^1/_2$ pounds boneless, skinless turkey breast
5 scallions (green onions)
5 small mushrooms
2 tablespoons butter
1 tablespoon regular or light vegetable oil
$^1/_4$ cup dry vermouth (or nonalcoholic white
    wine or chicken broth)
2 teaspoons dried sage
1 tablespoon flour
$^3/_4$ cup regular or low-fat plain yogurt
Seasoning to taste

Sesame Potatoes

1 can ($14^1/_2$ ounces) vegetable broth
1 cup water
$1^1/_4$ pounds small new red potatoes
2 tablespoons butter
1 tablespoon sesame seeds
Seasoning to taste

My Favorite Snap Peas

$^3/_4$ pound fresh sugar snap peas
2 tablespoons butter
$^1/_2$ teaspoon ground cinnamon
$^1/_2$ teaspoon dark brown sugar
Seasoning to taste

Cranberry Cake

1 frozen pound cake
2 kiwifruit
1 small container (8 ounces) frozen whipped
    topping
$^3/_4$ cup whole cranberry sauce reserved from
    Monday

EQUIPMENT

Large covered skillet
Medium skillet
Medium covered
  saucepan
Assorted kitchen knives
Measuring cups and
  spoons

Assorted cooking
  utensils
Whisk
Vegetable brush

COUNTDOWN

IN THE MORNING:
  Do Step 1 of the *Cranberry Cake*
BEFORE DINNER:
  1 Assemble the remaining ingredients and
     equipment
  2 Do Steps 2–4 of the *Cranberry Cake*
  3 Do Step 1 of *My Favorite Snap Peas*
  4 Do Step 1 of the *Hot-to-Trot Turkey*
  5 Do Steps 1–2 of the *Sesame Potatoes*
  6 Do Steps 2–4 of the *Hot-to-Trot Turkey*
  7 Do Step 3 of the *Sesame Potatoes*
  8 Do Step 5 of the *Hot-to-Trot Turkey*
  9 Do Step 2 of *My Favorite Snap Peas*

Hot-to-Trot Turkey

1 Cut the turkey breast into thin slices. Trim and slice the scallions. Wash, pat dry and slice the mushrooms.

2 Melt the butter with the oil in a large skillet. Add the turkey slices and sauté until they are lightly browned, 3 to 4 minutes per side.

3 Add the scallions and the mushrooms, and sauté 3 minutes more.

4 Remove the turkey and keep it warm.

5 Add the vermouth and the sage to the skillet and cook until the alcohol burns off, 2 to 3 minutes. Whisk in the flour and the yogurt. Season to taste. Bring the mixture to a boil and then remove the skillet from the heat. Return the turkey to the skillet and coat the slices in the sauce. Cover to keep warm.

Sesame Potatoes

1 Bring the broth and the water to a boil in a medium saucepan.

2 Scrub the potatoes and cook them in the broth until they are almost tender, 10 to 15 minutes.

3 Drain the potatoes. Melt the butter in the saucepan. Add the sesame seeds and sauté until they begin to brown, about 2 minutes. Return the potatoes to the saucepan and toss to coat them in the butter and seeds. Season to taste and cover to keep warm.

My Favorite Snap Peas

1 Trim and string the sugar snap peas.

2 Melt the butter in a medium skillet. Mix in the cinnamon and the brown sugar. Season to taste. Sauté the sugar snap peas until they are crisp-tender, 2 to 3 minutes.

Cranberry Cake

1 Set the pound cake in the refrigerator to thaw.

2 Peel and thinly slice the kiwifruit, reserving 4 slices.

3 Cut the cake into 3 horizontal layers.

4 Spread the bottom layer of the cake with a quarter of the whipped topping. Lay the remaining kiwi slices over the topping. Spread the cranberry sauce on the second layer and then another quarter of the whipped topping. Spread the top layer of the cake and the sides with the remaining whipped topping, and garnish with the reserved kiwi slices. Refrigerate the cake until you are ready to serve.

THURSDAY

Lazy Lasagna

1 medium onion
2 cloves garlic
1 tablespoon fresh parsley (when chopped)
1 pound lean ground beef
1 can (14$^1/_2$ ounces) herb-flavored tomato
    sauce
2 cups water
2 teaspoons dried basil
$^1/_2$ teaspoon dried oregano
8 ounces medium egg noodles
1 cup regular or low-fat small-curd cottage
    cheese
3 tablespoons grated Parmesan cheese
1 egg
Seasoning to taste

Pisa Salad

1 medium head lettuce
1 medium cucumber
$^1/_2$ pound fresh tomatoes
3 scallions (green onions)
1 jar (6$^1/_2$ ounces) marinated artichoke hearts
1 small jar (3 ounces) pimiento-stuffed green
    olives
1 clove garlic
1$^1/_2$ tablespoons red wine vinegar
1$^1/_2$ tablespoons lemon juice
1 teaspoon Dijon mustard
Seasoning to taste

Bob-Bob-Boboli

1 clove garlic
3 ounces sun-dried tomatoes
3 tablespoons regular or light olive oil
2 small (8-inch) Boboli breads (or English or
    Australian muffins)

Tutti-Fruitti Baked Cake

1 small can (8$^3/_4$ ounces) fruit cocktail
$^1/_2$ cup flour
$^1/_4$ cup granulated sugar
$^1/_2$ teaspoon baking soda
$^1/_4$ teaspoon salt
1 egg
$^1/_4$ cup dark brown sugar
$^1/_2$ cup pecan pieces

EQUIPMENT

Large covered skillet	Assorted kitchen knives
8x8-inch glass baking dish	Measuring cups and spoons
Cookie sheet	Assorted cooking utensils
2 large bowls	
2 medium bowls	Whisk
2 small bowls	Vegetable peeler

COUNTDOWN

1 Assemble the ingredients and equipment
2 Do Step 1 of the *Tutti-Fruitti Baked Cake*
3 Do Steps 1–3 of the *Lazy Lasagna*
4 Do Steps 2–5 of the *Tutti-Fruitti Baked Cake*
5 Do Step 4 of the *Lazy Lasagna*
6 Do Steps 1–2 of the *Pisa Salad*
7 Do Steps 1–3 of the *Bob-Bob-Boboli*
8 Do Step 3 of the *Pisa Salad*

Lazy Lasagna

1 Peel and chop the onion. Peel and mince the garlic. Chop the parsley.

2 In a large skillet, sauté the beef and the onion until the meat is browned, about 5 minutes. Drain off any fat.

3 Stir in the tomato sauce, the water, the garlic, the basil, the oregano and the noodles. Heat the mixture to boiling, stirring. Then reduce the heat, cover and simmer for 10 minutes.

4 In a medium bowl, combine the cheeses, the egg and the parsley. Season to taste. Spread the cheese mixture over the noodle mixture, cover and simmer for 15 minutes more.

Pisa Salad

1 Wash and dry the lettuce and tear it into bite-size pieces. Peel and slice the cucumber. Chop the tomatoes. Trim and slice the scallions. Drain the artichokes, reserving the oil. Drain the olives. Combine the ingredients in a large bowl.

2 Peel and mince the garlic. In a small bowl, whisk together the garlic, the reserved artichoke oil, the vinegar, the lemon juice and the mustard. Season to taste.

3 Toss the salad with the dressing.

Bob-Bob-Boboli

1 Preheat the oven to 400°F.

2 Peel and mince the garlic. Chop the tomatoes. Combine the garlic and the tomatoes with the olive oil in a small bowl.

3 Cut the Boboli breads into wedges and place them on an ungreased cookie sheet. Spread the bread with the tomato mixture and bake until the Boboli is golden, 5 to 6 minutes.

Tutti-Fruitti Baked Cake

1 Preheat the oven to 350°F. Grease an 8x8-inch glass baking dish.

2 Drain the fruit cocktail, reserving $1/4$ cup of the juice.

3 In a large bowl, combine the flour, the granulated sugar, the baking soda and the salt.

4 In a medium bowl, beat the egg until thick and lemon colored. Combine the fruit and the reserved juice with the egg, add the mixture to the dry ingredients and blend thoroughly.

5 Pour the batter into the baking dish. Sprinkle the top with the brown sugar and the nuts, and bake until a toothpick comes out of the center clean, 30 to 35 minutes.

FRIDAY

Shrimp & Scallop au Gratin

$^1/_2$ cup fresh parsley (when chopped)
1 scallion (green onion)
2 cloves garlic
$^3/_4$ cup plain bread crumbs
$^1/_2$ pound medium shrimp, shelled and
    deveined
$^1/_2$ pound scallops
6 tablespoons dry sherry (or nonalcoholic red
    wine or vegetable broth)
$^1/_4$ teaspoon dried oregano
Seasoning to taste
8 tablespoons butter

Sourpuss Noodles

1 scallion (green onion)
8 ounces fine egg noodles
2 tablespoons butter
$^1/_4$ cup regular or light sour cream
Seasoning to taste

Asparagus Crunch

$1^1/_2$ pounds fresh asparagus
2 tablespoons butter
1 tablespoon lemon juice
$^1/_2$ cup chopped walnuts
Seasoning to taste

Mocha-Noli

1 small container (8 ounces) frozen whipped
    topping
$^1/_4$ cup + 1 tablespoon sweetened cocoa
1 tablespoon instant or brewed coffee
1 teaspoon vanilla extract
$^1/_4$ cup confectioners' sugar
$^1/_2$ cup semisweet chocolate chips
4 cannoli shells

EQUIPMENT

Large covered skillet	Strainer
Large saucepan	Assorted kitchen knives
7x11-inch glass baking dish	Measuring cups and spoons
Cookie sheet	Assorted cooking utensils
Large bowl	Sifter
Medium bowl	

COUNTDOWN

1 Assemble the ingredients and equipment
2 Do Steps 1–2 of the *Shrimp & Scallop au Gratin*
3 Do Step 1 of the *Sourpuss Noodles*
4 Do Step 1 of the *Mocha-Noli*
5 Do Steps 3–6 of the *Shrimp & Scallop au Gratin*
6 Do Step 1 of the *Asparagus Crunch*
7 Do Step 2 of the *Sourpuss Noodles*
8 Do Step 2 of the *Asparagus Crunch*
9 Do Step 3 of the *Sourpuss Noodles*
10 Do Step 2 of the *Mocha-Noli*

Shrimp & Scallop au Gratin

1 Preheat the broiler. Grease a 7x11-inch glass baking dish.

2 Chop the parsley. Trim and chop the scallion. Peel and mince the garlic.

3 Spread the bread crumbs on an ungreased cookie sheet and place them under the broiler until they are lightly browned, about 2 minutes. Remove the crumbs and set the oven temperature to 400°F.

4 Rinse the shrimp. Rinse and pat dry the scallops. If you are using sea scallops, cut them in half. Combine the seafood in a large bowl and toss with the sherry. Spread the mixture in the baking dish.

5 In the same bowl, combine the toasted bread crumbs, the parsley, the scallion, the garlic and the oregano, and season to taste. Spread the mixture over the seafood.

6 Melt the butter and drizzle it over the bread crumb mixture, and bake until the casserole is hot and bubbly, 10 to 12 minutes.

Sourpuss Noodles

1 Bring water to a boil in a large saucepan. Chop the scallion.

2 Cook the noodles in the boiling water until they are almost tender, 3 to 5 minutes.

3 Drain the noodles, return them to the saucepan and toss them with the butter and the sour cream. Heat the mixture through, add the scallion, season to taste and cover to keep warm.

Asparagus Crunch

1 Rinse the asparagus, remove the tough ends and slice the spears into 1-inch diagonals.

2 Melt the butter in a large skillet. Add the asparagus and sauté for 4 minutes. Add the lemon juice and the walnuts, and toss them with the asparagus. Season to taste, cover the skillet, remove it from the heat and let the asparagus steam for 2 to 3 minutes.

Mocha-Noli

1 In a medium bowl, blend the whipped topping with 1/4 cup of the cocoa, the coffee, the vanilla, the confectioners' sugar and the chocolate chips, and refrigerate for at least 15 minutes.

2 Fill the cannoli shells with the chocolate cream mixture and dust them with the remaining cocoa.

MAY

WEEK FOUR

WEEK AT A GLANCE

Monday

VEGETARIAN STROGANOFF
TURMERIC RICE
SLEEK SALAD
LIME PUFFER

Tuesday

ROSY PORK
CLEVER COUSCOUS
CUTE CARROTS
ORANGE TANGO

Wednesday

RIO GRANDE CHICKEN
DEEP SOUTH CORN
VERANDAH SALAD
RICH REWARDS

Thursday

MACARONI PONY
YANKEE DOODLE SALAD
SECRET INGREDIENT BISCUITS
FAB FRUIT CREATION

Friday

FISHING FOR COMPLIMENTS
BILLY BUDS
BELL-RINGERS
STRAWBERRY DISCOVERY

CHECK STAPLES

- ☐ Butter
- ☐ Flour
- ☐ Cornstarch
- ☐ Bisquick
- ☐ Granulated sugar
- ☐ Dark brown sugar
- ☐ Confectioners' sugar
- ☐ Long-grain white rice
- ☐ Regular or light vegetable oil
- ☐ Regular or light olive oil
- ☐ Red wine vinegar
- ☐ Balsamic vinegar
- ☐ Lemon juice
- ☐ Grated fresh lemon peel
- ☐ Grated fresh orange peel
- ☐ Soy sauce
- ☐ Dijon mustard
- ☐ Honey
- ☐ Grated Parmesan cheese
- ☐ Chicken bouillon cubes
- ☐ Ground coriander
- ☐ Cream of tartar
- ☐ Dried rosemary
- ☐ Dried sage
- ☐ Turmeric
- ☐ Pepper
- ☐ Salt
- ☐ Almond extract
- ☐ Vanilla extract

SHOPPING NOTE

● If you are shopping once a week and cannot arrange to purchase fresh seafood on the day you plan to use it, you can purchase *not previously frozen* seafood and freeze it, placing it in the refrigerator to thaw the night before you are ready to use it. Or you can purchase *still frozen* seafood and keep it frozen until the night before you are ready to use it.

SHOPPING LIST

MEAT & POULTRY

1 1/2 pounds lean boneless pork loin (T)

4 boneless, skinless chicken breast halves (W)

FISH

1 1/2 pounds bass fillets (F)

1/2 pound medium shrimp, shelled and deveined (F)

FRESH PRODUCE

Vegetables

1 pound small new white potatoes (F)

1 medium bunch broccoli (M)

1 pound green beans (Th)

1 small zucchini (Th)

1/2 pound mushrooms (M)

2 medium carrots (M)

1 pound baby carrots (T)

2 large sweet onions (M)

2 medium onions—1 (Th), 1 (F)

1 small red onion (Th)

1 small leek (M)

4 scallions (green onions) (T)

1 head garlic (M, Th, F)

1 bunch parsley (M, T, Th)

1 small bunch basil (F)

1 medium head lettuce (W)

2 small heads lettuce—1 (M), 1 (Th)

3/4 pound tomatoes—1/2 pound (Th), 1/4 pound (F)

1 large cucumber (W)

2 medium red bell peppers (F)

2 medium green bell peppers (F)

1 medium daikon (or turnip) (W)

Fruit

1 medium banana (T)

1/2 pound cherries (T)

1 pint strawberries (F)

3 small limes (M)

1 medium lemon (W)

2 large oranges (T)

2 small pink grapefruit (Th)

CANS, JARS & BOTTLES

Soup

1 can (14 1/2 ounces) chicken broth (M)

1 can (14 1/2 ounces) vegetable broth (T)

Mexican Products

1/2 cup taco sauce (W)

Fruit

1 can (11 ounces) mandarin oranges (Th)

Condiments

1 small can (3.3 ounces) sliced black olives (M)

1 small jar (6 ounces) maraschino cherries (W)

PACKAGED GOODS

Pasta, Rice & Grains

16 ounces elbow macaroni (Th)

2 cups quick-cooking couscous (T)

Nuts & Seeds

1/2 cup pecan pieces (W)

1/4 pound pine nuts (Th)

Dessert & Baking Needs

1 small package (3.9 ounces) instant chocolate pudding mix (W)

WINES & SPIRITS

1/4 cup dry white wine (or nonalcoholic white wine or vegetable broth) (M)

1/4 cup dry white wine (or nonalcoholic white wine or clam juice) (F)

1/4 cup + 1 teaspoon Grand Marnier liqueur (or nonalcoholic Italian orange syrup)—1 teaspoon (T), 1/4 cup (F)

2 tablespoons whiskey (or nonalcoholic Italian praline syrup) (W)

REFRIGERATED PRODUCTS

Dairy

2 cups whole milk (W)

2 1/4 cups whole or low-fat milk—1 cup (M), 3/4 cup (T), 1/2 cup (Th)

2/3 cup buttermilk (Th)

1/2 cup whipping cream (W)

1 cup regular or light sour cream—1/2 cup (M), 1/2 cup (F)

3/4 cup regular or low-fat plain yogurt—1/4 cup (M), 1/2 cup (W)

6 eggs—4 (M), 2 (Th)

Cheese

1/2 cup regular or low-fat small-curd cottage cheese (M)

1 small container (15 ounces) regular or low-fat ricotta cheese (Th)

Juice

1/2 cup orange juice (F)

FROZEN GOODS

Vegetables

1 package (16 ounces) whole kernel corn (W)

Desserts

1 pint orange frozen yogurt (T)

MONDAY

Vegetarian Stroganoff

1 medium bunch broccoli
2 medium carrots
$^1/_2$ pound mushrooms
1 small leek
1 clove garlic
1 small can (3.3 ounces) sliced black olives
2 tablespoons butter
$1^1/_2$ tablespoons flour
1 chicken bouillon cube
1 cup whole or low-fat milk
1 tablespoon soy sauce
$^1/_4$ cup dry white wine (or nonalcoholic white wine or vegetable broth)
Seasoning to taste
$^1/_2$ cup regular or light sour cream
$^1/_2$ cup regular or low-fat small-curd cottage cheese
$^1/_4$ cup grated Parmesan cheese

Turmeric Rice

2 tablespoons fresh parsley (when chopped)
1 cup long-grain white rice
1 can ($14^1/_2$ ounces) chicken broth
$^1/_4$ cup water
$^1/_2$ teaspoon turmeric

Sleek Salad

1 small head lettuce
2 large sweet onions
2 teaspoons grated fresh orange peel
$^1/_4$ cup regular or low-fat plain yogurt
1 teaspoon sugar
1 teaspoon lemon juice
Seasoning to taste

Lime Puffer

4 eggs
3 small limes
8 tablespoons butter
$1^1/_4$ cups granulated sugar
1 tablespoon cornstarch
$^1/_2$ teaspoon cream of tartar
2 tablespoons flour
2 tablespoons confectioners' sugar

EQUIPMENT

Electric hand mixer	Measuring cups and
Large covered skillet	spoons
Large saucepan	Assorted cooking
Small saucepan	utensils
Double boiler	Juicer
$1^1/_2$-quart casserole	Sifter
2 medium bowls	Whisk
2 small bowls	Vegetable peeler
Colander	Citrus grater
Assorted kitchen knives	

COUNTDOWN

1 Assemble the ingredients and equipment
2 Do Step 1 of the *Turmeric Rice*
3 Do Steps 1–5 of the *Lime Puffer*
4 Do Steps 1–2 of the *Sleek Salad*
5 Do Step 1 of the *Vegetarian Stroganoff*
6 Do Step 6 of the *Lime Puffer*
7 Do Steps 2–5 of the *Vegetarian Stroganoff*
8 Do Step 3 of the *Sleek Salad*
9 Do Step 2 of the *Turmeric Rice*

Vegetarian Stroganoff

1 Trim and cut the broccoli into bite-size florets. Peel and thinly slice the carrots. Wash, pat dry and slice the mushrooms. Wash thoroughly, trim and slice the leek. Peel and mince the garlic. Drain the olives.

2 Bring water to a boil in a large saucepan. Cook the broccoli and the carrots in the boiling water until they are crisp-tender, about 5 minutes.

3 Melt the butter in a large skillet, and sauté the mushrooms, the leek and the garlic until the mushrooms are tender, about 5 minutes.

4 Drain the vegetables. Stir the flour and the bouillon cube into the mushroom mixture. Stir in the milk and the soy sauce. Cook and stir until the mixture is thick and bubbly. Cook, stirring, for 1 minute more. Stir in the broccoli, the carrots, the wine and the olives. Season to taste.

5 In a medium bowl, combine the sour cream, the cottage cheese and the Parmesan cheese. Gradually stir about 1 cup of the mushroom mixture into the sour cream mixture and return it to the skillet. Cook, covered, until the mixture is heated through, 2 to 4 minutes. Do not boil.

Turmeric Rice

1 Chop the parsley. Place the parsley, the rice, the broth, the water and the turmeric in the top of a double boiler. Bring water to a boil in the bottom of the double boiler. Reduce the heat, cover and simmer until all the liquid is absorbed and the rice is tender, 30 to 40 minutes.

2 Fluff the rice before serving.

Sleek Salad

1 Wash and dry the lettuce and place the leaves on individual salad plates.

2 Peel and thinly slice the sweet onions and place them over the lettuce.

3 In a small bowl, whisk together the orange peel, the yogurt, the sugar and the lemon juice. Season the dressing to taste and drizzle it over the salad.

Lime Puffer

1 Preheat the oven to 350°F.

2 Separate the eggs, placing the whites in a medium bowl and the yolks in a small bowl.

3 Grate 1 teaspoon of the lime peel and juice the limes to measure $1/3$ cup. Melt the butter in a small saucepan. Mix in $3/4$ cup of the granulated sugar and the cornstarch. Add the lime juice and the lime peel. Bring the mixture to a boil, whisking until it is slightly thickened, about 2 minutes. Pour it into a $1^1/_2$-quart casserole.

4 Beat the egg whites with the cream of tartar until stiff peaks form, about 4 minutes. Add the remaining granulated sugar and beat until the mixture is very stiff, about 3 minutes more.

5 Beat the egg yolks with the flour until the yolks are thickened, about 2 minutes. Fold the egg yolk mixture into the egg white mixture and spread it over the lime sauce. Bake until the egg whites are set, about 15 minutes.

6 Remove the puffer from the oven, dust it with the confectioners' sugar, and let it stand to cool until you are ready to serve.

TUESDAY

Rosy Pork

1 1/2 pounds lean boneless pork loin
1 tablespoon butter
1 tablespoon regular or light olive oil
2 tablespoons flour
3/4 cup whole or low-fat milk
3 tablespoons balsamic vinegar
1 1/2 teaspoons dried rosemary
Seasoning to taste

Clever Couscous

4 scallions (green onions)
2 tablespoons regular or light olive oil
2 cups quick-cooking couscous
1 can (14 1/2 ounces) vegetable broth
2 tablespoons water
2 teaspoons soy sauce
1 tablespoon butter
1 teaspoon sugar

Cute Carrots

2 tablespoons fresh parsley (when chopped)
1 pound baby carrots
2 tablespoons butter
1/2 teaspoon dark brown sugar
Seasoning to taste

Orange Tango

2 large oranges
1/2 pound fresh cherries
1 teaspoon Grand Marnier liqueur (or
    nonalcoholic Italian orange syrup)
1 medium banana
1 pint orange frozen yogurt

EQUIPMENT

Large covered skillet	Assorted cooking
Medium covered skillet	utensils
Medium covered	Whisk
saucepan	Ice cream scoop
Small saucepan	Mallet
Medium bowl	Waxed paper
Assorted kitchen knives	
Measuring cups and	
spoons	

COUNTDOWN

1 Assemble the ingredients and equipment
2 Do Step 1 of the *Orange Tango*
3 Do Step 1 of the *Clever Couscous*
4 Do Steps 1–3 of the *Rosy Pork*
5 Do Steps 1–2 of the *Cute Carrots*
6 Do Step 2 of the *Clever Couscous*
7 Do Step 3 of the *Cute Carrots*
8 Do Step 2 of the *Orange Tango*

Rosy Pork

1 Cut the pork loin into 8 slices, place them between sheets of waxed paper and pound them with a mallet to a ¹/₂-inch thickness.

2 Melt the butter with the oil in a large skillet. Place half the pork slices in the skillet and sauté until they are brown, about 3 minutes per side. Remove the pork and repeat the process with the remaining slices.

3 Reduce the heat under the skillet. Add the flour and whisk until smooth. Stir in the milk, the vinegar and the rosemary. Season to taste, cover the skillet and bring the mixture to a boil. Reduce the heat, return all the pork to the skillet, partially cover and cook, turning occasionally, until the meat is fork-tender and the sauce is caramel colored and has reduced to around ²/₃ cup, 15 to 20 minutes.

Clever Couscous

1 Trim and finely chop the scallions. Heat the oil in a medium saucepan and sauté the scallions until they are soft, about 3 minutes. Add the couscous and sauté for 4 to 5 minutes more.

2 In a small saucepan, combine the broth, the water, the soy sauce, the butter and the sugar. Bring the mixture to a boil and pour it over the couscous. Cover the couscous, remove it from the heat and let it stand until all the liquid is absorbed and the couscous is tender, about 10 minutes.

Cute Carrots

1 Chop the parsley. Trim the carrots, if necessary.

2 Bring a small amount of water to a boil in a medium skillet. Add the carrots, cover the skillet and cook until the carrots are crisp-tender, 10 to 12 minutes. Check to make sure the water does not boil away or the carrots will burn.

3 Pour off any remaining carrot water and reduce the heat. Add the butter and the brown sugar, and season to taste. Sauté until the carrots are glazed, 3 to 4 minutes. Sprinkle them with the parsley, remove the skillet from the heat and cover to keep warm.

Orange Tango

1 Peel and section the oranges, and cut the sections in half. Pit and halve the cherries. Combine the oranges and the cherries in a medium bowl and toss them with the Grand Marnier. Refrigerate until you are ready to use.

2 Peel and slice the banana, and add it to the oranges and cherries. Place scoops of frozen yogurt in individual bowls, and top them with the fruit mixture.

WEDNESDAY

Rio Grande Chicken

¹/₂ cup taco sauce
¹/₄ cup Dijon mustard
2 tablespoons lemon juice
4 boneless, skinless chicken breast halves
1 medium lemon
2 tablespoons butter
Seasoning to taste
¹/₂ cup regular or low-fat plain yogurt

Deep South Corn

1 package (16 ounces) frozen whole kernel corn
4 tablespoons butter
1 tablespoon dark brown sugar
2 tablespoons whiskey (or Italian praline syrup)
¹/₂ cup pecan pieces

Verandah Salad

3 tablespoons regular or light vegetable oil
2 tablespoons red wine vinegar
1 teaspoon sugar
Seasoning to taste
1 large cucumber
1 medium daikon (or turnip)
1 medium head lettuce

Rich Rewards

1 small jar (6 ounces) maraschino cherries
1 small package (3.9 ounces) instant chocolate pudding mix
2 cups whole milk
¹/₂ cup whipping cream
2 tablespoons confectioners' sugar

EQUIPMENT

Electric hand mixer	Assorted kitchen knives
Large covered skillet	Measuring cups and
Medium covered skillet	spoons
7x11-inch glass baking	Assorted cooking
dish	utensils
2 medium bowls	Whisk
Small bowl	Vegetable peeler

COUNTDOWN

1 Assemble the ingredients and equipment
2 Do Step 1 of the *Rio Grande Chicken*
3 Do Steps 1–3 of the *Rich Rewards*
4 Do Steps 1–2 of the *Verandah Salad*
5 Do Steps 2–4 of the *Rio Grande Chicken*
6 Do Steps 1–2 of the *Deep South Corn*
7 Do Step 3 of the *Verandah Salad*
8 Do Step 5 of the *Rio Grande Chicken*
9 Do Step 3 of the *Deep South Corn*
10 Do Step 4 of the *Rich Rewards*

Rio Grande Chicken

1 In a 7x11-inch glass baking dish, combine the taco sauce with the mustard and the lemon juice. Add the chicken and let it marinate for 30 minutes.

2 Cut the lemon into 4 slices.

3 Remove the chicken from the dish and reserve the marinade.

4 Melt the butter in a large skillet. Add the chicken and cook until it is lightly browned, 3 to 5 minutes per side. Add the reserved marinade to the skillet, reduce the heat and simmer, turning the chicken once or twice, until the breasts are fork-tender, 10 to 15 minutes.

5 When the chicken is tender, bring the marinade to a boil, season to taste and cook it for 1 minute. Cover until you are ready to serve. To serve, top each breast with a dollop of yogurt and a slice of lemon.

Deep South Corn

1 In a medium skillet, cook the corn with the butter until it is heated through, about 5 minutes.

2 Stir the brown sugar and the whiskey into the corn and cook, uncovered, stirring, until the mixture thickens, about 2 minutes. Remove the skillet from the heat and cover to keep warm.

3 Sprinkle the corn with the pecan pieces.

Verandah Salad

1 In a medium bowl, whisk together the oil, the vinegar and the sugar. Season to taste. Peel and thinly slice the cucumber. Peel and slice the daikon. Add them to the dressing, toss until well blended, and refrigerate until you are ready to serve.

2 Wash and dry the lettuce and place the leaves on individual salad plates.

3 Spoon the cucumber-daikon mixture over the lettuce leaves.

Rich Rewards

1 Drain the maraschino cherries, reserving 1 tablespoon of the juice and 4 whole cherries. Chop the remaining cherries.

2 In a medium bowl, beat the pudding mix and the milk together until well blended. Fold in the chopped cherries, pour the mixture into individual dessert dishes and refrigerate for at least 20 minutes.

3 In a small bowl, whip the cream until soft peaks form, about 3 minutes. Add the reserved cherry juice and the confectioners' sugar and beat until stiff, about 2 minutes more. Cover the bowl and refrigerate until you are ready to use.

4 Top the pudding with the whipped cream and garnish with the reserved cherries.

THURSDAY

Macaroni Pony

1 medium onion
1 small zucchini
$^1/_2$ pound fresh tomatoes
$^1/_2$ cup fresh parsley (when chopped)
1 clove garlic
16 ounces elbow macaroni
2 tablespoons butter
1 tablespoon regular or light vegetable oil
Seasoning to taste
1 container (15 ounces) regular or low-fat
    ricotta cheese
$^1/_2$ cup whole or low-fat milk
4 tablespoons grated Parmesan cheese

Yankee Doodle Salad

1 pound fresh green beans
1 small red onion
1 tablespoon fresh parsley (when chopped)
3 tablespoons regular or light vegetable oil
$1^1/_2$ tablespoons red wine vinegar
$1^1/_2$ tablespoons lemon juice
$^3/_4$ teaspoon sugar
Seasoning to taste
$^1/_4$ pound pine nuts
1 small head lettuce

Secret Ingredient Biscuits

$2^1/_4$ cups Bisquick
2 tablespoons butter
$^2/_3$ cup buttermilk
1 teaspoon ground coriander

Fab Fruit Creation

1 pink grapefruit
1 can (11 ounces) mandarin oranges
2 eggs
$^1/_8$ teaspoon salt
2 tablespoons sugar
2 tablespoons honey
2 teaspoons grated fresh lemon peel
$^1/_2$ teaspoon almond extract

EQUIPMENT

Electric hand mixer	Assorted kitchen knives
Stockpot	Measuring cups and
Large skillet	spoons
Medium saucepan	Assorted cooking
Small saucepan	utensils
1½-quart casserole	Pastry board
Cookie sheet	Whisk
3 medium bowls	Biscuit cutter
Colander	

COUNTDOWN

1 Assemble the ingredients and equipment
2 Do Step 1 of the *Macaroni Pony*
3 Do Steps 1–4 of the *Yankee Doodle Salad*
4 Do Steps 1–3 of the *Secret Ingredient Biscuits*
5 Do Steps 2–10 of the *Macaroni Pony*
6 Do Step 4 of the *Secret Ingredient Biscuits*
7 Do Steps 1–3 of the *Fab Fruit Creation*
8 Do Step 5 of the *Yankee Doodle Salad*
9 Do Step 4 of the *Fab Fruit Creation*

Macaroni Pony

1 Preheat the oven to 350°F. Grease a 1½-quart casserole.

2 Bring water to a boil in a stockpot.

3 Peel and chop the onion. Trim and slice the zucchini. Chop the tomatoes. Chop the parsley. Peel and crush the garlic.

4 Cook the macaroni in the boiling water until it is slightly underdone, about 6 minutes.

5 Melt the butter in a large skillet and sauté the onion for 5 minutes.

6 Drain the pasta, return it to the stockpot and toss it with the oil.

7 Add the zucchini to the onion and sauté for 5 minutes.

8 Stir the tomatoes, the parsley and the garlic into the skillet, season to taste and simmer, uncovered, for 5 minutes more. Stir in the ricotta, the milk and 3 tablespoons of the Parmesan cheese.

9 Combine the macaroni with the sauce and pour the mixture into the casserole. Sprinkle the top with the remaining Parmesan cheese.

10 Bake the macaroni until the top is lightly browned, about 20 minutes.

Yankee Doodle Salad

1 Bring water to a boil in a medium saucepan.

2 Trim and string the green beans and cut them into 1-inch pieces. Peel and slice the red onion. Chop the parsley.

3 Cook the beans in the boiling water until they are crisp-tender, 5 to 6 minutes.

4 In a medium bowl, whisk together the parsley, the oil, the vinegar, the lemon juice and the sugar. Season to taste.

5 Drain the beans and add them to the bowl. Add the pine nuts and the onion. Toss the mixture until well blended, and refrigerate until you are ready to serve.

6 Wash and dry the lettuce, and arrange the leaves on individual salad plates. Spoon the green bean mixture over the lettuce.

Secret Ingredient Biscuits

1 Preheat the oven to 350°F. Grease a cookie sheet.

2 Dust a pastry board with Bisquick. Melt the butter.

3 Combine the Bisquick and the buttermilk in a medium bowl. Fold in the coriander and the melted butter until a soft dough forms. Turn the dough out onto the pastry board and knead it gently 9 or 10 times. Pat the dough out into a ½-inch thickness, cut the biscuits with a floured biscuit cutter and place them on the cookie sheet.

4 Bake the biscuits until they are golden, 15 to 20 minutes.

Fab Fruit Creation

1 Peel and section the grapefruit. Drain the mandarin oranges. Distribute the fruit among individual dessert dishes and refrigerate until you are ready to serve.

2 Separate the eggs. Beat the whites in a medium bowl with the salt and the sugar until they are stiff, about 3 minutes. Refrigerate until you are ready to use.

3 Beat the yolks in a small saucepan. Add the honey and heat, whisking, until the mixture is warm, well blended, and slightly thickened, but not cooked, about 1 minute. Add the lemon peel to the yolk mixture and refrigerate until you are ready to use.

4 Fold the honey-yolk mixture into the egg whites, mix in the almond extract and spoon the sauce over the fruit.

FRIDAY

Fishing for Compliments

$^1/_4$ pound fresh tomatoes
1 medium onion
2 cloves garlic
3 tablespoons butter
$^1/_4$ cup dry white wine (or nonalcoholic white
    wine or clam juice)
Seasoning to taste
$^1/_2$ pound medium shrimp, shelled and
    deveined
$1^1/_2$ pounds bass fillets

Billy Buds

1 pound small new white potatoes
2 tablespoons butter
$^1/_2$ teaspoon dried rosemary
$^1/_2$ teaspoon dried sage
Seasoning to taste

Bell-Ringers

2 medium red bell peppers
2 medium green bell peppers
2 tablespoons fresh basil (when chopped)
1 tablespoon regular or light olive oil
1 tablespoon grated fresh lemon peel
2 teaspoons lemon juice
Seasoning to taste

Strawberry Discovery

1 pint fresh strawberries
$^1/_4$ cup Grand Marnier liqueur (or
    nonalcoholic Italian orange syrup)
$^1/_2$ cup orange juice
$^1/_2$ cup regular or light sour cream
1 teaspoon vanilla extract
4 tablespoons confectioners' sugar

EQUIPMENT

Large skillet	Shallow bowl
Medium skillet	Assorted kitchen knives
Large covered	Measuring cups and
saucepan	spoons
7x11-inch glass baking	Assorted cooking
dish	utensils
Large bowl	Whisk
Small bowl	Vegetable brush

COUNTDOWN

1 Assemble the ingredients and equipment
2 Do Step 1 of *Fishing for Compliments*
3 Do Steps 1–2 of the *Strawberry Discovery*
4 Do Step 1 of the *Billy Buds*
5 Do Steps 2–4 of *Fishing for Compliments*
6 Do Step 2 of the *Billy Buds*
7 Do Steps 1–2 of the *Bell–Ringers*
8 Do Step 3 of the *Strawberry Discovery*

Fishing for Compliments

1 Preheat the oven to 400°F.

2 Chop the tomatoes. Peel and chop the onion. Peel and mince the garlic.

3 Melt the butter in a medium skillet. Add the onion and the garlic, and sauté until limp, about 5 minutes. Add the tomatoes and the wine, and cook until hot. Season to taste.

4 Rinse the shrimp. Pat the bass fillets dry with paper towels and place the fillets, in a single layer, in a 7x11-inch glass baking dish. Top the fillets with the shrimp. Spoon the tomato mixture over the seafood, and bake until the shrimp turn pink and the bass is opaque but still moist in its thickest part, about 15 minutes.

Billy Buds

1 Scrub and quarter the potatoes. Place them in a large saucepan, cover them with water, bring them to a boil, reduce the heat, cover and cook until they are tender, about 10 minutes.

2 Drain the potatoes and return them to the saucepan. Toss with the butter, the rosemary and the sage. Season to taste and cover to keep warm.

Bell-Ringers

1 Seed the bell peppers and cut them into $1/4$-inch slices. Stem and chop the basil.

2 Heat the oil in a large skillet. Sauté the bell pepper slices with the basil and the lemon peel, tossing gently, until heated through, 3 to 5 minutes. Add the lemon juice and season to taste.

Strawberry Discovery

1 Wash and pat dry the strawberries. Reserve 4 berries with stems intact. Hull and slice the remaining berries and place them in a large bowl. Add the Grand Marnier and the orange juice and toss lightly. Cover and refrigerate until you are ready to use.

2 In a small bowl, whisk the sour cream with the vanilla and the confectioners' sugar until well blended. Cover and refrigerate until you are ready to use.

3 Drain the strawberries and spoon them into individual dessert dishes. Top each portion with a dollop of the sour cream mixture and garnish with a reserved berry.

MAY

WEEK FIVE

CHECK STAPLES

- ☐ Butter
- ☐ Flour
- ☐ Cornstarch
- ☐ Granulated sugar
- ☐ Dark brown sugar
- ☐ Chocolate syrup
- ☐ Long-grain white rice
- ☐ Regular or light vegetable oil
- ☐ Regular or light olive oil
- ☐ White wine vinegar
- ☐ Rice vinegar
- ☐ Apple cider vinegar
- ☐ Balsamic vinegar
- ☐ Lemon juice
- ☐ Lime juice
- ☐ Grated fresh lemon peel
- ☐ Tabasco sauce
- ☐ Dijon mustard
- ☐ Prepared horseradish
- ☐ Regular or low-fat mayonnaise
- ☐ Honey
- ☐ Grated Parmesan cheese
- ☐ Ground allspice
- ☐ Dried basil
- ☐ Celery seeds
- ☐ Ground cinnamon
- ☐ Ground cloves
- ☐ Dry mustard
- ☐ Ground nutmeg
- ☐ Dried rosemary
- ☐ Dried tarragon
- ☐ Pepper
- ☐ Salt
- ☐ Vanilla extract

SHOPPING NOTE

● If you are shopping once a week and cannot arrange to purchase fresh sole on the day you plan to use it, you can purchase *not previously frozen* sole and freeze it, placing it in the refrigerator to thaw the night before you are ready to use it. Or you can purchase *still frozen* sole and keep it frozen until the night before you are ready to use it.

MEAT & POULTRY

8 lean boneless veal slices (1 pound) (M)

1 pound lean cooked ham steak (W)

4 boneless, skinless chicken breast halves (Th)

FISH

1¼ pounds sole fillets (F)

FRESH PRODUCE

Vegetables

1 pound new red potatoes (F)

1 medium bunch broccoli (T)

1½ pounds asparagus (Th)

½ pound unshelled green peas (M)

2 stalks celery (W)

1 medium onion (W)

1 small onion (Th)

1 medium red onion (T)

1 small red onion (W)

10 scallions (green onions)— 4 (M), 6 (F)

1 head garlic (M, T, Th)

1 bunch parsley (M, T, Th)

1 small head red cabbage (F)

2 medium heads lettuce—1 (M), 1 (W)

1 medium head red leaf lettuce (T)

½ pound tomatoes (W)

1 medium cucumber (W)

1 small green bell pepper (W)

1 small bunch radishes (W)

Fruit

1 pound seedless red grapes (M)

1 pound pineapple chunks (or net weight canned) (W)

½ pint blueberries (F)

1 medium orange (F)

CANS, JARS & BOTTLES

Soup

1 can (10¾ ounces) beef broth (W, Th)

Vegetables

1 medium can (15 ounces) sliced beets (T)

1 small can (4 ounces) button mushrooms (M)

1 medium can (15½ ounces) butter beans (W)

2 medium cans (15½ ounces each) ranch-style (or plain) baked beans (W)

3 ounces sun-dried tomatoes (T)

Fruit

1 large can (29 ounces) sliced peaches in syrup (W)

Spreads

½ cup apricot preserves (W)

Dessert Needs

1 can (15¾ ounces) chocolate fudge pudding (T)

1 can (15¾ ounces) vanilla pudding (T)

PACKAGED GOODS

Pasta, Rice & Grains

8 ounces broad egg noodles (Th)

Nuts & Seeds

½ cup pine nuts (T)

½ cup chopped walnuts (F)

Dessert & Baking Needs

4 graham cracker tart shells (T)

1 angel food loaf cake (F)

¼ pound peanut brittle (Th)

½ cup flaked coconut (F)

WINES & SPIRITS

½ cup dry sherry (or nonalcoholic red wine or beef broth) (M)

1 tablespoon creme de cacao liqueur (or nonalcoholic Italian chocolate syrup) (T)

3 tablespoons marsala wine (or nonalcoholic red wine + 1 teaspoon sugar or omit) (Th)

REFRIGERATED PRODUCTS

Dairy

2 cups whole or low-fat milk (M)

½ cup + 3 tablespoons whipping cream—½ cup (Th), 3 tablespoons (F)

⅔ cup regular or light sour cream—⅓ cup (T), ⅓ cup (W)

¼ cup regular or low-fat plain yogurt (T)

4 eggs—2 (M, W), 2 (Th)

Juice

¼ cup orange juice (F)

Deli

12 ounces cheese ravioli (or frozen) (T)

8 thin slices prosciutto ham (M)

FROZEN GOODS

Vegetables

1 package (9 ounces) chopped spinach (M)

Desserts

1 pint butterscotch swirl (or similar) ice cream (Th)

MONDAY

Ferris Veal

1 clove garlic
3 tablespoons fresh parsley (when chopped)
$1/2$ teaspoon dried rosemary
Seasoning to taste
8 lean boneless veal slices (1 pound)
8 thin slices lean prosciutto ham
4 tablespoons regular or light olive oil
$1/2$ cup dry sherry (or nonalcoholic red wine or beef broth)
1 small can (4 ounces) button mushrooms

Merry-Go-Rice

1 cup long–grain white rice
2 cups water
1 package (9 ounces) frozen chopped spinach
$1/2$ cup butter
$1/2$ cup grated Parmesan cheese
$1/4$ teaspoon ground nutmeg

Trapeas Salad

1 medium head lettuce
4 scallions (green onions)
$1/2$ pound unshelled green peas
2 tablespoons balsamic vinegar
3 tablespoons regular or light olive oil
1 teaspoon Dijon mustard
Seasoning to taste

Bake-Off Parfait

1 pound seedless red grapes
2 eggs yolks*
$1/3$ cup sugar
2 tablespoons cornstarch
$1/8$ teaspoon salt
2 cups whole or low-fat milk
$1^1/2$ teaspoons vanilla extract
2 tablespoons butter
$1/2$ teaspoon ground cinnamon

EQUIPMENT

Large covered skillet	Assorted kitchen knives
2 medium saucepans	Measuring cups and
Double boiler	spoons
2 large bowls	Assorted cooking
3 small bowls	utensils
Strainer	Whisk

COUNTDOWN

1 Assemble the ingredients and equipment
2 Do Step 1 of the *Merry-Go-Rice*
3 Do Steps 1–3 of the *Bake-Off Parfait*
4 Do Steps 1–3 of the *Ferris Veal*
5 Do Steps 1–2 of the *Trapeas Salad*
6 Do Steps 2–3 of the *Merry-Go-Rice*
7 Do Step 3 of the *Trapeas Salad*
8 Do Step 4 of the *Bake-Off Parfait*

*Reserve the egg whites for use on Wednesday.

Ferris Veal

1 Peel and chop the garlic. Chop the parsley.

2 In a small bowl, combine the garlic, the parsley and the rosemary, and season to taste. Spread the mixture over the veal slices. Top each slice with a slice of prosciutto. Roll the veal slices up tightly and fasten them with toothpicks, if necessary.

3 Heat the oil in a large skillet. Brown the veal rolls quickly on both sides, about 5 minutes. Drain off any fat. Add the sherry, reduce the heat and simmer until the alcohol has evaporated, 2 to 3 minutes. Add the mushrooms and their liquid and simmer, covered, until the veal is tender, 15 to 20 minutes.

Merry-Go-Rice

1 Place the rice and the water in the top of a double boiler. Bring water to a boil in the bottom of the double boiler. Reduce the heat, cover and simmer until all the liquid is absorbed and the rice is tender, 30 to 40 minutes.

2 Bring ½-inch of water to a boil in a medium saucepan. Cook the spinach for a scant 5 minutes.

3 Drain the spinach. Melt the butter in the saucepan and return the spinach. Add the cooked rice. Stir in the cheese until it is well blended and sprinkle with the nutmeg.

Trapeas Salad

1 Wash and dry the lettuce. Reserve 4 leaves and tear the remaining leaves into bite-size pieces. Trim and slice the scallions. Shell the peas. Combine the ingredients in a large bowl.

2 In a small bowl, whisk together the vinegar, the oil and the mustard, and season to taste.

3 Place the reserved lettuce leaves on individual salad plates. Toss the pea mixture with the dressing and spoon it over the lettuce.

Bake-Off Parfait

1 Wash, dry and halve the grapes. In a small bowl, lightly beat the egg yolks.

2 Combine the sugar, the cornstarch and the salt in a medium saucepan. Gradually add the milk and blend well. Bring the mixture to a boil, stirring, and cook for 1 minute. Remove the saucepan from the heat. Stir half of the hot sauce into the egg yolks. Return the mixture to the saucepan and cook for 30 seconds more. Remove the saucepan from the heat, stir in the vanilla and the butter, and mix until the butter melts and the pudding is well blended.

3 Layer spoonfuls of grapes and pudding into individual dessert dishes. Refrigerate for at least 20 minutes.

4 Dust the pudding with the cinnamon.

TUESDAY

Nuts About Ravioli

12 ounces cheese ravioli (fresh or frozen)
3 cloves garlic
$1/4$ cup fresh parsley (when chopped)
3 ounces sun-dried tomatoes
4 tablespoons regular or light olive oil
$1/2$ cup pine nuts
$3/4$ teaspoon dried basil
Seasoning to taste
$1/4$ cup grated Parmesan cheese

Broccoli with a Kick

1 medium bunch broccoli
$1/4$ cup regular or low-fat mayonnaise
$1/4$ cup regular or low-fat plain yogurt
$1/4$ cup lime juice
$1/2$ teaspoon prepared horseradish
$1/2$ teaspoon Dijon mustard
Seasoning to taste

Red Red Salad

1 medium can (15 ounces) sliced beets
1 medium red onion
1 medium head red leaf lettuce
2 tablespoons rice vinegar
3 tablespoons regular or light vegetable oil
$1/4$ teaspoon dried tarragon
1 teaspoon grated fresh lemon peel
Seasoning to taste

Black-Bottom Tarts

1 can ($15^3/4$ ounces) chocolate fudge pudding
1 tablespoon crème de cacao liqueur (or
    nonalcoholic Italian chocolate syrup)
4 individual graham cracker tart shells
1 can ($15^3/4$ ounces) prepared vanilla pudding
$1/3$ cup regular or light sour cream
4 tablespoons chocolate syrup

EQUIPMENT

Stockpot	Assorted kitchen knives
Medium covered skillet	Measuring cups and
Medium saucepan	spoons
Small saucepan	Assorted cooking
Vegetable steamer	utensils
2 small bowls	Whisk
Colander	

COUNTDOWN

1 Assemble the ingredients and equipment
2 Do Step 1 of *Nuts About Ravioli*
3 Do Steps 1–3 of the *Black-Bottom Tarts*
4 Do Steps 1–3 of the *Red Red Salad*
5 Do Step 2 of *Nuts About Ravioli*
6 Do Steps 1–3 of the *Broccoli with a Kick*
7 Do Steps 3–4 of *Nuts About Ravioli*
8 Do Step 4 of the *Red Red Salad*
9 Do Step 4 of the *Broccoli with a Kick*

Nuts About Ravioli

1 Bring water to a boil in a stockpot.

2 Cook the ravioli in the boiling water until it is almost tender, about 10 minutes.

3 Peel and mince the garlic. Chop the parsley. Chop the tomatoes. Heat the oil in a medium skillet. Add the garlic and sauté for 2 minutes. Add the pine nuts and sauté for 1 minute more. Stir in the parsley, the tomatoes and the basil. Season to taste, cover the skillet and remove it from the heat.

4 Drain the ravioli and return it to the stockpot. Toss the pasta with the sauce and sprinkle with the cheese. Cover to keep warm.

Broccoli with a Kick

1 Cut the broccoli into spears.

2 Bring a small amount of water to a boil in a medium saucepan. Place the broccoli in a vegetable steamer over the boiling water and steam until the spears are barely tender, about 5 minutes.

3 Combine the mayonnaise, the yogurt, the lime juice, the horseradish and the mustard in a small saucepan. Heat through. Season to taste.

4 Drain the broccoli and top it with the sauce.

Red Red Salad

1 Drain the beets. Peel and thinly slice the red onion. Wash and dry the lettuce.

2 Distribute the lettuce leaves among individual salad plates. Arrange the beets and the onion over the lettuce.

3 In a small bowl, whisk together the vinegar, the oil, the tarragon and the lemon peel. Season to taste.

4 Drizzle the dressing over the salad.

Black-Bottom Tarts

1 In a small bowl, blend the chocolate fudge pudding with the creme de cacao. Spoon the mixture into the prepared tart shells.

2 In the same bowl, blend the vanilla pudding with the sour cream, and spoon it over the chocolate mixture.

3 Drizzle the chocolate syrup over each tart and refrigerate for at least 20 minutes.

WEDNESDAY

Texas Bean Bake

1 medium onion
1 pound lean cooked ham steak
1 medium can (15$^1/_2$ ounces) butter beans
1 pound fresh (or net weight canned)
    pineapple chunks
2 medium cans (15$^1/_2$ ounces each) ranch–
    style (or plain) baked beans
$^2/_3$ cup beef broth*
1 tablespoon white wine vinegar
$^1/_4$ teaspoon dry mustard
Seasoning to taste

El Paso Salad

1 small red onion
1 small bunch radishes
1 medium cucumber
$^1/_2$ pound fresh tomatoes
1 small green bell pepper
2 stalks celery
1 medium head lettuce
$^1/_3$ cup regular or light sour cream
1 tablespoon lemon juice
$^1/_2$ teaspoon Dijon mustard
1 teaspoon honey
Seasoning to taste

Spiced Peaches

1 large can (29 ounces) sliced peaches in syrup
1 tablespoon lemon juice
$^1/_2$ teaspoon ground cloves
$^1/_2$ teaspoon ground cinnamon
$^1/_2$ teaspoon ground nutmeg

*Reserve the balance of the can for use on Thursday.

Apricot Alamo

$^1/_2$ cup apricot preserves
2 teaspoons lemon juice
2 egg whites reserved from Monday
$^1/_8$ teaspoon salt
2 tablespoons sugar
$^1/_2$ teaspoon cornstarch

EQUIPMENT

Electric hand mixer	Small bowl
Medium covered saucepan	Assorted kitchen knives
Small saucepan	Measuring cups and spoons
2-quart casserole	Assorted cooking utensils
1-quart broiler-proof casserole	Whisk
Large bowl	Vegetable peeler
Medium bowl	

COUNTDOWN

1 Assemble the ingredients and equipment
2 Do Steps 1–4 of the *Texas Bean Bake*
3 Do Step 1 of the *El Paso Salad*
4 Do Steps 1–3 of the *Apricot Alamo*
5 Do Steps 1–2 of the *Spiced Peaches*
6 Do Step 2 of the *El Paso Salad*
7 Do Step 4 of the *Apricot Alamo*

Texas Bean Bake

1 Preheat the oven to 375°F.

2 Peel and chop the onion. Cube the ham.

3 Drain the butter beans. In a 2-quart casserole, combine the onion, the pineapple chunks, the ham, the butter beans, the undrained baked beans, the broth, the vinegar and the mustard. Season to taste. Mix thoroughly.

4 Bake, uncovered, until the mixture is hot and bubbly, about 35 minutes.

El Paso Salad

1 Peel and thinly slice the red onion. Trim and slice the radishes. Peel and slice the cucumber. Chop the tomatoes. Seed and chop the bell pepper. Trim and slice the celery. Wash and dry the lettuce and tear it into bite-size pieces. Combine the ingredients in a large bowl.

2 In a small bowl, whisk together the sour cream, the lemon juice, the mustard and the honey until well blended. Season to taste. Toss the salad with the dressing.

Spiced Peaches

1 Place the undrained peaches in a medium saucepan.

2 Add the lemon juice, the cloves, the cinnamon and the nutmeg. Bring the mixture just to a boil, then remove it from the heat and cover to keep warm.

Apricot Alamo

1 Butter and flour a 1-quart broiler-proof casserole and refrigerate it until you are ready to use.

2 Melt the preserves in a small saucepan. Stir in the lemon juice and remove the saucepan from the heat.

3 Beat the egg whites with the salt in a medium bowl until foamy, about 2 minutes. Add the sugar and the cornstarch, and continue beating until the whites are stiff and glossy, about 2 minutes more. Fold in the preserves and pour the mixture into the casserole. Preheat the oven to 350°F.

4 Just before sitting down to dinner, bake the Apricot Alamo until it is golden on top, about 15 minutes. Serve warm.

THURSDAY

Chicken Marsala

4 boneless, skinless chicken breast halves
1 small onion
2 cloves garlic
$1/2$ pound fresh mushrooms
2 eggs
3 tablespoons flour
Seasoning to taste
4 tablespoons butter
1 tablespoon regular or light vegetable oil
3 tablespoons marsala wine (or nonalcoholic
    red wine + 1 teaspoon sugar or omit)
$2/3$ cup beef broth reserved from Wednesday

Buttered-up Noodles

1 tablespoon fresh parsley (when chopped)
8 ounces broad egg noodles
2 tablespoons butter

Allspice Asparagus

$1^1/2$ pounds fresh asparagus
1 tablespoon butter
$1/2$ teaspoon ground allspice
Seasoning to taste

Butterscotch Crumbles

$1/4$ pound peanut brittle
2 tablespoons butter
$1/2$ cup whipping cream
$2/3$ cup dark brown sugar
1 teaspoon vanilla extract
1 pint butterscotch swirl (or similar) ice
    cream

EQUIPMENT

2 large covered skillets	Assorted cooking
Large covered	utensils
saucepan	Whisk
Small saucepan	Waxed paper
2 shallow bowls	Mallet
Colander	Ice cream scoop
Assorted kitchen knives	
Measuring cups and	
spoons	

COUNTDOWN

1 Assemble the ingredients and equipment
2 Do Step 1 of the *Buttered-up Noodles*
3 Do Steps 1–2 of the *Butterscotch Crumbles*
4 Do Steps 1–5 of the *Chicken Marsala*
5 Do Step 2 of the *Buttered-up Noodles*
6 Do Steps 1–2 of the *Allspice Asparagus*
7 Do Step 3 of the *Buttered-up Noodles*
8 Do Step 6 of the *Chicken Marsala*
9 Do Step 3 of the *Allspice Asparagus*
10 Do Step 3 of the *Butterscotch Crumbles*

Chicken Marsala

1 Place the chicken breasts between sheets of waxed paper and pound them with a mallet from the center out to a $1/2$-inch thickness.

2 Peel and chop the onion. Peel and chop the garlic. Wash, pat dry and slice the mushrooms.

3 Lightly beat the eggs in a shallow bowl. Put the flour in another shallow bowl and season to taste. Dip the chicken breasts in the egg, then dredge them in the flour, shaking off any excess.

4 Melt 2 tablespoons of the butter with the oil in a large skillet. Cook the chicken until it is lightly browned, about 4 minutes per side. Remove the chicken and keep it warm.

5 Add the onion and the garlic to the skillet and sauté until the onion is soft, about 5 minutes. Add the mushrooms and sauté until they are lightly browned, 3 to 5 minutes. Return the chicken to the skillet and stir in the marsala and the beef broth. Bring the mixture to a boil, reduce the heat and cook until the liquid reduces by one-third, about 4 minutes.

6 Whisk the remaining butter into the marsala mixture until well blended.

Buttered-up Noodles

1 Bring water to a boil in a large saucepan. Chop the parsley.

2 Cook the noodles in the boiling water until they are almost tender, 3 to 5 minutes.

3 Drain the noodles, return them to the saucepan and toss them with the butter and the parsley. Cover to keep warm.

Allspice Asparagus

1 Bring a small amount of water to a boil in a large skillet.

2 Remove the tough ends from the asparagus. Place the spears in the boiling water, cover and steam until crisp-tender, 3 to 8 minutes, depending on thickness.

3 Drain the asparagus, return it to the skillet and toss it with the butter and the allspice. Season to taste.

Butterscotch Crumbles

1 Crumble the peanut brittle.

2 Melt the butter in a small saucepan. Stir in the cream and the brown sugar. Bring the mixture almost to a boil, reduce the heat and simmer, stirring occasionally, until the sauce thickens, 3 to 4 minutes. Remove the saucepan from the heat and stir in the vanilla. Let the sauce cool.

3 Top scoops of ice cream with the sauce and sprinkle with the crumbled peanut brittle.

FRIDAY

Body & Sole

1¹/₄ pounds sole fillets
Seasoning to taste
¹/₄ cup orange juice
¹/₄ cup lime juice
1 medium orange
1 teaspoon cornstarch dissolved in 2
    tablespoons cold water

Laid-Back Potatoes

6 scallion greens
2 tablespoons regular or light vegetable oil
1 pound new red potatoes
¹/₂ teaspoon dried rosemary
Seasoning to taste

Slow-Down Slaw

2 tablespoons sugar
3 tablespoons apple cider vinegar
3 tablespoons regular or light vegetable oil
¹/₂ teaspoon celery seeds
¹/₄ teaspoon Tabasco sauce
Seasoning to taste
¹/₂ pint fresh blueberries
1 small head red cabbage
6 scallion whites

Memorable Cake

1 angel food loaf cake
2 tablespoons butter
¹/₂ cup flaked coconut
¹/₂ cup chopped walnuts
¹/₃ cup dark brown sugar
3 tablespoons whipping cream

EQUIPMENT

Large covered skillet	Assorted cooking
2 small saucepans	utensils
9x13-inch glass baking	Whisk
dish	Vegetable brush
Cookie sheet	Vegetable grater
Large bowl	Aluminum foil
Assorted kitchen knives	
Measuring cups and	
spoons	

COUNTDOWN

1 Assemble the ingredients and equipment
2 Do Step 1 of the *Body & Sole*
3 Do Steps 1–2 of the *Slow-Down Slaw*
4 Do Step 1 of the *Laid-Back Potatoes*
5 Do Step 2 of the *Body & Sole*
6 Do Step 2 of the *Laid-Back Potatoes*
7 Do Steps 3–4 of the *Body & Sole*
8 Do Steps 1–2 of the *Memorable Cake*
9 Do Step 5 of the *Body & Sole*
10 Do Step 3 of the *Memorable Cake*
11 Do Step 3 of the *Laid-Back Potatoes*
12 Do Step 3 of the *Slow-Down Slaw*
13 Do Step 6 of the *Body & Sole*

Body & Sole

1 Arrange the fish in a 9x13-inch glass baking dish in a single layer. Season to taste. Add the orange and the lime juices. Cover the dish and refrigerate it for 20 minutes.

2 Preheat the oven to 425°F.

3 Remove the fish from the refrigerator, cover the dish tightly with aluminum foil and bake until the fish is firm and opaque, 8 to 10 minutes.

4 Peel and section the orange.

5 Remove the fish from the oven.

6 Pour the cooking liquid from the fish into a small saucepan. Add the cornstarch mixture to the saucepan and bring it to a boil, stirring until it thickens, about 1 minute. Spoon the sauce over the fish and garnish with the orange sections.

Laid-Back Potatoes

1 Chop the scallion greens.

2 Heat the oil in a large skillet. Wash, dry and thinly slice, but do not peel, the potatoes. Sauté them in the oil until they are golden, about 15 minutes.

3 Add the scallion greens and the rosemary to the potatoes, season to taste and cook for 2 minutes more. Remove the skillet from the heat and cover to keep warm.

Slow-Down Slaw

1 In a large bowl, whisk together the sugar, the vinegar, the oil, the celery seeds and the Tabasco sauce. Season to taste.

2 Rinse and dry the blueberries. Grate the cabbage. Trim and chop the scallion whites. Add the cabbage and the scallion whites to the large bowl and toss with the dressing. Cover the bowl and refrigerate until you are ready to serve.

3 Sprinkle the blueberries over the slaw.

Memorable Cake

1 Set the angel food cake on a cookie sheet.

2 Melt the butter in a small saucepan. Stir in the coconut, the walnuts, the brown sugar and the cream. Spread the mixture over the cake.

3 Preheat the broiler. Place the cake under the broiler, 4 or 5 inches from the heat, and broil until the topping begins to bubble, 3 to 4 minutes.

JUNE
WEEK ONE

WEEK AT A GLANCE

Monday

SUPER SPANISH RICE
SEVILLE SALAD
ICE CREAM BOLERO

Tuesday

SALMON-CHANTED EVENING
AH SOBA
HAPPY SLAW
HONEY BUN CAKE

Wednesday

RAT-A-TATOUILLE
ALPHABETS YOU BET
QUICKIE CRESCENTS
NO-SKID BANANA PUDDING

Thursday

CONTEMPORARY CHICKEN
CLASSIC SALAD
CARAMEL CLOUD

Friday

TRAFFIC-STOPPING SHRIMP
GREEN LIGHT RICE
MISDEMEANOR SALAD
DOUBLE-TROUBLE CHOCOLATE

CHECK STAPLES

- ☐ Butter
- ☐ Granulated sugar
- ☐ Dark brown sugar
- ☐ Confectioners' sugar
- ☐ Chocolate syrup
- ☐ Long-grain white rice
- ☐ Regular or light vegetable oil
- ☐ Regular or light olive oil
- ☐ Sesame oil
- ☐ Red wine vinegar
- ☐ White wine vinegar
- ☐ Balsamic vinegar
- ☐ Rice vinegar
- ☐ Lemon juice
- ☐ Grated fresh lemon peel
- ☐ Soy sauce
- ☐ Dijon mustard
- ☐ Honey
- ☐ Dried basil
- ☐ Ground cumin
- ☐ Garlic powder
- ☐ Sesame seeds
- ☐ Pepper
- ☐ Salt
- ☐ Vanilla extract

SHOPPING NOTE

● If you are shopping once a week and cannot arrange to purchase fresh seafood on the day you plan to use it, you can purchase *not previously frozen* seafood and freeze it, placing it in the refrigerator to thaw the night before you are ready to use it. Or you can purchase *still frozen* seafood and keep it frozen until the night before you are ready to use it.

MEAT & POULTRY

1 pound lean ground beef (M)
4 boneless, skinless chicken
  breast halves (Th)

FISH

4 salmon fillets (1¼ pounds) (T)
1 pound medium shrimp,
  shelled and deveined (F)

FRESH PRODUCE

Vegetables

1 pound small new red
  potatoes (Th)
1 pound eggplant (W)
6 medium zucchini (W)
1½ pounds green beans (F)
20 Chinese snow peas (T)
4 medium mushrooms (T)
5 medium carrots (Th)
2 stalks celery (T)
3 medium onions—1 (M), 2 (W)
1 medium sweet onion (M)
1 small red onion (Th)
2 medium leeks (Th)
3 medium shallots (Th)
8 scallions (green onions)—
  6 (T), 2 (F)
1 head garlic (M–F)
1 bunch parsley (W, F)
1 bunch chives (W, F)
¼ pound bean sprouts (T)
1 small head Napa cabbage (T)
3 medium heads lettuce—1 (M),
  1 (Th), 1 (F)
1 small bunch watercress (M)
½ pound tomatoes (Th)
2 medium cucumbers—
  1 (Th), 1 (F)
1 medium green bell pepper (W)
1 medium red bell pepper (W)
1 small green bell pepper (M)
1 small red bell pepper (Th)

Fruit

2 medium bananas (W)
1 small orange (M)

CANS, JARS & BOTTLES

Soup

1 can (10¾ ounces) beef
  broth (M, Th)

Vegetables

2 large cans (28 ounces each)
  cut-up tomatoes—1 (M),
  1 (F)
1 medium can (14½ ounces)
  cut-up tomatoes (W)
2 small cans (6 ounces each)
  tomato paste—1 (M), 1 (W, F)

Mexican Foods

¼ cup diced green chilies (M)

Oriental Foods

1 can (8 ounces) sliced water
  chestnuts (T)
8 ounces Japanese soba
  noodles (T)

Fruit

1 can (11 ounces) mandarin
  oranges (T)

Condiments

1 small can (3½ ounces) pitted
  black olives (M)
4 maraschino cherries for
  garnish (F)

PACKAGED GOODS

Pasta, Rice & Grains

8 ounces alphabet pasta (W)

Nuts & Seeds

¼ cup pecan pieces (M)
¼ cup sliced almonds (W)

Dessert & Baking Needs

1 small package (3.4 ounces)
  instant banana cream
  pudding mix (W)
1 envelope unflavored
  gelatin (Th)
16 Oreo cookies (F)

WINES & SPIRITS

2 tablespoons dry white wine
  (or nonalcoholic white wine
  or clam juice) (F)
2 tablespoons dry sherry (or
  nonalcoholic red wine or
  soy sauce) (T)

REFRIGERATED PRODUCTS

Dairy

2 cups whole milk (W)
¾ cup + 3 tablespoons
  whipping cream —¾ cup
  (M), 3 tablespoons (T)
Whipped cream for garnish
  (Th, F)
6 eggs—5 (Th), 1 (F)

Cheese

1 cup shredded regular or low-
  fat cheddar cheese (W)
1 container (4 ounces) whipped
  cream cheese with garlic
  and herbs (W)

Deli

1 package (8) refrigerator
  crescent rolls (W)

FROZEN GOODS

Desserts

1 frozen pound cake (T)
1 medium container (12
  ounces) frozen whipped
  topping (Th)
1 pint butterscotch swirl (or
  similar) ice cream (M)
1 pint chocolate chip ice
  cream (F)

MONDAY

Super Spanish Rice

1 medium onion
1 small green bell pepper
1 pound lean ground beef
1 cup long-grain white rice
1 large can (28 ounces) cut-up tomatoes
1 small can (6 ounces) tomato paste
$^3/_4$ cup beef broth*
$^1/_4$ cup water
2 teaspoons ground cumin
$^1/_4$ cup canned diced green chilies
Seasoning to taste

Seville Salad

1 medium head lettuce
1 small bunch watercress
1 medium sweet onion
1 small orange
1 small can (3$^1/_2$ ounces) pitted black olives
1 clove garlic
3 tablespoons regular or light vegetable oil
2 tablespoons red wine vinegar
1 tablespoon lemon juice
$^1/_2$ teaspoon sugar
$^1/_2$ teaspoon Dijon mustard
Seasoning to taste

Ice Cream Bolero

3 tablespoons butter
$^3/_4$ cup whipping cream
1 cup dark brown sugar
1 teaspoon vanilla extract
1 pint butterscotch swirl (or similar) ice
    cream
$^1/_4$ cup pecan pieces

*Reserve the remainder of the can for use on Thursday.

EQUIPMENT

Large covered skillet	Assorted cooking
Medium saucepan	utensils
Large bowl	Whisk
Small bowl	Ice cream scoop
Assorted kitchen knives	
Measuring cups and	
spoons	

COUNTDOWN

1 Assemble the ingredients and equipment
2 Do Steps 1–2 of the *Super Spanish Rice*
3 Do Step 1 of the *Ice Cream Bolero*
4 Do Step 3 of the *Super Spanish Rice*
5 Do Steps 1–2 of the *Seville Salad*
6 Do Step 2 of the *Ice Cream Bolero*

Super Spanish Rice

1 Peel and chop the onion. Seed and chop the bell pepper.

2 In a large skillet, cook the beef, the onion and the bell pepper, stirring often, until the beef is browned, 8 to 10 minutes.

3 Drain off any fat. Stir in the rice, the undrained tomatoes, the tomato paste, the broth, the water, the cumin and the chilies. Season to taste. Bring the mixture to a boil, stirring occasionally. Reduce the heat, cover and simmer until the rice is tender, 30 to 35 minutes.

Seville Salad

1 Wash and dry the lettuce and tear it into bite-size pieces. Wash, dry and stem the watercress. Peel and thinly slice the sweet onion. Peel and section the orange. Drain the olives. Combine the ingredients in a large bowl.

2. Peel and mince the garlic. In a small bowl, whisk together the garlic, the oil, the vinegar, the lemon juice, the sugar and the mustard. Season to taste. Toss the dressing with the salad.

Ice Cream Bolero

1 Melt the butter in a medium saucepan. Add the cream and the brown sugar, and heat to boiling, stirring frequently. Reduce the heat and cook until the mixture is thickened, 3 to 4 minutes. Remove the saucepan from the heat and let the mixture cool.

2 Whisk the vanilla into the cooled cream mixture and pour it over scoops of ice cream. Top with the pecan pieces.

TUESDAY

Salmon-Chanted Evening

4 teaspoons sesame seeds
20 Chinese snow peas
4 salmon fillets (1¼ pounds)
Seasoning to taste
4 tablespoons regular or light vegetable oil
2 tablespoons soy sauce
2 tablespoons dry sherry (or nonalcoholic red wine or additional soy sauce)

Ah Soba

2 scallions (green onions)
8 ounces Japanese soba noodles
⅛ teaspoon sesame oil
Seasoning to taste

Happy Slaw

1 clove garlic
1 teaspoon sesame oil
3 tablespoons regular or light olive oil
2 teaspoons Dijon mustard
3 tablespoons rice vinegar
Seasoning to taste
4 scallions (green onions)
2 stalks celery
4 medium mushrooms
1 small head Napa cabbage
¼ pound fresh bean sprouts
1 can (8 ounces) sliced water chestnuts

Honey Bun Cake

1 frozen pound cake
1 can (11 ounces) mandarin oranges
½ cup confectioners' sugar
2 tablespoons honey
3 tablespoons whipping cream
⅛ teaspoon salt

EQUIPMENT

Large covered saucepan
Cookie sheet
Large bowl
Small bowl
Colander
Assorted kitchen knives
Measuring cups and spoons
Assorted cooking utensils
Whisk
Aluminum foil

COUNTDOWN

IN THE MORNING:
  Do Step 1 of the *Honey Bun Cake*
BEFORE DINNER:
  1 Assemble the remaining ingredients and equipment
  2 Do Steps 2–3 of the *Honey Bun Cake*
  3 Do Step 1 of the *Salmon-Chanted Evening*
  4 Do Step 1 of the *Ah Soba*
  5 Do Steps 1–2 of the *Happy Slaw*
  6 Do Step 2 of the *Ah Soba*
  7 Do Steps 2–6 of the *Salmon-Chanted Evening*
  8 Do Steps 3–4 of the *Ah Soba*
  9 Do Step 4 of the *Honey Bun Cake*

Salmon-Chanted Evening

1 Preheat the broiler.

2 Spread the sesame seeds on a cookie sheet. Place the cookie sheet under the broiler until lightly toasted, about 5 minutes.

3 Set the oven temperature to 425°F.

4 Stem and string the snow peas and cut them lengthwise into thin strips.

5 Tear off 4 sheets of aluminum foil, each about 12x15 inches. Lay each fillet flat on half of one sheet. Season to taste. Distribute the snow peas equally among the fillets and drizzle them with the oil, the soy sauce and the sherry. Sprinkle the fillets with the toasted sesame seeds.

6 Fold the top of the foil over the bottom, crimping all the edges tightly to seal. Arrange the fish packets in a single layer on the cookie sheet and bake until the foil is puffed and the fish is cooked through, 10 to 12 minutes.

Ah Soba

1 Chop the scallions.

2 Bring water to a boil in a large saucepan.

3 Cook the soba noodles until they are tender, about 1 minute, stirring to keep them from sticking. Be careful not to overcook them.

4 Drain the noodles, return them to the saucepan and toss them with the scallions and the sesame oil. Season to taste and cover to keep warm.

Happy Slaw

1 Peel and mince the garlic. In a large bowl, whisk together the garlic, both oils, the mustard and the vinegar. Season to taste.

2 Trim and chop the scallions. Trim and slice the celery diagonally. Trim and slice the mushrooms. Chop the cabbage. Rinse the bean sprouts. Drain the water chestnuts. Add the ingredients to the large bowl and toss with the dressing to combine. Refrigerate until you are ready to serve.

Honey Bun Cake

1 Set the pound cake out to thaw.

2 Drain the mandarin oranges.

3 In a small bowl, whisk together the confectioners' sugar, the honey, the cream and the salt until a glaze is formed. Set aside.

4 Drizzle the mixture over the cake and top with the oranges.

WEDNESDAY

Rat-a-Tatouille

2 medium onions
2 cloves garlic
1 pound eggplant
1 medium green bell pepper
1 medium red bell pepper
6 medium zucchini
$1/2$ cup fresh parsley (when chopped)
3 tablespoons regular or light olive oil
1 medium can ($14^1/2$ ounces) cut-up tomatoes
2 teaspoons dried basil
Seasoning to taste
$1/2$ small can (6 ounces) tomato paste*
1 cup shredded regular or low-fat cheddar
    cheese

Alphabets You Bet

$1/4$ cup fresh chives (when chopped)
8 ounces alphabet pasta
2 tablespoons butter
Seasoning to taste

Quickie Crescents

1 tablespoon fresh parsley (when minced)
1 tablespoon softened butter
1 container (4 ounces) whipped cream cheese
    with garlic and herbs
1 package (8) refrigerator crescent rolls

No-Skid Banana Pudding

1 small package (3.4 ounces) instant banana
    cream pudding mix
2 cups whole milk
2 medium bananas
$1/4$ cup sliced almonds

EQUIPMENT

Electric hand mixer	Strainer
Dutch oven	Assorted kitchen knives
Large covered	Measuring cups and
saucepan	spoons
Cookie sheet	Assorted cooking
Medium bowl	utensils
Small bowl	

COUNTDOWN

1 Assemble the ingredients and equipment
2 Do Step 1 of the *No-Skid Banana Pudding*
3 Do Steps 1–3 of the *Rat-a-Tatouille*
4 Do Steps 1–2 of the *Alphabets You Bet*
5 Do Steps 1–3 of the *Quickie Crescents*
6 Do Step 4 of the *Rat-a-Tatouille*
7 Do Steps 3–4 of the *Alphabets You Bet*
8 Do Step 5 of the *Rat-a-Tatouille*
9 Do Step 2 of the *No-Skid Banana Pudding*

---

*Reserve the remainder of the can for use on Friday.

Rat-a-Tatouille

1 Peel and chop the onions. Peel and crush the garlic. Wash, dry and chop the eggplant. Trim, seed and chop the bell peppers. Wash and slice the zucchini. Chop the parsley.

2 Heat the oil in a Dutch oven until it is hot but not smoking. Add the onions, the garlic, the eggplant and the peppers and cook, stirring often, until the onions are crisp-tender, about 5 minutes.

3 Stir the zucchini, the undrained tomatoes, the parsley and the basil into the Dutch oven. Bring the mixture to a boil, reduce the heat, cover and cook for 15 minutes.

4 Remove the cover from the Dutch oven and season to taste. Continue cooking, uncovered, for 10 minutes more.

5 Stir the tomato paste into the ratatouille. Top each serving with a sprinkling of the shredded cheese.

Alphabets You Bet

1 Chop the chives.

2 Bring water to a boil in a large saucepan.

3 Cook the alphabets until they are almost tender, 3 to 5 minutes.

4 Drain the pasta and return it to the saucepan. Toss it with the butter and the chives, season to taste and cover to keep warm.

Quickie Crescents

1 Preheat the oven to 375°F.

2 Mince the parsley. Blend the softened butter with the cream cheese and the parsley.

3 Separate the crescent rolls and open them into triangles. Spread the insides with the cheese mixture. Roll the rolls back up, place them on an ungreased cookie sheet, seam side down, and bake until they are golden, 10 to 12 minutes.

No-Skid Banana Pudding

1 In a medium bowl, combine the pudding mix and the milk and beat until well blended. Refrigerate for at least 20 minutes.

2 Peel and slice the bananas. Place half the banana slices in the bottom of individual dessert dishes. Cover with the pudding. Top with the remaining banana slices and sprinkle with the sliced almonds.

THURSDAY

Contemporary Chicken

1 pound small new red potatoes
3 medium shallots
2 medium leeks
5 medium carrots
1 small red bell pepper
1 tablespoon butter
4 boneless, skinless chicken breast halves
¹/₂ cup beef broth reserved from Monday
¹/₄ teaspoon garlic powder
¹/₄ cup balsamic vinegar
Seasoning to taste

Classic Salad

1 medium head lettuce
1 small red onion
¹/₂ pound fresh tomatoes
1 medium cucumber
1 clove garlic
3 tablespoons regular or light olive oil
2 tablespoons red wine vinegar
¹/₂ teaspoon sugar
¹/₂ teaspoon dried basil
Seasoning to taste

Caramel Cloud

5 eggs
11 tablespoons sugar
6 tablespoons water
1 envelope unflavored gelatin dissolved in
    3 tablespoons cold water
1 teaspoon vanilla extract
1 medium container (12 ounces) frozen
    whipped topping
Whipped cream for garnish

EQUIPMENT

Electric hand mixer	Measuring cups and
Large covered skillet	spoons
Medium saucepan	Assorted cooking
Large bowl	utensils
Medium bowl	Whisk
Small bowl	Vegetable peeler
Assorted kitchen knives	Vegetable brush

COUNTDOWN

1 Assemble the ingredients and equipment
2 Do Steps 1–2 of the *Caramel Cloud*
3 Do Step 1 of the *Contemporary Chicken*
4 Do Step 3 of the *Caramel Cloud*
5 Do Step 2 of the *Contemporary Chicken*
6 Do Steps 4–6 of the *Caramel Cloud*
7 Do Steps 3–5 of the *Contemporary Chicken*
8 Do Steps 1–2 of the *Classic Salad*
9 Do Step 6 of the *Contemporary Chicken*
10 Do Step 3 of the *Classic Salad*
11 Do Step 7 of the *Caramel Cloud*

Contemporary Chicken

1 Scrub and slice the potatoes. Peel and chop the shallots. Thoroughly wash the leeks and cut them into 2-inch slices. Peel the carrots and cut them into 2-inch strips. Seed the bell pepper and cut it into thin strips.

2 Melt the butter in a large skillet. Add the chicken and cook, turning, until it is golden brown on the outside and cooked on the inside, 8 to 10 minutes.

3 Remove the chicken and keep it warm.

4 Add the potatoes and the shallots to the skillet and cook, stirring frequently, until the shallots are soft and fragrant, 2 to 3 minutes.

5 Stir in the broth, scraping up any brown bits on the bottom of the skillet. Add the leeks, the carrots and the bell pepper. Bring the broth to a boil, reduce the heat, cover and simmer until the potatoes are tender, about 10 minutes.

6 Stir the garlic powder and the vinegar into the skillet. Season to taste. Bring the mixture to a boil. Return the chicken to the skillet, coat the pieces with the sauce and cook until heated through, 2 to 3 minutes.

Classic Salad

1 Wash and dry the lettuce and tear it into bite-size pieces. Distribute it on individual salad plates. Peel and thinly slice the red onion, chop the tomatoes, peel and slice the cucumber and arrange them over the lettuce.

2 Peel and mince the garlic. In a small bowl, whisk together the garlic, the oil, the vinegar, the sugar and the basil. Season to taste.

3 Drizzle the dressing over the salad.

Caramel Cloud

1 Separate the eggs, placing the yolks in a large bowl and the whites in a medium bowl.

2 In a medium saucepan, dissolve 9 tablespoons of the sugar in 2 tablespoons of the water. Bring the mixture to a boil and cook until the syrup turns a rich caramel color, about 5 minutes. Remove the syrup from the heat and let it cool for 5 minutes.

3 Gradually add the remaining $1/4$ cup of water, stirring to dilute the caramel. Be careful or the caramel might splatter. Let the mixture stand for 5 minutes.

4 Stir the gelatin mixture into the caramel mixture.

5 Beat the egg yolks with the remaining 2 tablespoons of sugar and the vanilla until they are light and creamy. Add the caramel mixture and continue beating until the mixture is fluffy. Fold in the whipped topping.

6 Beat the egg whites until stiff and fold them into the caramel. Pour the mixture into individual dessert dishes and refrigerate for at least 20 minutes.

7 Garnish each mousse with a dollop of whipped cream.

FRIDAY

Traffic-Stopping Shrimp

3 cloves garlic
1¹/₂ pounds fresh green beans
1 large can (28 ounces) cut-up tomatoes
1 pound medium shrimp, shelled and deveined
2 tablespoons regular or light olive oil
¹/₂ small can (6 ounces) tomato paste reserved
    from Wednesday
2 tablespoons dry white wine (or nonalcoholic
    white wine or clam juice)
Seasoning to taste
2 tablespoons lemon juice

Green Light Rice

¹/₄ cup fresh parsley (when chopped)
2 scallions (green onions)
1 cup long-grain white rice
2 cups water

Misdemeanor Salad

1 egg
1 medium head lettuce
3 tablespoons fresh chives (when chopped)
1 medium cucumber
1 clove garlic
3 tablespoons regular or light vegetable oil
2 tablespoons white wine vinegar
¹/₂ teaspoon sugar
¹/₂ teaspoon Dijon mustard
¹/₂ teaspoon grated fresh lemon peel
Seasoning to taste
2 tablespoons sesame seeds

Double-Trouble Chocolate

16 Oreo cookies
1 pint chocolate chip ice cream
Chocolate syrup for garnish
Whipped cream for garnish
4 maraschino cherries for garnish

EQUIPMENT

Large covered skillet	Assorted cooking
Double boiler	utensils
Small saucepan	Whisk
Large bowl	Vegetable peeler
Small bowl	Ice cream scoop
Assorted kitchen knives	
Measuring cups and	
spoons	

COUNTDOWN

1 Assemble the ingredients and equipment
2 Do Step 1 of the *Misdemeanor Salad*
3 Do Steps 1–2 of the *Green Light Rice*
4 Do Steps 1–3 of the *Traffic-Stopping Shrimp*
5 Do Steps 2–4 of the *Misdemeanor Salad*
6 Do Step 4 of the *Traffic-Stopping Shrimp*
7 Do Step 5 of the *Misdemeanor Salad*
8 Do Step 3 of the *Green Light Rice*
9 Do Steps 1–3 of the *Double-Trouble Chocolate*

Traffic-Stopping Shrimp

1 Peel and crush the garlic. Trim the green beans and cut them into 1-inch lengths. Drain the tomatoes. Rinse the shrimp.

2 Heat 1 tablespoon of the oil in a large skillet and sauté the garlic for 1 minute. Add the shrimp and sauté until they are pink and loosely curled, 1 to 2 minutes. Remove the shrimp and cover to keep warm.

3 Heat the remaining oil in the skillet and add the green beans, the tomatoes, the tomato paste and the wine. Season to taste. Bring the mixture to a boil, stirring once or twice. Reduce the heat, cover and simmer until the beans are crisp-tender, about 10 minutes.

4 Return the shrimp to the skillet, season to taste, stir in the lemon juice and cook until heated through, about 1 minute.

Green Light Rice

1 Chop the parsley. Trim and chop the scallions.

2 Combine the parsley, the scallions, the rice and the water in the top of a double boiler. Bring water to a boil in the bottom of the double boiler. Reduce the heat, cover and simmer until all the liquid is absorbed and the rice is tender, 30 to 40 minutes.

3 Fluff the rice before serving.

Misdemeanor Salad

1 Cover the egg with water in a small saucepan. Bring the water to a boil and hard-cook the egg, 10 to 12 minutes.

2 Wash and dry the lettuce and tear it into bite-size pieces. Chop the chives. Peel and slice the cucumber. Combine the ingredients in a large bowl.

3 Peel and mince the garlic. In a small bowl, whisk the garlic together with the oil, the vinegar, the sugar, the mustard and the lemon peel until well blended. Season to taste.

4 Drain the egg and place it in the freezer to chill for 10 minutes.

5 Peel and chop the egg. Toss the salad with the dressing and sprinkle with the chopped egg and the sesame seeds.

Double-Trouble Chocolate

1 Crumble 8 of the Oreo cookies into the bottom of individual dessert dishes. Add scoops of chocolate chip ice cream.

2 Place the remaining cookies on end around the edge of the ice cream.

3 Top with a dollop of chocolate syrup, a dollop of whipped cream and a maraschino cherry.

JUNE
WEEK TWO

WEEK AT A GLANCE

Monday

HARLEQUIN FOWL
GINGHAM SALAD
CRAZY QUILT FONDUE

Tuesday

PORK & CIRCUMSTANCE
BUTTERY SPIRALS
CARROT TOPS
FROZEN LEMON TARTS

Wednesday

ST. BART'S SCALLOPS
ARUBA RICE
HAITIAN SALAD
BANANAS CARIBBEAN

Thursday

ORANGE CHICKEN MARRAKECH
CURRANT COUSCOUS
CASBAH SALAD
COCONUT TOPPER

Friday

VEGETABLE CONSOMMÉ
CRABBY MACARONI
JUNE BREAD
JAZZY RAZZBERRY PUDDING

CHECK STAPLES

- ☐ Butter
- ☐ Flour
- ☐ Cornstarch
- ☐ Corn syrup
- ☐ Granulated sugar
- ☐ Dark brown sugar
- ☐ Long-grain white rice
- ☐ Regular or light vegetable oil
- ☐ Regular or light olive oil
- ☐ Sesame oil
- ☐ Red wine vinegar
- ☐ White wine vinegar
- ☐ Balsamic vinegar
- ☐ Rice vinegar
- ☐ Lemon juice
- ☐ Worcestershire sauce
- ☐ Tabasco sauce
- ☐ Soy sauce
- ☐ Dijon mustard
- ☐ Regular or low-fat mayonnaise
- ☐ Ketchup
- ☐ Honey
- ☐ Ground allspice
- ☐ Whole allspice
- ☐ Bay leaves
- ☐ Caraway seeds
- ☐ Cayenne pepper
- ☐ Ground cinnamon
- ☐ Ground cloves
- ☐ Ground coriander
- ☐ Ground ginger
- ☐ Ground nutmeg
- ☐ Paprika
- ☐ Dried tarragon
- ☐ Pepper
- ☐ Salt
- ☐ Vanilla extract

SHOPPING NOTE

● If you are shopping once a week and cannot arrange to purchase fresh seafood on the day you plan to use it, you can purchase *not previously frozen* seafood and freeze it, placing it in the refrigerator to thaw the night before you are ready to use it. Or you can purchase *still frozen* seafood and keep it frozen until the night before you are ready to use it. You can also purchase imitation crabmeat; however, canned crabmeat will significantly alter the recipe.

MEAT & POULTRY

1 pound lean boneless pork loin (T)
1½ pounds boneless turkey breast (M)
3 pounds chicken pieces (Th)

FISH

1 pound scallops (W)
1 pound cooked crabmeat (F)

FRESH PRODUCE

Vegetables

1 medium bunch broccoli (M)
1 small zucchini (F)
20 Chinese snow peas (W)
½ pound spinach (M)
6 medium carrots—5 (T), 1 (F)
3 stalks celery (F)
8 scallions (green onions)—2 (M), 3 (T), 3 (F)
1 medium onion (F)
1 small onion (W)
1 medium red onion (Th)
1 head garlic (M, T)
1 bunch parsley (T, W, F)
1 bunch chives (W, Th, F)
1 pound green cabbage (T)
3 medium heads lettuce—1 (M), 1 (Th), 1 (F)
1 ripe avocado (M)
½ pound tomatoes (M)
2 medium cucumbers (W)
1 medium red bell pepper (W)
1 small white radish (Th)

Fruit

1 small cantaloupe (M)
2 medium bananas (W)
1 pint raspberries (F)
1 medium orange (Th)

CANS, JARS & BOTTLES

Soup

1 can (10¾ ounces) chicken broth (Th)
1 can (10¾ ounces) beef broth (T)
1 can (14½ ounces) oriental broth (W)

2 cans (14½ ounces each) vegetable broth (F)

Vegetables

1 jar (6½ ounces) marinated artichoke hearts (M)

Oriental Foods

1 can (8 ounces) sliced water chestnuts (W)

Juice

1 cup tomato juice (F)

Condiments

1 small jar (3½ ounces) pitted green olives (M)
1 small jar (2 ounces) diced pimientos (F)

Spreads

2 tablespoons apricot preserves (M)
¼ cup raspberry preserves (F)

Dessert Needs

1 can (14 ounces) regular or low-fat sweetened condensed milk (T)

PACKAGED GOODS

Pasta, Rice & Grains

1 cup orzo (M)
8 ounces fusilli (spiral pasta) (T)
8 ounces small elbow macaroni (F)
1 cup quick-cooking couscous (Th)

Baked Goods

1 small loaf sourdough bread (F)
1 angel food loaf cake (M)

Fruit

½ cup dried currants (Th)

Nuts & Seeds

1 cup unshelled pistachio nuts (Th)

Dessert & Baking Needs

1 package Jiffy golden cake mix (Th)
4 prepared graham cracker tart shells (T)
1 small package (3.4 ounces) instant vanilla pudding mix (F)
1 cup semisweet chocolate chips (M)
1½ cups mini-marshmallows (M)
⅓ cup flaked coconut (Th)

WINES & SPIRITS

¼ cup dry sherry (or nonalcoholic red wine or omit) (F)

REFRIGERATED PRODUCTS

Dairy

1¼ cups whole milk (F)
½ cup low-fat milk (Th)
1 cup whipping cream (M)
1 cup regular or light sour cream—¼ cup (T), ¾ cup (F)
1¼ cups regular or low-fat plain yogurt—¼ cup (M), 1 cup (T)
1 egg (Th)

Juice

¾ cup orange juice—½ cup (W), ¼ cup (Th)

Deli

4 slices bacon (W)

FROZEN GOODS

Vegetables

1 package (9 ounces) peas and carrots (F)

Desserts

1 small container (8 ounces) frozen whipped topping (F)

MONDAY

Harlequin Fowl

1 medium bunch broccoli
1 jar (6^1/$_2$ ounces) marinated artichoke hearts
1 small jar (3^1/$_2$ ounces) pitted green olives
^{1}/$_2$ pound fresh tomatoes
2 scallions (green onions)
1 clove garlic
1^1/$_2$ pounds boneless turkey breast
1 cup orzo
^{1}/$_2$ pound fresh spinach
2 tablespoons regular or light olive oil
3 tablespoons red wine vinegar
Seasoning to taste

Gingham Salad

1 small cantaloupe
1 ripe avocado
1 medium head lettuce
^{1}/$_4$ cup regular or low-fat plain yogurt
2 tablespoons apricot preserves
1 tablespoon regular or low-fat mayonnaise
Seasoning to taste

Crazy Quilt Fondue

1 cup semisweet chocolate chips
1^1/$_2$ cups mini-marshmallows
1 cup whipping cream
1 angel food loaf cake
1 teaspoon vanilla extract

EQUIPMENT

Dutch oven	Assorted kitchen knives
Medium covered saucepan	Measuring cups and spoons
Medium saucepan	Assorted cooking utensils
Small bowl	
Strainer	Whisk

COUNTDOWN

1 Assemble the ingredients and equipment
2 Do Steps 1–3 of the *Gingham Salad*
3 Do Steps 1–7 of the *Harlequin Fowl*
4 Do Step 4 of the *Gingham Salad*
5 Do Step 8 of the *Harlequin Fowl*
6 Do Steps 1–3 of the *Crazy Quilt Fondue*

Harlequin Fowl

1 Bring water to a boil in a Dutch oven. Bring water to a boil in a medium saucepan.

2 Cut the broccoli into bite-size florets. Drain and chop the artichokes. Drain and chop the olives. Chop the tomatoes. Trim and chop the scallions. Peel and mince the garlic.

3 Cut the turkey breast into 4 portions and simmer them in the Dutch oven until they are opaque throughout, about 10 minutes.

4 Cook the orzo in the saucepan for 5 minutes. Add the broccoli and cook until the orzo and the broccoli are tender, about 5 minutes more.

5 Drain and cube the turkey.

6 Bring 2 inches of water to a boil in the Dutch oven.

7 Wash and stem the spinach, and cook until it is just wilted, about 3 minutes. Drain the spinach and distribute it among individual plates.

8 Drain the orzo and the broccoli well, and place them in the Dutch oven. Add the artichokes, the olives, the tomatoes, the scallions, the oil, the vinegar, the garlic and the turkey cubes, tossing well, until the mixture is heated through. Season to taste and serve over the spinach.

Gingham Salad

1 Seed the cantaloupe and cut it into 8 wedges, removing the rind. Pit, peel and slice the avocado.

2 Wash and dry the lettuce, tear it into bite-size pieces and distribute it on individual salad plates. Arrange the melon and avocado on top of the lettuce. Refrigerate until you are ready to serve.

3 In a small bowl, whisk together the yogurt, the apricot preserves and the mayonnaise. Season to taste.

4 Spoon the dressing over the salad.

Crazy Quilt Fondue

1 Combine the chocolate chips, the mini-marshmallows and the cream in a medium covered saucepan. Cover and simmer for 10 minutes, stirring occasionally to blend.

2 Cut the angel food cake into cubes.

3 Remove the chocolate mixture from the heat and quickly blend in the vanilla. Bring the hot sauce to the table and dip the cake cubes in it.

TUESDAY

Pork & Circumstance

1 pound lean boneless pork loin
Seasoning to taste
1 tablespoon flour
2 cloves garlic
1 tablespoon regular or light vegetable oil
2 tablespoons paprika
1 can (10³/₄ ounces) beef broth
1 teaspoon Worcestershire sauce
1 tablespoon caraway seeds
1 pound green cabbage
¹/₄ cup regular or light sour cream

Buttery Spirals

8 ounces fusilli (spiral pasta)
3 scallions (green onions)
2 tablespoons fresh parsley (when chopped)
2 tablespoons butter
Seasoning to taste

Carrot Tops

5 medium carrots
1 tablespoon butter
1 tablespoon honey
¹/₄ teaspoon ground ginger
¹/₈ teaspoon ground cinnamon
Seasoning to taste

Frozen Lemon Tarts

1 can (14 ounces) regular or low-fat
    sweetened condensed milk
¹/₄ cup lemon juice
1 cup regular or low-fat plain yogurt
¹/₂ teaspoon ground cinnamon
¹/₂ teaspoon ground nutmeg
4 prepared graham cracker tart shells

EQUIPMENT

Large covered skillet	Assorted kitchen knives
2 large covered saucepans	Measuring cups and spoons
Medium covered saucepan	Assorted cooking utensils
Vegetable steamer	Whisk
Medium bowl	Vegetable peeler
Shallow bowl	Vegetable grater
Colander	

COUNTDOWN

1 Assemble the ingredients and equipment
2 Do Steps 1–3 of the *Pork & Circumstance*
3 Do Steps 1–2 of the *Frozen Lemon Tarts*
4 Do Step 1 of the *Buttery Spirals*
5 Do Steps 1–2 of the *Carrot Tops*
6 Do Step 2 of the *Buttery Spirals*
7 Do Step 4 of the *Pork & Circumstance*
8 Do Step 3 of the *Carrot Tops*
9 Do Steps 3–4 of the *Buttery Spirals*
10 Do Step 5 of the *Pork & Circumstance*

Pork & Circumstance

1 Cut the pork into ³/₄-inch cubes, place them in a shallow bowl and season them to taste. Sprinkle flour over the meat and toss to coat lightly. Peel and mince the garlic.

2 Heat the oil in a large skillet. Add the pork and cook, tossing, until the cubes are lightly browned, about 5 minutes. Reduce the heat, add the garlic and the paprika and cook, stirring frequently, for 1 minute. Add the broth, the Worcestershire sauce and the caraway seeds, cover and simmer until the pork is tender, 25 to 30 minutes.

3 Coarsely grate the cabbage.

4 Bring a small amount of water to a boil in a large saucepan. Place the vegetable steamer in the saucepan. Place the cabbage in the steamer. Cover and steam the cabbage until it is tender but still firm, about 10 minutes.

5 Drain the cabbage and add it to the pork, tossing to combine. Remove the pork and cabbage mixture from the heat and stir in the sour cream.

Buttery Spirals

1 Bring water to a boil in a large saucepan.

2 Cook the pasta in the boiling water until it is almost tender, 8 to 9 minutes.

3 Trim and chop the scallions. Chop the parsley.

4 Drain the pasta, return it to the saucepan and toss it with the butter, the scallions and the parsley. Season to taste and cover to keep warm until you are ready to serve.

Carrot Tops

1 Bring water to a boil in a medium saucepan.

2 Peel and slice the carrots. Cook them in the boiling water until they are crisp-tender, 6 to 8 minutes.

3 Drain the carrots and return them to the saucepan. Add the butter, the honey, the ginger and the cinnamon and toss to coat well. Season to taste. Cover to keep warm.

Frozen Lemon Tarts

1 In a medium bowl, whisk together the condensed milk and the lemon juice. Fold in the yogurt, the cinnamon and the nutmeg. Spoon the mixture into individual tart shells.

2 Chill the tarts in the freezer for 30 minutes.

WEDNESDAY

St. Bart's Scallops

1 pound scallops
4 slices bacon
1 can (8 ounces) sliced water chestnuts
1 medium red bell pepper
20 Chinese snow peas
1 tablespoon soy sauce
3 tablespoons cornstarch
2 tablespoons water
1 cup oriental broth
Seasoning to taste

Aruba Rice

1 small onion
1 tablespoon butter
2 tablespoons fresh parsley (when chopped)
1 cup long-grain white rice
$3/4$ cup oriental broth
$1^1/_2$ cups water
$1/2$ teaspoon ground ginger

Haitian Salad

1 tablespoon balsamic vinegar
1 tablespoon sugar
1 teaspoon soy sauce
1 teaspoon sesame oil
$1/8$ teaspoon Tabasco sauce
Seasoning to taste
2 medium cucumbers
1 tablespoon fresh chives (when chopped)

Bananas Caribbean

2 medium bananas
$1/4$ cup dark brown sugar
$1/2$ cup orange juice
$1/4$ teaspoon ground nutmeg
$1/4$ teaspoon ground cinnamon
2 tablespoons butter

EQUIPMENT

Wok and wok utensils	Assorted kitchen knives
Small skillet	Measuring cups and
Double boiler	spoons
8x8-inch glass baking	Assorted cooking
dish	utensils
2 medium bowls	Whisk
Small bowl	Vegetable peeler

COUNTDOWN

1 Assemble the ingredients and equipment
2 Do Step 1 of the *Bananas Caribbean*
3 Do Steps 1–2 of the *Aruba Rice*
4 Do Steps 1–2 of the *Haitian Salad*
5 Do Steps 1–2 of the *St. Bart's Scallops*
6 Do Steps 2–3 of the *Bananas Caribbean*
7 Do Steps 3–5 of the *St. Bart's Scallops*
8 Do Step 3 of the *Aruba Rice*

St. Bart's Scallops

1 Wash the scallops and pat them dry with paper towels. If you are using sea scallops, cut them in half. Dice the bacon. Drain the water chestnuts. Seed the bell pepper and cut it into thin strips. Trim and string the snow peas.

2 In a medium bowl, whisk the soy sauce with 1 tablespoon of the cornstarch until well blended. Add the scallops and toss to coat.

3 Stir-fry the bacon in a wok until it is crisp and brown, about 5 minutes. Drain it on a paper towel.

4 Discard all but 2 tablespoons of the drippings from the wok. Add the scallops and stir-fry until they are opaque throughout, 3 to 5 minutes. Remove and reserve the scallops.

5 Add the water chestnuts, the bell pepper and the snow peas to the wok. Stir-fry until the peppers are crisp-tender, 1 to 2 minutes. Return the bacon and the scallops to the wok. Add the water and toss gently until the mixture is hot. Dissolve the remaining cornstarch in the vegetable broth. Make a center well in the wok and add the mixture. Stir-fry until the sauce is thick and bubbly, about 1 minute. Season to taste.

Aruba Rice

1 Peel and mince the onion. Melt the butter in a small skillet and sauté the onion until it is golden but not brown, about 5 minutes.

2 Chop the parsley. Place the onion, the parsley, the rice, the broth, the water and the ginger in the top of a double boiler. Bring water to a boil in the bottom of the double boiler, reduce the heat, cover and simmer until all the liquid is absorbed and the rice is tender, 30 to 40 minutes.

3 Fluff the rice before serving.

Haitian Salad

1 In a medium bowl, whisk together the vinegar, the sugar, the soy sauce, the sesame oil and the Tabasco sauce. Season to taste.

2 Peel and slice the cucumbers. Chop the chives. Add them to the bowl, toss gently to combine and refrigerate until you are ready to serve.

Bananas Caribbean

1 Preheat the oven to 450°F. Grease an 8x8-inch glass baking dish.

2 Peel the bananas and split them in half lengthwise. Place them in the dish.

3 In a small bowl, combine the brown sugar, the orange juice, the nutmeg, the cinnamon and the butter. Pour the mixture over the bananas and bake for 10 minutes, basting once. Serve warm.

THURSDAY

Orange Chicken Marrakech

1 medium orange
3 pounds chicken pieces
3 tablespoons flour
$^1/_2$ teaspoon ground coriander
$^1/_2$ teaspoon ground cinnamon
$^1/_4$ teaspoon cayenne pepper
Seasoning to taste
$^1/_4$ cup orange juice
$^1/_4$ cup chicken broth

Currant Couscous

1 cup chicken broth
$^1/_4$ cup water
$^1/_8$ teaspoon ground cinnamon
1 teaspoon regular or light vegetable oil
$^1/_2$ cup dried currants
Seasoning to taste
1 cup quick-cooking couscous

Casbah Salad

1 medium head lettuce
1 medium red onion
1 small white radish
1 cup unshelled pistachio nuts
1 teaspoon fresh chives (when chopped)
2 tablespoons white wine vinegar
3 tablespoons regular or light olive oil
$^1/_2$ teaspoon dried tarragon
Seasoning to taste

Coconut Topper

1 package Jiffy golden cake mix
1 egg
$^1/_2$ cup low-fat milk
$^1/_2$ teaspoon ground cinnamon
$^1/_2$ teaspoon ground nutmeg
$^1/_4$ teaspoon ground allspice
$^1/_4$ teaspoon ground cloves
$^1/_4$ teaspoon ground ginger
2 tablespoons butter
$^1/_4$ cup packed dark brown sugar
2 tablespoons corn syrup
$^1/_3$ cup flaked coconut

EQUIPMENT

Electric hand mixer	2 small bowls
Medium covered saucepan	Assorted kitchen knives
Small saucepan	Measuring cups and spoons
9x13-inch glass baking dish	Assorted cooking utensils
8x8-inch baking pan	Whisk
Large bowl	
Medium bowl	

COUNTDOWN

1 Assemble the ingredients and equipment
2 Do Steps 1–4 of the *Orange Chicken Marrakech*
3 Do Steps 1–2 of the *Coconut Topper*
4 Do Steps 1–2 of the *Currant Couscous*
5 Do Steps 1–3 of the *Casbah Salad*
6 Do Step 3 of the *Coconut Topper*

Orange Chicken Marrakech

1 Preheat the oven to 375°F. Grease a 9x13-inch baking dish.

2 Peel and slice the orange. Place the chicken pieces in the baking dish. Tuck the orange slices around the chicken.

3 In a small bowl, combine the flour, the coriander, the cinnamon and the cayenne pepper. Season to taste. Sprinkle the mixture over the chicken. Add the orange juice and the broth to the dish.

4 Bake, occasionally basting with the cooking juices, until the chicken is tender, about 45 minutes.

Currant Couscous

1 Place the broth, the water, the cinnamon, the oil and the currants in a medium saucepan. Season to taste. Bring the mixture to a boil. Stir in the couscous, cover the saucepan, remove it from heat and let it stand until you are ready to serve, at least 5 minutes.

2 Fluff the couscous before serving.

Casbah Salad

1 Wash and dry the lettuce and tear it into bite-size pieces. Peel and slice the red onion. Trim and chop the radish. Shell the pistachio nuts. Combine the ingredients in a large bowl and refrigerate until you are ready to serve.

2 Chop the chives. In a small bowl, whisk together the chives, the vinegar, the oil and the tarragon. Season to taste.

3 Toss the salad with the dressing.

Coconut Topper

1 Preheat the oven to 350°F. Grease and flour an 8x8-inch baking pan.

2 In a medium bowl, combine the cake mix, the egg, the milk, the cinnamon, the nutmeg, the allspice, the cloves and the ginger. Beat until the ingredients are well blended, about 2 minutes. Spread the mixture in the baking pan and bake until a toothpick stuck in the center comes out clean, about 25 minutes.

3 Melt the butter, the brown sugar and the corn syrup in a small saucepan, and cook until the mixture is bubbly. Drizzle the glaze over the cake and sprinkle with the coconut.

FRIDAY

Vegetable Consommé

1 medium onion
1 small zucchini
1 medium carrot
2 stalks celery
2 cans (14^1/$_2$ ounces each) vegetable broth
1 cup tomato juice
^{1}/$_4$ cup dry sherry (or nonalcoholic red wine or
    omit)
1 bay leaf
3 whole allspice
^{1}/$_2$ teaspoon ground nutmeg
Seasoning to taste

Crabby Macaroni

1 package (9 ounces) frozen peas & carrots
1 medium head lettuce
2 scallions (green onions)
1 stalk celery
1 small jar (2 ounces) diced pimientos
1 pound cooked crabmeat
8 ounces small elbow macaroni
^{1}/$_4$ cup rice vinegar
1 tablespoon balsamic vinegar
^{1}/$_2$ cup regular or low-fat mayonnaise
2 tablespoons ketchup
1 teaspoon sugar
2 tablespoons lemon juice
1 tablespoon Worcestershire sauce
^{1}/$_4$ teaspoon Tabasco sauce
Seasoning to taste

June Bread

2 tablespoons fresh parsley (when minced)
1 tablespoon fresh chives (when minced)
4 tablespoons softened butter
2 teaspoons Dijon mustard
^{1}/$_2$ teaspoon lemon juice
1 small loaf sourdough bread

Jazzy Razzberry Pudding

1^1/$_4$ cups whole milk
^{3}/$_4$ cup regular or light sour cream
1 small package (3.4 ounces) instant vanilla
    pudding mix
1 pint fresh raspberries
^{1}/$_4$ cup raspberry preserves
1 small container (8 ounces) frozen whipped
    topping

EQUIPMENT

Electric hand mixer	Strainer
Dutch oven	Assorted kitchen knives
Large covered saucepan	Measuring cups and spoons
Cookie sheet	Assorted cooking utensils
2 medium bowls	Vegetable peeler
2 small bowls	Whisk
Colander	

COUNTDOWN

1 Assemble the ingredients and equipment
2 Do Step 1 of the *June Bread*
3 Do Steps 1–2 of the *Crabby Macaroni*
4 Do Steps 1–2 of the *Vegetable Consommé*
5 Do Steps 1–2 of the *Jazzy Razzberry Pudding*
6 Do Steps 2–3 of the *June Bread*
7 Do Step 3 of the *Crabby Macaroni*
8 Do Steps 3–4 of the *Jazzy Razzberry Pudding*
9 Do Steps 4–5 of the *Crabby Macaroni*
10 Do Step 3 of the *Vegetable Consommé*

Vegetable Consommé

1 Peel and quarter the onion. Wash and quarter the zucchini. Peel and chunk the carrot. Trim and chunk the celery.

2 In a large saucepan, combine the vegetables, the broth, the tomato juice, the sherry, the bay leaf, the allspice and the nutmeg. Season to taste. Bring the mixture to a boil, reduce the heat, cover and simmer for 20 minutes.

3 Strain the soup, discarding the vegetables, the bay leaf and the allspice.

Crabby Macaroni

1 Bring water to a boil in a Dutch oven. Set out the package of peas and carrots to thaw.

2 Wash, dry and finely chop the lettuce. Trim and chop the scallions. Trim and chop the celery. Drain the pimientos. Flake the crabmeat.

3 Cook the macaroni in the boiling water until it is just tender, 8 to 9 minutes. Add the peas and carrots to the macaroni for the last 2 minutes of cooking.

4 Drain the macaroni and vegetables well and place them in the Dutch oven. Add the lettuce, the scallions, the celery, the pimientos and the crabmeat to the pasta mixture and combine.

5 In a small bowl, whisk together both vinegars, the mayonnaise, the ketchup, the sugar, the lemon juice, the Worcestershire sauce and the Tabasco sauce. Season to taste. Toss to mix well. Serve at room temperature.

June Bread

1 Preheat the oven to 350°F.

2 Chop the parsley. Chop the chives. In a small bowl, blend together the parsley, the chives, the softened butter, the mustard and the lemon juice.

3 Cut the sourdough loaf into 1-inch slices. Lightly spread each slice with the butter mixture. Arrange the slices on an ungreased cookie sheet and bake until crisp, 10 to 15 minutes.

Jazzy Razzberry Pudding

1 Combine the milk, the sour cream and the pudding mix in a medium bowl. Beat for 1 minute and then place the mixture in the refrigerator for 10 minutes.

2 Rinse and dry the berries and drain them on paper towels.

3 Fold the raspberry preserves into the whipped topping.

4 Reserve 12 berries. Layer the pudding, the remaining berries and the whipped topping into parfait glasses. Top with the reserved berries and refrigerate for at least 15 minutes.

JUNE
WEEK THREE

Monday

FANCY FLOUNDER
DANDY RICE
SWELL SLAW
STRAWBERRY PARFAIT

Tuesday

THIS LAMB IS MY LAMB
EVERYTHING'S COMING UP ORZO
SWEET & SOUR AVOCADOS
CHOCOLATE RETORT

Wednesday

CRAZY VEGETABLE PIE
BRIEF ONION SALAD
KEEP IT SIMPLE

Thursday

LOTSA PASTA
ENOUGH SALAD
A LITTLE BIT OF BREAD
SUGAR SHELL SURPRISE

Friday

ASPARAGUS SMOOTHIE
WARM PEAR & SCALLOP SALAD
LEMON DROP BISCUITS
CARAMEL CORN FLAKE RING

CHECK STAPLES

- ☐ Butter
- ☐ Bisquick
- ☐ Granulated sugar
- ☐ Dark brown sugar
- ☐ Confectioners' sugar
- ☐ Unsweetened cocoa
- ☐ Chocolate syrup
- ☐ Corn syrup
- ☐ Long-grain white rice
- ☐ Regular or light vegetable oil
- ☐ Regular or light olive oil
- ☐ Sesame oil
- ☐ Red wine vinegar
- ☐ Rice vinegar
- ☐ Lemon juice
- ☐ Worcestershire sauce
- ☐ Soy sauce
- ☐ Dijon mustard
- ☐ Prepared horseradish
- ☐ Regular or low-fat mayonnaise
- ☐ Ketchup
- ☐ Grated Parmesan cheese
- ☐ Dried basil
- ☐ Cayenne pepper
- ☐ Dried dill
- ☐ Garlic powder
- ☐ Italian seasoning
- ☐ Dried rosemary
- ☐ Pepper
- ☐ Salt
- ☐ Vanilla extract

SHOPPING NOTE

● If you are shopping once a week and cannot arrange to purchase fresh seafood on the day you plan to use it, you can purchase *not previously frozen* seafood and freeze it, placing it in the refrigerator to thaw the night before you are ready to use it. Or you can purchase *still frozen* seafood and keep it frozen until the night before you are ready to use it.

MEAT & POULTRY

4 lean lamb chops ($^3/_4$-inch thick) (T)

$^3/_4$ pound regular or light sweet Italian pork or turkey sausage (Th)

1 pound boneless, skinless chicken breasts (Th)

FISH

$1^1/_4$ pounds flounder fillets (M)

1 pound scallops (F)

FRESH PRODUCE

Vegetables

1 medium baking potato (F)

$^1/_2$ pound green beans (M)

$^3/_4$ pound asparagus (F)

2 medium zucchini—1 (W), 1 (F)

1 medium yellow squash (W)

1 medium fennel bulb (Th)

$^1/_2$ pound spinach (W)

3 medium carrots—1 (M), 2 (F)

4 stalks celery—2 (Th), 2 (F)

2 medium onions—1 (M), 1 (Th)

1 small onion (M)

1 large sweet onion (W)

2 scallions (green onions) (W)

1 head garlic (M, T, Th)

1 bunch parsley (M, T, Th)

1 small bunch basil (W, F)

1 small bunch mint leaves (W)

1 small head green cabbage (M)

2 medium heads lettuce—1 (W), 1 (Th)

1 small head lettuce (F)

2 ripe avocados (T)

$1^2/_3$ pounds tomatoes— $^1/_2$ pound (M), $^1/_3$ pound (W), $^1/_2$ pound (Th), $^1/_3$ pound (F)

1 medium cucumber (Th)

1 medium red bell pepper (Th)

1 medium green bell pepper (Th)

Fruit

3 medium pears (F)

2 small honeydew melons (W)

3 medium bananas—1 (M), 2 (W)

$^1/_2$ pound seedless green grapes (W)

1 pint strawberries (M)

1 pint raspberries (Th)

CANS, JARS & BOTTLES

Soup

1 can ($14^1/_2$ ounces) chicken broth (M)

1 can ($14^1/_2$ ounces) vegetable broth (F)

Vegetables

1 medium can ($14^1/_2$ ounces) cut-up tomatoes (T)

Condiments

2 tablespoons capers (M)

1 small can (3.3 ounces) sliced black olives (T)

Spreads

1 small jar (10 ounces) raspberry preserves for garnish (Th)

PACKAGED GOODS

Pasta, Rice & Grains

8 ounces orzo (T)

12 ounces rigatoni (Th)

2 cups corn flakes cereal (F)

Baked Goods

1 small loaf Italian bread (Th)

Nuts & Seeds

$^1/_4$ cup sliced almonds (M)

$^1/_2$ cup pecan pieces (F)

Dessert & Baking Needs

1 small package ($3^1/_2$ ounces) strawberry gelatin (M)

1 small package (6 ounces) semisweet chocolate chips (T)

WINES & SPIRITS

3 tablespoons dry red wine (or nonalcoholic red wine or vegetable broth) (T)

3 tablespoons dry white wine (or nonalcoholic white wine or vegetable broth) (Th)

1 tablespoon dry sherry (or nonalcoholic red wine or omit) (M)

3 tablespoons dry sherry (or nonalcoholic white wine or omit)—1 tablespoon (M), 2 tablespoons (F)

6 tablespoons Amaretto liqueur (or nonalcoholic Italian almond syrup) (T)

REFRIGERATED PRODUCTS

Dairy

$1^1/_2$ cups + 6 tablespoons whole or low-fat milk— $1^1/_2$ cups (W), 6 tablespoons (F)

$^1/_2$ cup whipping cream (M)

Whipped cream for garnish (Th)

4 tablespoons regular or low-fat plain yogurt— 2 tablespoons (Th), 2 tablespoons (F)

1 container (8 ounces) regular or low-fat lemon yogurt (F)

3 eggs (W)

Cheese

1 small container (15 ounces) regular or low-fat ricotta cheese (T)

Deli

4 slices bacon (T)

1 package (18 ounces) refrigerator sugar cookie dough (Th)

FROZEN GOODS

Vegetables

1 package (16 ounces) whole kernel corn (M)

Desserts

1 pound cake (T)

1 pint butter pecan ice cream (F)

MONDAY

Fancy Flounder

1/2 pound fresh tomatoes
2 tablespoons capers
1/2 pound fresh green beans
1 package (16 ounces) frozen whole kernel corn
Seasoning to taste
1 tablespoon regular or light vegetable oil
1 tablespoon dry sherry (or nonalcoholic red wine or omit)
1 1/4 pounds flounder fillets
2 teaspoons sesame oil

Dandy Rice

1 medium onion
1 tablespoon fresh parsley (when chopped)
2 tablespoons butter
1 cup long-grain white rice
1 can (14 1/2 ounces) chicken broth
2 tablespoons water
1 tablespoon dry sherry (or nonalcoholic white wine or omit)
1 tablespoon soy sauce
1/2 teaspoon garlic powder

Swell Slaw

2 cloves garlic
2 tablespoons regular or light vegetable oil
1 tablespoon sesame oil
2 tablespoons rice vinegar
1 teaspoon sugar
Seasoning to taste
1 small head green cabbage
1 small onion
1 medium carrot
1/4 cup sliced almonds

Strawberry Parfait

1 1/4 cups boiling water
1 small package (3 1/2 ounces) strawberry gelatin
1 pint fresh strawberries
1 medium banana
1/2 cup whipping cream
2 tablespoons sugar
1 teaspoon vanilla extract

EQUIPMENT

Electric hand mixer	Assorted kitchen knives
Medium covered saucepan	Measuring cups and spoons
Medium saucepan	Assorted cooking utensils
9x13-inch glass baking dish	Whisk
Large bowl	Vegetable grater
2 medium bowls	Vegetable peeler
Small bowl	Aluminum foil
Colander	

COUNTDOWN

1 Assemble the ingredients and equipment
2 Do Steps 1–4 of the *Strawberry Parfait*
3 Do Steps 1–2 of the *Dandy Rice*
4 Do Steps 1–2 of the *Swell Slaw*
5 Do Steps 1–6 of the *Fancy Flounder*
6 Do Step 3 of the *Dandy Rice*

Fancy Flounder

1 Preheat the oven to 400°F. Grease a 9x13-inch glass baking dish.

2 Bring water to a boil in a medium saucepan.

3 Dice the tomatoes. Rinse the capers.

4 Place the beans in the saucepan, return the water to a boil and cook for 5 minutes. Drain the beans, rinse them under cold water and then drain them again.

5 In a medium bowl, combine the beans, the corn, the capers and the tomatoes. Season to taste. Spoon the mixture into the baking dish and drizzle with the vegetable oil and the sherry.

6 Arrange the fish fillets on top of the bean mixture, overlapping if necessary. Drizzle the fish with the sesame oil. Cover the dish with aluminum foil and bake until the fish is tender and opaque throughout, about 10 minutes.

Dandy Rice

1 Peel and chop the onion. Chop the parsley. Melt the butter in a medium covered saucepan and sauté the onion and the rice until the onion is soft, about 10 minutes.

2 Add the broth, the water, the sherry, the soy sauce, the garlic powder and the parsley. Bring the mixture to a boil, reduce the heat, cover and simmer until all the liquid is absorbed and the rice is tender, about 25 minutes.

3 Fluff the rice before serving.

Swell Slaw

1 Peel and mince the garlic. In a large bowl, whisk together the garlic, the oils, the vinegar and the sugar. Season to taste.

2 Grate the cabbage. Peel and chop the onion. Peel and grate the carrot. Add the ingredients to the dressing, add the almonds and toss until the cabbage mixture is well coated. Refrigerate until you are ready to serve.

Strawberry Parfait

1 Bring the water to a boil. Combine it with the gelatin in a medium bowl and stir until the gelatin is dissolved. Let the mixture stand until it thickens slightly, stirring occasionally, about 5 minutes.

2 Wash, hull and slice the strawberries, reserving 4 whole berries. Peel and slice the banana.

3 In a small bowl, beat the cream until it is stiff, about 3 minutes. Blend in the sugar and the vanilla.

4 Spoon layers of gelatin, banana, strawberries and whipped cream into parfait glasses. Top the parfaits with the reserved berries, and refrigerate for at least 20 minutes.

TUESDAY

This Lamb Is My Lamb

4 lean lamb chops ($^3/_4$-inch thick)
1 clove garlic
1 medium can (14$^1/_2$ ounces) cut-up tomatoes
1 tablespoon regular or light olive oil
3 tablespoons dry red wine (or nonalcoholic
    red wine or vegetable broth)
1 tablespoon red wine vinegar
$^1/_2$ teaspoon dried basil
Seasoning to taste
1 small can (3.3 ounces) sliced black olives

Everything's Coming Up Orzo

2 tablespoons fresh parsley (when chopped)
8 ounces orzo
2 tablespoons butter
$^1/_2$ teaspoon dried rosemary
Seasoning to taste

Sweet & Sour Avocados

4 slices bacon
4 tablespoons butter
$^1/_4$ cup dark brown sugar
$^1/_4$ cup ketchup
$^1/_4$ cup red wine vinegar
1 tablespoon Worcestershire sauce
Seasoning to taste
2 ripe avocados
2 tablespoons lemon juice

Chocolate Retort

1 frozen pound cake
1 small container (15 ounces) regular or low-
    fat ricotta cheese

1 small package (6 ounces) semisweet
    chocolate chips
$^1/_2$ cup granulated sugar
1$^1/_2$ teaspoons vanilla extract
6 tablespoons Amaretto liqueur (or
    nonalcoholic Italian almond syrup)
2 tablespoons boiling water
1 tablespoon butter
1 cup confectioners' sugar
2 tablespoons unsweetened cocoa

EQUIPMENT

Large covered skillet	Assorted kitchen knives
Small covered skillet	Measuring cups and
Large covered	spoons
saucepan	Assorted cooking
Small saucepan	utensils
Large bowl	Whisk
Strainer	

COUNTDOWN

IN THE MORNING:
  Do Step 1 of the *Chocolate Retort*
BEFORE DINNER:
  1 Assemble the remaining ingredients and
     equipment
  2 Do Step 1 of *This Lamb Is My Lamb*
  3 Do Step 1 of *Everything's Coming Up Orzo*
  4 Do Steps 2–4 of the *Chocolate Retort*
  5 Do Steps 1–2 of the *Sweet & Sour Avocados*
  6 Do Steps 2–3 of *This Lamb Is My Lamb*
  7 Do Step 2 of *Everything's Coming Up Orzo*
  8 Do Steps 3–4 of the *Sweet & Sour Avocados*
  9 Do Step 3 of *Everything's Coming Up Orzo*
 10 Do Step 4 of *This Lamb Is My Lamb*
 11 Do Step 5 of the *Sweet & Sour Avocados*

RECIPES

This Lamb Is My Lamb

1 Preheat the broiler. Trim the lamb chops of any excess fat. Peel and mince the garlic. Drain the tomatoes.

2 Broil the chops to taste, turning once, 6 to 8 minutes per side for medium-rare.

3 Heat the oil in a large skillet. Add the garlic, the wine, the vinegar, the basil and the tomatoes. Season to taste, cover and simmer for 10 minutes.

4 Remove the chops. Drain the olives and add them to the sauce. Bring the sauce to a boil for 30 seconds and pour it over the chops.

Everything's Coming Up Orzo

1 Bring water to a boil in a large saucepan. Chop the parsley.

2 Cook the orzo until it is almost tender, about 7 minutes.

3 Drain the orzo, return it to the saucepan and toss it with the butter, the parsley and the rosemary. Season to taste and cover to keep warm.

Sweet & Sour Avocados

1 Sauté the bacon in a small skillet until it is crisp, about 5 minutes. Then drain it on a paper towel.

2 Wipe out the skillet and melt the butter in it. Add the brown sugar, the ketchup, the vinegar and the Worcestershire sauce. Season to taste. Stir until the sugar is dissolved and the mixture begins to bubble, about 5

minutes. Cover the skillet and remove it from the heat.

3 Halve and pit the avocados. Place them on individual plates and sprinkle them with the lemon juice.

4 Crumble the bacon and place a quarter of the amount in each avocado cavity.

5 Drizzle the sauce over the avocados.

Chocolate Retort

1 Set the pound cake in the refrigerator to thaw.

2 Cut the thawed pound cake into 3 horizontal layers.

3 In a large bowl, combine the ricotta, the chocolate chips, the sugar, the vanilla and the Amaretto, until the mixture is well blended. Spread the bottom layer of the cake with half of the cheese mixture. Cover with the second layer of cake and spread it with the remaining cheese mixture. Top with the third layer of cake.

4 Bring the water to a boil. Melt the butter in a small saucepan. Add the confectioners' sugar, the cocoa and the boiling water and whisk the mixture into a glaze. Pour the glaze over the cake, letting it drizzle down the sides. Refrigerate for at least 15 minutes.

WEDNESDAY

Crazy Vegetable Pie

1/3 pound fresh tomatoes
1 medium zucchini
1 medium yellow squash
1/2 pound fresh spinach
2 scallions (green onions)
1/4 cup grated Parmesan cheese
1 1/2 cups whole or low-fat milk
3/4 cup Bisquick
3 eggs
1 teaspoon Worcestershire sauce
2 teaspoons Dijon mustard
Seasoning to taste

Brief Onion Salad

1 medium head lettuce
1 large sweet onion
1 tablespoon fresh basil (when chopped)
3 tablespoons regular or light olive oil
2 tablespoons red wine vinegar
Seasoning to taste

Keep It Simple

1/2 pound seedless green grapes
2 small honeydew melons
1/2 cup fresh mint leaves
1/2 cup corn syrup
2 tablespoons lemon juice
1/8 teaspoon salt
2 medium bananas

EQUIPMENT

Blender	Measuring cups and
9-inch quiche or pie	spoons
plate	Assorted cooking
Medium bowl	utensils
Small bowl	Whisk
Assorted kitchen knives	

COUNTDOWN

1 Assemble the ingredients and equipment
2 Do Steps 1–5 of the *Crazy Vegetable Pie*
3 Do Steps 1–2 of the *Keep It Simple*
4 Do Steps 1–3 of the *Brief Onion Salad*
5 Do Step 3 of the *Keep It Simple*

Crazy Vegetable Pie

1 Preheat the oven to 400°F. Grease a 9-inch quiche or pie plate.

2 Chop the tomatoes. Trim and chop the zucchini. Trim and chop the squash. Wash, dry, stem and chop the spinach. Peel and chop the scallions.

3 Scatter the tomatoes, the zucchini, the squash, the spinach, the scallions and the cheese over the bottom of the quiche or pie plate.

4 In a medium bowl, whisk together the milk, the Bisquick, the eggs, the Worcestershire sauce and the mustard until smooth. Season to taste. Pour the mixture over the vegetables.

5 Bake until a knife inserted in the center of the pie comes out clean, about 30 minutes.

Brief Onion Salad

1 Wash and dry the lettuce. Distribute the leaves among individual salad plates. Peel and thinly slice the sweet onion. Arrange the slices over the lettuce.

2 Chop the basil. In a small bowl, whisk together the basil, the oil and the vinegar. Season to taste.

3 Drizzle the dressing over the salad.

Keep It Simple

1 Wash, dry, separate and halve the grapes. Cut the melons in half and discard the seeds. Place the melon halves on individual dessert dishes and fill the centers with the grapes. Refrigerate until you are ready to use.

2 Chop the mint leaves. Combine the corn syrup, the mint leaves, the lemon juice and the salt in a blender and process until well blended. Let the mixture stand for at least 15 minutes.

3 Peel and slice the bananas and add them to the grapes. Drizzle the sauce over the fruit.

THURSDAY

Lotsa Pasta

1 pound boneless, skinless chicken breasts
3/4 pound regular or light sweet Italian pork
    or turkey sausage
1 medium red bell pepper
1 medium green bell pepper
1 medium onion
1 medium fennel bulb
1/2 pound fresh tomatoes
1 clove garlic
12 ounces rigatoni
1 tablespoon regular or light vegetable oil
1 teaspoon dried basil
3 tablespoons dry white wine (or nonalcoholic
    white wine or vegetable broth)
Seasoning to taste

Enough Salad

1 medium head lettuce
1 medium cucumber
2 stalks celery
1/4 cup fresh parsley (when chopped)
2 teaspoons dried dill
1 teaspoon sugar
3 tablespoons red wine vinegar
3 tablespoons regular or light olive oil
1/2 teaspoon prepared horseradish
2 tablespoons ketchup
1 teaspoon Dijon mustard
2 tablespoons regular or low-fat plain yogurt

A Little Bit of Bread

1 small Italian bread loaf
1/3 cup regular or light mayonnaise
1 tablespoon Italian seasoning
1/3 cup grated Parmesan cheese

Sugar Shell Surprise

1 package (18 ounces) refrigerator sugar
    cookie dough
1 pint fresh raspberries
Whipped cream for garnish
1 jar (10 ounces) raspberry preserves for
    garnish

EQUIPMENT

Stockpot	Rolling pin
Large skillet	Assorted kitchen knives
Cookie sheet	Measuring cups and
Large 6-cup muffin tin	spoons
Large bowl	Assorted cooking
2 small bowls	utensils
Colander	Whisk
Pastry board	Vegetable peeler

COUNTDOWN

1 Assemble the ingredients and equipment
2 Do Steps 1–4 of the *Sugar Shell Surprise*
3 Do Step 1 of *A Little Bit of Bread*
4 Do Steps 1–2 of the *Lotsa Pasta*
5 Do Steps 1–2 of the *Enough Salad*
6 Do Steps 3–5 of the *Lotsa Pasta*
7 Do Steps 2–3 of *A Little Bit of Bread*
8 Do Step 6 of the *Lotsa Pasta*
9 Do Step 4 of *A Little Bit of Bread*
10 Do Step 7 of the *Lotsa Pasta*
11 Do Step 3 of the *Enough Salad*
12 Do Step 5 of the *Sugar Shell Surprise*

Lotsa Pasta

1 Bring water to a boil in a stockpot.

2 Cut the chicken breast into thin strips. Remove the sausage from its casing. Seed the bell peppers and cut them into thin strips. Peel and chop the onion. Trim and chop the fennel. Chop the tomatoes. Peel and mince the garlic.

3 Cook the rigatoni in the boiling water until it is almost tender, about 10 minutes.

4 In a large skillet, sauté the chicken and the sausage until the sausage is browned and cooked through, 10 to 12 minutes.

5 Drain the pasta, return it to the stockpot, toss it with the oil and cover to keep warm.

6 Drain off any fat from the skillet. Add the bell peppers, the onion, the fennel and the garlic to the skillet, and sauté until the onion is limp and the peppers are crisp-tender, 3 to 5 minutes. Stir in the tomatoes, the basil and the wine. Season to taste. Reduce the heat and cook until hot, 2 to 3 minutes.

7 Toss the sauce with the rigatoni.

Enough Salad

1 Wash and dry the lettuce and tear it into bite-size pieces. Peel and chop the cucumber. Trim and slice the celery. Chop the parsley. Combine the ingredients in a large bowl.

2 In a small bowl, whisk together the dill, the sugar, the vinegar, the oil, the horseradish, the ketchup, the mustard and the yogurt.

3 Toss the salad with the dressing.

A Little Bit of Bread

1 Preheat the broiler.

2 Cut the bread into 8 slices. Arrange the slices on an ungreased cookie sheet.

3 In a small bowl, combine the mayonnaise, the Italian seasoning and the Parmesan cheese. Spread the mixture over the bread slices.

4 Place the cookie sheet under the broiler, 3 or 4 inches from the heat, and broil until the bread is lightly toasted and the cheese mixture is melted, 2 to 3 minutes.

Sugar Shell Surprise

1 Preheat the oven to 375°F.

2 Divide the cookie dough into 4 sections. Roll out each section into a 4-inch round. Turn a large 6-cup muffin tin upside down and grease 4 of the backs. Press the dough over the outside of the cups to form shells. Bake the shells upside down until golden, about 7 minutes.

3 Rinse the raspberries, drain them on paper towels and then refrigerate them until you are ready to use.

4 Remove the cookie shells from the oven and let them cool.

5 Carefully lift the cooled cookie shells from the muffin tin. Fill them with the berries. Top them with a dollop of whipped cream and drizzle them with the raspberry preserves.

FRIDAY

Asparagus Smoothie

$^3/_4$ pound fresh asparagus
1 can (14$^1/_2$ ounces) vegetable broth
2 tablespoons dry sherry (or nonalcoholic
    white wine or omit)
$^1/_8$ teaspoon cayenne pepper
Seasoning to taste
2 tablespoons regular or low-fat plain yogurt

Warm Pear & Scallop Salad

2 medium carrots
2 stalks celery
1 medium zucchini
1 medium baking potato
3 medium pears
1 pound scallops
1 small head lettuce
$^1/_3$ pound fresh tomatoes
$^1/_2$ cup fresh basil (when chopped)
4 tablespoons red wine vinegar
6 tablespoons regular or light olive oil
2 teaspoons Dijon mustard
1 teaspoon sugar
Seasoning to taste
$^1/_2$ cup pecan pieces

Lemon Drop Biscuits

2 cups Bisquick
1 teaspoon sugar
1 container (8 ounces) regular or low-fat
    lemon yogurt
2 tablespoons whole or low-fat milk

Caramel Corn Flake Ring

$^1/_2$ cup dark brown sugar
1 tablespoon corn syrup
$^1/_4$ cup whole or low-fat milk
1$^1/_2$ tablespoons butter
$^1/_2$ teaspoon vanilla extract
2 cups corn flakes cereal
1 pint butter pecan ice cream
Chocolate syrup for garnish

EQUIPMENT

Blender	Colander
Large covered skillet	Strainer
Medium covered	Assorted kitchen knives
saucepan	Measuring cups and
2 small saucepans	spoons
Cookie sheet	Assorted cooking
1-quart ring mold	utensils
2 large bowls	Whisk
Medium bowl	Vegetable peeler
Small bowl	Ice cream scoop

COUNTDOWN

1 Assemble the ingredients and equipment
2 Do Steps 1–3 of the *Caramel Corn Flake Ring*
3 Do Step 1 of the *Lemon Drop Biscuits*
4 Do Steps 1–2 of the *Warm Pear & Scallop Salad*
5 Do Step 2 of the *Lemon Drop Biscuits*
6 Do Steps 1–3 of the *Asparagus Smoothie*
7 Do Step 3 of the *Lemon Drop Biscuits*
8 Do Steps 3–6 of the *Warm Pear & Scallop Salad*
9 Do Step 4 of the *Caramel Corn Flake Ring*

Asparagus Smoothie

1 Bring water to a boil in a medium saucepan.

2 Remove the tough ends from the asparagus and cut the remainder into 1-inch pieces. Cook the asparagus until it is crisp-tender, about 5 minutes. Drain the asparagus in a colander set over a medium bowl, reserving 2 cups of the cooking liquid.

3 Place the asparagus and the reserved cooking liquid in a blender and puree until smooth. Pour the puree back into the saucepan. Stir in the broth, the sherry and the cayenne pepper, and bring the mixture to a boil. Season to taste. Stir in the yogurt, remove the saucepan from the heat and cover to keep warm.

Warm Pear & Scallop Salad

1 Peel the carrots and cut them into thin strips. Trim and slice the celery. Trim the zucchini and cut it into thin strips. Peel the potato and cut it into thin strips. Core and chunk the pears. Rinse and pat dry the scallops. If you are using sea scallops, cut them in half.

2 Wash and dry the lettuce and distribute the leaves among individual salad plates.

3 In a large skillet, cover the carrots, the celery, the zucchini and the potato with cold water. Bring the water to a boil, then cover and cook the vegetables until they are just tender, 4 to 5 minutes.

4 Peel and dice the tomatoes. Chop the basil. In a small saucepan, combine the tomatoes and the basil with the vinegar, the oil, the mustard and the sugar. Season to taste. Bring the mixture to a simmer.

5 Add the scallops to the skillet and cook until they are opaque throughout, about 2 minutes. Drain the scallops and the vegetables and arrange them over the lettuce.

6 Remove the skillet from the heat. Add the pears and the pecans, and toss them with the warm dressing. Spoon the dressing over the scallops and the vegetables.

Lemon Drop Biscuits

1 Preheat the oven to 450°F. Grease a cookie sheet.

2 Combine the Bisquick and the sugar in a large bowl. In a small bowl, combine the yogurt and the milk. Add the yogurt mixture to the Bisquick mixture. Stir until the dough is well blended and clings together. Drop spoonfuls of the dough onto the cookie sheet.

3 Bake the biscuits until they are golden, 10 to 12 minutes.

Caramel Corn Flake Ring

1 Grease a large bowl and a 1-quart ring mold.

2 Combine the brown sugar, the corn syrup, the milk and the butter in a small saucepan and cook until just bubbly. Remove the saucepan from the heat and mix in the vanilla.

3 Place the corn flakes in the greased bowl. Add the syrup mixture and toss until the corn flakes are well coated. Pack the mixture into the greased mold and refrigerate for at least 20 minutes.

4 Unmold the corn flake ring by dipping the bottom into hot water for 30 seconds. Fill the center with small scoops of ice cream and drizzle the ring with chocolate syrup.

JUNE

WEEK FOUR

WEEK AT A GLANCE

Monday

TUNA & POTATO TOSS
BEGGERMAN'S SALAD
ENGLISH TIPPERS
APRICOT WHATNOT

Tuesday

RAINBOW PASTA
SUNBEAM SALAD
POTS O' GOLD

Wednesday

PIÑATA PIE
WARM SALSA CHIPS
MELON RUMBA

Thursday

OASIS CHICKEN
DESERT RICE
SHEIK SNAP PEAS
DARKS NIGHTS

Friday

NEPTUNE POT PIE
DE-VINE SALAD
SHIPWRECK SHERBET

CHECK STAPLES

- ☐ Butter
- ☐ Flour
- ☐ Cornstarch
- ☐ Granulated sugar
- ☐ Dark brown sugar
- ☐ Confectioners' sugar
- ☐ Sweetened cocoa
- ☐ Brown rice
- ☐ Regular or light vegetable oil
- ☐ Regular or light olive oil
- ☐ Sesame oil
- ☐ Red wine vinegar
- ☐ White wine vinegar
- ☐ Rice vinegar
- ☐ Lemon juice
- ☐ Lime juice
- ☐ Dijon mustard
- ☐ Regular or low-fat mayonnaise
- ☐ Honey
- ☐ Golden raisins
- ☐ Chili powder
- ☐ Ground cinnamon
- ☐ Ground cumin
- ☐ Dried dill
- ☐ Garlic powder
- ☐ Ground ginger
- ☐ Paprika
- ☐ Dried savory
- ☐ Sesame seeds
- ☐ Dried tarragon
- ☐ Pepper
- ☐ Salt
- ☐ Vanilla extract

SHOPPING NOTE

● If you are shopping once a week and cannot arrange to purchase fresh seafood on the day you plan to use it, you can purchase *not previously frozen* seafood and freeze it, placing it in the refrigerator to thaw the night before you are ready to use it. Or you can purchase *still frozen* seafood and keep it frozen until the night before you are ready to use it.

MEAT & POULTRY

$3/4$ pound lean cooked ham steak (T)
1 pound lean ground beef (W)
4 skinless, boneless chicken breast halves (Th)

FISH

1 pound scallops (F)
12 ounces medium shrimp, shelled and deveined (F)

FRESH PRODUCE

Vegetables

$3/4$ pound sugar snap peas (Th)
6 medium carrots—4 (T), 2 (F)
6 stalks celery—2 (M), 2 (T), 2 (F)
2 medium onions—1 (W), 1 (F)
1 small onion (Th)
1 medium red onion (M)
1 small red onion (T)
6 scallions (green onions)— 4 (T), 2 (Th)
1 head garlic (M, T, W)
1 bunch parsley (M)
3 medium heads lettuce—1 (M), 1 (T), 1 (F)
1 small head lettuce (W)
1 ripe avocado (W)
$1/2$ pound tomatoes (W)
1 medium red bell pepper (T)
1 small green bell pepper (W)
1 small jicama (or turnip) (T)
1 small bunch radishes (T)

Fruit

1 tart green apple (F)
1 large honeydew melon (W)
$1/4$ pound seedless green grapes (F)
$1/4$ pound seedless red grapes (F)
$1/2$ pint raspberries (Th)
1 medium orange (Th)

CANS, JARS & BOTTLES

Soup

1 can ($14^1/2$ ounces) chicken broth (Th)

Fish

1 can (6 ounces) solid white tuna (M)

Mexican Foods

1 medium can (16 ounces) refried beans (W)
1 small can (4.05 ounces) diced green chilies (W)
1 jar (16 ounces) salsa (W)

Fruit

1 can (11 ounces) mandarin oranges (M)
1 small can (8 ounces) crushed pineapple (M)

Juice

$1/2$ cup clam juice (F)

Condiments

1 small can (3.3 ounces) sliced black olives (W)

Dessert Needs

1 can (21 ounces) apricot (or peach) pie filling (M)

PACKAGED GOODS

Pasta, Rice & Grains

16 ounces rainbow pasta spirals (T)
1 package (14 ounces) tortilla chips (W)

Baked Goods

4 English muffins (M)
4 individual shortcake dessert cups (Th)

Nuts & Seeds

$1/4$ cup pecan pieces (Th)
$1/2$ cup chopped walnuts (F)

Dessert & Baking Needs

1 cup hard lemon candies (T)
$1/2$ cup soft caramel candies (Th)
4 individual graham cracker tart shells (T)
4 cinnamon sticks (F)

WINES & SPIRITS

2 cups dry white wine (or nonalcoholic white wine or clam juice) (F)
2 tablespoons rum (or nonalcoholic Italian orange syrup) (W)
1 tablespoon brandy (or nonalcoholic Italian praline syrup) (Th)

REFRIGERATED PRODUCTS

Dairy

$1^1/4$ cups whole or low-fat milk—1 cup (M), $1/4$ cup (F)
$1/2$ cup whipping cream (F)
1 cup regular or light sour cream—$3/4$ cup (W), $1/4$ cup (Th)

Cheese

1 container (4 ounces) whipped cream cheese (Th)
2 cups shredded regular or low-fat cheddar cheese—$1^1/2$ cups (M), $1/2$ cup (W)
$1/2$ cup shredded regular or low-fat Monterey Jack cheese (W)

Juice

$1/4$ cup orange juice (Th)

Deli

1 package (10) refrigerator biscuits (M)

FROZEN GOODS

Vegetables

1 package (24 ounces) frozen O'Brien potatoes with onions and peppers (M)
2 packages (9 ounces each) whole kernel corn—1 (M), 1 (F)
1 large package (16 ounces) green peas (T)
1 package (9 ounces) green peas (F)

Desserts

1 sheet frozen puff pastry (F)
1 pint lemon frozen yogurt (T)
1 pint grapefruit sherbet (F)

MONDAY

MENU

Tuna & Potato Toss

1 package (9 ounces) frozen whole kernel corn
1 package (24 ounces) frozen O'Brien potatoes
    with onions and peppers
1 cup whole or low-fat milk
1 can (6 ounces) solid white tuna
1 clove garlic
Seasoning to taste
1¹/₂ cups shredded regular or low-fat cheddar
    cheese

Beggarman's Salad

1 medium head lettuce
2 stalks celery
1 medium red onion
1 tablespoon fresh parsley (when chopped)
3 tablespoons rice vinegar
4 tablespoons regular or light vegetable oil
¹/₂ teaspoon dried tarragon
Seasoning to taste

English Tippers

4 English muffins
3 tablespoons softened butter
¹/₄ teaspoon dried savory
¹/₄ teaspoon dried dill
¹/₈ teaspoon paprika

Apricot Whatnot

1 can (11 ounces) mandarin oranges
1 small can (8 ounces) crushed pineapple
1 package (10) refrigerator biscuits
4 tablespoons butter
1 can (21 ounces) apricot (or peach) pie filling
2 tablespoons sugar
¹/₄ teaspoon ground cinnamon

EQUIPMENT

Large covered skillet	Assorted kitchen knives
Medium saucepan	Measuring cups and
9x9-inch glass baking	spoons
dish	Assorted cooking
Cookie sheet	utensils
Large bowl	Whisk
3 small bowls	

COUNTDOWN

1 Assemble the ingredients and equipment
2 Do Steps 1–6 of the *Apricot Whatnot*
3 Do Steps 1–2 of the *Tuna & Potato Toss*
4 Do Steps 1–2 of the *Beggarman's Salad*
5 Do Step 1 of the *English Tippers*
6 Do Steps 3–4 of the *Tuna & Potato Toss*
7 Do Steps 2–3 of the *English Tippers*
8 Do Step 3 of the *Beggarman's Salad*

Tuna & Potato Toss

1 Set the package of corn out to thaw.

2 Combine the frozen potatoes and the milk in a large skillet. Bring the mixture to a boil, stirring to break up the potatoes. Cover, reduce the heat and simmer until the potatoes are thawed and tender, 10 to 15 minutes.

3 Drain and flake the tuna. Peel and mince the garlic.

4 Remove the cover from the skillet and stir in the garlic, the corn and the tuna. Season to taste. Cook until the tuna is hot, 2 to 3 minutes. Stir in 1 cup of the cheese, mixing well. Sprinkle the remaining cheese over the top. Cover and simmer until the cheese is melted, 2 to 3 minutes.

Beggarman's Salad

1 Wash and dry the lettuce and tear it into bite-size pieces. Trim the celery and slice it into thin diagonals. Peel and thinly slice the red onion. Combine the ingredients in a large bowl.

2 Chop the parsley. In a small bowl, whisk together the parsley, the vinegar, the oil and the tarragon. Season to taste.

3 Toss the salad with the dressing.

English Tippers

1 Preheat the broiler.

2 Split the muffins and place them on an ungreased cookie sheet. Place the cookie sheet 3 or 4 inches from the heat and broil the muffins until they are lightly toasted, 1 to 2 minutes.

3 In a small bowl, combine the softened butter with the savory and the dill. Spread the mixture over the toasted muffins and lightly sprinkle them with the paprika.

Apricot Whatnot

1 Preheat the oven to 400°F. Grease a 9x9-inch glass baking dish.

2 Drain the oranges. Drain the pineapple.

3 Separate the biscuits and cut them into thirds.

4 Melt the butter in a medium saucepan. Reserve 2 tablespoons in a small bowl. Add the pie filling and the drained fruit to the remaining butter in the saucepan. Bring the mixture to a boil, stirring, and then pour it into the baking dish.

5 Dip the biscuit pieces into the reserved butter and arrange them over the fruit. Sprinkle the biscuits with the sugar and the cinnamon.

6 Bake until the biscuits are golden brown, 15 to 20 minutes.

TUESDAY

Rainbow Pasta

1 large package (16 ounces) frozen green peas
1 medium red bell pepper
4 medium carrots
4 scallions (green onions)
2 stalks celery
³/₄ pound lean cooked ham steak
1 clove garlic
16 ounces rainbow pasta spirals
¹/₄ cup regular or light olive oil
¹/₄ cup white wine vinegar
¹/₄ teaspoon dried tarragon
1 teaspoon sugar
¹/₂ teaspoon Dijon mustard
2 tablespoons regular or light vegetable oil
Seasoning to taste

Sunbeam Salad

1 medium head lettuce
1 small jicama (or turnip)
1 small red onion
1 small bunch radishes
2 tablespoons regular or light olive oil
1 tablespoon regular or light vegetable oil
2 tablespoons white wine vinegar
1 tablespoon honey
1 tablespoon lime juice
Seasoning to taste

Pots O' Gold

1 cup hard lemon candies
1 pint lemon frozen yogurt
4 individual graham cracker tart shells

EQUIPMENT

Stockpot	Assorted cooking
Large skillet	utensils
Large bowl	Whisk
2 small bowls	Vegetable peeler
Colander	Vegetable grater
Assorted kitchen knives	Plastic bag
Measuring cups and	Mallet
spoons	Ice cream scoop

COUNTDOWN

1 Assemble the ingredients and equipment
2 Do Step 1 of the *Pots O' Gold*
3 Do Steps 1–2 of the *Sunbeam Salad*
4 Do Steps 1–7 of the *Rainbow Pasta*
5 Do Step 3 of the *Sunbeam Salad*
6 Do Step 2 of the *Pots O' Gold*

Rainbow Pasta

1 Bring water to a boil in a stockpot. Set the package of peas out to thaw.

2 Seed and chop the bell pepper. Peel and grate the carrots. Trim and chop the scallions. Trim and chop the celery. Dice the ham. Peel and mince the garlic.

3 Cook the pasta in the boiling water until it is almost tender, 8 to 10 minutes.

4 In a small bowl, whisk the garlic together with the olive oil, the vinegar, the tarragon, the sugar and the mustard.

5 Heat the vegetable oil in a large skillet. Add the bell pepper, the carrots, the peas, the scallions and the celery and sauté for 2 minutes. Add the ham and sauté for 1 minute more.

6 Add the dressing, season to taste and toss quickly to combine. Remove the skillet from the heat.

7 Drain the pasta and return it to the stockpot. Toss the pasta with the sauce.

Sunbeam Salad

1 Wash and dry the lettuce and tear it into bite-size pieces. Peel and chunk the jicama. Peel and slice the red onion. Trim and slice the radishes. Combine the ingredients in a large bowl and refrigerate until you are ready to use.

2 In a small bowl, whisk together both oils, the vinegar, the honey and the lime juice. Season to taste.

3 Toss the salad with the dressing.

Pots O' Gold

1 Place the lemon candies in a plastic bag and crush them with a mallet.

2 Place scoops of frozen yogurt in the tart shells. Make a hole in the yogurt with a wooden spoon handle. Fill the holes with some of the crushed lemon candies and sprinkle the remaining lemon candies over the top.

WEDNESDAY

Piñata Pie

1 ripe avocado
2 tablespoons lemon juice
¼ teaspoon garlic powder
Seasoning to taste
1 package (14 ounces) tortilla chips
1 medium onion
½ pound fresh tomatoes
1 clove garlic
1 small can (3.3 ounces) sliced black olives
1 small green bell pepper
1 small head lettuce
1 pound lean ground beef
1 medium can (16 ounces) refried beans
1 small can (4.05 ounces) diced green chilies
¾ cup regular or light sour cream
½ teaspoon ground cumin
½ teaspoon chili powder
½ cup shredded regular or low-fat cheddar cheese
½ cup shredded regular or low-fat Monterey Jack cheese

Warm Salsa Chips

Tortilla chips reserved from the Piñata Pie
1 jar (16 ounces) salsa

Melon Rumba

1 large honeydew melon
2 tablespoons confectioners' sugar
2 tablespoons rum (or nonalcoholic Italian orange syrup)
2 tablespoons lime juice
⅛ teaspoon ground ginger

EQUIPMENT

Large covered skillet
Cookie sheet
2 small bowls
Assorted kitchen knives
Measuring cups and spoons

Assorted cooking utensils
Whisk

COUNTDOWN

1 Assemble the ingredients and equipment
2 Do Step 1 of the *Warm Salsa Chips*
3 Do Steps 1–2 of the *Piñata Pie*
4 Do Steps 1–2 of the *Melon Rumba*
5 Do Steps 2–3 of the *Warm Salsa Chips*
6 Do Steps 3–7 of the *Piñata Pie*

Piñata Pie

1 Peel, pit and mash the avocado. Blend in the lemon juice and the garlic powder. Season to taste.

2 Crush enough taco chips to make about 1 cup, reserving the remainder for the Warm Salsa Chips.

3 Peel and chop the onion. Chop the tomatoes. Peel and mince the garlic. Drain the olives. Seed and chop the bell pepper. Wash, dry and shred the lettuce.

4 In a large skillet, cook the beef, the onion and the garlic, stirring occasionally, until the beef is browned, about 5 minutes. Drain off any fat.

5 Stir in the refried beans and the chilies. Season to taste. Bring the mixture to a bubble, stirring occasionally. Remove the beans from the heat, scrape down the sides of the skillet and spread the mixture evenly around the skillet.

6 In a small bowl, combine the sour cream with the cumin and the chili powder and spread it over the beef mixture. Place the tomatoes in a circle around the outer edge of the pie. Place the olives in a circle inside the tomatoes and place the bell pepper in the center of the pie.

7 Sprinkle the pie with both cheeses. Top with the lettuce, the crushed tortilla chips and dollops of the guacamole.

Warm Salsa Chips

1 Preheat the oven to 250°F.

2 Spread the remaining tortilla chips on an ungreased cookie sheet.

3 Place the cookie sheet in the oven until the chips are heated through, about 10 minutes. Serve the chips with the salsa.

Melon Rumba

1 Seed and slice the melon and remove the rind. Distribute the slices among individual dessert plates.

2 In a small bowl, whisk together the sugar, the rum, the lime juice and the ginger. Drizzle the mixture over the melon and refrigerate until you are ready to serve.

THURSDAY

Oasis Chicken

1/2 pint fresh raspberries
1 medium orange
1 small onion
2 tablespoons butter
4 skinless, boneless chicken breast halves
1/4 cup orange juice
1/2 cup chicken broth
3 tablespoons red wine vinegar
2 tablespoons cornstarch dissolved in
   2 tablespoons cold water
1/2 cup golden raisins
Seasoning to taste

Desert Rice

2 scallions (green onions)
1 cup brown rice
1 1/4 cups chicken broth
3/4 cup water
1/2 teaspoon dried cumin

Sheik Snap Peas

3/4 pound sugar snap peas
2 tablespoons sesame oil
1 tablespoon sesame seeds
Seasoning to taste

Dark Nights

1 container (4 ounces) whipped cream cheese
1/4 cup regular or light sour cream
1 tablespoon dark brown sugar
1/2 teaspoon vanilla extract
4 individual shortcake dessert cups
1/4 cup pecan pieces
1/2 cup soft caramel candies
1 tablespoon butter
1 tablespoon brandy (or nonalcoholic Italian
   praline syrup)

EQUIPMENT

2 large skillets	Measuring cups and
Double boiler	spoons
Small saucepan	Assorted cooking
Small bowl	utensils
Assorted kitchen knives	Whisk

COUNTDOWN

1 Assemble the ingredients and equipment
2 Do Step 1 of the *Desert Rice*
3 Do Step 1 of the *Dark Nights*
4 Do Steps 1–2 of the *Oasis Chicken*
5 Do Step 1 of the *Sheik Snap Peas*
6 Do Steps 3–5 of the *Oasis Chicken*
7 Do Step 2 of the *Sheik Snap Peas*
8 Do Step 6 of the *Oasis Chicken*
9 Do Step 2 of the *Desert Rice*
10 Do Step 2 of the *Dark Nights*

Oasis Chicken

1 Rinse the raspberries and drain them on paper towels. Peel and section the orange. Peel and chop the onion.

2 Melt the butter in a large skillet. Sauté the onion until it is translucent, 3 to 4 minutes. Add the chicken breasts and cook, turning once, until they are golden outside and white throughout, about 10 minutes.

3 Remove the chicken and keep it warm.

4 In the same skillet, heat the orange juice with the broth and the vinegar until boiling. Whisk in the cornstarch mixture until it is well blended. Bring the sauce to a boil and cook, stirring constantly, until it is smooth and thickened, about 5 minutes.

5 Add the raspberries and the raisins to the sauce. Season to taste. Reduce the heat and simmer for 5 minutes more.

6 Gently stir in the orange sections and heat for 1 minute more. Return the chicken to the skillet and coat the pieces with the sauce.

Desert Rice

1 Trim and chop the scallions. Place the scallions, the rice, the broth, the water and the cumin in the top of a double boiler. Bring water to a boil in the bottom of the double boiler. Reduce the heat, cover and simmer until all the liquid is absorbed and the rice is tender, 35 to 45 minutes.

2 Fluff the rice before serving.

Sheik Snap Peas

1 Trim and string the sugar snap peas.

2 Heat the oil in a large skillet and stir in the sesame seeds. Stir-fry the snap peas until they are crisp-tender, 2 to 3 minutes. Season to taste.

Dark Nights

1 In a small bowl, mix the cream cheese, the sour cream, the brown sugar and the vanilla until well blended. Fill the dessert cups, sprinkle them with the pecans, and refrigerate until you are ready to use.

2 In a small saucepan, melt the caramels in the butter, stirring, about 5 minutes. Add the brandy and cook until the alcohol evaporates, about 3 minutes. Pour the sauce over the cakes.

FRIDAY

Neptune Pot Pie

1 package (9 ounces) frozen green peas
1 package (9 ounces) frozen whole kernel corn
1 sheet frozen puff pastry
2 cups dry white wine (or nonalcoholic white
    wine or clam juice)
12 ounces medium shrimp, shelled and
    deveined
1 pound scallops
1 tart green apple
1 medium onion
2 medium carrots
3 tablespoons butter
$^1/_2$ cup clam juice
$^1/_2$ cup whipping cream
2 tablespoons flour
$^1/_4$ cup whole or low-fat milk
Seasoning to taste

De-Vine Salad

1 medium head lettuce
$^1/_4$ pound seedless green grapes
$^1/_4$ pound seedless red grapes
2 stalks celery
4 tablespoons regular or low-fat mayonnaise
$^1/_2$ teaspoon lemon juice
1 teaspoon sugar
Seasoning to taste
$^1/_2$ cup chopped walnuts

Shipwreck Sherbet

2 tablespoons sweetened cocoa
2 tablespoons confectioners' sugar
1 pint grapefruit sherbet
4 cinnamon sticks

EQUIPMENT

Dutch oven	Assorted cooking
Medium saucepan	utensils
9x9-inch glass baking	Whisk
dish	Vegetable peeler
Large bowl	Sifter
2 small bowls	Ice cream scoop
Assorted kitchen knives	
Measuring cups and	
spoons	

COUNTDOWN

1 Assemble the ingredients and equipment
2 Do Steps 1–9 of the *Neptune Pot Pie*
3 Do Steps 1–2 of the *De-Vine Salad*
4 Do Steps 1–2 of the *Shipwreck Sherbet*

Neptune Pot Pie

1 Set the frozen peas, the corn and the puff pastry sheet out to thaw.

2 Preheat the oven to 350°F.

3 Bring the wine to a boil in a medium saucepan and cook until it is reduced by a third, about 7 minutes.

4 Rinse the shrimp. Rinse and pat dry the scallops. If you are using seas scallops, cut them in half. Core and chop the apple. Peel and chop the onion. Peel and chop the carrots.

5 Add the scallops to the wine, reduce the heat and simmer just until they turn opaque, 2 to 3 minutes.

6 Remove the scallops with a slotted spoon and reserve. Reserve the cooking liquid.

7 Melt the butter in a Dutch oven. Add the apple, the onion and the carrots and sauté until they are soft, 5 to 7 minutes. Add the reserved cooking liquid, the clam juice and the cream. Simmer the mixture for 5 minutes.

8 In a small bowl, combine the flour and the milk until a smooth paste forms. Slowly stir the paste into the simmering stock, whisking until the sauce thickens. Add the scallops, the shrimp, the peas and the corn, and simmer until the shrimp turn bright pink, about 2 minutes. Season to taste.

9 Turn the mixture into a 9x9-inch glass baking dish. Lay the pastry over the top, sealing the pie and trimming to fit. Cut several slits in the pastry with the tip of a knife. Bake until the pie is golden, about 30 minutes.

De-Vine Salad

1 Wash and dry the lettuce and tear it into bite-size pieces, reserving 4 leaves. Wash, separate and halve the grapes. Trim and diagonally slice the celery.

2 In a large bowl, whisk together the mayonnaise, the lemon juice and the sugar. Season to taste and toss the dressing lightly with the salad ingredients. Place the reserved lettuce leaves on individual salad plates and top with the grape mixture. Sprinkle with the walnuts.

Shipwreck Sherbet

1 In a small bowl, sift together the cocoa and the confectioners' sugar.

2 Place scoops of sherbet in individual dessert bowls. Sprinkle with the cocoa mixture, and place a cinnamon stick into the sherbet at a rakish angle.

JULY
WEEK ONE

Monday

BIG TOP TURKEY
SIDESHOW NOODLES
THREE-RING SALAD
CLOWNING AROUND DESSERT

Tuesday

HAMMING IT UP
SUPERSTAR SLAW
DEPTHS OF PLEASURE

Wednesday

ONE LIFE TO LIVER
AS THE RICE TURNS
THE BOLD & THE BROCCOLI
ANOTHER SHERBET

Thursday

PASTA PUTTANESCA
MOZZARELLA SALAD
BELLA BREAD
CHOCOLATE CHIP CLOUD

Friday

BUNKER HILL BISQUE
STAR SPANGLED SALAD
REVOLUTIONARY RYE BREAD
INDEPENDENCE PIE

- ☐ Butter
- ☐ Granulated sugar
- ☐ Sweetened cocoa
- ☐ Marshmallow topping
- ☐ Long-grain white rice
- ☐ Regular or light vegetable oil
- ☐ Regular or light olive oil
- ☐ Red wine vinegar
- ☐ Rice vinegar
- ☐ Lemon juice
- ☐ Tabasco sauce
- ☐ Prepared horseradish
- ☐ Regular or low-fat mayonnaise
- ☐ Honey
- ☐ Grated Parmesan cheese
- ☐ Dried basil
- ☐ Celery seeds
- ☐ Ground cinnamon
- ☐ Cream of tartar
- ☐ Dried dill
- ☐ Garlic powder
- ☐ Dried oregano
- ☐ Paprika
- ☐ Poppy seeds
- ☐ Red pepper flakes
- ☐ Dried sage
- ☐ Dried tarragon
- ☐ Dried thyme
- ☐ Pepper
- ☐ Salt
- ☐ Vanilla extract

MEAT & POULTRY

1¼ pounds lean cooked ham steak (T)

1½ pounds boneless turkey breast (M)

1 pound chicken livers (W)

FRESH PRODUCE

Vegetables

2 large sweet potatoes (T)

2 medium zucchini (F)

1 medium bunch broccoli (W)

6 medium mushrooms (W)

1 medium carrot (T)

1 stalk celery (F)

1 large sweet onion (M)

2 medium onions—1 (T), 1 (W)

2 small onions—1 (M), 1 (Th)

1 small red onion (F)

1 large leek (F)

8 scallions (green onions)— 2 (W), 2 (Th), 4 (F)

1 head garlic (W, Th)

1 bunch parsley (M, W, Th, F)

1 small (or half) head red cabbage (T)

1 medium head lettuce (F)

1 small head lettuce (M, Th)

1 ripe avocado (M)

2 large tomatoes (Th)

2 medium tomatoes (F)

1 medium cucumber (F)

2 small green bell peppers— 1 (T), 1 (F)

Fruit

2 large tart green apples (T)

1 medium nectarine (W)

1 medium banana (W)

½ pint blueberries (W)

1 pint blueberries (F)

1 pint raspberries (F)

4 medium oranges (M)

1 medium lemon (F)

CANS, JARS & BOTTLES

Soup

1 can (10¾ ounces) chicken broth (M)

1 can (14½ ounces) chicken broth (W)

2 cans (14½ ounces each) vegetable broth (F)

Vegetables

1 large can (28 ounces) cut-up tomatoes (Th)

1 medium can (14½ ounces) cut-up tomatoes (M)

Fish

1 can (2 ounces) anchovy fillets (Th)

1 large can (6.05 ounces) boneless, skinless salmon (F)

1 small jar (2 ounces) black caviar or lumpfish (optional) (F)

Fruit

1 can (11 ounces) mandarin oranges (M)

Condiments

1 small can (3.3 ounces) chopped black olives (Th)

2 teaspoons capers (Th)

PACKAGED GOODS

Pasta, Rice & Grains

8 ounces broad egg noodles (M)

16 ounces spaghetti (Th)

Baked Goods

1 French bread baguette (Th)

1 small loaf crusty rye bread (F)

Nuts & Seeds

½ cup pecan pieces (T)

2 tablespoons sunflower seeds (T)

Dessert & Baking Needs

1 package (13 ounces) coconut macaroons (M)

1 package (9 ounces) chocolate wafers (M)

1 small package (3½ ounces) lemon gelatin (T)

16 Hershey's Kisses (T)

1 package (12 ounces) semisweet chocolate chips (Th)

WINES & SPIRITS

1 cup + 3 tablespoons dry white wine (or nonalcoholic white wine or chicken broth)—1 cup (M), 3 tablespoons (W)

¼ cup dry sherry (or water) (W)

REFRIGERATED PRODUCTS

Dairy

1 cup half-and-half (M)

¼ cup regular or light sour cream (F)

1 cup regular or low-fat plain yogurt (F)

4 eggs—2 (M, Th), 2 (F)

Cheese

4 ounces sliced regular or low-fat mozzarella cheese (Th)

Juice

¾ cup orange juice (T)

Deli

4 ounces sliced dry salami (Th)

FROZEN GOODS

Vegetables

1 package (9 ounces) artichoke hearts (M)

Desserts

4 toaster waffles (F)

1 pint strawberry ice cream (M)

1 pint pineapple (or lemon) sherbet (W)

2 small containers (8 ounces each) frozen whipped topping—1 (Th), 1 (F)

MONDAY

Big Top Turkey

1 package (9 ounces) frozen artichoke hearts
1 small onion
1 can (14$\frac{1}{2}$ ounces) cut-up tomatoes
1$\frac{1}{2}$ pounds boneless turkey breast
Seasoning to taste
3 tablespoons regular or light olive oil
1 can (10$\frac{3}{4}$ ounces) chicken broth
1 cup dry white wine (or nonalcoholic white
    wine or additional chicken broth)
2 egg yolks*
1 cup half-and-half
$\frac{1}{2}$ teaspoon dried basil

Sideshow Noodles

1 tablespoon fresh parsley (when chopped)
8 ounces broad egg noodles
1 tablespoon butter
1 tablespoon lemon juice
Seasoning to taste

Three-Ring Salad

4 medium oranges
1 can (11 ounces) mandarin oranges
1 large sweet onion
1 ripe avocado
4 lettuce leaves*
3 tablespoons honey
3 tablespoons rice vinegar
3 tablespoons regular or light vegetable oil
1 tablespoon poppy seeds
Seasoning to taste

Clowning Around Dessert

1 package (13 ounces) coconut macaroons
1 package (9 ounces) chocolate wafers
1 pint strawberry ice cream
Marshmallow topping for garnish

EQUIPMENT

Large covered skillet	Assorted kitchen knives
Large covered saucepan	Measuring cups and spoons
Large bowl	Assorted cooking utensils
Medium bowl	Whisk
3 small bowls	Ice cream scoop
Strainer	

COUNTDOWN

1 Assemble the ingredients and equipment
2 Do Steps 1–2 of the *Big Top Turkey*
3 Do Steps 1–2 of the *Three-Ring Salad*
4 Do Step 1 of the *Sideshow Noodles*
5 Do Step 1 of the *Clowning Around Dessert*
6 Do Steps 3–4 of the *Big Top Turkey*
7 Do Step 2 of the *Sideshow Noodles*
8 Do Step 5 of the *Big Top Turkey*
9 Do Step 3 of the *Sideshow Noodles*
10 Do Step 3 of the *Three-Ring Salad*
11 Do Step 2 of the *Clowning Around Dessert*

---

*Reserve the egg whites and remaining lettuce for use on Thursday.

Big Top Turkey

1 Set the artichokes in a medium bowl of hot water to thaw. Peel and chop the onion. Drain the tomatoes. Slice the turkey into 4 portions, pat dry and season them to taste.

2 Heat the oil in a large skillet. Add the turkey portions and cook until they are lightly browned, 3 to 4 minutes per side. Drain off any excess fat and add the onion, the broth and the wine to the skillet. Reduce the heat, cover and simmer until the turkey is fork-tender, 15 to 20 minutes.

3 In a small bowl, lightly beat the egg yolks and combine them with the half-and-half.

4 Remove the turkey from the skillet and reserve. Boil the pan juices until they are reduced to $1/2$ cup, about 5 minutes. Add the tomatoes and the artichokes, and cook for 1 minute. Reduce the heat, add the half-and-half mixture and the basil, season to taste and simmer until the sauce is thickened and slightly reduced, 7 to 8 minutes.

5 Return the turkey to the skillet and heat in the sauce for 5 minutes.

Sideshow Noodles

1 Bring water to a boil in a large saucepan. Chop the parsley.

2 Cook the noodles in the boiling water until they are almost tender, 3 to 5 minutes.

3 Drain the noodles and return them to the saucepan. Toss them with the butter, the lemon juice and the parsley. Season to taste and cover to keep warm.

Three-Ring Salad

1 Peel and thinly slice the oranges. Drain the mandarin oranges, reserving the juice in a small bowl. Peel and slice the sweet onion and separate it into rings. Combine the ingredients in a large bowl. Peel and slice the avocado and toss it lightly with the reserved orange juice. Wash and dry 4 lettuce leaves and place them on individual salad plates.

2 Drain the avocado and add it to the large bowl. In a small bowl, whisk together the honey, the vinegar, the oil and the poppy seeds. Season to taste. Toss the salad lightly with the dressing and refrigerate until you are ready to serve.

3 Spoon the orange mixture over the lettuce leaves.

Clowning Around Dessert

1 Crumble the macaroons and the chocolate wafers. Place half of the macaroon crumbs in the bottom of individual dessert bowls.

2 Place scoops of ice cream over the crumbs. Add the chocolate wafer crumbs. Top with the marshmallow topping and sprinkle with the remaining macaroon crumbs.

TUESDAY

Hamming It Up

2 large sweet potatoes
2 large tart green apples
1 medium onion
1^1/$_4$ pounds lean cooked ham steak
^{3}/$_4$ cup orange juice
^{1}/$_2$ teaspoon ground cinnamon
^{1}/$_2$ cup pecan pieces

Superstar Slaw

^{1}/$_3$ cup regular or low-fat mayonnaise
2 tablespoons lemon juice
1 tablespoon sugar
Seasoning to taste
1 small (or half) head red cabbage
1 medium carrot
1 small green bell pepper
2 tablespoons sunflower seeds

Depths of Pleasure

1^1/$_4$ cups water
1 small package (3^1/$_2$ ounces) lemon gelatin
Ice cubes
16 Hershey's Kisses

EQUIPMENT

Blender	Assorted cooking
Large covered skillet	utensils
Large bowl	Whisk
Assorted kitchen knives	Vegetable peeler
Measuring cups and	Vegetable grater
spoons	

COUNTDOWN

1 Assemble the ingredients and equipment
2 Do Steps 1–4 of the *Depths of Pleasure*
3 Do Steps 1–2 of the *Superstar Slaw*
4 Do Steps 1–3 of *Hamming It Up*

Hamming It Up

1 Peel and thinly slice the sweet potatoes. Core and chop the apples. Peel and chop the onion. Dice the ham.

2 Combine the potatoes, the apples and the onion in a large skillet. Add ½ cup of the orange juice and bring the mixture to a boil. Reduce the heat, cover and steam until the potatoes are almost tender, 8 to 10 minutes.

3 Remove the cover, stir in the remaining orange juice, the cinnamon and the ham until the ingredients are well blended. Simmer until the mixture is hot, about 5 minutes. Sprinkle with the pecan pieces.

Superstar Slaw

1 In a large bowl, whisk together the mayonnaise, the lemon juice and the sugar until smooth. Season to taste.

2 Grate the cabbage. Peel and grate the carrot. Seed and slice the bell pepper into thin strips. Add the ingredients to the large bowl, add the sunflower seeds, toss with the dressing and refrigerate until you are ready to serve.

Depths of Pleasure

1 Bring ¾ cup of the water to a boil.

2 Pour the boiling water into a blender. Add the gelatin. Cover and blend on low speed until the gelatin is completely dissolved, about 30 seconds.

3 Combine the remaining ½ cup of cold water with enough ice cubes to make 1¼ cups. Add the ice to the gelatin and stir until it is partially melted. Then blend at high speed for 30 seconds.

4 Unwrap the Hershey's Kisses and place them in the bottom of individual dessert glasses. Pour the gelatin mixture over the chocolate and refrigerate for at least 30 minutes.

WEDNESDAY

One Life to Liver

1 pound chicken livers
1 medium onion
6 medium fresh mushrooms
2 tablespoons fresh parsley (when chopped)
4 tablespoons butter
Seasoning to taste
3 tablespoons dry white wine (or nonalcoholic
    white wine or chicken broth)
$^1/_2$ cup grated Parmesan cheese

As the Rice Turns

1 tablespoon fresh parsley (when chopped)
1 cup long-grain white rice
1 can (14$^1/_2$ ounces) chicken broth
$^1/_4$ cup dry sherry (or nonalcoholic white wine
    or water)

The Bold & the Broccoli

1 medium bunch broccoli
2 cloves garlic
2 scallions (green onions)
2 tablespoons regular or light olive oil
2 tablespoons water
1 teaspoon celery seeds
1 teaspoon dried thyme
Seasoning to taste

Another Sherbet

1 medium nectarine
$^1/_2$ pint fresh blueberries
$^1/_2$ pound fresh cherries
1 tablespoon lemon juice
1 medium banana
1 pint pineapple (or lemon) sherbet

EQUIPMENT

Large covered skillet	Measuring cups and
Medium covered skillet	spoons
Double boiler	Assorted cooking
Large bowl	utensils
Assorted kitchen knives	Ice cream scoop

COUNTDOWN

1 Assemble the ingredients and equipment
2 Do Step 1 of *One Life to Liver*
3 Do Step 1 of *As the Rice Turns*
4 Do Step 1 *The Bold & the Broccoli*
5 Do Step 1 of *Another Sherbet*
6 Do Step 2 of *One Life to Liver*
7 Do Steps 2–3 of *The Bold & the Broccoli*
8 Do Step 2 of *As the Rice Turns*
9 Do Step 3 of *One Life to Liver*
10 Do Step 2 of *Another Sherbet*

One Life to Liver

1 Wash, pat dry and cut the chicken livers in half. Peel and chop the onion. Wash, pat dry, trim and slice the mushrooms. Chop the parsley.

2 Melt the butter in a large skillet. Sauté the chicken livers, the onion and the mushrooms until the onion is limp and the livers are pink in the middle, 4 to 6 minutes. Season to taste. Reduce the heat, add the wine and simmer for 2 minutes more. Remove the skillet from the heat and cover to keep warm.

3 Sprinkle the livers with the parsley and the Parmesan cheese.

As the Rice Turns

1 Chop the parsley. Place the parsley, the rice, the chicken broth and the sherry in the top of a double boiler. Bring water to a boil in the bottom of the double boiler, reduce the heat, cover and simmer until all the liquid is absorbed and the rice is tender, 30 to 40 minutes.

2 Fluff the rice before serving.

The Bold & the Broccoli

1 Trim and cut the broccoli into bite-size florets. Peel and mince the garlic. Trim and chop the scallions.

2 Heat the oil in a medium skillet and sauté the garlic for 3 minutes. Add the broccoli, the scallions and the water. Cover and steam for 5 minutes.

3 Remove the skillet from the heat, and toss the broccoli with the celery seeds and the thyme. Season to taste and cover to keep warm.

Another Sherbet

1 Peel and slice the nectarine. Wash and dry the berries. Wash, stem, halve and pit the cherries. Place the fruit in a large bowl, sprinkle it with the lemon juice and refrigerate until you are ready to use.

2 Peel and slice the banana. Layer scoops of sherbet with scoops of the refrigerated fruit into individual dessert dishes. Top with the banana slices.

THURSDAY

Pasta Puttanesca

2 cloves garlic
2 tablespoons fresh parsley (when chopped)
1 small can (3.3 ounces) chopped black olives
2 teaspoons capers
4 tablespoons regular or light olive oil
1 large can (28 ounces) cut-up tomatoes
1 teaspoon red pepper flakes
1/2 teaspoon dried oregano
1 can (2 ounces) anchovy fillets
16 ounces spaghetti
Seasoning to taste

Mozzarella Salad

2 large tomatoes
2 scallions (green onions)
Lettuce reserved from Monday
4 ounces sliced regular or low-fat mozzarella
    cheese
4 ounces sliced dry salami
3 tablespoons regular or light olive oil
2 tablespoons red wine vinegar
1/8 teaspoon dried tarragon
Seasoning to taste

Bella Bread

1 small onion
2 tablespoons butter
1 small French bread baguette
1 teaspoon garlic powder

Chocolate Chip Cloud

2 egg whites reserved from Monday
1/2 teaspoon vanilla extract
1/4 teaspoon cream of tartar
1/3 cup sugar
1 package (12 ounces) semisweet chocolate
    chips
1 small container (8 ounces) frozen whipped
    topping
2 tablespoons sweetened cocoa

EQUIPMENT

Electric hand mixer	Colander
Stockpot	Assorted kitchen knives
Large skillet	Measuring cups and
Small skillet	spoons
2 cookie sheets	Assorted cooking
Large bowl	utensils
Small bowl	Whisk

COUNTDOWN

1 Assemble the ingredients and cooking
   equipment
2 Do Steps 1–2 of the *Chocolate Chip Cloud*
3 Do Steps 1–2 of the *Mozzarella Salad*
4 Do Steps 1–6 of the *Pasta Puttanesca*
5 Do Steps 1–3 of the *Bella Bread*
6 Do Steps 7–8 of the *Pasta Puttanesca*
7 Do Step 4 of the *Bella Bread*
8 Do Step 3 of the *Mozzarella Salad*
9 Do Step 3 of the *Chocolate Chip Cloud*

Pasta Puttanesca

1 Bring water to a boil in a stockpot.

2 Peel and mince the garlic. Chop the parsley. Drain the olives. Rinse the capers.

3 Heat 3 tablespoons of the oil in a large skillet. Add the garlic and sauté until it is soft but not brown, 1 to 2 minutes.

4 Stir in the undrained tomatoes, the olives, the capers, the red pepper flakes and the oregano. Simmer until the sauce thickens, about 15 minutes.

5 Drain the anchovies, blot them dry on paper towels and cut them into small pieces.

6 Cook the pasta in the boiling water until it is almost tender, 2 to 3 minutes if you are using fresh pasta and 6 to 7 minutes if you are using dried pasta.

7 Drain the pasta well, return it to the stockpot and toss it with the remaining oil. Cover to keep warm.

8 Stir the anchovies and the parsley into the skillet and simmer for 2 minutes more. Season to taste. Toss the sauce with the pasta.

Mozzarella Salad

1 Slice the tomatoes. Trim and chop the scallions. Wash and dry the lettuce leaves and place them on individual salad plates. Arrange the slices of tomato, cheese and salami over the lettuce. Refrigerate until you are ready to serve.

2 In a small bowl, whisk together the oil, the vinegar and the tarragon. Season to taste.

3 Drizzle the dressing over the salad and top with the chopped scallions.

Bella Bread

1 Preheat the broiler.

2 Peel and thinly slice the onion. Melt the butter in a small skillet and sauté the onion until it is limp, about 5 minutes.

3 Slice the baguette lengthwise and then in half, and place the quarters on an ungreased cookie sheet. Spread the cut sides of the bread with the onion-butter mixture. Sprinkle with the garlic powder.

4 Broil, 3 or 4 inches from the heat, until the onion is golden, 1 to 2 minutes.

Chocolate Chip Cloud

1 Preheat the oven to 325°F. Grease a cookie sheet.

2 In a large bowl, beat the egg whites with the vanilla and the cream of tartar until soft peaks form, about 2 minutes. Gradually beat in the sugar until stiff peaks form, about 2 minutes more. Fold in $1/2$ cup of the chocolate chips. Spoon the mixture onto the cookie sheet, forming shells with the bowl of a spoon. Bake for 10 minutes.

3 Fold the remaining chocolate chips into the whipped topping and fill the meringues. Sprinkle with the cocoa.

FRIDAY

Bunker Hill Bisque

2 medium zucchini
1 large leek
1 tablespoon fresh parsley (when chopped)
2 cans (14$^1/_2$ ounces each) vegetable broth
$^1/_4$ cup regular or light sour cream
$^1/_2$ teaspoon Tabasco sauce
Seasoning to taste

Star Spangled Salad

2 eggs
1 can (6.05 ounces) boneless, skinless salmon
1 stalk celery
1 small red onion
4 scallions (green onions)
Ice cubes
1 cup regular or low-fat plain yogurt
1 tablespoon dried dill
2 tablespoons red wine vinegar
Seasoning to taste
1 medium head lettuce
1 medium cucumber
1 small green bell pepper
2 medium tomatoes
1 medium lemon
1 small jar (2 ounces) black caviar or
    lumpfish (optional)

Revolutionary Rye Bread

1 small loaf crusty rye bread
4 tablespoons fresh parsley (when chopped)
3 tablespoons softened butter
1 tablespoon prepared horseradish
2 teaspoons dried sage
1 teaspoon paprika

Independence Pie

1 pint fresh blueberries
1 pint fresh raspberries
4 toaster waffles
1 small container (8 ounces) frozen whipped
    topping

EQUIPMENT

Blender	Assorted kitchen knives
Medium covered	Measuring cups and
saucepan	spoons
Small saucepan	Assorted cooking
Large bowl	utensils
2 small bowls	Vegetable peeler

COUNTDOWN

1 Assemble the ingredients and equipment
2 Do Steps 1–3 of the *Star Spangled Salad*
3 Do Steps 1–2 of the *Bunker Hill Bisque*
4 Do Step 1 of the *Independence Pie*
5 Do Steps 4–6 of the *Star Spangled Salad*
6 Do Steps 1–3 of the *Revolutionary Rye Bread*
7 Do Step 3 of the *Bunker Hill Bisque*
8 Do Step 7 of the *Star Spangled Salad*
9 Do Step 2 of the *Independence Pie*

Bunker Hill Bisque

1 Trim the zucchini and cut it into thick slices. Thoroughly wash the leek, split it lengthwise and cut it into thick slices. Chop the parsley.

2 Bring the broth to a boil in a medium saucepan. Add the zucchini and the leek and simmer, partially covered, until the vegetables are tender, 10 to 15 minutes.

3 Transfer the zucchini mixture to a blender and process until it is smooth. Return the mixture to the saucepan. Stir in the sour cream and the Tabasco, and season to taste. Heat until hot, but do not let boil. Garnish with the parsley.

Star Spangled Salad

1 Cover the eggs with water in a small saucepan. Bring the water to a boil and hard-cook the eggs, 10 to 12 minutes.

2 Drain and flake the salmon. Trim and chop the celery. Peel and chop the red onion.

3 Trim the scallions and cut off all but 1 inch of green stem. Quarter each scallion lengthwise about 1 inch from the end, leaving the bottom white part uncut. Place the scallions in a small bowl of cold water with ice cubes. They will form curly frills in about 30 minutes.

4 In a large bowl, combine the salmon, the celery, the onion, the yogurt, the dill and the vinegar. Season to taste. Cover the bowl and refrigerate until you are ready to use.

5 Drain and peel the hard-cooked eggs and place them in the freezer to chill for 10 minutes.

6 Wash and dry the lettuce and arrange the leaves on a platter. Peel, cut in half lengthwise and thinly slice the cucumber. Thinly slice the bell pepper. Quarter the tomatoes. Quarter the eggs. Cut the lemon in half and slice it thinly. Remove the scallions from the water and shake to dry them.

7 Mound the salmon mixture in the center of the lettuce. Sprinkle the caviar over the salmon, and garnish with the cucumber, the bell pepper, the egg quarters, the tomato quarters, the scallions and the lemon slices.

Revolutionary Rye Bread

1 Cut the bread into 1-inch-thick slices. Chop the parsley.

2 In a small bowl, combine the parsley with the softened butter, the horseradish and the sage.

3 Spread the bread with the parsley mixture and sprinkle with the paprika.

Independence Pie

1 Rinse and stem the blueberries, if necessary. Rinse the raspberries. Drain them on paper towels.

2 Lightly toast the waffles. Spread each waffle with a quarter of the whipped topping and arrange the berries over the topping in a pattern of stars and stripes.

JULY

WEEK TWO

Monday

TEX-MEX PASTA
SOUTH OF THE BORDER SALAD
SAND TARTS

Tuesday

COOL AS A CUCUMBER
TIPSY POTATOES
SWEET & SOUR CARROTS
HOPSCOTCH PUDDING

Wednesday

QUICK GREEK BEEF
OH-SO ORZO
TURNIP TOSS
CHOCOLATE CREAM

Thursday

CIOPPINO
SWEET ONION SALAD
CRUSTY ITALIAN BREAD
PEPPERMINT PIE

Friday

IT HASTA BE PASTA
SNAPPY SALAD
CHEESE BUNS
NECTARINE MELBA

- ☐ Butter
- ☐ Flour
- ☐ Cornstarch
- ☐ Granulated sugar
- ☐ Confectioners' sugar
- ☐ Chocolate syrup
- ☐ Chocolate sprinkles
- ☐ Regular or light vegetable oil
- ☐ Regular or light olive oil
- ☐ Red wine vinegar
- ☐ Rice vinegar
- ☐ Lemon juice
- ☐ Worcestershire sauce
- ☐ Dijon mustard
- ☐ Prepared horseradish
- ☐ Honey
- ☐ Dark raisins
- ☐ Grated Parmesan cheese
- ☐ Seasoned bread crumbs
- ☐ Instant coffee crystals
- ☐ Ground cinnamon
- ☐ Ground cumin
- ☐ Onion powder
- ☐ Dried thyme
- ☐ Pepper
- ☐ Salt
- ☐ Vanilla extract

SHOPPING NOTES

● If you are shopping once a week and cannot arrange to purchase fresh clams on the day you plan to use them, you can substitute 2 cans (10 ounces each) whole clams and omit cooking instructions.

● If you are shopping once a week and cannot arrange to purchase fresh seafood on the day you plan to use it, you can purchase *not previously frozen* seafood and freeze it, placing it in the refrigerator to thaw the night before you are ready to use it. Or you can purchase *still frozen* seafood and keep it frozen until the night before you are ready to use it.

MEAT & POULTRY
1 pound lean boneless sirloin steak (W)
4 boneless, skinless chicken breast halves (T)

FISH
24 hard-shelled clams (Th)
1 pound medium shrimp, shelled and deveined (Th)
$1/2$ pound scallops (Th)
2 pounds white fish fillets (Th)

FRESH PRODUCE
Vegetables
1 pound small new red potatoes (T)
2 medium turnips (W)
1 pound baby carrots (T)
1 large sweet onion (Th)
1 medium sweet onion (M)
3 medium onions—1 (M), 1 (W), 1 (Th)
2 small onions—1 (T), 1 (F)
2 small red onions—1 (W), 1 (F)
4 scallions (green onions) (T)
1 head garlic (W, Th, F)
1 bunch basil (Th, F)
1 bunch dill (T, W)
1 bunch parsley (M-F)
$1/4$ pound alfalfa sprouts (M)
3 medium heads lettuce—1 (M), 1 (W), 1 (F)
1 small head lettuce (Th)
$1^1/2$ pounds tomatoes—$1/2$ pound (M), 1 pound (Th)
2 large tomatoes (Th)
1 medium cucumber (T)
1 small green bell pepper (M)
1 small bunch radishes (F)

Fruit
4 large apricots (M)
2 medium nectarines (F)
$1/2$ pint raspberries (F)

CANS, JARS & BOTTLES
Soup
1 can ($10^3/4$ ounces) beef broth (W, Th)

Vegetables
1 medium can ($14^1/2$ ounces) cut-up tomatoes (Th)
1 small can (6 ounces) tomato paste (W)
1 small can ($8^3/4$ ounces) whole kernel corn (M)

Fish
1 can (2 ounces) anchovy fillets (F)
1 can ($3^3/4$ ounces) boneless, skinless sardines packed in oil (F)

Juice
1 small can ($5^1/2$ ounces) V-8 juice (M, F)
$1/4$ cup apple juice (T)
2 bottles (8 ounces each) clam juice (Th)

Condiments
$2/3$ cup picante sauce (M)
1 small can ($3^1/2$ ounces) pitted black olives (M)

Spreads
1 cup apricot preserves (M)
$1/2$ cup orange marmalade (M)

PACKAGED GOODS
Pasta, Rice & Grains
16 ounces fettuccine (M)
8 ounces orzo (W)
12 ounces bucatini or other small tubular pasta (F)

Baked Goods
4 taco shells (M)
1 small crusty Italian bread (Th)
2 hamburger buns (F)

Nuts & Seeds
12 whole pecans (T)
$1/2$ cup pine nuts (F)

Dessert Needs
1 small package (3.4 ounces) instant butterscotch pudding mix (T)

1 envelope unflavored gelatin (W)
1 small package (6 ounces) semisweet chocolate chips (W)
4 individual graham cracker tart shells (M)
1 prepared 9-inch chocolate pie shell (Th)

WINES & SPIRITS
$2/3$ cup dry white wine (or nonalcoholic white wine or chicken broth) (T)
$1/2$ cup dry white wine (or nonalcoholic white wine or water) (Th)
$1/2$ cup dry red wine (or nonalcoholic red wine or beef broth) (W)
$1^1/2$ cups dry red wine (or nonalcoholic red wine or tomato juice) (Th)
1 tablespoon Kirsch liqueur (or nonalcoholic Italian cherry syrup) (F)

REFRIGERATED PRODUCTS
Dairy
2 cups whole milk (T)
$1^1/2$ cups whole or low-fat milk (W)
1 cup whipping cream (W)
1 cup regular or light sour cream (M)
1 cup regular or low-fat plain yogurt (T)

Cheese
3 ounces feta cheese (W)

FROZEN GOODS
Vegetables
1 package (9 ounces) peas and carrots (W)

Desserts
1 small container (8 ounces) frozen whipped topping (M)
1 quart peppermint ice cream (Th)
1 pint vanilla ice cream (F)

MONDAY

Tex-Mex Pasta

1 medium onion
$^1/_2$ pound fresh tomatoes
2 tablespoons fresh parsley (when chopped)
16 ounces fettuccine
4 tablespoons butter
1 tablespoon regular or light vegetable oil
$^2/_3$ cup picante sauce
3 tablespoons V-8 juice*
$^2/_3$ cup grated Parmesan cheese
1 cup regular or light sour cream
Seasoning to taste

South of the Border Salad

1 medium head lettuce
1 medium sweet onion
1 small green bell pepper
1 small can (3$^1/_2$ ounces) pitted black olives
1 small can (8$^3/_4$ ounces) whole kernel corn
3 tablespoons regular or light olive oil
2 tablespoons red wine vinegar
$^1/_2$ teaspoon ground cumin
Seasoning to taste
4 taco shells
$^1/_4$ pound alfalfa sprouts

Sand Tarts

4 large fresh apricots
1 cup apricot preserves
$^1/_2$ cup orange marmalade
4 individual graham cracker tart shells
1 small container (8 ounces) frozen whipped
    topping
$^1/_4$ cup confectioners' sugar

*Reserve the remainder of the can for use on Friday.

EQUIPMENT	
Stockpot	Measuring cups and
Medium saucepan	spoons
Large bowl	Assorted cooking
2 small bowls	utensils
Colander	Whisk
Assorted kitchen knives	Sifter

COUNTDOWN

1 Assemble the ingredients and equipment
2 Do Steps 1–2 of the *South of the Border Salad*
3 Do Step 1 of the *Tex-Mex Pasta*
4 Do Steps 1–3 of the *Sand Tarts*
5 Do Steps 2–6 of the *Tex-Mex Pasta*
6 Do Step 3 of the *South of the Border Salad*
7 Do Step 4 of the *Sand Tarts*

Tex-Mex Pasta

1 Bring water to a boil in a stockpot.

2 Peel and chop the onion. Chop the tomatoes. Chop the parsley.

3 Cook the fettuccine in the boiling water until it is almost tender, 3 to 4 minutes if you are using fresh pasta and 6 to 7 minutes if you are using dried pasta.

4 Melt the butter in a medium saucepan and sauté the onion until it is limp, about 5 minutes.

5 Drain the pasta, return it to the stockpot and toss it with the oil. Cover to keep warm.

6 Add the tomatoes, the picante sauce, the V-8 juice and the cheese to the onion. Cook, stirring, until the mixture is hot. Stir in the sour cream. Season to taste. Toss the pasta with the sauce and sprinkle with the parsley.

South of the Border Salad

1 Wash and dry the lettuce and tear it into bite-size pieces. Peel and slice the sweet onion. Seed and slice the bell pepper. Drain the olives. Drain the corn. Combine the ingredients in a large bowl.

2 In a small bowl, whisk together the oil, the vinegar and the cumin. Season to taste.

3 Toss the salad with the dressing. Stuff the salad into taco shells and sprinkle with the alfalfa sprouts.

Sand Tarts

1 Wash and slice the apricots.

2 Combine the apricot preserves and the marmalade in a small bowl. Spoon the mixture into the graham cracker tart shells.

3 Top the tarts with the sliced apricots and the whipped topping and refrigerate until you are ready to serve.

4 Dust the tarts with the confectioners' sugar.

TUESDAY

Cool as a Cucumber

4 boneless, skinless chicken breast halves
1 medium cucumber
1 small onion
¼ cup fresh dill (when chopped)
1 cup regular or low-fat plain yogurt
Seasoning to taste

Tipsy Potatoes

1 pound small new red potatoes
3 tablespoons fresh parsley (when chopped)
4 tablespoons butter
⅔ cup dry white wine (or nonalcoholic white
*   wine or chicken broth)*
Seasoning to taste

Sweet & Sour Carrots

1 pound baby carrots
4 scallions (green onions)
¼ cup apple juice
2 tablespoons butter
2 tablespoons honey
1 tablespoon rice vinegar

Hopscotch Pudding

1 small package (3.4 ounces) instant
*   butterscotch pudding mix*
2 cups whole milk
Chocolate syrup for decorating
12 whole pecans

EQUIPMENT

Electric hand mixer	Measuring cups and
2 large skillets	spoons
Large covered	Assorted cooking
saucepan	utensils
Large saucepan	Vegetable brush
2 medium bowls	Vegetable peeler
Assorted kitchen knives	Vegetable grater

COUNTDOWN

1 Assemble the ingredients and equipment
2 Do Step 1 of the *Cool as a Cucumber*
3 Do Step 1 of the *Hopscotch Pudding*
4 Do Steps 2–5 of the *Cool as a Cucumber*
5 Do Steps 1–3 of the *Sweet & Sour Carrots*
6 Do Steps 1–2 of the *Tipsy Potatoes*
7 Do Step 6 of the *Cool as a Cucumber*
8 Do Step 2 of the *Hopscotch Pudding*

Cool as a Cucumber

1 Bring water to a boil in a large skillet.

2 Poach the chicken breasts until they are opaque throughout, 10 to 12 minutes.

3 Peel, seed and grate the cucumber. Peel and grate the onion. Chop the dill.

4 Drain the chicken and cover to keep warm.

5 In a medium bowl, combine the cucumber with the yogurt, the onion and the dill. Season to taste. Stir to mix well. Cover the bowl and let it stand.

6 Spoon the sauce over the chicken breasts.

Tipsy Potatoes

1 Bring water to a boil in a large saucepan. Scrub the potatoes. With a peeler, cut a thin strip of skin around the width of each potato. Cook the potatoes in the boiling water until they are tender, about 10 minutes. Drain.

2 Chop the parsley. Melt 2 tablespoons of the butter in a large skillet. Add the potatoes and roll them around the skillet until a light crust forms, but do not brown. Add the wine and the remaining butter and cook, stirring, until the wine is reduced and the sauce is thick, about 5 minutes. Season to taste. Sprinkle with the parsley.

Sweet & Sour Carrots

1 Bring water to a boil in a large covered saucepan. Trim the carrots, if necessary. Cook the carrots until they are crisp-tender, about 15 minutes.

2 Trim and chop the scallions.

3 Drain the carrots and return them to the saucepan. Add the scallions, the apple juice, the butter, the honey and the vinegar. Cover and simmer for 5 minutes. Remove the saucepan from the heat.

Hopscotch Pudding

1 In a medium bowl, beat the pudding mix and the milk with an electric beater until well blended. Pour the mixture into individual dessert bowls and refrigerate for at least 20 minutes.

2 Crisscross the pudding with thin lines of chocolate syrup to form squares. Fill in any three squares with the whole pecans.

WEDNESDAY

Quick Greek Beef

2 cloves garlic
3 tablespoons fresh parsley (when chopped)
1 medium onion
1 pound lean boneless sirloin steak
1 tablespoon regular or light vegetable oil
1 small can (6 ounces) tomato paste
$1/2$ cup dry red wine (or nonalcoholic red wine or beef broth)
$1/3$ cup water
2 tablespoons lemon juice
$1/8$ teaspoon ground cumin
$1/4$ teaspoon ground cinnamon
Seasoning to taste
3 ounces feta cheese

Oh-So Orzo

1 package (9 ounces) frozen peas and carrots
1 clove garlic
2 tablespoons fresh parsley (when chopped)
8 ounces orzo
$1/4$ cup beef broth*
$1/2$ teaspoon onion powder
Seasoning to taste

Turnip Toss

2 medium turnips
1 small red onion
1 medium head lettuce
1 clove garlic
$1/4$ cup fresh dill (when chopped)
2 tablespoons lemon juice
2 tablespoons red wine vinegar
3 tablespoons regular or light olive oil
1 teaspoon Dijon mustard
Seasoning to taste

*Reserve the balance of the can for use on Thursday.

Chocolate Cream

$1^{1}/_{2}$ cups whole or low-fat milk
1 envelope unflavored gelatin
$1/4$ cup cold water
1 tablespoon instant coffee crystals
1 small package (6 ounces) semisweet chocolate chips
2 tablespoons sugar
$1/2$ teaspoon vanilla extract
$1/8$ teaspoon salt
1 cup whipping cream

EQUIPMENT

Blender	Assorted kitchen knives
Large covered skillet	Measuring cups and
Large covered saucepan	spoons
Small saucepan	Assorted cooking utensils
Large bowl	Vegetable peeler
Small bowl	Whisk
Strainer	

COUNTDOWN

1 Assemble the ingredients and equipment
2 Do Steps 1–2 of the *Oh-So Orzo*
3 Do Step 1 of the *Quick Greek Beef*
4 Do Steps 1–3 of the *Chocolate Cream*
5 Do Steps 1–3 of the *Turnip Toss*
6 Do Step 2 of the *Quick Greek Beef*
7 Do Step 3 of the *Oh-So Orzo*
8 Do Step 3 of the *Quick Greek Beef*
9 Do Step 4 of the *Oh-So Orzo*
10 Do Step 4 of the *Turnip Toss*
11 Do Step 4 of the *Quick Greek Beef*

Quick Greek Beef

1 Peel and mince the garlic. Chop the parsley. Peel and halve the onion and cut it into thin wedges. Cut the steak diagonally across the grain into thin slices.

2 Heat the oil in a large skillet until hot. Add the beef and cook, stirring often, until the meat loses its redness, 3 to 5 minutes. Remove the meat and the drippings and cover to keep warm.

3 Add the onion and the garlic to the skillet and cook, stirring, until the onion is tender, about 5 minutes. Stir in the tomato paste, the wine, the water, the lemon juice, the cumin, the cinnamon and the parsley. Season to taste. Bring the mixture to a boil, stirring. Reduce the heat, cover and simmer for 10 minutes, stirring occasionally.

4 Return the beef and the drippings to the skillet and cook until heated through, 1 to 2 minutes. Crumble the cheese and sprinkle it on top.

Oh-So Orzo

1 Bring water to a boil in a large saucepan. Set the package of peas and carrots out to thaw.

2 Peel and mince the garlic. Chop the parsley.

3 Cook the orzo in the boiling water until it is just tender, 6 to 8 minutes.

4 Drain the orzo and return it to the saucepan. Toss with the parsley, the garlic, the thawed peas and carrots, the broth and the onion powder. Season to taste and simmer

until the broth reduces, about 3 minutes. Remove the saucepan from the heat and cover to keep warm.

Turnip Toss

1 Peel and slice the turnips. Peel and slice the red onion. Combine the ingredients in a large bowl. Refrigerate until you are ready to serve.

2 Wash and dry the lettuce and arrange the leaves on individual salad plates.

3 Peel and mince the garlic. Chop the dill. In a small bowl, whisk the garlic and the dill with the lemon juice, the vinegar, the oil and the mustard. Season to taste.

4 Toss the vegetables with the dressing and spoon over the lettuce.

Chocolate Cream

1 In a small saucepan, heat $1/2$ cup of the milk until hot but not boiling.

2 Place the gelatin, the cold water and the coffee crystals in a blender. Cover and process for 20 seconds. Add the hot milk and blend until the gelatin dissolves. Add the chocolate chips, the sugar, the vanilla and the salt. Cover and blend until the mixture is smooth, about 20 seconds. Add the remaining milk, cover and process until the mixture is blended, about 20 seconds. With the blender running, add the cream through the lid and process for 20 seconds more.

3 Pour the mixture into individual dessert dishes and refrigerate for at least 30 minutes.

THURSDAY

Cioppino

1 medium onion
1 clove garlic
1 pound fresh tomatoes
1 tablespoon fresh parsley (when chopped)
$^1/_4$ cup regular or light olive oil
1 medium can (14$^1/_2$ ounces) cut-up tomatoes
$^1/_4$ cup flour
2 bottles (8 ounces each) clam juice
1 cup beef broth reserved from Wednesday
2 cups dry red wine (or nonalcoholic red wine
    or tomato juice)
1 teaspoon dried thyme
Seasoning to taste
24 small hard-shelled clams (or 2 cans [10
    ounces each] whole clams)
$^1/_2$ cup dry white wine (or nonalcoholic white
    wine or water)
2 pounds white fish fillets
1 pound medium shrimp, shelled and deveined
$^1/_2$ pound scallops

Sweet Onion Salad

1 large sweet onion
2 large tomatoes
1 small head lettuce
$^1/_4$ cup fresh basil (when chopped)
3 tablespoons regular or light olive oil
2 tablespoons red wine vinegar
Seasoning to taste

Crusty Italian Bread

Peppermint Pie

1 quart peppermint ice cream
1 prepared 9-inch chocolate pie shell
Chocolate sprinkles for garnish

EQUIPMENT

Dutch oven	Measuring cups and
Large saucepan	spoons
Large bowl	Assorted cooking
2 small bowls	utensils
Fine sieve	Whisk
Assorted kitchen knives	Vegetable brush

COUNTDOWN

1 Assemble the ingredients and equipment
2 Do Step 1 of the *Peppermint Pie*
3 Do Steps 1–2 of the *Sweet Onion Salad*
4 Do Steps 1–3 of the *Cioppino*
5 Do Step 2 of the *Peppermint Pie*
6 Do Steps 4–10 of the *Cioppino*
7 Do Step 3 of the *Sweet Onion Salad*
8 Do Step 3 of the *Peppermint Pie*

Cioppino

1 Peel and chop the onion. Peel and mince the garlic. Chop the tomatoes. Chop the parsley.

2 Heat the oil in a large saucepan. Add the onion and the garlic, and sauté until they are softened, about 5 minutes. Add the canned tomatoes, bring the mixture to a boil, and cook until it is thickened, 3 to 5 minutes.

3 Sprinkle the flour into the saucepan and whisk to blend. Add the clam juice, the beef broth, the fresh tomatoes and the red wine. Bring the mixture to a boil, stirring frequently. Add the thyme and the parsley, and season to taste. Reduce the heat and simmer until the mixture is thickened, about 20 minutes.

4 Scrub the clams, discarding any that are open and do not close when tapped. In a Dutch oven, combine the clams with the white wine. Cook, stirring, until the wine comes to a boil, about 2 minutes. Cover, reduce the heat and simmer until the clams have opened, 5 to 7 minutes.

5 Cut the fish fillets into 2-inch cubes. Rinse the shrimp. Rinse the scallops. If you are using sea scallops, cut them in half.

6 Remove the clams to a large bowl, discarding any that have not opened.

7 Strain the cooking liquid through a fine sieve into a small bowl. Rinse out the Dutch oven and pour in the strained liquid. Add the white fish and gently poach until it is firm, about 5 minutes.

8 Add the shrimp and the scallops to the Dutch oven. Cover and cook until the shrimp are bright pink and the scallops are firm, 2 to 3 minutes.

9 Remove the Dutch oven from the heat.

10 Add the hot soup to the seafood. If you are using canned clams, add them now. Stir lightly to combine and simmer until hot. Serve with chunks of crusty Italian bread.

Sweet Onion Salad

1 Peel and thinly slice the sweet onion. Thinly slice the tomatoes. Wash and dry the lettuce, and place the leaves on individual plates. Arrange layers of onion and tomato over the lettuce.

2 Chop the basil. In a small bowl, whisk together the basil, the oil and the vinegar. Season to taste.

3 Drizzle the dressing over the onion and tomatoes.

Peppermint Pie

1 Set the ice cream out to soften.

2 Pack the softened ice cream into the pie shell. Return the pie to the freezer for at least 30 minutes.

3 Before serving, top the pie with the sprinkles.

FRIDAY

It Hasta Be Pasta

1 tablespoon dark raisins
$^1/_4$ cup seasoned bread crumbs
1 small onion
$^1/_4$ cup fresh parsley (when chopped)
1 can (2 ounces) anchovy fillets
1 can (3$^3/_4$ ounces) boneless, skinless sardines
    packed in oil
12 ounces bucatini or other small tubular
    pasta
5 tablespoons regular or light olive oil
$^1/_2$ cup pine nuts
Seasoning to taste

Snappy Salad

1 medium head lettuce
1 small red onion
1 small bunch radishes
1 clove garlic
2 tablespoons V–8 juice reserved from Monday
1 tablespoon lemon juice
1 tablespoon red wine vinegar
$^1/_8$ teaspoon Worcestershire sauce
1 teaspoon honey
1 tablespoon regular or light olive oil
$^1/_2$ teaspoon prepared horseradish
Seasoning to taste

Cheese Buns

2 hamburger buns
1$^1/_2$ teaspoons fresh basil (when chopped)
4 tablespoons softened butter
1 tablespoon grated Parmesan cheese

Nectarine Melba

$^1/_2$ pint fresh raspberries
2 teaspoons cornstarch
2 tablespoons sugar
2 medium nectarines
1 tablespoon lemon juice
1 pint vanilla ice cream
1 tablespoon Kirsch liqueur (or nonalcoholic
    Italian cherry syrup)

EQUIPMENT

Blender	Assorted kitchen knives
Stockpot	Measuring cups and
Large skillet	spoons
Small skillet	Assorted cooking
2 small saucepans	utensils
2 small bowls	Whisk
Colander	Ice cream scoop

COUNTDOWN

1 Assemble the ingredients and equipment
2 Do Steps 1–2 of It Hasta Be Pasta
3 Do Step 1 of the Nectarine Melba
4 Do Steps 3–4 of It Hasta Be Pasta
5 Do Steps 1–2 of the Snappy Salad
6 Do Step 1 of the Cheese Buns
7 Do Step 2 of the Nectarine Melba
8 Do Steps 5–7 of It Hasta Be Pasta
9 Do Step 2 of the Cheese Buns
10 Do Step 3 of the Snappy Salad
11 Do Step 3 of the Nectarine Melba

It Hasta Be Pasta

1 Bring water to a boil in a stockpot.

2 Bring water to a boil in a small saucepan. Remove the saucepan from the heat, add the raisins and soak them for 10 minutes.

3 Place the bread crumbs in a small skillet and toss them over a heated burner until they are lightly toasted, about 5 minutes.

4 Peel and chop the onion. Chop the parsley. Drain the anchovies, blot them dry on paper towels and finely chop them. Drain the sardines and pat dry. Drain the raisins.

5 Cook the pasta in the boiling water until it is almost tender, about 10 minutes.

6 Heat the oil in a large skillet. Add the onion and sauté until it is golden, about 5 minutes. Add the anchovies and sauté until they are dissolved. Add the parsley, the pine nuts, the raisins and the sardines. Season to taste. Heat through, stirring gently, about 5 minutes.

7 Drain the pasta, return it to the stockpot. Sprinkle the pasta with the bread crumbs, and toss with the sauce. Cover to keep warm.

Snappy Salad

1 Wash and dry the lettuce and tear it into bite-size pieces. Peel and thinly slice the red onion. Trim and slice the radishes. Arrange the ingredients on individual salad plates.

2 Peel and mince the garlic. In a small bowl, whisk the garlic together with the V–8 juice, the lemon juice, the vinegar, the Worcestershire sauce, the honey, the oil and the horseradish. Season to taste.

3 Drizzle the dressing over the salad.

Cheese Buns

1 Split the hamburger buns. Chop the basil. In a small bowl, blend the softened butter with the Parmesan cheese and the basil. Spread the mixture on the cut sides of the buns. Place the buns on an unheated broiler pan.

2 Preheat the broiler. Broil the cheese buns, 3 or 4 inches from the heat, until lightly browned, 2 to 3 minutes.

Nectarine Melba

1 Rinse the raspberries and puree them in a blender. Scrape the berries into a small saucepan, add the cornstarch and the sugar and bring the mixture to a boil. Cook, stirring constantly, until the mixture is thickened, about 5 minutes. Remove the saucepan from the heat and let cool.

2 Peel, halve and pit the nectarines. Place one half of a nectarine in each dessert dish and sprinkle with the lemon juice to keep them from browning.

3 Top the nectarine halves with scoops of ice cream. Stir the Kirsch into the raspberry sauce and spoon it over the ice cream.

JULY

WEEK THREE

WEEK AT A GLANCE

Monday

HONORABLE HALIBUT
RICKSHAW RICE
BEIJING BROCCOLI
ORANGE MACAO

Tuesday

HOT DIGGITY DOGS
SUPER BAKED BEANS
SPECIAL KRAUT
DANISH DOUBLES

Wednesday

SEAFOOD BISQUE
ROCK 'N' ROLLS
SLY SLAW
BLUEBERRY HILL

Thursday

UPTOWN CHICKEN
RIVERSIDE RICE
SOPHISTICATED SALAD
PISTACHIO PARFAIT

Friday

MARCO POLO PASTA
HALE CAESAR SALAD
BUBBLY BOBOLI
PRALINE POMPEII

CHECK STAPLES

- ☐ Butter
- ☐ Cornstarch
- ☐ Granulated sugar
- ☐ Dark brown sugar
- ☐ Multicolored sprinkles
- ☐ Molasses
- ☐ Long-grain white rice
- ☐ Brown rice
- ☐ Regular or light vegetable oil
- ☐ Regular or light olive oil
- ☐ White wine vinegar
- ☐ Red wine vinegar
- ☐ Rice vinegar
- ☐ Lemon juice
- ☐ Tabasco sauce
- ☐ Soy sauce
- ☐ Dijon mustard
- ☐ Yellow mustard
- ☐ Ketchup
- ☐ Sweet pickle relish
- ☐ Grated Parmesan cheese
- ☐ Grated Romano cheese
- ☐ Whole allspice
- ☐ Bay leaves
- ☐ Caraway seeds
- ☐ Chinese five-spice powder
- ☐ Ground coriander
- ☐ Dried dill
- ☐ Ground ginger
- ☐ Italian seasoning
- ☐ Dry mustard
- ☐ Ground nutmeg
- ☐ Pepper
- ☐ Salt
- ☐ Vanilla extract

SHOPPING NOTE

● If you are shopping once a week and cannot arrange to purchase fresh seafood on the day you plan to use it, you can purchase *not previously frozen* seafood and freeze it, placing it in the refrigerator to thaw the night before you are ready to use it. Or you can purchase *still frozen* seafood and keep it frozen until the night before you are ready to use it. You can also purchase substitute crabmeat; however, canned crabmeat will significantly alter the recipe.

MEAT & POULTRY
3 pounds chicken pieces (Th)

FISH
4 halibut steaks (1-inch thick) (M)
$1/2$ pound medium shrimp, shelled and deveined (W)
$1/2$ pound cooked crabmeat (W)

FRESH PRODUCE
Vegetables
$1 1/2$ pounds broccoli—$3/4$ pound (M), $3/4$ pound (F)
$1/4$ pound spinach (Th)
1 medium carrot (Th)
1 stalk celery (T)
1 large onion (Th)
2 medium onions—1 (M), 1 (Th)
1 small onion (T)
1 large sweet onion (T)
1 small red onion (W)
5 scallions (green onions)— 2 (M), 3 (F)
1 head garlic (M, W, Th, F)
1 small bunch basil (Th, F)
1 small bunch chives (W)
1 bunch parsley (M, Th, F)
4 mint sprigs (optional) (Th)
1 small (or half) head red cabbage (W)
1 large head romaine (F)
1 small head lettuce (Th)
$1/2$ pound tomatoes (F)
1 large cucumber (Th)
1 small red bell pepper (W)
1 small bunch radishes (W)

Fruit
2 large tart green apples (Th)
$1/2$ pint blueberries (W)
5 large oranges (M)

CANS, JARS & BOTTLES
Soup
1 can ($10^3/4$ ounces) chicken broth (Th)
1 can ($14^1/2$ ounces) chicken broth (M)
2 cans ($10^3/4$ ounces each) vichyssoise (or cream of potato soup) (W)

Vegetables
2 medium cans ($15^1/2$ ounces each) baked beans (T)
1 large jar (32 ounces) sauerkraut (T)
1 medium can (15 ounces) sliced pickled beets (Th)
1 jar ($6^1/2$ ounces) marinated artichoke hearts (Th)

Oriental Foods
1 can (8 ounces) sliced water chestnuts (M)

Juice
2 tablespoons apple cider (Th)

Condiments
1 small jar (2 ounces) diced pimientos (Th)

Dessert Needs
1 can (14 ounces) regular or low-fat sweetened condensed milk (W)
1 jar ($12^1/4$ ounces) caramel topping (F)

PACKAGED GOODS
Pasta, Rice & Grains
16 ounces linguine (F)
1 package (11 ounces) potato chips (T)

Baked Goods
8 hot dog buns (T)
4 hoagie-style rolls (W)
2 small (8-inch) Boboli breads (or English or Australian muffins) (F)
1 angel food loaf cake (F)
$1/2$ cup croutons (F)

Nuts & Seeds
$1/4$ cup pecan pieces (F)

Dessert & Baking Needs
1 prepared 9-inch shortbread pie shell (M)
4 individual graham cracker tart shells (W)
4 Danish-style (extra-large sugar) ice cream cones (T)

1 package (9 ounces) chocolate wafers (Th)

WINES & SPIRITS
$1/4$ cup dry sherry (or nonalcoholic white wine or clam juice) (M)
3 tablespoons dry sherry (or nonalcoholic white wine or omit) (W)
2 tablespoons brandy (or apple cider) (Th)
1 tablespoon brandy (or nonalcoholic Italian praline syrup) (F)
2 tablespoons creme de menthe liqueur (or nonalcoholic Italian peppermint syrup) (Th)
2 tablespoons creme de cacao liqueur (or nonalcoholic Italian chocolate syrup) (Th)

REFRIGERATED PRODUCTS
Dairy
1 cup half-and-half (Th)
1 cup whipping cream (W)
Whipped cream for garnish (M)
$1/4$ cup regular or light sour cream (F)
1 cup regular or low-fat plain yogurt (W)
1 egg (F)

Cheese
1 container (8 ounces) soft cream cheese with pineapple (M)
1 container (4 ounces) whipped cream cheese (F)

Juice
1 cup orange juice (M)

Deli
3 slices bacon (T)
8 all-beef hot dogs (T)

FROZEN GOODS
Desserts
1 quart of your favorite ice cream (T)
1 small container (8 ounces) frozen whipped topping (Th)

MONDAY

Honorable Halibut

$1/2$ cup cornstarch
4 halibut steaks (1-inch thick)
1 clove garlic
$1/2$ cup soy sauce
$1/4$ cup dry sherry (or nonalcoholic white wine or clam juice)
2 teaspoons rice vinegar
$1/8$ teaspoon ground ginger
1 tablespoon sugar
Seasoning to taste
1 tablespoon regular or light vegetable oil

Rickshaw Rice

2 scallions (green onions)
$1/4$ cup fresh parsley (when chopped)
1 cup long-grain white rice
1 can ($14^1/2$ ounces) chicken broth
$1/4$ cup soy sauce

Beijing Broccoli

$3/4$ pound broccoli
1 can (8 ounces) sliced water chestnuts
1 medium onion
1 tablespoon regular or light vegetable oil
1 teaspoon Chinese five-spice powder
Seasoning to taste

Orange Macao

5 large oranges
$1/2$ cup sugar
2 tablespoons cornstarch
1 cup orange juice
1 container (8 ounces) soft cream cheese with pineapple
1 prepared 9-inch shortbread pie shell
Whipped cream for garnish
$1/2$ teaspoon ground nutmeg

EQUIPMENT

Large covered skillet	Assorted kitchen knives
Large skillet	Measuring cups and
Small saucepan	spoons
Double boiler	Assorted cooking
Large bowl	utensils
Small bowl	Whisk
Shallow bowl	

COUNTDOWN

1 Assemble the ingredients and equipment
2 Do Step 1 of the *Rickshaw Rice*
3 Do Step 1 of the *Orange Macao*
4 Do Step 1 of the *Beijing Broccoli*
5 Do Steps 1–2 of the *Honorable Halibut*
6 Do Steps 2–3 of the *Orange Macao*
7 Do Step 2 of the *Beijing Broccoli*
8 Do Steps 3–4 of the *Honorable Halibut*
9 Do Step 2 of the *Rickshaw Rice*
10 Do Step 4 of the *Orange Macao*

Honorable Halibut

1 Place the cornstarch in a shallow bowl. Add the fish steaks and turn to coat well.

2 Peel and mince the garlic. In a small bowl, combine the garlic with the soy sauce, the sherry, the vinegar, the ginger and the sugar. Season to taste.

3 Heat the oil in a large skillet and sauté the halibut, turning once, until the fish is lightly browned and crisp, about 1½ minutes per side.

4 Pour the soy sauce mixture over the fish and cook until the fish is opaque throughout and the sauce is thickened, 5 to 7 minutes.

Rickshaw Rice

1 Trim and chop the scallion. Chop the parsley. Place the rice, the broth, the soy sauce, the scallion and the parsley in the top of the double boiler. Bring water to a boil in the bottom of the double boiler, cover, reduce the heat and simmer until all the liquid is absorbed and the rice is tender, 30 to 40 minutes.

2 Fluff the rice before serving.

Beijing Broccoli

1 Trim and cut the broccoli into bite-size florets. Drain the water chestnuts. Peel and slice the onion.

2 Heat the oil in a large covered skillet. Add the broccoli, the water chestnuts, the onion and the five-spice powder, season to taste and cook, covered, until the vegetables are just tender, gently tossing once or twice, 5 to 7 minutes.

Orange Macao

1 Peel and section 4 of the oranges. Place them in a large bowl, sprinkle them with the sugar and let them stand for 15 minutes. Peel and section the remaining orange and reserve.

2 In a small saucepan, whisk the cornstarch with the orange juice until well blended. Cook, stirring, until the mixture is thick and clear, about 4 minutes. Place the saucepan in the refrigerator to cool.

3 Spread the cream cheese in the pie shell. Layer the oranges on top of the cream cheese.

4 Drizzle the cooled orange glaze over the pie and top with dollops of whipped cream and the reserved orange sections. Sprinkle with the nutmeg.

TUESDAY

Hot Diggity Dogs

1 large sweet onion
8 all-beef hot dogs
8 hot dog buns
Sweet pickle relish
Ketchup
Yellow mustard

Super Baked Beans

3 slices bacon
1 small onion
1 stalk celery
2 medium cans (15½ ounces each) baked
*   beans*
2 tablespoons molasses
2 tablespoons dark brown sugar

Special Kraut

1 large jar (32 ounces) sauerkraut
1 tablespoon caraway seeds
2 teaspoons sugar
1 bay leaf
3 whole allspice

Danish Doubles

Multicolored sprinkles
4 Danish-style (extra-large sugar) ice cream
*   cones*
1 quart of your favorite ice cream

EQUIPMENT

Small skillet	Assorted kitchen knives
Large covered saucepan	Measuring cups and spoons
Medium covered saucepan	Assorted cooking utensils
Shallow bowl	Ice cream scoop

COUNTDOWN

1 Assemble the ingredients and equipment
2 Do Step 1 of the *Hot Diggity Dogs*
3 Do Steps 1–4 of the *Super Baked Beans*
4 Do Step 2 of the *Hot Diggity Dogs*
5 Do Step 1 of the *Special Kraut*
6 Do Step 3 of the *Hot Diggity Dogs*
7 Do Step 2 of the *Special Kraut*
8 Do Step 4 of the *Hot Diggity Dogs*
9 Do Steps 1–2 of the *Danish Doubles*

Hot Diggity Dogs

1 Prepare the grill.

2 Peel and chop the sweet onion.

3 Grill the hot dogs and toast the buns to taste.

4 Serve the hot dogs in the buns with the onion, the relish, the ketchup and the mustard.

Super Baked Beans

1 Chop the bacon. In a small skillet, sauté the bacon until it is crisp, about 5 minutes.

2 Peel and chop the onion. Trim and thinly slice the celery.

3 Drain the bacon on a paper towel and sauté the onion and the celery in the bacon drippings until they are limp, 5 to 7 minutes.

4 In a large saucepan, combine the baked beans, the molasses, the brown sugar, the bacon, the onion, the celery and the drippings. Cover and simmer for 30 minutes. Do not let boil.

Special Kraut

1 In a medium saucepan, combine the undrained sauerkraut, the caraway seeds, the sugar, the bay leaf and the allspice. Cover and simmer for 20 minutes. Do not let boil.

2 Remove and discard the bay leaf and the allspice before serving.

Danish Doubles

1 Place the sprinkles in a shallow bowl.

2 Pack the ice cream cones with ice cream and dip them in the sprinkles.

WEDNESDAY

Seafood Bisque

$1/4$ cup fresh chives (when chopped)
$1/2$ pound cooked crabmeat
$1/2$ pound medium shrimp, shelled and deveined
2 cans ($10^3/4$ ounces each) vichyssoise (or cream of potato) soup
1 cup whipping cream
3 tablespoons dry sherry (or nonalcoholic white wine or omit)
$1/8$ teaspoon ground nutmeg
Seasoning to taste

Rock 'n' Rolls

4 cloves garlic
$1/4$ cup regular or light olive oil
4 hoagie-style rolls
$1/3$ cup grated Parmesan cheese

Sly Slaw

3 tablespoons regular or light vegetable oil
2 tablespoons rice vinegar
1 tablespoon Dijon mustard
$1/2$ teaspoon dried dill
1 teaspoon sugar
Seasoning to taste
1 small (or half) head red cabbage
1 small red onion
1 small red bell pepper
1 small bunch radishes

Blueberry Hill

1 can (14 ounces) regular or low-fat sweetened condensed milk
$1/4$ cup lemon juice
1 cup regular or low-fat plain yogurt
4 individual graham cracker tart shells
$1/2$ pint fresh blueberries

EQUIPMENT

Large saucepan	Assorted cooking
Large bowl	utensils
Medium bowl	Whisk
Small bowl	Vegetable grater
Assorted kitchen knives	Pastry brush
Measuring cups and	
spoons	

COUNTDOWN

1 Assemble the ingredients and equipment
2 Do Steps 1–2 of the *Sly Slaw*
3 Do Steps 1–2 of the *Blueberry Hill*
4 Do Steps 1–2 of the *Rock 'n' Rolls*
5 Do Steps 1–2 of the *Seafood Bisque*
6 Do Step 3 of the *Rock 'n' Rolls*
7 Do Step 3 of the *Seafood Bisque*
8 Do Step 3 of the *Blueberry Hill*

Seafood Bisque

1 Chop the chives. Flake the crabmeat. Rinse the shrimp.

2 In a large saucepan, bring the soup and the cream to a simmer. Add the crab, the shrimp, the sherry and the nutmeg. Season to taste. Cook until the shrimp are bright pink, about 5 minutes.

3 Garnish the bisque with the chopped chives.

Rock 'n' Rolls

1 Peel and mash the garlic. Blend it with the oil in a small bowl.

2 Split the rolls, and place them on a broiler tray. Brush the cut sides with the garlic-oil mixture and sprinkle them with the Parmesan cheese.

3 Preheat the broiler. Place the rolls under the broiler, 3 or 4 inches from the heat, until they are lightly browned and the cheese begins to bubble, 2 to 3 minutes.

Sly Slaw

1 In a large bowl, whisk together the oil, the vinegar, the mustard, the dill and the sugar until well blended. Season to taste.

2 Grate the cabbage. Peel and grate the red onion. Trim, seed and chop the bell pepper. Trim and chop the radishes. Add the ingredients to the large bowl, toss with the dressing and refrigerate until you are ready to serve.

Blueberry Hill

1 In a medium bowl, combine the condensed milk and the lemon juice. Fold in the yogurt. Spoon the mixture into individual tart shells and refrigerate them for at least 20 minutes.

2 Rinse and stem the blueberries as necessary.

3 Top the tarts with the blueberries.

THURSDAY

Uptown Chicken

Seasoning to taste
3 pounds chicken pieces
3 tablespoons butter
2 large tart green apples
1 large onion
2 tablespoons apple cider
2 tablespoons brandy (or additional apple
    cider)
1 cup half-and-half

Riverside Rice

1 medium onion
1 medium carrot
1 tablespoon butter
$^1/_2$ cup brown rice
1 can ($10^3/_4$ ounces) chicken broth
1 teaspoon ground coriander
$^1/_4$ cup water

Sophisticated Salad

1 small head lettuce
$^1/_4$ pound fresh spinach
1 medium can (15 ounces) sliced pickled beets
1 jar ($6^1/_2$ ounces) marinated artichoke hearts
1 large cucumber
1 small jar (2 ounces) diced pimientos
1 clove garlic
2 tablespoons fresh basil (when chopped)
$^1/_4$ cup fresh parsley (when chopped)
2 tablespoons white wine vinegar
Seasoning to taste

Pistachio Parfait

1 package (9 ounces) chocolate wafers
1 small container (8 ounces) frozen whipped
    topping
2 tablespoons green creme de menthe liqueur
    (or nonalcoholic Italian peppermint syrup)
1 tablespoon creme de cacao liqueur (or
    nonalcoholic Italian chocolate syrup)
4 fresh mint sprigs (optional)

EQUIPMENT

Large covered skillet	Measuring cups and
Medium covered	spoons
saucepan	Assorted cooking
Medium bowl	utensils
Small bowl	Whisk
Small strainer	Vegetable grater
Assorted kitchen knives	Vegetable peeler

COUNTDOWN

1 Assemble the ingredients and equipment
2 Do Step 1 of the *Riverside Rice*
3 Do Steps 1–3 of the *Pistachio Parfait*
4 Do Steps 1–5 of the *Uptown Chicken*
5 Do Step 1 of the *Sophisticated Salad*
6 Do Step 6 of the *Uptown Chicken*
7 Do Step 2 of the *Sophisticated Salad*
8 Do Step 2 of the *Riverside Rice*
9 Do Step 4 of the *Pistachio Parfait*

Uptown Chicken

1 Season the chicken pieces to taste.

2 Melt the butter in a large skillet. Add the chicken and cook until the pieces are brown on all sides, about 10 minutes.

3 Peel, core and chop the apples. Peel and chop the onion.

4 Remove the chicken from the skillet and cover to keep warm.

5 Add the apples and the onion to the skillet and sauté until the onion is tender, 3 to 5 minutes. Return the chicken to the skillet, add the apple cider and the brandy, season to taste, reduce the heat, cover and simmer for 20 minutes.

6 Stir the half-and-half into the chicken mixture and simmer, covered, until the chicken pieces are tender, about 10 minutes.

Riverside Rice

1 Peel and chop the onion. Peel and grate the carrot. Melt the butter in a medium saucepan and sauté the onion and the carrot for 2 minutes. Add the rice, the broth, the coriander and the water. Bring the mixture to a boil, reduce the heat, cover and simmer until all the liquid is absorbed and the rice is tender, 30 to 40 minutes.

2 Fluff the rice before serving.

Sophisticated Salad

1 Wash and dry the lettuce and arrange the leaves in the bottom of a salad bowl. Stem and tear the spinach into bite-size pieces and place it on top of the lettuce. Drain and rinse the beets and arrange them around the edge of the spinach. Drain the artichokes, reserving the oil, and arrange them inside the beets. Peel and slice the cucumber and arrange it inside the artichokes. Drain the pimientos and arrange them in the center.

2 Peel and mince the garlic. Chop the basil. Chop the parsley. In a small bowl, whisk together the garlic, the basil, the parsley, the reserved artichoke oil and the vinegar. Season to taste and drizzle the mixture over the salad.

Pistachio Parfait

1 Reserve 4 chocolate wafers, and crumble the rest.

2 In a medium bowl, combine the whipped topping, the creme de menthe and the creme de cacao.

3 Layer the mixture into parfait glasses, using 2 tablespoons of cookie crumbs between each of 3 layers. Refrigerate the parfaits for at least 20 minutes.

4 Garnish the parfaits with an upright cookie and a mint sprig, if desired.

FRIDAY

Marco Polo Pasta

$^3/_4$ pound fresh broccoli
$^1/_2$ pound fresh tomatoes
3 scallions (green onions)
$^1/_4$ cup fresh basil (when chopped)
$^1/_4$ cup fresh parsley (when chopped)
16 ounces linguine
3 tablespoons red wine vinegar
3 tablespoons regular or light olive oil
Seasoning to taste
$^1/_4$ cup grated Parmesan cheese

Hale Caesar Salad

1 clove garlic
1 egg
3 tablespoons regular or light olive oil
1 tablespoon lemon juice
$^1/_8$ teaspoon Tabasco sauce
$^1/_2$ teaspoon dry mustard
Seasoning to taste
1 large head romaine
$^1/_2$ cup croutons
$^1/_2$ cup grated Romano cheese

Bubbly Boboli

2 cloves garlic
2 tablespoons softened butter
1 tablespoon Italian seasoning
2 small (8-inch) Boboli breads (or English or
    Australian muffins)

Praline Pompeii

1 angel food loaf cake
1 container (4 ounces) whipped cream cheese
$^1/_4$ cup regular or light sour cream
2 tablespoons sugar
1 teaspoon vanilla extract
1 tablespoon brandy (or nonalcoholic Italian
    praline syrup)
$^1/_4$ cup pecan pieces
$^1/_2$ cup caramel topping

EQUIPMENT

Stockpot	Colander
Medium saucepan	Assorted kitchen knives
Small saucepan	Measuring cups and
Cookie sheet	spoons
Large bowl	Assorted cooking
Medium bowl	utensils
Small bowl	Whisk

COUNTDOWN

1 Assemble the ingredients and equipment
2 Do Step 1 of the *Praline Pompeii*
3 Do Steps 1–4 of the *Hale Caesar Salad*
4 Do Step 1 of the *Bubbly Boboli*
5 Do Steps 1–6 of the *Marco Polo Pasta*
6 Do Steps 2–3 of the *Bubbly Boboli*
7 Do Step 5 of the *Hale Caesar Salad*
8 Do Step 7 of the *Marco Polo Pasta*
9 Do Step 2 of the *Praline Pompeii*

Marco Polo Pasta

1 Bring water to a boil in a stockpot. Bring water to a boil in a medium saucepan.

2 Trim and cut the broccoli into small florets. Chop the tomatoes. Trim and chop the scallions. Chop the basil. Chop the parsley.

3 Cook the pasta in the stockpot until it is almost tender, 2 to 3 minutes if you are using fresh pasta and 6 to 7 minutes if you are using dried pasta.

4 Cook the broccoli until it is crisp-tender, about 5 minutes.

5 Drain the pasta and return it to the stockpot. Drain the broccoli and add it to the pasta. Add the tomatoes, the vinegar, the oil, the scallions, the basil and the parsley. Season to taste and toss to combine. Cover to keep warm.

6 Sprinkle with the Parmesan cheese.

Hale Caesar Salad

1 Peel and mash the garlic. Rub it around the inside of a large bowl.

2 Bring water to a boil in a small saucepan. Add the egg and cook for 1 minute only. Remove the egg and break it into the large bowl.

3 Whisk the garlic, the oil, the lemon juice, the Tabasco sauce and the dry mustard into the egg until well blended. Season to taste.

4 Wash, dry and tear the romaine into bite-size pieces. Add it to the large bowl. Toss the romaine with the dressing.

5 Add the croutons and the Romano cheese to the romaine and toss again to combine.

Bubbly Boboli

1 Peel and mince the garlic. In a small bowl, combine the garlic with the softened butter and the Italian seasoning. Spread the mixture on the Boboli breads and place them on an ungreased cookie sheet.

2 Preheat the broiler.

3 Broil, 3 or 4 inches from the heat, until the Boboli breads are bubbly, 1 to 2 minutes.

Praline Pompeii

1 Hollow out and reserve a $1\frac{1}{2}$-inch-deep section from the top of the angel food loaf, being careful to leave a $\frac{1}{2}$-inch border all around. In a medium bowl, whisk together the whipped cream cheese, the sour cream, the sugar, the vanilla and the brandy. Spoon the mixture into the hollowed-out section of the cake. Sprinkle the pecans on top and refrigerate the cake for at least 20 minutes.

2 Crumble the reserved section of the cake. Top the cake with the crumbs and drizzle it with the caramel topping.

JULY

WEEK FOUR

WEEK AT A GLANCE

Monday

STEAK ON A STICK
FIVE-SPICE RICE
STOP & GO SALAD
PEACHY KEEN CAKES

Tuesday

ECHO SOUP
BOWL 'EM OVER SALAD
BAGEL TREATS
BANANA PUDDING CRUMBLE

Wednesday

PICTURESQUE PASTA
CHEESE BAGUETTES
OPEN-FACED CREAMWICHES

Thursday

HOT-SPOT CHICKEN SALAD
STONE COLD SOBA
RED DRAGONS
FIRESTICKS

Friday

SEASIDE SAUTÉ
RICING AROUND
SNOWBODY'S BABY
SORT-OF BAKED ALASKA

CHECK STAPLES

- ☐ Butter
- ☐ Granulated sugar
- ☐ Marshmallow topping
- ☐ Long-grain white rice
- ☐ Regular or light vegetable oil
- ☐ Regular of light olive oil
- ☐ Sesame oil
- ☐ Red wine vinegar
- ☐ Lemon juice
- ☐ Lime juice
- ☐ Fresh ginger
- ☐ Worcestershire sauce
- ☐ Soy sauce
- ☐ Dijon mustard
- ☐ Prepared horseradish
- ☐ Regular or low-fat mayonnaise
- ☐ Ketchup
- ☐ Honey
- ☐ Ground allspice
- ☐ Bay leaves
- ☐ Dried chervil
- ☐ Chili powder
- ☐ Curry powder
- ☐ Garlic powder
- ☐ Dried oregano
- ☐ Dried tarragon
- ☐ Dried thyme
- ☐ Red pepper flakes
- ☐ Saffron threads
- ☐ Pepper
- ☐ Salt
- ☐ Vanilla extract

SHOPPING NOTE

● If you are shopping once a week and cannot arrange to purchase fresh seafood on the day you plan to use it, you can purchase *not previously frozen* seafood and freeze it, placing it in the refrigerator to thaw the night before you are ready to use it. Or you can purchase *still frozen* seafood and keep it frozen until the night before you are ready to use it.

MEAT & POULTRY
1¼ pounds lean boneless sirloin steak (M)
1¼ pounds boneless, skinless chicken breasts (Th)

FISH
½ pound scallops (W)
1½ pounds cod steaks (F)

FRESH PRODUCE
Vegetables
1 small head cauliflower (T)
½ pound spinach (Th)
½ pound green beans (M)
20 Chinese snow peas (F)
10 medium mushrooms—8 (M), 2 (F)
1 medium carrot (T)
½ pound baby carrots (F)
2 medium onions (M)
3 small onions—1 (T), 1 (Th), 1 (F)
2 small red onions—1 (T), 1 (W)
5 scallions (green onions)— 2 (T), 3 (Th)
1 head garlic (M, T, W, Th)
1 small bunch basil (M, W)
1 bunch chives (T, Th)
1 bunch dill (M, W, F)
1 bunch parsley (T, W, F)
2 medium heads lettuce (T)
2 small heads lettuce—1 (M), 1 (Th)
1½ pounds tomatoes—½ pound (M), ¾ pound (T), ¼ pound (W)
4 large tomatoes (Th)
1 large cucumber (T)
1 medium cucumber (W)
1 large red bell pepper (M)
1 small green bell pepper (W)
1 small red bell pepper (W)
1 small bunch radishes (T)

Fruit
4 sweet red apples (F)
4 large peaches (M)
1 large banana (T)
¼ small watermelon (Th)
1 medium cantaloupe (Th)
1 small honeydew melon (Th)
½ pound pineapple chunks (or net weight canned) (Th)

CANS, JARS & BOTTLES
Soup
1 can (14½ ounces) beef broth (M)
2 cans (14½ ounces each) vegetable broth—1 (T), 1 (F)

Vegetables
1 small can (8¾ ounces) whole kernel corn (W)

Fruit
1 can (11 ounces) mandarin oranges (Th)

Juice
1 small can (5½ ounces) V-8 juice (M, T)
1 cup apple cider (F)

Spreads
½ cup orange marmalade (W)

PACKAGED GOODS
Pasta, Rice & Grains
12 ounces rotelle (W)

Baked Goods
4 bagels (T)
4 individual sourdough French bread baguettes (W)
8 individual shortcake dessert cups—4 (M), 4 (F)

Oriental Products
12 ounces Japanese soba noodles (Th)

Nuts & Seeds
¼ cup pecan pieces (W)
¼ cup sliced almonds (Th)

Dessert & Baking Needs
1 small package (3.4 ounces) instant banana cream pudding mix (T)
1 small package (10 ounces) oatmeal cookies (T)
¼ cup flaked coconut (Th)

WINES & SPIRITS
1 tablespoon dry sherry (or nonalcoholic red wine or omit) (M)
2 tablespoons + 1 teaspoon dry sherry (or nonalcoholic white wine or omit)— 2 tablespoons (T), 1 teaspoon (Th)
1 tablespoon Amaretto liqueur (or nonalcoholic Italian almond syrup) (M)

REFRIGERATED PRODUCTS
Dairy
2 cups whole milk (T)
1 cup half-and-half (T)
Whipped cream for garnish (M)
7 eggs—4 (T), 3 (F)

Cheese
¼ pound sliced regular or low-fat Swiss cheese (T)
6 ounces shredded regular or low-fat Monterey Jack cheese (W)
1 container (8 ounces) regular or light soft cream cheese (T)

Deli
½ pound thinly sliced deli turkey breast (T)
½ pound thinly sliced deli baked ham (T)
½ pound thinly sliced deli roast beef (T)

FROZEN GOODS
Vegetables
1 package (9 ounces) green peas (T)
1 package (9 ounces) chopped spinach (T)

Desserts
4 toaster waffles (W)
1 pint peach ice cream (M)
1 pint vanilla ice cream (W)
1 pint orange frozen yogurt (F)

MONDAY

Steak on a Stick

1¼ pounds lean boneless sirloin steak
1 tablespoon regular or light olive oil
1 bay leaf
½ teaspoon dried oregano
1 tablespoon dry sherry (or nonalcoholic red wine or omit)
1 tablespoon red wine vinegar
2 tablespoons beef broth
Seasoning to taste
2 medium onions
8 medium mushrooms
1 large red bell pepper

Five-Spice Rice

1 cup long-grain white rice
½ cup water
1½ cups beef broth
½ teaspoon garlic powder
¼ teaspoon dried thyme
1 teaspoon saffron threads
¼ teaspoon dried oregano
½ teaspoon ground allspice

Stop & Go Salad

½ pound green beans
1 clove garlic
3 tablespoons fresh basil (when chopped)
2 tablespoons fresh dill (when chopped)
1 tablespoon regular or light olive oil
3 tablespoons V-8 juice*
Seasoning to taste
1 small head lettuce
½ pound fresh tomatoes

*Reserve the remainder of the can for use on Tuesday.

Peachy Keen Cakes

4 large peaches
1 tablespoon lemon juice
1 tablespoon Amaretto liqueur (or nonalcoholic Italian almond syrup)
4 individual shortcake dessert cups
1 pint peach ice cream
Whipped cream for garnish

EQUIPMENT

Medium saucepan	Assorted cooking
Double boiler	utensils
3 medium bowls	8 skewers
Small bowl	Whisk
Assorted kitchen knives	Ice cream scoop
Measuring cups and spoons	

COUNTDOWN

1 Assemble the ingredients and equipment
2 Do Step 1 of the *Steak on a Stick*
3 Do Step 1 of the *Five-Spice Rice*
4 Do Step 1 of the *Peachy Keen Cakes*
5 Do Steps 1–3 of the *Stop & Go Salad*
6 Do Steps 2–4 of the *Steak on a Stick*
7 Do Step 5 of the *Stop & Go Salad*
8 Do Step 2 of the *Five-Spice Rice*
9 Do Step 2 of the *Peachy Keen Cakes*

Steak on a Stick

1 Cut the meat into 1-inch cubes. In a medium bowl, combine the oil, the bay leaf, the oregano, the sherry, the vinegar and the broth. Season to taste. Add the beef cubes and tumble about to coat well. Let stand 30 minutes.

2 Prepare the grill.

3 Peel and quarter the onions. Wash, pat dry and trim the mushrooms. Seed the bell pepper and cut it into 8 pieces.

4 Thread the steak, the onions, the mushrooms, and the pepper onto skewers, alternating the ingredients. Grill, turning and basting the skewers several times with the marinade, until the beef is cooked, about 7 minutes for medium-rare.

Five-Spice Rice

1 Combine the rice, the water, the broth, the garlic powder, the thyme, the saffron, the oregano and the allspice in the top of a double boiler. Bring water to a boil in the bottom of the double boiler, reduce the heat, cover and simmer until all the liquid is absorbed and the rice is tender, 30 to 40 minutes.

2 Fluff the rice before serving.

Stop & Go Salad

1 Bring water to a boil in a medium saucepan. Trim the green beans and cut them into 1-inch diagonals. Cook the beans in the boiling water until they are almost tender, 3 to 5 minutes.

2 Peel and mince the garlic. Chop the basil. Chop the dill. Whisk the herbs in a small bowl with the oil and the V-8 juice. Season to taste.

3 Wash and dry the lettuce and arrange the leaves on individual salad plates.

4 Remove the beans to a medium bowl, reserving the cooking liquid. Add the tomatoes to the bean liquid for 10 to 20 seconds to loosen the skins. Remove the tomatoes and rinse them in cold water. Peel and dice the tomatoes and add them to the beans.

5 Toss the bean mixture gently with the dressing. Spoon the beans over the lettuce and serve at room temperature.

Peachy Keen Cakes

1 Peel, pit and slice the peaches and place them in a medium bowl. Sprinkle them with the lemon juice and the Amaretto. Cover and refrigerate them until you are ready to use.

2 Fill each dessert cup with scoops of peach ice cream. Top with the sliced peaches and a dollop of whipped cream.

TUESDAY

Echo Soup

1 small onion
1 tablespoon fresh parsley (when chopped)
1 package (9 ounces) frozen green peas
1 package (9 ounces) frozen chopped spinach
1 bay leaf
$1/4$ teaspoon dried chervil
$1/4$ teaspoon dried tarragon
1 can ($14^1/2$ ounces) vegetable broth
1 cup half-and-half
2 tablespoons dry sherry (or nonalcoholic
  white wine or omit)
$1/4$ teaspoon curry powder
Seasoning to taste

Bowl 'em Over Salad

4 eggs
2 medium heads lettuce
1 large cucumber
$3/4$ pound fresh tomatoes
1 small head cauliflower
1 medium carrot
1 small red onion
1 small bunch radishes
$1/2$ pound thinly sliced deli turkey breast
$1/2$ pound thinly sliced deli baked ham
$1/2$ pound thinly sliced deli roast beef
$1/4$ pound sliced regular or low-fat Swiss
  cheese
1 clove garlic
3 tablespoons fresh chives (when chopped)
2 tablespoons V-8 juice reserved from Monday
2 tablespoons red wine vinegar
1 tablespoon lemon juice
4 tablespoons regular or light olive oil
2 teaspoons Dijon mustard
1 tablespoon ketchup
$1/4$ teaspoon Worcestershire sauce
Seasoning to taste

Bagel Treats

4 bagels
2 scallions (green onions)
1 container (8 ounces) regular or light soft
  cream cheese
$1/2$ teaspoon prepared horseradish

Banana Pudding Crumble

1 small package (3.4 ounces) instant banana
  cream pudding mix
2 cups whole milk
$1/2$ teaspoon vanilla extract
1 package (10 ounces) oatmeal cookies
1 large banana

EQUIPMENT

Electric hand mixer	Measuring cups and
Blender	spoons
Medium covered	Assorted cooking
saucepan	utensils
Small saucepan	Whisk
Medium bowl	Vegetable peeler
2 small bowls	Vegetable grater
Assorted kitchen knives	

COUNTDOWN

1 Assemble the ingredients and equipment
2 Do Step 1 of the *Bowl 'em Over Salad*
3 Do Step 1 of the *Banana Pudding Crumble*
4 Do Step 1 of the *Echo Soup*
5 Do Steps 2–6 of the *Bowl 'em Over Salad*
6 Do Step 2 of the *Echo Soup*
7 Do Steps 1–2 of the *Bagel Treats*
8 Do Step 7 of the *Bowl 'em Over Salad*
9 Do Step 2 of the *Banana Pudding Crumble*

Echo Soup

1 Peel and chop the onion. Chop the parsley. Combine the onion, the peas, the spinach, the bay leaf, the chervil, the tarragon and the broth in a medium saucepan. Bring the mixture to a boil, reduce the heat and simmer, covered, for 20 minutes.

2 Remove the bay leaf. Process the soup in a blender until pureed. Return it to the saucepan. Add the half-and-half, the sherry and the curry powder. Season to taste. Bring the soup to a simmer and sprinkle with the parsley.

Bowl 'em Over Salad

1 Cover the eggs with water in a small saucepan. Bring the water to a boil and hard-cook the eggs, 10 to 12 minutes.

2 Wash and dry the lettuce and tear it into bite-size pieces. Arrange it on a large platter.

3 Peel and slice the cucumber. Cut the tomatoes into thin wedges. Trim and cut the cauliflower into bite-size florets. Peel and grate the carrot. Peel and thinly slice the red onion. Trim and slice the radishes.

4 Drain and peel the eggs and place them in the freezer to chill for 10 minutes.

5 Cut the turkey, the ham and the roast beef into thin strips. Dice the cheese. Arrange the meat over the lettuce. Top the meat with the vegetables. Sprinkle with the cheese.

6 Peel and mince the garlic. Chop the chives. Whisk the garlic and the chives in a small bowl with the V-8 juice, the vinegar, the lemon juice, the oil, the mustard, the ketchup and the Worcestershire sauce. Season to taste.

7 Slice the eggs and arrange them over the salad. Drizzle the salad with the dressing.

Bagel Treats

1 Slice the bagels and lightly toast them.

2 Trim and chop the scallions. In a small bowl, blend the scallions, the cream cheese and the horseradish. Spread the mixture liberally on the toasted bagels.

Banana Pudding Crumble

1 In a medium bowl, beat the pudding mix, the milk and the vanilla until well blended. Pour the mixture into individual dessert dishes and refrigerate for at least 20 minutes.

2 Crumble the oatmeal cookies. Layer the crumbs over the pudding. Peel and slice the banana and arrange the slices over the cookie crumbs. Garnish with a dollop of marshmallow topping.

WEDNESDAY

Picturesque Pasta

1 small red onion
1 small green bell pepper
1 small red bell pepper
2 tablespoons regular or light olive oil
12 ounces rotelle
$^1/_2$ pound scallops
$^1/_4$ pound fresh tomatoes
1 medium cucumber
2 cloves garlic
2 tablespoons fresh parsley (when chopped)
2 tablespoons fresh basil (when chopped)
1 small can (8$^3/_4$ ounces) whole kernel corn
3 tablespoons lime juice
Seasoning to taste

Cheese Baguettes

2 cloves garlic
$^1/_4$ cup fresh dill (when chopped)
$^1/_3$ pound shredded regular or low-fat
    Monterey Jack cheese
1 tablespoon regular or low-fat mayonnaise
4 individual sourdough French bread
    baguettes

Open-Faced Creamwiches

4 toaster waffles
$^1/_2$ cup orange marmalade
1 pint vanilla ice cream
$^1/_4$ cup pecan pieces

EQUIPMENT

Large covered skillet	Assorted cooking
Large saucepan	utensils
Small bowl	Vegetable peeler
Colander	Ice cream scoop
Assorted kitchen knives	
Measuring cups and	
spoons	

COUNTDOWN

1 Assemble the ingredients and equipment
2 Do Steps 1–4 of the *Picturesque Pasta*
3 Do Steps 1–3 of the *Cheese Baguettes*
4 Do Steps 5–7 of the *Picturesque Pasta*
5 Do Step 4 of the *Cheese Baguettes*
6 Do Steps 1–2 of the *Open-Faced
   Creamwiches*

Picturesque Pasta

1 Bring water to a boil in a large saucepan.

2 Peel and chop the onion. Seed and dice the bell peppers.

3 Heat the oil in a large skillet and sauté the onion and the peppers until they are tender, about 7 minutes.

4 Rinse and pat dry the scallops. If you are using sea scallops, cut them in quarters. Chop the tomatoes. Peel and chop the cucumber. Peel and crush the garlic. Chop the parsley. Chop the basil. Drain the corn.

5 Cook the pasta in the boiling water until it is almost tender, 8 to 10 minutes.

6 Add the scallops and the corn to the onion and peppers. Sauté, until the scallops are just tender, about 3 minutes. Remove the skillet from the heat and stir in the tomatoes, the cucumber, the garlic, the lime juice, the parsley and the basil. Season to taste.

7 Drain the pasta, return it to the saucepan and toss it with the scallop mixture. Cover to keep warm.

Cheese Baguettes

1 Peel and mince the garlic. Chop the dill. Combine the garlic, the dill, the cheese and the mayonnaise in a small bowl.

2 Split the baguettes and place them on an unheated broiler tray. Spread the cut sides generously with the cheese mixture.

3 Preheat the broiler.

4 Broil the baguettes, 3 to 4 inches from the heat, until they are bubbly, 2 to 3 minutes.

Open-Faced Creamwiches

1 Toast the waffles and let them cool slightly.

2 Spread the waffles with the marmalade. Top with scoops of vanilla ice cream and sprinkle with the pecan pieces.

THURSDAY

Hot-Spot Chicken Salad

1 small head lettuce
1/2 pound fresh spinach
1 can (11 ounces) mandarin oranges
1 1/4 pounds boneless, skinless chicken breasts
1 small onion
1 clove garlic
1/2 teaspoon fresh ginger (when grated)
3 tablespoons soy sauce
1 tablespoon honey
3 tablespoons water
3 tablespoons regular or light vegetable oil
Seasoning to taste
1/4 cup sliced almonds

Stone Cold Soba

3 scallions (green onions)
2 teaspoons sesame oil
2 tablespoons soy sauce
1 teaspoon dry sherry (or nonalcoholic white
 wine or omit)
12 ounces fresh Japanese soba noodles
Seasoning to taste

Red Dragons

2 tablespoons fresh chives (when chopped)
4 large tomatoes
1 tablespoon red pepper flakes
1/4 teaspoon chili powder
2 tablespoons sesame oil
Seasoning to taste

Firesticks

1/4 small watermelon
1 medium cantaloupe
1 small honeydew melon
1/2 pound fresh (or net weight canned)
 pineapple chunks
1/4 cup flaked coconut

EQUIPMENT

Large skillet	Assorted cooking
Large saucepan	utensils
2 large bowls	4 skewers
2 small bowls	Citrus grater
Strainer	Whisk
Assorted kitchen knives	
Measuring cups and	
spoons	

COUNTDOWN

1 Assemble the ingredients and equipment
2 Do Step 1 of the *Firesticks*
3 Do Steps 1–2 of the *Red Dragons*
4 Do Steps 1–3 of the *Stone Cold Soba*
5 Do Steps 1–6 of the *Hot-Spot Chicken Salad*
6 Do Step 3 of the *Red Dragons*
7 Do Step 2 of the *Firesticks*

Hot-Spot Chicken Salad

1 Wash and dry the lettuce and tear it into bite-size pieces. Wash, dry and stem the spinach and tear it into bite-size pieces. Drain the mandarin oranges. Combine the ingredients in a large bowl.

2 Cut the chicken into 1-inch pieces. Peel and chop the onion. Peel and mince the garlic. Grate the ginger.

3 In a small bowl, whisk together the soy sauce, the honey, the ginger and the water.

4 Heat the oil in a large skillet. Add the chicken and the onion and sauté until the chicken is opaque throughout, 3 to 4 minutes. Add the garlic. Season to taste. Sauté for 1 minute more.

5 Add the soy sauce mixture to the skillet and cook, tossing, until it is heated through, about 30 seconds.

6 Pour the chicken and the sauce over the greens and oranges, and toss to combine. Sprinkle the sliced almonds on top.

Stone Cold Soba

1 Bring water to a boil in a large saucepan.

2 Peel and chop the scallions. In a large bowl, combine the scallions, the sesame oil, the soy sauce and the sherry.

3 Cook the soba until the noodles rise, about 30 seconds. Drain and rinse the noodles under cold water, add them to the bowl and toss them lightly with the dressing. Season to taste and refrigerate until you are ready to serve.

Red Dragons

1 Chop the chives. Slice the tomatoes and arrange them on individual salad plates.

2 In a small bowl, combine the red pepper flakes, the chili powder and the sesame oil. Season to taste.

3 Drizzle the dressing over the tomatoes. Sprinkle with the chives.

Firesticks

1 Seed and chunk the melons, removing the rinds. Thread the chunks alternately onto skewers with the pineapple and refrigerate until you are ready to serve.

2 Sprinkle the firesticks with the coconut.

FRIDAY

Seaside Sauté

4 sweet red apples
1¹/₂ pounds cod steaks
2 tablespoons butter
2 tablespoons regular or light vegetable oil
1 cup apple cider
Seasoning to taste

Ricing Around

1 teaspoon fresh parsley (when chopped)
1 cup long-grain white rice
1 can (14¹/₂ ounces) vegetable broth
¹/₄ cup water
¹/₈ teaspoon dried thyme
1 small onion
2 medium mushrooms
3 egg yolks
1 tablespoon butter

Snowbody's Baby

¹/₂ pound baby carrots
20 Chinese snow peas
2 tablespoons fresh dill (when chopped)
2 tablespoons butter
Seasoning to taste

Sort-of Baked Alaska

4 individual shortcake dessert cups
3 egg whites
¹/₄ cup sugar
¹/₈ teaspoon salt
1 pint orange frozen yogurt

EQUIPMENT

Electric hand mixer	Measuring cups and
2 large skillets	spoons
Medium covered	Assorted cooking
saucepan	utensils
Double boiler	Ice cream scoop
Large bowl	Aluminum foil
Assorted kitchen knives	Vegetable peeler

COUNTDOWN

IN THE MORNING:
   Do Step 1 of the *Sort-of Baked Alaska*
BEFORE DINNER:
   1 Assemble the remaining ingredients and equipment
   2 Do Steps 1–2 of the *Ricing Around*
   3 Do Steps 1–2 of *Snowbody's Baby*
   4 Do Steps 1–3 of the *Seaside Sauté*
   5 Do Step 3 of *Snowbody's Baby*
   6 Do Step 2 of the *Sort-of Baked Alaska*
   7 Do Step 4 of the *Seaside Sauté*
   8 Do Step 4 of *Snowbody's Baby*
   9 Do Steps 3–4 of the *Ricing Around*
   10 Do Step 3 of the *Sort-of Baked Alaska*

Seaside Sauté

1 Peel, core and quarter the apples. Cut the fish into 1-inch pieces.

2 In a large skillet, melt the butter with the oil. Add the apples and sauté until they are lightly browned, 3 to 4 minutes. Remove the apples and keep them warm.

3 Add the fish pieces to the skillet and cook until they are lightly browned, 2 to 3 minutes per side. Remove the fish pieces and keep them warm.

4 Add the cider to the skillet and bring the mixture to a boil. Cook, stirring to scrape up any bits left on the bottom, until the mixture is reduced by half, about 4 minutes. Return the apples and the fish to the skillet and cook, stirring gently, until the fish is cooked through and the liquid turns thick and syrupy, 3 to 5 minutes. Season to taste.

Ricing Around

1 Chop the parsley. Combine the parsley, the rice, the broth, the water, and the thyme in the top of a double boiler. Bring water to a boil in the bottom of the double boiler. Reduce the heat, cover and simmer until all the liquid is absorbed and the rice is tender, 30 to 40 minutes.

2 Peel and mince the onion. Wash, pat dry and chop the mushrooms. Lightly beat the egg yolks.

3 Melt the butter in a large skillet. Sauté the onion for 2 minutes. Add the mushrooms and sauté for 3 minutes more. Add the beaten egg yolks to the skillet in a thin stream. Sauté until the mixture is cooked through. Add the rice and toss until combined.

4 Fluff the rice before serving.

Snowbody's Baby

1 Bring water to a boil in a medium saucepan.

2 Trim the carrots, if necessary. String the snow peas. Chop the dill.

3 Cook the carrots in the boiling water until they are crisp-tender, 10 to 15 minutes.

4 Add the snow peas to the carrots and cook for 30 seconds more. Drain the vegetables and return them to the saucepan. Toss them with the dill and the butter, season to taste and cover to keep warm.

Sort-of Baked Alaska

1 Place the dessert cups in the refrigerator to chill.

2 In a large bowl, whip the egg whites until soft peaks form, about 5 minutes. Gradually add the sugar and the salt and continue beating until stiff peaks form, about 5 minutes more. Seal the bowl and let it stand.

3 Preheat the broiler. Cover the broiler pan with a sheet of aluminum foil. Place a scoop of frozen yogurt in the center of each cold dessert shell. Spread the egg mixture over each cake, carefully sealing the entire cake right down to the foil. Place the cakes under the broiler, 3 to 4 inches from the heat, until golden, about 2 minutes.

JULY

WEEK FIVE

Monday

CHARLIE'S FETTUCCINE
SNAP HAPPY PEAS
PITA PATTER
BLUE BUNNIES

Tuesday

ORIENTAL ONION SOUP
MANDARIN CHICKEN SALAD
EMPRESS ICE CREAM

Wednesday

MEDITERRANEAN KABOBS
CONTINENTAL COUSCOUS
TOMATOES ON THE SIDE
NAUGHTY NECTARINES

Thursday

SLEIGHT OF HAM
PINEAPPLE TOASTIES
TRIFLING AROUND

Friday

SAMPAN SALMON
RUBY POTATOES
ORANGE & ONION SALAD
FROOT TOOTIES

CHECK STAPLES

- ☐ Butter
- ☐ Cornstarch
- ☐ Granulated sugar
- ☐ Confectioners' sugar
- ☐ Regular or light vegetable oil
- ☐ Regular or light olive oil
- ☐ Sesame oil
- ☐ Red wine vinegar
- ☐ White wine vinegar
- ☐ Rice vinegar
- ☐ Raspberry vinegar
- ☐ Lemon juice
- ☐ Grated fresh orange peel
- ☐ Fresh ginger
- ☐ Tabasco sauce
- ☐ Soy sauce
- ☐ Dijon mustard
- ☐ Regular or low-fat mayonnaise
- ☐ Honey
- ☐ Beef bouillon cubes
- ☐ Ground allspice
- ☐ Chili powder
- ☐ Chinese Five-Spice powder
- ☐ Ground ginger
- ☐ Dried marjoram
- ☐ Dried oregano
- ☐ Poppy seeds
- ☐ Dried rosemary
- ☐ Sesame seeds
- ☐ Dried thyme
- ☐ Pepper
- ☐ Salt
- ☐ Vanilla extract

SHOPPING NOTE

● If you are shopping once a week and cannot arrange to purchase fresh salmon on the day you plan to use it, you can purchase *not previously frozen* salmon and freeze it, placing it in the refrigerator to thaw the night before you are ready to use it. Or you can purchase *still frozen* salmon and keep it frozen until the night before you are ready to use it.

MEAT & POULTRY
1 pound lean boneless lamb (W)
1¼ pounds lean cooked ham steak (Th)
1½ pounds boneless, skinless chicken breasts (T)

FISH
4 salmon steaks (1½ pounds) (F)

FRESH PRODUCE
Vegetables
12 small new red potatoes (F)
1 medium bunch broccoli (Th)
1 medium zucchini (Th)
2 pounds unshelled green peas (Th)
¾ pound sugar snap peas (M)
8 medium mushrooms (W)
3 medium carrots—1 (T), 1 (W), 1 (Th)
4 stalks celery—2 (T), 2 (Th)
2 large onions (M)
1 large sweet onion (T)
2 medium onions (W)
3 medium sweet onions—1 (Th), 2 (F)
1 small red onion (M)
14 scallions (green onions)—4 (M), 4 (T), 2 (W), 4 (Th)
1 head garlic (M, W, Th, F)
1 bunch dill (M, F)
1 bunch parsley (T, W, F)
1 large head lettuce (T)
2 medium heads lettuce (Th, F)
4 large tomatoes (W)
1 medium cucumber (T)
1 medium red bell pepper (M)
1 medium yellow bell pepper (M)
1 large green bell pepper (W)
1 small jicama (or turnip) (T)

Fruit
4 large nectarines (W)
2 large peaches (F)
2 medium bananas (F)
¼ pound pineapple chunks (or net weight canned) (W)
1 pint blueberries (M)
¼ pound seedless red grapes (T)
3 medium oranges (F)

CANS, JARS & BOTTLES
Soup
1 can (10¾ ounces) chicken broth (W)

2 cans (14½ ounces each) chicken broth (T)
1 can (14½ ounces) vegetable broth (F)

Vegetables
1 small can (8¾ ounces) whole kernel corn (M)

Fish
1 can (6 ounces) solid white tuna (M)

Oriental Foods
1 small can (5 ounces) Chinese chow mein noodles (T)
2 cans (8 ounces each) sliced water chestnuts—1 (T), 1 (Th)

Fruit
1 can (11 ounces) mandarin oranges (T)
1 small can (8 ounces) crushed pineapple (Th)

Condiments
8 maraschino cherries—4 (T), 4 (Th)
3 tablespoons maraschino cherry juice (T)

Spreads
3 tablespoons raspberry preserves (Th)

PACKAGED GOODS
Pasta, Rice & Grains
12 ounces fettuccine (M)
1 cup quick-cooking couscous (W)

Baked Goods
2 small pita breads (M)
4 French rolls (Th)
1 package (3 ounces) ladyfingers (M, Th)

Fruit
½ cup chopped dates (W)

Nuts & Seeds
⅔ cup sliced almonds (T)
⅔ cup unsalted cashew pieces (Th)

Dessert & Baking Needs
1 small package (10 ounces) macaroons (W)

1 small package (3.4 ounces) instant vanilla pudding mix (Th)
1 small package (3½ ounces) lime-flavored gelatin (F)

WINES & SPIRITS
1 cup dry white wine (or nonalcoholic white wine or clam juice) (M)
¼ cup dry sherry (or nonalcoholic white wine or omit) (T)
2 tablespoons dry sherry (or 1 tablespoon water + 1 tablespoon dark brown sugar) (F)
1 tablespoon sweet sherry (or nonalcoholic Italian cherry syrup) (Th)
2 tablespoons Grand Marnier liqueur (or nonalcoholic Italian orange syrup) (T)
2 tablespoons rum (or 2 teaspoons rum extract) (W)

REFRIGERATED PRODUCTS
Dairy
1¼ cups whole milk (Th)
1 cup whipping cream (W)
¾ cup regular or light sour cream (Th)
3 eggs (Th)

Cheese
4 ounces regular or low-fat Swiss cheese (M)
1 container (8 ounces) regular or light soft cream cheese (Th)

Juice
2 tablespoons orange juice (Th)

FROZEN GOODS
Vegetables
1 package (9 ounces) green peas (T)

Desserts
1 pint lemon sherbet (M)
1 pint vanilla ice cream (T)
1 small container (8 ounces) frozen whipped topping (Th)

MONDAY

Charlie's Fettuccine

1 medium red bell pepper
1 medium yellow bell pepper
4 scallions (green onions)
2 cloves garlic
2 tablespoons fresh dill (when chopped)
1 can (6 ounces) solid white tuna
1 cup dry white wine (or nonalcoholic white
    wine or clam juice)
12 ounces fettuccine
$2^1/_2$ teaspoons Dijon mustard
Seasoning to taste

Snap Happy Peas

$^3/_4$ pound sugar snap peas
1 small red onion
1 can ($8^3/_4$ ounces) whole kernel corn
2 tablespoons butter
$^1/_2$ teaspoon ground allspice
Seasoning to taste

Pita Patter

2 large onions
2 small pita breads
2 tablespoons regular or light olive oil
4 ounces shredded regular or low-fat Swiss
    cheese

Blue Bunnies

1 pint fresh blueberries
1 pint lemon sherbet
8 whole ladyfingers*
$^1/_4$ cup confectioners' sugar

*Reserve the remainder of the package for use on
Thursday.

EQUIPMENT

2 large skillets	Measuring cups and
Large saucepan	spoons
Medium covered	Assorted cooking
saucepan	utensils
Colander	Ice cream scoop
Assorted kitchen knives	Sifter

COUNTDOWN

1 Assemble the ingredients and equipment
2 Do Step 1 of the *Charlie's Fettuccine*
3 Do Step 1 of the *Blue Bunnies*
4 Do Step 1 of the *Snap Happy Peas*
5 Do Steps 1–2 of the *Pita Patter*
6 Do Steps 2–7 of the *Charlie's Fettuccine*
7 Do Step 2 of the *Snap Happy Peas*
8 Do Steps 3–4 of the *Pita Patter*
9 Do Step 2 of the *Blue Bunnies*

Charlie's Fettuccine

1 Bring water to a boil in a large saucepan.

2 Seed the bell peppers and cut them into thin strips. Trim and chop the scallions. Peel and mince the garlic. Chop the dill.

3 Drain and flake the tuna.

4 In a medium saucepan, combine the peppers, the scallions, the garlic and 3/4 cup of the wine. Heat the mixture to boiling, stirring. Reduce the heat, cover and simmer for 5 minutes.

5 Cook the pasta until it is almost tender, 2 to 3 minutes if you are using fresh pasta and 6 to 7 minutes if you are using dried pasta.

6 Stir the dill, the remaining wine, the mustard and the tuna into the bell pepper mixture. Season to taste and heat through.

7 Drain the pasta and return it to the saucepan and toss it with the sauce.

Snap Happy Peas

1 String the sugar snap peas. Peel and chop the red onion. Drain the corn.

2 Melt the butter in a large skillet. Add the sugar snap peas, the onions, the corn and the allspice. Season to taste and stir-fry until the vegetables are crisp-tender, 2 to 3 minutes.

Pita Patter

1 Peel and thinly slice the onions. Cut the pita breads in half.

2 Heat the oil in a large skillet. Sauté the onions until they are golden, about 10 minutes.

3 Sprinkle the cheese over the onions and cook until the cheese is just melted, 1 to 2 minutes.

4 Stuff the pita halves with the onion-cheese mixture.

Blue Bunnies

1 Rinse and stem the blueberries as necessary, and refrigerate until you are ready to use.

2 Place scoops of lemon sherbet in individual dessert bowls. Place 2 ladyfingers upright into each dish of sherbet, one on each side. Cover the sherbet with the blueberries. Sprinkle the ladyfinger "ears" and the berries with the confectioners' sugar.

TUESDAY

Oriental Onion Soup

1 package (9 ounces) frozen green peas
1 large sweet onion
1 can (8 ounces) sliced water chestnuts
2 teaspoons sesame oil
2 cans (14$1/2$ ounces each) chicken broth
1 tablespoon soy sauce
1 teaspoon sugar
2 teaspoons ground ginger
$1/4$ cup dry sherry (or nonalcoholic white wine
   or omit)
Seasoning to taste

Mandarin Chicken Salad

1 can (11 ounces) mandarin oranges
1$1/2$ pounds boneless, skinless chicken breasts
1 large head lettuce
1 medium cucumber
1 medium carrot
2 stalks celery
1 small jicama (or turnip)
4 scallions (green onions)
1 tablespoon fresh parsley (when chopped)
$1/4$ pound seedless red grapes
4 tablespoons regular or light vegetable oil
1 teaspoon sesame oil
1 tablespoon red wine vinegar
2 tablespoons rice vinegar
$1/2$ teaspoon grated fresh orange peel
Seasoning to taste
$2/3$ cup sliced almonds
1 can (5 ounces) Chinese chow mein noodles

Empress Ice Cream

1 tablespoon cornstarch
Orange juice reserved from the Mandarin
   Chicken Salad
2 tablespoons honey
3 tablespoons maraschino cherry juice
$1/8$ teaspoon Chinese five-spice powder
2 tablespoons Grand Marnier liqueur (or
   nonalcoholic Italian orange syrup)
1 pint vanilla ice cream
4 maraschino cherries for garnish

EQUIPMENT

Large saucepan	Assorted cooking
Medium saucepan	utensils
Small saucepan	Whisk
Large bowl	Vegetable peeler
Small bowl	Vegetable grater
Assorted kitchen knives	Ice cream scoop
Measuring cups and	
spoons	

COUNTDOWN

IN THE MORNING:
   Do Step 1 of the *Mandarin Chicken Salad*
BEFORE DINNER:
   1 Assemble the remaining ingredients and
      equipment
   2 Do Step 1 of the *Oriental Onion Soup*
   3 Do Steps 2–4 of the *Mandarin Chicken
      Salad*
   4 Do Step 1 of the *Empress Ice Cream*
   5 Do Steps 5–7 of the *Mandarin Chicken
      Salad*
   6 Do Steps 2–3 of the *Oriental Onion Soup*
   7 Do Step 2 of the *Empress Ice Cream*

Oriental Onion Soup

1 Set the package of peas out to thaw. Peel and chop the onion. Drain the water chestnuts.

2 Heat the sesame oil in a large saucepan and sauté the onion until it is limp, about 5 minutes.

3 Add the thawed peas, the water chestnuts, the broth, the soy sauce, the sugar, the ginger and the sherry. Season to taste and simmer for 5 minutes.

Mandarin Chicken Salad

1 Place the can of mandarin oranges in the refrigerator to chill.

2 Bring water to a boil in a medium saucepan.

3 Cut the chicken breasts in strips and boil until they are opaque throughout, 5 to 6 minutes.

4 Drain the chicken and run the strips under cold water several times to cool. Place the chicken in the refrigerator for 10 minutes.

5 Wash and dry the lettuce and tear it into bite-size pieces. Peel and chop the cucumber. Peel and grate the carrot. Trim and slice the celery. Peel and chop the jicama. Trim and slice the scallions. Chop the parsley. Wash, separate and halve the grapes. Drain the chilled mandarin oranges, reserving the juice. Combine the ingredients in a large bowl.

6 In a small bowl, whisk together both oils, both vinegars, the parsley and the orange peel. Season to taste.

7 Chop the chicken and add it to the salad. Add the almonds. Toss the salad with the dressing and sprinkle with the chow mein noodles.

Empress Ice Cream

1 In a small saucepan, dissolve the cornstarch in the reserved orange juice. Add the honey, the maraschino cherry juice, the Chinese five-spice powder and the Grand Marnier. Bring the mixture to a boil and cook until slightly thickened, about 3 minutes. Let the sauce cool at room temperature.

2 Place scoops of ice cream in individual dessert bowls. Top with the sauce and garnish with a maraschino cherry.

WEDNESDAY

Mediterranean Kabobs

1 pound lean boneless lamb
1 clove garlic
$1/4$ cup red wine vinegar
1 tablespoon regular or light olive oil
$1/4$ cup chicken broth
$1/2$ teaspoon dried rosemary
$1/2$ teaspoon dried oregano
Seasoning to taste
2 medium onions
1 large green bell pepper
8 medium mushrooms

Continental Couscous

1 medium carrot
2 scallions (green onions)
2 tablespoons fresh parsley (when chopped)
1 cup chicken broth
$1/4$ cup water
1 beef bouillon cube
1 cup quick-cooking couscous
Seasoning to taste

Tomatoes on the Side

4 large fresh tomatoes
$1/4$ cup fresh parsley (when chopped)
1 clove garlic
$1/2$ teaspoon dried oregano
1 teaspoon sugar
3 tablespoons regular or light olive oil
2 tablespoons red wine vinegar
2 teaspoons Dijon mustard
Seasoning to taste

Naughty Nectarines

4 large nectarines
2 tablespoons lemon juice
1 small package (10 ounces) macaroons
$1/4$ pound fresh pineapple chunks (or net
    weight canned)
$1/2$ cup chopped dates
2 tablespoons rum (or 2 teaspoons rum
    extract)

EQUIPMENT

Electric hand mixer	Assorted cooking
Blender	utensils
Medium covered	8 skewers
saucepan	Whisk
2 medium bowls	Vegetable grater
Small bowl	Citrus grater
Large shallow bowl	Vegetable peeler
Assorted kitchen knives	
Measuring cups and	
spoons	

COUNTDOWN

1 Assemble the ingredients and equipment
2 Do Steps 1–2 of the Mediterranean Kabobs
3 Do Steps 1–4 of the Naughty Nectarines
4 Do Steps 1–2 of the Tomatoes on the Side
5 Do Steps 1–3 of the Continental Couscous
6 Do Step 3 of the Mediterranean Kabobs
7 Do Step 5 of the Naughty Nectarines

Mediterranean Kabobs

1 Cut the lamb into 1-inch cubes and place them in a medium bowl. Peel and mince the garlic. Add the garlic, the vinegar, the oil, the broth, the rosemary and the oregano to the lamb, and season to taste. Toss to coat the meat with the marinade and let the mixture stand, tossing occasionally, for 30 minutes.

2 Prepare the grill.

3 Quarter the onions. Seed the bell pepper and cut it into $1^1/_2$-inch squares. Wash, pat dry and trim the mushrooms. Thread the lamb, the onions, the mushrooms and the bell pepper onto skewers. Grill the skewers, turning and basting with the marinade several times, until the meat is browned outside but still pink and juicy inside and the vegetables are crisp-tender, 10 to 12 minutes.

Continental Couscous

1 Peel and finely grate the carrot. Trim and finely chop the scallions. Chop the parsley.

2 In a medium saucepan, bring the broth, the water, the bouillon cube and the carrot to a boil. Add the couscous and the scallions. Season to taste. Cover the saucepan and remove it from the heat, letting it stand until all the liquid has been absorbed, at least 5 minutes.

3 Fluff the couscous before serving and toss it with the parsley.

Tomatoes on the Side

1 Wash and slice the tomatoes. Arrange them in a large shallow bowl.

2 Chop the parsley. Peel and mince the garlic. In a small bowl, whisk together the parsley, the garlic, the oregano, the sugar, the oil, the vinegar and the mustard. Season the mixture to taste and pour it over the tomatoes. Toss gently to coat. Cover the bowl and let it stand until you are ready to serve.

Naughty Nectarines

1 Wash and slice the nectarines and distribute them among individual dessert bowls. Sprinkle them with the lemon juice and refrigerate until you are ready to use.

2 Crumble the macaroons.

3 In a blender, combine 1 cup of the crumbled macaroons, the pineapple chunks, the chopped dates and the rum, and process until pureed, about 1 minute.

4 Whip the cream in a medium bowl until stiff, about 5 minutes. Fold the pureed mixture into the whipped cream and refrigerate until you are ready to use.

5 Spoon the whipped cream mixture over the nectarines, and top with the remaining crumbled macaroons.

THURSDAY

Sleight of Ham

3 eggs
1¹/₄ pounds lean cooked ham steak
2 pounds unshelled green peas
1 medium bunch broccoli
1 medium zucchini
1 medium carrot
2 stalks celery
1 medium sweet onion
4 scallions (green onions)
1 clove garlic
1 can (8 ounces) sliced water chestnuts
²/₃ cup unsalted cashew pieces
2 medium heads lettuce*
¹/₂ cup regular or low-fat mayonnaise
¹/₂ teaspoon Tabasco sauce
1 teaspoon chili powder
2 tablespoons white wine vinegar
¹/₄ teaspoon dried marjoram
¹/₄ teaspoon dried thyme
1 teaspoon Dijon mustard
Seasoning to taste

Pineapple Toasties

1 small can (8 ounces) crushed pineapple
4 French rolls
1 container (8 ounces) regular or light soft
    cream cheese
1 tablespoon poppy seeds

Trifling Around

4 ladyfingers reserved from Monday
2 tablespoons orange juice
3 tablespoons raspberry preserves
1 tablespoon water
1 small package (3.4 ounces) instant vanilla
    pudding mix
1¹/₄ cups whole milk
³/₄ cup regular or light sour cream
1 small container (8 ounces) frozen whipped
    topping
1 tablespoon sweet sherry (or nonalcoholic
    Italian cherry syrup)
4 maraschino cherries for garnish

EQUIPMENT

Electric hand mixer	Measuring cups and
Small saucepan	spoons
Cookie sheet	Assorted cooking
Large bowl	utensils
Medium bowl	Whisk
Small bowl	Vegetable peeler
Assorted kitchen knives	

COUNTDOWN

1 Assemble the ingredients and equipment
2 Do Steps 1–2 of *Trifling Around*
3 Do Steps 1–5 of the *Sleight of Ham*
4 Do Steps 1–2 of the *Pineapple Toasties*
5 Do Step 6 of the *Sleight of Ham*
6 Do Step 3 of *Trifling Around*

---

*Reserve 4 large leaves for use on Friday.

Sleight of Ham

1 Cover the eggs with water in a small saucepan, bring the water to a boil and hard-cook the eggs, 10 to 12 minutes.

2 Dice the ham. Shell the peas. Trim the broccoli and cut it into bite-size pieces. Trim and chop the zucchini. Peel and thinly slice the carrot. Trim and slice the celery. Peel and chop the sweet onion. Trim and chop the scallions. Peel and mince the garlic. Drain and chop the water chestnuts. Combine the ingredients in a large bowl with half of the cashew pieces.

3 Drain the eggs and place them in the freezer to chill for 10 minutes.

4 Wash and dry the lettuce, reserving 4 large lettuce leaves. Pull off 8 large leaves. Place them on a platter. Shred the remaining lettuce and arrange it on top of the lettuce leaves.

5 In a small bowl, whisk the garlic with the mayonnaise, the Tabasco sauce, the chili powder, the vinegar, the marjoram, the thyme and the mustard. Season to taste.

6 Peel and chop the eggs. Toss the ham mixture with the dressing and spoon it over the lettuce. Sprinkle with the chopped eggs and the remaining cashew pieces.

Pineapple Toasties

1 Preheat the broiler. Drain the pineapple well.

2 Split the French rolls and place them on an ungreased cookie sheet. Spread the cut sides of the rolls liberally with the cream cheese, top with a layer of pineapple and sprinkle them with the poppy seeds. Place the rolls under the broiler, 3 or 4 inches from the heat, and broil until the topping is bubbly, 1 to 2 minutes.

Trifling Around

1 Cube the ladyfingers and distribute them among individual sherbet glasses. Sprinkle the cubes with the orange juice. Combine the preserves and the water and spoon the mixture over the cake cubes.

2 In a medium bowl, beat together the pudding mix, the milk and the sour cream until well blended. Blend in 1 cup of the whipped topping and the sherry. Spoon the mixture over the cake and refrigerate for at least 20 minutes.

3 Top the trifles with the remaining whipped topping and garnish with the maraschino cherries.

FRIDAY

Sampan Salmon

1 clove garlic
1 tablespoon fresh ginger (when grated)
$1/3$ cup soy sauce
2 tablespoons dry sherry (or 1 tablespoon
    water + 1 tablespoon dark brown sugar)
1 teaspoon sesame oil
Seasoning to taste
4 salmon steaks ($1^1/2$ pounds)
2 tablespoons butter

Ruby Potatoes

12 small new red potatoes
1 tablespoon fresh dill (when chopped)
1 tablespoon fresh parsley (when chopped)
1 can ($14^1/2$ ounces) vegetable broth
2 tablespoons butter
Seasoning to taste

Orange & Onion Salad

$1/2$ teaspoon sesame oil
1 tablespoon sesame seeds
4 lettuce leaves reserved from Thursday
3 medium oranges
2 medium sweet onions
3 tablespoons regular or light vegetable oil
2 tablespoons raspberry vinegar
$1/4$ teaspoon ground ginger
Seasoning to taste

Froot Tooties

$1^1/4$ cups water
2 large peaches
$1/2$ teaspoon lemon juice
2 medium bananas
1 package ($3^1/2$ ounces) lime gelatin
Ice cubes

EQUIPMENT

Blender	Measuring cups and
Large covered skillet	spoons
Small skillet	Assorted cooking
Large saucepan	utensils
7x11-inch glass baking	Whisk
dish	Vegetable brush
2 small bowls	Citrus grater
Assorted kitchen knives	

COUNTDOWN

1 Assemble the ingredients and equipment
2 Do Step 1 of the *Froot Tooties*
3 Do Step 1 of the *Sampan Salmon*
4 Do Steps 2–3 of the *Froot Tooties*
5 Do Steps 1–2 of the *Ruby Potatoes*
6 Do Steps 1–3 of the *Orange & Onion Salad*
7 Do Step 2 of the *Sampan Salmon*
8 Do Step 3 of the *Ruby Potatoes*
9 Do Step 4 of the *Orange & Onion Salad*
10 Do Step 4 of the *Froot Tooties*

Sampan Salmon

1 Peel and mince the garlic. Grate the ginger. In a 7x11-inch glass baking dish, combine the garlic, the ginger, the soy sauce, the sherry and the oil. Season to taste. Place the salmon steaks in the dish and marinate them for 30 minutes, turning occasionally.

2 Melt the butter in a large skillet. Sauté the salmon steaks until they are almost firm and opaque, 4 to 5 minutes per side. Remove the skillet from the heat and cover to keep warm.

Ruby Potatoes

1 Scrub the potatoes. Chop the dill. Chop the parsley.

2 In a large saucepan, combine the potatoes and the broth. Cook until the potatoes are tender, about 20 minutes.

3 Drain the potatoes. Return them to the saucepan and toss gently with the butter, the dill and the parsley. Season to taste.

Orange & Onion Salad

1 Heat the sesame oil in a small skillet. Add the sesame seeds and toss over the heat until lightly toasted, about 5 minutes.

2 Wash, dry and place the lettuce leaves on individual salad plates. Peel and slice the oranges. Peel and thinly slice the sweet onions. Arrange the orange and onion slices over the lettuce leaves. Refrigerate until you are ready to serve.

3 In a small bowl, whisk together the oil, the vinegar and the ginger. Season to taste.

4 Drizzle the dressing over the salad and sprinkle with the toasted sesame seeds.

Froot Tooties

1 Bring $3/4$ cup of the water to a boil.

2 Peel, pit and slice the peaches, place them in a small bowl and sprinkle them with the lemon juice to keep them from browning. Peel and slice the bananas.

3 Pour the boiling water into a blender. Add the gelatin. Cover and blend at low speed until the gelatin is dissolved, about 30 seconds. Combine the remaining $1/2$ cup of water and the ice cubes to make $1^1/4$ cups. Add it to the blender, stir until the ice is partially melted and then blend at high speed for 30 seconds. Pour the mixture into individual parfait glasses. Spoon in the fruit, reserving 4 peach slices. Refrigerate for at least 30 minutes. The fruit will layer as it chills.

4 Drape a reserved peach slice over the edge of each glass.

AUGUST
WEEK ONE

Monday

INTOXICATING TOMATO SOUP
CURRIED CHICKEN SALAD
NOTHIN' MUFFINS
FRESH FRUIT PLATTER

Tuesday

FISH ON THE GRILL
CORN IN THE CRADLE
B & B SALAD
NECTARINE SHORTCAKE

Wednesday

RICH LITTLE POOR BOY
CONFETTI ORZO SALAD
SUMMER MIST

Thursday

STIR-FRIED BEEF & BROCCOLI
FLUFFY STEAMED WHITE RICE
SUN LUCK SALAD
PINEAPPLE BOATS

Friday

TITANIC SOUP
ICEBERG SALAD
SOP-UP BREAD
CHOCOLATE FLOATS

CHECK STAPLES

- ☐ Butter
- ☐ Flour
- ☐ Cornstarch
- ☐ Granulated sugar
- ☐ Dark brown sugar
- ☐ Chocolate syrup
- ☐ Chocolate sprinkles
- ☐ Long-grain white rice
- ☐ Regular or light vegetable oil
- ☐ Regular or light olive oil
- ☐ Sesame oil
- ☐ Red wine vinegar
- ☐ White wine vinegar
- ☐ Rice vinegar
- ☐ Lemon juice
- ☐ Grated fresh lemon peel
- ☐ Worcestershire sauce
- ☐ Soy sauce
- ☐ Dijon mustard
- ☐ Prepared horseradish
- ☐ Regular or low-fat mayonnaise
- ☐ Honey
- ☐ Dark raisins
- ☐ Golden raisins
- ☐ Whole allspice
- ☐ Bay leaves
- ☐ Celery seeds
- ☐ Ground cinnamon
- ☐ Curry powder
- ☐ Ground ginger
- ☐ Paprika
- ☐ Seasoning salt
- ☐ Dried thyme
- ☐ Turmeric
- ☐ Pepper
- ☐ Salt
- ☐ Vanilla extract

SHOPPING NOTE

• If you are shopping once a week and cannot arrange to purchase fresh seafood on the day you plan to use it, you can purchase *not previously frozen* seafood and freeze it, placing it in the refrigerator to thaw the night before you are ready to use it. Or you can purchase *still frozen* seafood and keep it frozen until the night before you are ready to use it.

• If you are shopping once a week and cannot arrange to purchase fresh clams and mussels on the day you plan to use them, you may substitute 4 cans (10 ounces each) whole clams and their juice for the fresh clams and mussels and omit the cooking instruction.

MEAT & POULTRY

1 pound lean boneless sirloin steak (Th)
$1^1/_2$ pounds boneless, skinless chicken breasts (M)

FISH

4 firm red snapper fillets ($1^1/_4$ pounds) (T)
1 pound medium shrimp, shelled and deveined (F)
36 small hard-shelled clams (F)
12 mussels (F)

FRESH PRODUCE

Vegetables

1 small bunch broccoli (Th)
4 ears sweet corn (T)
6 ounces green beans (T)
12 Chinese snow peas (Th)
$^1/_4$ pound mushrooms (Th)
1 medium carrot (W)
1 large onion (F)
1 medium onion (Th)
1 small sweet onion (W)
2 small red onions—1 (W), 1 (F)
7 scallions (green onions)—
    1(M), 4 (W), 2 (Th)
1 head garlic (T, W, Th, F)
1 small bunch basil (M, T)
1 small bunch dill (T, F)
1 small bunch parsley (W, F)
$^3/_4$ pound bean sprouts (Th)
1 small head lettuce (T, W)
1 head iceberg lettuce (F)
3 large tomatoes—1 (M), 2 (F)
2 medium tomatoes (W)
$^1/_2$ pound tomatoes (T)
2 medium cucumbers—1 (W), 1 (F)
2 small green bell peppers—
    1 (M), 1 (W)
2 small red bell peppers—1 (M), 1 (W)
1 small yellow bell pepper (W)

Fruit

8 small nectarines (T)
1 small honeydew melon (M)
1 small cantaloupe (M)
1 large pineapple (Th)
$^1/_2$ pound seedless red grapes (M)
$^1/_2$ pint blueberries (M)
$^1/_2$ pint raspberries (W)
2 medium oranges (W)

CANS, JARS & BOTTLES

Soup

1 can ($10^3/_4$ ounces) beef broth (M, Th)
1 can ($14^1/_2$ ounces) chicken broth (M)

Oriental Products

1 can (5 ounces) sliced bamboo shoots (Th)
1 can (11 ounces) lychees in syrup (Th)

Juice

$2^1/_2$ cups tomato juice (M)
1 bottle (8 ounces) clam juice (F)

Condiments

3 tablespoons capers (T)
1 small jar (11 ounces) bread and butter pickles (W)

PACKAGED GOODS

Pasta, Rice & Grains

16 ounces orzo (W)

Baked Goods

4 English muffins (M)
1 loaf Italian bread (W)
1 small loaf sourdough bread (F)

Nuts & Seeds

$^1/_2$ cup walnuts (M)

WINES & SPIRITS

$^1/_4$ cup dry red wine (or nonalcoholic red wine or beef broth) (M)
4 cups dry white wine (or nonalcoholic white wine or vegetable broth) (F)
2 tablespoons dry sherry (or nonalcoholic red wine or omit) (Th)
1 tablespoon Grand Marnier liqueur (or nonalcoholic Italian orange syrup) (M)
2 tablespoons Amaretto liqueur (or nonalcoholic Italian almond syrup) (W)

REFRIGERATED PRODUCTS

Dairy

1 quart whole or low-fat milk (F)
2 cups whipping cream—
    1 cup (T), 1 cup (F)
Whipped cream for garnish (F)
$^1/_4$ cup regular or light sour cream (M)

Cheese

1 container (4 ounces) whipped cream cheese (M)
$^1/_4$ pound sliced regular or low-fat Swiss cheese (W)

Deli

$^1/_4$ pound sliced deli baked ham (W)
$^1/_4$ pound sliced deli turkey (W)
$^1/_4$ pound dry salami (W)

FROZEN GOODS

Desserts

1 pound cake (T)
1 pint lemon frozen yogurt (W)
1 quart chocolate ice cream (F)

MONDAY

Intoxicating Tomato Soup

1 large fresh tomato
2 tablespoons fresh basil (when chopped)
1 scallion (green onion)
2¹/₂ cups tomato juice
1 tablespoon Worcestershire sauce
1 cup beef broth*
¹/₄ cup dry red wine (or nonalcoholic red wine
    or additional beef broth)
1 teaspoon sugar
¹/₂ teaspoon dried thyme
Seasoning to taste

Curried Chicken Salad

1 cup long-grain white rice
1 can (14¹/₂ ounces) chicken broth
1 teaspoon curry powder
¹/₄ teaspoon ground ginger
¹/₄ teaspoon turmeric
1 cup water
1 small green bell pepper
1 small red bell pepper
1¹/₂ pounds boneless, skinless chicken breasts
2 tablespoons regular or light olive oil
2 tablespoons lemon juice
¹/₄ cup regular or low-fat mayonnaise
¹/₄ cup regular or light sour cream
¹/₄ cup dark raisins
¹/₄ cup golden raisins
Seasoning to taste

Nothin' Muffins

¹/₂ cup walnuts
4 English muffins
1 container (4 ounces) whipped cream cheese

Fresh Fruit Platter

¹/₂ pound seedless red grapes
1 small honeydew melon
1 small cantaloupe
¹/₂ pint fresh blueberries
1 tablespoon lemon juice
1 tablespoon honey
1 tablespoon Grand Marnier liqueur (or
    nonalcoholic Italian orange syrup)

EQUIPMENT

Blender	Assorted kitchen knives
Large saucepan	Measuring cups and
Medium saucepan	spoons
Double boiler	Assorted cooking
2 large bowls	utensils
2 small bowls	Whisk

COUNTDOWN

1 Assemble the ingredients and equipment
2 Do Steps 1–5 of the *Curried Chicken Salad*
3 Do Steps 1–2 of the *Intoxicating Tomato
   Soup*
4 Do Step 1 of the *Fresh Fruit Platter*
5 Do Steps 6–7 of the *Curried Chicken Salad*
6 Do Steps 1–3 of the *Nothin' Muffins*
7 Do Step 3 of the *Intoxicating Tomato Soup*
8 Do Step 8 of the *Curried Chicken Salad*
9 Do Step 2 of the *Fresh Fruit Platter*

*Reserve the balance of the can for use on Thursday.

Intoxicating Tomato Soup

1 Chop the tomato. Chop the basil. Trim and chop the scallion. Combine them in a large saucepan with the tomato juice, the Worcestershire sauce, the broth, the wine, the sugar and the thyme. Season to taste.

2 Bring the mixture to a boil, reduce the heat and simmer, uncovered, for 20 minutes.

3 Place the soup in a blender and process until it is pureed. Return it to the saucepan and reheat.

Curried Chicken Salad

1 In the top of a double boiler, combine the rice, the broth, the curry powder, the ginger, the turmeric and the water. Bring water to a boil in the bottom of the double boiler, reduce the heat, cover and simmer until all the liquid is absorbed and the rice is tender, 30 to 40 minutes.

2 Bring water to a boil in a medium saucepan.

3 Seed and chop the bell peppers.

4 Cut the chicken breasts into strips and poach them in the boiling water until they are opaque throughout, 5 to 7 minutes.

5 Drain the chicken, rinse it in cold water, drain it again and refrigerate.

6 In a large bowl, combine the oil and the lemon juice. Transfer the rice to the bowl and toss it with the dressing. Cover and refrigerate until you are ready to serve.

7 In a small bowl, combine the mayonnaise and the sour cream. In a second large bowl, combine the raisins and the bell peppers. Add the mayonnaise mixture and mix well. Season to taste. Chop the chicken and add it to the raisin mixture.

8 Arrange the rice on a platter. Top it with the chicken mixture.

Nothin' Muffins

1 Place the walnuts in a blender and process until they are coarsely ground.

2 Split and toast the muffins.

3 Spread the muffins lightly with cream cheese and top with the ground walnuts.

Fresh Fruit Platter

1 Wash and separate the grapes. Quarter, seed, and slice the melons, removing the rinds. Rinse the blueberries and stem as necessary. Combine the fruit on a platter and refrigerate until you are ready to serve.

2 In a small bowl, whisk the lemon juice, the honey and the Grand Marnier together and spoon it over the fruit.

TUESDAY

Fish on the Grill

3 tablespoons capers
4 firm red snapper fillets (1 1/4 pounds)
4 teaspoons lemon juice
Seasoning to taste
1 clove garlic
3 tablespoons Dijon mustard
1/2 teaspoon prepared horseradish
1/2 teaspoon paprika

Corn in the Cradle

4 large ears sweet corn
4 tablespoons softened butter
1 teaspoon seasoning salt

B & B Salad

1/3 pound green beans
4 leaves from 1 small head lettuce*
1/2 pound fresh tomatoes
1 clove garlic
3 tablespoons fresh basil (when chopped)
1 tablespoon fresh dill (when chopped)
2 tablespoons regular or light olive oil
2 tablespoons red wine vinegar
1 teaspoon Dijon mustard
Seasoning to taste

Nectarine Shortcake

1 frozen pound cake
8 small nectarines
1/2 cup sugar
2 tablespoons lemon juice
1 cup whipping cream
1 teaspoon vanilla extract

* Reserve the remainder of the lettuce for use on Wednesday.

EQUIPMENT

Electric hand mixer	Measuring cups and
Medium saucepan	spoons
3 medium bowls	Assorted cooking
3 small bowls	utensils
Strainer	Whisk
Assorted kitchen knives	Aluminum foil

COUNTDOWN

1 Assemble the ingredients and equipment
2 Do Step 1 of the *Nectarine Shortcake*
3 Do Step 1 of the *Fish on the Grill*
4 Do Steps 2–4 of the *Nectarine Shortcake*
5 Do Steps 1–5 of the *B & B Salad*
6 Do Steps 2–3 of the *Fish on the Grill*
7 Do Steps 2–3 of the *Corn in the Cradle*
8 Do Step 4 of the *Fish on the Grill*
9 Do Step 4 of the *Corn in the Cradle*
10 Do Step 5 of the *Nectarine Shortcake*

Fish on the Grill

1 Prepare the grill. Cover half the surface with a sheet of aluminum foil.

2 Drain the capers. Rinse and pat dry the snapper and sprinkle it with the lemon juice. Season to taste.

3 Peel and mince the garlic. In a small bowl, whisk together the garlic, the mustard and the horseradish. Spread the mixture over the snapper.

4 Grill the fish on the foil until it is opaque but still moist, 5 to 7 minutes. Sprinkle it with the paprika and the capers.

Corn in the Cradle

1 Carefully preserving the outer husks of the corn, remove the inner leaves and the cornsilk.

2 In a small bowl, blend 2 tablespoons of the softened butter with the seasoning salt. Spread the mixture on the corn. Close the outer husks back around the ears.

3 Cook the corn directly over the grill for 10 minutes, turning occasionally.

4 Remove the outer husks of the corn and spread the ears with the remaining butter.

B & B Salad

1 Bring a small amount of water to a boil in a medium saucepan.

2 String the green beans and cut them into 1-inch lengths. Cook the beans in the boiling water until they are just tender, 5 to 7 minutes.

3 Wash and dry 4 lettuce leaves and arrange them on individual salad plates.

4 Dice the tomatoes. Peel and mince the garlic. Chop the basil. Chop the dill. In a medium bowl, whisk the tomatoes, the garlic, the basil and the dill with the oil, the vinegar and the mustard. Season to taste.

5 Plunge the beans into cold water, drain them and add them to the tomatoes. Toss gently to blend. Spoon the mixture over the lettuce and refrigerate until you are ready to serve.

Nectarine Shortcake

1 Set the pound cake out to thaw.

2 Pit and coarsely chop 4 nectarines. Place them in a medium bowl and sprinkle them with 1/4 cup of the sugar. Cover the bowl and let it stand for 30 minutes.

3 Cut the pound cake into 8 slices. Pit and slice the remaining nectarines. Place them in a small bowl, drizzle them with the lemon juice and refrigerate until you are ready to use.

4 In a medium bowl, whip the cream, the remaining sugar and the vanilla until stiff peaks form. Refrigerate until you are ready to use.

5 Place 1 slice of pound cake on each of 4 individual plates. Spoon the chopped nectarines and juices over the cake. Spoon half of the whipped cream over the nectarines. Top with the remaining slices of cake. Place the sliced nectarines over the cake and top with the remaining whipped cream.

WEDNESDAY

Rich Little Poor Boy

Lettuce reserved from Tuesday
1 small sweet onion
2 medium tomatoes
1 loaf Italian bread
2 tablespoons regular or low-fat mayonnaise
2 tablespoons Dijon mustard
1/4 pound sliced deli baked ham
1/4 pound sliced Swiss cheese
1/4 pound sliced dry salami
1 small jar (11 ounces) bread and butter
  pickles
1/4 pound sliced deli turkey
Seasoning to taste

Confetti Orzo Salad

16 ounces orzo
1 medium carrot
1 small green bell pepper
1 small red bell pepper
1 small yellow bell pepper
1 medium cucumber
4 scallions (green onions)
1 small red onion
2 cloves garlic
1/4 cup fresh parsley (when chopped)
1/2 cup regular or light olive oil
4 tablespoons lemon juice
1/2 teaspoon grated fresh lemon peel
Seasoning to taste

Summer Mist

1/2 pint fresh raspberries
2 medium oranges
2 tablespoons Amaretto liqueur (or
  nonalcoholic Italian almond syrup)
1 teaspoon dark brown sugar
1/4 teaspoon vanilla extract
1 pint lemon frozen yogurt

EQUIPMENT

Large saucepan	Assorted cooking
Large bowl	utensils
Medium bowl	Whisk
2 small bowls	Vegetable peeler
Strainer	Ice cream scoop
Assorted kitchen knives	
Measuring cups and	
spoons	

COUNTDOWN

1 Assemble the ingredients and equipment
2 Do Steps 1–5 of the *Confetti Orzo Salad*
3 Do Steps 1–2 of the *Summer Mist*
4 Do Steps 1–2 of the *Rich Little Poor Boy*
5 Do Step 3 of the *Summer Mist*

Rich Little Poor Boy

1 Wash, dry and shred the lettuce. Peel and slice the sweet onion. Slice the tomatoes.

2 Slice the bread in half lengthwise. Spread one cut side with the mayonnaise. Spread the other cut side with the mustard. Layer the ham, the cheese, the onion, the salami, the pickles, the turkey, the tomatoes and the lettuce over the mustard. Season to taste. Place the mayonnaise-spread side of the bread over the sandwich and slice into 4 portions.

Confetti Orzo Salad

1 Bring water to a boil in a large saucepan. Cook the orzo until it is tender, 8 to 10 minutes.

2 Peel and dice the carrot. Seed and finely chop the bell peppers. Peel, seed and dice the cucumber. Trim and chop the scallions. Peel and chop the red onion. Peel and mince the garlic. Chop the parsley. Combine the ingredients in a large bowl.

3 In a small bowl, whisk together the oil, the lemon juice, the lemon peel and the garlic until well blended. Season to taste.

4 Drain the orzo, rinse it under cold water and drain it again. Combine it with the vegetables.

5 Toss the salad with the dressing and serve at room temperature.

Summer Mist

1 Rinse and drain the raspberries and dry on paper towels. Peel and section the oranges. Place the fruit in a medium bowl and refrigerate until you are ready to use.

2 In a small bowl, whisk the Amaretto with the brown sugar and the vanilla until the sugar is dissolved.

3 Place scoops of frozen yogurt in individual dessert dishes. Top with the raspberries and orange sections and drizzle with the Amaretto mixture.

THURSDAY

Stir-Fried Beef & Broccoli

1 pound lean boneless sirloin steak
1 clove garlic
1 medium onion
1 small bunch broccoli
¼ pound fresh mushrooms
1 can (5 ounces) sliced bamboo shoots
2 tablespoons dry sherry (or nonalcoholic red wine or omit)
3 tablespoons soy sauce
1 tablespoon dark brown sugar
½ teaspoon ground ginger
2 tablespoons cornstarch
2 tablespoons beef broth reserved from Monday
Seasoning to taste
2 tablespoons sesame oil

Fluffy Steamed White Rice

1 cup long-grain white rice
2 cups water

Sun Luck Salad

12 fresh Chinese snow peas
2 scallions (green onions)
¾ pound fresh bean sprouts
1 tablespoon soy sauce
2 teaspoons sesame oil
1 tablespoon rice vinegar
Seasoning to taste

Pineapple Boats

1 can (11 ounces) lychees in syrup
2 tablespoons dark brown sugar
2 teaspoons ground ginger
1 large pineapple

EQUIPMENT

Wok and wok utensils	Assorted kitchen knives
Medium saucepan	Measuring cups and
Small saucepan	spoons
Double boiler	Assorted cooking
Medium bowl	utensils
2 small bowls	Whisk

COUNTDOWN

1 Assemble the ingredients and equipment
2 Do Step 1 of the *Fluffy Steamed White Rice*
3 Do Steps 1–3 of the *Pineapple Boats*
4 Do Steps 1–2 of the *Stir-Fried Beef & Broccoli*
5 Do Steps 1–3 of the *Sun Luck Salad*
6 Do Steps 3–4 of the *Stir-Fried Beef & Broccoli*
7 Do Step 2 of the *Fluffy Steamed White Rice*
8 Do Step 4 of the *Pineapple Boats*

Stir-Fried Beef & Broccoli

1 Cut the steak across the grain into thin strips. Peel and mince the garlic. Peel and slice the onion. Trim the broccoli and cut it into bite-size florets. Wash, pat dry and slice the mushrooms. Drain the bamboo shoots.

2 In a small bowl, combine the garlic, the sherry, the soy sauce, the brown sugar, the ginger, the cornstarch and the broth. Season to taste.

3 Heat $1\frac{1}{2}$ tablespoons of the oil in a wok until hot, swirling to coat all the sides. Add the beef and stir-fry until the meat loses its redness, 2 to 3 minutes. Remove the beef and cover to keep warm.

4 Heat the remaining oil in the wok. Add the broccoli and the onion and stir-fry until they are crisp-tender, 2 to 3 minutes. Add the mushrooms and the bamboo shoots and stir-fry for 2 minutes. Return the beef to the wok. Stir the soy sauce mixture into the wok, season to taste and cook, stirring, until the sauce boils and thickens, 3 to 4 minutes.

Fluffy Steamed White Rice

1 Place the rice and the water in the top of a double boiler. Bring water to a boil in the bottom of the double boiler. Reduce the heat, cover and simmer until all the liquid is absorbed and the rice is tender, 30 to 40 minutes.

2 Fluff the rice before serving.

Sun Luck Salad

1 Bring water to a boil in a medium saucepan. Trim and string the Chinese snow peas. Plunge the snow peas into the boiling water for 10 seconds. Then drain and rinse them in cold water to stop the cooking.

2 Slice the snow peas into $\frac{1}{4}$-inch diagonals. Trim and chop the scallions. Toss the snow peas and the scallions in the saucepan with the bean sprouts.

3 In a small bowl, whisk together the soy sauce, the oil and the vinegar. Season to taste and toss the salad with the dressing.

Pineapple Boats

1 Drain the lychees into a medium bowl, reserving the syrup. Refrigerate the lychees until you are ready to use. In a small saucepan, heat the reserved syrup with the brown sugar and the ginger until the sugar and ginger are dissolved, about 5 minutes.

2 Cut the pineapple into quarters. Remove the center core, while retaining the top leaves. With a serrated knife, carefully cut along the base of the pineapple until the fruit is free. Slice the pineapple into chunks, but do not remove them from the shell. Refrigerate until you are ready to serve.

3 Remove the syrup from the heat and allow it to cool.

4 Top the pineapple boats with the lychees and the syrup.

FRIDAY

Titanic Soup

36 small hard-shelled clams (or 4 cans
    [10 ounces each] whole clams)
12 mussels
1 pound medium shrimp, shelled and deveined
1 large onion
3 cloves garlic
1 tablespoon fresh parsley (when chopped)
4 cups dry white wine (or nonalcoholic white
    wine or vegetable broth)
2 bay leaves
3 whole allspice
4 tablespoons butter
6 tablespoons flour
1 bottle (8 ounces) clam juice
1 teaspoon curry powder
1 cup whipping cream
2 tablespoons lemon juice
Seasoning to taste

Iceberg Salad

1 head iceberg lettuce
2 large tomatoes
1 small red onion
1 medium cucumber
1 tablespoon fresh dill (when chopped)
3 tablespoons regular or light vegetable oil
2 tablespoons white wine vinegar
$1/2$ teaspoon Worcestershire sauce
$1/4$ teaspoon celery seeds
Seasoning to taste

Sop-up Bread

Chocolate Floats

1 quart chocolate ice cream
1 cup whole or low-fat milk
$1/3$ cup chocolate syrup
$3/4$ teaspoon ground cinnamon
$1/2$ teaspoon vanilla extract
Whipped cream for garnish
Chocolate sprinkles for garnish

EQUIPMENT

Blender	Assorted cooking
Dutch oven	utensils
Large bowl	Whisk
Medium bowl	Vegetable brush
Small bowl	Vegetable peeler
Fine sieve	Ice cream scoop
Assorted kitchen knives	
Measuring cups and	
spoons	

COUNTDOWN

1 Assemble the ingredients and equipment
2 Do Steps 1–2 of the *Iceberg Salad*
3 Do Steps 1–4 of the *Titanic Soup*
4 Do Step 3 of the *Iceberg Salad*
5 Do Step 5 of the *Titanic Soup*
6 Do Steps 1–3 of the *Chocolate Floats*

Titanic Soup

1 Scrub the clams. Scrub the mussels and remove the beards. Discard any that are open and do not close when tapped. Rinse the shrimp. Peel and finely chop the onion. Peel and mince the garlic. Chop the parsley.

2 In a Dutch oven, combine the clams, the mussels, the onion, the wine, the bay leaves and the allspice. Bring the mixture to a boil, cover and cook, stirring, just until the clams and mussels open, 5 to 7 minutes. Remove the clams and mussels, reserving the cooking liquid. Separate the clams and mussels from their shells, discarding any that have not opened, and reserve them in a medium bowl.

3 Strain the cooking liquid through a fine sieve into a large bowl.

4 Melt the butter in the Dutch oven. Add the flour and whisk until the mixture turns lemon colored, 1 to 2 minutes. Whisk in the strained cooking liquid and the clam juice, bring the mixture to a boil, and whisk until the soup is thick and smooth. Stir in the garlic and the curry powder. Bring the soup to a boil and cook until it is slightly reduced, about 5 minutes.

5 Remove the stockpot from the heat and stir in the cream. Add the reserved shellfish and the shrimp to the soup. If you are using canned clams, add them now. Return the Dutch oven to the heat and simmer the soup until the shrimp turn bright pink, about 3 minutes. Add the lemon juice. Season to taste. Garnish with the parsley. Sop up the soup with chunks of sourdough bread.

Iceberg Salad

1 Wash and dry the lettuce and tear it into bite-size pieces. Arrange it on individual plates. Slice the tomatoes. Peel and thinly slice the red onion. Peel and slice the cucumber. Arrange the tomato, the onion and the cucumber over the lettuce. Chop the dill and sprinkle it over the salad. Refrigerate until you are ready to serve.

2 In a small bowl, whisk together the oil, the vinegar, the Worcestershire sauce and the celery seeds. Season to taste.

3 Drizzle the dressing over the salad.

Chocolate Floats

1 Place one third of the ice cream, half of the milk, half of the chocolate syrup, half of the cinnamon and half of the vanilla in a blender.

2 Cover and blend until the mixture is thick and smooth, and then pour into 2 tall glasses. Repeat the process.

3 Add a scoop of ice cream to each glass and top the floats with a dollop of whipped cream and the sprinkles.

AUGUST
WEEK TWO

Monday

SOUSED AMERICAN CHICKEN
LIMA RICE
INCA SALAD
MACHU PEACHES

Tuesday

GARLIC SOUP
PASTA SALAD VINAIGRETTE
BANANA BUGGIES

Wednesday

PORK BARREL STIR-FRY
STIRRED-UP NOODLES
ANGEL TIERS

Thursday

SENTIMENTAL SALMON
DO-DAH ONIONS
SOFT-SPOKEN ASPARAGUS
LEMON-LIME SURE-BET

Friday

GAZPACHO
SIESTA SLAW
GOUDANOUGH BREAD
CREAM CAKE FROM CASTILE

CHECK STAPLES

- ☐ Butter
- ☐ Cornstarch
- ☐ Granulated sugar
- ☐ Dark brown sugar
- ☐ Long-grain white rice
- ☐ Regular or light vegetable oil
- ☐ Regular or light olive oil
- ☐ Sesame oil
- ☐ White wine vinegar
- ☐ Rice vinegar
- ☐ Apple cider vinegar
- ☐ Lemon juice
- ☐ Lime juice
- ☐ Grated fresh lemon peel
- ☐ Worcestershire sauce
- ☐ Tabasco sauce
- ☐ Soy sauce
- ☐ Dijon mustard
- ☐ Regular or low-fat mayonnaise
- ☐ Chili sauce
- ☐ Honey
- ☐ Golden raisins
- ☐ Ground allspice
- ☐ Bay leaves
- ☐ Cayenne pepper
- ☐ Chinese five-spice powder
- ☐ Cream of tartar
- ☐ Ground cinnamon
- ☐ Whole cloves
- ☐ Ground cumin
- ☐ Garlic powder
- ☐ Ground ginger
- ☐ Italian seasoning
- ☐ Dry mustard
- ☐ Onion powder
- ☐ Paprika
- ☐ Poppy seeds
- ☐ Pepper
- ☐ Salt
- ☐ Almond extract

SHOPPING NOTE

⚬ If you are shopping once a week and cannot arrange to purchase fresh salmon on the day you plan to use it, you can purchase *not previously frozen* salmon and freeze it, placing it in the refrigerator to thaw the night before you are ready to use it. Or you can purchase *still frozen* salmon and keep it frozen until the night before you are ready to use it.

SHOPPING LIST

MEAT & POULTRY
1 pound lean boneless pork
  loin (W)
4 chicken breast halves (M)

FISH
4 salmon steaks (1½
  pounds) (Th)

FRESH PRODUCE
Vegetables
1½ pounds asparagus (Th)
1 pound spinach (W)
1 medium carrot (F)
4 stalks celery—1 (W), 3 (F)
1 large sweet onion (F)
4 medium sweet onions (Th)
1 small onion (M)
1 small red onion (T)
4 scallions (green onions)—
  2 (W), 2 (Th)
1 head garlic (M, T, Th, F)
1 bunch basil (T)
1 bunch chives (Th)
1 bunch parsley (M, T, F)
1 pound Napa cabbage (W)
1 small (or half) head green
  cabbage (F)
1 small head lettuce (M)
2½ pounds tomatoes—
  ½ pound (T), 2 pounds (F)
2 medium cucumbers (F)
3 medium red bell peppers—
  1 (W), 2 (F)
1 small green bell pepper (T)

Fruit
3 large peaches (T)
2 medium bananas (M)
½ pound pineapple chunks (or
  net weight canned) (W)
4 medium oranges (M)

CANS, JARS & BOTTLES
Soup
2 cans (14½ ounces each)
  chicken broth (M)

2 cans (14½ ounces each)
  vegetable broth (T)
1 can (14½ ounces) oriental
  broth (W)

Fish
1 can (3¾ ounces) boneless,
  skinless sardines packed in
  oil (T)

Fruit
1 can (11 ounces) mandarin
  oranges (W)

Juice
2 cups tomato juice (F)

Condiments
1 small can (3½ ounces) pitted
  black olives (M)

PACKAGED GOODS
Pasta, Rice & Grains
12 ounces small shell pasta (T)

Baked Goods
1 large loaf Italian bread (T, F)
1 angel food loaf cake (W)

Oriental Products
8 ounces soft Chinese-style
  noodles (W)

Nuts & Seeds
½ cup sliced almonds (M)

Dessert & Baking Needs
1 small package (3.4 ounces)
  instant banana cream
  pudding mix (T)
1 small package (3.4 ounces)
  instant vanilla pudding
  mix (F)
1 small package (4 ounces)
  Oreo cookies (Th)
1 small package (6 ounces)
  semisweet chocolate
  chips (F)

4 individual graham cracker
  tart shells (T)

WINES & SPIRITS
1¼ cups dry white wine (or
  nonalcoholic white wine or
  chicken broth) (M)
1 tablespoon dry white wine (or
  nonalcoholic white wine or
  omit) (F)
6 tablespoons dry red wine (or
  nonalcoholic red wine or
  water) (T)
3 tablespoons bourbon (or
  lemon juice) (Th)

REFRIGERATED PRODUCTS
Dairy
2 cups + 2 tablespoons whole
  milk—1 cup (M), 1 cup +
  2 tablespoons (F)
¼ cup whole or low-fat
  milk (W)
½ cup half-and-half (M)
2 tablespoons regular or light
  sour cream (F)
2 eggs (M, T)

Cheese
1 small package (3 ounces)
  cream cheese (W)
6 ounces sliced Gouda cheese (F)

FROZEN GOODS
Vegetables
1 package (9 ounces) baby lima
  beans (M)

Desserts
1 pound cake (F)
1 small container (8 ounces)
  frozen whipped topping
  (T, W)
1 pint vanilla ice cream (M)
1 pint lemon sherbet (Th)
1 pint lime sherbet (Th)

MONDAY

Soused American Chicken

1 small onion
2 tablespoons butter
4 chicken breast halves
4 whole cloves
1 bay leaf
$^1/_2$ teaspoon ground cumin
1 cup chicken broth
$1^1/_4$ cups dry white wine (or nonalcoholic
    white wine or additional chicken broth)
$^1/_2$ cup golden raisins
$^1/_2$ cup half-and-half
2 egg yolks*
$^1/_2$ cup sliced almonds
Seasoning to taste

Lima Rice

1 package (9 ounces) frozen baby lima beans
2 tablespoons fresh parsley (when chopped)
1 clove garlic
1 cup long-grain white rice
2 tablespoons butter
1 teaspoon grated fresh lemon peel
$^1/_4$ teaspoon ground ginger
$^3/_4$ cup chicken broth
$1^1/_4$ cups water
1 tablespoon lemon juice

Inca Salad

1 tablespoon fresh parsley (when chopped)
1 clove garlic
3 tablespoons regular or light olive oil
2 tablespoons lemon juice

*Reserve the egg whites for use on Tuesday.

$^1/_2$ teaspoon sugar
Seasoning to taste
1 small head lettuce
1 small can ($3^1/_2$ ounces) pitted black olives
4 medium oranges

Machu Peaches

3 large peaches
2 teaspoons lime juice
$^1/_4$ teaspoon ground cinnamon
1 tablespoon sugar
1 pint vanilla ice cream

EQUIPMENT

Large covered skillet	Assorted cooking
Double boiler	utensils
2 medium bowls	Whisk
2 small bowls	Ice cream scoop
Assorted kitchen knives	
Measuring cups and	
spoons	

COUNTDOWN

1 Assemble the ingredients and equipment
2 Do Steps 1–2 of the *Lima Rice*
3 Do Step 1 of the *Inca Salad*
4 Do Step 1 of the *Machu Peaches*
5 Do Steps 1–3 of the *Soused American Chicken*
6 Do Step 2 of the *Inca Salad*
7 Do Step 3 of the *Lima Rice*
8 Do Step 4 of the *Soused American Chicken*
9 Do Step 3 of the *Inca Salad*
10 Do Step 4 of the *Lima Rice*
11 Do Step 2 of the *Machu Peaches*

Soused American Chicken

1 Peel and chop the onion.

2 Melt the butter in a large skillet. Brown the chicken breasts lightly, about 4 minutes on each side. Add the onion, the cloves, the bay leaf, the cumin and the broth. Bring the mixture to a boil, reduce the heat and simmer for 10 minutes.

3 Add 1 cup of the wine and the raisins. Cook, partially covered, until the chicken is tender but still juicy, 20 to 25 minutes.

4 In a small bowl, whisk together the half-and-half, the egg yolks and the remaining wine. Stir a small amount of the chicken sauce into the egg yolk mixture and return it to the skillet. Add the almonds. Stir until the sauce is thickened, but do not let it boil. Season to taste.

Lima Rice

1 Place the lima beans in a medium bowl of hot water to thaw.

2 Chop the parsley. Mince the garlic. Place the garlic, the rice, the butter, the lemon peel, the ginger, the broth, the water and the lemon juice in the top of a double boiler. Bring water to a boil in the bottom of the double boiler, reduce the heat, cover and simmer until all the liquid is absorbed and the rice is tender, 30 to 40 minutes.

3 Fold the thawed lima beans into the rice. Cover and let stand for 5 minutes.

4 Fluff the rice and sprinkle it with the parsley.

Inca Salad

1 Chop the parsley. Peel and mince the garlic. In a small bowl, whisk together the garlic, the parsley, the oil, the lemon juice and the sugar. Season to taste.

2 Wash and dry the lettuce, tear it into bite-size pieces and distribute it among individual salad plates. Drain the olives. Peel and slice the oranges and arrange them over the lettuce. Arrange the olives over the oranges.

3 Drizzle the dressing over the salad.

Machu Peaches

1 Peel, pit and slice the peaches. Place them in a medium bowl and sprinkle them with the lime juice, the cinnamon and the sugar. Refrigerate until you are ready to use.

2 Place scoops of ice cream in individual dessert dishes. Top with the peach mixture.

TUESDAY

Garlic Soup

8 cloves garlic
1 tablespoon fresh basil (when chopped)
1 tablespoon fresh parsley (when chopped)
$1/3$ large loaf Italian bread*
2 tablespoons butter
2 teaspoons regular or light olive oil
6 tablespoons dry red wine (or nonalcoholic red wine or water)
2 cans ($14^1/2$ ounces each) vegetable broth
1 tablespoon Italian seasoning
Seasoning to taste

Pasta Salad Vinaigrette

$1/2$ pound fresh tomatoes
1 small red onion
1 small green bell pepper
$1/4$ cup fresh parsley (when chopped)
12 ounces small shell pasta
4 tablespoons regular or light olive oil
1 tablespoon white wine vinegar
1 tablespoon lemon juice
1 tablespoon Dijon mustard
Seasoning to taste
1 can ($3^3/4$ ounces) boneless, skinless sardines packed in oil

Banana Buggies

1 small package (3.4 ounces) instant banana cream pudding mix
1 cup whole milk
2 egg whites reserved from Monday
2 tablespoons sugar
$1/4$ teaspoon cream of tartar
$1/2$ small container (8 ounces) frozen whipped topping**
4 individual graham cracker tart shells
2 medium bananas

EQUIPMENT

Electric hand mixer	Colander
Large saucepan	Assorted kitchen knives
Medium covered saucepan	Measuring cups and spoons
2 large bowls	Assorted cooking utensils
Medium bowl	Whisk
Small bowl	

COUNTDOWN

1 Assemble the ingredients and equipment
2 Do Steps 1–3 of the *Banana Buggies*
3 Do Steps 1–2 of the *Pasta Salad Vinaigrette*
4 Do Step 1 of the *Garlic Soup*
5 Do Steps 3–6 of the *Pasta Salad Vinaigrette*
6 Do Step 2 of the *Garlic Soup*
7 Do Step 4 of the *Banana Buggies*

---

*Freeze the remainder of the bread for use on Friday.
**Reserve the remainder of the container for use on Wednesday.

Garlic Soup

1 Peel and mince the garlic. Chop the basil. Chop the parsley. Cut the bread into 4 slices and cut the slices into cubes.

2 Melt the butter with the oil in a medium saucepan. Add the garlic and sauté until it is golden but not brown, 3 to 4 minutes. Add the bread cubes to the saucepan and toss. Add the wine, the broth, the basil, the parsley and the Italian seasoning. Bring the mixture to a boil, reduce the heat, cover and simmer for 10 minutes. Season to taste.

Pasta Salad Vinaigrette

1 Bring water to a boil in a large saucepan.

2 Chop the tomatoes. Peel and dice the red onion. Seed and dice the bell pepper. Chop the parsley.

3 Cook the pasta in the boiling water until it is almost tender, 7 to 8 minutes.

4 In a small bowl, whisk together the oil, the vinegar, the lemon juice and the mustard. Season to taste.

5 Drain and flake the sardines.

6 Drain the pasta, rinse it in cold water to cool and then drain it again. Place it in a large bowl and toss it with the dressing. Add the tomatoes, the onion, the bell pepper and the parsley and toss lightly. Add the sardines and toss lightly to combine. Refrigerate until you are ready to serve.

Banana Buggies

1 In a large bowl, beat the pudding mix and milk together until well blended, about 1 minute.

2 Beat the egg whites in a medium bowl until frothy. Gradually add the sugar and the cream of tartar and beat until stiff. Fold in $3/4$ cup of the whipped topping. Fold the mixture into the pudding.

3 Pour the pudding into individual tart shells and refrigerate them for at least 30 minutes.

4 Slice the bananas over the tarts and top with the remaining whipped topping.

WEDNESDAY

Pork Barrel Stir-Fry

1 pound lean boneless pork loin
1 medium red bell pepper
1 stalk celery
1 pound fresh spinach
1 pound Napa cabbage
1 tablespoon cornstarch
3 tablespoons chili sauce
2 tablespoons rice vinegar
1 tablespoon regular or light vegetable oil
1 tablespoon soy sauce
$^1/_2$ cup oriental broth
$^1/_4$ teaspoon garlic powder
Seasoning to taste

Stirred-up Noodles

1 quart water
1$^1/_4$ cups oriental broth
2 scallions (green onions)
8 ounces soft Chinese-style noodles
1 teaspoon sesame oil
$^1/_4$ teaspoon Chinese five-spice powder
Seasoning to taste

Angel Tiers

1 small package (3 ounces) cream cheese
1 angel food loaf cake
$^1/_4$ cup whole or low-fat milk
$^1/_2$ cup sugar
1 teaspoon almond extract
$^1/_2$ small container (8 ounces) frozen whipped
    topping reserved from Tuesday
1 can (11 ounces) mandarin oranges
$^1/_2$ pound fresh (or net weight canned)
    pineapple chunks

EQUIPMENT

Electric hand mixer	Assorted kitchen knives
Wok and wok utensils	Measuring cups and
Large covered	spoons
saucepan	Assorted cooking
Large bowl	utensils
Medium bowl	Whisk
Small bowl	Vegetable grater
Strainer	

COUNTDOWN

1 Assemble the ingredients and equipment
2 Do Steps 1–4 of the *Angel Tiers*
3 Do Step 1 of the *Stirred-up Noodles*
4 Do Steps 1–3 of the *Pork Barrel Stir-Fry*
5 Do Steps 2–3 of the *Stirred-up Noodles*
6 Do Steps 4–6 of the *Pork Barrel Stir-Fry*
7 Do Step 5 of the *Angel Tiers*

Pork Barrel Stir-Fry

1 Trim the pork of any excess fat and cut the meat into thin strips.

2 Seed and chop the bell pepper. Trim and thinly slice the celery. Chop the spinach. Grate the cabbage.

3 In a small bowl, combine the cornstarch with the chili sauce and the vinegar.

4 Heat the oil in a wok until hot. Add the pork and stir-fry until it is browned, 2 to 3 minutes.

5 Add the bell pepper, the celery, the spinach and the cabbage and stir-fry until the vegetables are crisp-tender, 2 to 3 minutes.

6 Add the soy sauce, the broth, the garlic powder and the cornstarch mixture to the wok and stir-fry until the sauce begins to thicken, 1 to 2 minutes. Season to taste.

Stirred-up Noodles

1 Bring the water and the broth to a boil in a large saucepan. Trim and chop the scallions.

2 Cook the noodles, stirring and watching carefully for them to begin to rise, about 1 minute. Drain them immediately and return them to the saucepan.

3 Toss the noodles with the scallions, the oil and the Chinese five-spice powder. Season to taste and cover to keep warm.

Angel Tiers

1 Mash the cream cheese in a medium bowl.

2 Tear the angel food cake into small pieces and place them in a large bowl.

3 Add the milk, the sugar, the almond extract and the whipped topping to the cream cheese. Spoon the mixture over the cake pieces and combine. Refrigerate until you are ready to serve.

4 Drain the mandarin oranges and refrigerate them until you are ready to serve.

5 Top the cake mixture with the orange segments and the pineapple chunks.

THURSDAY

Sentimental Salmon

1 clove garlic
2 scallions (green onions)
$^1/_4$ cup dark brown sugar
3 tablespoons bourbon (or lemon juice)
2 tablespoons soy sauce
2 tablespoons regular or light vegetable oil
Seasoning to taste
4 salmon steaks (1$^1/_2$ pounds)

Do-Dah Onions

4 medium sweet onions
4 tablespoons butter
2 tablespoons Dijon mustard
1 tablespoon honey
1 tablespoon white wine vinegar
$^1/_4$ teaspoon paprika
$^1/_4$ teaspoon ground allspice
Seasoning to taste

Soft-Spoken Asparagus

$^1/_3$ cup fresh chives (when chopped)
1$^1/_2$ pounds fresh asparagus
4 tablespoons butter
$^1/_4$ cup lemon juice
2 teaspoons Dijon mustard
$^1/_4$ teaspoon Worcestershire sauce
Seasoning to taste

Lemon-Lime Sure-Bet

1 small package (4 ounces) Oreo cookies
1 pint lemon sherbet
1 pint lime sherbet

EQUIPMENT

Large covered skillet	Assorted cooking
2 small saucepans	utensils
7x11-inch glass baking	Whisk
dish	Ice cream scoop
2 small bowls	Pastry brush
Assorted kitchen knives	Aluminum foil
Measuring cups and	
spoons	

COUNTDOWN

1 Assemble the ingredients and equipment
2 Do Steps 1–3 of the *Sentimental Salmon*
3 Do Steps 1–2 of the *Do-Dah Onions*
4 Do Step 1 of the *Lemon–Lime Sure-Bet*
5 Do Step 4 of the *Sentimental Salmon*
6 Do Step 3 of the *Do-Dah Onions*
7 Do Steps 1–4 of the *Soft-Spoken Asparagus*
8 Do Step 2 of the *Lemon–Lime Sure-Bet*

Sentimental Salmon

1 Peel and mince the garlic. Trim and chop the scallions. Place the garlic and the scallions in a small bowl. Add the brown sugar, the bourbon, the soy sauce and the oil. Season to taste.

2 Wash and pat dry the salmon steaks and place them in a 7x11-inch glass baking dish. Add the marinade and turn the fish to coat evenly. Refrigerate for 20 minutes.

3 Prepare the grill. Cover half the grill with a sheet of aluminum foil.

4 Place the salmon steaks on the foil and grill, basting with the marinade, until they are opaque throughout, 15 to 20 minutes.

Do-Dah Onions

1 Peel and halve the onions.

2 Melt the butter in a small saucepan. Blend in the mustard, the honey, the vinegar, the paprika and the allspice. Season to taste.

3 Place the onions directly on the grill. Brush them with the mustard mixture while they roast, 5 to 7 minutes per side.

Soft-Spoken Asparagus

1 Bring 2 inches of water to a boil in a large skillet.

2 Chop the chives. Remove the tough ends from the asparagus, and cook, covered, until the stalks are crisp-tender, 3 to 8 minutes depending on thickness.

3 Melt the butter in a small saucepan. Add the lemon juice, the chives, the mustard and the Worcestershire sauce. Season to taste.

4 Drain the asparagus and drizzle it with the lemon-butter mixture.

Lemon-Lime Sure-Bet

1 Reserve 4 whole Oreo cookies and crumble the rest.

2 Alternate scoops of lemon sherbet, cookie crumbs and lime sherbet in parfait glasses. Garnish with the reserved whole cookies, standing on end across the top.

FRIDAY

Gazpacho

2 cups tomato juice
2 pounds fresh tomatoes
2 medium cucumbers
3 stalks celery
2 medium red bell peppers
1 large sweet onion
3 cloves garlic
3 tablespoons regular or light vegetable oil
$3/8$ teaspoon Worcestershire sauce
$3/8$ teaspoon Tabasco sauce
$1^1/2$ teaspoons sugar
Seasoning to taste

Siesta Slaw

2 tablespoons regular or light sour cream
1 tablespoon apple cider vinegar
1 teaspoon honey
1 tablespoon poppy seeds
Seasoning to taste
1 small (or half) head green cabbage
1 medium carrot

Goudanough Bread

$2/3$ loaf Italian bread reserved from Tuesday
$1^1/2$ tablespoons fresh parsley (when chopped)
$1/4$ cup regular or low-fat mayonnaise
1 tablespoon dry white wine (or nonalcoholic
   white wine or omit)
$1^1/2$ teaspoons dry mustard
$1/4$ teaspoon Worcestershire sauce
$1/4$ teaspoon cayenne pepper
$1/8$ teaspoon onion powder
6 ounces sliced Gouda cheese

Cream Cake from Castile

1 frozen pound cake
1 small package (3.4 ounces) instant vanilla
   pudding mix
1 cup + 2 tablespoons whole milk
1 small package (6 ounces) semisweet
   chocolate chips

EQUIPMENT

Electric hand mixer	Measuring cups and
Blender	spoons
Small saucepan	Assorted cooking
Cookie sheet	utensils
Large bowl	Whisk
Medium bowl	Vegetable peeler
Small bowl	Vegetable grater
Assorted kitchen knives	

COUNTDOWN

IN THE MORNING:

  1 Do Step 1 of the Gazpacho
  2 Do Step 1 of the Goudanough Bread
  3 Do Step 1 of the Cream Cake from Castile

BEFORE DINNER:

  1 Assemble the remaining ingredients and
    equipment
  2 Do Steps 2–4 of the Cream Cake from
    Castile
  3 Do Steps 1–2 of the Siesta Slaw
  4 Do Steps 2–4 of the Gazpacho
  5 Do Steps 2–5 of the Goudanough Bread
  6 Do Step 5 of the Gazpacho

Gazpacho

1 Place the tomato juice in the refrigerator to chill.

2 Peel and chop the tomatoes. Peel and chop the cucumbers. Trim and chop the celery. Seed and chop the bell peppers. Peel and chop the sweet onion. Peel and mince the garlic.

3 Reserve for garnish $1/2$ cup each of the chopped tomato, the chopped cucumber, the chopped celery, the chopped bell pepper and the chopped onion.

4 Place a third of the remaining vegetables in a blender. Add 1 tablespoon of the oil, $2/3$ cup of the tomato juice, a third of the garlic, $1/8$ teaspoon of the Worcestershire sauce, $1/8$ teaspoon of the Tabasco sauce and $1/2$ teaspoon of the sugar. Season to taste. Puree until the mixture is blended but not quite smooth. Transfer the soup to a tureen. Repeat the process two more times. Cover the tureen and refrigerate until you are ready to serve.

5 Serve the soup chilled, garnished with the reserved vegetables.

Siesta Slaw

1 In a large bowl, whisk together the sour cream, the vinegar, the honey and the poppy seeds. Season to taste.

2 Grate the cabbage. Peel and grate the carrot. Combine the cabbage and the carrot with the dressing and refrigerate until you are ready to serve.

Goudanough Bread

1 Set the bread out to thaw.

2 Slice the bread in half horizontally and place the halves on an ungreased cookie sheet.

3 Chop the parsley. In a small bowl, combine the parsley, the mayonnaise, the wine, the mustard, the Worcestershire sauce, the cayenne pepper and the onion powder. Spread the mixture over the cut sides of the bread.

4 Preheat the broiler. Toast the bread, 3 or 4 inches from the heat, for 2 minutes.

5 Add slices of cheese to cover the bread, and broil until bubbly, 1 to 2 minutes more.

Cream Cake from Castile

1 Set the pound cake out to thaw.

2 In a medium bowl, beat together the pudding mix and 1 cup of the milk until the pudding starts to thicken. Let it stand.

3 In a small saucepan, melt the chocolate chips in the remaining milk, stirring until the mixture is smooth. Remove the saucepan from the heat.

4 Slice the pound cake into 3 horizontal layers. Spread half of the pudding mixture evenly over the bottom layer. Cover with the second layer and spread it with the remaining pudding mixture. Cover with the top layer of cake and spread it with the melted chocolate, allowing it to drip down the sides. Refrigerate for at least 20 minutes.

AUGUST
WEEK THREE

WEEK AT A GLANCE

Monday

DEEP SEA STIR-FRY
REFRESHING RICE
ORANGE WATERFALL

Tuesday

HAMBURGER STUFFS
RED POTATO SALAD
BARBECUE CHIPS
OLD-FASHIONED ROOT BEER FlOATS

Wednesday

UP FRONT SALAD
RIBBON FETTUCCINE
NECTARINE NUT

Thursday

LEMON CHICKEN BROTH
PATIO SALAD
BUNDERFULS
BLACK BEAUTIES

Friday

DEVILISH SHELLS
HODGEPODGE SALAD
BUTTERSCOTCH LADDIES

CHECK STAPLES

- ☐ Butter
- ☐ Cornstarch
- ☐ Granulated sugar
- ☐ Confectioners' sugar
- ☐ Unsweetened cocoa
- ☐ Chocolate sprinkles
- ☐ Long-grain white rice
- ☐ Regular or light vegetable oil
- ☐ Regular or light olive oil
- ☐ Sesame oil
- ☐ Red wine vinegar
- ☐ White wine vinegar
- ☐ Rice vinegar
- ☐ Apple cider vinegar
- ☐ Lemon juice
- ☐ Lime juice
- ☐ Grated fresh orange peel
- ☐ Soy sauce
- ☐ Dijon mustard
- ☐ Regular or low-fat mayonnaise
- ☐ Ketchup
- ☐ Honey
- ☐ Grated Parmesan cheese
- ☐ Dried basil
- ☐ Ground ginger
- ☐ Dried oregano
- ☐ Red pepper flakes
- ☐ Pepper
- ☐ Salt
- ☐ Almond extract
- ☐ Vanilla extract

SHOPPING NOTE

• If you are shopping once a week and cannot arrange to purchase fresh seafood on the day you plan to use it, you can purchase *not previously frozen* seafood and freeze it, placing it in the refrigerator to thaw the night before you are ready to use it. Or you can purchase *still frozen* seafood and keep it frozen until the night before you are ready to use it.

SHOPPING LIST

MEAT & POULTRY
2 pounds lean ground beef (T)
1 1/2 pounds boneless, skinless
   chicken breasts (Th)

FISH
1 1/2 pounds orange roughy (or
   sole) fillets (M)
1/2 pound medium shrimp,
   shelled and deveined (F)

FRESH PRODUCE
Vegetables
6 medium red potatoes (T)
1 small bunch broccoli (F)
1 small head cauliflower (W)
3 small zucchini (W)
20 Chinese snow peas (M)
3 medium carrots (W)
7 stalks celery—2 (M), 2 (T),
   1 (W), 2 (Th)
1 large onion (F)
2 small sweet onions—1 (T),
   1 (W)
2 small red onions (Th)
10 scallions (green onions)—
   2 (M), 4 (T), 4 (F)
1 head garlic (W, F)
1 bunch parsley (T, W, Th, F)
1 small head Napa cabbage (M)
2 medium heads lettuce—1 (W),
   1 (Th)
1 package (16 ounces) mixed
   salad greens (F)
2 ripe avocados (Th)
1 large tomato (T)
1 pound tomatoes—1/2 pound
   (W), 1/2 pound (F)
2 medium cucumbers—1 (W),
   1 (F)
1 medium red bell pepper (M)
1 small bunch radishes (F)

Fruit
4 large nectarines (W)
1 medium cantaloupe (M)
1/2 pint blackberries (M)
2 small pink grapefruit (Th)

4 small oranges (Th)
1 small lemon (Th)

CANS, JARS & BOTTLES
Soup
3 cans (14 1/2 ounces each)
   chicken broth—1 (M), 2 (Th)

Vegetables
1 medium can (15 ounces)
   tomato sauce (F)
1 small jar (4 ounces)
   marinated mushrooms (W)

Oriental Products
2 cans (8 ounces each) sliced
   water chestnuts—1 (M),
   1 (Th)

Condiments
1 small jar (3 1/2 ounces)
   pimiento-stuffed green
   olives (W)
1/2 cup hamburger relish (T)
1 small jar (11 ounces) sliced
   sweet pickles (T)

Beverages
1 quart root beer (T)

PACKAGED GOODS
Pasta, Rice & Grains
12 ounces spinach fettuccine
   (W)
12 ounces small shell pasta (F)
1 package (14 ounces) barbecue
   chips (T)

Baked Goods
1 cup croutons (W)
8 hamburger buns—4 (T), 4 (Th)

Nuts & Seeds
1/4 cup sliced almonds (Th)

Dessert & Baking Needs
1/2 cup flaked coconut (W)

1 small package (3.4 ounces)
   instant butterscotch
   pudding mix (F)
1 cup peanut brittle (F)

WINES & SPIRITS
4 tablespoons dry red wine (or
   nonalcoholic red wine or
   water) (F)
2 tablespoons dry sherry (or
   nonalcoholic white wine or
   omit) (Th)
1/4 cup creme de cacao liqueur
   (or nonalcoholic Italian
   chocolate syrup) (Th)

REFRIGERATED PRODUCTS
Dairy
1 1/4 cups whole milk (F)
Whipped cream for garnish (T)
1 3/4 cups + 2 tablespoons
   regular or light sour
   cream—1 cup (T), 3/4 cup +
   2 tablespoons (F)
4 eggs—2 (T), 2 (Th, F)

Cheese
2 containers (8 ounces each)
   soft cream cheese—1 (M), 1
   (Th)
1 cup shredded regular or low-
   fat cheddar cheese (T)

Juice
1/2 cup + 2 tablespoons orange
   juice—1/2 cup (M),
   2 tablespoons (Th)

Deli
1/4 pound sliced dry salami (W)

FROZEN GOODS
Desserts
1 pint vanilla ice cream (T)
1 quart chocolate ice cream (Th)
2 small containers (8 ounces
   each) frozen whipped
   topping—1 (W), 1 (Th)

MONDAY

Deep Sea Stir-Fry

$1^{1}/_{2}$ pounds orange roughy (or sole) fillets
3 tablespoons rice vinegar
3 tablespoons soy sauce
1 medium red bell pepper
2 stalks celery
1 small head Napa cabbage
2 scallions (green onions)
20 Chinese snow peas
1 can (8 ounces) sliced water chestnuts
3 tablespoons sesame oil
2 teaspoons cornstarch
$^{1}/_{2}$ cup chicken broth
Seasoning to taste

Refreshing Rice

1 cup long-grain white rice
$1^{1}/_{4}$ cups chicken broth
$^{1}/_{4}$ cup lime juice
$^{1}/_{2}$ cup water

Orange Waterfall

1 medium cantaloupe
$^{1}/_{2}$ pint fresh blackberries
1 container (8 ounces) regular or light soft
    cream cheese
$^{1}/_{2}$ cup orange juice
2 tablespoons confectioners' sugar
$^{1}/_{2}$ teaspoon ground ginger

EQUIPMENT

Electric hand mixer	Measuring cups and
Wok and wok utensils	spoons
Double boiler	Assorted cooking
2 large bowls	utensils
Small bowl	Whisk
Assorted kitchen knives	

COUNTDOWN

1 Assemble the ingredients and equipment
2 Do Step 1 of the *Refreshing Rice*
3 Do Step 1 of the *Deep Sea Stir-Fry*
4 Do Steps 1–2 of the *Orange Waterfall*
5 Do Steps 2–5 of the *Deep Sea Stir-Fry*
6 Do Step 2 of the *Refreshing Rice*
7 Do Step 3 of the *Orange Waterfall*

Deep Sea Stir-Fry

1 Cut the orange roughy crosswise into ½-inch-wide strips. In a large bowl, combine the vinegar and the soy sauce. Add the fish and stir to coat. Cover and marinate for 20 minutes.

2 Seed the bell pepper and cut it into thin strips. Trim and slice the celery. Chop the cabbage. Trim and slice the scallions. Stem and string the Chinese snow peas. Drain the water chestnuts.

3 Heat 2 tablespoons of the oil in a wok until hot but not smoking. Add the bell pepper, the celery, the cabbage, the scallions, the snow peas and the water chestnuts. Stir-fry until the vegetables are slightly softened, about 2 minutes. Remove them to a large bowl and keep them warm.

4 Remove the fish from the marinade, reserving the liquid. Add the remaining oil to the wok. Add the fish and stir-fry until it is opaque throughout, about 2 minutes. Return the vegetables to the wok.

5 Add the cornstarch and the broth to the reserved marinade and whisk until the cornstarch is dissolved. Pour the mixture over the fish and vegetables. Season to taste and cook, stirring, until the sauce thickens, 1 to 2 minutes.

Refreshing Rice

1 Place the rice, the broth, the lime juice and the water in the top of a double boiler. Bring water to a boil in the bottom of the double boiler. Reduce the heat, cover and simmer until all the liquid is absorbed and the rice is tender, 30 to 40 minutes.

2 Fluff the rice before serving.

Orange Waterfall

1 Halve and seed the melon and cut it into slices, removing the rind. Refrigerate. Rinse the berries and drain them on paper towels.

2 In a small bowl, blend the cream cheese with the orange juice, the confectioners' sugar and the ginger until smooth. Cover and let stand.

3 Arrange the melon slices and the berries on individual dessert plates and serve with the orange sauce.

TUESDAY

Hamburger Stuffs

2 pounds lean ground beef
Seasoning to taste
1 large tomato
1 small sweet onion
$^1/_2$ cup hamburger relish
1 cup shredded regular or low-fat cheddar
    cheese
4 hamburger buns*
Ketchup
1 jar (11 ounces) sliced sweet pickles

Red Potato Salad

2 eggs
6 medium red potatoes
4 scallions (green onions)
2 stalks celery
$^1/_4$ cup fresh parsley (when chopped)
1 cup regular or light sour cream
1 tablespoon regular or low-fat mayonnaise
1 teaspoon apple cider vinegar
$^1/_2$ teaspoon sugar
Seasoning to taste

Barbecue Chips

Old-Fashioned Root Beer Floats

1 quart root beer
1 pint vanilla ice cream
Whipped cream for garnish

*Reserve the remaining buns for use on Thursday.

EQUIPMENT

Large covered saucepan	Assorted cooking utensils
Small saucepan	Whisk
Small bowl	Vegetable brush
Assorted kitchen knives	Ice cream scoop
Measuring cups and spoons	

COUNTDOWN

IN THE MORNING:
  Do Step 1 of the *Old-Fashioned Root Beer Floats*

BEFORE DINNER:
1. Assemble the remaining ingredients and equipment
2. Do Step 1 of the *Hamburger Stuffs*
3. Do Steps 1–8 of the *Red Potato Salad*
4. Do Steps 2–6 of the *Hamburger Stuffs*
5. Do Step 2 of the *Old-Fashioned Root Beer Floats*

Hamburger Stuffs

1 Prepare the grill.

2 Divide the ground beef into 8 hamburger patties, about 4 ounces each and about $1/4$-inch thick. Season to taste.

3 Cut the tomato into 4 slices. Peel and cut the sweet onion into 4 slices. Lay a slice of tomato and a slice onion on each of 4 patties. Top with relish and cheese.

4 Place the second patty over the first, and crimp around the edges to seal the ingredients inside.

5 Grill the hamburgers until they are done to taste, preferably using a grill cage to preserve the stuffing.

6 Lay the hamburger buns on the coolest part of the grill for 2 minutes to toast while the hamburgers complete cooking. Serve the hamburgers with the ketchup and the pickle slices.

Red Potato Salad

1 Cover the eggs with water in a small saucepan. Bring the water to a boil and hard-cook the eggs, 10 to 12 minutes.

2 Bring water to a boil in a large saucepan.

3 Scrub but do not peel the potatoes and cut them unto $1/2$-inch cubes. Cook, covered, until the potatoes are tender, about 10 minutes.

4 Drain the eggs and place them in the freezer to chill for 10 minutes.

5 Trim and chop the scallions. Trim and chop the celery. Chop the parsley.

6 Drain the potatoes, rinse them with cold water until they are cool and return them to the saucepan.

7 In a small bowl, combine the sour cream, the mayonnaise, the vinegar and the sugar. Season to taste.

8 Peel and chop the eggs. Add the eggs, the scallions, the celery and the parsley to the potatoes and toss the mixture with the dressing. Season to taste and refrigerate until you are ready to serve.

Old-Fashioned Root Beer Floats

1 Place the root beer in the refrigerator to chill.

2 Place scoops of ice cream in each of 4 tall glasses. Top with the cold root beer and a dollop of whipped cream.

WEDNESDAY

Up Front Salad

1 medium head lettuce
$^1/_2$ pound fresh tomatoes
1 small sweet onion
1 small head cauliflower
1 medium cucumber
$^1/_4$ pound sliced dry salami
1 small jar (3$^1/_2$ ounces) pimiento-stuffed
    green olives
1 small jar (4 ounces) marinated mushrooms
1 clove garlic
3 tablespoons regular or light olive oil
2 tablespoons red wine vinegar
$^1/_2$ teaspoon dried oregano
Seasoning to taste
1 cup croutons

Ribbon Fettuccine

3 small zucchini
3 medium carrots
1 stalk celery
2 tablespoons fresh parsley (when chopped)
12 ounces spinach fettuccine
6 tablespoons butter
Seasoning to taste
$^1/_4$ cup grated Parmesan cheese

Nectarine Nut

4 large nectarines
1 tablespoon lemon juice
$^1/_2$ cup flaked coconut
1 small container (8 ounces) frozen whipped
    topping
2 teaspoons almond extract
2 teaspoons confectioners' sugar

EQUIPMENT

Large skillet	Measuring cups and
Large saucepan	spoons
Medium bowl	Assorted cooking
2 small bowls	utensils
Colander	Whisk
Assorted kitchen knives	Vegetable peeler

COUNTDOWN

1 Assemble the ingredients and equipment
2 Do Steps 1–2 of the *Up Front Salad*
3 Do Step 1 of the *Nectarine Nut*
4 Do Steps 1–5 of the *Ribbon Fettuccine*
5 Do Step 3 of the *Up Front Salad*
6 Do Step 2 of the *Nectarine Nut*

Up Front Salad

1 Wash and dry the lettuce. Chop the tomatoes. Peel and slice the sweet onion. Trim and cut the cauliflower into bite-size florets. Peel and slice the cucumber. Place the lettuce leaves on a platter and arrange the vegetables and the salami over the lettuce. Drain the olives and the mushrooms and arrange them over the vegetables. Refrigerate until you are ready to serve.

2 Peel and mince the garlic. In a small bowl, whisk together the garlic, the oil, the vinegar and the oregano. Season to taste.

3 Drizzle the salad with the dressing and top it with the croutons.

Ribbon Fettuccine

1 Bring water to a boil in a large saucepan.

2 Wash and trim the zucchini. Trim and peel the carrots. With a peeler, slice down the zucchini and the carrots in wide, thin, full-length strips. Trim and thinly slice the celery on the diagonal. Chop the parsley.

3 Cook the spinach fettuccine in the boiling water until it is almost tender, 2 to 3 minutes if you are using fresh pasta and 6 to 7 minutes if you are using dried pasta.

4 Melt the butter in a large skillet. Stir in the zucchini and carrot ribbons and the celery. Sauté until the vegetables are crisp-tender, about 2 minutes. Season to taste.

5 Drain the pasta and return it to the saucepan. Toss it with the parsley and the vegetable mixture. Sprinkle with the Parmesan cheese.

Nectarine Nut

1 Wash, dry, pit and slice the nectarines. Place them in a medium bowl and sprinkle them with the lemon juice to keep them from browning. Refrigerate until you are ready to use.

2 Sprinkle the nectarines with the coconut. In a small bowl, blend the whipped topping with the almond extract and the confectioners' sugar. Fold the mixture into the nectarines.

THURSDAY

Lemon Chicken Broth

2 cans (14^1/$_2$ ounces each) chicken broth
^{1}/$_4$ cup lemon juice
1 teaspoon sugar
2 tablespoons dry sherry (or nonalcoholic
    white wine or omit)
1 tablespoon fresh parsley (when chopped)
1 small lemon

Patio Salad

1^1/$_2$ pounds boneless, skinless chicken breasts
2 small pink grapefruit
4 small oranges
2 small red onions
2 stalks celery
1 can (8 ounces) sliced water chestnuts
2 ripe avocados
2 tablespoons lime juice
2 egg yolks*
2 teaspoons Dijon mustard
^{1}/$_2$ cup regular or light vegetable oil
1 teaspoon grated fresh orange peel
2 tablespoons orange juice
Seasoning to taste
1 medium head lettuce

Bunderfuls

4 hamburger buns reserved from Tuesday
2 tablespoons honey
1 container (8 ounces) regular or light soft
    cream cheese
^{1}/$_4$ cup sliced almonds

*Reserve the egg whites for use on Friday.

Black Beauties

1 quart chocolate ice cream
^{1}/$_4$ cup creme de cacao liqueur (or nonalcoholic
    Italian chocolate syrup)
1 teaspoon vanilla extract
1 small container (8 ounces) frozen whipped
    topping
^{1}/$_4$ cup unsweetened cocoa
Chocolate sprinkles for garnish

EQUIPMENT

Blender	Assorted kitchen knives
Medium covered saucepan	Measuring cups and spoons
Medium saucepan	Assorted cooking utensils
Small saucepan	Whisk
Medium bowl	
Shallow bowl	

COUNTDOWN

1 Assemble the ingredients and equipment
2 Do Steps 1–5 of the *Patio Salad*
3 Do Step 1 of the *Lemon Chicken Broth*
4 Do Steps 1–2 of the *Bunderfuls*
5 Do Steps 6–7 of the *Patio Salad*
6 Do Step 2 of the *Lemon Chicken Broth*
7 Do Steps 1–2 of the *Black Beauties*

Lemon Chicken Broth

1 In a medium covered saucepan, combine the chicken broth, the lemon juice, the sugar and the sherry. Cover and simmer until hot.

2 Chop the parsley. Slice the lemon. Float both in the soup before serving.

Patio Salad

1 Bring water to a boil in a medium saucepan.

2 Cut the chicken into thick strips and poach them until they are opaque throughout, 5 to 7 minutes.

3 Peel and section the grapefruit. Peel and section the oranges. Peel and thinly slice the red onions. Trim and slice the celery. Drain and rinse the water chestnuts. Peel, pit and slice the avocados, place them in a shallow bowl and sprinkle them with 1 tablespoon of the lime juice to keep them from browning.

4 Drain the chicken strips, place them in a medium bowl, and refrigerate to cool.

5 In a small saucepan, whisk together the egg yolks, the mustard and the remaining lime juice until hot. Remove the saucepan from the heat and slowly whisk in half of the oil until the mixture begins to thicken. Gradually whisk in the remaining oil. Blend in the orange peel and the orange juice. Season to taste. Cover and refrigerate until you are ready to use.

6 Wash and dry the lettuce and arrange the leaves on a platter, stems toward the center. Arrange an alternating ring of avocado slices and grapefruit sections on the lettuce around the outside edge of the platter. Arrange an alternating ring of orange sections and red onion slices on the lettuce inside the avocado and grapefruit. Place the celery and the water chestnuts inside the oranges and the red onions.

7 Chop the cooled chicken. Toss it with $1/3$ cup of the mayonnaise mixture and mound it in the center of the salad. Pass the remaining mayonnaise separately.

Bunderfuls

1 Split the hamburger buns in half and lightly toast them.

2 Brush the buns with the honey. Spread them with the cream cheese. Top them with the sliced almonds.

Black Beauties

1 Process the ice cream, the creme de cacao and the vanilla in a blender until smooth.

2 Pour the ice cream mixture into individual parfait glasses. Fold the cocoa into the whipped topping, and top the ice cream with the topping and the sprinkles.

FRIDAY

Devilish Shells

1 large onion
2 cloves garlic
12 ounces small shell pasta
1 tablespoon regular or light olive oil
4 tablespoons dry red wine (or nonalcoholic red wine or water)
1/4 teaspoon red pepper flakes
2 tablespoons fresh parsley (when chopped)
1 teaspoon dried basil
1 teaspoon dried oregano
Seasoning to taste
1 medium can (15 ounces) tomato sauce
1/2 pound medium shrimp, shelled and deveined

Hodgepodge Salad

1 small bunch broccoli
4 scallions (green onions)
1/2 pound fresh tomatoes
1 medium cucumber
1 small bunch radishes
1 package (16 ounces) mixed salad greens
1 clove garlic
2 tablespoons regular or low-fat mayonnaise
2 tablespoons regular or light sour cream
2 tablespoons white wine vinegar
2 tablespoons grated Parmesan cheese
Seasoning to taste

Butterscotch Laddies

1 cup peanut brittle (when crumbled)
1 1/4 cups whole milk
3/4 cup regular or light sour cream
1 small package (3.4 ounces) instant butterscotch pudding mix
2 egg whites reserved from Thursday
2 teaspoons sugar

EQUIPMENT

Electric hand mixer	Measuring cups and
Stockpot	spoons
2 medium saucepans	Assorted cooking
2 large bowls	utensils
Medium bowl	Whisk
2 small bowls	Vegetable peeler
Colander	Plastic bag
Assorted kitchen knives	Mallet

COUNTDOWN

1 Assemble the ingredients and equipment
2 Do Steps 1–3 of the *Butterscotch Laddies*
3 Do Steps 1–3 of the *Devilish Shells*
4 Do Steps 1–3 of the *Hodgepodge Salad*
5 Do Steps 3–7 of the *Devilish Shells*
6 Do Step 4 of the *Hodgepodge Salad*

Devilish Shells

1 Bring water to a boil in a stockpot.

2 Peel and chop the onion. Peel and mince the garlic.

3 Cook the pasta in the boiling water until it is tender but still firm, 8 to 10 minutes.

4 Heat the oil in a medium saucepan. Add the onion and the garlic and sauté until they are soft but not brown, about 5 minutes. Add the wine, the red pepper flakes, the parsley, the basil and the oregano. Season to taste and cook for 2 minutes.

5 Stir in the tomato sauce and simmer for 2 minutes more.

6 Rinse the shrimp and add them to the sauce, mixing to combine, and cook until the shrimp turn bright pink, about 2 minutes.

7 Drain the pasta and return it to the stockpot. Pour the sauce over the pasta and toss gently.

Hodgepodge Salad

1 Bring a small amount of water to a boil in a medium saucepan. Trim and cut the broccoli into bite-size florets and blanch in the boiling water for 1 minute. Drain and rinse in cold water.

2 Trim and chop the scallions. Chop the tomatoes. Peel and slice the cucumber. Trim and slice the radishes. Rinse and dry the mixed salad greens. Combine the ingredients with the broccoli in a large bowl and refrigerate until you are ready to serve.

3 Peel and mince the garlic. In a small bowl, whisk together the garlic, the mayonnaise, the sour cream, the vinegar and the cheese. Season to taste.

4 Toss the salad with the dressing.

Butterscotch Laddies

1 Place the peanut brittle in a plastic bag and crumble with a mallet.

2 In a medium bowl, blend the milk into the sour cream. Add the pudding mix and beat until well blended, about 2 minutes.

3 In a small bowl, beat the egg whites until frothy, about 3 minutes. Add the sugar and beat until stiff. Fold the egg white mixture into the pudding mixture. Fold in half of the peanut brittle. Pour the mixture into individual dishes. Top with the remaining peanut brittle and refrigerate for at least 20 minutes.

AUGUST
WEEK FOUR

WEEK AT A GLANCE

Monday

BROADWAY CHICKEN
COMPANY RICE
SIDE-BY-SIDE BY VEGETABLES
CATS' CREAM

Tuesday

SPICY SCALLOP KABOBS
EDITH PILAF
BEETS ME SALAD
PINEAPPLE FLARES

Wednesday

SEAFARER SALAD
LOVE THAT CORN
TWO-BIT BREAD
ICE SCREAMERS

Thursday

SASSY SOUP
CAPRICIOUS SALAD
WRY BREAD
MOONBEAMS

Friday

PRESTO PESTO PASTA
LATE SUMMER SALAD
MICKEY MOUSSE

CHECK STAPLES

☐ Butter
☐ Flour
☐ Granulated sugar
☐ Dark brown sugar
☐ Confectioners' sugar
☐ Marshmallow topping
☐ Chocolate sprinkles
☐ Long-grain white rice
☐ Regular or light vegetable oil
☐ Regular or light olive oil
☐ White wine vinegar
☐ Raspberry vinegar
☐ Tarragon vinegar
☐ Lemon juice
☐ Grated fresh lemon peel
☐ Grated fresh orange peel
☐ Worcestershire sauce
☐ Tabasco sauce

☐ Dijon mustard
☐ Regular or low-fat mayonnaise
☐ Honey
☐ Grated Parmesan cheese
☐ Ground allspice
☐ Dried basil
☐ Bouquet Garni
☐ Caraway seeds
☐ Ground cinnamon
☐ Ground cumin
☐ Curry powder
☐ Garlic powder
☐ Dried marjoram
☐ Ground nutmeg
☐ Instant minced onion
☐ Dried oregano
☐ Paprika
☐ Dried tarragon
☐ Pepper
☐ Salt
☐ Almond extract
☐ Vanilla extract

SHOPPING NOTE

● If you are shopping once a week and cannot arrange to purchase fresh scallops on the day you plan to use them, you can purchase *not previously frozen* scallops and freeze them, placing them in the refrigerator to thaw the night before you are ready to use them. Or you can purchase *still frozen* scallops and keep them frozen until the night before you are ready to use them.

MEAT & POULTRY

4 boneless, skinless chicken breast halves (M)
1 whole boneless, skinless chicken breast (Th)

FISH

1¼ pounds sea scallops (T)

FRESH PRODUCE

Vegetables

2 medium baking potatoes (F)
2 medium zucchini (M)
2 small summer squash (M)
4 ears sweet corn (W)
½ pound green beans (F)
1 pound unshelled green peas (W)
¼ pound Swiss chard (or spinach) (Th)
8 medium mushrooms (T)
3 medium carrots—2 (M), 1 (Th)
7 stalks celery—2 (M), 3 (W), 2 (Th)
6 medium onions—3 (M), 2 (T), 1 (Th)
1 medium sweet onion (F)
1 small red onion (W)
2 medium shallots (M)
3 scallions (green onions) (Th)
1 head garlic (M, T, F)
1 large bunch basil (F)
1 bunch parsley (M, W)
2 medium heads lettuce—1 (T), 1 (F)
1 small head romaine (Th)
1 small bunch arugula (Th)
2 large tomatoes (F)
½ pound tomatoes (W)
1 medium cucumber (F)
1 large green bell pepper (T)
1 small white radish (or turnip) (F)

Fruit

1 tart green apple (Th)
4 large nectarines (Th)
2 medium bananas (M)
1 large pineapple (T)
1 pint blackberries (M)
2 large oranges (T)

CANS, JARS & BOTTLES

Soup

3 cans (14½ ounces each) chicken broth—1 (M), 2 (Th)
1 can (14½ ounces) vegetable broth (T)

Vegetables

1 medium can (15 ounces) sliced pickled beets (T)

Fish

1 can (6 ounces) solid white tuna (W)
1 can (2 ounces) anchovy fillets (W)

Fruit

1 small can (8 ounces) crushed pineapple (T)

Condiments

1 small can (3½ ounces) pitted black olives (W)
2 tablespoons capers (W)

PACKAGED GOODS

Pasta, Rice & Grains

½ cup dried capellini (angel hair pasta) (T)
12 ounces penne (W)
16 ounces bucatini or other tubular pasta (F)

Baked Goods

4 sesame seed sandwich rolls (W)
1 small loaf sliced dark rye bread (Th)

Nuts & Seeds

½ cup sliced almonds (T)
½ cup unsalted cashew pieces (Th)
2 tablespoons pine nuts (F)

Dessert & Baking Needs

1 small package hot cinnamon candies (W)

WINES & SPIRITS

¼ cup dry sherry (or nonalcoholic white wine or water) (T)
3 tablespoons dry sherry (or nonalcoholic white wine or omit) (Th)
2 tablespoons brandy (or 1 tablespoon Worcestershire sauce + 1 tablespoon lemon juice) (M)
1 tablespoon rum (or nonalcoholic Italian hazelnut syrup) (T)

REFRIGERATED PRODUCTS

Dairy

1½ cups half-and-half (Th)
2 cups whipping cream (F)
1¼ cups regular or light sour cream—1 cup (M), ¼ cup (Th)
½ cup + 2 tablespoons regular or low-fat plain yogurt—½ cup (W), 2 tablespoons (Th)
6 eggs—2 (W), 4 (Th, F)

Juice

4 tablespoons orange juice—2 (M), 1 (T), 1 (Th)

Deli

4 slices bacon (T)

FROZEN GOODS

Desserts

1 pint peppermint ice cream (W)

MONDAY

Broadway Chicken

¹/₂ cup flour
Seasoning to taste
4 boneless, skinless chicken breast halves
2 medium shallots
2 tablespoons fresh parsley (when chopped)
2 tablespoons butter
1 tablespoon regular or light vegetable oil
2 tablespoons lemon juice
*2 tablespoons brandy (or 1 tablespoon
    Worcestershire sauce + 1 tablespoon
    lemon juice)*

Company Rice

1 medium onion
2 tablespoons butter
1 cup long-grain white rice
1 can (14¹/₂ ounces) chicken broth
2 tablespoons orange juice
¹/₄ cup water
1 tablespoon grated fresh orange peel
¹/₄ teaspoon ground allspice

Side-By-Side By Vegetables

2 medium zucchini
2 small summer squash
2 medium onions
2 medium carrots
2 stalks celery
2 cloves garlic
2 tablespoons regular or light vegetable oil
2 teaspoons Bouquet Garni
Seasoning to taste

Cats' Cream

1 cup regular or light sour cream
3 tablespoons confectioners' sugar
1 tablespoon almond extract
1 pint fresh blackberries
2 medium bananas

EQUIPMENT

Large covered skillet	Measuring cups and
Large skillet	spoons
Medium skillet	Assorted cooking
Double boiler	utensils
Medium bowl	Vegetable peeler
Shallow bowl	Waxed paper
Assorted kitchen knives	Mallet

COUNTDOWN

1 Assemble the ingredients and equipment
2 Do Steps 1–2 of the *Company Rice*
3 Do Steps 1–2 of the *Cats' Cream*
4 Do Step 1 of the *Side-By-Side By Vegetables*
5 Do Steps 1–5 of the *Broadway Chicken*
6 Do Step 2 of the *Side-By-Side By Vegetables*
7 Do Step 3 of the *Company Rice*
8 Do Step 6 of the *Broadway Chicken*
9 Do Step 3 of the *Cats' Cream*

Broadway Chicken

1 Place the flour in a shallow bowl and season it to taste. Place the chicken breasts between sheets of waxed paper and pound them with a mallet to a $1/2$-inch thickness. Dip the chicken in the seasoned flour to coat lightly.

2 Peel and mince the shallots. Chop the parsley.

3 Melt the butter with the oil in a large covered skillet. Add the chicken and cook, turning, until it is opaque throughout, about 10 minutes. Remove the chicken and cover to keep warm.

4 Add the shallots to the skillet and cook until they are soft, about 3 minutes. Return the chicken to the skillet with any juices that have collected.

5 Bring the liquid to a bubble. Add the lemon juice and the brandy. Ignite the brandy carefully with a match. After the flames subside, cover the skillet and remove it from the heat.

6 Top the chicken with the sauce and sprinkle with the parsley.

Company Rice

1 Peel and chop the onion. Melt the butter in a medium skillet and sauté the onion until it is limp, about 5 minutes.

2 Place the onion in the top of a double boiler. Add the rice, the broth, the orange juice, the water, the orange peel and the allspice. Bring water to a boil in the bottom of the double boiler. Reduce the heat, cover and simmer until all the liquid is absorbed and the rice is tender, 30 to 40 minutes.

3 Fluff the rice before serving.

Side-By-Side By Vegetables

1 Trim and slice the zucchini. Trim and chunk the squash. Peel and chunk the onions. Peel and slice the carrots. Trim and slice the celery. Peel and mince the garlic.

2 Heat the oil with the Bouquet Garni in a large skillet. Add the garlic and the onions and sauté for 2 minutes. Add the carrots and the celery and sauté for 3 minutes. Add the zucchini and the squash and sauté for another 2 minutes. Season to taste.

Cats' Cream

1 In a medium bowl, combine the sour cream, the confectioners' sugar and the almond extract until well blended. Cover and refrigerate until you are ready to use.

2 Rinse the blackberries and drain them on paper towels.

3 Peel and slice the bananas into individual dishes. Top with the sour cream mixture and the blackberries.

TUESDAY

Spicy Scallop Kabobs

1¹/₄ pounds sea scallops
1 clove garlic
1 tablespoon instant minced onion
¹/₄ cup regular or light vegetable oil
¹/₄ cup white wine vinegar
2 tablespoons lemon juice
¹/₄ teaspoon dried basil
¹/₂ teaspoon Tabasco sauce
Seasoning to taste
4 slices bacon
2 medium onions
8 medium mushrooms
1 large green bell pepper

Edith Pilaf

4 tablespoons butter
¹/₂ cup sliced almonds
¹/₂ cup dried capellini (angel hair pasta)
1 cup long-grain white rice
1 can (14¹/₂ ounces) vegetable broth
2 tablespoons water
¹/₄ cup dry sherry (or nonalcoholic white wine
    or additional water)
1¹/₂ teaspoons dried tarragon

Beets Me Salad

1 medium head lettuce
2 large oranges
1 medium can (15 ounces) sliced pickled beets
2 tablespoons regular or light vegetable oil
1 tablespoon white wine vinegar
1 tablespoon orange juice
1 teaspoon honey
¹/₈ teaspoon ground nutmeg
Seasoning to taste

Pineapple Flares

1 large pineapple
2 tablespoons butter
1 tablespoon rum (or nonalcoholic Italian
    hazelnut syrup)
1 small can (8 ounces) crushed pineapple
¹/₂ teaspoon ground cinnamon

EQUIPMENT

Large covered skillet	Assorted cooking
Small saucepan	utensils
Large bowl	Whisk
Small bowl	4 long skewers
Strainer	Pastry brush
Assorted kitchen knives	Pineapple corer
Measuring cups and	
spoons	

COUNTDOWN

1 Assemble the ingredients and equipment
2 Do Steps 1–3 of the *Spicy Scallop Kabobs*
3 Do Steps 1–3 of the *Edith Pilaf*
4 Do Step 1 of the *Pineapple Flares*
5 Do Step 1 of the *Beets Me Salad*
6 Do Steps 4–5 of the *Spicy Scallop Kabobs*
7 Do Step 2 of the *Beets Me Salad*
8 Do Step 4 of the *Edith Pilaf*
9 Do Step 2 of the *Pineapple Flares*

Spicy Scallop Kabobs

1 Prepare the grill.

2 Wash and pat dry the scallops and place them in a large bowl. Peel and mince the garlic. Add the garlic to the scallops. Add the instant minced onion, the oil, the vinegar, the lemon juice, the basil and the Tabasco sauce. Season to taste. Toss lightly until the scallops are evenly coated with the marinade. Cover and let stand, tossing occasionally, for at least 30 minutes.

3 Cut the bacon slices into 2-inch pieces. Peel and quarter the onions. Wash, pat dry and trim the mushrooms. Seed the bell pepper and cut it into $1^1/_2$-inch squares.

4 Drain the scallops, reserving the marinade. Thread the scallops, the bacon, the onions, the mushrooms and the bell pepper onto skewers.

5 Grill, turning and basting with the marinade several times, until the scallops are cooked through, the bacon is brown and the vegetables are crisp-tender, 7 to 8 minutes.

Edith Pilaf

1 Melt 1 tablespoon of the butter in a large skillet and sauté the almonds until lightly toasted, about 3 minutes. Remove them from the skillet and reserve.

2 Break the capellini into 1-inch pieces and sauté them in the skillet for 2 minutes. Remove the capellini and the almonds and reserve them.

3 Melt the remaining butter in the skillet. Add the rice and sauté until it is lightly browned, about 5 minutes. Return the al-monds and the capellini to the skillet, add the broth, the water, the sherry and the tarragon, bring the mixture to a boil, reduce the heat, cover and simmer until all the liquid is absorbed and the rice is tender, about 20 minutes.

4 Fluff the pilaf before serving.

Beets Me Salad

1 Wash and dry the lettuce and arrange the leaves on individual salad plates. Peel and slice the oranges. Drain and rinse the beets well. Alternate the beet and the orange slices on the lettuce.

2 In a small bowl, whisk together the oil, the vinegar, the juice, the honey and the nutmeg. Season to taste and drizzle the dressing over the salad.

Pineapple Flares

1 Peel and core the pineapple and slice it into 8 rings. Distribute the pineapple among individual dessert plates. Refrigerate until you are ready to use.

2 Melt the butter with the rum in a small saucepan. Add the undrained crushed pineapple and the cinnamon. Heat the mixture thoroughly and spoon it over the pineapple rings.

WEDNESDAY

Seafarer Salad

2 eggs
1 can (6 ounces) solid white tuna
1 small can (2 ounces) anchovy fillets
1/2 cup regular or low-fat plain yogurt
1/4 cup regular or low-fat mayonnaise
1/2 teaspoon paprika
1 1/2 tablespoons lemon juice
Seasoning to taste
12 ounces penne
1 pound unshelled peas
1 small red onion
3 stalks celery
1/4 cup fresh parsley (when chopped)
2 tablespoons capers
1 small can (3 1/2 ounces) pitted black olives
1/2 pound fresh tomatoes

Love That Corn

2 tablespoons softened butter
3/4 teaspoon garlic powder
Seasoning to taste
4 large ears sweet corn

Two-Bit Bread

4 sesame seed sandwich rolls
2 tablespoons softened butter
2 teaspoons dried marjoram
1 tablespoon instant minced onion

Ice Screamers

1 small package hot cinnamon candies
1 cup marshmallow topping
1 quart peppermint ice cream

EQUIPMENT

Blender	Assorted kitchen knives
Stockpot	Measuring cups and
Large saucepan	spoons
Small saucepan	Assorted cooking
Cookie sheet	utensils
Large bowl	Ice cream scoop
2 small bowls	Plastic bag
Colander	Mallet

COUNTDOWN

1 Assemble the ingredients and equipment
2 Do Step 1 of the *Seafarer Salad*
3 Do Step 1 of the *Ice Screamers*
4 Do Steps 2–8 of the *Seafarer Salad*
5 Do Steps 1–2 of the *Love That Corn*
6 Do Step 1 of the *Two–Bit Bread*
7 Do Step 3 of the *Love That Corn*
8 Do Step 2 of the *Two–Bit Bread*
9 Do Step 2 of the *Ice Screamers*

Seafarer Salad

1 Cover the eggs with water in a small saucepan. Bring the water to a boil and hard-cook the eggs, 10 to 12 minutes.

2 Drain the eggs and place them in the freezer to chill for 10 minutes.

3 Bring water to a boil in a stockpot. Bring a small amount of water to a boil in the egg saucepan.

4 Drain and flake the tuna. Drain, blot dry, and chop the anchovies. Place the tuna, the yogurt, the mayonnaise, the paprika, the anchovies and the lemon juice in a blender. Season to taste and puree.

5 Cook the pasta in the stockpot until it is almost tender, 8 to 10 minutes.

6 Shell the peas. Cook them in the saucepan until they are crisp-tender, 2 to 3 minutes. Drain and turn them into a large bowl.

7 Peel and dice the red onion. Trim and chop the celery. Chop the parsley. Drain the capers. Drain the olives. Chop the tomatoes.

8 Drain the pasta and add it to the peas. Toss the pasta and the peas with the tuna sauce, the onion, the celery, the parsley and the capers. Peel and slice the eggs. Top the salad with the eggs, the tomatoes and the olives. Serve at room temperature.

Love That Corn

1 Bring water to a boil in a large saucepan.

2 In a small bowl, combine the softened butter with the garlic powder. Season to taste.

3 Shuck the corn. Cook the corn until it is crisp-tender, not more than 2 to 3 minutes. Spread the ears with the garlic butter.

Two-Bit Bread

1 Preheat the broiler. Split the sandwich rolls in half and place them on an ungreased cookie sheet. Spread the cut sides with the softened butter. Sprinkle with the marjoram and the minced onion.

2 Broil the rolls, 3 or 4 inches from the heat, until they are lightly browned, 1 to 2 minutes.

Ice Screamers

1 Place the cinnamon candies in a plastic bag and crush them with a mallet. Combine them in a small bowl with the marshmallow topping.

2 Place a scoop of ice cream in each parfait glass. Add a layer of the marshmallow-cinnamon mixture. Repeat.

THURSDAY

Sassy Soup

1 whole boneless, skinless chicken breast
1 medium onion
2 stalks celery
1 medium carrot
1 tart green apple
$^1/_4$ pound Swiss chard (or spinach)
2 tablespoons butter
2 teaspoons curry powder
$^1/_2$ teaspoon ground cumin
2 tablespoons lemon juice
2 cans (14$^1/_2$ ounces each) chicken broth
Seasoning to taste
1$^1/_2$ cups half-and-half
4 egg yolks*
2 tablespoons grated fresh lemon peel
3 tablespoons dry sherry (or nonalcoholic
    white wine or omit)

Capricious Salad

1 small bunch arugula
1 small head romaine
3 scallions (green onions)
$^1/_2$ cup unsalted cashew pieces
3 tablespoons regular or light vegetable oil
2 tablespoons tarragon vinegar
2 tablespoons regular or low-fat plain yogurt
$^1/_2$ teaspoon Worcestershire sauce
2 teaspoons Dijon mustard
1 teaspoon sugar
Seasoning to taste

Wry Bread

3 tablespoons softened butter
1 tablespoon orange juice
1 tablespoon grated fresh orange peel
2 teaspoons caraway seeds
1 small loaf sliced dark rye bread

Moonbeams

4 large nectarines
2 teaspoons lemon juice
$^1/_4$ cup regular or light sour cream
1 teaspoon dark brown sugar
$^1/_8$ teaspoon ground nutmeg

EQUIPMENT

Dutch oven	Assorted cooking
Medium saucepan	utensils
Large bowl	Whisk
4 small bowls	Vegetable peeler
Assorted kitchen knives	
Measuring cups and	
spoons	

COUNTDOWN

1 Assemble the ingredients and equipment
2 Do Steps 1–2 of the *Capricious Salad*
3 Do Step 1 of the *Wry Bread*
4 Do Steps 1–2 of the *Moonbeams*
5 Do Steps 1–6 of the *Sassy Soup*
6 Do Step 3 of the *Capricious Salad*
7 Do Step 2 of the *Wry Bread*
8 Do Step 3 of the *Moonbeams*

*Reserve the egg whites for use on Friday.

Sassy Soup

1 Bring water to a boil in a medium saucepan.

2 Cut the chicken breast into 1-inch strips. Cook the strips until they are opaque throughout, 5 to 6 minutes.

3 Peel and chop the onion. Trim and slice the celery. Peel and slice the carrot. Peel, core and slice the apple. Wash and chop the Swiss chard.

4 Drain the chicken, rinse it in cold water to cool and chop.

5 Melt the butter in a Dutch oven. Add the onion, the carrot, the celery and the apple, and cook until the onion is tender, about 5 minutes. Stir in the curry powder and the cumin. Add the lemon juice, the broth and the chicken. Season to taste. Bring the soup to a boil and reduce the heat. Add the Swiss chard and simmer.

6 In a small bowl, whisk the half-and-half into the egg yolks until well blended. Gradually beat in 1/2 cup of the hot soup. Stir the mixture into the Dutch oven, but do not let the soup boil or the eggs will curdle. Add the lemon peel and the sherry, cover and keep the soup warm until you are ready to serve.

Capricious Salad

1 Wash and dry the arugula and the romaine and tear them into bite-size pieces. Trim and chop the scallions. Combine the ingredients in a large bowl with the cashew pieces. Refrigerate until you are ready to serve.

2 In a small bowl, whisk together the oil, the vinegar, the yogurt, the Worcestershire sauce, the mustard and the sugar. Season to taste.

3 Toss the salad with the dressing.

Wry Bread

1 In a small bowl, combine the softened butter with the orange juice, the orange peel and the caraway seeds until well blended.

2 Spread the orange butter on the bread slices.

Moonbeams

1 Pit and slice the nectarines and arrange them on individual plates. Sprinkle them with lemon juice to keep them from browning and refrigerate until you are ready to use.

2 In a small bowl, combine the sour cream with the brown sugar. Refrigerate until you are ready to use.

3 Top the nectarines with a dollop of the sour cream mixture and sprinkle with the nutmeg.

FRIDAY

Presto Pesto Pasta

2 medium baking potatoes
$1/2$ pound green beans
16 ounces bucatini or other small tubular
    pasta
2 cloves garlic
2 cups fresh basil leaves
$1/4$ cup grated Parmesan cheese
2 tablespoons pine nuts
$1/2$ cup regular or light olive oil
3 tablespoons butter
Seasoning to taste

Late Summer Salad

1 medium head lettuce
2 large tomatoes
1 medium cucumber
1 medium sweet onion
1 small white radish (or turnip)
$1/2$ teaspoon dried tarragon
$1/4$ teaspoon dried oregano
2 tablespoons raspberry vinegar
3 tablespoons regular or light vegetable oil
1 teaspoon honey
Seasoning to taste

Mickey Mousse

4 tablespoons water
4 egg whites reserved from Thursday
1 cup confectioners' sugar
$1^{1/2}$ teaspoons vanilla extract
2 cups whipping cream
Chocolate sprinkles for garnish

EQUIPMENT	
Electric hand mixer	Colander
Blender	Assorted kitchen knives
Stockpot	Measuring cups and
Large skillet	spoons
Large saucepan	Assorted cooking
Large bowl	utensils
Medium bowl	Whisk
Small bowl	Vegetable peeler

COUNTDOWN

1 Assemble the ingredients and equipment
2 Do Steps 1–2 of the *Mickey Mousse*
3 Do Step 1 of the *Presto Pesto Pasta*
4 Do Steps 1–3 of the *Late Summer Salad*
5 Do Steps 2–7 of the *Presto Pesto Pasta*
6 Do Step 4 of the *Late Summer Salad*
7 Do Step 3 of the *Mickey Mousse*

Presto Pesto Pasta

1 Bring water to a boil in a stockpot. Bring water to a boil in a large saucepan.

2 Peel the potatoes and cut them into ¹/₂-inch cubes. Trim the green beans and cut them into 1-inch pieces.

3 Cook the pasta in the stockpot until it is almost tender, 8 to 10 minutes.

4 Cook the potatoes and the beans in the saucepan until they are tender, about 6 minutes.

5 Peel and chop the garlic. Rinse, dry and stem the basil leaves. In a blender, process the garlic, the basil leaves, the cheese, the pine nuts and 7 tablespoons of the oil.

6 Drain and rinse the pasta, return it to the stockpot and toss it with the remaining olive oil. Cover to keep warm. Drain the potatoes and the beans.

7 Melt the butter in a large skillet and sauté the potatoes and the beans for 3 minutes. Add the mixture to the pasta. Add the pesto to the pasta and toss to mix. Season to taste. Serve with additional Parmesan cheese, if desired.

Late Summer Salad

1 Wash and dry the lettuce and arrange the leaves on individual salad plates.

2 Slice the tomatoes. Peel and slice the cucumber. Peel and slice the sweet onion. Peel and julienne the white radish. Arrange the vegetables over the lettuce. Refrigerate until you are ready to serve.

3 In a small bowl, whisk together the tarragon, the oregano, the vinegar, the oil and the honey. Season to taste.

4 Drizzle the dressing over the salad.

Mickey Mousse

1 In a medium bowl, combine the water and the egg whites and beat until soft peaks form, about 3 minutes. Gradually add the confectioners' sugar and the vanilla and beat until stiff, about 5 minutes.

2 In a large bowl, beat the cream until thick. Fold the egg white mixture into the cream and spoon it into individual dessert dishes. Refrigerate for at least 30 minutes.

3 Top each mousse with a generous amount of chocolate sprinkles.

SEPTEMBER
WEEK ONE

Monday

ROCKING CHAIR MACARONI
LAZY DAY SALAD
TIME ON OUR BRANS
DO-ALMOST-NOTHING DESSERT

Tuesday

I WOK ALONE
SALAD DAZE
SIDE-SPLITTERS

Wednesday

TURKEY IN THE STRAWGANOFF
HEY NOODLES
GREEN-JEANS SALAD
TOFFEE PARFAIT

Thursday

APRICOT PORK CHOPS
SASS-SQUASH
SLAP-APPLES
TRIPLE-BERRY DELIGHT

Friday

DRUNKEN SHRIMP
ARTICHOKE SALAD
PRALINE PEARS

- ☐ Butter
- ☐ Flour
- ☐ Baking powder
- ☐ Granulated sugar
- ☐ Dark brown sugar
- ☐ Brown rice
- ☐ Regular or light vegetable oil
- ☐ Regular or light olive oil
- ☐ Red wine vinegar
- ☐ White wine vinegar
- ☐ Balsamic vinegar
- ☐ Apple cider vinegar
- ☐ Lemon juice
- ☐ Worcestershire sauce
- ☐ Dijon mustard
- ☐ Regular or low-fat mayonnaise
- ☐ Ketchup
- ☐ Instant coffee crystals
- ☐ Dried basil
- ☐ Celery seeds
- ☐ Ground cinnamon
- ☐ Whole cloves
- ☐ Dried dill
- ☐ Garlic powder
- ☐ Ground ginger
- ☐ Dried marjoram
- ☐ Dry mustard
- ☐ Onion powder
- ☐ Dried oregano
- ☐ Paprika
- ☐ Dried sage
- ☐ Dried thyme
- ☐ Pepper
- ☐ Salt
- ☐ Vanilla extract

SHOPPING NOTE

● If you are shopping once a week and cannot arrange to purchase fresh seafood on the day you plan to use it, you can purchase *not previously frozen* seafood and freeze it, placing it in the refrigerator to thaw the night before you are ready to use it. Or you can purchase *still frozen* seafood and keep it frozen until the night before you are ready to use it.

MEAT & POULTRY

1 pound lean ground beef (M)
4 loin pork chops (1-inch thick) (Th)
1 1/2 pounds boneless, skinless turkey breast (W)

FISH

1 1/4 pounds sole fillets (T)
3/4 pound medium shrimp, shelled and deveined (F)

FRESH PRODUCE

Vegetables

1 small head cauliflower (M)
1 large bunch broccoli (T)
2 medium acorn squash (Th)
1 medium zucchini (T)
1/4 pound small mushrooms (W)
4 stalks celery—2 (T), 2 (F)
1 medium onion (T)
2 small onions—1 (M), 1 (W)
1 small red onion (M)
8 scallions (green onions)—
    3 (T), 2 (W), 3 (F)
1 head garlic (T, W, F)
1 bunch chives (W, Th, F)
1 bunch parsley (T, W, F)
2 medium heads lettuce—
    1 (M), 1 (T)
1 small head lettuce (W)
1/2 pound tomatoes (W)
1 large cucumber (F)
1 medium red bell pepper (M)
1 small bunch radishes (F)

Fruit

2 large peaches (T)
4 medium pears (F)
4 large tart green apples (Th)
2 small cantaloupes (M)
2 medium bananas (T)
1/2 pound seedless red grapes (M)
1/2 pint blackberries (Th)

CANS, JARS & BOTTLES

Soup

1 can (10 3/4 ounces) cream of celery soup (W)

Vegetables

1 medium can (14 1/2 ounces) stewed tomatoes (T)
1 small can (8 ounces) tomato sauce (M)
1 medium can (15 1/2 ounces) baby lima beans (Th)
1 jar (6 1/2 ounces) marinated artichoke hearts (F)

Fruit

1 large can (16 ounces) jellied cranberry sauce (M)

Juice

1 1/4 cups clam juice (T)

Spreads

1 small jar (10 ounces) raspberry jam (Th)

Dessert Needs

1 jar (12 1/4 ounces) butterscotch topping (T)
1 can (12 ounces) chocolate fudge topping (W)

PACKAGED GOODS

Pasta, Rice & Grains

12 ounces elbow macaroni (M)
8 ounces medium egg noodles (W)
12 ounces spaghetti (F)
1 cup All-Bran cereal (M)

Soup

1 package (1.8 ounces) dried onion soup mix (W)

Fruit

4 large dried apricots (Th)

Nuts & Seeds

1 cup pecan pieces (F)

Dessert & Baking Needs

1 small package (3.4 ounces) instant vanilla pudding mix (W)

2 large (7 ounces each) chocolate-covered toffee bar (W)

WINES & SPIRITS

3/4 cup dry white wine (or nonalcoholic white wine or beef broth) (Th)
1 cup dry white wine (or nonalcoholic white wine or clam juice) (F)
1/2 teaspoon Grand Marnier liqueur (or nonalcoholic Italian orange syrup) (M)
1 tablespoon Amaretto liqueur (or nonalcoholic Italian almond syrup) (T)

REFRIGERATED PRODUCTS

Dairy

2 cups whole milk (W)
1 cup buttermilk (M)
1/2 cup whipping cream (F)
Whipped cream for garnish (W)
1 1/2 cups + 3 tablespoons regular or light sour cream—3 tablespoons (M), 1 cup (W), 1/2 cup (Th)
2 eggs (M)

Cheese

1 container (8 ounces) soft cream cheese (F)

Deli

4 slices prosciutto ham (Th)

FROZEN GOODS

Vegetables

1 package (9 ounces) cut green beans (W)

Desserts

1 pound cake (Th)
1 pint maple nut (or similar) ice cream (T)
1 pint strawberry frozen yogurt (Th)

MONDAY

Rocking Chair Macaroni

1 small onion
1 pound lean ground beef
1 small can (8 ounces) tomato sauce
1 large can (16 ounces) jellied cranberry sauce
2 tablespoons ketchup
2 tablespoons Worcestershire sauce
$1/2$ teaspoon ground ginger
$1/4$ teaspoon ground cinnamon
Seasoning to taste
12 ounces elbow macaroni

Lazy Day Salad

1 egg yolk
3 tablespoons regular or light sour cream
2 tablespoons regular or low-fat mayonnaise
1 tablespoon apple cider vinegar
1 teaspoon Dijon mustard
1 teaspoon dried dill
$1/2$ teaspoon garlic powder
1 teaspoon onion powder
Seasoning to taste
1 medium head lettuce
1 small red onion
1 medium red bell pepper
1 small head cauliflower

Time on Our Brans

2 tablespoons butter
1 egg
1 cup buttermilk
1 cup All-Bran cereal
1 cup flour
1 tablespoon baking powder
$1/4$ cup dark brown sugar

Do-Almost-Nothing Dessert

2 small cantaloupes
$1/2$ pound seedless red grapes
1 egg white
$1/2$ teaspoon Grand Marnier liqueur (or nonalcoholic Italian orange syrup)
$1/4$ cup sugar

EQUIPMENT

Large skillet	Assorted kitchen knives
Large saucepan	Measuring cups and
12-cup muffin tin	spoons
2 large bowls	Assorted cooking
Medium bowl	utensils
Small bowl	Whisk
Colander	Plastic bag

COUNTDOWN

1 Assemble the ingredients and equipment
2 Do Steps 1–2 of *Time on Our Brans*
3 Do Steps 1–2 of the *Lazy Day Salad*
4 Do Steps 1–4 of the *Rocking Chair Macaroni*
5 Do Step 3 of *Time on Our Brans*
6 Do Steps 1–3 of the *Do-Almost-Nothing Dessert*
7 Do Step 5 of the *Rocking Chair Macaroni*

Rocking Chair Macaroni

1 Bring water to a boil in a large saucepan.

2 Peel and chop the onion.

3 Sauté the beef and the onion in a large skillet until the beef is browned and the onion is translucent, about 6 minutes. Drain any excess fat from the skillet and stir in the tomato sauce, the cranberry sauce, the ketchup, the Worcestershire sauce, the ginger and the cinnamon. Season to taste and cook, uncovered, stirring occasionally, until the flavors are combined, 15 to 20 minutes.

4 Cook the macaroni in the boiling water until it is almost tender, 7 to 9 minutes.

5 Drain the pasta, return it to the saucepan and toss it with the sauce.

Lazy Day Salad

1 In a large bowl, whisk together the egg yolk, the sour cream, the mayonnaise, the vinegar, the mustard, the dill, the garlic powder and the onion powder. Season to taste.

2 Wash and dry the lettuce and tear it into bite-size pieces. Peel and thinly slice the red onion. Seed and chop the bell pepper. Trim and cut the cauliflower into bite-size florets. Add the ingredients to the dressing and toss to combine. Refrigerate until you are ready to serve.

Time on Our Brans

1 Preheat the oven to 375°F. Grease a 12-cup muffin tin.

2 Melt the butter. In a large bowl, lightly beat the egg. Add the butter, the buttermilk and the All-Bran and combine. Add the flour, the baking powder and the brown sugar and fold until well blended.

3 Fill the muffin cups 2/3 full and bake until the muffins are lightly browned, 15 to 20 minutes.

Do-Almost-Nothing Dessert

1 Halve and seed the melons and place them in individual dessert dishes.

2 Wash and separate the grapes and cut them in half.

3 Combine the egg white and the Grand Marnier in a medium bowl. Place the sugar in a plastic bag. Add the grapes to the egg white mixture and toss to coat. Remove the grapes with a slotted spoon and place them in the plastic bag. Shake the bag to coat the grapes. Fill the melon centers with the coated grapes and refrigerate until you are ready to serve.

TUESDAY

I Wok Alone

1 medium onion
2 stalks celery
2 tablespoons regular or light olive oil
1 medium can ($14^1/_2$ ounces) stewed tomatoes
$1^1/_4$ cups clam juice
2 tablespoons white wine vinegar
Seasoning to taste
1 cup brown rice
$1^1/_4$ pounds sole fillets

Salad Daze   add lettuce

1 large bunch broccoli
1 medium zucchini
3 scallions (green onions)
3 cloves garlic
2 tablespoons fresh parsley (when chopped)
$^1/_4$ cup regular or light vegetable oil
3 tablespoons white wine vinegar
1 teaspoon Dijon mustard
$^1/_2$ teaspoon dried basil
$^1/_2$ teaspoon dried oregano
Seasoning to taste

Side-Splitters

1 jar ($12^1/_4$ ounces) butterscotch topping
1 tablespoon Amaretto liqueur (or
    nonalcoholic Italian almond syrup)
2 medium bananas
2 large peaches
1 pint maple nut (or similar) ice cream

EQUIPMENT

Wok and wok utensils	Measuring cups and
Medium saucepan	spoons
Small saucepan	Assorted cooking
Colander	utensils
Large bowl	Whisk
Small bowl	Ice scream scoop
Assorted kitchen knives	

COUNTDOWN

1 Assemble the ingredients and equipment
2 Do Steps 1–3 of *I Wok Alone*
3 Do Steps 1–2 of the *Salad Daze*
4 Do Step 4 of *I Wok Alone*
5 Do Step 3 of the *Salad Daze*
6 Do Steps 1–3 of the *Side-Splitters*

---

1 Wok Alone

1 Peel and chop the onion. Trim and slice the celery.

2 Heat the oil in a wok until hot. Add the onion and the celery and stir-fry until the onion is soft, about 5 minutes.

3 Add the stewed tomatoes, the clam juice and the vinegar. Season to taste. Bring the mixture to a boil and then reduce the heat. Add the rice and stir to combine. Cover and cook for 15 minutes.

4 Uncover the wok, top the rice with the fish fillets, re-cover the wok, and simmer until the fish is opaque throughout, the rice is tender, and almost all of the liquid is absorbed, about 10 minutes.

Salad Daze

1 Bring a small amount of water to a boil in a medium saucepan. Trim and cut the broccoli into bite-size florets and blanch it in the boiling water for 1 minute. Drain and rinse in cold water.

2 Trim and slice the zucchini. Trim and chop the scallions. Combine the ingredients with the broccoli in a large bowl.

3 Peel and mince the garlic. Chop the parsley. In a small bowl, whisk together the garlic, the parsley, the oil, the vinegar, the mustard, the basil and the oregano. Season to taste. Toss the salad with the dressing.

Side-Splitters

1 Heat the butterscotch topping and the Amaretto in a small saucepan.

2 Peel and slice the bananas and distribute them among individual dessert dishes. Peel, pit and chop the peaches.

3 Place a scoop of ice cream over the bananas. Drizzle the ice cream with the warm butterscotch topping, and top with the chopped peaches.

WEDNESDAY

Turkey in the Strawganoff

1 small onion
$1/4$ pound small fresh mushrooms
1 clove garlic
1 tablespoon fresh parsley (when chopped)
1 tablespoon fresh chives (when chopped)
$1^1/2$ pounds boneless, skinless turkey breast
1 package (1.8 ounces) dried onion soup mix
2 tablespoons butter
2 tablespoons flour
1 can ($10^3/4$ ounces) cream of celery soup
Seasoning to taste
1 cup regular or light sour cream
1 teaspoon paprika

Hey Noodles

8 ounces medium egg noodles
1 tablespoon butter
2 teaspoons dried sage
Seasoning to taste

Green-Jeans Salad

1 package (9 ounces) frozen cut green beans
$1/2$ pound fresh tomatoes
2 scallions (green onions)
3 tablespoons regular or light olive oil
2 tablespoons balsamic vinegar
1 teaspoon Dijon mustard
2 teaspoons dried dill
1 teaspoon dried marjoram
1 tablespoon celery seeds
Seasoning to taste
1 small head lettuce

Toffee Parfait

2 chocolate-covered toffee bars (7 ounces each)
1 tablespoon instant coffee crystals
2 cups whole milk
1 small package (3.4 ounces) instant vanilla
    pudding mix
1 jar (12 ounces) chocolate fudge topping
Whipped cream for garnish

EQUIPMENT

Electric hand mixer	Measuring cups and
Large skillet	spoons
Large covered	Assorted cooking
saucepan	utensils
2 medium saucepans	Whisk
2 medium bowls	Plastic bag
Colander	Mallet
Assorted kitchen knives	

COUNTDOWN

1 Assemble the ingredients and equipment
2 Do Steps 1–3 of the *Toffee Parfait*
3 Do Steps 1–3 of the *Green-Jeans Salad*
4 Do Steps 1–3 of the *Turkey in the Strawganoff*
5 Do Step 1 of the *Hey Noodles*
6 Do Steps 4–5 of the *Turkey in the Strawganoff*
7 Do Step 4 of the *Green-Jeans Salad*
8 Do Step 6 of the *Turkey in the Strawganoff*
9 Do Steps 2–3 of the *Hey Noodles*

Turkey in the Strawganoff

1 Bring water to a boil in a medium saucepan.

2 Peel and chop the onion. Wash, pat dry, trim and chop the mushrooms. Peel and mince the garlic. Chop the parsley. Chop the chives. Cut the turkey breast into 1-inch strips.

3 Add the dried soup mix to the boiling water. Add the turkey strips and cook until they are opaque throughout, 8 to 10 minutes.

4 Drain the turkey and run it under cold water to cool. Cut the strips into cubes.

5 Melt the butter in a large skillet and sauté the onion and the mushrooms until the onion is limp, about 5 minutes. Stir in the turkey cubes, the garlic, the flour, the parsley and the chives. Add the canned soup, season to taste and simmer, uncovered, for 10 minutes.

6 Stir the sour cream into the turkey mixture and simmer until heated through, about 5 minutes. Sprinkle with the paprika.

Hey Noodles

1 Bring water to a boil in a large saucepan.

2 Cook the noodles until they are almost tender, 3 to 5 minutes.

3 Drain the noodles and return them to the saucepan, toss them with the butter and the sage, season to taste and cover to keep warm.

Green-Jeans Salad

1 Run the green beans under hot water to thaw.

2 Bring a small amount of water to a boil in a medium saucepan. Chop the tomatoes. Trim and chop the scallions. Cook the beans in the boiling water for 2 minutes. Remove them from the saucepan and run them under cold water to stop the cooking.

3 In a medium bowl, combine the oil, the vinegar, the mustard, the dill, the marjoram and the celery seeds. Season to taste. Add the beans, the tomatoes and the scallions, toss to combine and refrigerate until you are ready to serve.

4 Wash and dry the lettuce and arrange the leaves on individual salad plates. Spoon the bean mixture over the lettuce.

Toffee Parfait

1 Place the toffee bars in a plastic bag and crush them with a mallet.

2 In a medium bowl, dissolve the coffee crystals in the milk. Add the pudding mix and beat until well blended.

3 In 4 parfait glasses, layer half the pudding mixture, half the fudge topping and half the crushed candy. Repeat. Top the parfaits with a dollop of whipped cream and refrigerate for at least 20 minutes.

THURSDAY

Apricot Pork Chops

4 loin pork chops (1-inch thick)
Seasoning to taste
4 slices prosciutto ham
4 large dried apricots
1 tablespoon regular or light olive oil
³/₄ cup dry white wine (or nonalcoholic white
*   wine or beef broth)*
¹/₃ cup water
1 teaspoon dry mustard

Sass-Squash

2 medium acorn squash
1 medium can (15¹/₂ ounces) baby lima beans
2 tablespoons fresh chives (when chopped)
3 tablespoons butter
¹/₂ cup regular or light sour cream
Seasoning to taste

Slap-Apples

4 large tart green apples
3 tablespoons butter
4 whole cloves
1 tablespoon dark brown sugar

Triple-Berry Delight

1 frozen pound cake
¹/₂ pint fresh blackberries
1 pint strawberry frozen yogurt
1 jar (10 ounces) raspberry jam

EQUIPMENT

Large covered skillet	Assorted kitchen knives
Medium covered skillet	Measuring cups and
9x13-inch glass baking	spoons
dish	Assorted cooking
Strainer	utensils
Medium bowl	Apple corer

COUNTDOWN

IN THE MORNING:
  Do Step 1 of the *Triple-Berry Delight*
BEFORE DINNER:
  1 Assemble the remaining ingredients and
     equipment
  2 Do Step 1 of the *Sass-Squash*
  3 Do Steps 1–2 of the *Apricot Pork Chops*
  4 Do Steps 2–3 of the *Sass-Squash*
  5 Do Step 3 of the *Apricot Pork Chops*
  6 Do Steps 2–3 of the *Triple-Berry Delight*
  7 Do Steps 1–2 of the *Slap-Apples*
  8 Do Step 4 of the *Sass-Squash*
  9 Do Step 4 of the *Triple-Berry Delight*

Apricot Pork Chops

1 Trim any excess fat from the chops and season them to taste. With a sharp knife, slit a pocket in the meaty part of each chop, cutting toward the bone. Stuff each chop with a slice of prosciutto and an apricot.

2 Heat the oil in a large skillet. Add the chops and cook until they are browned on both sides, 5 to 6 minutes.

3 Add the wine, the water and the dry mustard to the skillet, and bring the liquid to a boil. Reduce the heat, cover and simmer until the pork is tender and white throughout, 25 to 30 minutes.

Sass-Squash

1 Preheat the oven to 400°F. Bring water to a boil.

2 Cut the squash in half. Scoop out and discard the seeds and place the halves in a 9x13-inch glass baking dish, cut side down. Add boiling water to a 1/4-inch depth and bake for 25 minutes.

3 Drain the lima beans. Chop the chives.

4 Melt the butter. Remove the squash from the oven and reduce the temperature to 350°F. Turn the squash right side up and brush the tops with the melted butter. In a medium bowl, mix the lima beans with the sour cream and the chives and season to taste. Fill the squash halves with the lima bean mixture. Return the squash to the oven and bake until heated through, about 5 minutes.

Slap-Apples

1 Peel, core and slice the apples.

2 Melt the butter in a medium skillet and sauté the apples with the cloves and the brown sugar until the slices are lightly caramelized, but still crisp, 6 to 7 minutes. Remove the cloves. Remove the skillet from the heat and cover to keep warm.

Triple-Berry Delight

1 Set the pound cake out to thaw.

2 Rinse the blackberries and drain them on paper towels. Cut the pound cake into 12 thin slices.

3 Set the frozen yogurt out to soften.

4 Place 1 slice of cake on each of 4 plates and spread with the softened yogurt. Add a second slice of cake and spread with the blackberries. Add the top slice of cake and spread with the jam, allowing it to drizzle down the sides.

FRIDAY

Drunken Shrimp

3 cloves garlic
12 ounces spaghetti
2 tablespoons regular or light olive oil
3/4 pound medium shrimp, shelled and
    deveined
1 cup dry white wine (or nonalcoholic white
    wine or clam juice)
1 teaspoon dried basil
1 teaspoon dried thyme
Seasoning to taste

Artichoke Salad

1 medium head lettuce
1 large cucumber
2 stalks celery
3 scallions (green onions)
1 small bunch radishes
1 jar (6 1/2 ounces) marinated artichoke hearts
1 tablespoon fresh chives (when chopped)
1 tablespoon fresh parsley (when chopped)
2 tablespoons red wine vinegar
1/4 teaspoon Worcestershire sauce
1/2 teaspoon sugar
Seasoning to taste

EQUIPMENT

Stockpot	Measuring cups and
Large covered skillet	spoons
Small saucepan	Assorted cooking
Large bowl	utensils
Small bowl	Whisk
Shallow bowl	Vegetable peeler
Colander	Plastic bag
Assorted kitchen knives	Mallet

Praline Pears

4 medium pears
2 tablespoons lemon juice
1 cup pecan pieces
1 container (8 ounces) soft cream cheese
1 tablespoon butter
1/2 cup whipping cream
1 teaspoon vanilla extract
2/3 cup dark brown sugar

COUNTDOWN

1 Assemble the ingredients and equipment
2 Do Steps 1–3 of the *Artichoke Salad*
3 Do Steps 1–3 of the *Praline Pears*
4 Do Steps 1–7 of the *Drunken Shrimp*
5 Do Step 4 of the *Artichoke Salad*
6 Do Step 4 of the *Praline Pears*

Drunken Shrimp

1 Bring water to a boil in a stockpot.

2 Peel and mince the garlic.

3 Cook the spaghetti until it is almost tender, 2 to 3 minutes if you are using fresh pasta and 6 to 7 minutes if you are using dried pasta.

4 Drain the pasta, reserve $1/2$ cup of the pasta cooking liquid, return the pasta to the stockpot and toss with 1 tablespoon of the oil. Cover to keep warm.

5 In a large skillet, sauté the shrimp and the garlic in the remaining oil until the shrimp turn bright pink, a scant 3 minutes.

6 Add the wine, the basil, the thyme and the reserved pasta liquid. Season to taste, cover, reduce the heat and simmer for 2 minutes.

7 Toss the spaghetti with the sauce.

Artichoke Salad

1 Wash and dry the lettuce and tear it into bite-size pieces. Peel and slice the cucumber. Trim and slice the celery. Trim and chop the scallions. Trim and slice the radishes. Combine the ingredients in a large bowl.

2 Drain the artichokes, reserving the oil. Add the artichokes to the salad.

3 Chop the chives. Chop the parsley. In a small bowl, whisk together the artichoke oil, the chives, the parsley, the vinegar, the Worcestershire sauce and the sugar. Season to taste.

4 Toss the salad with the dressing.

Praline Pears

1 Peel, core and halve the pears. Set the halves on individual dessert plates and sprinkle them with the lemon juice to keep them from browning.

2 Place the pecans in a plastic bag and crush them with a mallet.

3 Divide the cream cheese into 8 pieces and roll each piece into a ball. Place the crushed pecans in a shallow bowl and roll the cheese balls in the nuts until they are well coated. Place a cheese ball in each pear half and refrigerate until you are ready to serve.

4 Heat the butter, the cream and the vanilla in a small saucepan. Add the brown sugar and any remaining crushed pecans and cook until the sugar is dissolved and the sauce begins to bubble. Spoon the sauce over the pears.

SEPTEMBER
WEEK TWO

WEEK AT A GLANCE

Monday

PARMESAN VEAL
PORTOFINO POTATOES
OLD-WORLD EGGPLANT
NOT-SO-SOUR GRAPES

Tuesday

CRAZY CABBAGE SOUP
SEPTEMBER SALAD
GRAND PRIZES
CHOCOLATE ABSURDITY

Wednesday

POCKET STEAKS
CORNYCOPIA
HONEY TARTS

Thursday

THE PASTA CAPER
INDISCREET SALAD
SNOWONDERS

Friday

PEKING PERCH
IMPERIAL RICE
SWEET & SOUR CUCUMBERS
FIVE-TREASURE PUDDING

CHECK STAPLES

- ☐ Butter
- ☐ Flour
- ☐ Cornstarch
- ☐ Granulated sugar
- ☐ Dark brown sugar
- ☐ Unsweetened cocoa
- ☐ Marshmallow topping
- ☐ Long-grain white rice
- ☐ Regular or light vegetable oil
- ☐ Regular or light olive oil
- ☐ Sesame oil
- ☐ White wine vinegar
- ☐ Red wine vinegar
- ☐ Apple cider vinegar
- ☐ Lemon juice
- ☐ Grated fresh orange peel
- ☐ Soy sauce
- ☐ Honey
- ☐ Golden raisins
- ☐ Grated Parmesan cheese
- ☐ Seasoned bread crumbs
- ☐ Dried basil
- ☐ Bay leaves
- ☐ Bouquet Garni
- ☐ Italian seasoning
- ☐ Dry mustard
- ☐ Ground nutmeg
- ☐ Dried oregano
- ☐ Dried tarragon
- ☐ Dried thyme
- ☐ Pepper
- ☐ Salt
- ☐ Almond extract
- ☐ Vanilla extract

SHOPPING NOTE

● If you are shopping once a week and cannot arrange to purchase fresh perch on the day you plan to use it, you can purchase *not previously frozen* perch and freeze it, placing it in the refrigerator to thaw the night before you are ready to use it. Or you can purchase *still frozen* perch and keep it frozen until the night before you are ready to use it.

MEAT & POULTRY

$1^1/_2$ pounds ground veal (or chicken) (M)

4 beef cube steaks ($1^1/_4$ pounds) (W)

$^1/_2$ pound regular or light sweet Italian pork or turkey sausage (T)

FISH

$1^1/_4$ pounds perch (or cod) fillets (F)

FRESH PRODUCE

Vegetables

1 pound small new white potatoes (M)

2 medium eggplant (M)

$^1/_4$ pound spinach (T)

20 Chinese snow peas (F)

$^1/_2$ pound mushrooms (F)

2 medium carrots (T)

4 stalks celery—1 (T), 1 (W), 2 (Th)

3 medium onions—1 (M), 1 (T), 1 (W)

1 medium red onion (Th)

2 small red onions—1 (T), 1 (W)

8 scallions (green onions)—4 (Th), 4 (F)

1 head garlic (M, T, Th, F)

1 bunch chives (M, Th)

1 bunch parsley (M, T, Th, F)

1 head Belgian endive (T)

1 small head green cabbage (T)

1 small head lettuce (W)

1 package (16 ounces) mixed salad greens (Th)

$^3/_4$ pound tomatoes—$^1/_2$ pound (M), $^1/_4$ pound (W)

2 large cucumbers (F)

1 small cucumber (W)

2 medium green bell peppers (M)

1 small green bell pepper (W)

Fruit

1 medium red apple (T)

1 pound seedless green grapes (M)

2 medium white grapefruit (Th)

CANS, JARS & BOTTLES

Soup

2 cans ($14^1/_2$ ounces each) beef broth (T)

2 cans ($14^1/_2$ ounces each) vegetable broth (T)

Vegetables

1 medium can ($14^1/_2$ ounces) cut-up tomatoes (Th)

1 can (15 ounces) tomato sauce (M)

1 can (11 ounces) whole kernel corn (W)

Fish

1 small can (6 ounces) solid white tuna (Th)

Oriental Products

1 can (8 ounces) sliced water chestnuts (F)

Fruit

1 can (11 ounces) mandarin oranges (F)

Condiments

1 small jar (2 ounces) diced pimientos (W)

$^1/_2$ cup sweet pickles (W)

3 tablespoons capers (Th)

PACKAGED GOODS

Pasta, Rice & Grains

16 ounces spaghetti (Th)

Baked Goods

2 large pita breads (W)

1 angel food loaf cake (Th)

Nuts & Seeds

$^2/_3$ cup pecan pieces (W)

Dessert & Baking Needs

1 small package (8 ounces) caramels (T)

1 small package (6 ounces) semisweet chocolate chips (T)

1 small package (3.4 ounces) instant banana cream pudding mix (F)

2 ounces white chocolate (Th)

$^1/_4$ cup flaked coconut (Th)

1 small package ($5^1/_2$ ounces) almond cookies (F)

WINES & SPIRITS

$^1/_2$ cup dry white wine (or nonalcoholic white wine or vegetable broth) (Th)

1 tablespoon dry sherry (or nonalcoholic white wine or omit) (F)

2 tablespoons rum (or nonalcoholic Italian chocolate syrup) (T)

REFRIGERATED PRODUCTS

Dairy

2 cups whole milk (F)

$^1/_4$ cup whipping cream (T)

$^3/_4$ cup + 1 tablespoon regular or light sour cream—$^3/_4$ cup (M), 1 tablespoon (Th)

5 eggs—2 (M), 2 (W), 1 (F)

Cheese

$^3/_4$ cup shredded regular or low-fat mozzarella cheese (M)

4 slices regular or low-fat Swiss cheese (W)

Juice

$^1/_3$ cup orange juice (F)

Deli

1 small package (5) large refrigerator buttermilk biscuits (T)

16 ounces spinach ravioli (or frozen) (T)

FROZEN GOODS

Desserts

4 individual pastry shells (W)

2 small containers (8 ounces each) frozen whipped topping—1 (T), 1 (F)

1 pint French vanilla ice cream (Th)

MONDAY

Parmesan Veal

$1^1/_2$ pounds ground veal (or chicken)
Seasoning to taste
$^1/_3$ cup flour
2 eggs
2 tablespoons water
1 cup seasoned bread crumbs
$^1/_2$ teaspoon dried oregano
$^1/_4$ cup regular or light olive oil
1 can (15 ounces) tomato sauce
$^3/_4$ cup shredded regular or low–fat
    mozzarella cheese
$^1/_2$ cup grated Parmesan cheese

Portofino Potatoes

1 tablespoon fresh parsley (when chopped)
1 tablespoon fresh chives (when chopped)
1 pound small new white potatoes
2 tablespoons butter
Seasoning to taste

Old-World Eggplant

2 medium eggplant
$^1/_2$ pound fresh tomatoes
2 medium green bell peppers
1 medium onion
2 cloves garlic
2 tablespoons fresh parsley (when chopped)
4 tablespoons olive oil
3 tablespoons lemon juice
1 teaspoon dried tarragon
$^1/_2$ teaspoon dried oregano

Not-So-Sour Grapes

1 pound seedless green grapes
$^3/_4$ cup regular or light sour cream
$^1/_2$ teaspoon ground nutmeg
$^1/_2$ teaspoon almond extract
$^1/_2$ cup dark brown sugar

EQUIPMENT

Large covered skillet	2 small bowls
Large skillet	3 shallow bowls
Large covered saucepan	Assorted kitchen knives
9x13-inch glass baking dish	Measuring cups and spoons
8x8-inch glass baking dish	Assorted cooking utensils
Cookie sheet	Whisk
	Vegetable brush

COUNTDOWN

1 Assemble the ingredients and equipment
2 Do Steps 1–3 of the *Not–So–Sour Grapes*
3 Do Steps 1–5 of the *Parmesan Veal*
4 Do Steps 1–2 of the *Portofino Potatoes*
5 Do Steps 1–2 of the *Old–World Eggplant*
6 Do Step 3 of the *Portofino Potatoes*
7 Do Steps 2–5 of the *Old–World Eggplant*
8 Do Step 4 of the *Portofino Potatoes*

Parmesan Veal

1 Divide the veal into 8 patties and season them to taste.

2 Spread the flour in a shallow bowl. Beat the eggs with the water in a second shallow bowl. Combine the bread crumbs and the oregano in a third shallow bowl and season to taste.

3 Dredge the patties in the flour, dip them in the egg and coat them with the bread crumb mixture. Pat the crumbs gently to help them stick.

4 Heat the oil in a large skillet. Cook the patties, turning, until they are browned on both sides, 5 to 7 minutes. Remove them to a 9x13-inch glass baking dish.

5 Preheat the oven to 350°F. Spoon the tomato sauce over the veal. Top with the mozzarella cheese and sprinkle with the Parmesan cheese. Bake until the cheese is bubbly, about 20 minutes.

Portofino Potatoes

1 Bring water to a boil in a large saucepan.

2 Chop the parsley. Chop the chives. Scrub the potatoes and cook them in the boiling water for 10 minutes.

3 Drain the potatoes, run them under cold water to cool and quarter them.

4 Melt the butter in the saucepan. Add the parsley, the chives and the potatoes and sauté until the potatoes are lightly browned, about 5 minutes. Season to taste and cover to keep warm.

Old-World Eggplant

1 Preheat the broiler. Cut each eggplant in half lengthwise. Place the 4 halves, cut side down, on an ungreased cookie sheet and broil until the skins blacken and are crisp, 8 to 10 minutes.

2 Chop the tomatoes. Seed and chop the bell peppers. Peel and chop the onion. Peel and mince the garlic. Chop the parsley.

3 Heat 2 tablespoons of the oil in a large covered skillet. Sauté the onion and the garlic for 3 minutes. Add the bell pepper and sauté for 3 minutes more. Add the tomato and heat through.

4 Rub the skin off the eggplant halves with damp paper towels. Chop the pulp. Add the pulp to the skillet and heat through.

5 In a small bowl, combine the parsley with the lemon juice, the remaining oil, the tarragon and the oregano. Toss the dressing with the eggplant mixture. Remove the skillet from the heat and cover to keep warm.

Not-So-Sour Grapes

1 Preheat the broiler.

2 Wash and separate the grapes, drain them on paper towels and place them in an 8x8-inch glass baking dish. In a small bowl, combine the sour cream, the nutmeg and the almond extract. Spread the mixture over the grapes. Sprinkle them with the brown sugar, place them under the broiler and broil until the sour cream mixture is bubbly, 3 to 4 minutes.

3 Remove the grapes from the oven and refrigerate until you are ready to serve.

TUESDAY

Crazy Cabbage Soup

$1/2$ pound regular or light sweet Italian pork
    or turkey sausage
1 medium onion
2 cloves garlic
2 medium carrots
2 tablespoons fresh parsley (when chopped)
1 small head green cabbage
2 tablespoons regular or light olive oil
2 cans ($14^1/2$ ounces) beef broth
2 cans ($14^1/2$ ounces) vegetable broth
1 bay leaf
1 teaspoon Italian seasoning
Seasoning to taste
16 ounces spinach ravioli, fresh or frozen
$1/2$ cup grated Parmesan cheese

September Salad

1 medium red apple
1 stalk celery
1 small red onion
$1/4$ pound fresh spinach
1 head Belgian endive
3 tablespoons regular or light olive oil
1 teaspoon sugar
1 tablespoon white wine vinegar
1 tablespoon lemon juice
Seasoning to taste

Grand Prizes

1 small package (5) large refrigerator
    buttermilk biscuits
2 tablespoons butter
1 teaspoon dried thyme

Chocolate Absurdity

1 small package (8 ounces) caramels
1 small package (6 ounces) semisweet
    chocolate chips
$1/4$ cup whipping cream
2 tablespoons rum (or nonalcoholic Italian
    chocolate syrup)
$1/4$ cup unsweetened cocoa
1 small container (8 ounces) frozen whipped
    topping

EQUIPMENT

Dutch oven	Assorted cooking
Double boiler	utensils
Cookie sheet	Whisk
2 large bowls	Pastry brush
Small bowl	Vegetable peeler
Assorted kitchen knives	Vegetable grater
Measuring cups and	
spoons	

COUNTDOWN

1 Assemble the ingredients and equipment
2 Do Step 1 of the *Chocolate Absurdity*
3 Do Steps 1–2 of the *September Salad*
4 Do Step 1 of the *Grand Prizes*
5 Do Step 2 of the *Chocolate Absurdity*
6 Do Steps 2–3 of the *Grand Prizes*
7 Do Steps 1–5 of the *Crazy Cabbage Soup*
8 Do Step 3 of the *Grand Prizes*
9 Do Step 6 of the *Crazy Cabbage Soup*
10 Do Step 3 of the *September Salad*

Crazy Cabbage Soup

1 Cut the sausage into $1/2$-inch slices and sauté the slices in a Dutch oven until they are well browned, about 10 minutes.

2 Peel and chop the onion. Peel and mince the garlic. Peel and grate the carrots. Chop the parsley. Grate the cabbage.

3 Drain the sausage and set aside. Heat the oil in the Dutch oven and sauté the onion, the garlic and the carrots until the onion is translucent, about 5 minutes.

4 Add the beef broth, the vegetable broth, the cabbage, the parsley, the bay leaf and the Italian seasoning to the Dutch oven. Return the sausage. Season to taste and bring the mixture to a boil.

5 Add the ravioli, reduce the heat, and simmer until the ravioli is tender, 10 to 12 minutes.

6 Remove the bay leaf and sprinkle the soup with the Parmesan cheese.

September Salad

1 Core and chop the apple. Trim and slice the celery. Peel and thinly slice the red onion. Wash and dry the spinach and tear it into bite-size pieces. Trim, core and julienne the Belgian endive. Combine the ingredients in a large bowl.

2 In a small bowl, whisk together the oil, the sugar, the vinegar and the lemon juice. Season to taste.

3 Toss the salad with the dressing.

Grand Prizes

1 Preheat the oven 375°F.

2 Open the biscuits onto an ungreased cookie sheet.

3 Melt the butter. Mix in the thyme. Brush the biscuits with the butter mixture and bake until they are golden, 12 to 14 minutes.

Chocolate Absurdity

1 Heat the caramels, the chocolate chips and the cream in the top of a double boiler over hot water, stirring, until the caramels are melted and the mixture is smooth, about 10 minutes. Stir in the rum, then pour the mixture into a large bowl and let it cool.

2 Fold the cocoa into the whipped topping. Fold the topping into the caramel mixture, spoon it into individual dessert dishes, and refrigerate for at least 20 minutes.

WEDNESDAY

Pocket Steaks

1 medium onion
1 small cucumber
$^1/_4$ pound fresh tomatoes
1 small head lettuce
2 large pita breads
2 tablespoons regular or light olive oil
1 tablespoon red wine vinegar
$^1/_2$ teaspoon Bouquet Garni
Seasoning to taste
4 beef cube steaks (1$^1/_2$ pounds)
4 slices regular or low-fat Swiss cheese

Cornycopia

1 can (11 ounces) whole kernel corn
1 small jar (2 ounces) diced pimientos
1 stalk celery
1 small red onion
$^1/_2$ cup sweet pickles
1 small green bell pepper
$^1/_4$ cup regular or light vegetable oil
2 tablespoons red wine vinegar
$^1/_2$ teaspoon sugar
2 tablespoons lemon juice
Seasoning to taste
1 teaspoon cornstarch dissolved in 1
     tablespoon cold water
$^1/_2$ teaspoon dry mustard

Honey Tarts

4 frozen individual pastry shells
2 eggs
$^1/_2$ cup honey
$^1/_4$ cup dark brown sugar
$^1/_4$ teaspoon salt
1 teaspoon vanilla extract
$^2/_3$ cup pecan pieces

EQUIPMENT

Electric hand mixer	Measuring cups and
Large skillet	spoons
Small saucepan	Assorted cooking
2 cookie sheets	utensils
3 large bowls	Wire rack
Small bowl	Whisk
Assorted kitchen knives	Vegetable peeler

COUNTDOWN

IN THE MORNING:
  Do Step 1 of the *Honey Tarts*
BEFORE DINNER:
  1 Assemble the remaining ingredients and equipment
  2 Do Steps 2–3 of the *Honey Tarts*
  3 Do Steps 1–3 of the *Cornycopia*
  4 Do Step 4 of the *Honey Tarts*
  5 Do Steps 1–5 of the *Pocket Steaks*

Pocket Steaks

1 Preheat the oven to 200°F. Peel and slice the onion. Peel and chop the cucumber. Chop the tomatoes. Wash, dry and shred the lettuce. Combine the ingredients in a large bowl.

2 Cut the pita bread rounds in half crosswise, place them on an ungreased cookie sheet and warm them in the oven.

3 In a small bowl, combine 1 tablespoon of the oil with the vinegar and the Bouquet Garni. Season to taste.

4 In a large skillet, heat the remaining oil and sauté the onion until limp but not brown, about 5 minutes. Push the onions to the side of the skillet and sauté the beef steaks until the meat loses its pinkness, 2 to 3 minutes. Turn the steaks, top them with the cheese, and cook them for another 2 to 3 minutes.

5 Place a steak and some of the onions inside each warm pita half. Toss the dressing with the salad and spoon portions of it into the pita breads over the meat and the onions.

Cornycopia

1 Drain the corn well. Drain the pimientos. Trim and chop the celery. Peel and chop the red onion. Trim and chop the pickles. Seed and chop the bell pepper. Combine the ingredients in a large bowl.

2 In a small saucepan, combine the oil, the vinegar, the sugar and the lemon juice. Season to taste. Bring the mixture to a boil, and stir in the cornstarch mixture and the dry mustard. Reduce the heat and whisk until the sauce is smooth and slightly thick.

3 Pour the sauce over the salad and toss to combine. Serve at room temperature.

Honey Tarts

1 Set the pastry shells out to thaw.

2 Preheat the oven to 400°F.

3 In a large bowl, beat the eggs until frothy. Blend in the honey, the brown sugar, the salt, the vanilla and the pecans. Pour the mixture into the pastry shells and place them on an ungreased cookie sheet. Bake until the filling is set, 15 to 18 minutes.

4 Remove the tarts and set them on a wire rack to cool until you are ready to serve.

THURSDAY

The Pasta Caper

1 small can (6 ounces) solid white tuna
4 scallions (green onions)
3 cloves garlic
2 tablespoons fresh parsley (when chopped)
2 tablespoons capers
16 ounces spaghetti
1 tablespoon butter
2 tablespoons regular or light olive oil
1 medium can ($14^1/2$ ounces) cut-up tomatoes
$^1/_2$ cup dry white wine (or nonalcoholic white
    wine or vegetable broth)
2 teaspoons dried basil
1 teaspoon dried oregano
1 teaspoon Italian seasoning
Seasoning to taste
$^1/_2$ cup grated Parmesan cheese

Indiscreet Salad

1 package (16 ounces) mixed salad greens
2 medium white grapefruit
1 medium red onion
2 stalks celery
2 tablespoons fresh chives (when chopped)
3 tablespoons regular or light vegetable oil
2 tablespoons red wine vinegar
1 tablespoon regular or light sour cream
$^1/_2$ teaspoon sugar
Seasoning to taste

Snowonders

2 ounces white chocolate
1 angel food loaf cake
1 pint French vanilla ice cream
$^1/_2$ cup marshmallow topping
$^1/_4$ cup flaked coconut for garnish

EQUIPMENT

Stockpot	Assorted cooking
Large skillet	utensils
Large bowl	Whisk
Small bowl	Ice cream scoop
Colander	Cheese grater
Assorted kitchen knives	
Measuring cups and	
spoons	

COUNTDOWN

1 Assemble the ingredients and equipment
2 Do Step 1 of the *Indiscreet Salad*
3 Do Step 1 of *The Pasta Caper*
4 Do Step 1 of the *Snowonders*
5 Do Steps 2–5 of *The Pasta Caper*
6 Do Step 2 of the *Indiscreet Salad*
7 Do Step 6 of *The Pasta Caper*
8 Do Step 2 of the *Snowonders*

The Pasta Caper

1 Bring water to a boil in a stockpot.

2 Drain and chunk the tuna. Trim and chop the scallions. Peel and mince the garlic. Chop the parsley. Rinse the capers.

3 Cook the pasta in the boiling water until it is almost tender, 2 to 3 minutes if you are using fresh pasta and 6 to 7 minutes if you are using dried pasta.

4 Melt the butter with 1 tablespoon of the oil in a large skillet. Add the scallions and the garlic and sauté for 2 minutes. Add the tomatoes, the wine, the capers, the basil, the oregano and the Italian seasoning, and cook until the sauce is slightly reduced, 3 to 5 minutes.

5 Drain the pasta, return it to the stockpot, toss it with the remaining olive oil and cover to keep warm.

6 Add the tuna and the parsley to the skillet. Season to taste and stir to mix well. Toss the pasta with the sauce, and sprinkle with the Parmesan cheese.

Indiscreet Salad

1 Rinse and dry the salad greens. Peel and section the grapefruit, reserving 2 tablespoons of the juice. Peel and thinly slice the red onion. Trim and thinly slice the celery. Combine the ingredients in a large bowl and refrigerate until you are ready to serve.

2 Chop the chives. In a small bowl, whisk together the reserved grapefruit juice, the chives, the oil, the vinegar, the sour cream and the sugar. Season to taste and toss the salad with the dressing.

Snowonders

1 Using a cheese grater, grate the white chocolate.

2 Slice the cake and arrange the slices on individual plates. Top the slices with scoops of ice cream and a dollop of marshmallow topping, and sprinkle with the white chocolate and the coconut.

FRIDAY

Peking Perch

20 Chinese snow peas
1/2 pound fresh mushrooms
2 scallions (green onions)
1 clove garlic
1/2 cup cornstarch
1 teaspoon grated fresh orange peel
Seasoning to taste
1 egg
1 1/4 pounds perch (or cod) fillets
4 1/2 tablespoons regular or light olive oil
1/3 cup orange juice
1 tablespoon soy sauce
1 teaspoon sesame oil

Imperial Rice

1 can (8 ounces) sliced water chestnuts
2 scallions (green onions)
2 tablespoons fresh parsley (when chopped)
1 cup long-grain white rice
2 cups water
2 tablespoons soy sauce
1 tablespoon dry sherry (or nonalcoholic white
    wine or omit)

Sweet & Sour Cucumbers

2 large cucumbers
1/2 teaspoon salt
2 tablespoons dark brown sugar
2 tablespoons apple cider vinegar
1/2 teaspoon soy sauce
1/2 teaspoon sesame oil

Five-Treasure Pudding

1 small package (5 1/2 ounces) almond cookies
1 small container (8 ounces) frozen whipped
    topping
1 small package (3.4 ounces) instant banana
    cream pudding mix
2 cups whole milk
1 can (11 ounces) mandarin oranges
1 cup golden raisins

EQUIPMENT

Electric hand mixer	Assorted kitchen knives
Wok and wok utensils	Measuring cups and
Double boiler	spoons
2 medium bowls	Assorted cooking
Small bowl	utensils
2 shallow bowls	Whisk
Strainer	Vegetable peeler

COUNTDOWN

1 Assemble the ingredients and equipment
2 Do Step 1 of the *Imperial Rice*
3 Do Step 1 of the *Sweet & Sour Cucumbers*
4 Do Steps 1–3 of the *Five-Treasure Pudding*
5 Do Steps 1–2 of the *Peking Perch*
6 Do Step 2 of the *Sweet & Sour Cucumbers*
7 Do Steps 3–6 of the *Peking Perch*
8 Do Step 2 of the *Imperial Rice*

Peking Perch

1 Stem and string the Chinese snow peas. Wash, pat dry, trim, and slice the mushrooms. Trim and slice the scallions. Peel and mince the garlic.

2 In a shallow bowl, combine the cornstarch and the orange peel. Season to taste. In a second shallow bowl, beat the egg. Dip the perch fillets in the egg and then dredge them in the seasoned cornstarch to coat. Shake off any excess.

3 Heat 1 tablespoon of the oil in a wok. Add the snow peas and stir-fry until they are bright green and crisp-tender, about 1 minute. Remove the snow peas and reserve them.

4 Heat another 1½ tablespoons of the oil in the wok. Add the mushrooms, the scallions and the garlic and stir-fry until the mushrooms are lightly browned, about 3 minutes. Remove the mushrooms and reserve them.

5 Heat the remaining oil in the wok, swirling to coat the sides. Add the fish fillets, arranging them up the sides of the wok without overlapping. Fry the fillets, turning them once, until they are golden brown on both sides and opaque in the middle, 5 to 7 minutes.

6 Return the vegetables to the wok. Arrange the fish over the vegetables. Add the orange juice, the soy sauce and the sesame oil. Season to taste, cover and cook until heated through, about 1 minute.

Imperial Rice

1 Drain and chop the water chestnuts. Trim and chop the scallions. Chop the parsley. Combine the rice, the water, the water chestnuts, the scallions, the parsley, the soy sauce and the sherry in the top of a double boiler. Bring water to a boil in the bottom of the double boiler, reduce the heat, cover and simmer until all the liquid is absorbed and the rice is tender, 30 to 40 minutes.

2 Fluff the rice before serving.

Sweet & Sour Cucumbers

1 Peel and slice the cucumbers, put them in a medium bowl, toss them with the salt and let them stand for 15 minutes.

2 Drain the cucumbers. In a small bowl, whisk together the brown sugar, the vinegar, the soy sauce and the oil until the sugar is dissolved. Toss the mixture with the cucumbers and refrigerate until you are ready to serve.

Five-Treasure Pudding

1 Crumble the cookies and fold the crumbs into the whipped topping.

2 In a medium bowl, beat the pudding mix and the milk until well blended.

3 Drain the mandarin oranges. In 4 parfait glasses, layer the pudding, the mandarin oranges and the whipped topping mixture. Sprinkle with the raisins and refrigerate for at least 20 minutes.

SEPTEMBER
WEEK THREE

WEEK AT A GLANCE

Monday

SIMPLE SALMON
SILLY BEANS
ACCOMMODATING SLAW
PEACH TUMBLE

Tuesday

LUCKY EWE
UNIVERSAL NOODLES
GO IN PEAS
POUND CAKEWICH

Wednesday

CRISPY CRITTERS
BARELY BARLEY
CRAZY MIXED-UP SALAD
NUTTY TOP-OFFS

Thursday

WHITE FISH WIZARDRY
POTATO SORCERY
BEWITCHING BROCCOLI
HAPPY FACE PUDDING

Friday

NITTY-GRITTY ZITI
SOMEBODY'S SALAD
BISCUIT DIPS
PIE IN THE SKY

CHECK STAPLES

- ☐ Butter
- ☐ Granulated sugar
- ☐ Dark brown sugar
- ☐ Corn syrup
- ☐ Marshmallow topping
- ☐ Multicolored sprinkles
- ☐ Regular or light vegetable oil
- ☐ Regular or light olive oil
- ☐ White wine vinegar
- ☐ Red wine vinegar
- ☐ Tarragon vinegar
- ☐ Lemon juice
- ☐ Grated fresh lemon peel
- ☐ Grated fresh orange peel
- ☐ Worcestershire sauce
- ☐ Tabasco sauce
- ☐ Dijon mustard
- ☐ Regular or low-fat mayonnaise
- ☐ Honey
- ☐ Seasoned bread crumbs
- ☐ Ground allspice
- ☐ Celery seeds
- ☐ Ground cinnamon
- ☐ Ground cumin
- ☐ Curry powder
- ☐ Garlic powder
- ☐ Dried marjoram
- ☐ Instant minced onion
- ☐ Dry mustard
- ☐ Ground nutmeg
- ☐ Red pepper flakes
- ☐ Dried sage
- ☐ Dried thyme
- ☐ Pepper
- ☐ Salt
- ☐ Vanilla extract

SHOPPING NOTE

● If you are shopping once a week and cannot arrange to purchase fresh seafood on the day you plan to use it, you can purchase *not previously frozen* seafood and freeze it, placing it in the refrigerator to thaw the night before you are ready to use it. Or you can purchase *still frozen* seafood and keep it frozen until the night before you are ready to use it.

MEAT & POULTRY

2 pounds lean boneless lamb (T)
2 Cornish game hens (W)

FISH

4 salmon fillets (1½ pounds) (M)
4 white fish fillets (1¼ pounds) (Th)

FRESH PRODUCE

Vegetables

3 medium red potatoes (M)
1 pound small new white potatoes (Th)
1 pound green beans (M)
1 large bunch broccoli (Th)
½ pound spinach (F)
1 small carrot (W)
3 stalks celery—1 (W), 2 (F)
1 medium onion (M)
1 small onion (W)
1 medium red onion (F)
1 small red onion (T)
2 small leeks (Th)
1 head garlic (M, Th, F)
1 bunch dill (M, W, F)
1 bunch chives (M, W, F)
1 bunch parsley (M, T, Th)
1 small (or half) head green cabbage (M)
1 medium head lettuce (F)
1 package (16 ounces) mixed salad greens (W)
1 pint cherry tomatoes (F)
1 medium cucumber (F)
1 small daikon radish (or small bunch radishes) (F)

Fruit

1 tart green apple (W)
3 medium peaches (M)
2 medium pears (T)

CANS, JARS & BOTTLES

Soup

1 can (10¾ ounces) chicken broth (W)

Vegetables

1 large can (28 ounces) cut-up tomatoes (F)
1 small can (6 ounces) tomato paste (T, F)
1 jar (6½ ounces) marinated artichoke hearts (W)

Fruit

1 small can (8 ounces) crushed pineapple (M)

Juice

¼ cup clam juice (Th)

PACKAGED GOODS

Pasta, Rice & Grains

8 ounces broad egg noodles (T)
12 ounces ziti (F)
¾ cup quick-cooking barley (W)
½ cup graham cracker crumbs (M)

Nuts & Seeds

¼ cup pecan pieces (W)

Dessert & Baking Needs

1 small package (3.4 ounces) instant coconut cream pudding mix (Th)
8 M&M plain candies (Th)
4 M&M peanut candies (Th)
1 small package (6 ounces) butterscotch chips (T)
1 strip red licorice (Th)
½ cup flaked coconut (Th)
1 prepared 9-inch chocolate pie shell (F)

WINES & SPIRITS

½ cup dry white wine (or nonalcoholic white wine or chicken broth) (W)
½ cup dry white wine (or nonalcoholic white wine or clam juice) (Th)
½ cup dry sherry (or nonalcoholic white wine or orange juice) (M)

REFRIGERATED PRODUCTS

Dairy

2 cups whole milk (Th)
2 tablespoons whole or low-fat milk (W)
½ cup half-and-half (Th)

Cheese

1 small package (3 ounces) cream cheese (F)

Juice

⅓ cup orange juice (M)

Deli

2 slices bacon (T)
1 package (10) refrigerator biscuits (F)

FROZEN GOODS

Vegetables

1 package (9 ounces) green peas (T)

Desserts

1 pound cake (T)
1 pint vanilla ice cream (W)
1 quart chocolate frozen yogurt (F)
1 small container (8 ounces) frozen whipped topping (T)

MONDAY

Simple Salmon

3 medium red potatoes
1 medium onion
1 clove garlic
2 tablespoons fresh parsley (when chopped)
1 tablespoon butter
2 tablespoons regular or light vegetable oil
$^1/_3$ cup orange juice
$^1/_2$ cup dry sherry (or nonalcoholic white wine
    or additional orange juice)
4 salmon fillets (1$^1/_2$ pounds)
1 teaspoon grated fresh orange peel
Seasoning to taste

Silly Beans

1 pound green beans
1 tablespoon fresh dill (when chopped)
1 tablespoon fresh chives (when chopped)
1 tablespoon butter
$^1/_2$ teaspoon ground allspice
Seasoning to taste

Accommodating Slaw

1 small (or half) head green cabbage
1 small can (8 ounces) crushed pineapple
$^1/_3$ cup regular or low-fat mayonnaise
1 tablespoon white wine vinegar
Seasoning to taste

Peach Tumble

3 medium peaches
6 tablespoons dark brown sugar
$^1/_2$ teaspoon vanilla extract
$^1/_2$ cup graham cracker crumbs
$^1/_4$ teaspoon ground cinnamon
$^1/_4$ teaspoon ground nutmeg
3 tablespoons softened butter

EQUIPMENT

Large covered skillet	Measuring cups and
Medium saucepan	spoons
9x5-inch loaf pan	Assorted cooking
Steamer insert	utensils
Large bowl	Vegetable brush
Medium bowl	Vegetable grater
Small bowl	Whisk
Assorted kitchen knives	

COUNTDOWN

1 Assemble the ingredients and equipment
2 Do Steps 1–3 of the *Peach Tumble*
3 Do Steps 1–2 of the *Accommodating Slaw*
4 Do Steps 1–4 of the *Simple Salmon*
5 Do Steps 1–4 of the *Silly Beans*

Simple Salmon

1 Scrub and thinly slice the potatoes. Peel and thinly slice the onion. Peel and mince the garlic. Chop the parsley.

2 Melt the butter with the oil in a large skillet. Add the potatoes, the onion and the garlic and cook, stirring, until the potatoes are translucent, 4 to 6 minutes. Add the orange juice and the sherry, cover and cook for 10 minutes.

3 Wash and pat dry the salmon fillets and remove the skin, if necessary.

4 Arrange the salmon on top of the potatoes. Sprinkle with the parsley and the orange peel. Season to taste. Reduce the heat, cover and cook until the fish is opaque throughout and almost all the liquid is absorbed, 8 to 10 minutes.

Silly Beans

1 Bring a small amount of water to a boil in a medium saucepan.

2 Wash, trim and string the green beans. Place the steamer insert in the saucepan and steam the beans until they are crisp-tender, 4 to 5 minutes.

3 Chop the dill. Chop the chives.

4 Drain the beans and melt the butter in the saucepan. Return the beans to the saucepan, sprinkle with the dill, the chives and the allspice. Season to taste and toss to coat.

Accommodating Slaw

1 Grate the cabbage into a large bowl. Drain the pineapple, reserving the juice. Add the pineapple to the cabbage and toss to combine.

2 In a small bowl, combine the mayonnaise, the vinegar and the reserved pineapple juice. Season to taste and toss the dressing with the cabbage mixture until thoroughly blended. Refrigerate until you are ready to serve.

Peach Tumble

1 Preheat the oven to 375°F.

2 Peel, pit and slice the peaches. In a medium bowl, toss the peaches with the brown sugar and the vanilla and turn them into a 9x5-inch loaf pan.

3 In the same bowl, combine the graham cracker crumbs, the cinnamon, the nutmeg and the softened butter. Sprinkle the topping evenly over the peaches and bake until the peaches are soft and the top is bubbly, 20 to 25 minutes.

TUESDAY

Lucky Ewe

2 pounds lean boneless lamb
Seasoning to taste
3 tablespoons regular or light olive oil
$^1/_2$ small can (6 ounces) tomato paste*
1 cup water
$^1/_2$ cup red wine vinegar
2 teaspoons dark brown sugar

Universal Noodles

8 ounces broad egg noodles
1 tablespoon fresh parsley (when chopped)
2 tablespoons butter
$^1/_8$ teaspoon ground cumin
$^1/_8$ teaspoon curry powder
Seasoning to taste

Go in Peas

1 package (9 ounces) frozen green peas
2 slices bacon
1 small red onion
Seasoning to taste

Pound Cakewich

1 frozen pound cake
2 medium pears
1 small package (6 ounces) butterscotch chips
1 small container (8 ounces) frozen whipped
    topping
1 tablespoon grated fresh orange peel

*Reserve the balance of the can for use on Friday.

EQUIPMENT

Large covered skillet	Assorted kitchen knives
Medium skillet	Measuring cups and
Large covered	spoons
saucepan	Assorted cooking
Colander	utensils

COUNTDOWN

IN THE MORNING:
  Do Step 1 of the *Pound Cakewich*
BEFORE DINNER:
  1 Assemble the remaining ingredients and
     equipment
  2 Do Steps 2–4 of the *Pound Cakewich*
  3 Do Step 1 of the *Go in Peas*
  4 Do Steps 1–3 of the *Lucky Ewe*
  5 Do Step 1 of the *Universal Noodles*
  6 Do Steps 2–4 of the *Go in Peas*
  7 Do Step 4 of the *Lucky Ewe*
  8 Do Steps 2–4 of the *Universal Noodles*
  9 Do Step 5 of the *Go in Peas*

Lucky Ewe

1 Trim any excess fat from the lamb and cut the meat into 1-inch cubes. Season to taste.

2 Heat the oil in a large skillet, and cook the meat until it is browned on all sides, about 5 minutes.

3 Add the tomato paste, the water, the vinegar and the brown sugar. Bring the mixture to a boil, reduce the heat, cover and simmer until the lamb is fork-tender, about 20 minutes.

4 Uncover the lamb, return the liquid to a boil and cook until the sauce begins to thicken, about 5 minutes.

Universal Noodles

1 Bring water to a boil in a large saucepan.

2 Cook the noodles in the boiling water until they are almost tender, 3 to 5 minutes.

3 Chop the parsley.

4 Drain the noodles, return them to the saucepan and toss them with the butter, the parsley, the cumin and the curry. Season to taste and cover to keep warm.

Go in Peas

1 Set the peas out to thaw.

2 Chop the bacon and sauté it in a medium skillet until it is crisp, about 5 minutes.

3 Drain the bacon on a paper towel, reserving 2 teaspoons of the drippings in the skillet.

4 Peel and chop the red onion and sauté it in the bacon drippings until golden, about 10 minutes.

5 Add the peas and the bacon to the onions, season to taste and toss to heat through.

Pound Cakewich

1 Set the pound cake out to thaw.

2 Cut the pound cake in half horizontally.

3 Peel, core and chop the pears. Fold the butterscotch chips into the whipped topping.

4 Lay the pears over the bottom layer of the cake. Spread with a third of the whipped topping mixture. Place the second layer of cake over the filling and spread it with the remaining whipped topping mixture, swirling the topping down the sides. Sprinkle with the orange peel and refrigerate until you are ready to serve.

WEDNESDAY

Crispy Critters

2 Cornish game hens
4 tablespoons butter
2 cups seasoned bread crumbs
1 tablespoon dry mustard
Seasoning to taste
1 tablespoon fresh dill (when chopped)
$1/4$ cup chicken broth
$1/2$ cup dry white wine (or nonalcoholic white
    wine or additional chicken broth)
1 tablespoon Dijon mustard

Barely Barley

1 small onion
1 stalk celery
1 small carrot
1 cup chicken broth
$1/2$ cup water
$3/4$ cup quick-cooking barley
1 tablespoon regular or light vegetable oil
$1/2$ teaspoon Worcestershire sauce
1 tablespoon lemon juice
Seasoning to taste

Crazy Mixed-up Salad

1 jar ($6^{1/2}$ ounces) marinated artichokes
1 large tart green apple
2 tablespoons fresh chives (when chopped)
1 package (16 ounces) mixed salad greens
3 tablespoons white wine vinegar
$1/2$ teaspoon sugar
$1/4$ teaspoon Worcestershire sauce
Seasoning to taste

Nutty Top-offs

3 tablespoons corn syrup
2 tablespoons whole or low-fat milk
2 teaspoons butter
$1/4$ cup pecan pieces
$1/2$ teaspoon vanilla extract
1 pint vanilla ice cream

EQUIPMENT

Medium covered skillet	Measuring cups and
Medium covered	spoons
saucepan	Assorted cooking
2 small saucepans	utensils
9x13-inch baking pan	Whisk
Large bowl	Vegetable peeler
Small bowl	Vegetable grater
2 shallow bowls	Ice cream scoop
Assorted kitchen knives	

COUNTDOWN

1 Assemble the ingredients and equipment
2 Do Steps 1–4 of the *Crispy Critters*
3 Do Step 1 of the *Nutty Top-offs*
4 Do Steps 1–2 of the *Barely Barley*
5 Do Steps 1–2 of the *Crazy Mixed-up Salad*
6 Do Step 5 of the *Crispy Critters*
7 Do Step 3 of the *Barely Barley*
8 Do Step 3 of the *Crazy Mixed-up Salad*
9 Do Step 2 of the *Nutty Top-offs*

Crispy Critters

1 Preheat the oven to 425°F. Grease a 9x13-inch baking pan.

2 Split the game hens in half lengthwise.

3 Melt the butter and turn it into a shallow bowl. Combine the bread crumbs and the dry mustard in a second shallow bowl and season to taste.

4 Chop the dill. Dip the hens in the melted butter and roll them in the bread crumb mixture. Place the hens in the baking pan, skin side up, sprinkle them with the dill and bake them until well browned, about 30 minutes.

5 In a small saucepan, combine the broth, the wine, and the Dijon mustard. Bring the mixture to a boil and cook until the sauce is reduced to about ½ cup. Spoon the sauce over the hens.

Barely Barley

1 Peel and chop the onion. Trim and chop the celery. Peel and grate the carrot.

2 In a medium saucepan, bring the broth and the water to a boil. Stir in the barley, reduce the heat and simmer, covered, until it is tender, 10 to 12 minutes.

3 Heat the oil in a medium skillet, and sauté the onion, the celery and the carrot for 3 minutes. Drain the barley and add it to the vegetables. Add the Worcestershire sauce and the lemon juice. Season to taste and cover to keep warm.

Crazy Mixed-up Salad

1 Drain the artichoke hearts, reserving the oil in a small bowl. Core and chop the apple. Chop the chives. Rinse and dry the salad greens and place them in a large bowl with the artichokes, the apple and the chives.

2 Whisk the vinegar, the sugar and the Worcestershire sauce into the reserved artichoke oil. Season to taste.

3 Toss the salad with the dressing.

Nutty Top-offs

1 Blend the corn syrup, the milk and the butter in a small saucepan. Cook, stirring, for 2 minutes. Remove the saucepan from the heat, fold in the pecans and the vanilla, and let the mixture cool.

2 Pour the nutty sauce over scoops of ice cream.

THURSDAY

White Fish Wizardry

4 white fish fillets (1$^1/_4$ pounds)
1 clove garlic
2 small leeks
3 tablespoons regular or light olive oil
$^1/_4$ cup clam juice
$^1/_2$ cup dry white wine (or nonalcoholic white
    wine or additional clam juice)
1 tablespoon honey
1 tablespoon Dijon mustard
Seasoning to taste
$^1/_2$ cup half-and-half

Potato Sorcery

1 pound small new white potatoes
1 tablespoon fresh parsley (when chopped)
1 tablespoon butter
1 teaspoon grated fresh lemon peel
1$^1/_2$ tablespoons lemon juice

Bewitching Broccoli

1 large bunch broccoli
3 tablespoons regular or light vegetable oil
2 tablespoons tarragon vinegar
1 teaspoon garlic powder
$^1/_2$ teaspoon dried thyme
Seasoning to taste

Happy Face Pudding

2 cups whole milk
1 small package (3.4 ounces) instant coconut
    cream pudding mix
$^1/_2$ cup flaked coconut
8 M&M plain candies
4 M&M peanut candies
1 red licorice strip

EQUIPMENT

Electric hand mixer	Cookie sheet
Large covered skillet	Medium bowl
Medium skillet	Assorted kitchen knives
Large covered saucepan	Measuring cups and spoons
Medium covered saucepan	Assorted cooking utensils
Small saucepan	Vegetable brush

COUNTDOWN

1 Assemble the ingredients and equipment
2 Do Steps 1–3 of the *Happy Face Pudding*
3 Do Steps 1–2 of the *White Fish Wizardry*
4 Do Step 1 of the *Potato Sorcery*
5 Do Step 1 of the *Bewitching Broccoli*
6 Do Steps 3–4 of the *White Fish Wizardry*
7 Do Steps 2–3 of the *Bewitching Broccoli*
8 Do Step 2 of the *Potato Sorcery*
9 Do Step 5 of the *White Fish Wizardry*
10 Do Step 4 of the *Happy Face Pudding*

White Fish Wizardry

1 Wash and pat dry the fish fillets and remove the skin, if necessary.

2 Peel and mince the garlic. Thoroughly wash, trim and chop the leeks, discarding the tough green ends.

3 Heat 1 tablespoon of the oil in a large skillet. Add the fillets in a single layer and cook, turning once, until they are opaque and cooked through, 6 to 8 minutes. Remove the skillet from the heat and cover to keep warm.

4 Heat the remaining oil in a medium skillet. Add the garlic and the leeks and sauté until they are softened, about 5 minutes. Add the clam juice, the wine, the honey and the mustard. Season to taste and mix well. Bring the mixture to a boil and cook for 3 minutes. Add the half-and-half and cook, stirring, until the sauce is reduced by half, about 5 minutes.

5 Spoon the honey mustard sauce over the fish.

Potato Sorcery

1 Scrub and quarter the potatoes. Place them in a large saucepan and cover them with water. Bring the water to a boil and cook until the potatoes are tender, 10 to 12 minutes.

2 Chop the parsley. Drain the potatoes, return them to the saucepan and toss them with the butter, the lemon peel, the lemon juice and the parsley. Cover to keep warm.

Bewitching Broccoli

1 Bring water to a boil in a medium saucepan. Trim the broccoli, cut it into bite-size florets and cook in the boiling water until crisp-tender, 6 to 8 minutes.

2 In a small saucepan, combine the oil, the vinegar, the garlic powder and the thyme. Season to taste. Bring the mixture to a boil and cook for 1 minute.

3 Drain the broccoli, return it to the saucepan and toss it with the dressing. Cover to keep warm.

Happy Face Pudding

1 Preheat the oven to 350°F.

2 In a medium bowl, beat the milk and the pudding mix until well blended. Pour the mixture into individual dessert bowls and refrigerate for at least 20 minutes.

3 Spread the coconut on an ungreased cookie sheet and toast it in the oven until it is golden, 6 to 8 minutes, stirring occasionally.

4 Decorate the pudding to make faces, using the toasted coconut for the hair, the M&M plain candies for the eyes, the M&M peanut candies for the noses, and pieces of red licorice for the mouths.

FRIDAY

Nitty-Gritty Ziti

1 large can (28 ounces) cut-up tomatoes
$^1/_2$ small can (6 ounces) tomato paste reserved
    from Tuesday
$^1/_4$ teaspoon red pepper flakes
Seasoning to taste
12 ounces ziti
$^1/_2$ pound fresh spinach
1 small package (3 ounces) cream cheese
$^1/_2$ teaspoon ground nutmeg

Somebody's Salad

1 medium head lettuce
1 medium red onion
1 medium cucumber
2 stalks celery
1 pint cherry tomatoes
1 small daikon radish (or small bunch
    radishes)
2 tablespoons fresh chives (when chopped)
1 clove garlic
$^1/_2$ teaspoon Dijon mustard
$^1/_4$ teaspoon dried thyme
$^1/_2$ teaspoon dried marjoram
2 tablespoons red wine vinegar
$^1/_2$ teaspoon Tabasco sauce
3 tablespoons regular or light olive oil
$^1/_2$ teaspoon sugar
Seasoning to taste

Biscuit Dips

$^1/_4$ teaspoon fresh dill (when chopped)
$^1/_4$ teaspoon instant minced onion
$^1/_4$ teaspoon dried sage
$^1/_4$ teaspoon celery seeds
2 tablespoons butter
1 package (10) refrigerator biscuits

Pie in the Sky

1 quart chocolate frozen yogurt
1 prepared 9-inch chocolate pie shell
1 cup marshmallow topping
Multicolored sprinkles

EQUIPMENT

Stockpot	Assorted kitchen knives
Medium saucepan	Measuring cups and
Small saucepan	spoons
Cookie sheet	Assorted cooking
Large bowl	utensils
Small bowl	Whisk
Shallow bowl	Vegetable peeler
Colander	

COUNTDOWN

1 Assemble the ingredients and equipment
2 Do Step 1 of the *Pie in the Sky*
3 Do Steps 1–2 of *Somebody's Salad*
4 Do Steps 1–2 of the *Biscuit Dips*
5 Do Step 1 of the *Nitty-Gritty Ziti*
6 Do Step 2 of the *Pie in the Sky*
7 Do Step 3 of the *Biscuit Dips*
8 Do Steps 2–5 of the *Nitty-Gritty Ziti*
9 Do Step 3 of *Somebody's Salad*
10 Do Step 3 of the *Pie in the Sky*

Nitty-Gritty Ziti

1 Bring water to a boil in a stockpot.

2 In a medium saucepan, combine the undrained tomatoes with the tomato paste and the red pepper flakes. Season to taste and heat through, but do not boil.

3 Cook the pasta in the boiling water until it is almost tender, 8 to 10 minutes.

4 Rinse, dry and coarsely chop the spinach.

5 Drain the pasta and return it to the stockpot. Add the spinach, the cream cheese and the nutmeg and simmer, stirring, until the spinach wilts, 1 to 2 minutes. Pour the tomato sauce over the spinach and ziti, season to taste, and stir gently to mix.

Somebody's Salad

1 Wash and dry the lettuce and tear it into bite-size pieces. Peel and thinly slice the red onion. Peel and slice the cucumber. Trim and slice the celery. Halve the cherry tomatoes. Trim and slice the daikon. Chop the chives. Combine the ingredients in a large bowl.

2 Peel and mince the garlic. In a small bowl, whisk together the garlic, the mustard, the thyme, the marjoram, the vinegar, the Tabasco sauce, the oil and the sugar. Season to taste.

3 Toss the salad with the dressing.

Biscuit Dips

1 Preheat the oven to 375°F.

2 Chop the dill. In a shallow bowl, combine the dill, the minced onion, the sage and the celery seeds.

3 Melt the butter in a small saucepan. Separate the biscuits. Dip the tops into the melted butter and then coat them in the herb mix. Place the biscuits on an ungreased cookie sheet and bake until they are golden, 10 to 12 minutes.

Pie in the Sky

1 Set the frozen yogurt out to soften.

2 Pack the softened yogurt as evenly as possible into the pie shell. Place the pie in the freezer for at least 20 minutes.

3 Spread the marshmallow topping over the frozen yogurt and top with the sprinkles.

SEPTEMBER
WEEK FOUR

WEEK AT A GLANCE

Monday

CLASSY CHICKEN
UNUSUAL RICE
REAL COOL CAULIFLOWER
FOREVER AMBER

Tuesday

RAINY DAY SOUP
UMBRELLA BREAD
MUD PUDDLES

Wednesday

PORK & PEPPER STEW
CABBAGE PATCH SALAD
HEIRLOOM CAKE

Thursday

FLASH IN THE PAN
EASY ON THE ORZO
PRETTY PERKY KALE
FROSTED MELON SLICES

Friday

SAUCY SALMON
NEAR EAST RICE
SWEET & SOUR SALAD
HUGS & KISSES PUDDING

CHECK STAPLES

- ☐ Butter
- ☐ Cornstarch
- ☐ Confectioners' sugar
- ☐ Long-grain white rice
- ☐ Brown rice
- ☐ Regular or light vegetable oil
- ☐ Regular or light olive oil
- ☐ Sesame oil
- ☐ Red wine vinegar
- ☐ Apple cider vinegar
- ☐ Rice vinegar
- ☐ Lemon juice
- ☐ Lime juice
- ☐ Grated fresh orange peel
- ☐ Fresh ginger
- ☐ Worcestershire sauce
- ☐ Dijon mustard
- ☐ Soy sauce
- ☐ Honey
- ☐ Candied ginger
- ☐ Ground allspice
- ☐ Dried basil
- ☐ Caraway seeds
- ☐ Ground cinnamon
- ☐ Ground coriander
- ☐ Garlic powder
- ☐ Ground nutmeg
- ☐ Dried sage
- ☐ Sesame seeds
- ☐ Dried tarragon
- ☐ Pepper
- ☐ Salt

SHOPPING NOTE

● If you are shopping once a week and cannot arrange to purchase fresh salmon on the day you plan to use it, you can purchase *not previously frozen* salmon and freeze it, placing it in the refrigerator to thaw the night before you are ready to use it. Or you can purchase *still frozen* salmon and keep it frozen until the night before you are ready to use it.

MEAT & POULTRY

2 pounds lean boneless pork loin (W)

8 chicken thighs (M)

4 boneless, skinless chicken breast halves (Th)

FISH

4 salmon fillets (1½ pounds) (F)

FRESH PRODUCE

Vegetables

1 pound small new white potatoes (W)

1 medium head cauliflower (M)

2 large zucchini (T)

16 Chinese snow peas (F)

¾ pound mushrooms— ½ pound (M), ¼ pound (F)

1 small carrot (M)

3 stalks celery—2 (W), 1 (F)

2 large onions—1 (T), 1 (W)

4 medium onions (T)

1 small onion (Th)

2 medium shallots (M)

7 scallions (green onions)— 4 (M), 3 (F)

1 head garlic (M, W)

1 bunch chives (W, Th)

1 bunch parsley (M, W)

2 ounces bean sprouts (F)

1 pound kale (Th)

1 small (or half) head green cabbage (W)

1 medium head lettuce (F)

½ pound tomatoes (M)

1 large green bell pepper (T)

2 large red bell peppers (W)

Fruit

2 medium sweet red apples (W)

1 large honeydew melon (Th)

CANS, JARS & BOTTLES

Soup

1 can (14½ ounces) beef broth (M)

1 can (14½ ounces) vegetable broth (T)

1 can (14½ ounces) oriental broth (F)

Vegetables

1 large can (28 ounces) cut-up tomatoes (T)

2 medium cans (14½ ounces each) stewed tomatoes (W)

1 can (11 ounces) whole kernel corn (T)

Oriental Products

1 can (8 ounces) sliced water chestnuts (F)

Fruit

1 large can (29 ounces) sliced peaches (M)

Juice

2 cups V-8 juice (T)

PACKAGED GOODS

Pasta, Rice & Grains

8 ounces orzo (Th)

Baked Goods

1 small loaf sliced pumpernickel bread (T)

Fruit

¼ pound dried apricots (F)

Nuts & Seeds

¾ cup pecan pieces (Th)

Dessert & Baking Needs

8 large macaroons (M)

1 small package (3.4 ounces) instant French vanilla pudding mix (F)

1 small package (3.9 ounces) instant chocolate pudding mix (F)

1 cup chocolate-covered raisins (T)

1 small package (1.69 ounces) M&M plain candies (T)

12 Hershey's Hugs (F)

12 Hershey's Kisses (F)

½ cup flaked coconut (W)

WINES & SPIRITS

½ cup dry white wine (or nonalcoholic white wine or beef broth) (M)

½ cup dry white wine (or nonalcoholic white wine or clam juice) (F)

2 tablespoons Grand Marnier liqueur (or nonalcoholic Italian orange syrup) (W)

REFRIGERATED PRODUCTS

Dairy

1 quart whole milk (F)

Whipped cream for garnish (M)

⅔ cup regular or light sour cream (Th)

Cheese

8 slices regular or low-fat Swiss cheese (T)

Juice

3 tablespoons orange juice— 2 (M), 1 (W)

Deli

2 slices bacon (Th)

FROZEN GOODS

Desserts

1 pound cake (W)

1 pint chocolate sherbet (or frozen yogurt) (T)

MONDAY

Classy Chicken

2 medium shallots
$^1/_2$ pound fresh mushrooms
1 clove garlic
$^1/_2$ pound fresh tomatoes
1 tablespoon butter
2 tablespoons regular or light vegetable oil
8 chicken thighs
$^1/_2$ teaspoon dried tarragon
Seasoning to taste
$^1/_2$ cup beef broth
$^1/_2$ cup dry white wine (or nonalcoholic white
    wine or additional beef broth)
1 tablespoon cornstarch dissolved in 2
    tablespoons cold water

Unusual Rice

1 small carrot
1 tablespoon fresh parsley (when chopped)
1 cup long-grain white rice
1$^1/_4$ cups beef broth
$^3/_4$ cup water
$^1/_2$ teaspoon dried sage

Real Cool Cauliflower

1 medium head cauliflower
4 scallions (green onions)
2 teaspoons butter
1 teaspoon lime juice
Seasoning to taste

Forever Amber

8 large coconut macaroons
1 large can (29 ounces) sliced peaches
2 tablespoons orange juice
2 teaspoons grated fresh orange peel
$^1/_2$ teaspoon ground cinnamon
$^1/_8$ teaspoon ground nutmeg
1 tablespoon butter
Whipped cream for garnish

EQUIPMENT

Large covered skillet	Assorted kitchen knives
Medium covered saucepan	Measuring cups and spoons
Double boiler	Assorted cooking utensils
8x8-inch glass baking dish	Vegetable peeler

COUNTDOWN

1 Assemble the ingredients and equipment
2 Do Step 1 of the *Unusual Rice*
3 Do Steps 1–3 of the *Classy Chicken*
4 Do Step 1 of the *Forever Amber*
5 Do Step 4 of the *Classy Chicken*
6 Do Step 2 of the *Forever Amber*
7 Do Steps 1–2 of the *Real Cool Cauliflower*
8 Do Step 5 of the *Classy Chicken*
9 Do Step 2 of the *Unusual Rice*
10 Do Step 3 of the *Forever Amber*

Classy Chicken

1 Peel and chop the shallots. Wash, pat dry, trim and quarter the mushrooms. Peel and mince the garlic. Chop the tomatoes.

2 Melt the butter with the oil in a large skillet. Add the chicken thighs and sauté until they are browned all over, 12 to 15 minutes. Remove the chicken and reserve.

3 Add the shallots to the pan drippings and sauté until softened, 2 to 3 minutes. Add the mushrooms and sauté until they are lightly browned, about 3 minutes. Add the garlic, the tomatoes and the tarragon. Season to taste. Reduce the heat and simmer for 5 minutes.

4 Add the broth and the wine to the skillet. Bring the mixture to a boil. Return the chicken, reduce the heat, cover and simmer until the chicken is tender, 15 to 20 minutes.

5 Remove the chicken and reserve. Stir the cornstarch mixture into the sauce. Bring the mixture to a boil and cook until the sauce is thickened, 1 to 2 minutes. Return the chicken to the skillet and coat with the sauce.

Unusual Rice

1 Peel and chop the carrot. Chop the parsley. Place the rice, the broth, the water, the parsley and the sage in the top of a double boiler. Bring water to a boil in the bottom of the double boiler. Reduce the heat, cover and simmer until all the liquid is absorbed and the rice is tender, 30 to 40 minutes.

2 Fluff the rice before serving.

Real Cool Cauliflower

1 Bring water to a boil in a medium saucepan. Trim and cut the cauliflower into bite-size florets. Trim and chop the scallions. Cook the cauliflower in the boiling water until it is crisp-tender, 5 to 6 minutes.

2 Drain the cauliflower. Melt the butter in the saucepan with the lime juice, and sauté the scallions for 1 minute. Return the cauliflower to the saucepan and toss it with the lime-butter sauce. Season to taste and cover to keep warm.

Forever Amber

1 Preheat the oven to 400°F. Grease an 8x8-inch glass baking dish. Crumble the macaroons.

2 Drain the peaches and place them in the baking dish. Sprinkle them with the orange juice, the orange peel, the cinnamon and the nutmeg. Spread the crumbled macaroons evenly over the peaches. Dot with the butter and bake until the macaroons are golden, 10 to 15 minutes.

3 Top the warm peaches with dollops of whipped cream.

TUESDAY

Rainy Day Soup

1 large onion
1 large green bell pepper
2 large zucchini
1 can (11 ounces) whole kernel corn
2 tablespoons regular or light olive oil
2 cups V-8 juice
1 can (14$^1/_2$ ounces) vegetable broth
1 large can (28 ounces) cut-up tomatoes
1 teaspoon dried basil
$^1/_2$ teaspoon ground allspice
1 tablespoon Worcestershire sauce
Seasoning to taste

Umbrella Bread

4 medium onions
3 tablespoons butter
1 small loaf sliced pumpernickel bread
2 tablespoons Dijon mustard
1 teaspoon garlic powder
8 slices regular or low-fat Swiss cheese

Mud Puddles

1 small package (1.69 ounces) M&M plain
    candies
1 pint chocolate sherbet (or frozen yogurt)
1 cup chocolate-covered raisins

EQUIPMENT	
Dutch oven	Assorted cooking
Medium skillet	utensils
Cookie sheet	Whisk
Small bowl	Vegetable grater
Assorted kitchen knives	Plastic bag
Measuring cups and	Mallet
spoons	Ice cream scoop

COUNTDOWN

1 Assemble the ingredients and equipment
2 Do Steps 1–3 of the *Rainy Day Soup*
3 Do Step 1 of the *Mud Puddles*
4 Do Steps 1–6 of the *Umbrella Bread*
5 Do Step 2 of the *Mud Puddles*

Rainy Day Soup

1 Peel and chop the onion. Trim, seed and chop the bell pepper. Wash, dry and grate the zucchini. Drain the corn.

2 Heat the oil in a Dutch oven. Add the onion and the bell pepper and sauté until the onion is softened, about 5 minutes.

3 Add the V-8 juice and the broth. Bring the mixture to a boil. Add the zucchini, the un-drained tomatoes, the corn, the basil, the allspice and the Worcestershire sauce. Season to taste, reduce the heat, cover and simmer for 15 minutes.

Umbrella Bread

1 Preheat the broiler.

2 Peel and thinly slice the onions and separate them into rings.

3 Melt the butter in a medium skillet and sauté the onions until they are golden, about 10 minutes.

4 Place the bread slices on an ungreased cookie sheet and toast them lightly, turning once.

5 In a small bowl, combine the mustard and the garlic powder. Spread each slice of the bread with the mustard mixture. Add the onions. Top with the cheese.

6 Return the bread to the broiler and broil until the cheese is melted, about 1 minute.

Mud Puddles

1 Place the M&Ms in a plastic bag and crush them with a mallet.

2 Place scoops of sherbet in individual dessert dishes. Top with the chocolate-covered raisins and sprinkle with the crushed M&Ms.

WEDNESDAY

Pork & Pepper Stew

2 pounds lean boneless pork loin
Seasoning to taste
1 large onion
2 large red bell peppers
1 clove garlic
1 pound small new white potatoes
2 tablespoons fresh parsley (when chopped)
2 tablespoons regular or light olive oil
2 medium cans (14^1/$_2$ ounces each) stewed
    tomatoes
2 teaspoons dried basil

Cabbage Patch Salad

1 small (or half) head green cabbage
2 medium sweet red apples
2 stalks celery
1 tablespoon fresh chives (when chopped)
^{1}/$_4$ cup honey
1 teaspoon Dijon mustard
^{1}/$_4$ cup apple cider vinegar
1 teaspoon caraway seeds
Seasoning to taste

Heirloom Cake

1 frozen pound cake
1 tablespoon butter
1 cup confectioners' sugar
2 tablespoons Grand Marnier liqueur (or
    nonalcoholic Italian orange syrup)
1 tablespoon orange juice
^{1}/$_2$ cup flaked coconut

EQUIPMENT

Dutch oven	Assorted cooking
2 small saucepans	utensils
Large bowl	Whisk
Small bowl	Vegetable brush
Assorted kitchen knives	Vegetable grater
Measuring cups and	
spoons	

COUNTDOWN

1 Assemble the ingredients and equipment
2 Do Step 1 of the *Heirloom Cake*
3 Do Steps 1–2 of the *Cabbage Patch Salad*
4 Do Steps 1–4 of the *Pork & Pepper Stew*
5 Do Step 2 of the *Heirloom Cake*
6 Do Step 5 of the *Pork & Pepper Stew*

Pork & Pepper Stew

1 Trim any excess fat from the pork and cut the meat into 1-inch cubes. Season to taste.

2 Peel and chop the onion. Seed and chop the bell peppers. Peel and mince the garlic. Scrub the potatoes. Chop the parsley.

3 Heat the oil in the Dutch oven. Add the pork and the garlic and sauté until the pork cubes are lightly browned on all sides, 4 to 6 minutes.

4 Add the onion, the bell peppers and the potatoes and sauté until the onion is softened, about 5 minutes. Add the undrained tomatoes and bring the mixture to a boil. Reduce the heat, cover and simmer until the pork is tender, about 20 minutes.

5 Add the parsley and the basil to the pork, season to taste, and stir to blend.

Cabbage Patch Salad

1 Grate the cabbage. Core and chop the apples. Trim and thinly slice the celery. Chop the chives. Combine the ingredients in a large bowl.

2 In a small saucepan, heat the honey, the mustard and the vinegar, whisking until the mixture is smooth. Fold in the caraway seeds. Season to taste and pour the dressing over the cabbage mixture, tossing well. Refrigerate until you are ready to serve.

Heirloom Cake

1 Set the pound cake out to thaw.

2 Melt the butter in a small saucepan. Place the confectioners' sugar in a small bowl. Gradually add the Grand Marnier, the orange juice and the melted butter to the sugar and whisk until the mixture is smooth. Drizzle the glaze over the pound cake, letting it drip down the sides. Sprinkle the cake with the coconut and let it stand until you are ready to serve.

THURSDAY

Flash in the Pan

³/₄ cup pecan pieces
4 tablespoons butter
3 tablespoons Dijon mustard
4 boneless, skinless chicken breast halves
1 tablespoon regular or light vegetable oil
²/₃ cup regular or light sour cream
Seasoning to taste

Easy on the Orzo

2 tablespoons fresh chives (when chopped)
8 ounces orzo
1 tablespoon butter
Seasoning to taste

Pretty Perky Kale

1 pound kale
1 small onion
2 slices bacon
1 tablespoon butter
¹/₄ teaspoon ground allspice
1 tablespoon red wine vinegar
Seasoning to taste

Frosted Melon Slices

3 pieces candied ginger
¹/₄ teaspoon ground nutmeg
¹/₄ teaspoon ground cinnamon
1 tablespoon honey
2 teaspoons lime juice
1 large honeydew melon
2 tablespoons confectioners' sugar

EQUIPMENT

Blender	Measuring cups and
2 large covered skillets	spoons
Small skillet	Assorted cooking
Large covered	utensils
saucepan	Whisk
Small bowl	Sifter
Shallow bowl	Waxed paper
Strainer	Mallet
Assorted kitchen knives	

COUNTDOWN

1 Assemble the ingredients and equipment
2 Do Step 1 of the *Frosted Melon Slices*
3 Do Steps 1–3 of the *Flash in the Pan*
4 Do Step 1 of the *Easy on the Orzo*
5 Do Steps 1–2 of the *Pretty Perky Kale*
6 Do Step 2 of the *Easy on the Orzo*
7 Do Steps 4–5 of the *Flash in the Pan*
8 Do Step 3 of the *Easy on the Orzo*
9 Do Step 6 of the *Flash in the Pan*
10 Do Step 3 of the *Pretty Perky Kale*
11 Do Step 2 of the *Frosted Melon Slices*

Flash in the Pan

1 Process the pecans in a blender until finely ground and put them in a shallow bowl.

2 Melt 2 tablespoons of the butter in a small skillet. Whisk in 2 tablespoons of the mustard until blended.

3 Place the chicken breasts between sheets of waxed paper and pound them with a mallet to a 1/4-inch thickness.

4 Dip the chicken breasts in the butter mixture, and then dredge them in the pecans.

5 In a large skillet, heat the remaining butter with the oil. Add the chicken and cook until it is lightly browned, 3 to 4 minutes per side. Remove the chicken and cover to keep warm.

6 Discard all but 2 tablespoons of the fat from the skillet and reduce the heat. Add the sour cream, whisk in the remaining mustard, season to taste and blend well. Cook the sauce just until it is heated through—do not boil, and spoon it over the chicken.

Easy on the Orzo

1 Bring water to a boil in a large saucepan. Chop the chives.

2 Cook the orzo until it is almost tender, 6 to 8 minutes.

3 Drain the orzo, return it to the saucepan and toss it with the butter and chives. Season to taste and cover to keep warm.

Pretty Perky Kale

1 Rinse, stem and coarsely chop the kale. Peel and finely chop the onion. Dice the bacon and sauté it in a large skillet until it is crisp. Drain the bacon on a paper towel.

2 Add the butter to the bacon drippings. Add the onion and sauté until it is soft, about 5 minutes. Add the kale and cook, covered, until it is tender, about 15 minutes.

3 Add the allspice and the vinegar to the skillet. Season to taste, and sprinkle with the diced bacon.

Frosted Melon Slices

1 Process the candied ginger, the nutmeg and the cinnamon in a blender until finely ground. Turn the mixture into a small bowl and fold in the honey and the lime juice.

2 Quarter and seed the melon, removing the rind. Place the melon on individual dessert plates and cut the quarters into 1/2-inch slices. Spoon the sauce over the melon and dust with the confectioners' sugar.

FRIDAY

Saucy Salmon

4 salmon fillets (1$^1/_2$ pounds)
$^1/_4$ pound fresh mushrooms
3 scallions (green onions)
2 teaspoons fresh ginger (when grated)
3 tablespoons regular or light vegetable oil
$^1/_2$ cup dry white wine (or nonalcoholic white wine or clam juice)
2 tablespoons soy sauce
Seasoning to taste

Near East Rice

$^1/_4$ pound dried apricots
1 stalk celery
1 cup brown rice
1 can (14$^1/_2$ ounces) oriental broth
$^1/_4$ cup water
$^1/_2$ teaspoon ground coriander

Sweet & Sour Salad

2 tablespoons sesame seeds
16 Chinese snow peas
1 medium head lettuce
1 can (8 ounces) sliced water chestnuts
2 ounces fresh bean sprouts
1 teaspoon grated fresh orange peel
1 tablespoon soy sauce
1$^1/_2$ teaspoons rice vinegar
1 tablespoon lemon juice
1 tablespoon honey
1 teaspoon sesame oil
2 tablespoons regular or light vegetable oil
Seasoning to taste

Hugs & Kisses Pudding

12 Hershey's Hugs
12 Hershey's Kisses
1 quart whole milk
1 small package (3.4 ounces) instant French vanilla pudding mix
1 small package (3.9 ounces) instant chocolate pudding mix

EQUIPMENT

Electric hand mixer	Assorted kitchen knives
Blender	Measuring cups and
2 large covered skillets	spoons
Double boiler	Assorted cooking
Small saucepan	utensils
Large bowl	Citrus grater
2 medium bowls	Whisk
Small bowl	

COUNTDOWN

1 Assemble the ingredients and equipment
2 Do Step 1 of the *Near East Rice*
3 Do Steps 1–2 of the *Hugs & Kisses Pudding*
4 Do Steps 1–5 of the *Sweet & Sour Salad*
5 Do Steps 1–5 of the *Saucy Salmon*
6 Do Step 6 of the *Sweet & Sour Salad*
7 Do Step 2 of the *Near East Rice*

Saucy Salmon

1 Rinse and pat dry the salmon fillets, removing the skin, if necessary.

2 Rinse, pat dry, trim and slice the mushrooms. Trim and slice the scallions. Grate the ginger.

3 Heat 2 tablespoons of the oil in a large skillet. Add the salmon fillets in a single layer and cook until they are lightly browned, 4 to 5 minutes per side.

4 Add the wine to the skillet, cover and cook until the fish is opaque in the center, about 2 minutes. Remove the salmon and reserve it along with any cooking liquid and brown bits.

5 Heat the remaining oil in the skillet. Add the mushrooms, the scallions and the ginger and cook until the mushrooms are tender, 3 to 5 minutes. Add the soy sauce and the reserved cooking liquid and brown bits from the salmon. Season to taste. Cook, stirring, for 3 minutes. Return the salmon to the skillet and cook until it is heated through, 1 to 2 minutes.

Near East Rice

1 Dice the apricots. Trim and chop the celery. Place the rice, the broth, the water, the apricots, the celery and the coriander in the top of a double boiler. Bring water to a boil in the bottom of the double boiler. Reduce the heat, cover and simmer until all the liquid is absorbed and the rice is tender, 40 to 45 minutes.

2 Fluff the rice before serving.

Sweet & Sour Salad

1 Place the sesame seeds in a large skillet and toss over a heated burner to toast, 3 to 4 minutes.

2 Bring a small amount of water to a boil in a small saucepan. String the snow peas, blanch them in the boiling water for 30 seconds, and then drain them and run them under cold water to stop further cooking. Pat them dry and slice them diagonally. Place them in a large bowl.

3 Wash and dry the lettuce. Reserve 4 whole leaves and tear the remainder into bite-size pieces. Place the whole leaves on individual salad plates. Add the torn lettuce to the snow peas.

4 Drain the water chestnuts and add them to the snow peas. Add the bean sprouts. Add the orange peel.

5 In a small bowl, whisk together the soy sauce, the vinegar, the lemon juice, the honey, and both oils. Season to taste.

6 Toss the snow pea mixture with the dressing and spoon the mixture onto the whole lettuce leaves. Sprinkle with the toasted sesame seeds.

Hugs & Kisses Pudding

1 Place 8 Hugs in a blender and process until they are coarsely chopped. Remove and reserve them. Then repeat the process with the Kisses.

2 In a medium bowl, beat 2 cups of the milk and the French vanilla pudding mix until well blended. In a second medium bowl, beat the remaining milk and the chocolate pudding mix until well blended. Fold the chopped Kisses into the vanilla pudding. Fold the chopped Hugs into the chocolate pudding. Alternate layers of pudding in parfait glasses. Garnish with the remaining whole Hugs and Kisses and refrigerate for at least 20 minutes.

OCTOBER

WEEK ONE

Monday

FETTUCCINE FIRENZE
MEDICI SALAD
HOT BOBOLI
MOCHA-TONI

Tuesday

CHICKEN PIQUANT
FLUFFY STEAMED WHITE RICE
SPROUTS & ONIONS
ICE CREAM DREAMERS

Wednesday

CREOLE EGGS
PLANTATION SALAD
STEAMBOAT BISCUITS
BAYOU BANANAS

Thursday

SABLE & CHAMPAGNE
GREEN BEAN DE MENTHE
OPULENT FRUIT TARTS

Friday

AUTUMN MACARONI
HARVEST MOON SALAD
PISTACHIO AMERICANA

CHECK STAPLES

- ☐ Butter
- ☐ Granulated sugar
- ☐ Dark brown sugar
- ☐ Confectioners' sugar
- ☐ Unsweetened cocoa
- ☐ Multicolored sprinkles
- ☐ Long-grain white rice
- ☐ Regular or light vegetable oil
- ☐ Regular or light olive oil
- ☐ White wine vinegar
- ☐ Balsamic vinegar
- ☐ Raspberry vinegar
- ☐ Lemon juice
- ☐ Lime juice
- ☐ Tabasco sauce
- ☐ Dijon mustard
- ☐ Chili sauce
- ☐ Instant coffee crystals
- ☐ Grated Parmesan cheese
- ☐ Ground allspice
- ☐ Dried basil
- ☐ Dried dill
- ☐ Ground nutmeg
- ☐ Onion powder
- ☐ Dried oregano
- ☐ Paprika
- ☐ Red pepper flakes
- ☐ Dried tarragon
- ☐ Pepper
- ☐ Salt
- ☐ Almond extract

SHOPPING NOTE

● If you are shopping once a week and cannot arrange to purchase fresh cod on the day you plan to use it, you can purchase *not previously frozen* cod and freeze it, placing it in the refrigerator to thaw the night before you are ready to use it. Or you can purchase *still frozen* cod and keep it frozen until the night before you are ready to use it.

MEAT & POULTRY

4 boneless, skinless chicken
    breast halves (T)

FISH

4 sablefish (black cod)
    steaks (Th)

FRESH PRODUCE

Vegetables

2 large baking potatoes (Th)
1 pound Brussels sprouts (T)
1 pound green beans (or
    frozen) (Th)
1 medium zucchini (M)
1 pound small zucchini (F)
$^1/_2$ pound mushrooms (M)
2 stalks celery (W)
1 large onion (W)
2 medium onions—1 (T), 1 (F)
1 small onion (M)
1 medium red onion (M)
3 medium shallots (Th)
5 scallions (green onions)—
    2 (W), 3 (Th)
1 head garlic (M, T, F)
1 small bunch basil (F)
1 bunch chives (M, W, F)
1 bunch parsley (M, T, Th)
2 ounces bean sprouts (Th)
2 medium heads lettuce—
    1 (M), 1 (W, F)
1 ripe avocado (W)
$1^1/_4$ pounds tomatoes—
    $^1/_4$ pound (M), 1 pound (F)
2 medium cucumbers (W)
1 large green bell pepper (W)
1 large yellow bell pepper (F)
1 small red bell pepper (M)

Fruit

4 small bananas (W)
2 medium pears (Th)
2 kiwifruit (Th)
$^1/_4$ pound seedless red
    grapes (Th)
6 medium oranges—2 (T), 4 (F)

CANS, JARS & BOTTLES

Soup

2 cans ($10^3/_4$ ounces each)
    chicken broth—1 (T), 1 (Th)

Vegetables

1 medium can (15 ounces)
    tomato sauce (W)
1 can (11 ounces) whole kernel
    corn (W)

Fruit

1 can (11 ounces) mandarin
    oranges (M)

Condiments

1 small can ($3^1/_2$ ounces) pitted
    black olives (M)

Spreads

10 tablespoons currant jelly—
    6 (T), 4 (Th)

PACKAGED GOODS

Pasta, Rice & Grains

12 ounces fettuccine (M)
16 ounces elbow macaroni (F)

Baked Goods

2 small (8-inch) Boboli breads
    (or English or Australian
    muffins) (M)
1 cup coarse bread crumbs (F)

Nuts & Seeds

$^1/_2$ cup sliced almonds (M)

Dessert & Baking Needs

4 individual graham cracker
    tart shells (M)
4 individual shortcake dessert
    cups (Th)
1 small package (3.4 ounces)
    instant vanilla pudding mix
    (Th)
1 small package (3.4 ounces)
    instant pistachio pudding
    mix (F)
$^1/_2$ cup flaked coconut (W)

WINES & SPIRITS

1 cup champagne (or sparkling
    apple cider) (Th)
2 tablespoons Amaretto liqueur
    (or nonalcoholic Italian
    almond syrup) (T)
2 tablespoons rum (or 2
    teaspoons rum extract) (W)
3 tablespoons creme de menthe
    (or nonalcoholic Italian
    peppermint syrup) (Th)

REFRIGERATED PRODUCTS

Dairy

$3^1/_4$ cups whole milk—$1^1/_4$ cups
    (Th), 2 cups (F)
1 cup whipping cream (M)
$1^1/_4$ cups regular or light sour
    cream—$^1/_2$ cup (W), $^3/_4$ cup
    (Th)
8 eggs (W)

Cheese

1 cup regular or low-fat small-
    curd cottage cheese (F)
2 ounces shredded regular or
    low-fat mozzarella
    cheese (M)

Juice

2 tablespoons orange juice (T)

Deli

2 slices bacon (W)
1 package (10) refrigerator
    biscuits (W)

FROZEN GOODS

Vegetables

1 package (9 ounces) green
    peas (M)

Desserts

1 pound cake (F)
1 pint vanilla ice cream (T)

MONDAY

Fettuccine Firenze

1 package (9 ounces) frozen green peas
$1/2$ pound fresh mushrooms
1 small onion
$1/2$ cup fresh parsley (when chopped)
4 tablespoons butter
$1/4$ cup regular or light olive oil
$1/4$ teaspoon red pepper flakes
$1/2$ teaspoon ground nutmeg
Seasoning to taste
12 ounces fettuccine
$1/4$ cup grated Parmesan cheese

Medici Salad

1 medium head lettuce
1 medium zucchini
1 small red bell pepper
$1/4$ cup fresh chives (when chopped)
1 can (11 ounces) mandarin oranges
1 small can ($3^1/2$ ounces) pitted black olives
3 tablespoons regular or light olive oil
2 tablespoons raspberry vinegar
$1/4$ teaspoon dried oregano
$1/4$ teaspoon dried basil
$1/4$ teaspoon paprika
Seasoning to taste

Hot Boboli

2 cloves garlic
$1/4$ pound fresh tomatoes
1 medium red onion
2 small (8–inch) Boboli breads (or English or
   Australian muffins)
2 tablespoons regular or light olive oil
Seasoning to taste
2 ounces shredded regular or low–fat
   mozzarella cheese

Mocha-Toni

1 cup whipping cream
$1/4$ cup confectioners' sugar
1 tablespoon unsweetened cocoa
1 tablespoon instant coffee crystals
$1/4$ teaspoon almond extract
4 individual graham cracker tart shells
$1/2$ cup sliced almonds

EQUIPMENT

Electric hand mixer	Assorted kitchen knives
Large covered skillet	Measuring cups and
Large saucepan	spoons
Cookie sheet	Assorted cooking
Large bowl	utensils
Medium bowl	Whisk
Small bowl	Pastry brush
Colander	

COUNTDOWN

1 Assemble the ingredients and equipment
2 Do Step 1 of the *Fettuccine Firenze*
3 Do Steps 1–2 of the *Mocha-Toni*
4 Do Steps 1–2 of the *Medici Salad*
5 Do Steps 1–3 of the *Hot Boboli*
6 Do Steps 2–5 of the *Fettuccine Firenze*
7 Do Step 3 of the *Medici Salad*
8 Do Step 6 of the *Fettuccine Firenze*
9 Do Step 3 of the *Mocha-Toni*

Fettuccine Firenze

1 Set the peas out to thaw.

2 Bring water to a boil in a large saucepan.

3 Wash, pat dry, trim and slice the mushrooms. Peel and chop the onion. Chop the parsley.

4 Melt the butter with the oil in a large skillet. Sauté the mushrooms and the onion until the onion is soft, about 5 minutes. Add the parsley, the red pepper flakes, the nutmeg and season to taste. Add the peas and simmer, covered, until heated through, about 2 minutes.

5 Cook the pasta in the boiling water until it is almost tender, 2 to 3 minutes if you are using fresh pasta and 6 to 7 minutes if you are using dried pasta.

6 Drain the pasta, return it to the saucepan and toss it with the sauce. Sprinkle with the Parmesan cheese.

Medici Salad

1 Wash and dry the lettuce and tear it into bite-size pieces. Trim and slice the zucchini. Seed and chop the bell pepper. Chop the chives. Drain the oranges. Drain the olives. Combine the ingredients in a large bowl.

2 In a small bowl, whisk together the oil, the vinegar, the oregano, the basil and the paprika. Season to taste.

3 Lightly toss the salad with the dressing.

Hot Boboli

1 Heat the oven to 400°F.

2 Peel and mince the garlic. Chop the tomatoes. Peel and chop the onion.

3 Place the Boboli breads on an ungreased cookie sheet and brush them generously with the oil. Sprinkle the garlic over the breads. Season to taste. Spread the chopped tomatoes and the onions on the breads. Top with the cheese. Bake the Boboli breads until they are brown and crusty, about 15 minutes.

Mocha-Toni

1 In a medium bowl, whip the cream until it is stiff. Fold in the sugar, the cocoa, the coffee crystals and the almond extract.

2 Spoon the mixture into the tart shells and refrigerate them for 30 minutes.

3 Sprinkle the sliced almonds over the tarts.

TUESDAY

Chicken Piquant

2 tablespoons regular or light vegetable oil
4 boneless, skinless chicken breast halves
$3/4$ cup chicken broth
6 tablespoons currant jelly
1 tablespoon chili sauce
2 teaspoons Dijon mustard
Seasoning to taste

Fluffy Steamed White Rice

1 cup long-grain white rice
2 cups water

Sprouts & Onions

1 medium onion
1 clove garlic
1 tablespoon fresh parsley (when chopped)
1 pound fresh Brussels sprouts
$1/4$ cup regular or light olive oil
$1/2$ cup chicken broth
Seasoning to taste

Ice Cream Dreamers

2 medium oranges
1 pint vanilla ice cream
2 tablespoons orange juice
2 tablespoons Amaretto liqueur (or
    nonalcoholic Italian almond syrup)
2 tablespoons confectioners' sugar

EQUIPMENT

Blender
2 large covered skillets
Double boiler
Large saucepan
Small bowl
Strainer
Assorted kitchen knives

Measuring cups and
    spoons
Assorted cooking
    utensils
Whisk
Ice cream scoop

COUNTDOWN

1 Assemble the ingredients and equipment
2 Do Step 1 of the *Fluffy Steamed White Rice*
3 Do Steps 1–2 of the *Ice Cream Dreamers*
4 Do Step 1 of the *Chicken Piquant*
5 Do Steps 1–4 of the *Sprouts & Onions*
6 Do Steps 2–3 of the *Chicken Piquant*
7 Do Step 2 of the *Fluffy Steamed White Rice*
8 Do Step 4 of the *Chicken Piquant*
9 Do Step 3 of the *Ice Cream Dreamers*

Chicken Piquant

1 Heat the oil in a large skillet. Add the chicken and cook, turning, until it is browned on all sides, 8 to 10 minutes. Discard any fat, add the broth to the skillet and simmer, covered, until the chicken is fork-tender, 15 to 20 minutes.

2 Remove the chicken and cover to keep warm.

3 In a small bowl, whisk together the currant jelly, the chili sauce and the mustard. Stir the mixture into the skillet, season to taste, and bring the sauce to a boil, stirring constantly.

4 Return the chicken to the skillet and coat the pieces with the sauce.

Fluffy Steamed White Rice

1 Place the rice and the water in the top of a double boiler. Bring water to a boil in the bottom of the double boiler. Reduce the heat, cover and simmer until all the liquid is absorbed and the rice is tender, 30 to 40 minutes.

2 Fluff the rice before serving.

Sprouts & Onions

1 Bring water to a boil in a large saucepan.

2 Peel and chop the onion. Peel and mince the garlic. Chop the parsley. Trim the Brussels sprouts, and cut Xs in the bottom of the stems. Cook the sprouts until they are crisp-tender, 8 to 10 minutes.

3 Heat the oil in a large skillet and sauté the onion and the garlic until they are golden, about 10 minutes.

4 Drain the sprouts well, add them to the skillet and brown them lightly. Add the broth and the parsley. Season to taste, and cook until the sprouts are thoroughly heated, 3 to 4 minutes. Remove the skillet from the heat and cover to keep warm.

Ice Cream Dreamers

1 Peel and section the oranges and refrigerate them until you are ready to use.

2 Process 2 tablespoons of the ice cream in a blender with the orange juice, the Amaretto and the sugar until it is smooth. Refrigerate the mixture until you are ready to use.

3 Top scoops of ice cream with the sectioned oranges and drizzle them with the sauce.

WEDNESDAY

Creole Eggs

1 large green bell pepper
1 large onion
4 teaspoons butter
1 medium can (15 ounces) tomato sauce
$1/2$ teaspoon dried tarragon
$1/8$ teaspoon Tabasco sauce
$1/2$ teaspoon ground allspice
Seasoning to taste
8 eggs

Plantation Salad

1 medium head lettuce*
2 medium cucumbers
1 ripe avocado
2 stalks celery
2 scallions (green onions)
1 can (11 ounces) whole kernel corn
3 tablespoons white wine vinegar
1 tablespoon lemon juice
$1/2$ teaspoon sugar
3 tablespoons regular or light vegetable oil
Seasoning to taste
1 tablespoon fresh chives (when chopped)

Steamboat Biscuits

2 slices bacon
2 tablespoons butter
1 package (10) refrigerator biscuits
$1/2$ teaspoon onion powder

Bayou Bananas

4 small bananas
$1^1/2$ tablespoons lime juice
2 tablespoons dark brown sugar
$1/2$ cup regular or light sour cream
2 tablespoons rum (or 2 teaspoons rum
 extract)
$1/2$ cup flaked coconut
Multicolored sprinkles

EQUIPMENT

Large covered skillet	Assorted cooking
Small skillet	utensils
9-inch pie plate	Whisk
3 small bowls	Vegetable peeler
Assorted kitchen knives	
Measuring cups and spoons	

COUNTDOWN

1 Assemble the ingredients and utensils
2 Do Step 1 of the *Steamboat Biscuits*
3 Do Steps 1–2 of the *Bayou Bananas*
4 Do Steps 1–2 of the *Plantation Salad*
5 Do Step 1 of the *Creole Eggs*
6 Do Steps 2–5 of the *Steamboat Biscuits*
7 Do Steps 2–4 of the *Creole Eggs*
8 Do Step 3 of the *Plantation Salad*

*Reserve the remaining lettuce for use on Friday.

Creole Eggs

1 Seed and dice the bell pepper. Peel and finely chop the onion.

2 Combine the bell pepper, the onion and the butter in a large skillet and cook until the vegetables are slightly softened, about 3 minutes.

3 Add the tomato sauce, the tarragon, the Tabasco sauce and the allspice to the skillet. Season to taste. Cook for 2 minutes.

4 With a spoon, make 8 nests in the sauce. Break the eggs and drop them, one at a time, into the nests. Reduce the heat and simmer, covered, until the eggs are firm, 5 to 8 minutes. Bring the skillet to the table.

Plantation Salad

1 Wash and dry 4 large lettuce leaves and reserve the remaining lettuce. Arrange the leaves on individual salad plates. Peel and slice the cucumbers. Peel, pit and slice the avocado. Trim and slice the celery. Trim and slice the scallions. Drain the corn. Arrange the vegetables over the lettuce leaves.

2 In a small bowl, whisk together the vinegar, the lemon juice, the sugar and the oil. Season to taste. Chop the chives.

3 Drizzle the dressing over the salad and sprinkle with the chives.

Steamboat Biscuits

1 Preheat the oven to 450°F.

2 Dice the bacon and sauté it in a small skillet until crisp, about 5 minutes, and then drain it on a paper towel.

3 Place the butter in a 9-inch pie plate. Place the plate in the heating oven until the butter is melted.

4 Remove the biscuits from the package and cut each of them into 4 pieces.

5 Stir the onion powder into the melted butter. Add the biscuit pieces, coating all sides in the butter mixture. Sprinkle the bacon over the biscuits and bake until they are golden, 8 to 10 minutes.

Bayou Bananas

1 Peel the bananas and cut them into 1-inch chunks.

2 Place the lime juice in a small bowl. Blend the brown sugar with the sour cream. Fold in the rum. Place the mixture in a small bowl. Dip the banana chunks into the lime juice and then into the sour cream mixture. Place the bananas on individual dessert plates, sprinkle with the coconut and the multicolored sprinkles and refrigerate until you are ready to serve.

THURSDAY

Sable & Champagne

2 large baking potatoes
3 medium shallots
2 tablespoons butter
2 tablespoons regular or light vegetable oil
1 cup champagne (or sparkling apple cider)
1 can (10³/₄ ounces) chicken broth
4 sablefish (black cod) steaks (1¹/₄ pounds)
1¹/₂ teaspoons dried dill
Seasoning to taste

Green Bean de Menthe

3 scallions (green onions)
1 tablespoon fresh parsley (when chopped)
1 pound green beans
3 tablespoons butter
3 tablespoons creme de menthe (or
    nonalcoholic Italian peppermint syrup)
Seasoning to taste

Opulent Fruit Tarts

1¹/₄ cups whole milk
³/₄ cup regular or light sour cream
1 small package (3.4 ounces) instant vanilla
    pudding mix
4 individual shortcake dessert cups
2 medium pears
1 tablespoon lemon juice
¹/₄ pound seedless red grapes
2 kiwifruit
4 tablespoons currant jelly

EQUIPMENT

Electric hand mixer	Measuring cups and
Large covered skillet	spoons
Medium saucepan	Assorted cooking
Medium bowl	utensils
Strainer	Vegetable peeler
Assorted kitchen knives	

COUNTDOWN

1 Assemble the ingredients and equipment
2 Do Steps 1–2 of the *Opulent Fruit Tarts*
3 Do Steps 1–3 of the *Sable & Champagne*
4 Do Steps 1–2 of the *Green Bean de Menthe*
5 Do Steps 4–5 of the *Sable & Champagne*
6 Do Step 3 of the *Green Bean de Menthe*
7 Do Step 3 of the *Opulent Fruit Tarts*

Sable & Champagne

1 Peel and thinly slice the potatoes. Peel and chop the shallots.

2 Melt the butter with the oil in a large skillet. Add the potatoes and the shallots and cook, stirring, until the potatoes are translucent, 4 to 6 minutes.

3 Add the champagne and the broth. Bring the mixture to a boil, reduce the heat, cover and simmer for 10 minutes.

4 Rinse and pat dry the cod steaks, removing the skin, if necessary.

5 Arrange the fish on top of the potatoes. Sprinkle with the dill, season to taste and cook, covered, until the fish is opaque throughout, 10 to 12 minutes.

Green Bean de Menthe

1 Bring water to a boil in a medium saucepan.

2 Trim and chop the scallions. Chop the parsley. Rinse and trim the green beans and cut them diagonally into 1-inch pieces. Cook the beans in the boiling water for 5 minutes. Drain the beans and rinse them under cold water. Then drain them again.

3 Melt the butter in the saucepan. Sauté the scallions until they are limp, about 2 minutes. Return the beans, add the parsley and the creme de menthe and continue to cook, stirring frequently, for 5 minutes. Season to taste.

Opulent Fruit Tarts

1 In a medium bowl, beat together the milk, the sour cream and the pudding mix until well blended. Pour the mixture into the shortcake dessert cups and refrigerate for at least 20 minutes.

2 Core, halve and slice the pears and sprinkle them with the lemon juice to keep them from browning. Rinse and separate the grapes and cut them in half. Peel and slice the kiwifruit. Refrigerate the fruit until you are ready to use.

3 Melt the currant jelly. Arrange the pear slices, the grapes and the kiwi slices on the tarts and drizzle the melted jelly over the fruit.

FRIDAY

MENU

Autumn Macaroni

1 medium onion
1 large yellow bell pepper
1 pound small zucchini
2 cloves garlic
1 pound fresh tomatoes
1 tablespoon fresh basil (when chopped)
3 tablespoons regular or light olive oil
$^1/_2$ teaspoon dried oregano
Seasoning to taste
16 ounces elbow macaroni
1 cup coarse bread crumbs
1 cup grated Parmesan cheese

Harvest Moon Salad

Lettuce reserved from Wednesday
4 medium oranges
3 tablespoons fresh basil (when chopped)
1 tablespoon fresh chives (when chopped)
2 tablespoons balsamic vinegar
1 cup regular or low-fat small-curd cottage
    cheese
Seasoning to taste

Pistachio Americana

1 frozen pound cake
2 cups whole milk
1 small package (3.4 ounces) instant
    pistachio pudding mix
$^1/_2$ cup confectioners' sugar

EQUIPMENT

Electric hand mixer	Small bowl
Stockpot	Colander
Large covered	Assorted kitchen knives
saucepan	Measuring cups and
Small skillet	spoons
2-quart casserole	Assorted cooking
Medium bowl	utensils

COUNTDOWN

IN THE MORNING:
  Do Step 1 of the *Pistachio Americana*
BEFORE DINNER:
  1 Assemble the remaining ingredients and
    equipment
  2 Do Steps 1–2 of the *Autumn Macaroni*
  3 Do Steps 2–4 of the *Pistachio Americana*
  4 Do Steps 3–4 of the *Autumn Macaroni*
  5 Do Step 5 of the *Pistachio Americana*
  6 Do Steps 5–7 of the *Autumn Macaroni*
  7 Do Steps 1–2 of the *Harvest Moon Salad*

Autumn Macaroni

1 Preheat the oven to 350°F.

2 Bring water to a boil in a stockpot. Lightly grease a 2-quart casserole.

3 Peel and chop the onion. Stem, seed and chop the bell pepper. Wash the zucchini and cut it into $1/2$-inch slices. Peel and mince the garlic. Chop the tomatoes. Chop the basil.

4 Heat 2 tablespoons of the oil in a large saucepan. Add the onion and sauté until it is golden, about 10 minutes. Stir in the bell pepper, the zucchini and half of the garlic and sauté until the vegetables are crisp-tender, about 5 minutes. Stir in the tomatoes, the basil and the oregano, season to taste and simmer, covered, until the vegetables are tender, about 7 minutes.

5 Cook the pasta until it is almost tender, 8 to 10 minutes.

6 Heat the remaining oil in a small skillet and sauté the remaining garlic for 1 minute. Stir in the bread crumbs and sauté until the crumbs are golden, about 5 minutes.

7 Drain the pasta and combine it with the vegetables and the cheese. Pour it into the casserole, sprinkle the top with the garlic bread crumbs and bake until the casserole is bubbly and the top is lightly browned, about 20 minutes.

Harvest Moon Salad

1 Wash and dry the lettuce, and place the leaves on individual salad plates. Peel and slice the oranges. Chop the basil. Chop the chives. Arrange the orange slices over the lettuce. Sprinkle the vinegar over the oranges.

2 In a small bowl, blend the cheese with the basil and the chives. Season to taste. Top the orange slices with dollops of the cheese mixture.

Pistachio Americana

1 Set the pound cake out to thaw.

2 With the handle of a wooden spoon, poke holes in the pound cake at 1-inch intervals.

3 In a medium bowl, beat together the milk, the pudding mix and the sugar until well blended.

4 Pour half of the mixture over the top of the cake and into the holes. Refrigerate the remaining pudding until it has thickened slightly, about 10 minutes.

5 Spoon the remaining pudding over the top of the cake and swirl to frost it. Refrigerate for at least 20 minutes.

WEEK AT A GLANCE

Monday

HEIDELBERG STEW
APPLE-ONION SAUTÉ
LOADED PUMPERNICKEL
LIME SUBLIME

Tuesday

SOUP OF THE SEA
SALAD OF THE LAND
CUMIN THROUGH THE RYE
CHERRIES ON TOP

Wednesday

WORLD SERIES CHICKEN
HOME RUN RICE
PINCH-HITTING PEARS
DOUBLE PLAY PUDDING

Thursday

SKINNY PASTA
A SLIP OF A SALAD
RED BREAD
IMPOSSIBLE PIE

Friday

FLASHY FLOUNDER
FEISTY POTATOES
SNAPPY PEAS & CARROTS
PINEAPPLE SPLASH

CHECK STAPLES

- Butter
- Flour
- Bisquick
- Cornstarch
- Granulated sugar
- Dark brown sugar
- Confectioners' sugar
- Long-grain white rice
- Regular or light vegetable oil
- Regular or light olive oil
- Lemon juice
- Lime juice
- Dijon mustard
- Yellow mustard
- Chili sauce
- Honey
- Grated Parmesan cheese
- Bouquet Garni
- Caraway seeds
- Cayenne pepper
- Ground cinnamon
- Ground cloves
- Ground cumin
- Ground ginger
- Ground nutmeg
- Dried oregano
- Paprika
- Poppy seeds
- Red pepper flakes
- Dried tarragon
- Pepper
- Salt
- Vanilla extract

SHOPPING NOTE

● If you are shopping once a week and cannot arrange to purchase fresh seafood on the day you plan to use it, you can purchase *not previously frozen* seafood and freeze it, placing it in the refrigerator to thaw the night before you are ready to use it. Or you can purchase *still frozen* seafood and keep it frozen until the night before you are ready to use it.

MEAT & POULTRY

1 pound lean boneless sirloin
steak (M)
4 boneless, skinless chicken
breast halves (W)

FISH

2 pounds assorted fish fillets
(halibut, snapper, cod) (T)
4 flounder fillets (1¼ pounds)
(F)

FRESH PRODUCE

Vegetables

4 medium new red potatoes (M)
1 pound small new red
potatoes (F)
½ pound sugar snap peas (F)
½ pound spinach (M)
½ pound mushrooms (Th)
2 medium carrots (T)
½ pound medium carrots (F)
2 stalks celery (T)
2 large onions (M)
3 medium onions—1 (M), 1 (T),
1 (Th)
1 small onion (W)
2 medium shallots (F)
5 scallions (green onions)—
3 (T), 2 (Th)
1 head garlic (T, W, Th, F)
1 small bunch basil (W, Th)
1 bunch parsley (T, Th, F)
2 ounces bean sprouts (Th)
2 medium heads lettuce—
1 (T, W), 1 (Th)
1 ripe avocado (T)
2 small red bell peppers—
1 (W), 1 (F)
1 small bunch radishes (T)

Fruit

2 large tart green apples (M)
4 medium pears (W)
2 small honeydew melons (M)
1 pound pineapple chunks (or
net weight canned) (F)

CANS, JARS & BOTTLES

Soup

1 can (10¾ ounces) chicken
broth (T)
1 can (14½ ounces) chicken
broth (W)

Vegetables

1 large can (28 ounces) cut-up
tomatoes (T)
1 large can (28 ounces) crushed
tomatoes (Th)
1 small can (6 ounces) tomato
paste (Th)
1 can (11 ounces) whole kernel
corn (W)
1 large jar (32 ounces)
sauerkraut (M)

Fish

1 can (2 ounces) anchovy
fillets (T)
1 tube (1.58 ounces) anchovy
paste (Th)

Juice

2 bottles (8 ounces each) clam
juice (T)
⅓ cup apple juice (F)

Condiments

1 large jar (4 ounces) diced
pimientos (Th)

Dessert Needs

1 can (21 ounces) cherry pie
filling (T)
1 medium can (16 ounces)
pumpkin (W)

PACKAGED GOODS

Pasta, Rice & Grains

16 ounces capellini (angel hair
pasta) (Th)

Baked Goods

1 small loaf unsliced
pumpernickel bread (M)

1 small loaf unsliced rye
bread (T)
1 small loaf Italian bread (Th)

Nuts & Seeds

2 tablespoons sunflower
seeds (T)

Dessert & Baking Needs

1 small package (6 ounces)
semisweet chocolate
chips (Th)

WINES & SPIRITS

1 can (12 ounces) beer (or
nonalcoholic beer or beef
broth) (M)
¼ cup dry white wine (or
nonalcoholic white wine or
chicken broth) (W)
1½ tablespoons Kirsch liqueur
(or nonalcoholic Italian
cherry syrup) (F)

REFRIGERATED PRODUCTS

Dairy

1 cup whole or low-fat milk (Th)
Whipped cream for garnish (Th)
1 cup regular or light sour
cream (T)
4 eggs—2 (T), 2 (Th)

Cheese

¼ pound shredded regular or
low-fat Monterey Jack
cheese (M)
4 slices regular or low-fat
mozzarella cheese (W)

Deli

4 slices prosciutto ham (W)

FROZEN GOODS

Fruit

1 package (12 ounces)
raspberries (F)

Desserts

1 pint lime sherbet (M)
1 small container (8 ounces)
frozen whipped topping (W)

MONDAY

Heidelberg Stew

1 pound lean boneless sirloin steak
1 medium onion
4 medium new red potatoes
$^1/_2$ pound fresh spinach
1 large jar (32 ounces) sauerkraut
2 tablespoons regular or light vegetable oil
1 can (12 ounces) beer (or nonalcoholic beer or
    beef broth)
$^1/_2$ teaspoon caraway seeds
Seasoning to taste

Apple-Onion Sauté

2 large onions
2 large tart green apples
2 tablespoons butter
1 teaspoon dark brown sugar
$^1/_2$ teaspoon ground nutmeg
1 tablespoon water

Loaded Pumpernickel

2 tablespoons yellow mustard
1 teaspoon ground cloves
1 small loaf unsliced pumpernickel bread
$^1/_4$ pound shredded regular or low-fat
    Monterey Jack cheese

Lime Sublime

2 tablespoons lime juice
2 tablespoons confectioners' sugar
2 small honeydew melons
1 pint lime sherbet

EQUIPMENT	
Large covered skillet	Assorted cooking
Medium covered skillet	utensils
Small saucepan	Vegetable brush
Strainer	Whisk
Assorted kitchen knives	Apple corer
Measuring cups and	Ice cream scoop
spoons	Aluminum foil

COUNTDOWN

1 Assemble the ingredients and equipment
2 Do Steps 1–3 of the *Heidelberg Stew*
3 Do Steps 1–3 of the *Loaded Pumpernickel*
4 Do Steps 1–2 of the *Apple-Onion Sauté*
5 Do Step 4 of the *Heidelberg Stew*
6 Do Steps 1–2 of the *Lime Sublime*

Heidelberg Stew

1 Trim the beef of any fat and cut it diagonally across the grain into ¼-inch slices. Cut the slices in half. Peel and slice the onion. Scrub and slice the potatoes. Rinse, stem and chop the spinach. Drain the sauerkraut.

2 Heat the oil in a large skillet. Add the beef and cook, stirring, until it loses its redness, 3 to 4 minutes. Remove the beef and all the drippings and cover to keep warm.

3 Add the onion to the skillet and cook, stirring, until golden, about 10 minutes. Add the beer, the sauerkraut, the potatoes and the caraway seeds. Season to taste and stir to blend well. Heat the mixture to boiling, then reduce the heat, cover and simmer until the potatoes are tender, 15 to 20 minutes.

4 Stir in the spinach, re-cover and cook for 5 minutes more. Return the beef to the skillet and simmer until hot, 1 to 2 minutes.

Apple-Onion Sauté

1 Peel and slice the onion. Core and slice the apples.

2 Melt the butter in a medium skillet. Separate the onion into rings and sauté until they are limp, about 5 minutes. Add the apple slices, the brown sugar, the nutmeg and the water. Cover and simmer until the apples are just soft, 10 to 12 minutes.

Loaded Pumpernickel

1 Preheat the oven to 400°F.

2 Blend the mustard with the ground cloves. Slice the bread in half lengthwise and spread the cut sides with the mustard mixture. Sprinkle with the cheese. Replace the top half of the bread and wrap it in aluminum foil.

3 Place the pumpernickel in the oven until it is hot throughout, 15 to 20 minutes.

Lime Sublime

1 Heat the lime juice with the confectioners' sugar in a small saucepan, whisking until the sugar is completely dissolved. Refrigerate to cool slightly.

2 Halve and seed the melons. Fill the center of each melon with a scoop of lime sherbet and drizzle with the cooled sauce.

TUESDAY

Soup of the Sea

2 pounds assorted fish fillets (halibut,
    snapper, cod)
1 medium onion
2 medium carrots
2 stalks celery
2 cloves garlic
1 can (2 ounces) anchovy fillets
2 tablespoons fresh parsley (when chopped)
3 tablespoons regular or light olive oil
2 bottles (8 ounces each) clam juice
1 can ($10^3/4$ ounces) chicken broth
$1/4$ cup water
1 large can (28 ounces) cut-up tomatoes
$1/2$ teaspoon cayenne pepper
$1/2$ teaspoon Bouquet Garni
Seasoning to taste

Salad of the Land

2 eggs
1 medium head lettuce*
3 scallions (green onions)
1 small bunch radishes
1 ripe avocado
3 tablespoons lemon juice
3 tablespoons regular or light vegetable oil
$1/4$ teaspoon paprika
$1/4$ teaspoon dried tarragon
$1/2$ teaspoon sugar
Seasoning to taste
2 tablespoons sunflower seeds

Cumin Through the Rye

4 tablespoons softened butter
2 teaspoons ground cumin
1 tablespoon caraway seeds
1 small loaf unsliced rye bread

Cherries on Top

1 cup regular or light sour cream
1 tablespoon sugar
1 teaspoon vanilla extract
1 can (21 ounces) cherry pie filling

EQUIPMENT

Dutch oven	Assorted cooking
Small saucepan	utensils
Large bowl	Whisk
3 small bowls	Vegetable peeler
Assorted kitchen knives	Aluminum foil
Measuring cups and	
spoons	

COUNTDOWN

1 Assemble the ingredients and equipment
2 Do Steps 1–3 of *Cumin Through the Rye*
3 Do Step 1 of the *Salad of the Land*
4 Do Steps 1–4 of the *Soup of the Sea*
5 Do Steps 2–4 of the *Salad of the Land*
6 Do Step 5 of the *Soup of the Sea*
7 Do Steps 1–3 of the *Cherries on Top*
8 Do Step 5 of the *Salad of the Land*
9 Do Step 6 of the *Soup of the Sea*

---

* Reserve 4 large lettuce leaves for use on Wednesday.

Soup of the Sea

1 Rinse, pat dry and cut the fish into 2-inch pieces.

2 Peel and chop the onion. Peel and chop the carrots. Trim and chop the celery. Peel and chop the garlic. Drain and finely chop the anchovies. Chop the parsley.

3 Heat the oil in a Dutch oven. Add the onion and sauté until it is soft, about 5 minutes. Add the carrots, the celery and the garlic and sauté until the onion is just beginning to turn golden, about 7 minutes.

4 Stir in the anchovies, the clam juice, the broth, the water, the undrained tomatoes, the cayenne and the Bouquet Garni. Bring the mixture to a boil, reduce the heat and cook, uncovered, until the flavors combine, about 10 minutes.

5 Add the fish to the Dutch oven and cover. Reduce the heat and simmer until the fish is opaque throughout, about 15 minutes.

6 Season the soup to taste and sprinkle with the parsley.

Salad of the Land

1 Cover the eggs with water in a small saucepan. Bring the water to a boil and hard-cook the eggs, 10 to 12 minutes.

2 Drain the eggs and place them in the freezer to chill for 10 minutes.

3 Reserve 4 large lettuce leaves. Wash and dry the remaining lettuce and tear it into bite-size pieces. Trim and slice the scallions. Trim and slice the radishes. Combine the in-gredients in a large bowl and refrigerate until you are ready to use. Peel, pit and slice the avocado and sprinkle it with 1 tablespoon of the lemon juice to keep it from browning.

4 In a small bowl, whisk together the oil, the remaining lemon juice, the paprika, the tarragon and the sugar. Season to taste.

5 Add the avocado to the salad. Peel and chop the eggs and add them to the salad. Sprinkle the salad with the sunflower seeds and toss it with the dressing.

Cumin Through the Rye

1 Preheat the oven to 350°F.

2 In a small bowl, blend together the softened butter, the cumin and the caraway seeds.

3 Slice the bread down, without cutting through the bottom crust. Spread the cumin butter along the cut sides of the bread. Wrap the loaf in aluminum foil and heat until you are ready to serve, 15 to 20 minutes.

Cherries on Top

1 In a small bowl, whisk together the sour cream, the sugar and the vanilla.

2 Reserving 4 whole cherries, place a layer of cherry pie filling in the bottom of 4 parfait glasses. Add a layer of the sour cream mixture. Repeat.

3 Top with the reserved cherries and refrigerate for at least 15 minutes.

WEDNESDAY

World Series Chicken

4 boneless, skinless chicken breast halves
2 tablespoons butter
1 teaspoon dried oregano
Seasoning to taste
4 slices prosciutto ham
4 slices regular or low-fat mozzarella cheese
$1/4$ cup dry white wine (or nonalcoholic white
    wine or chicken broth)

Home Run Rice

1 small onion
1 clove garlic
1 small red bell pepper
2 tablespoons fresh basil (when chopped)
1 can (11 ounces) whole kernel corn
1 tablespoon regular or light olive oil
1 cup long-grain white rice
1 can ($14^1/2$ ounces) chicken broth
$1/2$ cup water

Pinch-Hitting Pears

4 medium pears
2 tablespoons lemon juice
4 lettuce leaves reserved from Tuesday
1 tablespoon honey
2 teaspoons poppy seeds

Double Play Pudding

1 medium can (16 ounces) pumpkin
$1/2$ teaspoon ground cinnamon
$1/4$ teaspoon ground nutmeg
$1/4$ teaspoon ground ginger
1 teaspoon vanilla extract
1 small container (8 ounces) frozen whipped
    topping

EQUIPMENT

Large covered skillet	Measuring cups and
Medium skillet	spoons
Double boiler	Assorted cooking
Large bowl	utensils
Medium bowl	Waxed paper
Assorted kitchen knives	Mallet

COUNTDOWN

1 Assemble the ingredients and equipment
2 Do Steps 1–2 of the *Home Run Rice*
3 Do Steps 1–2 of the *Double Play Pudding*
4 Do Step 1 of the *Pinch-Hitting Pears*
5 Do Steps 1–3 of the *World Series Chicken*
6 Do Step 2 of the *Pinch-Hitting Pears*
7 Do Step 3 of the *Home Run Rice*
8 Do Step 3 of the *Double Play Pudding*

World Series Chicken

1 Place the chicken between sheets of waxed paper and pound them with a mallet to a 1/2-inch thickness.

2 Melt the butter in a large skillet. Add the chicken and sauté until lightly browned, about 4 minutes per side. Sprinkle with the oregano and season to taste.

3 Place a slice of prosciutto and then a slice of cheese on each breast. Drizzle the wine over the chicken. Cover the skillet and cook until the cheese is melted and the chicken is cooked through, about 5 minutes.

Home Run Rice

1 Peel and chop the onion. Peel and mince the garlic. Seed and chop the bell pepper. Chop the basil. Drain the corn. Heat the oil in a medium skillet and sauté the onion, the garlic and the peppers until they are limp, about 5 minutes. Add the corn and sauté for 1 minute more.

2 Combine the rice, the broth, the water, the basil, the onion, the garlic, the bell pepper and the corn in the top of a double boiler. Bring water to a boil in the bottom of the double boiler. Reduce the heat, cover and simmer until all the liquid is absorbed and the rice is tender, 30 to 40 minutes.

3 Fluff the rice before serving.

Pinch-Hitting Pears

1 Core and slice the pears. Place them in a medium bowl and sprinkle them with the lemon juice to keep them from browning. Refrigerate until you are ready to use.

2 Wash and dry the lettuce leaves, place them on individual salad plates and top them with the pear slices. Drizzle the pears with the honey and sprinkle with the poppy seeds.

Double Play Pudding

1 In a large bowl, blend together the pumpkin, the cinnamon, the nutmeg, the ginger and the vanilla. Gently fold in half of the whipped topping to achieve a streaky look.

2 Spoon the mixture into individual dessert dishes and refrigerate for at least 20 minutes.

3 Garnish the pudding with dollops of the remaining whipped topping.

THURSDAY

Skinny Pasta

1 medium onion
2 cloves garlic
$1/4$ cup fresh parsley (when chopped)
1 tablespoon fresh basil (when chopped)
3 tablespoons regular or light olive oil
1 large can (28 ounces) crushed tomatoes
1 small can (6 ounces) tomato paste
1 teaspoon dried oregano
2 teaspoons sugar
$1/8$ teaspoon red pepper flakes
1 cup water
Seasoning to taste
16 ounces capellini (angel hair pasta)
$1/4$ cup grated Parmesan cheese

A Slip of a Salad

1 medium head lettuce
2 scallions (green onions)
$1/2$ pound fresh mushrooms
2 ounces fresh bean sprouts
2 tablespoons lemon juice
3 tablespoons regular or light olive oil
$1/4$ teaspoon dried tarragon
$1/4$ teaspoon sugar
Seasoning to taste

Red Bread

1 clove garlic
1 large jar (4 ounces) diced pimientos
1 small loaf Italian bread
1 tube (1.58 ounces) anchovy paste
1 tablespoon regular or light olive oil

Impossible Pie

$1/2$ cup semisweet chocolate chips
4 tablespoons butter
2 eggs
1 cup whole or low-fat milk
$1/2$ cup sugar
1 teaspoon vanilla extract
$1/2$ cup Bisquick
Whipped cream for garnish

EQUIPMENT

Blender	Assorted kitchen knives
Large covered skillet	Measuring cups and
Large saucepan	spoons
Small saucepan	Assorted cooking
9-inch pie plate	utensils
Large bowl	Whisk
2 small bowls	Aluminum foil
Colander	

COUNTDOWN

1 Assemble the ingredients and equipment
2 Do Steps 1–3 of the *Impossible Pie*
3 Do Steps 1–4 of the *Skinny Pasta*
4 Do Steps 1–3 of the *Red Bread*
5 Do Steps 1–2 of *A Slip of a Salad*
6 Do Step 4 of the *Impossible Pie*
7 Do Steps 5–6 of the *Skinny Pasta*
8 Do Step 5 of the *Impossible Pie*
9 Do Step 3 of *A Slip of a Salad*

Skinny Pasta

1 Peel and chop the onion. Peel and mince the garlic. Chop the parsley. Chop the basil.

2 Heat the oil in a large skillet. Add the onion and the garlic and sauté until they are soft, about 5 minutes.

3 Add the crushed tomatoes, the tomato paste, the parsley, the basil, the oregano, the sugar, the red pepper flakes and the water. Season to taste. Bring the mixture to a boil, partially cover, reduce the heat, and cook until the liquid is reduced by a third, 15 to 20 minutes.

4 Bring water to a boil in a large saucepan.

5 Cook the pasta in the boiling water until it is almost tender, 1 to 2 minutes if you are using fresh pasta and 3 to 4 minutes if you are using dried pasta.

6 Drain the pasta, return it to the saucepan and toss it with the sauce. Sprinkle with the Parmesan cheese.

A Slip of a Salad

1 Wash and dry the lettuce and tear it into bite-size pieces. Trim and chop the scallions. Wash, pat dry, trim and slice the mushrooms. Combine the ingredients in a large bowl. Add the sprouts and toss lightly.

2 In a small bowl, whisk together the lemon juice, the oil, the tarragon and the sugar. Season to taste.

3 Toss the salad with the dressing.

Red Bread

1 Preheat the oven to 350°F.

2 Peel and mince the garlic. Drain the pimientos. Slice the bread in half lengthwise.

3 In a small bowl, combine the garlic, the pimientos, the anchovy paste and the oil. Spread the mixture on the bottom cut side of the bread. Replace the top half. Wrap the bread in aluminum foil and heat it in the oven until you are ready to serve.

Impossible Pie

1 Preheat the oven to 350°F. Grease a 9-inch pie plate.

2 In a small saucepan, melt the chocolate chips with the butter.

3 Combine the eggs, the milk, the sugar, the vanilla and the Bisquick in a blender. Add the chocolate mixture and process until smooth. Pour the mixture into the pie plate and bake until the pie is set, about 30 minutes.

4 Remove the pie from the oven and let it cool.

5 Garnish the cooled pie with dollops of whipped cream.

FRIDAY

MENU

Flashy Flounder

1 clove garlic
2 medium shallots
1 small red bell pepper
3 tablespoons flour
1 teaspoon dried tarragon
Seasoning to taste
4 flounder fillets (1$^1/_4$ pounds)
2 tablespoons olive oil
3 tablespoons chili sauce
$^1/_3$ cup apple juice

Feisty Potatoes

1 pound small new red potatoes
$^1/_3$ cup fresh parsley (when chopped)
3 tablespoons butter
1$^1/_2$ tablespoons Dijon mustard
$^1/_4$ teaspoon paprika
Seasoning to taste

Snappy Peas & Carrots

$^1/_2$ pound sugar snap peas
$^1/_2$ pound medium carrots
2 tablespoons butter
$^1/_2$ teaspoon ground cinnamon
Seasoning to taste

Pineapple Splash

1 package (12 ounces) frozen raspberries
1 tablespoon cornstarch
$^1/_4$ cup sugar
1$^1/_2$ tablespoons Kirsch liqueur (or
    nonalcoholic Italian cherry syrup)
1 pound fresh pineapple chunks (or net weight
    canned)

EQUIPMENT

2 large skillets	Assorted kitchen knives
Large covered saucepan	Measuring cups and spoons
Small covered saucepan	Assorted cooking utensils
9x13-inch baking pan	Vegetable brush
Shallow bowl	Vegetable peeler
Colander	Aluminum foil

COUNTDOWN

IN THE MORNING:
  Do Step 1 of the *Pineapple Splash*
BEFORE DINNER:
  1 Assemble the remaining ingredients and equipment
  2 Do Steps 2–3 of the *Pineapple Splash*
  3 Do Steps 1–6 of the *Flashy Founder*
  4 Do Steps 1–2 of the *Feisty Potatoes*
  5 Do Step 1 of the *Snappy Peas & Carrots*
  6 Do Step 7 of the *Flashy Flounder*
  7 Do Step 3 of the *Feisty Potatoes*
  8 Do Step 2 of the *Snappy Peas & Carrots*
  9 Do Step 4 of the *Pineapple Splash*

Flashy Flounder

1 Peel and mince the garlic. Peel and thinly slice the shallots. Seed and thinly slice the bell pepper.

2 Preheat the oven to 375°F. Line a 9x13-inch baking pan with aluminum foil.

3 In a shallow bowl, combine the flour with the tarragon. Season to taste. Pat dry the fish fillets and coat them in the mixture.

4 Heat the oil in a large skillet. Add the garlic and the shallots and sauté for 1 minute. Add the fish fillets and brown them quickly, about 2 minutes per side.

5 Transfer the fillets, the garlic and the shallots to the baking pan.

6 Add the chili sauce and the apple juice to the skillet and bring to a boil, scraping up any browned bits. Pour the mixture over the fish and top with the bell pepper slices. Cover the pan tightly with aluminum foil.

7 Bake the fish until it flakes with a fork, 10 to 12 minutes.

Feisty Potatoes

1 Bring water to a boil in a large saucepan. Scrub the potatoes. Chop the parsley.

2 Boil the potatoes until they are tender, 10 to 15 minutes.

3 Drain the potatoes. Melt the butter in the saucepan. Stir in the parsley, the mustard and the paprika. Roll the potatoes around until they are well coated. Season to taste and cover to keep warm.

Snappy Peas & Carrots

1 Trim and string the sugar snap peas. Peel and slice the carrots.

2 Melt the butter with the cinnamon in a large skillet. Sauté the carrots for 5 minutes. Add the snap peas and sauté until they are crisp-tender, 2 to 3 minutes. Season to taste.

Pineapple Splash

1 Set the package of frozen raspberries in the refrigerator to thaw.

2 In a small saucepan, combine the thawed raspberries, the cornstarch and the sugar. Cook until the sauce turns clear and begins to thicken, about 5 minutes.

3 Remove the saucepan from the heat, stir in the Kirsch, cover and refrigerate until you are ready to serve.

4 Distribute the pineapple chunks among individual dessert bowls. Top with the raspberry sauce.

OCTOBER

WEEK THREE

Monday

NIÑA SNAPPER
PINTA PILAF
SANTA MARIA SALAD
NEW WORLD PEAR LOAF

Tuesday

MANHATTAN CHICKEN
TRUMPED-UP RICE
BROOKLYN BEANS
MIDTOWN DECADENCE

Wednesday

OCTOBER OMELET
PEPPY POTATOES
GREAT GREENS
SOMETHING LEMONY

Thursday

GARLIC-GARLIC PORK
FOOL'S GOLD
IMPECCABLE PEPPERS
VERY BERRY CROISSANTS

Friday

UP IN SMOKE
SWAYING PALM SALAD
MAPLE CRUNCHIES

CHECK STAPLES

- ☐ Butter
- ☐ Flour
- ☐ Cornstarch
- ☐ Granulated sugar
- ☐ Dark brown sugar
- ☐ Confectioners' sugar
- ☐ Maple syrup
- ☐ Chocolate sprinkles
- ☐ Long-grain white rice
- ☐ Regular or light vegetable oil
- ☐ Regular or light olive oil
- ☐ Walnut oil
- ☐ White wine vinegar
- ☐ Rice vinegar
- ☐ Tarragon vinegar
- ☐ Lemon juice
- ☐ Grated fresh lemon peel
- ☐ Worcestershire sauce
- ☐ Dijon mustard
- ☐ Seasoned bread crumbs
- ☐ Ground allspice
- ☐ Celery seeds
- ☐ Ground cinnamon
- ☐ Dried dill
- ☐ Ground nutmeg
- ☐ Dried oregano
- ☐ Paprika
- ☐ Dried rosemary
- ☐ Saffron threads
- ☐ Sesame seeds
- ☐ Pepper
- ☐ Salt
- ☐ Rum extract
- ☐ Vanilla extract

SHOPPING NOTE

● If you are shopping once a week and cannot arrange to purchase fresh fish on the day you plan to use it, you can purchase *not previously frozen* fish and freeze it, placing it in the refrigerator to thaw the night before you are ready to use it. Or you can purchase *still frozen* seafood and keep it frozen until the night before you are ready to use it.

MEAT & POULTRY

$1^1/_4$ pounds lean boneless pork loin (Th)
4 boneless, skinless chicken breast halves (T)

FISH

4 red snapper fillets ($1^1/_4$ pounds) (M)
1 salmon fillet (1 pound) (F)

FRESH PRODUCE

Vegetables

1 pound medium baking potatoes (W)
3 large sweet potatoes (Th)
1 pound green beans (T)
1 small bunch broccoli (W)
$^1/_2$ pound mushrooms (T)
2 medium carrots (Th)
4 large stalks celery (W)
2 medium onions—1 (M), 1 (W)
2 small onions—1 (T), 1 (Th)
6 scallions (green onions)—3 (T), 3 (F)
1 head garlic (M, T, W, Th)
1 bunch chives (T, Th)
1 small head lettuce (F)
1 ripe avocado (F)
$^3/_4$ pound tomatoes—$^1/_4$ pound (M), $^1/_2$ pound (F)
2 medium cucumbers (M)
3 medium red bell peppers (Th)

Fruit

2 large pears (M)
3 large tart green apples (W)

CANS, JARS & BOTTLES

Soup

1 can ($14^1/_2$ ounces) chicken broth (T)
1 can ($10^3/_4$ ounces) chicken broth (Th)

Vegetables

1 can (14 ounces) hearts of palm (F)

Fish

1 can ($6^1/_2$ ounces) chopped clams (M)

Juice

$^1/_4$ cup clam juice (M)

Condiments

1 small can (3.3 ounces) sliced black olives (M)
2 tablespoons capers (M)
3 tablespoons liquid smoke (F)

Dessert Needs

1 can (14 ounces) regular or low-fat sweetened condensed milk (T)

PACKAGED GOODS

Pasta, Rice & Grains

8 ounces capellini (angel hair pasta) (M)
12 ounces spaghetti (F)
1 cup corn flakes cereal (F)

Baked Goods

4 small croissants (Th)
8 slices white bread (F)
1 loaf cake (M)

Nuts & Seeds

$^1/_4$ cup sliced almonds (M)
$^1/_2$ cup chopped walnuts (F)

Dessert & Baking Needs

1 small package (3.4 ounces) instant lemon pudding mix (W)
8 lemon cookies (W)

WINES & SPIRITS

1 cup dry red wine (or nonalcoholic red wine or clam juice) (M)
$^1/_3$ cup dry white wine (or nonalcoholic white wine or chicken broth) (T)
$^3/_4$ cup dry white wine (or nonalcoholic white wine or clam juice) (F)

REFRIGERATED PRODUCTS

Dairy

1 cup whole milk (W)
3 tablespoons whole or low-fat milk (W)
$1^1/_4$ cups half-and-half—$^1/_4$ cup (Th), 1 cup (F)
Whipped cream for garnish (F)
$^1/_2$ cup regular or light sour cream (M)
9 eggs—1 (T), 8 (W)

Cheese

1 cup regular or low-fat small-curd cottage cheese (W)
4 slices regular or low-fat Swiss cheese (T)
$^1/_2$ cup shredded regular or low-fat cheddar cheese (W)
$^1/_4$ cup shredded regular or low-fat mozzarella cheese (F)

FROZEN GOODS

Vegetables

1 package (9 ounces) chopped spinach (T)

Fruit

1 package (10 ounces) sweetened strawberries (Th)

Desserts

1 pint strawberry frozen yogurt (Th)
1 small container (8 ounces) frozen whipped topping (T)

MONDAY

Niña Snapper

1 medium onion
1 clove garlic
$^1/_4$ pound fresh tomatoes
1 small can (3.3 ounces) sliced black olives
2 tablespoons capers
$^1/_2$ cup flour
$^1/_2$ teaspoon dried oregano
Seasoning to taste
4 red snapper fillets (1$^1/_4$ pounds)
$^1/_4$ cup regular or light olive oil
1 can (6$^1/_2$ ounces) chopped clams
$^1/_4$ cup clam juice
1 cup dry red wine (or nonalcoholic red wine
    or additional clam juice)

Pinta Pilaf

2 cloves garlic
3 tablespoons butter
Seasoning to taste
8 ounces capellini (angel hair pasta)

Santa Maria Salad

2 medium cucumbers
2 tablespoons fresh chives (when chopped)
$^1/_2$ cup regular or light sour cream
1 tablespoon rice vinegar
1 teaspoon lemon juice
Seasoning to taste
$^1/_4$ cup sliced almonds

New World Pear Loaf

2 large pears
1 tablespoon lemon juice
3 tablespoons butter
$^1/_2$ cup dark brown sugar
2 tablespoons flour
2 tablespoons water
1 teaspoon vanilla extract
1 loaf cake

EQUIPMENT

Large covered skillet	Strainer
Medium skillet	Assorted kitchen knives
Small skillet	Measuring cups and
Large covered	spoons
saucepan	Assorted cooking
Small saucepan	utensils
Cookie sheet	Whisk
2 medium bowls	Vegetable peeler
Shallow bowl	

COUNTDOWN

1 Assemble the ingredients and equipment
2 Do Steps 1–2 of the *Santa Maria Salad*
3 Do Steps 1–4 of the *New World Pear Loaf*
4 Do Steps 1–3 of the *Niña Snapper*
5 Do Step 1 of the *Pinta Pilaf*
6 Do Steps 4–6 of the *Niña Snapper*
7 Do Steps 2–4 of the *Pinta Pilaf*
8 Do Step 7 of the *Niña Snapper*
9 Do Step 3 of the *Santa Maria Salad*

Niña Snapper

1 Peel and chop the onion. Peel and mince the garlic. Chop the tomatoes. Drain the olives. Drain the capers.

2 Combine the flour and the oregano in a shallow bowl. Season to taste. Dredge the snapper to coat lightly on both sides and shake off any excess.

3 Heat 2 tablespoons of the oil in a large skillet. Add the fish in a single layer and cook, turning once, until the fillets are golden outside and opaque throughout, about 8 minutes.

4 Cover the skillet and remove it from the heat.

5 Heat the remaining oil in a medium skillet. Add the onion and the garlic and sauté until they are softened, about 5 minutes. Add the tomatoes and the olives and cook, stirring, for 1 minute more.

6 Add the capers, the undrained clams, the clam juice and the wine. Bring the mixture to a boil and cook until the liquid reduces by a third, about 3 minutes.

7 Arrange the fish over the pilaf and pour the clam sauce over it.

Pinta Pilaf

1 Bring water to a boil in a large saucepan.

2 Peel and mince the garlic. Melt the butter in a small skillet. Sauté the garlic until it is golden, about 5 minutes. Season to taste.

3 Cook the pasta until it is almost tender, 1 to 2 minutes if you are using fresh pasta and 3 to 4 minutes if you are using dried pasta.

4 Drain the pasta, return it to the saucepan and toss it with the butter mixture. Cover to keep warm.

Santa Maria Salad

1 Peel and slice the cucumbers. Chop the chives.

2 In a medium bowl, whisk together the sour cream, the chives, the vinegar and the lemon juice. Season to taste. Toss with the cucumbers and refrigerate until you are ready to serve.

3 Sprinkle with the sliced almonds.

New World Pear Loaf

1 Peel, core and slice the pears. Place them in a medium bowl and sprinkle them with the lemon juice to keep them from browning. Let them stand.

2 Preheat the broiler. Lightly grease a cookie sheet.

3 Melt the butter in a small saucepan. Add the brown sugar, the flour, the water and the vanilla and whisk until a glaze forms.

4 Place the loaf cake on the cookie sheet. Arrange the pear slices on top of the cake. Drizzle the glaze over the pears. Place the cake under the broiler, 3 or 4 inches from the heat, and broil until the glaze begins to bubble, 2 to 3 minutes. Let cool before serving.

TUESDAY

Manhattan Chicken

1 package (9 ounces) frozen chopped spinach
1 small onion
$1/2$ pound fresh mushrooms
1 clove garlic
4 boneless, skinless chicken breast halves
1 egg
$3/4$ cup seasoned bread crumbs
Seasoning to taste
2 tablespoons regular or light vegetable oil
2 tablespoons butter
$1/2$ teaspoon ground nutmeg
4 slices regular or low-fat Swiss cheese
$1/3$ cup dry white wine (or nonalcoholic white
   wine or chicken broth)

Trumped-up Rice

3 scallions (green onions)
2 tablespoons butter
1 cup long-grain white rice
1 teaspoon saffron threads
$1/4$ cup water
1 can ($14^{1}/_{2}$ ounces) chicken broth
$1/4$ teaspoon ground allspice

Brooklyn Beans

1 pound green beans
4 teaspoons butter
1 teaspoon Worcestershire sauce
1 teaspoon lemon juice
Seasoning to taste
1 teaspoon grated fresh lemon peel

Midtown Decadence

3 ounces semisweet chocolate chips
1 can (14 ounces) regular or low-fat
   sweetened condensed milk
$1/2$ teaspoon rum extract
$1/2$ teaspoon vanilla extract
1 small container (8 ounces) frozen whipped
   topping
Chocolate sprinkles

EQUIPMENT

Large covered skillet	2 shallow bowls
Medium covered skillet	Strainer
Double boiler	Assorted kitchen knives
Large covered	Measuring cups and
saucepan	spoons
Small saucepan	Assorted cooking
Steamer insert	utensils
Large bowl	Waxed paper
Medium bowl	Mallet

COUNTDOWN

1 Assemble the ingredients and equipment
2 Do Step 1 of the *Midtown Decadence*
3 Do Steps 1–2 of the *Trumped-up Rice*
4 Do Step 2 of the *Midtown Decadence*
5 Do Step 1 of the *Brooklyn Beans*
6 Do Steps 1–7 of the *Manhattan Chicken*
7 Do Steps 2–3 of the *Brooklyn Beans*
8 Do Step 3 of the *Trumped-up Rice*
9 Do Step 3 of the *Midtown Decadence*

Manhattan Chicken

1 Set the package of spinach in a medium bowl of hot water to thaw.

2 Peel and chop the onion. Wash, pat dry, trim and slice the mushrooms. Peel and mince the garlic. Drain the spinach.

3 Place the chicken breasts between sheets of waxed paper and pound them with a mallet to a $1/4$-inch thickness.

4 Lightly beat the egg in a shallow bowl. Place the bread crumbs in a second shallow bowl and season to taste. Dip the chicken breasts in the egg and then dredge them in the bread crumbs to coat.

5 Heat the oil in a large skillet. Add the chicken and cook until it is lightly browned, about 3 minutes per side. Remove the chicken and cover to keep warm.

6 Melt the butter in the skillet. Add the onion and sauté it for 2 minutes. Add the mushrooms and the garlic and sauté until the mushrooms are tender, about 5 minutes. Add the spinach and the nutmeg. Season to taste. Mix well and cook until the mixture is heated through, about 3 minutes.

7 Remove the mixture from the skillet. Return the chicken to the skillet, and place $1/4$ of the mushroom-spinach mixture on each breast. Top with a slice of cheese. Add the wine, cover and cook until the cheese is melted and the chicken is tender, 6 to 7 minutes.

Trumped-up Rice

1 Trim and chop the scallions. Melt the butter in a medium skillet and sauté the scallions for 1 minute. Add the rice and sauté for 3 minutes more.

2 Stir the saffron into the water in the top of a double boiler. Add the rice mixture, the broth and the allspice. Bring water to a boil in the bottom of the double boiler, reduce the heat, cover and simmer until all the liquid is absorbed and the rice is tender, 30 to 40 minutes.

3 Fluff the rice before serving.

Brooklyn Beans

1 Trim and string the green beans and cut them diagonally into 1-inch pieces.

2 Bring water to a boil in a large saucepan. Place a steamer insert in the saucepan, add the beans and steam until they are crisp-tender, about 5 minutes.

3 Drain the beans. Melt the butter in the saucepan. Add the Worcestershire sauce and the lemon juice. Season to taste. Return the beans to the saucepan and stir to coat. Heat through, 1 to 2 minutes. Garnish with the lemon peel.

Midtown Decadence

1 Melt the chocolate chips in the condensed milk in a small saucepan, stirring until smooth. Remove the saucepan from the heat. Stir in the rum and vanilla extracts. Place the mixture in a large bowl and chill in the freezer for 10 minutes.

2 Remove the chocolate mixture from the freezer. Reserving half of the whipped topping, fold the remainder into the mixture, and pour the mixture into individual dessert dishes. Refrigerate for at least 20 minutes.

3 Garnish the chocolate creams with the reserved whipped topping and the chocolate sprinkles.

WEDNESDAY

October Omelet

1 medium onion
3 large tart green apples
1 1/2 tablespoons lemon juice
1/4 teaspoon ground nutmeg
1/4 teaspoon ground cinnamon
4 tablespoons butter
8 eggs
3 tablespoons whole or low-fat milk
Seasoning to taste
1/2 cup shredded regular or low-fat cheddar
    cheese

Peppy Potatoes

1 pound medium baking potatoes
1 teaspoon dried rosemary
2 tablespoons butter
2 tablespoons regular or light vegetable oil
2 tablespoons sesame seeds
1/8 teaspoon cayenne pepper
Seasoning to taste

Great Greens

1 small bunch broccoli
4 large stalks celery
2 cloves garlic
2 tablespoons regular or light vegetable oil
1/2 teaspoon celery seeds
2 tablespoons water
Seasoning to taste

Something Lemony

1 cup regular or low-fat small-curd cottage
    cheese
1 cup whole milk
1 small package (3.4 ounces) instant lemon
    pudding mix
4 teaspoons lemon juice
8 lemon cookies

EQUIPMENT

Blender	Assorted kitchen knives
Large covered skillet	Measuring cups and
Large skillet	spoons
Medium covered	Assorted cooking
saucepan	utensils
Medium saucepan	Apple corer
9x13-inch baking pan	Whisk
2 medium bowls	

COUNTDOWN

1 Assemble the ingredients and equipment
2 Do Step 1 of *Something Lemony*
3 Do Steps 1–4 of the *Peppy Potatoes*
4 Do Step 1 of the *October Omelet*
5 Do Steps 1–2 of the *Great Greens*
6 Do Steps 2–5 of the *October Omelet*
7 Do Step 3 of the *Great Greens*
8 Do Step 6 of the *October Omelet*
9 Do Step 2 of *Something Lemony*

RECIPES

October Omelet

1 Peel and chop the onion. Peel, core and slice the apples. Place the apples in a medium bowl with the lemon juice, the nutmeg and the cinnamon. Toss to coat and let the apples stand.

2 Melt 2 tablespoons of the butter in a large covered skillet. Add the apples and the onion, and sauté until the apples begin to brown, 6 to 8 minutes.

3 In a medium bowl, whisk the eggs with the milk. Season to taste.

4 Melt the remaining butter in a large skillet and pour in the eggs. Cook gently until the eggs are set, lifting the edges to let the uncooked part flow to the bottom of the skillet, about 5 minutes.

5 Remove the apple-onion mixture from the heat and cover to keep warm.

6 When the eggs are set, spoon half of the apple-onion mixture down the center of the omelet. Add the cheese. Fold a third of the omelet over the filling and remove it to a large plate. Flip the folded portion of the omelet over the remaining third of the omelet. Top with the remaining apple-onion mixture.

Peppy Potatoes

1 Preheat the oven to 350°F.

2 Bring water to a boil in a medium saucepan. Peel the potatoes and dice them into 1-inch cubes. Crush the rosemary. Boil the potatoes for 5 minutes.

3 Place the butter with the oil in a 9x13-inch baking pan and melt the mixture in the oven.

4 Drain the potatoes and place them in the pan, tossing to coat. Sprinkle the potatoes with the rosemary, the sesame seeds and the cayenne. Season to taste and bake until the potatoes are crisp and golden, turning them occasionally, 20 to 25 minutes.

Great Greens

1 Trim and cut the broccoli into bite-size florets. Trim and diagonally slice the celery. Peel and crush the garlic.

2 Heat the oil in a medium covered saucepan. Add the garlic and sauté for 1 minute. Add the broccoli, the celery and the celery seeds, and sauté for 5 minutes. Cover, remove from the heat and let stand.

3 Add the water to the broccoli and celery mixture, season to taste, return to the heat, cover and cook gently for 2 to 3 minutes.

Something Lemony

1 In a blender, process the cottage cheese for 5 seconds. Add the milk, the lemon pudding mix and the lemon juice and process until the mixture is smooth, about 1 minute. Refrigerate for at least 20 minutes.

2 Place a cookie in the bottom of individual dessert dishes. Spoon the lemon mixture over the cookie. Finish with the remaining cookies, set into the pudding on their sides.

THURSDAY

Garlic-Garlic Pork

4 cloves garlic
1 1/4 pounds lean boneless pork loin
Seasoning to taste
2 tablespoons regular or light vegetable oil
1 can (10 3/4 ounces) chicken broth
1 teaspoon Dijon mustard
1 tablespoon cornstarch dissolved in 2
    tablespoons water

Fool's Gold

1 tablespoon fresh chives (when chopped)
2 medium carrots
3 large sweet potatoes
1 small onion
2 tablespoons butter
1/4 cup half-and-half
Seasoning to taste

Impeccable Peppers

3 medium red bell peppers
1 1/2 tablespoons butter
1/2 teaspoon ground allspice
Seasoning to taste

Very Berry Croissants

1 package (10 ounces) frozen sweetened
    strawberries
4 small croissants
1 pint strawberry frozen yogurt
1/4 cup confectioners' sugar

EQUIPMENT

Electric hand mixer	Assorted kitchen knives
Blender	Measuring cups and
Large skillet	spoons
Medium covered skillet	Assorted cooking
Large covered	utensils
saucepan	Whisk
Strainer	Vegetable peeler
Medium bowl	Sifter

COUNTDOWN

1 Assemble the ingredients and equipment
2 Do Step 1 of the *Very Berry Croissants*
3 Do Steps 1–2 of the *Fool's Gold*
4 Do Step 1 of the *Impeccable Peppers*
5 Do Steps 1–4 of the *Garlic-Garlic Pork*
6 Do Step 3 of the *Fool's Gold*
7 Do Step 2 of the *Impeccable Peppers*
8 Do Step 5 of the *Garlic-Garlic Pork*
9 Do Steps 2–3 of the *Very Berry Croissants*

Garlic-Garlic Pork

1 Peel and mince the garlic.

2 Trim any excess fat from the pork and cut the meat into 8 slices. Rub the garlic into the pork slices and season to taste.

3 Heat the oil in a large skillet. Sauté the pork until all the slices are well browned on both sides, about 10 minutes. Add more oil if necessary. Remove the pork and keep warm.

4 Add the broth and the mustard to the skillet, stirring to scrape up any browned bits. Bring the mixture to a boil. Whisk in the cornstarch mixture. Cook, stirring, until the sauce reduces slightly and begins to thicken, 8 to 10 minutes.

5 Return the pork to the skillet and coat the slices with the sauce.

Fool's Gold

1 Chop the chives. Peel and slice the carrots. Peel and cube the sweet potatoes. Peel and halve the onion.

2 Cover the carrots, the potatoes and the onion with water in a large saucepan. Bring the water to a boil, cover and cook until the vegetables are very tender, 15 to 20 minutes.

3 Drain the carrots and the potatoes. Discard the onion. Return the carrots and the potatoes to the saucepan and beat them with the butter and the half–and–half until the mixture is well blended. For color, pieces of carrot should remain. Season to taste, garnish with the chopped chives and cover to keep warm.

Impeccable Peppers

1 Seed the peppers and cut them into thin strips.

2 Melt the butter with the allspice in a medium skillet and sauté the peppers until they are crisp-tender, about 5 minutes. Season to taste, remove the skillet from the heat and cover to keep warm.

Very Berry Croissants

1 Set the package of strawberries in a medium bowl of hot water to thaw.

2 Process the thawed strawberries in a blender until pureed.

3 Cut a lengthwise slit down the inside of the croissants and fill them with the frozen yogurt. Spoon the pureed berries over the croissants and dust them with the confectioners' sugar.

FRIDAY

Up in Smoke

1 salmon fillet (1 pound)
3 tablespoons liquid smoke
3 scallions (green onions)
2 tablespoons white wine vinegar
1 cup half-and-half
$^3/_4$ cup dry white wine (or nonalcoholic white
    wine or clam juice)
1 tablespoon Dijon mustard
Seasoning to taste
12 ounces spaghetti
$^1/_4$ cup shredded regular or low-fat
    mozzarella cheese
$^1/_4$ teaspoon paprika

Swaying Palm Salad

$^1/_2$ pound fresh tomatoes
1 ripe avocado
2 tablespoons lemon juice
1 small head lettuce
1 can (14 ounces) hearts of palm
3 tablespoons olive oil
2 tablespoons tarragon vinegar
$^1/_2$ teaspoon sugar
$^1/_2$ teaspoon Worcestershire sauce
1 teaspoon dried dill
Seasoning to taste
$^1/_2$ cup chopped walnuts

Maple Crunchies

4 tablespoons butter
8 slices white bread
2 tablespoons maple syrup
1 cup corn flakes cereal
Whipped cream for garnish

EQUIPMENT	
Small roasting pan with rack	Measuring cups and spoons
Stockpot	Assorted cooking utensils
Medium skillet	
Small saucepan	Whisk
12-cup muffin tin	Pastry brush
Small bowl	Rolling pin
Colander	3-inch biscuit cutter
Assorted kitchen knives	Aluminum foil

COUNTDOWN

1 Assemble the ingredients and equipment
2 Do Steps 1–5 of the *Maple Crunchies*
3 Do Steps 1–3 of the *Swaying Palm Salad*
4 Do Steps 1–7 of the *Up in Smoke*
5 Do Step 4 of the *Swaying Palm Salad*
6 Do Step 6 of the *Maple Crunchies*

Up in Smoke

1 Preheat the oven to 350°F. Bring water to a boil in a stockpot.

2 Skin the salmon fillet, if necessary, and cut it into ½-inch strips.

3 Pour the liquid smoke into a small roasting pan. Set a rack in the pan. Arrange the salmon strips on the rack. Cover the pan tightly with aluminum foil and bake until the fish can be flaked easily with a fork, 10 to 12 minutes.

4 Trim and chop the scallions. Combine the scallions and the vinegar in a medium skillet. Bring the vinegar to a boil and cook until it has evaporated, about 1 minute. Blend in the half-and-half, the wine and the mustard. Season to taste. Bring the mixture to a boil and cook until the sauce has thickened slightly, 5 to 7 minutes.

5 Cook the spaghetti until it is almost tender, 2 to 3 minutes if you are using fresh pasta and 7 to 8 minutes if you are using dried pasta.

6 Drain the pasta and return it to the stockpot. Add the cream mixture and toss to coat. Sprinkle with the cheese and the paprika.

7 Arrange the salmon strips over the pasta.

Swaying Palm Salad

1 Chop the tomatoes. Peel, pit and slice the avocado, place it in a small bowl and toss it with the lemon juice. Wash and dry the lettuce and place the leaves on individual salad plates. Drain and thinly slice the hearts of palm.

2 Arrange the hearts of palm, the avocados and the tomatoes over the lettuce.

3 In the avocado bowl, whisk together any residual lemon juice with the oil, the vinegar, the sugar, the Worcestershire sauce and the dill. Season to taste.

4 Drizzle the dressing over the salad. Top with the chopped walnuts.

Maple Crunchies

1 Preheat the oven to 425°F.

2 Melt the butter in a small saucepan.

3 Flatten the bread with a rolling pin and cut out a 3-inch circle from each slice

4 Brush 1 side of the bread with the melted butter. Press the circle into a 12-cup muffin tin, buttered side down, and brush the inside of the bread with the remaining butter.

5 Warm the syrup in the butter saucepan. Crush the corn flakes lightly with your hands and add them to the syrup. Stir well and spoon the mixture into the bread cups. Half fill the unused muffin cups with water. Bake the tarts until they are crispy, about 10 minutes.

6 Top the crunchies with a dollop of whipped cream.

OCTOBER
WEEK FOUR

WEEK AT A GLANCE

Monday

TURKEY SINGS THE BLUES
NOT-SO-PLAIN JANE RICE
PEAS PLEASE
WHITE ON WHITE

Tuesday

GREEN HORNET LASAGNA
KATO SALAD
LICKETY SPLITS

Wednesday

CHUCKWAGON BEEF & BEANS
BACK AT THE RANCH SALAD
BRANDED PEARS
CORRAL CAKE

Thursday

REGGAE CHICKEN
COUSIN COUSCOUS
SAMBA SALAD
ALMOND MERENGUE

Friday

RED ORANGE ROUGHY
SPICED YELLOW SQUASH
GREEN GREEN SALAD
SNAP, CRACKLE & POP PIE

CHECK STAPLES

- ☐ Butter
- ☐ Flour
- ☐ Baking powder
- ☐ Baking soda
- ☐ Corn syrup
- ☐ Granulated sugar
- ☐ Dark brown sugar
- ☐ Confectioners' sugar
- ☐ Brown rice
- ☐ Regular or light vegetable oil
- ☐ Regular or light olive oil
- ☐ Red wine vinegar
- ☐ Lemon juice
- ☐ Grated fresh orange peel
- ☐ Worcestershire sauce
- ☐ Tabasco sauce
- ☐ Yellow mustard
- ☐ Prepared horseradish
- ☐ Regular or low-fat mayonnaise
- ☐ Honey
- ☐ Creamy-style peanut butter
- ☐ Grated Parmesan cheese
- ☐ Dried basil
- ☐ Ground cinnamon
- ☐ Ground nutmeg
- ☐ Dried oregano
- ☐ Paprika
- ☐ Red pepper flakes
- ☐ Pepper
- ☐ Salt
- ☐ Almond extract
- ☐ Vanilla extract

SHOPPING NOTE

● If you are shopping once a week and cannot arrange to purchase fresh orange roughy on the day you plan to use it, you can purchase *not previously frozen* orange roughy and freeze it, placing it in the refrigerator to thaw the night before you are ready to use it. Or you can purchase *still frozen* orange roughy and keep it frozen until the night before you are ready to use it.

MEAT & POULTRY

1 pound lean ground beef (W)
1½ pounds lean boneless
    turkey breast (M)
4 boneless, skinless chicken
    breast halves (Th)

FISH

4 orange roughy (or sole)
    fillets (F)

FRESH PRODUCE

Vegetables

2 medium carrots (W)
1 small carrot (F)
3 stalks celery—1 (M), 2 (W)
1 medium onion (F)
1 small onion (M)
3 small red onions—1 (T), 1 (W),
    1 (Th)
1 medium shallot (M)
7 scallions (green onions)—
    2 (T), 2 (Th), 3 (F)
1 head garlic (M, W, Th, F)
1 bunch parsley (W, F)
2 medium heads lettuce—1 (W),
    1 (Th)
2 small heads lettuce—1 (T),
    1 (F)
2 ripe avocados (F)
1 medium tomato (M)
½ pound tomatoes (Th)
1 large cucumber (T)
1 medium cucumber (Th)
1 large red bell pepper (T)
1 small green bell pepper (W)

Fruit

6 medium pears (W)
2 medium bananas (Th)
4 small bananas (T)
1 medium orange (Th)

CANS, JARS & BOTTLES

Soup

1 can (10¾ ounces) cream of
    chicken soup (M)
1 can (10¾ ounces) chicken
    broth (Th)

1 can (14½ ounces) vegetable
    broth (M)

Vegetables

1 medium can (14½ ounces)
    cut-up tomatoes (F)
1 jar (16 ounces) marinara
    sauce (T)
⅓ cup barbecue sauce (W)
1 can (15½ ounces) ranch-style
    (or regular) baked beans (W)
1 can (15 ounces) white
    beans (W)
1 jar (6½ ounces) marinated
    artichoke hearts (F)

Condiments

1 small can (3.3 ounces) sliced
    black olives (T)
1 tablespoon capers (Th)

Dessert Needs

1 jar (12 ounces) chocolate
    fudge topping (T)

PACKAGED GOODS

Pasta, Rice & Grains

8 ounces lasagna noodles (T)
1 cup couscous (Th)
1 small package (6 ounces) blue
    corn chips (M)
1¼ cups Rice Krispies cereal (F)

Nuts & Seeds

½ cup chopped unsalted
    cashews (M)
½ cup unsalted peanuts (T)
½ cup pecan pieces (W)
¼ cup sliced almonds (Th)

Dessert & Baking Needs

1 package (13 ounces) almond
    macaroons (Th)
1 cup white chocolate chips (M)
½ cup flaked coconut (T)

WINES & SPIRITS

½ cup dry white wine (or
    nonalcoholic white wine or
    clam juice) (F)

¼ cup dry sherry (or
    nonalcoholic white wine or
    water) (M)
2 tablespoons rum (or
    nonalcoholic Italian almond
    syrup) (Th)

REFRIGERATED PRODUCTS

Dairy

½ cup whole or low-fat
    milk—¼ cup (M), ¼ cup (W)
¼ cup buttermilk (W)
6 eggs—2 (T), 2 (W), 2 (Th)

Cheese

1 small container (15 ounces)
    regular or low-fat ricotta
    cheese (T)
1 container (8 ounces) regular
    or light soft cream
    cheese (W)
8 slices regular or low-fat Swiss
    cheese (M)
¾ pound sliced regular or low-
    fat Monterey Jack cheese (T)

Deli

4 slices (½ pound) deli baked
    ham (M)
1 package (10) refrigerator
    biscuits (W)

FROZEN GOODS

Vegetables

1 package (9 ounces) green
    peas (M)
2 packages (9 ounces each)
    chopped spinach (T)
1 package (9 ounces) yellow
    squash (F)

Desserts

1 pint almond-flavored (or
    other) frozen yogurt (Th)
1 pint vanilla ice cream (M)
1 quart rocky road (or similar)
    ice cream (F)
1 small container (8 ounces)
    frozen whipped topping (M)

MONDAY

Turkey Sings the Blues

1 medium tomato
1 pound boneless turkey breast
1 small package (6 ounces) blue corn chips
8 slices regular or low-fat Swiss cheese
4 slices ($^1/_2$ pound) deli baked ham
1 can (10$^3/_4$ ounces) cream of chicken soup
$^1/_4$ cup whole or low-fat milk
Seasoning to taste

Not-So-Plain Jane Rice

1 small onion
1 clove garlic
1 stalk celery
1 tablespoon regular or light vegetable oil
1 cup brown rice
1$^1/_2$ cups vegetable broth
$^1/_4$ cup water
$^1/_4$ cup dry sherry (or nonalcoholic white wine
   or water)

Peas Please

1 package (9 ounces) frozen green peas
1 medium shallot
1 tablespoon butter
$^1/_4$ cup vegetable broth
2 teaspoons honey
$^1/_8$ teaspoon Worcestershire sauce
Seasoning to taste
$^1/_2$ cup chopped unsalted cashews

White on White

1 cup white chocolate chips
1 small container (8 ounces) frozen whipped
   topping
1 pint vanilla ice cream
2 teaspoons confectioners' sugar

EQUIPMENT

Large skillet	Assorted cooking
Medium covered	utensils
saucepan	Ice cream scoop
7x11-inch baking pan	Aluminum foil
Small bowl	Whisk
Assorted kitchen knives	Sifter
Measuring cups and	
spoons	

COUNTDOWN

1 Assemble the ingredients and equipment
2 Do Step 1 of the *Peas Please*
3 Do Steps 1–3 of the *Turkey Sings the Blues*
4 Do Steps 1–2 of the *Not-So-Plain Jane Rice*
5 Do Step 2 of the *Peas Please*
6 Do Step 4 of the *Turkey Sings the Blues*
7 Do Steps 3–4 of the *Peas Please*
8 Do Step 3 of the *Not-So-Plain Jane Rice*
9 Do Steps 1–2 of the *White on White*

Turkey Sings the Blues

1 Preheat the oven to 375°F.

2 Cut the tomato into 4 slices. Cut the turkey breast into 4 portions. Crumble half of the blue corn chips. Place the turkey slices in a 7x11-inch baking pan and top them with the crumbled corn chips, a slice of cheese and a slice of ham.

3 In a small bowl, combine the soup and the milk. Season to taste and pour the mixture over the turkey. Cover the pan with aluminum foil and bake until the turkey is cooked through, about 30 minutes.

4 Remove the foil, top the turkey with the remaining cheese slices, the tomato, and the remaining corn chips. Bake, uncovered, for 5 minutes.

Not-So-Plain Jane Rice

1 Peel and chop the onion. Peel and mince the garlic. Trim and chop the celery.

2 Heat the oil in a medium saucepan. Sauté the onion, the garlic and the celery until they are soft, about 5 minutes. Add the rice, the broth, the water and the sherry, cover tightly and simmer until all the liquid is absorbed and the rice is tender, 30 to 35 minutes.

3 Fluff the rice before serving.

Peas Please

1 Set the frozen peas out to thaw.

2 Peel and mince the shallot.

3 Melt the butter in a large skillet. Add the shallot and sauté for 3 minutes. Add the broth and the honey and combine. Stir in the peas and cook, stirring constantly, until the liquid has evaporated and the peas are tender, about 3 minutes.

4 Add the Worcestershire sauce. Season to taste. Stir in the cashews and combine. Heat through.

White on White

1 Fold the white chocolate chips into the whipped topping.

2 Spoon the whipped mixture over scoops of vanilla ice cream and dust with the confectioners' sugar.

TUESDAY

Green Hornet Lasagna

2 packages (9 ounces each) frozen chopped
    spinach
8 ounces lasagna noodles
2 scallions (green onions)
2 eggs
1 small container (15 ounces) regular or low-
    fat ricotta cheese
1 teaspoon dried oregano
Seasoning to taste
1 jar (16 ounces) marinara sauce
$^3/_4$ pound sliced regular or low-fat Monterey
    Jack cheese
$^1/_2$ cup grated Parmesan cheese

Kato Salad

3 tablespoons regular or light olive oil
2 tablespoons lemon juice
$^1/_2$ teaspoon dried basil
Seasoning to taste
1 large cucumber
1 large red bell pepper
1 small red onion
1 small can (3.3 ounces) sliced black olives
1 small head lettuce

Lickety Splits

$^1/_4$ cup unsalted peanuts
1 jar (12 ounces) chocolate fudge topping
$^1/_2$ cup flaked coconut
4 small bananas

EQUIPMENT

Large saucepan	Assorted kitchen knives
Small saucepan	Measuring cups and
7x11-inch deep baking	spoons
pan	Assorted cooking
7x11-inch shallow	utensils
baking pan	4 skewers
Large bowl	Whisk
Medium bowl	Vegetable peeler
Small bowl	Waxed paper
Shallow bowl	Plastic bag
Colander	Mallet

COUNTDOWN

1 Assemble the ingredients and equipment
2 Do Steps 1–5 of the *Lickety Splits*
3 Do Steps 1–8 of the *Green Hornet Lasagna*
4 Do Steps 1–4 of the *Kato Salad*

Green Hornet Lasagna

1 Set the spinach in a medium bowl of hot water to thaw.

2 Preheat the oven to 375°F.

3 Bring water to a boil in a large saucepan.

4 Cook the lasagna noodles until they are almost tender, 9 to 12 minutes.

5 Grease a 7x11-inch deep baking pan. Trim and chop the scallions. In a small bowl, lightly beat the eggs.

6 In the spinach bowl, combine the ricotta cheese, the eggs, the thawed spinach, the scallions and the oregano. Season to taste.

7 Drain the pasta well. Layer half of the noodles in the bottom of the pan. Top with half of the cheese mixture, half of the marinara sauce, half of the Monterey Jack cheese, and half of the Parmesan cheese. Repeat with a second layer, ending with the Parmesan cheese.

8 Bake the lasagna until it is hot and bubbly, about 25 minutes.

Kato Salad

1 In a large bowl, whisk together the oil, the lemon juice and the basil. Season to taste.

2 Peel and thinly slice the cucumber. Seed the bell pepper and cut it into strips. Peel and thinly slice the onion. Drain the olives. Add the ingredients to the large bowl and toss with the dressing.

3 Wash and dry the lettuce and arrange the leaves on individual salad plates.

4 Spoon the cucumber-pepper mixture over the lettuce.

Lickety Splits

1 Place the peanuts in a plastic bag and crush them with a mallet.

2 In a small saucepan, heat the fudge topping until it is just runny and pour it into a shallow bowl.

3 Line a 7x11-inch shallow baking pan with waxed paper and spread the coconut and the crushed peanuts on it.

4 Peel the bananas and skewer them lengthwise. Roll the bananas in the fudge topping to coat. Then roll them in the coconut mixture until well coated.

5 Place the skewers on the baking pan and refrigerate for at least 20 minutes.

WEDNESDAY

Chuckwagon Beef & Beans

1 small green bell pepper
1 can (15 ounces) white beans
1 pound lean ground beef
1 can (15$^{1}/_{2}$ ounces) ranch–style (or regular)
    baked beans
$^{1}/_{3}$ cup barbecue sauce
2 tablespoons yellow mustard
1 teaspoon Worcestershire sauce
$^{1}/_{2}$ cup water
Seasoning to taste
1 package (10) refrigerator biscuits

Back at the Ranch Salad

1 medium head lettuce
1 small red onion
2 medium carrots
2 stalks celery
1 tablespoon fresh parsley (when chopped)
1 clove garlic
$^{1}/_{4}$ cup buttermilk
2 tablespoons regular or low-fat mayonnaise
$^{1}/_{4}$ teaspoon Tabasco sauce
$^{1}/_{4}$ teaspoon paprika
Seasoning to taste

Branded Pears

6 medium pears
1$^{1}/_{2}$ cups water
$^{1}/_{2}$ cup dark brown sugar
2 teaspoons almond extract
1 teaspoon ground nutmeg

Corral Cake

$^{1}/_{2}$ cup pecan pieces
$^{1}/_{3}$ cup packed dark brown sugar
2 cups flour
$^{1}/_{2}$ teaspoon ground cinnamon
10 tablespoons butter
1 container (8 ounces) regular or light soft
    cream cheese
1 cup granulated sugar
2 eggs
1 teaspoon vanilla extract
1 teaspoon baking powder
$^{1}/_{2}$ teaspoon baking soda
$^{1}/_{4}$ teaspoon salt
$^{1}/_{4}$ cup whole or low-fat milk

EQUIPMENT

Electric hand mixer	Measuring cups and
Large covered skillet	spoons
Medium saucepan	Assorted cooking
9x13-inch baking pan	utensils
2 large bowls	Whisk
2 medium bowls	Pastry blender
Small bowl	Vegetable peeler
Strainer	Vegetable grater
Assorted kitchen knives	

COUNTDOWN

1 Assemble the ingredients and equipment
2 Do Step 1 of the *Branded Pears*
3 Do Steps 1–5 of the *Corral Cake*
4 Do Steps 1–2 of the *Back at the Ranch Salad*
5 Do Steps 1–4 of the *Chuckwagon Beef & Beans*
6 Do Step 2 of the *Branded Pears*
7 Do Step 3 of the *Back at the Ranch Salad*

Chuckwagon Beef & Beans

1 Seed and chop the bell pepper. Drain, rinse and drain the white beans.

2 In a large skillet, cook the beef until it is browned, 6 to 8 minutes. Drain off any fat. Add the bell pepper, the undrained baked beans, the drained white beans, the barbecue sauce, the mustard, the Worcestershire sauce and the water to the meat. Season to taste and bring the mixture to a boil, stirring.

3 Arrange the biscuits over the meat mixture to cover the skillet.

4 Reduce the heat, cover and simmer until the biscuits are cooked in the center (they will be like dumplings and will not brown), 12 to 15 minutes.

Back at the Ranch Salad

1 Wash and dry the lettuce and tear it into bite-size pieces. Peel and thinly slice the red onion. Peel and grate the carrots. Trim and thinly slice the celery. Combine the ingredients in a large bowl. Refrigerate until you are ready to use.

2 Chop the parsley. Peel and mince the garlic. In a small bowl, whisk together the parsley, the garlic, the buttermilk, the mayonnaise, the Tabasco sauce and the paprika. Season to taste.

3 Toss the salad with the dressing.

Branded Pears

1 Peel, core and quarter the pears and place them in a medium saucepan. Cover them with the water and cook until they are soft, 15 to 20 minutes.

2 Remove the pears from the heat. Blend in the brown sugar, the almond extract and the nutmeg. Serve warm.

Corral Cake

1 Preheat the oven to 350°F. Grease and flour a 9x13-inch baking pan.

2 In a medium bowl, combine the nuts, the brown sugar, $1/4$ cup of the flour and the cinnamon. Cut in 4 tablespoons of the butter until the mixture resembles coarse crumbs.

3 In a large bowl, combine the cream cheese with the granulated sugar and the remaining butter, beating until the ingredients are well blended. Blend in the eggs and the vanilla.

4 In a medium bowl, combine the remaining flour, the baking powder, the baking soda and the salt. Add the mixture to the cheese mixture in small amounts, alternating with small amounts of milk and mixing well after each addition.

5 Pour the batter into the baking pan, top with the crumb mixture and bake until a toothpick inserted in the center comes out clean, about 30 minutes.

THURSDAY

Reggae Chicken

1 medium orange
$^1/_2$ cup flour
Seasoning to taste
4 boneless, skinless chicken breast halves
2 tablespoons regular or light vegetable oil
2 medium bananas
2 tablespoons butter
$^1/_2$ teaspoon ground cinnamon
$^1/_2$ cup flaked coconut

Cousin Couscous

2 scallions (green onions)
2 egg yolks
1 can (10$^3/_4$ ounces) chicken broth
2 tablespoons water
$^1/_4$ teaspoon red pepper flakes
1 cup couscous

Samba Salad

1 clove garlic
1 tablespoon capers
1 medium head lettuce
1 medium cucumber
1 small red onion
$^1/_2$ pound fresh tomatoes
2 tablespoons red wine vinegar
3 tablespoons regular or light olive oil
$^1/_2$ teaspoon prepared horseradish
$^1/_4$ teaspoon Worcestershire sauce
Seasoning to taste

Almond Merengue

1 package (13 ounces) almond macaroons
2 egg whites
2 tablespoons sugar
2 tablespoons rum (or nonalcoholic Italian almond syrup)
1 pint almond-flavored (or other) frozen yogurt
$^1/_4$ cup sliced almonds

EQUIPMENT

Electric hand mixer	Assorted kitchen knives
Large skillet	Measuring cups and
Medium covered	spoons
saucepan	Assorted cooking
Large bowl	utensils
Medium bowl	Whisk
Small bowl	Citrus grater
Shallow bowl	Ice cream scoop

COUNTDOWN

1 Assemble the ingredients and equipment
2 Do Steps 1–2 of the *Almond Merengue*
3 Do Steps 1–3 of the *Samba Salad*
4 Do Steps 1–2 of the *Reggae Chicken*
5 Do Steps 1–2 of the *Cousin Couscous*
6 Do Steps 3–4 of the *Reggae Chicken*
7 Do Step 4 of the *Samba Salad*
8 Do Step 3 of the *Cousin Couscous*
9 Do Step 3 of the *Almond Merengue*

Reggae Chicken

1 Grate 1 tablespoon of orange peel and reserve. Slice the orange and remove the rind. Reserve.

2 Place the flour in a shallow bowl and season to taste. Dredge the chicken breasts lightly in the flour. Heat the oil in a large skillet. Sauté the chicken breasts until they are browned on all sides, 8 to 10 minutes.

3 Remove the chicken and cover to keep warm. Peel and slice the bananas. Melt half the butter in the skillet with the cinnamon and sauté the bananas until they are lightly browned on both sides, 2 to 3 minutes. With a slotted spoon, remove the bananas, arrange them around the chicken and keep warm.

4 Melt the remaining butter in the skillet, add the orange peel and the coconut and sauté until the coconut is golden brown, 2 to 3 minutes. Top the chicken and the bananas with the coconut and garnish with the orange slices.

Cousin Couscous

1 Trim and chop the scallions. In a medium saucepan, lightly beat the egg yolks. Add the scallions, the broth, the water and the red pepper flakes and bring the liquid to a boil.

2 Add the couscous, cover the saucepan and remove it from the heat. Let it stand until all the liquid has been absorbed, at least 5 minutes.

3 Fluff the couscous before serving.

Samba Salad

1 Peel and mince the garlic. Drain the capers.

2 Wash and dry the lettuce and tear it into bite-size pieces. Peel and slice the cucumber. Peel and slice the red onion. Chop the tomatoes. Combine the ingredients in a large bowl. Sprinkle with the capers.

3 In a small bowl, whisk together the garlic, the vinegar, the oil, the horseradish and the Worcestershire sauce. Season to taste.

4 Toss the salad with the dressing.

Almond Merengue

1 Crumble the macaroons.

2 In a medium bowl, whip the egg whites until frothy. Gradually add the sugar, a tablespoon at a time, until stiff peaks form, about 5 minutes. Fold the macaroon crumbs into the whipped egg whites. Fold the rum into the mixture, cover and refrigerate until you are ready to use.

3 Place scoops of frozen yogurt in individual dessert dishes. Spoon the whipped egg white mixture over the yogurt and sprinkle with the sliced almonds.

FRIDAY

Red Orange Roughy

1 medium onion
1 small carrot
1 clove garlic
1 medium can (14$^1/_2$ ounces) cut-up tomatoes
$^1/_4$ cup fresh parsley (when chopped)
2 tablespoons regular or light olive oil
$^1/_2$ cup dry white wine (or nonalcoholic white
    wine or clam juice)
1 teaspoon sugar
$^1/_2$ teaspoon dried oregano
Seasoning to taste
4 orange roughy (or sole) fillets (1$^1/_4$ pounds)

Spiced Yellow Squash

1 package (9 ounces) frozen yellow squash
$^1/_3$ cup water
1$^1/_2$ tablespoons butter
1$^1/_2$ tablespoons dark brown sugar
$^1/_4$ teaspoon salt
$^1/_4$ teaspoon ground nutmeg
1 tablespoon grated fresh orange peel

Green Green Salad

1 jar (6$^1/_2$ ounces) marinated artichoke hearts
3 scallions (green onions)
1 small head lettuce
2 ripe avocados
1 tablespoon lemon juice

Snap, Crackle & Pop Pie

1 quart rocky road (or similar) ice cream
3 tablespoons creamy-style peanut butter
$^1/_4$ cup corn syrup
1$^1/_4$ cups Rice Krispies cereal
$^1/_2$ teaspoon vanilla extract

EQUIPMENT

Large covered skillet	Assorted cooking
Medium saucepan	utensils
9-inch pie plate	Vegetable peeler
2 medium bowls	Vegetable grater
Assorted kitchen knives	
Measuring cups and	
spoons	

COUNTDOWN

1 Assemble the ingredients and equipment
2 Do Step 1 of the *Snap, Crackle & Pop Pie*
3 Do Steps 1–3 of the *Red Orange Roughy*
4 Do Steps 2–5 of the *Snap, Crackle & Pop Pie*
5 Do Steps 1–3 of the *Green Green Salad*
6 Do Step 4 of the *Red Orange Roughy*
7 Do Steps 1–3 of the *Spiced Yellow Squash*
8 Do Step 4 of the *Green Green Salad*

Red Orange Roughy

1 Peel and chop the onion. Peel and grate the carrot. Peel and mince the garlic. Drain and chop the tomatoes. Chop the parsley.

2 Heat the oil in a large skillet. Add the onion, the carrot and the garlic and sauté until they are softened, about 5 minutes.

3 Add the tomatoes, the wine, the parsley, the sugar and the oregano. Season to taste. Reduce the heat, cover and simmer until the sauce is slightly reduced, 15 to 20 minutes.

4 Pat dry the fish fillets with paper towels. Add them to the skillet, spooning the sauce over them. Cook until the fish is opaque throughout, 8 to 10 minutes.

Spiced Yellow Squash

1 Place the frozen squash in a medium saucepan with the water. Bring the water to a boil and cook until the squash is soft, about 5 minutes.

2 Drain off any excess liquid from the squash. Fold in the butter, the brown sugar, the salt and the nutmeg.

3 Sprinkle with the orange peel.

Green Green Salad

1 Drain and quarter the artichokes, reserving the oil. Peel and chop the scallions. Combine the artichokes and the scallions in a medium bowl. Toss with the reserved oil.

2 Wash and dry the lettuce and arrange the leaves on individual salad plates.

3 Peel and pit the avocados, cut them in half lengthwise and sprinkle them with the lemon juice.

4 Arrange the avocado halves, cut side up, on the lettuce. Top each avocado half with some of the artichoke-onion mixture.

Snap, Crackle & Pop Pie

1 Set the ice cream out to soften.

2 Lightly grease a 9-inch pie plate.

3 In a medium bowl, combine the peanut butter, the corn syrup, the Rice Krispies and the vanilla.

4 Pat the mixture evenly into the bottom and sides of the pie plate, using wet fingers so you will not stick to the crust.

5 Spoon the softened ice cream into the pie crust and freeze for at least 20 minutes.

OCTOBER

WEEK FIVE

WEEK AT A GLANCE

Monday

SAILOR'S DELIGHT
SEA BREEZE SALAD
SUNSET SNOWBALLS

Tuesday

ATYPICAL LAMB STEW
OUT-OF-THE-ORDINARY ORZO
UNCOMMON COMPOTE

Wednesday

THE SOLE OF DISCRETION
POLITICALLY CORRECT POTATOES
NEAT BEET SALAD
BLACK-OUT CAKE

Thursday

TOP HAT CHICKEN
PUTTIN' ON THE RICE
MAD ABOUT ZUCCHINI
CANDY ANGEL

Friday

MONSTER MINESTRONE
GOBBLIN' SALAD
RAGAMUFFINS
SPOOKY PUDDING

CHECK STAPLES

- □ Butter
- □ Flour
- □ Baking powder
- □ Baking soda
- □ Dark brown sugar
- □ Sweetened cocoa
- □ Molasses
- □ Long-grain white rice
- □ Regular or light vegetable oil
- □ Regular or light olive oil
- □ Sesame oil
- □ Rice vinegar
- □ Apple cider vinegar
- □ Lemon juice
- □ Lime juice
- □ Grated fresh orange peel
- □ Worcestershire sauce
- □ Tabasco sauce
- □ Soy sauce
- □ Dijon mustard
- □ Honey
- □ Dark raisins
- □ Golden raisins
- □ Candied ginger
- □ Grated Parmesan cheese
- □ Dried basil
- □ Bay leaves
- □ Dried chervil
- □ Ground cumin
- □ Dried dill
- □ Ground nutmeg
- □ Dried oregano
- □ Poppy seeds
- □ Sesame seeds
- □ Dried tarragon
- □ Dried thyme
- □ Pepper
- □ Salt
- □ Vanilla extract

SHOPPING NOTE

● If you are shopping once a week and cannot arrange to purchase fresh sole on the day you plan to use it, you can purchase *not previously frozen* sole and freeze it, placing it in the refrigerator to thaw the night before you are ready to use it. Or you can purchase *still frozen* sole and keep it frozen until the night before you are ready to use it.

MEAT & POULTRY
3 pounds lean lamb stew meat (T)
4 boneless, skinless chicken breast halves (Th)

FISH
1¹/₂ pounds sole fillets (W)

FRESH PRODUCE
Vegetables
1 pound small new red potatoes (W)
1 pound green beans (T)
3 medium zucchini—2 (Th), 1 (F)
1 medium head cauliflower (W)
2 small turnips (F)
1 large carrot (F)
4 stalks celery—2 (Th), 2 (F)
2 medium onions (F)
4 small onions—1 (M), 1 (T), 1 (W), 1 (Th)
1 medium sweet onion (F)
1 small red onion (M)
7 scallions (green onions)—3 (T), 2 (W), 2 (Th)
1 head garlic (M–F)
1 small bunch chives (W)
1 bunch parsley (M, T, W, F)
¹/₄ pound bean sprouts (M)
1 small (or half) head green cabbage (F)
1 medium head lettuce (W)
2 small heads lettuce—1 (M), 1 (F)
1 medium cucumber (M)

Fruit
1 large pear (T)
1 medium melon (T)
1 pound seedless red grapes (T)
1 small pink grapefruit (M)
4 medium oranges (F)
3 small limes (W)

CANS, JARS & BOTTLES
Soup
1 can (14¹/₂ ounces) chicken broth (M)

2 cans (14¹/₂ ounces each) vegetable broth (F)

Vegetables
2 medium cans (14¹/₂ ounces each) cut-up tomatoes—1 (T), 1 (F)
1 medium can (15¹/₂ ounces) kidney beans (F)
1 small can (8 ounces) julienne pickled beets (W)

Fish
1 can (6 ounces) solid white tuna (M)

Oriental Products
1 can (8 ounces) sliced water chestnuts (M)

Juice
1 cup tomato juice (F)

Condiments
1 small can (3¹/₂ ounces) pitted black olives (F)

Dessert Needs
1 can (21 ounces) blackberry pie filling (W)
1 jar (11³/₄ ounces) strawberry topping (M)

PACKAGED GOODS
Pasta, Rice & Grains
1 cup orzo (T)
8 ounces medium shell pasta (F)
2¹/₄ cups All-Bran cereal (F)

Baked Goods
1 chocolate loaf cake (W)
1 angel food loaf cake (Th)

Fruit
8 pitted prunes (T)
8 dried apricots (T)

Nuts & Seeds
1 cup pecan pieces (M)
3 tablespoons chopped walnuts (F)

Dessert & Baking Needs
1 small package (3.4 ounces) instant vanilla pudding mix (Th)
1 small package (3.9 ounces) instant chocolate pudding mix (F)
2 chocolate-covered toffee candy bars (7 ounces each) (Th)
1 small package (6 ounces) semisweet chocolate chips (F)
20 pieces candy corn (F)
16 mini-marshmallows (F)

WINES & SPIRITS
1 cup dry white wine (or nonalcoholic white wine or chicken broth) (Th)
1 cup dry red wine (or nonalcoholic red wine or water) (F)

REFRIGERATED PRODUCTS
Dairy
3¹/₄ cups whole milk—2 cups (Th), 1¹/₄ cups (F)
1 cup buttermilk (F)
1 cup regular or light sour cream—¹/₄ cup (Th), ³/₄ cup (F)
1 egg (F)

Juice
1³/₄ cups orange juice—1 cup (T), ³/₄ cup (Th)

FROZEN GOODS
Vegetables
1 package (9 ounces) chopped spinach (T)
1 package (9 ounces) cut green beans (F)

Desserts
2 small containers (8 ounces each) frozen whipped topping—1 (W), 1 (Th)
1 quart vanilla ice cream (M)

MONDAY

Sailor's Delight

1 small onion
1 clove garlic
1 can (8 ounces) sliced water chestnuts
1 tablespoon sesame seeds
2 tablespoons butter
1 cup long-grain white rice
1 can (14$^1/_2$ ounces) chicken broth
1 tablespoon soy sauce
$^3/_4$ cup water
Seasoning to taste
1 can (6 ounces) solid white tuna

Sea Breeze Salad

1 small head lettuce
1 medium cucumber
1 small red onion
1 small pink grapefruit
$^1/_4$ pound fresh bean sprouts
1 tablespoon fresh parsley (when chopped)
1 tablespoon soy sauce
1 tablespoon rice vinegar
2 tablespoons sesame oil
Seasoning to taste

Sunset Snowballs

1 quart vanilla ice cream
1 cup pecan pieces
1 jar (11$^3/_4$ ounces) strawberry topping

EQUIPMENT	
Large covered saucepan	Assorted cooking utensils
Cookie sheet	Whisk
Large bowl	Vegetable peeler
Small bowl	Ice cream scoop
Shallow bowl	Plastic bag
Assorted kitchen knives	Mallet
Measuring cups and spoons	

COUNTDOWN

1 Assemble the ingredients and equipment
2 Do Step 1 of the *Sunset Snowballs*
3 Do Steps 1–3 of the *Sailor's Delight*
4 Do Steps 2–3 of the *Sunset Snowballs*
5 Do Steps 1–2 of the *Sea Breeze Salad*
6 Do Steps 4–6 of the *Sailor's Delight*
7 Do Step 3 of the *Sea Breeze Salad*
8 Do Step 4 of the *Sunset Snowballs*

Sailor's Delight

1 Peel and chop the onion. Peel and mince the garlic. Drain the water chestnuts.

2 Place the sesame seeds in a large saucepan and toss them until they are lightly toasted, about 3 minutes. Remove and reserve.

3 Melt the butter in the saucepan. Add the onion and the garlic and sauté until the onion is soft, about 5 minutes. Add the rice and cook, stirring, for 1 minute. Add the water chestnuts, the broth, the soy sauce and the water. Season to taste. Cover, reduce the heat and simmer until all the liquid is absorbed and the rice is tender, about 20 minutes.

4 Drain and flake the tuna.

5 Remove the rice mixture from the heat, stir to fluff, re-cover and let it stand for 5 minutes.

6 Stir the tuna and the reserved sesame seeds into the rice. Return the saucepan to the heat and simmer, stirring, until the tuna is heated through, about 2 minutes.

Sea Breeze Salad

1 Wash and dry the lettuce and tear it into bite-size pieces. Peel and slice the cucumber. Peel and chop the onion. Peel and section the grapefruit. Combine the ingredients in a large bowl. Add the bean sprouts and toss lightly.

2 Chop the parsley. In a small bowl, whisk together the parsley, the soy sauce, the vinegar and the oil. Season to taste.

3 Toss the salad with the dressing.

Sunset Snowballs

1 Scoop out ice cream balls. Set them on an ungreased cookie sheet and return them to the freezer until you are ready to use.

2 Place the pecans in a plastic bag and crush them with a mallet.

3 Place the crushed nuts in a shallow bowl. Roll the ice cream balls in the nuts to coat them. Return the ice cream balls to the freezer for at least 20 minutes.

4 Place the snowballs in individual dessert dishes and drizzle them with the strawberry topping.

TUESDAY

Atypical Lamb Stew

3 pounds lean lamb stew meat
Seasoning to taste
3 cloves garlic
1 small onion
1 medium can (14$^1/_2$ ounces) cut-up
    tomatoes*
1 pound green beans
2 tablespoons regular or light olive oil
1 cup water
$^3/_4$ teaspoon ground cumin

Out-of-the-Ordinary Orzo

1 package (9 ounces) frozen chopped spinach
3 scallions (green onions)
$^1/_4$ cup fresh parsley (when minced)
1 cup orzo
3 tablespoons butter
$^3/_4$ teaspoon dried basil
Reserved tomato juice
Seasoning to taste

Uncommon Compote

2 pieces candied ginger
8 pitted prunes
8 dried apricots
1 cup orange juice
1 medium melon
1 large pear
1 pound seedless red grapes
1 tablespoon honey
$^1/_2$ teaspoon ground nutmeg

*Reserve the juice to use in the Out-of-the-Ordinary
Orzo.

EQUIPMENT	
Dutch oven	Assorted kitchen knives
Large covered skillet	Measuring cups and
Medium saucepan	spoons
Large bowl	Assorted cooking
Medium bowl	utensils
Small bowl	Whisk
Strainer	

COUNTDOWN

1 Assemble the ingredients and equipment
2 Do Steps 1–3 of the *Out-of-the-Ordinary Orzo*
3 Do Steps 1–3 of the *Atypical Lamb Stew*
4 Do Step 4 of the *Out-of-the-Ordinary Orzo*
5 Do Steps 1–2 of the *Uncommon Compote*
6 Do Step 4 of the *Atypical Lamb Stew*
7 Do Steps 5–6 of the *Out-of-the Ordinary Orzo*
8 Do Step 3 of the *Uncommon Compote*

Atypical Lamb Stew

1 Trim any excess fat from the lamb and cut the meat into 1-inch cubes. Season to taste. Peel and chop the garlic. Peel and chop the onion. Drain the tomatoes, reserving the juice. Trim and string the green beans.

2 Heat the oil in a Dutch oven. Add the lamb and cook, turning, until the cubes are lightly browned, about 5 minutes.

3 Add the garlic and the onion to the Dutch oven and sauté for 3 minutes. Add the water and the tomatoes, bring the mixture to a boil, reduce the heat, cover and simmer for 20 minutes.

4 Add the green beans and the cumin to the stew. Season to taste. Simmer for 10 minutes more.

Out-of-the-Ordinary Orzo

1 Set the package of spinach in a medium bowl of hot water to thaw.

2 Bring water to a boil in a medium saucepan.

3 Trim and chop the scallions. Mince the parsley. Drain the spinach.

4 Cook the orzo until it is almost tender, 9 to 12 minutes.

5 In a large skillet, melt the butter and sauté the scallions for 2 minutes. Add the parsley, the spinach and the basil and sauté for 3 minutes. Add the reserved tomato juice, season to taste and bring the mixture to a boil.

6 Drain the orzo and combine it with the spinach mixture. Remove the skillet from the heat and cover to keep warm.

Uncommon Compote

1 Chop the ginger. Place the prunes, the apricots and the ginger in a small bowl. Cover with the orange juice and let stand until you are ready to use.

2 Seed and chunk the melon, removing the rind. Core and chunk the pear. Wash and separate the grapes. Combine the fruit in a large bowl and refrigerate until you are ready to use.

3 Drain the prunes and the apricots, reserving the liquid. Add the prunes and the apricots to the melon mixture. Combine the reserved liquid with the honey and the nutmeg and drizzle it over the fruit.

WEDNESDAY

The Sole of Discretion

3 small limes
2 tablespoons fresh parsley (when chopped)
2 tablespoons fresh chives (when minced)
1 small onion
1$^1/_2$ pounds sole fillets
Seasoning to taste
4 tablespoons butter
$^1/_2$ teaspoon dried tarragon
$^1/_4$ teaspoon dried chervil
2 tablespoons lime juice

Politically Correct Potatoes

1 pound small new red potatoes
2 tablespoons regular or light olive oil
$^1/_2$ teaspoon Tabasco sauce
$^1/_2$ teaspoon dried dill
Seasoning to taste

Neat Beet Salad

1 medium head lettuce
1 medium head cauliflower
2 scallions (green onions)
$^1/_4$ cup golden raisins
1 small can (8 ounces) julienne pickled beets
1 clove garlic
2 tablespoons apple cider vinegar
3 tablespoons regular or light olive oil
1 teaspoon Dijon mustard
1 teaspoon dried thyme
Seasoning to taste

Black-out Cake

1 chocolate loaf cake
$^1/_4$ cup sweetened cocoa
1 small container (8 ounces) frozen whipped
    topping
1 can (21 ounces) blackberry pie filling

EQUIPMENT

Large covered skillet	Assorted kitchen knives
Small skillet	Measuring cups and
9x13-inch glass baking	spoons
dish	Assorted cooking
Large bowl	utensils
Small bowl	Whisk
Strainer	Vegetable brush

COUNTDOWN

1 Assemble the ingredients and equipment
2 Do Step 1 of *The Sole of Discretion*
3 Do Steps 1–2 of the *Black-out Cake*
4 Do Steps 1–3 of the *Neat Beet Salad*
5 Do Step 1 of the *Politically Correct Potatoes*
6 Do Steps 2–4 of *The Sole of Discretion*
7 Do Step 2 of the *Politically Correct Potatoes*
8 Do Step 4 of the *Neat Beet Salad*

The Sole of Discretion

1 Preheat the oven 350°F.

2 Cut the limes into thin slices. Chop the parsley. Mince the chives. Peel and mince the onion. Pat dry the sole fillets and season to taste.

3 Melt half the butter in a small skillet and sauté the onion until it is soft, about 5 minutes. Blend in the remaining butter, the parsley, the chives, the tarragon and the chervil. Blend in the lime juice and season to taste.

4 Line the bottom of a 9x13-inch glass baking dish with the lime slices. Arrange the fish fillets over the limes, spoon the butter sauce over the fish and bake until the fish flakes easily with a fork, 10 to 12 minutes.

Politically Correct Potatoes

1 Bring water to a boil in a large skillet. Scrub and halve the potatoes and boil them until they are almost tender, 8–12 minutes.

2 Drain the potatoes. Heat the oil with the Tabasco sauce and the dill in the skillet. Season to taste and toss the potatoes in the oil until they are well coated. Cover to keep warm.

Neat Beet Salad

1 Wash and dry the lettuce and tear it into bite-size pieces. Trim and cut the cauliflower into bite-size florets. Trim and slice the scallions. Combine the ingredients in a large bowl. Add the raisins.

2 Drain the beets well.

3 Peel and mince the garlic. In a small bowl, whisk together the garlic, the vinegar, the oil, the mustard and the thyme. Season to taste.

4 Toss the salad with the dressing and sprinkle with the beets.

Black-out Cake

1 Slice the cake into 3 horizontal layers. Fold the cocoa into the whipped topping.

2 Spread half of the blackberry pie filing on the bottom layer of the cake. Top with a third of the whipped topping. Lay the second cake layer over the first and repeat. Lay the top layer of the cake over the second and frost the with the remaining whipped topping. Refrigerate until you are ready to serve.

THURSDAY

Top Hat Chicken

1 clove garlic
1 cup dry white wine (or nonalcoholic white
    wine or chicken broth)
1 tablespoon Worcestershire sauce
4 tablespoons regular or light vegetable oil
2 tablespoons lemon juice
4 boneless, skinless chicken breast halves
$1/2$ cup flour
Seasoning to taste
$1/4$ cup honey

Puttin' on the Rice

2 stalks celery
2 scallions (green onions)
4 tablespoons butter
$1^1/2$ cups water
1 tablespoon grated fresh orange peel
$3/4$ cup orange juice
$1/8$ teaspoon dried thyme
1 cup long-grain white rice
1 tablespoon poppy seeds

Mad About Zucchini

2 medium zucchini
1 small onion
1 tablespoon butter
$1/4$ cup regular or light sour cream
Seasoning to taste

Candy Angel

1 small container (8 ounces) frozen whipped
    topping
2 chocolate-covered toffee candy bars
    (7 ounces each)
1 angel food loaf cake
2 cups whole milk
1 small package (3.4 ounces) instant vanilla
    pudding mix
1 teaspoon vanilla extract

EQUIPMENT

Electric hand mixer	Shallow bowl
Large covered skillet	Assorted kitchen knives
Medium covered skillet	Measuring cups and
Medium covered	spoons
saucepan	Assorted cooking
9x13-inch glass baking	utensils
dish	Whisk
9x9-inch glass baking	Plastic bag
dish	Mallet
Medium bowl	

COUNTDOWN

1 Assemble the ingredients and equipment
2 Do Step 1 of the *Candy Angel*
3 Do Step 1 of the *Top Hat Chicken*
4 Do Steps 2–5 of the *Candy Angel*
5 Do Step 1 of *Puttin' on the Rice*
6 Do Steps 2–4 of the *Top Hat Chicken*
7 Do Steps 2–3 of *Puttin' on the Rice*
8 Do Steps 1–3 of the *Mad About Zucchini*
9 Do Step 4 of *Puttin' on the Rice*

Top Hat Chicken

1 Peel and mince the garlic. Combine the garlic, the wine, the Worcestershire sauce, 1 tablespoon of the oil and the lemon juice in a 9x13-inch glass baking dish. Add the chicken and turn the pieces in the mixture to coat them evenly. Cover and refrigerate for at least 15 minutes.

2 Drain the chicken, reserving the marinade.

3 Put the flour in a shallow bowl and season it to taste. Dredge the chicken in the seasoned flour until lightly coated.

4 Heat the remaining oil in a large skillet. Sauté the chicken until it is browned on all sides, 8 to 10 minutes. Combine the honey with the reserved marinade and pour the mixture over the chicken. Season to taste. Cover, reduce the heat and simmer until the chicken is tender, 20 to 25 minutes.

Puttin' on the Rice

1 Trim and chop the celery. Trim and chop the scallions.

2 Melt the butter in a medium saucepan and sauté the celery and the scallions until they are tender, about 5 minutes.

3 Add the water, the orange peel, the orange juice and the thyme. Bring the mixture to a boil. Stir in the rice and the poppy seeds. Reduce the heat, cover and simmer until all the liquid is absorbed and the rice is tender, about 20 minutes.

4 Fluff the rice before serving.

Mad About Zucchini

1 Trim and chop the zucchini. Peel and mince the onion.

2 Melt the butter in a medium skillet and sauté the onion until it is soft, about 5 minutes. Add the zucchini, cover, reduce the heat and simmer for 2 minutes.

3 Add the sour cream to the skillet and toss lightly to coat. Season to taste, remove from the heat and cover to keep warm.

Candy Angel

1 Set the whipped topping out to soften.

2 Place the candy bars in a plastic bag and crush them with a mallet.

3 Crumble the angel food cake and place it in a 9x9-inch glass baking dish.

4 In a medium bowl, beat together the milk and the pudding mix until well blended. Spoon the mixture over the crumbled cake.

5 Fold the vanilla into the whipped topping, spread the mixture over the pudding, top with the crushed candy and refrigerate for at least 20 minutes.

FRIDAY

Monster Minestrone

2 medium onions
3 cloves garlic
1 large carrot
2 small turnips
2 stalks celery
1 medium zucchini
1 small (or half) head green cabbage
$^1/_2$ cup fresh parsley (when chopped)
3 tablespoons regular or light olive oil
1 medium can (14$^1/_2$ ounces) cut-up tomatoes
2 cans (14$^1/_2$ ounces each) vegetable broth
1 cup dry red wine (or nonalcoholic red wine
    or water)
1 cup tomato juice
1 bay leaf
1 teaspoon dried oregano
1 medium can (15$^1/_2$ ounces) kidney beans
1 package (9 ounces) frozen cut green beans
8 ounces medium shell pasta
Seasoning to taste
$^1/_4$ cup grated Parmesan cheese

Gobblin' Salad

4 medium oranges
1 small head lettuce
1 medium sweet onion
1 small can (3$^1/_2$ ounces) pitted black olives
3 tablespoons regular or light olive oil
2 tablespoons lemon juice
$^1/_2$ teaspoon Dijon mustard
$^1/_4$ teaspoon Worcestershire sauce
Seasoning to taste

Ragamuffins

2$^1/_4$ cups All-Bran cereal
1 cup buttermilk
$^1/_3$ cup molasses
$^1/_4$ cup firmly packed dark brown sugar

1 cup flour
2 teaspoons baking powder
1 teaspoon baking soda
$^1/_2$ teaspoon salt
1 egg
$^1/_4$ cup regular or light vegetable oil
3 tablespoons chopped walnuts
$^1/_2$ cup dark raisins

Spooky Pudding

1 small package (3.9 ounces) instant
    chocolate pudding mix
1$^1/_4$ cups whole milk
$^3/_4$ cup regular or light sour cream
1 small package (6 ounces) semisweet
    chocolate chips
20 pieces candy corn
16 mini-marshmallows

EQUIPMENT

Electric hand mixer	Measuring cups and
Dutch oven	spoons
12-cup muffin tin	Assorted cooking
Large bowl	utensils
2 medium bowls	Whisk
2 small bowls	Vegetable peeler
Assorted kitchen knives	Vegetable grater

COUNTDOWN

1 Assemble the ingredients and equipment
2 Do Step 1 of the *Ragamuffins*
3 Do Steps 1–2 of the *Spooky Pudding*
4 Do Steps 1–2 of the *Monster Minestrone*
5 Do Steps 2–5 of the *Ragamuffins*
6 Do Step 3 of the *Monster Minestrone*
7 Do Steps 1–3 of the *Gobblin' Salad*
8 Do Step 4 of the *Monster Minestrone*
9 Do Step 3 of the *Spooky Pudding*

Monster Minestrone

1 Peel and chop the onions. Peel and mince the garlic. Peel and slice the carrot. Peel and dice the turnips. Trim and chop the celery. Trim and slice the zucchini. Trim and grate the cabbage. Chop the parsley.

2 Heat the oil in a Dutch oven. Add the onion and the garlic and sauté for 5 minutes. Add the carrot, the turnips, the celery, the zucchini and the cabbage. Add the undrained tomatoes, the broth, the wine, the tomato juice, the bay leaf and the oregano. Bring the soup to a boil, cover and cook for 15 minutes.

3 Add the undrained kidney beans, the frozen green beans and the pasta to the Dutch oven. Cover and simmer for 15 minutes.

4 Remove the bay leaf from the soup, season to taste and sprinkle with the Parmesan cheese.

Gobblin' Salad

1 Peel and slice the oranges. Wash and dry the lettuce, arrange the leaves on individual plates and arrange the orange slices on top.

2 Peel and thinly slice the onion, and separate the slices into rings. Drain the olives. Scatter the onion rings and the olives over the orange slices.

3 In a small bowl, whisk the oil, the lemon juice, the mustard and the Worcestershire sauce until well blended. Season to taste and drizzle over the salad.

Ragamuffins

1 Preheat the oven to 400°F. Grease a 12-cup muffin tin.

2 In a large bowl, combine the All-Bran, the buttermilk, the molasses and the brown sugar.

3 In a medium bowl, combine the flour, the baking powder, the baking soda and the salt. Add the dry ingredients to the bran mixture.

4 In a small bowl, beat the egg lightly and add the oil. Add the egg mixture to the bran mixture and combine until the batter is evenly moist. Fold in the nuts and the raisins.

5 Fill the muffin cups 2/3 full and bake until the muffins are lightly browned on top, about 20 minutes.

Spooky Pudding

1 In a medium bowl, combine the pudding mix, the milk and the sour cream and beat until well blended. Fold in the chocolate chips.

2 Pour the mixture into individual dessert dishes and refrigerate for at least 20 minutes.

3 Decorate the pudding with the candy corn and the mini-marshmallows.

NOVEMBER
WEEK ONE

WEEK AT A GLANCE

Monday

SMART & SPICY PORK CHOPS
SPUDS MacKENZIE
PETTY SALAD
PINEAPPLE DRIZZLE

Tuesday

PRIMARY PASTA
CONVENTIONAL CAULIFLOWER
BIPARTISAN BOBOLI
MAPLE LANDSLIDE

Wednesday

ALMOST WINTER BEEF & VEGGIES
NEARLY PILAF
MERELY TANGERINES

Thursday

FARMERS' MARKET SOUP
JUST GREEN SALAD
CRANBERRY COBBLER

Friday

SONORA SNAPPER
TIJUANA SALAD
MEXICAN SUNSET

CHECK STAPLES

- ☐ Butter
- ☐ Cornstarch
- ☐ Granulated sugar
- ☐ Dark brown sugar
- ☐ Maple syrup
- ☐ Regular or light vegetable oil
- ☐ Regular or light olive oil
- ☐ Red wine vinegar
- ☐ Balsamic vinegar
- ☐ Lemon juice
- ☐ Grated fresh orange peel
- ☐ Worcestershire sauce
- ☐ Dijon mustard
- ☐ Prepared horseradish
- ☐ Chili sauce
- ☐ Grated Parmesan cheese
- ☐ Beef bouillon cubes
- ☐ Dried basil
- ☐ Celery seeds
- ☐ Garlic powder
- ☐ Dry mustard
- ☐ Ground nutmeg
- ☐ Instant minced onion
- ☐ Dried oregano
- ☐ Paprika
- ☐ Poppy seeds
- ☐ Dried sage
- ☐ Dried thyme
- ☐ Pepper
- ☐ Salt
- ☐ Lemon extract

SHOPPING NOTE

● If you are shopping once a week and cannot arrange to purchase fresh snapper on the day you plan to use it, you can purchase *not previously frozen* snapper and freeze it, placing it in the refrigerator to thaw the night before you are ready to use it. Or you can purchase *still frozen* snapper and keep it frozen until the night before you are ready to use it.

MEAT & POULTRY

4 lean loin pork chops ($3/4$-inch thick) (M)
1 pound lean boneless sirloin steak (W)
1 pound boneless, skinless chicken breasts (Th)

FISH

$1^1/4$ pounds red snapper fillets (F)

FRESH PRODUCE

Vegetables

4 medium baking potatoes (M)
1 pound baking potatoes (Th)
1 medium head cauliflower (T)
1 small bunch broccoli (Th)
$1/2$ pound green beans (W)
3 medium turnips (W)
$1/4$ pound mushrooms (F)
9 medium carrots—5 (W), 4 (Th)
8 stalks celery—2 (M), 4 (W), 2 (Th)
1 large onion (Th)
1 medium onion (M)
1 small onion (F)
1 small sweet onion (T)
1 medium shallot (T)
10 scallions (green onions)— 2 (M), 5 (Th), 3 (F)
1 head garlic (T, Th)
1 bunch parsley (M, T, W, Th)
1 package (16 ounces) mixed salad greens (M)
1 large head lettuce (Th)
1 medium head lettuce (F)
$1/2$ pound tomatoes (F)
1 medium cucumber (Th)
1 large yellow bell pepper (T)
1 small white radish (M)
1 bunch radishes (W)

Fruit

1 large pineapple (M)
1 package (12 ounces) cranberries (Th)
8 seedless tangerines (W)

CANS, JARS & BOTTLES

Soup

1 can ($10^3/4$ ounces) beef broth (W)
3 cans ($14^1/2$ ounces each) chicken broth (Th)

Vegetables

1 small can (6 ounces) tomato paste (T, F)
1 small can ($8^3/4$ ounces) whole kernel corn (Th)
1 medium can (15 ounces) western-style chili beans (F)

Juice

1 cup apple cider (M)

Condiments

1 jar ($15^1/2$ ounces) roasted red peppers (T)
$1/4$ cup capers (T)
1 small can (3.3 ounces) sliced black olives (F)

PACKAGED GOODS

Pasta, Rice & Grains

16 ounces linguine (T)
1 cup quick-cooking barley (W)
1 small package (6 ounces) corn chips (F)

Baked Goods

2 small (8-inch) Boboli breads (or English or Australian muffins) (T)
1 small loaf French bread (Th)

Nuts & Seeds

$1/4$ cup sliced almonds (M)
$1/3$ cup chopped walnuts (Th)

Dessert & Baking Needs

10 hot cinnamon candies (F)

WINES & SPIRITS

$1/4$ cup dry red wine (or nonalcoholic red wine or vegetable broth) (T)
3 tablespoons dry sherry (or omit) (Th)
2 tablespoons Amaretto liqueur (or nonalcoholic Italian almond syrup) (M)
1 tablespoon rum (or 1 teaspoon rum extract) (F)

REFRIGERATED PRODUCTS

Dairy

2 cups + 2 tablespoons whole or low-fat milk—2 tablespoons (M), 2 cups (T)
Whipped cream for garnish (T)
$1/4$ cup regular or light sour cream (F)
4 eggs (T)

Cheese

$3/4$ pound Gouda cheese (Th)
$3/4$ cup shredded regular or low-fat Monterey Jack cheese (F)

Juice

1 cup orange juice (Th)

Deli

2 slices prosciutto ham (T)
1 package (8) refrigerator cinnamon rolls (Th)

FROZEN GOODS

Vegetables

2 packages (9 ounces each) chopped spinach (F)

Fruit

1 package (10 ounces) sweetened raspberries (F)

Desserts

1 pint orange frozen yogurt (or sherbet) (F)

MONDAY

Smart & Spicy Pork Chops

2 tablespoons regular or light vegetable oil
4 lean loin pork chops (³/₄-inch thick)
1 teaspoon dried sage
1 tablespoon prepared horseradish
2 teaspoons dry mustard
1 cup apple cider
1 tablespoon cornstarch
Seasoning to taste

Spuds MacKenzie

1 medium onion
2 stalks celery
4 medium baking potatoes
2 teaspoons fresh parsley (when chopped)
4 tablespoons butter
2 tablespoons whole or low-fat milk
Seasoning to taste

Petty Salad

1 package (16 ounces) mixed salad greens
2 scallions (green onions)
1 small white radish
3 tablespoons regular or light vegetable oil
2 tablespoons red wine vinegar
¹/₄ teaspoon sugar
¹/₂ teaspoon Dijon mustard
2 teaspoons poppy seeds
Seasoning to taste

Pineapple Drizzle

1 large pineapple
2 tablespoons Amaretto liqueur (or
  nonalcoholic Italian almond syrup)
2 tablespoons dark brown sugar
¹/₄ cup sliced almonds

EQUIPMENT

Electric hand mixer	Assorted kitchen knives
Large skillet	Measuring cups and
Large covered	spoons
saucepan	Assorted cooking
9x13-inch glass baking	utensils
dish	Whisk
Small bowl	Vegetable peeler

COUNTDOWN

1 Assemble the ingredients and equipment
2 Do Steps 1–3 of the *Petty Salad*
3 Do Steps 1–3 of the *Pineapple Drizzle*
4 Do Step 1 of the *Smart & Spicy Pork Chops*
5 Do Steps 1–3 of the *Spuds MacKenzie*
6 Do Steps 2–3 of the *Smart & Spicy Pork Chops*
7 Do Step 4 of the *Pineapple Drizzle*
8 Do Step 4 of the *Spuds MacKenzie*
9 Do Step 4 of the *Smart & Spicy Pork Chops*
10 Do Step 4 of the *Petty Salad*

Smart & Spicy Pork Chops

1 Heat the oil in a large skillet. Sear the pork chops quickly on all sides. Reduce the heat, add the sage and simmer, turning once, until the chops are tender, about 8 minutes per side.

2 Remove the chops and cover to keep warm.

3 Add the horseradish, the mustard and all but 1 tablespoon of the cider to the skillet. Dissolve the cornstarch in the remaining cider and whisk it into the skillet. Season to taste. Bring the mixture to a boil and cook the sauce until it thickens, about 3 minutes.

4 Return the chops to the skillet and coat them with the sauce.

Spuds MacKenzie

1 Bring water to a boil. Peel and chop the onion. Trim and chop the celery. Peel and chop the potatoes. Chop the parsley.

2 Melt 2 tablespoons of the butter in a large saucepan. Add the onion, the celery and the potatoes and sauté until they are soft, about 5 minutes.

3 Add enough boiling water to just cover. Reduce the heat and simmer until the vegetables are very soft, about 10 minutes.

4 Drain the vegetables and return them to the saucepan. Blend in the remaining butter and the milk and beat until the mixture is almost smooth. Season to taste and sprinkle with the parsley. Cover to keep warm.

Petty Salad

1 Rinse and drain the salad greens and arrange them on individual salad plates.

2 Trim and chop the scallions, peel and grate the radish, and arrange them over the greens.

3 In a small bowl, whisk together the oil, the vinegar, the sugar, the mustard and the poppy seeds. Season to taste.

4 Drizzle the dressing over the salad.

Pineapple Drizzle

1 Preheat the oven to 400°F.

2 Quarter the pineapple lengthwise and remove the core. Loosen the pineapple flesh from the skin with a sharp knife and cut it into bite-size pieces, keeping the quarters whole.

3 Place the quarters in a 9x13-inch glass baking dish. Drizzle them with the Amaretto, sprinkle them with the brown sugar and top them with the sliced almonds.

4 Bake the pineapple until the almonds are golden brown and the sugar is caramelized, about 15 minutes. Let the pineapple cool slightly before serving.

TUESDAY

Primary Pasta

2 cloves garlic
3 tablespoons fresh parsley (when chopped)
1 large yellow bell pepper
1 small sweet onion
1 jar (15½ ounces) roasted red peppers
¼ cup capers
16 ounces linguine
¼ cup regular or light olive oil
1 teaspoon dried oregano
1 tablespoon sugar
Seasoning to taste
¼ cup dry red wine (or nonalcoholic red wine
   or vegetable broth)
¼ cup grated Parmesan cheese

Conventional Cauliflower

1 medium head cauliflower
1 medium shallot
2 tablespoons butter
½ teaspoon celery seeds
Seasoning to taste
¼ teaspoon paprika

Bipartisan Boboli

2 cloves garlic
2 slices prosciutto ham
2 small (8-inch) Boboli breads (or English or
   Australian muffins)
2 tablespoons regular or light olive oil
½ small can (6 ounces) tomato paste*
1 teaspoon dried basil

*Reserve the remainder of the can for use on Friday.

Maple Landslide

4 eggs
2 cups whole or low-fat milk
½ cup maple syrup
½ teaspoon salt
Whipped cream for garnish
¼ teaspoon ground nutmeg

EQUIPMENT

Electric hand mixer
Stockpot
Large covered skillet
Medium skillet
9x13-inch baking pan
4 custard cups
Cookie sheet
Colander

Medium bowl
Assorted kitchen knives
Measuring cups and
   spoons
Assorted cooking
   utensils
Pastry brush

COUNTDOWN

1 Assemble the ingredients and equipment
2 Do Steps 1–5 of the *Maple Landslide*
3 Do Steps 1–2 of the *Primary Pasta*
4 Do Steps 1–2 of the *Bipartisan Boboli*
5 Do Steps 1–3 of the *Conventional Cauliflower*
6 Do Steps 3–4 of the *Bipartisan Boboli*
7 Do Steps 3–6 of the *Primary Pasta*
8 Do Step 6 of the *Maple Landslide*

Primary Pasta

1 Bring water to a boil in a stockpot.

2 Peel and mince the garlic. Chop the parsley. Seed the bell pepper and cut it into strips. Peel and chop the sweet onion. Drain the roasted red peppers and cut them in $1/2$-inch slices. Rinse and drain the capers.

3 Cook the pasta until it is almost tender, 2 to 3 minutes if you are using fresh pasta and 5 to 6 minutes if you are using dried pasta.

4 Drain the pasta, return it to the stockpot, and toss it with 1 tablespoon of the oil. Cover to keep warm.

5 Heat the remaining oil in a medium skillet. Add the garlic, the parsley, the peppers, the onion, the capers, the oregano and the sugar. Season to taste and sauté for 2 minutes. Add the wine and cook for 2 minutes more.

6 Add the sauce to the pasta and toss to coat. Sprinkle with the Parmesan cheese.

Conventional Cauliflower

1 Trim and cut the cauliflower into bite-size florets. Peel and chop the shallot.

2 Melt the butter in a large skillet. Sauté the shallot until it is soft, about 5 minutes. Add the cauliflower and the celery seeds, and sauté until the cauliflower is crisp-tender, 7 to 8 minutes. Season to taste.

3 Sprinkle the cauliflower with the paprika and cover to keep warm.

Bipartisan Boboli

1 Peel and mince the garlic. Chop the prosciutto.

2 Brush the Bobolis with the oil, spread them lightly with the tomato paste and sprinkle with the garlic, the prosciutto and the basil.

3 Preheat the oven to 350°F.

4 Place the Bobolis on an ungreased cookie sheet and bake until they are hot and the topping is bubbly, 7 to 8 minutes.

Maple Landslide

1 Preheat the oven to 325°F. Bring water to a boil.

2 Beat the eggs in a medium bowl. Add the milk, the syrup and the salt and beat until well blended.

3 Pour the mixture into individual custard cups.

4 Place the custard cups in a 9x13-inch baking pan. Pour boiling water into the pan around the custard cups to a depth of about 1 inch.

5 Bake until the tip of a sharp knife inserted in the center of the custard comes out clean, 30 to 35 minutes.

6 Top each custard with a dollop of whipped cream and a sprinkle of nutmeg.

WEDNESDAY

Almost Winter Beef & Veggies

1 pound lean boneless sirloin steak
4 stalks celery
5 medium carrots
1 bunch radishes
3 medium turnips
$^1/_2$ pound green beans
3 tablespoons regular or light vegetable oil
2 beef bouillon cubes
$^3/_4$ cup water
Seasoning to taste
2 tablespoons cornstarch

Nearly Pilaf

1 cup water
1 can (10$^3/_4$ ounces) beef broth
1 cup quick-cooking barley
1 teaspoon instant minced onion
$^1/_4$ teaspoon dried thyme
$^1/_4$ teaspoon garlic powder
1 tablespoon fresh parsley (when chopped)
1 tablespoon butter
Seasoning to taste

Merely Tangerines

8 seedless tangerines
1 tablespoon butter
2 teaspoons lemon extract
3 tablespoons dark brown sugar

EQUIPMENT

Large covered skillet	Measuring cups and
Medium covered skillet	spoons
Medium covered	Assorted cooking
saucepan	utensils
9x9-inch glass baking	Whisk
dish	Vegetable peeler
Assorted kitchen knives	Citrus grater

COUNTDOWN

1 Assemble the ingredients and equipment
2 Do Step 1 of the *Nearly Pilaf*
3 Do Steps 1–4 of the *Almost Winter Beef & Veggies*
4 Do Step 2 of the *Nearly Pilaf*
5 Do Steps 1–3 of the *Merely Tangerines*
6 Do Steps 5–6 of the *Almost Winter Beef & Veggies*
7 Do Step 3 of the *Nearly Pilaf*
8 Do Steps 4–6 of the *Merely Tangerines*

Almost Winter Beef & Veggies

1 Trim the steak of any excess fat and cut the meat diagonally across the grain into 1/4-inch slices. Trim the celery and thinly slice it on the diagonal. Peel the carrots and thinly slice them on the diagonal. Trim and thinly slice the radishes. Peel, quarter and thinly slice the turnips. Trim the green beans and cut them diagonally into 1-inch pieces.

2 Heat 2 tablespoons of the oil in a large skillet. Add the beef and sauté until it is medium-rare, about 2 minutes. Remove the beef with any drippings and reserve.

3 Add the remaining oil to the skillet and heat until hot. Add the celery, the carrots, the radishes, the turnips and the green beans and sauté until they are crisp-tender, 3 to 5 minutes.

4 Stir in the bouillon cubes and 1/2 cup of the water. Season to taste. Heat the mixture to boiling, stirring. Reduce the heat, cover and cook until the turnips and the beans are fork-tender, 15 to 20 minutes.

5 Dissolve the cornstarch in the remaining water and stir it into the skillet. Heat, stirring often, until the sauce thickens, 2 to 3 minutes.

6 Return the beef and the drippings to the skillet and stir until heated through, 1 to 2 minutes.

Nearly Pilaf

1 Bring the water and the broth to a boil in a medium saucepan.

2 Stir in the barley, the instant minced onion, the thyme and the garlic powder. Return the mixture to a boil, reduce the heat, cover and simmer, stirring occasionally, until the barley is tender and the liquid is absorbed, 20 to 25 minutes.

3 Chop the parsley. Stir the butter and the parsley into the barley. Season to taste.

Merely Tangerines

1 Finely grate the peel of 2 tangerines and then remove the rinds. Peel the remaining 2 tangerines.

2 Melt the butter in a medium skillet with the lemon extract and 2 tablespoons of the brown sugar.

3 Add the whole fruit and the shredded peel. Cover and cook for 3 minutes. Remove the skillet from the heat and leave it covered.

4 Preheat the broiler. Grease a 9x9-inch glass baking dish.

5 Place the tangerines with the sauce in the baking dish and sprinkle with the remaining brown sugar.

6 Place the dish under the broiler and broil just until the sugar begins to caramelize, about 3 minutes. Serve hot.

THURSDAY

Farmers' Market Soup

1 pound boneless, skinless chicken breasts
1 pound baking potatoes
1 small bunch broccoli
4 medium carrots
2 stalks celery
1 large onion
2 cloves garlic
1 small can (8³/₄ ounces) whole kernel corn
4 tablespoons butter
3 cans (14¹/₂ ounces each) chicken broth
3 tablespoons dry sherry (or omit)
1 small loaf French bread
³/₄ pound Gouda cheese
Seasoning to taste

Just Green Salad

1 large head lettuce
1 medium cucumber
5 scallions (green onions)
1 tablespoon fresh parsley (when chopped)
2 tablespoons balsamic vinegar
¹/₄ teaspoon Worcestershire sauce
Seasoning to taste
3 tablespoons regular or light olive oil

Cranberry Cobbler

1 package (12 ounces) fresh cranberries
1 cup dark brown sugar
1 teaspoon grated fresh orange peel
1 cup orange juice
¹/₂ cup water
1 package (8) refrigerator cinnamon rolls
¹/₃ cup chopped walnuts

EQUIPMENT

Dutch oven	Assorted kitchen knives
Medium saucepan	Measuring cups and
Cookie sheet	spoons
8x8-inch glass baking	Assorted cooking
dish	utensils
Large bowl	Whisk
Small bowl	Vegetable peeler

COUNTDOWN

1 Assemble the ingredients and equipment
2 Do Steps 1–4 of the *Farmers' Market Soup*
3 Do Steps 1–4 of the *Cranberry Cobbler*
4 Do Steps 1–2 of the *Just Green Salad*
5 Do Step 5 of the *Cranberry Cobbler*
6 Do Steps 5–6 of the *Farmers' Market Soup*
7 Do Step 3 of the *Just Green Salad*

Farmers' Market Soup

1 Cut the chicken into 1-inch cubes. Peel and cube the potatoes. Trim and cut the broccoli into bite-size florets. Peel and slice the carrots. Trim and slice the celery. Peel and chop the onion. Peel and mince the garlic. Drain the corn.

2 Melt 1 tablespoon of the butter in a Dutch oven. Sauté the chicken until it is opaque throughout, about 5 minutes. Remove and reserve.

3 Melt the remaining butter in the Dutch oven. Add the potatoes, the broccoli, the carrots, the celery, the onion and the garlic and sauté until the onion is golden, about 8 minutes.

4 Add the broth, the corn and the sherry to the Dutch oven. Return the chicken, reduce the heat, cover and simmer until the vegetables are tender, about 30 minutes.

5 Preheat the broiler. Slice the French bread and place it on an ungreased cookie sheet. Peel and slice the Gouda. Lay the cheese slices over the bread and broil, 3 or 4 inches from the heat, until the cheese is bubbly, 1 to 2 minutes.

6 Season the soup to taste. Top each serving with slices of the cheese bread.

Just Green Salad

1 Wash and dry the lettuce and tear it into bite-size pieces. Peel and slice the cucumber. Trim and slice the scallions. Combine the ingredients in a large bowl.

2 Chop the parsley. In a small bowl, whisk together the parsley, the vinegar and the Worcestershire sauce. Season to taste. Gradually whisk in the oil until the vinaigrette is thoroughly blended.

3 Toss the salad with the dressing.

Cranberry Cobbler

1 Preheat the oven to 400°F. Grease an 8x8-inch glass baking dish.

2 Rinse the cranberries, discarding any that are soft or discolored, and place them in a medium saucepan. Add the brown sugar, the orange peel, the orange juice and the water. Bring the mixture to a boil, reduce the heat and cook until the cranberries pop, 5 to 7 minutes.

3 Turn the cranberry mixture into the baking dish.

4 Separate the cinnamon rolls, reserving the icing packet, and place them over the cranberry mixture. Sprinkle with the nuts. Bake until the rolls are lightly browned, about 15 minutes.

5 Drizzle the cobbler with the reserved icing.

FRIDAY

Sonora Snapper

2 packages (9 ounces each) frozen chopped
    spinach
$^1/_4$ pound fresh mushrooms
3 scallions (green onions)
$^1/_2$ small can (6 ounces) tomato paste reserved
    from Tuesday
$^1/_4$ cup chili sauce
$1^1/_4$ pounds red snapper fillets
Seasoning to taste
$^3/_4$ cup shredded regular or low-fat Monterey
    Jack cheese

Tijuana Salad

1 medium head lettuce
$^1/_2$ pound fresh tomatoes
1 small onion
1 medium can (15 ounces) western-style chili
    beans
1 small can (3.3 ounces) sliced black olives
$^1/_4$ cup regular or light sour cream
2 tablespoons lemon juice
Seasoning to taste
1 small package (6 ounces) corn chips

Mexican Sunset

1 package (10 ounces) frozen sweetened
    raspberries
10 hot cinnamon candies
1 tablespoon rum (or 1 teaspoon rum extract)
1 pint orange frozen yogurt (or sherbet)

EQUIPMENT

Small saucepan	Assorted cooking
9x13-inch glass baking	utensils
dish	Whisk
Large bowl	Ice cream scoop
Small bowl	Plastic bag
Assorted kitchen knives	Mallet
Measuring cups and	
spoons	

COUNTDOWN

IN THE MORNING:
  1 Do Step 1 of the *Sonora Snapper*
  2 Do Step 1 of the *Mexican Sunset*
BEFORE DINNER:
  1 Assemble the remaining ingredients and
     equipment
  2 Do Steps 2–6 of the *Sonora Snapper*
  3 Do Steps 2–3 of the *Mexican Sunset*
  4 Do Steps 1–2 of the *Tijuana Salad*
  5 Do Step 7 of the *Sonora Snapper*
  6 Do Step 3 of the *Tijuana Salad*
  7 Do Step 4 of the *Mexican Sunset*

Sonora Snapper

1 Set the spinach in the refrigerator to thaw.

2 Preheat the oven to 375°F. Grease a 9x13-inch glass baking dish.

3 Squeeze the thawed spinach until it is dry. Rinse, pat dry, trim and slice the mushrooms. Trim and chop the scallions.

4 Line the bottom of the baking dish with the spinach. Sprinkle the mushrooms over the spinach. Sprinkle the scallions over the mushrooms.

5 Combine the tomato paste with the chili sauce and pour half of the mixture over the scallions. Lay the fish in a single layer on top of the sauce. Cover with the remaining tomato mixture and season to taste.

6 Bake until the fish is opaque throughout and flakes easily with a fork, 10 to 15 minutes.

7 Sprinkle the fish with the cheese and return it to the oven just until the cheese melts, 2 to 3 minutes.

Tijuana Salad

1 Wash and dry the lettuce and tear it into bite-size pieces. Chop the tomatoes. Peel and chop the onion. Drain the chili beans. Drain the olives. Combine the ingredients in a large bowl.

2 In a small bowl, combine the sour cream and the lemon juice. Season to taste.

3 Toss the salad with the dressing and top it with the corn chips, crumbled by hand.

Mexican Sunset

1 Set the raspberries in the refrigerator to thaw.

2 Place the hot cinnamon candies in a plastic bag and crush them with a mallet.

3 In a small saucepan, bring the raspberries and their syrup to a slow boil. Add the rum and the crushed candies and cook for 2 minutes. Let the mixture cool.

4 Place scoops of frozen yogurt in individual dessert dishes and drizzle with the raspberry sauce.

NOVEMBER
WEEK TWO

WEEK AT A GLANCE

Monday

SOLDIER'S SOUP
VETERAN'S VEGETABLE PASTA
POPPY BREAD
PROUD PUDDING

Tuesday

SHRIMP SCAMPER
LEMONY RICE
LITTLE SPROUT SALAD
PICTURESQUE PEACHES

Wednesday

STEAK-OUT
GUILTY SWEETS
PEAS PATROL
UNDERCOVER CAKE

Thursday

STRUTTIN' CHICKEN
VEGETABLE VARIATIONS
AMARETTO APPLES

Friday

IMPOSING ONION PASTA
EXCEPTIONAL SALAD
INDESCRIBABLE BREAD
COCONUT DREAM PIE

CHECK STAPLES

- [ ] Butter
- [ ] Flour
- [ ] Granulated sugar
- [ ] Confectioners' sugar
- [ ] Sweetened cocoa
- [ ] Multicolored sprinkles
- [ ] Long-grain white rice
- [ ] Regular or light vegetable oil
- [ ] Regular or light olive oil
- [ ] Rice vinegar
- [ ] Balsamic vinegar
- [ ] Lemon juice
- [ ] Grated fresh lemon peel
- [ ] Worcestershire sauce
- [ ] Dijon mustard
- [ ] Regular or low-fat mayonnaise
- [ ] Honey
- [ ] Chunky-style peanut butter
- [ ] Grated Parmesan cheese
- [ ] Ground allspice
- [ ] Whole allspice
- [ ] Dried basil
- [ ] Cayenne pepper
- [ ] Ground cloves
- [ ] Curry powder
- [ ] Garlic powder
- [ ] Dry mustard
- [ ] Dried oregano
- [ ] Whole black peppercorns
- [ ] Poppy seeds
- [ ] Dried rosemary
- [ ] Dried thyme
- [ ] Turmeric
- [ ] Pepper
- [ ] Salt
- [ ] Vanilla extract

SHOPPING NOTE

● If you are shopping once a week and cannot arrange to purchase fresh shrimp on the day you plan to use them, you can purchase *not previously frozen* shrimp and freeze them, placing them in the refrigerator to thaw the night before you are ready to use them Or you can purchase *still frozen* shrimp and keep them frozen until the night before you are ready to use them.

MEAT & POULTRY

$1^1/_2$ pounds lean flank steak (W)
3 pounds chicken legs and
    thighs (Th)

FISH

1 pound medium shrimp,
    shelled and deveined (T)

FRESH PRODUCE

Vegetables

2 pounds yams (W)
1 medium zucchini (M)
1 small rutabaga (M)
$1/_4$ pound mushrooms (Th)
$1^1/_2$ pounds carrots (M)
1 medium carrot (Th)
2 stalks celery—1 (W), 1 (Th)
4 large sweet onions (F)
2 medium onions—1 (M), 1 (Th)
1 small onion (W)
1 medium leek (M)
1 medium shallot (T)
12 scallions (green onions) (Th)
1 head garlic (T, W, Th)
1 bunch parsley (M, T, Th, F)
$1/_4$ pound bean sprouts (T)
1 package (16 ounces) mixed
    salad greens (T)
1 medium head lettuce (F)
1 ripe avocado (F)
$1/_2$ pound tomatoes (F)
1 medium cucumber (F)
1 small yellow bell pepper (M)

Fruit

4 large tart green apples (Th)
2 kiwifruit (W)
1 medium orange (Th)

CANS, JARS & BOTTLES

Soup

2 cans ($14^1/_2$ ounces each)
    chicken broth (M)
1 can ($10^3/_4$ ounces) chicken
    broth (Th)

1 can ($14^1/_2$ ounces) vegetable
    broth (Th)

Vegetables

1 medium can ($14^1/_2$ ounces)
    cut-up tomatoes (F)

Fruit

1 medium can (15 ounces)
    peach halves (T)

Condiments

1 jar ($6^1/_2$ ounces) marinated
    artichoke hearts (F)

Dessert Needs

1 can (21 ounces) coconut
    cream pie filling (F)

PACKAGED GOODS

Pasta, Rice & Grains

12 ounces medium egg
    noodles (M)
16 ounces linguine (F)

Baked Goods

1 medium foccacia (or any
    flat) bread (M)
1 small loaf French bread (F)

Nuts & Seeds

$1/_2$ cup sliced almonds (T)

Dessert & Baking Needs

1 small package (10 ounces)
    coconut macaroons (T)
1 small package (3.9 ounces)
    instant chocolate pudding
    mix (M)
1 package (3 ounces)
    ladyfingers (or angel food
    cake) (W)
1 prepared 9-inch shortbread
    pie shell (F)
$1/_2$ cup white chocolate chips (T)

1 cup flaked coconut—$1/_2$ cup
    (W), $1/_2$ cup (F)

WINES & SPIRITS

$1/_2$ cup dry white wine (or
    nonalcoholic white wine or
    vegetable broth) (T)
$1/_4$ cup dry white wine (or
    nonalcoholic white wine or
    chicken broth) (Th)
2 tablespoons dry red wine (or
    nonalcoholic red wine or red
    wine vinegar) (W)
1 tablespoon Grand Marnier
    liqueur (or nonalcoholic
    Italian orange syrup) (W)
$1/_4$ cup Amaretto liqueur (or
    nonalcoholic Italian almond
    syrup) (Th)

REFRIGERATED PRODUCTS

Dairy

$2^1/_2$ cups + 2 tablespoons
    whole milk (M)
$1/_2$ cup whole or low-fat
    milk (M)
$1/_2$ cup half-and-half (Th)
1 cup whipping cream (W)
1 egg (Th)

Cheese

1 package (5 ounces) herb and
    garlic cheese spread (M)

FROZEN GOODS

Vegetables

1 large package (16 ounces)
    green peas (W)

Desserts

1 quart vanilla ice cream (F)
1 medium container (12
    ounces) frozen whipped
    topping—4 ounces (M), 8
    ounces (F)

MONDAY

Soldier's Soup

1¹/₂ pounds carrots
1 tablespoon fresh parsley (when chopped)
2 cans (14¹/₂ ounces each) chicken broth
1 teaspoon curry powder
2 tablespoons lemon juice
1 teaspoon sugar
¹/₂ teaspoon cayenne pepper
Seasoning to taste

Veteran's Vegetable Pasta

1 medium leek
1 small rutabaga
1 medium zucchini
1 small yellow bell pepper
1 tablespoon butter
1 tablespoon regular or light vegetable oil
12 ounces medium egg noodles
1 container (5 ounces) herb and garlic cheese
    spread
¹/₂ cup whole or low-fat milk
Seasoning to taste

Poppy Bread

1 medium onion
3 tablespoons regular or light olive oil
1 medium foccaccia (or any flat) bread
¹/₂ teaspoon dried basil
2 tablespoons poppy seeds

Proud Pudding

4 ounces frozen whipped topping*
2 tablespoons sweetened cocoa
2 cups + 2 tablespoons whole milk
2 tablespoons chunky-style peanut butter
1 small package (3.9 ounces) instant
    chocolate pudding mix

EQUIPMENT

Electric hand mixer	Small bowl
Blender	Colander
Stockpot	Assorted kitchen knives
Large covered skillet	Measuring cups and
Medium covered skillet	spoons
Large covered	Assorted cooking
saucepan	utensils
Cookie sheet	Vegetable peeler
Medium bowl	Pastry brush

COUNTDOWN

1 Assemble the ingredients and equipment
2 Do Step 1 of the *Proud Pudding*
3 Do Step 1 of the *Soldier's Soup*
4 Do Steps 2–4 of the *Proud Pudding*
5 Do Steps 1–2 of the *Veteran's Vegetable
   Pasta*
6 Do Steps 2–3 of the *Soldier's Soup*
7 Do Steps 1–2 of the *Poppy Bread*
8 Do Steps 3–6 of the *Veteran's Vegetable
   Pasta*
9 Do Step 3 of the *Poppy Bread*

---

*Reserve the balance of the container for use on Friday.

Soldier's Soup

1 Peel and chunk the carrots. Chop the parsley. Place both in a large saucepan. Add the broth and the curry powder and bring the mixture to a boil. Reduce the heat, cover and simmer until the carrots are soft, about 20 minutes.

2 Stir the lemon juice into the carrot mixture. Place a portion at a time in a blender and process until the soup is pureed. Add the sugar. Add the cayenne pepper. Season to taste.

3 Return the soup to the saucepan and reheat. Sprinkle with the parsley and cover to keep warm.

Veteran's Vegetable Pasta

1 Bring water to a boil in a stockpot.

2 Thoroughly wash the leek and cut it into thin shreds. Peel and julienne the rutabaga. Trim and julienne the zucchini. Seed the bell pepper and cut it into fine strips.

3 Melt the butter with the oil in a large skillet. Add the rutabaga and stir to coat. Cover, reduce the heat and cook for 3 minutes. Add the remaining vegetables and sauté until they are crisp-tender, 3 to 4 minutes.

4 Cook the noodles until they are almost tender, 3 to 5 minutes.

5 Add the cheese spread and the milk to the skillet and stir to combine. Cook until the cheese has melted and the sauce has become creamy. Season to taste.

6 Drain the noodles, return them to the stockpot, and toss them with the sauce. Cover to keep warm.

Poppy Bread

1 Preheat the broiler.

2 Peel and mince the onion. Heat 2 tablespoons of the oil in a medium skillet and sauté the onion until soft, about 5 minutes. Remove the skillet from the heat and cover to keep warm.

3 Place the foccaccia bread on an ungreased cookie sheet and brush it with the remaining oil. Spread the sautéed onions over the bread, sprinkle with the basil and the poppy seeds and broil until hot, 2 to 3 minutes, being careful not to let the onions burn.

Proud Pudding

1 Set 4 ounces of frozen whipped topping out to thaw.

2 Fold the cocoa into the whipped topping. In a small bowl, combine 2 tablespoons of the milk with the peanut butter and blend well. Stir in the whipped topping.

3 In a medium bowl, beat the remaining milk with the pudding mix until well blended.

4 Spoon the pudding mixture into individual dessert dishes. Top with the whipped topping mixture and refrigerate for at least 20 minutes.

TUESDAY

Shrimp Scamper

1 medium shallot
1 clove garlic
2 teaspoons fresh parsley (when chopped)
1 pound medium shrimp, shelled and deveined
1 tablespoon regular or light vegetable oil
$1/2$ cup dry white wine (or nonalcoholic white
    wine or vegetable broth)
3 teaspoons lemon juice
$1/2$ teaspoon dried thyme
Seasoning to taste

Lemony Rice

4 tablespoons butter
$1/2$ teaspoon dry mustard
1 teaspoon turmeric
Seasoning to taste
1 cup long-grain white rice
2 cups water
1 tablespoon lemon juice
1 teaspoon grated fresh lemon peel

Little Sprout Salad

1 package (16 ounces) mixed salad greens
$1/4$ pound fresh bean sprouts
3 tablespoons regular or light olive oil
2 tablespoons rice vinegar
1 tablespoon honey
Seasoning to taste

Picturesque Peaches

1 medium can (15 ounces) peach halves
1 cup coconut macaroons (when crumbled)
$1/2$ cup white chocolate chips
$1/2$ cup sliced almonds
1 teaspoon almond extract
1 tablespoon butter

EQUIPMENT

Large skillet
Medium covered
    saucepan
8x8-inch glass baking
    dish
Large bowl
2 small bowls

Assorted kitchen knives
Measuring cups and
    spoons
Assorted cooking
    utensils
Whisk

COUNTDOWN

1 Assemble the ingredients and equipment
2 Do Steps 1–2 of the *Lemony Rice*
3 Do Steps 1–2 of the *Little Sprout Salad*
4 Do Steps 1–6 of the *Picturesque Peaches*
5 Do Steps 1–4 of the *Shrimp Scamper*
6 Do Step 3 of the *Little Sprout Salad*
7 Do Step 3 of the *Lemony Rice*

Shrimp Scamper

1 Peel and chop the shallot. Peel and mince the garlic. Chop the parsley. Rinse the shrimp.

2 Heat the oil in a large skillet. Add the shallot and the garlic and sauté until they are soft but not browned, about 5 minutes.

3 Add the shrimp and cook, stirring, until they are just pink and loosely curled, 1 to 2 minutes.

4 Stir in the wine, the lemon juice, the thyme and the parsley. Season to taste. Cook, stirring to coat the shrimp, until the sauce is heated through, about 2 minutes.

Lemony Rice

1 Melt the butter in a medium saucepan. Stir in the mustard and the turmeric. Season to taste and cook, stirring occasionally, for 5 minutes.

2 Stir the rice, the water, the lemon juice and the lemon peel into the saucepan. Reduce the heat, cover and simmer until all the liquid is absorbed and the rice is tender, 20 to 25 minutes.

3 Fluff the rice before serving.

Little Sprout Salad

1 Rinse the salad greens. Place them in a large bowl and toss them with the bean sprouts.

2 In a small bowl, whisk together the oil, the vinegar and the honey. Season to taste.

3 Toss the salad with the dressing.

Picturesque Peaches

1 Preheat the oven to 350°F.

2 Drain the peaches, reserving 6 tablespoons of the syrup.

3 Crumble the macaroons.

4 Place the peaches, cut side up, in an 8x8-inch glass baking dish.

5 In a small bowl, combine the crumbled macaroons, the white chocolate chips, the sliced almonds and half of the reserved peach syrup. Mix in the almond extract. Spoon the mixture into the peach halves. Dot with the butter. Drizzle the remaining syrup over the peaches.

6 Bake the peaches until the tops are lightly browned and the chocolate is almost melted, 15 to 20 minutes. Serve warm.

WEDNESDAY

Steak-out

1 tablespoon whole peppercorns
1 tablespoon whole allspice
1 1/2 pounds lean flank steak
Seasoning to taste
1 tablespoon regular or light vegetable oil

Guilty Sweets

2 pounds yams
4 tablespoons butter
2 tablespoons dry red wine (or red wine
    vinegar)
Seasoning to taste

Peas Patrol

1 large package (16 ounces) frozen green peas
1 clove garlic
1 small onion
1 stalk celery
2 tablespoons butter
1/2 teaspoon Dijon mustard
1/4 teaspoon sugar
Seasoning to taste

Undercover Cake

1 cup whipping cream
1 teaspoon vanilla extract
1 tablespoon confectioners' sugar
1 tablespoon Grand Marnier liqueur (or
    nonalcoholic Italian orange syrup)
2 kiwifruit
1 package (3 ounces) ladyfingers (or angel
    food cake)
1/2 cup flaked coconut

EQUIPMENT

Electric hand mixer	Measuring cups and
Large skillet	spoons
Medium covered	Assorted cooking
saucepan	utensils
9x13-inch baking pan	Vegetable peeler
Medium bowl	Plastic bag
Assorted kitchen knives	Mallet

COUNTDOWN

1 Assemble the ingredients and equipment
2 Do Steps 1–4 of the *Guilty Sweets*
3 Do Step 1 of the *Undercover Cake*
4 Do Steps 1–4 of the *Peas Patrol*
5 Do Steps 1–5 of the *Steak-out*
6 Do Step 5 of the *Guilty Sweets*
7 Do Steps 2–3 of the *Undercover Cake*

Steak-out

1 Place the peppercorns and the allspice in a plastic bag and crush them with a mallet.

2 Trim the flank steak of any excess fat and cut the meat into 4 portions.

3 Press the peppercorn mixture into all sides of the steaks. Season to taste.

4 Heat the oil in a large skillet. Add the steaks and cook, turning once, until they are well browned on the outside and cooked to taste on the inside (3 to 4 minutes for rare).

5 Remove the steaks and cover to keep warm.

Guilty Sweets

1 Preheat the oven to 450°F.

2 Peel and cut the yams into $1/2$-inch cubes.

3 Place the butter in a 9x13-inch baking pan and set it in the oven to melt.

4 Add the yams to the melted butter, toss lightly to coat, season to taste and bake until the yams are lightly browned, about 30 minutes.

5 Add the wine to the steak skillet and stir, scraping up any browned bits. Season to taste and lightly toss the potatoes in the skillet to coat.

Peas Patrol

1 Peel and mince the garlic. Peel and mince the onion. Trim and thinly slice the celery.

2 Bring $1/2$-inch of water to a boil in a medium saucepan. Cook the peas for a scant 4 minutes.

3 Melt the butter in the saucepan. Sauté the garlic, the onion and the celery until soft, about 4 minutes. Drain the peas.

4 Add the mustard and the sugar and stir to combine. Season to taste. Return the peas to the saucepan and toss to coat. Cover to keep warm.

Undercover Cake

1 In a medium bowl, whip the cream until it is stiff. Fold in the vanilla, the confectioners' sugar and the Grand Marnier. Refrigerate the mixture until you are ready to use.

2 Peel and thinly slice the kiwifruit. Divide them among individual dessert dishes. Split the ladyfingers and cover the kiwifruit with them.

3 Spoon the whipped cream mixture over the ladyfingers and sprinkle with the coconut.

THURSDAY

Struttin' Chicken

1 clove garlic
3 pounds chicken legs and thighs
$1/2$ cup flour
$1/8$ teaspoon ground allspice
Seasoning to taste
4 tablespoons butter
1 tablespoon regular or light vegetable oil
12 scallions (green onions)
$1/4$ cup fresh parsley (when chopped)
1 can ($10^3/4$ ounces) chicken broth
*$1/4$ cup dry white wine (or nonalcoholic white
    wine or additional chicken broth)*
1 egg
$1/2$ cup half-and-half
$1/8$ teaspoon ground cloves

Vegetable Variations

1 medium onion
1 medium carrot
1 stalk celery
$1/4$ pound fresh mushrooms
2 tablespoons butter
1 cup long-grain white rice
1 can ($14^1/2$ ounces) vegetable broth
$1/4$ cup water
Seasoning to taste

Amaretto Apples

1 medium orange
1 cup sugar
*$1/4$ cup Amaretto liqueur (or nonalcoholic
    Italian almond syrup)*
4 large firm tart green apples

EQUIPMENT

Dutch oven	Measuring cups and
Large covered skillet	spoons
Large skillet	Assorted cooking
Medium covered	utensils
saucepan	Whisk
Medium bowl	Citrus grater
Small bowl	Juicer
Fine strainer	Vegetable peeler
Assorted kitchen knives	Plastic bag

COUNTDOWN

1 Assemble the ingredients and equipment
2 Do Steps 1–4 of the *Struttin' Chicken*
3 Do Steps 1–3 of the *Vegetable Variations*
4 Do Steps 5–6 of the *Struttin' Chicken*
5 Do Steps 1–2 of the *Amaretto Apples*
6 Do Steps 7–10 of the *Struttin' Chicken*
7 Do Step 4 of the *Vegetable Variations*

Struttin' Chicken

1 Cut the garlic in half and rub the chicken pieces with it. Discard the garlic.

2 Combine the flour and the allspice in a plastic bag and season to taste. Add the chicken, several pieces at a time. Shake well to coat and reserve the excess flour.

3 Heat 3 tablespoons of the butter with the oil in a large skillet. Sauté the chicken until the pieces are deep golden brown on all sides, 10 to 12 minutes.

4 Transfer the chicken to a Dutch oven, cover and let stand. Trim and chop 4 of the scallions. Chop the parsley.

5 Remove all but 1 tablespoon of the drippings from the skillet. Add the remaining butter and the chopped scallions and sauté for 2 minutes. Stir in 2 tablespoons of the reserved flour mixture and cook, whisking constantly, for 2 minutes. Whisk in the broth and the wine. Heat the mixture to boiling and pour it over the chicken.

6 Reheat the chicken until the liquid boils. Then reduce the heat, cover and simmer for 15 minutes.

7 Trim the remaining scallions, leaving $1\frac{1}{2}$ inches of stem. Add them to the chicken, covering them with the broth. Cook, covered, until the chicken is tender, about 5 minutes more. The scallions should still be slightly crunchy.

8 Remove the chicken and the scallions and cover to keep warm.

9 Strain the sauce into a medium bowl, pour it into the skillet, bring it to a boil and cook until it is slightly thickened, about 5 minutes. Remove the skillet from the heat.

10 Lightly beat the egg in a small bowl. Combine the half-and-half with the egg. Add the cloves and stir the mixture into the sauce. Return the skillet to the heat and simmer for 2 minutes. (Do not let the sauce boil or it will curdle.) Pour the sauce over the chicken and scallions and sprinkle with the parsley.

Vegetable Variations

1 Peel and chop the onion. Peel and chop the carrot. Peel and chop the celery. Wash, pat dry, trim and chop the mushrooms.

2 Melt the butter in a medium saucepan. Add the vegetables and sauté until they are softened, about 5 minutes.

3 Add the rice, tossing to coat it with the butter. Add the broth and the water. Season to taste. Reduce the heat, cover and simmer until all the liquid is absorbed and the rice and the vegetables are tender, 20 to 25 minutes.

4 Fluff the rice before serving.

Amaretto Apples

1 Grate the peel from the orange and then squeeze the juice. Combine the peel and the juice with the sugar and the Amaretto in a large covered skillet.

2 Peel, core and thickly slice the apples. Add them to the skillet and simmer until they are tender and the liquid has evaporated. Cover the skillet and refrigerate it until you are ready to serve.

FRIDAY

Imposing Onion Pasta

4 large sweet onions
2 tablespoons fresh parsley (when chopped)
1/4 cup regular or light olive oil
1 medium can (14*1/2* ounces) cut-up tomatoes
1/4 teaspoon dried rosemary
1/2 teaspoon dried basil
Seasoning to taste
16 ounces linguine
1/2 cup grated Parmesan cheese

Exceptional Salad

1 medium head lettuce
1/2 pound fresh tomatoes
1 medium cucumber
1 ripe avocado
2 teaspoons lemon juice
1 jar (6*1/2* ounces) marinated artichoke hearts
1/4 teaspoon garlic powder
2 tablespoons balsamic vinegar
1/4 teaspoon Worcestershire sauce
1/4 teaspoon Dijon mustard
Seasoning to taste

Indescribable Bread

1 small loaf French bread
1/4 cup regular or light olive oil
2 tablespoons regular or low-fat mayonnaise
1/2 teaspoon dried oregano
1/2 teaspoon dried rosemary

Coconut Dream Pie

1 can (21 ounces) coconut cream pie filling
1 prepared 9-inch shortbread pie shell
1/2 cup flaked coconut
8 ounces frozen whipped topping reserved
    from Monday
Multicolored sprinkles

EQUIPMENT

Stockpot	Measuring cups and
Large skillet	spoons
Cookie sheet	Assorted cooking
Large bowl	utensils
2 small bowls	Whisk
Colander	Vegetable peeler
Assorted kitchen knives	Pastry brush

COUNTDOWN

1 Assemble the ingredients and equipment
2 Do Steps 1–2 of the *Coconut Dream Pie*
3 Do Steps 1–3 of the *Exceptional Salad*
4 Do Steps 1–4 of the *Imposing Onion Pasta*
5 Do Steps 1–3 of the *Indescribable Bread*
6 Do Steps 5–6 of the *Imposing Onion Pasta*
7 Do Step 4 of the *Indescribable Bread*
8 Do Step 4 of the *Exceptional Salad*

Imposing Onion Pasta

1 Bring water to a boil in a stockpot.

2 Peel and thinly slice the onions. Chop the parsley.

3 Heat the oil in a large skillet. Sauté the onions until they are very soft but not brown, about 7 minutes.

4 Add the undrained tomatoes, the rosemary and the basil. Season to taste. Cook until the flavors are combined, about 10 minutes.

5 Cook the pasta until it is almost tender, 2 to 3 minutes if you are using fresh pasta and 6 to 7 minutes if you are using dried pasta.

6 Drain the pasta and return it to the stockpot, tossing it with the sauce and $1/4$ cup of the cheese. Pass the remaining cheese.

Exceptional Salad

1 Wash and dry the lettuce and tear it into bite-size pieces. Chop the tomatoes. Peel and slice the cucumber. Combine the ingredients in a large bowl. Peel, pit and chop the avocado and sprinkle it with the lemon juice.

2 Drain the artichoke hearts, reserving the oil.

3 In a small bowl, whisk the reserved artichoke oil with the garlic powder, the vinegar, the Worcestershire sauce and the mustard until well blended. Season to taste.

4 Add the avocado to the salad. Toss the artichokes with the salad. Toss the salad with the dressing.

Indescribable Bread

1 Preheat the broiler.

2 Cut the bread into 1-inch slices. Arrange the slices on an ungreased cookie sheet.

3 In a small bowl, combine the oil, the mayonnaise, the oregano and the rosemary. Brush the mixture on the bread slices.

4 Broil the bread, 3 or 4 inches from the heat, until it is lightly toasted, 2 to 3 minutes.

Coconut Dream Pie

1 Spread the pie filling evenly into the prepared pie shell.

2 Fold the flaked coconut into the whipped topping and spread it over the pie filling. Top the pie with the sprinkles and chill it in the refrigerator for at least 30 minutes.

NOVEMBER

WEEK THREE

WEEK AT A GLANCE

Monday

HAPPY HUSBAND CHICKEN
WILD WIFE PILAF
RELATED VEGETABLES
KID CRISP

Tuesday

HAMMED-UP FETTUCCINE
SPOTLIGHT SPINACH SALAD
BACKSTAGE BREAD
PLUM ANXIOUS

Wednesday

THE THREE P'S
RED ON RED
MOCHA MADNESS

Thursday

FLOUNDERING AROUND
THE SPICE OF RICE
TURNIP YOUR NOSE
IN THE PINK

Friday

GREEN BEAN BISQUE
CAPELLINI CAKE
QUITE NICE SALAD
JUST A TRIFLE

CHECK STAPLES

- ☐ Butter
- ☐ Flour
- ☐ Baking soda
- ☐ Cornstarch
- ☐ Granulated sugar
- ☐ Dark brown sugar
- ☐ Brown rice
- ☐ Regular or light vegetable oil
- ☐ Regular or light olive oil
- ☐ Red wine vinegar
- ☐ Apple cider vinegar
- ☐ Lemon juice
- ☐ Dijon mustard
- ☐ Grated Parmesan cheese
- ☐ Instant coffee crystals
- ☐ Golden raisins
- ☐ Ground allspice
- ☐ Dried basil
- ☐ Ground cinnamon
- ☐ Ground cloves
- ☐ Italian seasoning
- ☐ Ground nutmeg
- ☐ Dried oregano
- ☐ Paprika
- ☐ Dried thyme
- ☐ Pepper
- ☐ Salt
- ☐ Vanilla extract

SHOPPING NOTE

● If you are shopping once a week and cannot arrange to purchase fresh flounder on the day you plan to use it, you can purchase *not previously frozen* flounder and freeze it, placing it in the refrigerator to thaw the night before you are ready to use it. Or you can purchase *still frozen* flounder and keep it frozen until the night before you are ready to use it.

MEAT & POULTRY

$1^1/_2$ pounds lean boneless pork loin (W)

4 boneless, skinless chicken breast halves (M)

FISH

$1^1/_4$ pounds flounder fillets (Th)

FRESH PRODUCE

Vegetables

12 small new white potatoes (W)

1 pound green beans (F)

$^1/_2$ pound sugar snap peas (M)

4 medium turnips (Th)

1 pound spinach (T)

3 medium carrots (M)

4 stalks celery—1 (M), 1 (T), 2 (Th)

6 medium onions—2 (M), 1 (T), 2 (Th), 1 (F)

1 medium red onion (W)

2 medium shallots (W)

8 scallions (green onions)— 2 (M), 3 (Th), 3 (F)

1 head garlic (M, T, F)

1 bunch parsley (F)

1 medium head red cabbage (W)

1 small head lettuce (F)

1 pound tomatoes—$^1/_2$ pound (Th), $^1/_2$ pound (F)

2 medium cucumbers (F)

Fruit

10 large plums (T)

1 small red apple (W)

4 small pink grapefruit (Th)

CANS, JARS & BOTTLES

Soup

1 can ($10^3/_4$ ounces) chicken broth (M)

1 can ($10^3/_4$ ounces) beef broth (M, W)

1 can ($14^1/_2$ ounces) chicken broth (Th)

2 cans ($14^1/_2$ ounces each) vegetable broth (F)

Vegetables

1 small can (4 ounces) sliced mushrooms (M)

Mexican Foods

$^1/_4$ cup mild salsa (F)

Fruit

1 large can (16 ounces) whole cranberry sauce (M)

Juice

$^1/_2$ cup apple juice (W)

Condiments

4 maraschino cherries + 2 tablespoons syrup (Th)

PACKAGED GOODS

Pasta, Rice & Grains

16 ounces fettuccine (T)

12 ounces capellini (angel hair pasta) (F)

$^1/_2$ cup wild rice (M)

1 cup quick-cooking oats (M)

Baked Goods

1 small loaf sourdough bread (T)

1 angel food loaf cake (F)

Fruit

12 moist pitted prunes (W)

Nuts & Seeds

$^1/_3$ cup chopped walnuts (Th)

$^1/_4$ cup sliced almonds (F)

Dessert & Baking Needs

$^1/_2$ cup semisweet chocolate chips (W)

1 small package (3.4 ounces) instant vanilla pudding (F)

WINES & SPIRITS

$^3/_4$ cup Madeira wine (or beef broth) (W)

4 teaspoons brandy (or nonalcoholic Italian coffee syrup) (W)

4 teaspoons sweet sherry (or nonalcoholic Italian cherry syrup) (Th)

$^1/_4$ cup rum (or nonalcoholic Italian praline syrup) (F)

REFRIGERATED PRODUCTS

Dairy

2 cups whole milk (F)

$1^3/_4$ cups half-and-half— $1^1/_2$ cups (T), $^1/_4$ cup (W)

$^1/_2$ cup whipping cream (F)

1 cup creme fraîche (W)

$1^1/_4$ cups regular or light sour cream—$^1/_4$ cup (W), 1 cup (F)

1 cup regular or low-fat plain yogurt (M)

4 eggs—1 (T), 3 (F)

Deli

6 ounces sliced prosciutto ham (T)

6 slices bacon (T)

FROZEN GOODS

Vegetables

1 package (9 ounces) green peas (T)

Desserts

1 pint vanilla ice cream (M)

MONDAY

Happy Husband Chicken

2 medium onions
2 cloves garlic
1 tablespoon regular or light vegetable oil
4 boneless, skinless chicken breast halves
1 can (10³/₄ ounces) chicken broth
2 tablespoons Dijon mustard
1 cup regular or low-fat plain yogurt
Seasoning to taste

Wild Wife Pilaf

1 stalk celery
2 scallions (green onions)
1 small can (4 ounces) sliced mushrooms
¹/₂ cup wild rice
¹/₂ cup beef broth*
³/₄ cup water
1 teaspoon lemon juice
¹/₄ teaspoon dried thyme
Seasoning to taste

Related Vegetables

3 medium carrots
¹/₂ pound sugar snap peas
1 tablespoon butter
¹/₂ teaspoon ground cloves
Seasoning to taste

Kid Crisp

4 tablespoons butter
1 cup quick-cooking oats
¹/₂ cup dark brown sugar
1 large can (16 ounces) whole cranberry sauce
1 pint vanilla ice cream

*Reserve the remainder of the can for use on Wednesday.

EQUIPMENT

Large covered skillet
2 medium covered
  saucepans
Small saucepan
8x8-inch glass baking
  dish
Small bowl
Assorted kitchen knives

Measuring cups and
  spoons
Assorted cooking
  utensils
Whisk
Vegetable peeler
Ice cream scoop

COUNTDOWN

1 Assemble the ingredients and equipment
2 Do Steps 1–3 of the *Wild Wife Pilaf*
3 Do Steps 1–3 of the *Kid Crisp*
4 Do Steps 1–4 of the *Happy Husband Chicken*
5 Do Step 4 of the *Kid Crisp*
6 Do Steps 1–3 of the *Related Vegetables*
7 Do Steps 5–7 of the *Happy Husband Chicken*
8 Do Step 4 of the *Wild Wife Pilaf*
9 Do Step 5 of the *Kid Crisp*

Happy Husband Chicken

1 Peel and finely chop the onions. Peel and mince the garlic.

2 Heat the oil in a large skillet. Add the chicken and sauté until the pieces are lightly browned, 4 to 5 minutes. Remove the chicken and reserve.

3 Add the onions and the garlic to the skillet and reduce the heat. If the pan is dry, add 2 tablespoons of the broth. Sauté until the onions are translucent, about 5 minutes. Add the broth and bring it to a boil. Whisk in the mustard until well blended.

4 Return the chicken to the skillet with any juices that have accumulated. Reduce the heat, cover and simmer, turning occasionally, until the chicken is cooked through, 12 to 15 minutes.

5 Remove the chicken and keep warm.

6 Boil the sauce until it reduces slightly, 2 to 3 minutes. Place the yogurt in a small bowl and gradually whisk in 1/4 cup of the sauce. Stir the yogurt mixture into the skillet and simmer until the sauce is hot, about 1 minute. Do not let the sauce boil or the yogurt will curdle. Season to taste.

7 Return the chicken to the skillet and coat the pieces with the sauce.

Wild Wife Pilaf

1 Trim and chop the celery. Trim and chop the scallions. Drain the mushrooms.

2 In a medium saucepan, combine the wild rice, the broth, the water, the celery, the scallions, the mushrooms, the lemon juice and the thyme. Season to taste.

3 Bring the mixture to a boil, reduce the heat, cover and simmer until all the liquid is absorbed and the rice is tender, about 40 minutes.

4 Fluff the pilaf before serving.

Related Vegetables

1 Bring water to a boil in a medium saucepan.

2 Peel and thinly slice the carrots. Trim and string the snap peas. Cook the vegetables until they are crisp-tender, about 4 minutes.

3 Drain the vegetables, return them to the saucepan and, over heat, toss them with the butter and the ground cloves until well coated. Season to taste, remove the saucepan from the heat and cover to keep warm.

Kid Crisp

1 Preheat the oven to 350°F. Grease an 8x8 inch glass baking dish.

2 Melt the butter in a small saucepan. Stir in the oats and the brown sugar, and sauté until the oats are well coated.

3 Pour the mixture into the baking dish and bake for 10 minutes.

4 Place the dish in the refrigerator for at least 20 minutes.

5 Crumble the cooled oat mixture. Divide half of the cranberry sauce into 4 parfait glasses. Top with half of the crumbled oat mixture. Add scoops of ice cream, the remaining cranberry sauce, and the remaining oat mixture.

TUESDAY

Hammed-up Fettuccine

1 package (9 ounces) frozen green peas
6 ounces sliced prosciutto ham
4 tablespoons butter
1 1/2 cups half-and-half
16 ounces fettuccine
Seasoning to taste
1/2 cup grated Parmesan cheese

Spotlight Spinach Salad

1 pound fresh spinach
1 stalk celery
1 medium onion
6 slices bacon
2 tablespoons dark brown sugar
2 teaspoons Dijon mustard
1/4 cup red wine vinegar
Seasoning to taste

Backstage Bread

1 small loaf sourdough bread
3 cloves garlic
2 tablespoons regular or light olive oil
1 teaspoon Italian seasoning

Plum Anxious

10 large fresh plums
1/4 cup dark brown sugar
1/4 teaspoon ground cinnamon
1 egg
1 tablespoon butter
1/2 cup granulated sugar
1/4 teaspoon baking soda
1 teaspoon vanilla extract
1/2 cup flour

EQUIPMENT

Stockpot	2 small bowls
Medium skillet	Colander
Small covered skillet	Assorted kitchen knives
8x8-inch glass baking dish	Measuring cups and spoons
Cookie sheet	Assorted cooking utensils
Large bowl	Whisk
2 medium bowls	

COUNTDOWN

1 Assemble the ingredients and equipment
2 Do Step 1 of the *Hammed-up Fettuccine*
3 Do Steps 1–6 of the *Plum Anxious*
4 Do Steps 1–5 of the *Spotlight Spinach Salad*
5 Do Steps 1–2 of the *Backstage Bread*
6 Do Steps 2–7 of the *Hammed-up Fettuccine*
7 Do Step 3 of the *Backstage Bread*
8 Do Step 6 of the *Spotlight Spinach Salad*

Hammed-up Fettuccine

1 Set the package of peas out to thaw.

2 Bring water to a boil in a stockpot.

3 Cut the prosciutto slices into slivers.

4 Melt the butter in a medium skillet. Add the half-and-half and heat, being careful not to boil, until the mixture begins to thicken, about 3 minutes.

5 Cook the pasta in the stockpot until it is almost tender, 2 to 3 minutes if you are using fresh pasta and 6 to 7 minutes if you are using dried pasta.

6 Add the peas and the prosciutto to the skillet and cook for 2 minutes. Season to taste, remove the skillet from the heat and stir in 2 tablespoons of the Parmesan cheese.

7 Drain the pasta and return it to the stockpot. Toss it with the cream sauce, sprinkle with the remaining Parmesan cheese, and cover to keep warm.

Spotlight Spinach Salad

1 Wash and dry the spinach and tear it into bite-size pieces. Trim and thinly slice the celery. Place both ingredients in a large bowl and let stand until you are ready to use.

2 Peel and chop the onion.

3 Chop the bacon and sauté it in a small skillet until it is crisp, about 5 minutes.

4 Remove the bacon, reserving the drippings, and drain it on a paper towel.

5 Sauté the onion in the bacon drippings until it is translucent, about 5 minutes.

Whisk in the brown sugar, the mustard and the vinegar. Season to taste, remove the skillet from the heat and cover to keep warm.

6 Add the bacon to the spinach and celery, and toss the mixture with the warm dressing.

Backstage Bread

1 Split the sourdough loaf in half horizontally and then cut each half in half.

2 Peel and mince the garlic. In a small bowl, combine the garlic, the oil and the Italian seasoning. Spread the mixture over the cut sides of the bread. Place the bread quarters on an ungreased cookie sheet.

3 Preheat the broiler. Broil the bread, 3 or 4 inches from the heat, until it is golden, 2 to 3 minutes.

Plum Anxious

1 Preheat the oven to 400°F. Grease an 8x8-inch glass baking dish.

2 Pit and slice the plums and place them in the baking dish.

3 In a medium bowl, combine the brown sugar and the cinnamon, and sprinkle the mixture over the plums.

4 In a small bowl, lightly beat the egg.

5 In the brown sugar bowl, cream together the butter and the granulated sugar. Stir in the beaten egg, the baking soda, the vanilla and the flour. Spread the batter evenly over the plums.

6 Bake until the top is golden, about 20 minutes.

WEDNESDAY

The Three P's

12 small new white potatoes
1¹/₂ pounds lean boneless pork loin
2 medium shallots
³/₄ cup beef broth reserved from Monday
³/₄ cup Madeira wine (or additional beef
    broth)
2 tablespoons red wine vinegar
2 teaspoons cornstarch
¹/₂ teaspoon ground cloves
2 tablespoons butter
Seasoning to taste
12 moist pitted prunes

Red on Red

1 medium head red cabbage
1 small red apple
1 medium red onion
2 teaspoons regular or light vegetable oil
¹/₂ cup apple juice
¹/₂ cup water
Seasoning to taste
¹/₄ cup apple cider vinegar
2 teaspoons dark brown sugar

Mocha Madness

¹/₂ cup semisweet chocolate chips
¹/₃ cup half-and-half
4 teaspoons brandy (or nonalcoholic Italian
    coffee syrup)
1 cup creme fraîche
¹/₄ cup regular or low-fat sour cream
2 teaspoons instant coffee crystals dissolved
    in 2 teaspoons hot water
1¹/₂ tablespoons sugar

EQUIPMENT

Large skillet	Measuring cups and
Large covered	spoons
saucepan	Assorted cooking
Medium saucepan	utensils
Small saucepan	Whisk
Medium bowl	Vegetable brush
2 small bowls	Vegetable grater
Assorted kitchen knives	

COUNTDOWN

1 Assemble the ingredients and equipment
2 Do Steps 1–3 of the *Mocha Madness*
3 Do Steps 1–5 of *The Three P's*
4 Do Steps 1–2 of the *Red on Red*
5 Do Steps 6–7 of *The Three P's*
6 Do Step 3 of the *Red on Red*
7 Do Steps 8–9 of *The Three P's*

The Three P's

1 Bring water to a boil in a medium saucepan.

2 Scrub the potatoes and cut them in half.

3 Trim the pork of any excess fat and cut the meat into 8 slices. Peel and chop the shallots.

4 In a medium bowl, combine the broth, the Madeira, the vinegar, the cornstarch and the cloves.

5 Boil the potatoes in the saucepan until they are tender, about 15 minutes.

6 Melt the butter in a large skillet. Sauté the pork slices, turning once, until they are well browned on the outside but still white in the center, 6 to 8 minutes. Remove the pork and cover to keep warm.

7 Drain the potatoes.

8 Add the shallots to the skillet and cook, stirring, until they are limp, about 3 minutes.

9 Add the Madeira mixture and any accumulated pork juices to the skillet. Season to taste and bring the mixture to a boil. Reduce the heat. Return the pork to the skillet, turning to coat the slices in the sauce. Add the prunes and the potatoes and cook, turning, until the flavors are combined, about 4 minutes.

Red on Red

1 Coarsely grate the cabbage. Core and slice the apple. Peel and chop the onion.

2 Heat the oil in a large saucepan. Add the onion and sauté until it is softened, about 5 minutes. Add the cabbage and the apple and toss to coat them with the oil. Add the apple juice and the water. Season to taste. Cover and cook until the cabbage and the apple are crisp-tender, 5 to 7 minutes.

3 In a small bowl, combine the vinegar and the brown sugar, add it to cabbage mixture and cook, stirring occasionally, to heat through. Cover to keep warm.

Mocha Madness

1 Melt the chocolate in a small saucepan. Add the half-and-half and the brandy and cook, whisking gently, until the sauce is smooth.

2 Whisk together the creme fraîche and the sour cream in a small bowl. Add the dissolved coffee crystals and the sugar.

3 Distribute the chocolate sauce among individual dessert dishes. Add the coffee mixture and, with a spoon, swirl the mixture to create a marbled effect. Refrigerate for at least 20 minutes.

THURSDAY

Floundering Around

3 scallions (green onions)
$1/2$ pound fresh tomatoes
$1^1/4$ pounds flounder fillets
4 tablespoons lemon juice
$1/8$ teaspoon dried basil
Seasoning to taste
1 tablespoon butter

The Spice of Rice

1 medium onion
2 stalks celery
1 tablespoon butter
1 cup brown rice
1 can ($14^1/2$ ounces) chicken broth
$1/4$ cup water
$1/2$ teaspoon ground allspice
$1/3$ cup chopped walnuts

Turnip Your Nose

4 medium turnips
1 medium onion
$1/2$ cup water
3 tablespoons butter
$1/2$ teaspoon ground nutmeg
$1/4$ teaspoon sugar
Seasoning to taste

In the Pink

4 small pink grapefruit
$1^1/2$ tablespoons dark brown sugar
4 teaspoons sweet sherry (or nonalcoholic
    Italian cherry syrup)
2 tablespoons maraschino cherry syrup
4 maraschino cherries

EQUIPMENT

Medium covered saucepan	Assorted kitchen knives
Medium saucepan	Measuring cups and spoons
9x13-inch glass baking dish	Assorted cooking utensils
9x9-inch glass baking dish	Vegetable peeler

COUNTDOWN

1 Assemble the ingredients and equipment
2 Do Steps 1–3 of *The Spice of Rice*
3 Do Steps 1–4 of the *Floundering Around*
4 Do Steps 1–2 of the *Turnip Your Nose*
5 Do Step 5 of the *Floundering Around*
6 Do Step 3 of the *Turnip Your Nose*
7 Do Step 4 of *The Spice of Rice*
8 Do Steps 1–4 of *In the Pink*

Floundering Around

1 Preheat the oven to 375°F. Grease a 9x13-inch glass baking dish.

2 Trim and thinly slice the scallions. Chop the tomatoes.

3 Arrange the fish fillets in the baking dish in a single layer.

4 Drizzle the lemon juice over the flounder. Top with the scallions, the tomatoes and the basil. Season to taste.

5 Dot the fish with the butter and bake until the fillets are just opaque throughout, 10 to 12 minutes.

The Spice of Rice

1 Peel and chop the onion. Trim and chop the celery.

2 Melt the butter in a medium covered saucepan and sauté the onion and the celery until they are soft, about 5 minutes.

3 Add the rice, the broth, the water and the allspice to the saucepan. Bring the mixture to a boil, reduce the heat, cover and simmer until all the liquid is absorbed and the rice is tender, about 35 minutes.

4 Fluff the rice and toss it with the walnuts.

Turnip Your Nose

1 Peel and slice the turnips. Peel and slice the onion.

2 Combine the turnips, the onion and the water in a medium saucepan and simmer until the turnips are tender, about 10 minutes.

3 Drain the vegetables, stir in the butter, the nutmeg and the sugar. Season to taste.

In the Pink

1 Preheat the broiler.

2 Cut the grapefruit in half. Loosen the sections with a grapefruit knife and place the halves in a 9x9-inch glass baking dish.

3 Sprinkle the grapefruit halves with the brown sugar, the sherry and the maraschino cherry syrup. Put a cherry in each center.

4 Place the grapefruit under the broiler, 3 or 4 inches from the heat, and broil until the topping begins to bubble, 2 to 3 minutes.

FRIDAY

Green Bean Bisque

1 pound green beans
1 medium onion
2 tablespoons fresh parsley (when chopped)
2 tablespoons butter
2 cans (14^1/$_2$ ounces each) vegetable broth
1 cup regular or light sour cream
Seasoning to taste
^{1}/$_4$ cup mild salsa

Capellini Cake

12 ounces capellini (angel hair pasta)
3 eggs
3 scallions (green onions)
^{1}/$_4$ teaspoon paprika
^{3}/$_4$ cup grated Parmesan cheese
Seasoning to taste
2 tablespoons regular or light olive oil

Quite Nice Salad

2 medium cucumbers
^{1}/$_2$ pound fresh tomatoes
1 clove garlic
^{1}/$_4$ cup regular or light olive oil
3 tablespoons red wine vinegar
1 teaspoon dried oregano
1 teaspoon dried basil
Seasoning to taste
1 small head lettuce

Just a Trifle

1 angel food loaf cake
^{1}/$_4$ cup rum (or nonalcoholic Italian praline syrup)
^{1}/$_3$ cup golden raisins
^{1}/$_4$ cup sliced almonds
^{1}/$_2$ cup whipping cream
1 small package (3.4 ounces) instant vanilla pudding mix
2 cups whole milk

EQUIPMENT

Electric hand mixer	2 small bowls
Blender	Strainer
Stockpot	Assorted kitchen knives
Medium ovenproof skillet	Measuring cups and spoons
Medium covered saucepan	Assorted cooking utensils
2 large bowls	Vegetable peeler
2 medium bowls	

COUNTDOWN

1 Assemble the ingredients and equipment
2 Do Steps 1–6 of *Just a Trifle*
3 Do Step 1 of the *Quite Nice Salad*
4 Do Steps 1–2 of the *Capellini Cake*
5 Do Steps 1–3 of the *Green Bean Bisque*
6 Do Steps 3–6 of the *Capellini Cake*
7 Do Steps 4–5 of the *Green Bean Bisque*
8 Do Step 2 of the *Quite Nice Salad*
9 Do Step 7 of the *Capellini Cake*

Green Bean Bisque

1 Trim the green beans and cut them into 1-inch pieces. Peel and chop the onion. Chop the parsley.

2 Melt the butter in a medium saucepan. Add the onion and the beans and sauté until the onion is translucent, about 5 minutes.

3 Add the broth. Cover and simmer until the beans are tender, about 10 minutes.

4 Puree the bean mixture in a blender, then return it to the saucepan. Blend in the sour cream. Season to taste. Cover and warm through.

5 Top each bowl of soup with a dollop of salsa and a sprinkle of parsley.

Capellini Cake

1 Bring water to a boil in a stockpot.

2 Preheat the oven to 375°F.

3 Break the pasta into 2-inch pieces and cook until it is almost tender, 1 to 2 minutes if you are using fresh pasta and 3 to 4 minutes if you are using dried pasta.

4 Lightly beat the eggs in a large bowl. Trim and chop the scallions and add them to the eggs.

5 Drain the pasta and add it to the eggs. Add the paprika and the Parmesan cheese. Season to taste. Mix well.

6 Heat the oil in a medium ovenproof skillet, swirling to coat the bottom. Add the noodle mixture, spreading it evenly and packing it down. Cook until the cake is lightly browned on the bottom, 2 to 3 minutes. Slip a spatula around the edges and the bottom of the cake to keep the crust from sticking. Place the skillet in the oven and bake until the cake is firm to the touch when you press a finger in the center, about 15 minutes.

7 Slip the spatula around the edges and the bottom to loosen. Place a large plate over the top of the skillet, carefully invert it and unmold the cake. Cut the cake into wedges to serve.

Quite Nice Salad

1 Peel and slice the cucumbers. Chop the tomatoes. Peel and mince the garlic. Combine the ingredients in a medium bowl. Add the oil, the vinegar, the oregano and the basil. Season to taste, toss to combine and refrigerate until you are ready to serve.

2 Wash and dry the lettuce and arrange the leaves on individual salad plates. Drain the cucumber-tomato mixture and spoon it over the lettuce.

Just a Trifle

1 Cut the angel food cake into 1-inch cubes.

2 In a small bowl, combine the rum, the raisins and the almonds.

3 In another small bowl, whip the cream until stiff.

4 In a medium bowl, combine the pudding mix and the milk and beat until the mixture is well blended and beginning to thicken, about 5 minutes.

5 Fold half of the whipped cream into the pudding mixture.

6 In a large bowl, layer half of the cake cubes, half of the rum mixture and half of the pudding mixture. Repeat. Top with the remaining whipped cream. Cover and refrigerate for at least 20 minutes.

NOVEMBER
WEEK FOUR

CHECK STAPLES

- ☐ Butter
- ☐ Flour
- ☐ Cornstarch
- ☐ Baking powder
- ☐ Baking soda
- ☐ Granulated sugar
- ☐ Dark brown sugar
- ☐ Confectioners' sugar
- ☐ Maple syrup
- ☐ Long-grain white rice
- ☐ Regular or light vegetable oil
- ☐ Regular or light olive oil
- ☐ Red wine vinegar
- ☐ White wine vinegar
- ☐ Apple cider vinegar
- ☐ Lime juice
- ☐ Worcestershire sauce
- ☐ Dijon mustard
- ☐ Yellow mustard
- ☐ Prepared horseradish
- ☐ Regular or low-fat mayonnaise
- ☐ Honey
- ☐ Grated Parmesan cheese
- ☐ Instant coffee crystals
- ☐ Dried chervil
- ☐ Ground cinnamon
- ☐ Ground cloves
- ☐ Ground coriander
- ☐ Ground cumin
- ☐ Ground ginger
- ☐ Ground nutmeg
- ☐ Dried oregano
- ☐ Paprika
- ☐ Red pepper flakes
- ☐ Poppy seeds
- ☐ Dried sage
- ☐ Dried tarragon
- ☐ Dried thyme
- ☐ Pepper
- ☐ Salt
- ☐ Vanilla extract

SHOPPING NOTE

● If you are shopping once a week and cannot arrange to purchase fresh fish on the day you plan to use it, you can purchase *not previously frozen* fish and freeze it, placing it in the refrigerator to thaw the night before you are ready to use it. Or you can purchase *still frozen* fish and keep it frozen until the night before you are ready to use it.

SHOPPING LIST

MEAT & POULTRY

1 pound lean boneless sirloin steak (T)
8 boneless, skinless chicken thighs (M)
1 1/2 pounds boneless turkey breast (Th)

FISH

4 firm white fish steaks (1 1/4 pounds) (W)

FRESH PRODUCE

2 large baking potatoes (M)
1 pound Brussels sprouts (W)
3/4 pound spinach (M)
1 small kohlrabi (or turnip) (W)
1/4 pound mushrooms (Th)
5 medium carrots—2 (M), 3 (F)
5 stalks celery—2 (M), 1 (W), 2 (F)
3 large onions—1 (T), 2 (W)
3 medium onions—1 (M), 1 (Th), 1 (F)
1 small onion (T)
1 small red onion (W)
2 large leeks (F)
1 head garlic (M–F)
1 bunch parsley (W, Th, F)
1 medium head lettuce (W)
1 small head lettuce (Th)
1 ripe avocado (T)
1/2 pound tomatoes (T)
1 large red bell pepper (T)
1 small yellow bell pepper (W)
1 small green bell pepper (F)
2 green chilies (T)

Fruit

1 small tart green apple (Th)
1 small lime (T)

CANS, JARS & BOTTLES

Soup

3 cans (14 1/2 ounces each) chicken broth—1 (M), 2 (Th)

2 cans (14 1/2 ounces each) vegetable broth—1 (T), 1 (F)

Vegetables

1 medium can (14 1/2 ounces) stewed tomatoes (T, F)
1 medium can (14 1/2 ounces) Cajun-style stewed tomatoes (F)

Fruit

1 large can (29 ounces) sliced pears (M)
1 can (11 ounces) mandarin oranges (Th)
1 large can (16 ounces) jellied cranberry sauce (Th)

Condiments

1 small can (3.3 ounces) sliced black olives (W)

Dessert Needs

1 small can (16 ounces) pumpkin (Th, F)
1 can (14 ounces) regular or low-fat sweetened condensed milk (F)

PACKAGED GOODS

Pasta, Rice & Grains

16 ounces spaghetti (F)
1 package long-grain and wild rice mix (Th)

Baked Goods

1 sourdough bread loaf (F)

Nuts & Seeds

1/2 cup chopped cashews (W)
1/4 cup pine nuts (Th)
1/2 cup chopped walnuts (F)

Dessert & Baking Needs

1 1/2 cups graham cracker crumbs (F)
1/2 cup white chocolate chips (M)
1 package (12 ounces) semisweet chocolate chips (F)

WINES & SPIRITS

1/2 cup dry red wine (or nonalcoholic red wine or chicken broth) (M)
1/4 cup dry white wine (or nonalcoholic white wine or chicken broth) (Th)
4 tablespoons Kahlua liqueur (or nonalcoholic Italian coffee syrup) (T)

REFRIGERATED PRODUCTS

Dairy

1 1/2 cups + 1 tablespoon whole or low-fat milk—1 1/2 cups (T), 1 tablespoon (F)
Whipped cream for garnish (T, Th)
1/2 cup regular or light sour cream (T)
5 eggs—2 (T), 2 (Th), 1 (F)

Deli

8 flour tortillas (T)
4 slices bacon (W)

FROZEN GOODS

Vegetables

1 package (9 ounces) cut green beans (Th)

Desserts

4 frozen puff pastry shells (W)
1 pint vanilla ice cream (W)

MONDAY

Château Chicken

1 medium onion
2 medium carrots
2 stalks celery
1$^1/_2$ cups chicken broth
$^1/_2$ cup dry red wine (or nonalcoholic red wine
*   or additional chicken broth)*
2 teaspoons dried tarragon
Seasoning to taste
8 boneless, skinless chicken thighs
$^1/_2$ teaspoon yellow mustard
$^1/_2$ teaspoon prepared horseradish

Potatoes San Souci

2 large baking potatoes
$^3/_4$ pound fresh spinach
2 cloves garlic
$^1/_4$ cup regular or light vegetable oil
2 teaspoons ground coriander
$^1/_2$ teaspoon ground ginger
$^1/_4$ cup chicken broth
Seasoning to taste

Slice of Heaven

1 large can (29 ounces) sliced pears
$^1/_4$ cup granulated sugar
$^1/_2$ cup dark brown sugar
1$^1/_4$ cups flour
$^1/_4$ teaspoon salt
$^1/_2$ teaspoon ground nutmeg
4 tablespoons butter
1 teaspoon vanilla extract
$^1/_2$ cup white chocolate chips
2 tablespoons confectioners' sugar

EQUIPMENT

Dutch oven	Assorted cooking
Large covered skillet	utensils
8x8-inch glass baking	Whisk
dish	Vegetable peeler
Medium bowl	Pastry blender
Assorted kitchen knives	Sifter
Measuring cups and	
spoons	

COUNTDOWN

1 Assemble the ingredients and equipment
2 Do Steps 1–4 of the *Slice of Heaven*
3 Do Steps 1–2 of the *Château Chicken*
4 Do Step 1 of the *Potatoes San Souci*
5 Do Step 3 of the *Château Chicken*
6 Do Steps 2–4 of the *Potatoes San Souci*
7 Do Step 4 of the *Château Chicken*
8 Do Step 5 of the *Slice of Heaven*

Château Chicken

1 Peel and thinly slice the onion. Peel and slice the carrots. Trim and slice the celery.

2 In a Dutch oven, combine the onion, the carrots, the celery, the broth, the wine and the tarragon. Season to taste. Bring the mixture to a boil, reduce the heat and simmer for 10 minutes.

3 Add the chicken and simmer until the thighs are cooked, 15 to 20 minutes.

4 Remove the chicken and vegetables with a slotted spoon and keep them warm. Whisk the mustard and the horseradish into the sauce and spoon it over the chicken and vegetables.

Potatoes San Souci

1 Peel and thinly slice the potatoes. Wash, stem and coarsely chop the spinach. Peel and mince the garlic.

2 Heat 3 tablespoons of the oil in a large skillet. Add the potatoes and sauté until they are browned, about 10 minutes.

3 Add the remaining oil, the garlic, the coriander and the ginger to the skillet and sauté for 2 minutes. Add the broth, cover and simmer until the potatoes are tender, about 5 minutes. Add more broth if necessary to prevent sticking.

4 Add the spinach, increase the heat and cook until the spinach is wilted and almost all the liquid has evaporated, about 2 minutes. Season to taste.

Slice of Heaven

1 Preheat the oven to 350°F. Grease an 8x8-inch glass baking dish.

2 Drain the pears and arrange them in the baking dish.

3 In a medium bowl, combine the granulated sugar, the brown sugar, the flour, the salt and the nutmeg. Cut the butter into the mixture until it is the consistency of small peas. Blend in the vanilla and the white chocolate chips.

4 Spread the mixture over the pears and bake until lightly golden, about 30 minutes.

5 Dust the crisp with the confectioners' sugar.

TUESDAY

Easy Fajitas

1 pound lean boneless sirloin steak
2 cloves garlic
1 large onion
2 fresh green chilies (or canned)
1 large red bell pepper
$^1/_2$ pound fresh tomatoes
8 flour tortillas
3 tablespoons regular or light vegetable oil
2 teaspoons ground cumin
3 tablespoons lime juice
1 teaspoon cornstarch
Seasoning to taste
1 ripe avocado
1 small lime
$^1/_2$ cup regular or light sour cream

Mexican Rice

1 small onion
1 clove garlic
2 tablespoons regular or light vegetable oil
1 cup long-grain white rice
1 cup stewed tomatoes*
2 teaspoons chili powder
Seasoning to taste
1 can (14$^1/_2$ ounces) vegetable broth
$^1/_4$ cup water

Cafe-Cali

1$^1/_2$ cups whole or low-fat milk
2 eggs
4 tablespoons sugar
$^1/_8$ teaspoon salt
2 tablespoons instant coffee crystals
$^1/_2$ teaspoon vanilla extract
4 tablespoons Kahlua liqueur (or nonalcoholic
  Italian coffee syrup)
Whipped cream for garnish

EQUIPMENT

Electric hand mixer	Small bowl
Large skillet	Assorted kitchen knives
Medium covered saucepan	Measuring cups and spoons
Small saucepan	Assorted cooking utensils
4 custard cups	
9x9-inch glass baking dish	Whisk
Medium bowl	Aluminum foil

COUNTDOWN

1 Assemble the ingredients and equipment
2 Do Steps 1–4 of the *Cafe-Cali*
3 Do Steps 1–2 of the *Mexican Rice*
4 Do Steps 1–7 of the *Easy Fajitas*
5 Do Step 3 of the *Mexican Rice*
6 Do Step 5 of the *Cafe-Cali*

*Reserve the remainder of the can for use on Friday.

Easy Fajitas

1 Cut the steak into thin strips. Peel and mince the garlic. Peel and slice the onion. Stem, seed and mince the chilies. Seed the bell pepper and cut it into strips. Dice the tomatoes.

2 Preheat the oven to 200°F. Stack the tortillas, wrap them in aluminum foil and place them in the oven to heat through, about 10 minutes.

3 Heat the oil in a large skillet. Add the beef strips and sauté until they are lightly browned, 3 to 4 minutes. Remove and reserve the beef with any accumulated juices.

4 Add the garlic, the onion, the chilies and the bell pepper to the skillet and sauté until the onion is crisp-tender, about 5 minutes.

5 In a small bowl, combine the cumin, the lime juice and the cornstarch. Add the mixture to the skillet. Add the tomatoes. Stir to blend. Return the beef and any accumulated juices to the skillet and toss to combine. Season to taste. Bring the mixture to a boil, then remove the skillet from the heat and cover to keep warm.

6 Peel, pit and dice the avocado. Quarter the lime.

7 Spoon the beef mixture into the center of the tortillas, and garnish with the avocado, the sour cream, and the lime.

Mexican Rice

1 Peel and chop the onion. Peel and mince the garlic.

2 Heat the oil in a medium saucepan. Add the rice, the onion and the garlic, and sauté until the rice begins to turn brown and soft, about 10 minutes. Add the tomatoes and the chili powder. Season to taste. Add the broth and the water. Reduce the heat, cover and simmer until all the liquid is absorbed and the rice is tender, about 20 minutes.

3 Fluff the rice before serving.

Cafe-Cali

1 Preheat the oven to 375°F.

2 Scald the milk in a small saucepan.

3 Lightly beat the eggs in a medium bowl. Add the sugar, the salt, the coffee crystals, the vanilla and the Kahlua and blend well. Gradually add the milk and beat until the mixture is well blended.

4 Pour the mixture into individual custard cups and sit them in a 9x9-inch glass baking dish. Put about 1 inch of water into the bottom of the dish and bake until the custard is firm on top, about 25 minutes.

5 Top with dollops of whipped cream.

WEDNESDAY

Fortunate Fish

2 large onions
2 cloves garlic
1 tablespoon fresh parsley (when chopped)
1 small can (3.3 ounces) sliced black olives
3 tablespoons regular or light olive oil
2 tablespoons red wine vinegar
1 teaspoon dried oregano
Seasoning to taste
4 firm white fish steaks (1¼ pounds)

Kaleidosprouts

1 pound Brussels sprouts
4 slices bacon
1 small red onion
1 small yellow bell pepper
Seasoning to taste

Hot & Cold Salad

1 medium head lettuce
1 stalk celery
1 small kohlrabi (or turnip)
3 tablespoons regular or light olive oil
½ cup cashew pieces
2 tablespoons white wine vinegar
¾ teaspoon Dijon mustard
¾ teaspoon honey
Seasoning to taste

Maple Top-offs

4 frozen puff pastry shells
2 tablespoons butter
1 cup maple syrup
1 pint vanilla ice cream

EQUIPMENT

Large covered skillet	Assorted kitchen knives
Large skillet	Measuring cups and
Small skillet	spoons
Medium saucepan	Assorted cooking
Small saucepan	utensils
9x13-inch glass baking	Vegetable peeler
dish	Whisk
Cookie sheet	Ice cream scoop
Large bowl	Aluminum foil
Strainer	

COUNTDOWN

IN THE MORNING:
  Do Step 1 of the *Maple Top-offs*
BEFORE DINNER:
  1 Assemble the remaining ingredients and equipment
  2 Do Step 2 of the *Maple Top-offs*
  3 Do Step 1 of the *Fortunate Fish*
  4 Do Step 1 of the *Hot & Cold Salad*
  5 Do Step 3 of the *Maple Top-offs*
  6 Do Steps 2–4 of the *Fortunate Fish*
  7 Do Step 4 of the *Maple Top-offs*
  8 Do Steps 1–6 of the *Kaleidosprouts*
  9 Do Steps 2–4 of the *Hot & Cold Salad*
  10 Do Step 5 of the *Fortunate Fish*
  11 Do Steps 5–6 of the *Maple Top-offs*

Fortunate Fish

1 Peel and thinly slice the onions. Peel and mince the garlic. Chop the parsley. Drain the olives.

2 Preheat the oven to 350°F.

3 Heat 2 tablespoons of the oil in a large skillet. Add the onion and the garlic and sauté until the onions are soft but not browned, about 5 minutes. Add the olives, the vinegar and the oregano. Season to taste and cook, stirring, for 2 minutes.

4 Brush the bottom of a 9x13-inch glass baking dish with the remaining oil. Add the fish steaks. Spoon the sauce over the fish. Cover the dish with aluminum foil and bake until the steaks are opaque throughout but still moist, 15 to 20 minutes.

5 Sprinkle the fish with the parsley.

Kaleidosprouts

1 Bring water to a boil in a medium saucepan.

2 Trim the Brussels sprouts and cut small X's in the stems. Dice the bacon. Peel and chop the onion. Seed and chop the bell pepper.

3 Cook the sprouts in the boiling water for 10 minutes.

4 Sauté the bacon in a large skillet until crisp, about 5 minutes. Remove the bacon from the skillet and drain it on a paper towel.

5 Sauté the onion and the bell pepper in the bacon drippings until they are soft, about 5 minutes.

6 Drain the sprouts and plunge them into cold water. Then drain them again. Add the sprouts to the skillet and sauté until they are well coated and heated through, about 5 minutes. Season to taste and sprinkle with the crisp bacon. Cover to keep warm.

Hot & Cold Salad

1 Wash and dry the lettuce and tear it into bite-size pieces. Trim and slice the celery. Peel and dice the kohlrabi. Combine the ingredients in a large bowl.

2 Heat the oil in a small skillet. Add the cashews and sauté until they are golden, about 5 minutes.

3 Add the vinegar, the mustard and the honey, season to taste and heat until the mixture is hot.

4 Pour the hot dressing over the salad and toss to combine.

Maple Top-offs

1 Place the pastry shells in the refrigerator to thaw.

2 Preheat the oven to 425°F.

3 Place the pastry shells on an ungreased cookie sheet and bake until they are golden, about 15 minutes.

4 Remove the shells from the oven and let them cool.

5 Melt the butter in a small saucepan. Add the maple syrup and bring the mixture to a boil, cooking until the sauce begins to thicken, 2 to 3 minutes. Remove the sauce from the heat and let it cool.

6 Place a scoop of ice cream in each pastry shell and pour the sauce over the ice cream.

THURSDAY

Timely Turkey

1½ pounds boneless turkey breast
2 cloves garlic
1 medium onion
¼ cup fresh parsley (when chopped)
Seasoning to taste
¼ cup regular or light vegetable oil
2 tablespoons flour
½ teaspoon paprika
1 teaspoon dried sage
1 teaspoon dried thyme
1¼ cups chicken broth
¼ cup dry white wine (or nonalcoholic white
    wine or additional chicken broth)

Wild Stuff

¼ pound fresh mushrooms
¼ cup fresh parsley (when chopped)
2 tablespoons regular or light vegetable oil
1 package long-grain and wild rice mix
2¼ cups chicken broth
¼ cup pine nuts

Wanna Beans

1 package (9 ounces) frozen cut green beans
1 tablespoon butter
½ teaspoon dried chervil
Seasoning to taste

Cranberry Parade

1 small head lettuce
1 large can (16 ounces) jellied cranberry sauce
1 small tart green apple
1 can (11 ounces) mandarin oranges
¼ cup regular or low-fat mayonnaise
1 tablespoon honey
1 tablespoon apple cider vinegar
¼ teaspoon poppy seeds
Seasoning to taste

*Reserve the balance of the can for use on Friday.

Square Pumpkins

2 eggs
½ small can (16 ounces) pumpkin*
¾ cup sugar
½ cup regular or light vegetable oil
1 teaspoon vanilla extract
1 cup flour
¼ teaspoon salt
½ teaspoon baking powder
½ teaspoon baking soda
½ teaspoon ground cinnamon
½ teaspoon ground nutmeg
½ teaspoon ground cloves

EQUIPMENT

Electric hand mixer	2 small bowls
Large covered skillet	Assorted kitchen knives
2 medium covered saucepans	Measuring cups and spoons
9x9-inch glass baking dish	Assorted cooking utensils
Large bowl	Whisk
Medium bowl	

COUNTDOWN

1 Assemble the ingredients and equipment
2 Do Steps 1–4 of the *Square Pumpkins*
3 Do Steps 1–3 of the *Timely Turkey*
4 Do Steps 1–3 of the *Wild Stuff*
5 Do Step 5 of the *Square Pumpkins*
6 Do Steps 4–6 of the *Timely Turkey*
7 Do Steps 1–4 of the *Cranberry Parade*
8 Do Steps 1–2 of the *Wanna Beans*
9 Do Step 4 of the *Wild Stuff*
10 Do Step 7 of the *Timely Turkey*
11 Do Step 6 of the *Square Pumpkins*

Timely Turkey

1 Cut the turkey breast into 4 portions. Peel and quarter the garlic. Peel and thinly slice the onion. Chop the parsley.

2 Season the turkey portions to taste.

3 Heat the oil in a large skillet and sauté the onion and the garlic until the onion is translucent and the garlic is golden, about 5 minutes. Remove the onion and reserve. Discard the garlic.

4 Sauté the turkey portions in the onion-garlic oil until they are lightly browned, about 10 minutes.

5 In a small bowl, combine the flour, the paprika, the sage and the thyme. Sprinkle the mixture over the turkey.

6 Return the onion to the skillet. Stir in the broth and the wine. Season to taste, cover and simmer until the turkey is tender, about 20 minutes.

7 Sprinkle with the parsley.

Wild Stuff

1 Wash, pat dry, trim and chop the mushrooms. Chop the parsley.

2 Heat the oil in a medium saucepan. Add the mushrooms and sauté for 3 minutes. Add the rice mix and sauté for 2 minutes.

3 Blend in the broth and the seasoning packet for the rice. Cover and simmer until all the liquid is absorbed and the rice is tender, about 25 minutes.

4 Fluff the rice and stir in the parsley and the pine nuts.

Wanna Beans

1 Bring water to a boil in a medium saucepan and cook the beans a scant 4 minutes.

2 Drain the beans, return them to the saucepan and toss them with the butter and the chervil. Season to taste and cover to keep warm.

Cranberry Parade

1 Wash and dry the lettuce and arrange the leaves on individual salad plates.

2 Slice the cranberry sauce and arrange the slices over the lettuce.

3 Core and slice the apple. Drain the mandarin oranges. Scatter the apple slices and the oranges over the cranberry sauce.

4 In a small bowl, whisk together the mayonnaise, the honey, the vinegar and the poppy seeds. Season to taste.

5 Spoon the dressing over the salad.

Square Pumpkins

1 Preheat the oven to 350°F. Grease a 9x9-inch glass baking dish.

2 In a medium bowl, beat together the eggs, the pumpkin, the sugar, the oil and the vanilla.

3 In a large bowl, combine the flour, the salt, the baking powder, the baking soda, the cinnamon, the nutmeg and the cloves. Gradually add the pumpkin mixture to the dry ingredients and beat well.

4 Pour the mixture into the baking dish and bake until a toothpick inserted in the center comes out clean, about 20 minutes.

5 Remove the pumpkin from the oven and let it cool.

6 Cut the pumpkin into squares and top them with dollops of whipped cream.

FRIDAY

Friday Soup

3 medium carrots
2 stalks celery
2 large leeks
2 tablespoons butter
3/4 cup stewed tomatoes reserved from Tuesday
1 can (14 1/2 ounces) Cajun-style stewed
    tomatoes
1/2 small can (16 ounces) pumpkin reserved
    from Thursday
1 can (14 1/2 ounces) vegetable broth
2 teaspoons Worcestershire sauce
1/2 teaspoon chili powder
Seasoning to taste

Spaghetti Forgetti

1 small green bell pepper
1 medium onion
1 clove garlic
2 tablespoons fresh parsley (when chopped)
16 ounces spaghetti
3 tablespoons regular or light olive oil
1/2 teaspoon red pepper flakes
1 teaspoon dried oregano
Seasoning to taste
1/2 cup grated Parmesan cheese

Sourdough Bread

Big Brown Bears

1 package (12 ounces) semisweet chocolate
    chips
1 tablespoon whole or low-fat milk
1 egg
1 1/2 cups graham cracker crumbs
1 can (14 ounces) regular or low-fat
    sweetened condensed milk
1 teaspoon vanilla extract
1/2 cup chopped walnuts
2 tablespoons confectioners' sugar

EQUIPMENT

Blender	Assorted kitchen knives
Stockpot	Measuring cups and
Medium skillet	spoons
Large covered	Assorted cooking
saucepan	utensils
Medium saucepan	Whisk
9x9-inch glass baking	Vegetable peeler
dish	Sifter
Colander	

COUNTDOWN

1 Assemble the ingredients and equipment
2 Do Steps 1–5 of the *Big Brown Bears*
3 Do Steps 1–3 of the *Friday Soup*
4 Do Steps 1–5 of the *Spaghetti Forgetti*
5 Do Step 4 of the *Friday Soup*
6 Do Step 6 of the *Big Brown Bears*

Friday Soup

1 Peel and finely chop the carrots. Peel and finely chop the celery. Thoroughly wash, trim and thinly slice the leeks.

2 Melt the butter in a large saucepan. Add the carrots, the celery and the leeks and sauté until the leeks are softened, but not browned, about 5 minutes.

3 Add the undrained tomatoes, the pumpkin, the broth, the Worcestershire sauce and the chili powder. Season to taste. Bring the soup to a boil, reduce the heat, cover and simmer until all the vegetables are tender, 15 to 20 minutes.

4 Pour half of the soup into a blender and puree until it is smooth. Return the puree to the saucepan and blend it with the remaining soup. Rewarm the soup, if necessary, and serve with chunks of sourdough bread.

Spaghetti Forgetti

1 Bring water to a boil in a stockpot.

2 Seed and dice the bell pepper. Peel and chop the onion. Peel and mince the garlic. Chop the parsley.

3 Cook the pasta until it is almost tender, 2 to 3 minutes if you are using fresh pasta and 5 to 6 minutes if you are using dried pasta.

4 Heat the oil in a medium skillet. Add the bell pepper, the garlic, the onion, the parsley, the red pepper flakes and the oregano. Season to taste and cook, stirring, for 2 minutes.

5 Drain the pasta and return it to the stock pot. Toss it with the sauce and half of the Parmesan cheese. Cover to keep warm. Pass the remaining cheese.

Big Brown Bears

1 Preheat the oven to 350°F. Grease and flour a 9x9-inch glass baking dish.

2 Melt 1 cup of the chocolate chips in a medium saucepan with the milk.

3 Slightly beat the egg. Add the graham cracker crumbs, the condensed milk, the beaten egg and the vanilla to the melted chocolate.

4 Stir in the remaining chocolate chips and the walnuts.

5 Pour the mixture into the baking dish and bake until the brownie is firm to the touch but still moist, 30 to 35 minutes.

6 Let the brownie cool slightly and then cut it into large squares. Dust with the confectioners' sugar.

DECEMBER

WEEK ONE

WEEK AT A GLANCE

Monday

PENNE SERENADE
SWANK SPINACH SALAD
PUCKER PIE

Tuesday

HALF MOON MEMORY
SURF SALAD
MONTEREY BREAD
ORANGE CONCOCTION

Wednesday

A WING AND A PRAYER
HIGH FLYING RICE
COPILOTS
BANANA LANDING

Thursday

MOROCCAN MEDLEY
ALMOND COUSCOUS
DESERT BREAD
CASABLANCA KIWI

Friday

ORANGE RUFFIAN
WAYWARD NOODLES
VAGABOND VEGETABLES
CHOCOLATE DRIFTERS

CHECK STAPLES

- ☐ Butter
- ☐ Cornstarch
- ☐ Granulated sugar
- ☐ Confectioners' sugar
- ☐ Unsweetened cocoa
- ☐ Long-grain white rice
- ☐ Regular or light vegetable oil
- ☐ Regular or light olive oil
- ☐ Sesame oil
- ☐ Red wine vinegar
- ☐ Balsamic vinegar
- ☐ Rice vinegar
- ☐ Lemon juice
- ☐ Grated fresh lemon peel
- ☐ Soy sauce
- ☐ Dijon mustard
- ☐ Honey
- ☐ Dried basil
- ☐ Ground cinnamon
- ☐ Ground cumin
- ☐ Garlic powder
- ☐ Ground ginger
- ☐ Ground nutmeg
- ☐ Paprika
- ☐ Dried rosemary
- ☐ Saffron threads
- ☐ Sesame seeds
- ☐ Dried thyme
- ☐ Pepper
- ☐ Salt
- ☐ Vanilla extract

SHOPPING NOTES

• If you are shopping once a week and cannot arrange to purchase fresh orange roughy on the day you plan to use it, you can purchase *not previously frozen* orange roughy and freeze it, placing it in the refrigerator to thaw the night before you are ready to use it. Or you can purchase *still frozen* orange roughy and keep it frozen until the night before you are ready to use it.

• If you are shopping once a week and cannot arrange to purchase fresh clams on the day you plan to use them, you can substitute 3 cans (10 ounces each) whole clams and omit cooking instructions.

MEAT & POULTRY

1 pound lean ground lamb (or beef) (M)
1/2 pound linguisa (or chorizo) sausage (T)
3 pounds chicken pieces (W)

FISH

36 small steamer clams (T)
1 1/4 pounds orange roughy (or snapper) fillets (F)

FRESH PRODUCE

Vegetables

1 pound small new red potatoes (Th)
1 medium bunch broccoli (F)
4 medium parsnips (W)
2 small turnips (Th)
1 pound spinach (M)
4 medium mushrooms (T)
7 medium carrots—4 (W), 3 (Th)
3 stalks celery—1 (Th), 2 (F)
3 medium onions—1 (T), 2 (Th)
2 small onions—1 (M), 1 (W)
6 scallions (green onions)— 3 (M), 3 (T)
1 head garlic (M, T, W, Th)
1 bunch parsley (M, T, Th)
1 small bunch cilantro (T, Th)
1 medium head lettuce (T)
1 ripe avocado (T)
1 small cucumber (T)
1 large red bell pepper (T)
1 small bunch radishes (M)

Fruit

2 medium bananas (W)
4 large kiwifruit (Th)
4 medium oranges (T)
4 seedless tangerines (Th)
1 medium lemon (F)

CANS, JARS & BOTTLES

Soup

2 cans (14 1/2 ounces each) chicken broth—1 (T), 1 (W)
1 can (14 1/2 ounces) vegetable broth (Th)

Vegetables

1 medium can (14 1/2 ounces) cut-up tomatoes (M)

Fish

1 small can (2 ounces) anchovy fillets (T)

Oriental Foods

1 can (8 ounces) sliced water chestnuts (M)
1 small can (5 1/2 ounces) baby corn (F)

Juice

1 bottle (8 ounces) clam juice (T)

Condiments

1 small jar (3 ounces) pimiento-stuffed green olives (Th)
4 maraschino cherries for garnish (F)

PACKAGED GOODS

Pasta, Rice & Grains

16 ounces penne (M)
4 ounces dried capellini (angel hair pasta) (T)
8 ounces medium egg noodles (F)
1 cup instant couscous (Th)

Baked Goods

1 cup croutons (M)
1 small loaf French bread (T)
2 small pita breads (Th)

Nuts & Seeds

2 tablespoons sliced almonds (Th)

Dessert & Baking Needs

1 small package (3.9 ounces) instant chocolate pudding mix (M)
1 small package (6 ounces) semisweet chocolate chips (M)
1 prepared 9-inch chocolate pie shell (M)
1 small package (10 ounces) sugar cookies (W)

WINES & SPIRITS

1 cup dry red wine (or nonalcoholic red wine or beef broth) (M)
3/4 cup dry white wine (or nonalcoholic white wine or clam juice) (T)
1/2 cup dry white wine (or nonalcoholic white wine or chicken broth) (W)
1 tablespoon rum (or 1 teaspoon rum extract) (W)
1 teaspoon creme de menthe liqueur (or nonalcoholic Italian peppermint syrup) (F)

REFRIGERATED PRODUCTS

Dairy

1 cup whole milk (M)
1 tablespoon whole or low-fat milk (F)
1 cup whipping cream (F)
2/3 cup regular or light sour cream—1/3 cup (M), 1/3 cup (F)
2 eggs—1 (M), 1 (F)

Cheese

1 cup shredded regular or low-fat Monterey Jack cheese (T)
1 container (8 ounces) regular or light soft cream cheese (T)

Juice

1/3 cup orange juice (T)

Deli

2 slices bacon (W)

FROZEN GOODS

Dessert

1 small container (8 ounces) frozen whipped topping (M, W)
1 pint lemon frozen yogurt (W)
1 pint mint chocolate chip ice cream (F)

MONDAY

Penne Serenade

1 small onion
2 cloves garlic
2 teaspoons fresh parsley (when chopped)
1 tablespoon regular or light olive oil
1 pound lean ground lamb (or beef)
1 cup dry red wine (or nonalcoholic red wine
    or beef broth)
1 medium can (14$^1/_2$ ounces) cut-up tomatoes
$^1/_2$ teaspoon dried rosemary
$^1/_2$ cup hot water
Seasoning to taste
16 ounces penne

Swank Spinach Salad

1 egg
1 tablespoon butter
1 teaspoon garlic powder
1 cup croutons
1 pound fresh spinach
1 small bunch radishes
3 scallions (green onions)
1 can (8 ounces) sliced water chestnuts
3 tablespoons regular or light vegetable oil
1 tablespoon red wine vinegar
1 tablespoon lemon juice
$^1/_2$ teaspoon sugar
$^1/_2$ teaspoon Dijon mustard
Seasoning to taste

Pucker Pie

1 small package (6 ounces) semisweet
    chocolate chips
1 small package (3.9 ounces) instant
    chocolate pudding mix
1 cup whole milk
$^1/_3$ cup regular or light sour cream
2 tablespoons unsweetened cocoa
$^1/_2$ small container (8 ounces) frozen whipped
    topping*
1 prepared 9-inch chocolate pie shell

EQUIPMENT

Electric hand mixer	Assorted kitchen knives
Stockpot	Measuring cups and
Small skillet	spoons
Large covered	Assorted cooking
saucepan	utensils
Small saucepan	Whisk
2 large bowls	Plastic bag
Small bowl	Mallet
Colander	

COUNTDOWN

1 Assemble the ingredients and equipment
2 Do Steps 1–3 of the *Pucker Pie*
3 Do Step 1 of the *Swank Spinach Salad*
4 Do Steps 1–4 of the *Penne Serenade*
5 Do Steps 2–5 of the *Swank Spinach Salad*
6 Do Step 5 of the *Penne Serenade*
7 Do Steps 6–7 of the *Swank Spinach Salad*
8 Do Step 6 of the *Penne Serenade*

*Reserve the balance of the container for use on Wednesday.

Penne Serenade

1 Peel and chop the onion. Peel and chop the garlic. Chop the parsley.

2 Heat the oil in a large saucepan. Add the onion and the garlic and sauté until the onion is soft, about 5 minutes. Add the lamb and cook, stirring, until the meat loses its pinkness, about 7 minutes.

3 Add the wine, increase the heat and cook, stirring occasionally, for 2 minutes. Add the undrained tomatoes, the rosemary, and the hot water. Season to taste. Reduce the heat and simmer, partially covered, stirring occasionally, until the sauce is thick, 25 to 30 minutes.

4 Bring water to a boil in a stockpot.

5 Cook the penne until it is tender but still firm, 9 to 11 minutes.

6 Drain the pasta, return it to the stockpot, toss it with the sauce and sprinkle with the parsley.

Swank Spinach Salad

1 Cover the egg with water in a small saucepan. Bring the water to a boil and hard-cook the egg, 10 to 12 minutes.

2 Drain the egg and place it in the freezer to chill for 10 minutes.

3 Melt the butter in a small skillet. Add the garlic powder. Sauté the croutons in the garlic butter until they are golden, about 5 minutes.

4 Rinse, dry and stem the spinach and tear it into bite-size pieces. Trim and slice the radishes. Trim and chop the scallions. Drain the water chestnuts. Combine the ingredients in a large bowl.

5 In a small bowl, whisk together the oil, the vinegar, the lemon juice, the sugar and the mustard. Season to taste.

6 Toss the salad with the dressing.

7 Peel and chop the egg and sprinkle it over the salad. Top with the croutons.

Pucker Pie

1 Place the chocolate chips in a plastic bag and crush them with a mallet.

2 In a large bowl, combine the pudding mix, the milk and the sour cream and beat until well blended. Fold the cocoa into the whipped topping, and fold the topping into the pudding mixture. Stir in $3/4$ cup of the crushed chocolate chips. Turn the mixture into the pie shell.

3 Sprinkle the top with the remaining crushed chocolate chips, and refrigerate for at least 20 minutes.

TUESDAY

Half Moon Memory

1 medium onion
1 large red bell pepper
1 clove garlic
1 tablespoon fresh parsley (when chopped)
$^1/_2$ pound linguisa (or chorizo) sausage
36 small steamer clams (or 3 cans [10 ounces each] whole clams)
2 cups water
1 bottle (8 ounces) clam juice
1 can (14$^1/_2$ ounces) chicken broth
$^3/_4$ cup dry white wine (or nonalcoholic white wine or additional clam juice)
4 ounces dried capellini (angel hair pasta)
$^1/_2$ teaspoon dried basil
Seasoning to taste

Surf Salad

1 medium head lettuce
4 medium mushrooms
1 small cucumber
3 scallions (green onions)
1 ripe avocado
3 tablespoons lemon juice
1 tablespoon fresh parsley (when chopped)
1 tablespoon fresh cilantro (when chopped)
1 small can (2 ounces) anchovy fillets
3 tablespoons regular or light olive oil
$^1/_4$ teaspoon dried thyme
$^1/_4$ teaspoon dried rosemary
$^1/_4$ teaspoon garlic powder
Seasoning to taste

Monterey Bread

1 small loaf French bread
1 clove garlic
2 tablespoons regular or light olive oil
1 teaspoon dried basil
1 cup shredded regular or low-fat Monterey Jack cheese

Orange Concoction

4 medium oranges
1 container (8 ounces) regular or light soft cream cheese
$^1/_3$ cup orange juice
3 tablespoons confectioners' sugar

EQUIPMENT

Dutch oven	Whisk
Large bowl	Vegetable brush
3 small bowls	Vegetable peeler
Assorted kitchen knives	Citrus grater
Measuring cups and spoons	Aluminum foil
Assorted cooking utensils	

COUNTDOWN

1 Assemble the ingredients and equipment
2 Do Steps 1–3 of the *Orange Concoction*
3 Do Steps 1–4 of the *Monterey Bread*
4 Do Steps 1–3 of the *Half Moon Memory*
5 Do Steps 1–2 of the *Surf Salad*
6 Do Step 4 of the *Half Moon Memory*
7 Do Step 3 of the *Surf Salad*
8 Do Step 5 of the *Half Moon Memory*

Half Moon Memory

1 Peel and chop the onion. Seed and dice the bell pepper. Peel and mince the garlic. Chop the parsley. Cut the sausage into ¼-inch slices. Scrub the clams, discarding any that are open and do not close when tapped.

2 In a Dutch oven, sauté the sausage until it is lightly browned, about 7 minutes. Add the onion, the bell pepper and the garlic and sauté until the onion is soft, about 5 minutes.

3 Add the water, the juice, the broth, the wine, the pasta and the basil to the Dutch oven. Season to taste, bring the mixture to a boil, reduce the heat, cover and simmer until the pasta is almost tender, 7 to 9 minutes.

4 Skim the fat from the broth. Add the clams. Cover and bring the mixture to a boil. Reduce the heat and simmer until the clams open, 5 to 7 minutes. If you are using canned clams, add them now and heat them through.

5 Remove the clams, discarding any that have not opened, and distribute them among individual bowls. Ladle the broth over the clams. Lightly sprinkle each serving with the parsley.

Surf Salad

1 Wash and dry the lettuce and tear it into bite-size pieces. Wash, pat dry, trim and slice the mushrooms. Peel and slice the cucumber. Trim and slice the scallions. Combine the ingredients in a large bowl. Peel, pit and chop the avocado and sprinkle it with 1 tablespoon of the lemon juice.

2 Chop the parsley. Chop the cilantro. Drain and finely chop the anchovies. In a small bowl, whisk together the parsley, the cilantro, the anchovies, the oil, the remaining lemon juice, the thyme, the rosemary, and the garlic powder. Season to taste.

3 Toss the salad with the dressing. Add the avocado and toss lightly to combine.

Monterey Bread

1 Preheat the oven to 350°F.

2 Slice the French loaf down almost to the crust and place it on a large sheet of aluminum foil.

3 Peel and mince the garlic. Combine the garlic in a small bowl with the oil and the basil. Spread the mixture between the bread slices. Sprinkle the cheese between the bread slices.

4 Wrap the foil around the bread and bake until it is hot and the cheese is bubbly, about 20 minutes.

Orange Concoction

1 Grate 1 tablespoon of peel from an orange and reserve. Then peel and section the oranges and distribute them among individual dessert dishes.

2 In a small bowl, combine the cream cheese, the orange juice and the confectioners' sugar until well blended.

3 Top the oranges with the cream cheese mixture and sprinkle with the orange peel. Refrigerate until you are ready to serve.

WEDNESDAY

A Wing and a Prayer

3 pounds chicken pieces
2 tablespoons regular or light olive oil
$^1/_2$ cup chicken broth
$^1/_2$ cup dry white wine (or nonalcoholic white
    wine or additional chicken broth)
$^1/_2$ cup balsamic vinegar
Seasoning to taste
2 tablespoons butter

High Flying Rice

2 slices bacon
1 small onion
1 cup long-grain white rice
1$^1/_4$ cups chicken broth
$^3/_4$ cup water

Copilots

2 cloves garlic
4 medium carrots
4 medium parsnips
4 tablespoons butter
2 tablespoons lemon juice
2 tablespoons honey
Seasoning to taste

Banana Landing

1 pint lemon frozen yogurt
2 medium bananas
1 tablespoon lemon juice
1 tablespoon rum (or 1 teaspoon rum extract)
2 tablespoons confectioners' sugar
$^1/_2$ small container (8 ounces) frozen whipped
    topping reserved from Monday
1 small package (10 ounces) sugar cookies

EQUIPMENT

Blender	Assorted kitchen knives
Large skillet	Measuring cups and
Medium covered skillet	spoons
Small saucepan	Assorted cooking
8x8-inch glass baking	utensils
dish	Vegetable peeler
Large bowl	

COUNTDOWN

1 Assemble the ingredients and equipment
2 Do Step 1 of the *Banana Landing*
3 Do Steps 1–3 of *A Wing and a Prayer*
4 Do Steps 1–4 of the *Copilots*
5 Do Steps 1–3 of the *High Flying Rice*
6 Do Step 2 of the *Banana Landing*
7 Do Steps 4–6 of *A Wing and a Prayer*
8 Do Step 4 of the *High Flying Rice*
9 Do Step 3 of the *Banana Landing*

A Wing and a Prayer

1 Rinse and pat dry the chicken.

2 Heat the oil in a large skillet. Add the chicken and cook, turning, until it is browned on all sides, about 10 minutes.

3 Add the broth to the skillet. Bring it to a boil, reduce the heat and simmer until the chicken is cooked throughout, but still juicy, 20 to 25 minutes.

4 Remove the chicken and cover to keep warm.

5 Add the wine and the vinegar to the skillet. Season to taste, bring the liquid to a boil, scraping up any browned bits from the bottom of the skillet, and cook until the sauce is reduced to $1/2$ cup, 2 to 3 minutes.

6 Remove the skillet from the heat. Whisk in the butter until it is melted and smooth. Pour the sauce over the chicken.

High Flying Rice

1 Chop the bacon. Peel and chop the onion.

2 Sauté the bacon in a medium skillet until it is half-cooked, 2 to 3 minutes. Add the onion and the rice and sauté until the rice is lightly browned, about 5 minutes.

3 Add the broth and the water, bring the mixture to a boil, reduce the heat, cover and simmer until all the liquid is absorbed and the rice is tender, about 20 minutes.

4 Fluff the rice before serving.

Copilots

1 Preheat the oven to 350°F.

2 Peel and mince the garlic. Peel and slice the carrots. Peel and slice the parsnips.

3 Melt the butter in a small saucepan. Add the garlic and sauté for 2 minutes. Stir in the lemon juice and the honey and mix well.

4 Place the parsnips and the carrots in an 8x8-inch glass baking dish. Pour the honey mixture over the vegetables, season to taste and bake until they are crisp-tender, 20 to 25 minutes.

Banana Landing

1 Set the frozen yogurt out to soften.

2 Peel and slice the bananas into a blender. Add the softened yogurt, the lemon juice, the rum and the sugar, and process until the mixture is smooth. Scrape the mixture into a large bowl and fold in the whipped topping. Cover the bowl and place it in the freezer until you are ready to serve, at least 30 minutes.

3 Crumble the sugar cookies into individual dessert dishes and spoon the banana cream over the crumbled cookies.

THURSDAY

Moroccan Medley

1 medium onion
1 clove garlic
3 medium carrots
2 small turnips
1 stalk celery
1 pound small new red potatoes
$1/2$ cup fresh parsley (when chopped)
$1/4$ cup fresh cilantro (when chopped)
1 small jar (3 ounces) pimiento-stuffed green
    olives
2 tablespoons regular or light olive oil
1 cup vegetable broth
1 tablespoon lemon juice
1 teaspoon paprika
$1/3$ cup water
1 tablespoon grated fresh lemon peel
Seasoning to taste

Almond Couscous

1 medium onion
4 tablespoons butter
2 tablespoons sliced almonds
$3/4$ cup vegetable broth
$1/2$ cup water
$1/2$ teaspoon saffron threads
1 cup instant couscous
1 teaspoon ground cinnamon
$1/4$ teaspoon ground nutmeg

Desert Bread

1 tablespoon lemon juice
3 tablespoons regular or light olive oil
1 teaspoon ground cumin
$1/4$ teaspoon pepper
2 small pita breads

Casablanca Kiwi

4 seedless tangerines
4 large kiwifruit
4 tablespoons sugar
4 tablespoons water
$1/2$ teaspoon ground ginger
$1/2$ teaspoon cornstarch
$1/4$ teaspoon vanilla extract

EQUIPMENT

Blender	Assorted kitchen knives
Dutch oven	Measuring cups and
Medium skillet	spoons
Medium covered	Assorted cooking
saucepan	utensils
Small saucepan	Whisk
Cookie sheet	Vegetable peeler
Small bowl	Vegetable brush

COUNTDOWN

1 Assemble the ingredients and equipment
2 Do Steps 1–3 of the *Moroccan Medley*
3 Do Steps 1–2 of the *Casablanca Kiwi*
4 Do Step 4 of the *Moroccan Medley*
5 Do Steps 1–4 of the *Almond Couscous*
6 Do Steps 1–3 of the *Desert Bread*
7 Do Step 3 of the *Casablanca Kiwi*

Moroccan Medley

1 Peel and slice the onion. Peel and mince the garlic. Peel and slice the carrots. Peel and quarter the turnips. Trim and slice the celery. Scrub and quarter the potatoes. Chop the parsley. Chop the cilantro. Drain and rinse the olives.

2 Heat the oil in a Dutch oven. Add the onion and the garlic and sauté until the onion is soft, about 5 minutes.

3 Add the carrots, the turnips, the celery, the potatoes and the broth. Cover and cook, stirring occasionally, until the turnips are tender, 15 to 20 minutes.

4 Combine the parsley, the cilantro, the lemon juice, the paprika and the water in a blender and process until smooth. Add the mixture to the Dutch oven. Add the lemon peel and the olives. Season to taste. Reduce the heat and simmer, covered, stirring occasionally, for 15 minutes.

Almond Couscous

1 Peel and chop the onion.

2 Melt 2 tablespoons of the butter in a medium skillet. Add the onions and the almonds and sauté until the onions are golden and the almonds are lightly toasted, about 10 minutes.

3 In a medium saucepan, bring the broth, the water, the remaining butter and the saffron to a boil. Stir in the couscous. Remove the saucepan from the heat, cover and let it stand for at least 5 minutes.

4 Fluff the couscous and toss it with the onion-almond mixture, the cinnamon and the nutmeg.

Desert Bread

1 Preheat the broiler.

2 In a small bowl, combine the lemon juice, the oil, the cumin and the pepper.

3 Cut the pita breads into triangles and brush them with the oil mixture. Place the triangles on an ungreased cookie sheet and broil, 3 or 4 inches from the heat, until lightly toasted, 2 to 3 minutes.

Casablanca Kiwi

1 Peel and section the tangerines. Peel and slice the kiwi. Arrange the fruit in individual dessert dishes and refrigerate until you are ready to use.

2 In a small saucepan, whisk together the sugar, the water, the ginger and the cornstarch. Bring the mixture to a boil and cook until it turns to syrup, 2 to 3 minutes. Remove the saucepan from the heat. Stir in the vanilla and let it cool.

3 Drizzle the ginger sauce over the fruit.

FRIDAY

Orange Ruffian

2 tablespoons regular or light vegetable oil
1 egg white
$^1/_3$ cup sesame seeds
1 medium lemon
$1^1/_4$ pounds orange roughy (or snapper) fillets
Seasoning to taste
2 tablespoons soy sauce

Wayward Noodles

8 ounces medium egg noodles
1 tablespoon butter
1 egg yolk
$^1/_3$ cup regular or light sour cream
1 tablespoon whole or low-fat milk
$^1/_2$ teaspoon soy sauce
Seasoning to taste

Vagabond Vegetables

1 medium bunch broccoli
2 stalks celery
1 small can ($5^1/_2$ ounces) baby corn
1 tablespoon sesame oil
1 teaspoon rice vinegar
Seasoning to taste

Chocolate Drifters

1 cup whipping cream
2 tablespoons confectioners' sugar
1 teaspoon creme de menthe liqueur (or
    nonalcoholic Italian peppermint syrup)
1 pint mint chocolate chip ice cream
4 maraschino cherries for garnish

EQUIPMENT

Electric hand mixer	Colander
Large covered saucepan	Assorted kitchen knives
Medium saucepan	Measuring cups and spoons
9x13-inch glass baking dish	Assorted cooking utensils
Steamer insert	Whisk
Medium bowl	Ice cream scoop
2 shallow bowls	

COUNTDOWN

1 Assemble the ingredients and equipment
2 Do Step 1 of the *Chocolate Drifters*
3 Do Step 1 of the *Wayward Noodles*
4 Do Steps 1–2 of the *Vagabond Vegetables*
5 Do Steps 1–4 of the *Orange Ruffian*
6 Do Step 2 of the *Wayward Noodles*
7 Do Step 3 of the *Vagabond Vegetables*
8 Do Steps 3–4 of the *Wayward Noodles*
9 Do Step 4 of the *Vagabond Vegetables*
10 Do Step 2 of the *Chocolate Drifters*

Orange Ruffian

1 Preheat the oven to 400°F.

2 Place the oil in a 9x13-inch glass baking dish and heat it in the oven for 5 minutes.

3 Beat the egg white in a shallow bowl. Place the sesame seeds in a second shallow bowl.

4 Slice the lemon. Rinse and pat dry the fish. Dip one side of the fillets in the egg and then in the sesame seeds. Lay the fillets, seed side down, in the baking dish. Season to taste, drizzle the soy sauce over the fish and top with the lemon slices. Bake until the fish is just opaque, but still moist inside, 10 to 12 minutes.

Wayward Noodles

1 Bring water to a boil in a large saucepan.

2 Cook the noodles until they are almost tender, 3 to 5 minutes.

3 Drain the noodles. Melt the butter in the saucepan. Add the egg yolk, the sour cream, the milk and the soy sauce and whisk to combine. Season to taste.

4 Return the noodles to the saucepan, combine them with the sauce and cover to keep warm.

Vagabond Vegetables

1 Bring a small amount of water to a boil in a medium saucepan.

2 Trim and cut the broccoli into bite-size pieces. Trim and slice the celery in diagonals. Drain the corn.

3 Place the steamer insert in the saucepan and steam the vegetables, covered, until they are crisp-tender, about 5 minutes.

4 Drain the vegetables and return them to the saucepan, tossing them with the oil and the vinegar. Season to taste.

Chocolate Drifters

1 In a medium bowl, whip the cream with the confectioners' sugar until stiff. Fold in the creme de menthe and refrigerate for at least 15 minutes.

2 Layer scoops of ice cream with the whipped cream into parfait glasses. End with the whipped cream. Top with a maraschino cherry.

DECEMBER
WEEK TWO

WEEK AT A GLANCE

Monday

WINTER SOLESTICE
BREATHLESS BAKED ONIONS
DRESSY GREEN BEANS
PUMPKIN WHIP

Tuesday

MIDDLE AMERICAN MACARONI
VEGETABLE PATCH SALAD
JOHNNY APPLE PUFFS

Wednesday

LEMON-CAPER PORK
PEACHY KEEN BEANS
LETTUCE ALONE
RUMBLE CAKE

Thursday

CHICKEN LA SCALA
PAVAROTTI PASTA
PUCCINI ZUCCHINI
PINEAPPLE ARIAS

Friday

PUGET SOUND CHOWDER
OYSTER CRACKERS
THE LAST SLAW
FEATHERBREAD

CHECK STAPLES

- ☐ Butter
- ☐ Flour
- ☐ Baking soda
- ☐ Cornmeal
- ☐ Granulated sugar
- ☐ Confectioners' sugar
- ☐ Corn syrup
- ☐ Molasses
- ☐ Marshmallow topping
- ☐ Regular or light vegetable oil
- ☐ Regular or light olive oil
- ☐ Red wine vinegar
- ☐ Balsamic vinegar
- ☐ Apple cider vinegar
- ☐ Lemon juice
- ☐ Grated fresh orange peel
- ☐ Dijon mustard
- ☐ Ketchup

- ☐ Honey
- ☐ Grated Parmesan cheese
- ☐ Plain bread crumbs
- ☐ Seasoned bread crumbs
- ☐ Dried basil
- ☐ Cayenne pepper
- ☐ Celery seeds
- ☐ Ground cinnamon
- ☐ Ground cloves
- ☐ Garlic powder
- ☐ Ground ginger
- ☐ Dried marjoram
- ☐ Dry mustard
- ☐ Ground nutmeg
- ☐ Dried oregano
- ☐ Paprika
- ☐ Dried thyme
- ☐ Pepper
- ☐ Salt
- ☐ Vanilla extract

SHOPPING NOTE

● If you are shopping once a week and cannot arrange to purchase fresh seafood on the day you plan to use it, you can purchase *not previously frozen* seafood and freeze it, placing it in the refrigerator to thaw the night before you are ready to use it. Or you can purchase *still frozen* seafood and keep it frozen until the night before you are ready to use it.

SHOPPING LIST

MEAT & POULTRY

$1\frac{1}{2}$ pounds lean boneless pork
loin (W)

1 pound boneless, skinless
chicken breasts (Th)

FISH

$1\frac{1}{4}$ pounds sole fillets (M)

2 pounds salmon fillets (F)

FRESH PRODUCE

Vegetables

1 pound green beans (M)

4 small zucchini (Th)

1 medium yellow squash (T)

4 medium mushrooms (T)

$\frac{1}{4}$ pound mushrooms (Th)

3 stalks celery—1 (T), 2 (F)

2 medium onions—1 (Th), 1 (F)

5 small onions—3 (T), 1 (W),
1 (Th)

2 large red onions (M)

1 small red onion (F)

3 scallions (green onions)—
1 (M), 2 (W)

1 head garlic (Th)

1 bunch parsley (M, Th)

1 small (or half) head green
cabbage (F)

1 large head lettuce (W)

1 medium head lettuce (T)

1 ripe avocado (T)

$\frac{3}{4}$ pound tomatoes—$\frac{1}{4}$ pound
(M), $\frac{1}{2}$ pound (T)

1 medium cucumber (T)

2 small green bell peppers—
1 (T), 1 (Th)

1 small yellow bell pepper (F)

1 small bunch radishes (T)

Fruit

2 small lemons (W)

CANS, JARS & BOTTLES

Soup

1 can ($14\frac{1}{2}$ ounces) vegetable
broth (F)

Vegetables

1 medium can ($14\frac{1}{2}$ ounces)
crushed tomatoes with
puree (Th)

1 large can (28 ounces) cut-up
tomatoes (F)

1 large can (28 ounces) baked
beans (W)

Fish

1 can (10 ounces) whole clams
(F)

Fruit

1 small can (8 ounces) crushed
pineapple (Th)

1 medium can (16 ounces)
sliced peaches (W)

Juice

1 bottle (8 ounces) clam juice (F)

Condiments

3 tablespoons capers (W)

Dessert Needs

1 small can (16 ounces)
pumpkin (M)

1 can (21 ounces) apple pie
filling (T)

PACKAGED GOODS

Pasta, Rice & Grains

8 ounces spaghetti (Th)

12 ounces elbow macaroni (T)

1 package oyster crackers (F)

Nuts & Seeds

$\frac{3}{4}$ cup chopped walnuts (W)

8 whole walnuts (W)

Dessert & Baking Needs

25 vanilla wafers (W)

$\frac{1}{4}$ cup flaked coconut (Th)

WINES & SPIRITS

2 tablespoons dry red wine (or
nonalcoholic red wine or
water) (Th)

1 cup dry white wine (or
nonalcoholic white wine or
clam juice) (F)

3 tablespoons rum (or
nonalcoholic Italian
hazelnut syrup) (W)

2 tablespoons Amaretto liqueur
(or nonalcoholic Italian
almond syrup) (Th)

1 tablespoon brandy (optional)
(F)

REFRIGERATED PRODUCTS

Dairy

$1\frac{1}{2}$ cups whole milk (F)

$3\frac{1}{4}$ cups whole or low-fat
milk—$\frac{1}{2}$ cup (M), $2\frac{1}{4}$ cups
(T), $\frac{1}{2}$ cup (F)

$\frac{1}{4}$ cup half-and-half (T)

1 cup regular or low-fat plain
yogurt (M)

5 eggs—1 (T), 2 (W), 1 (Th), 1 (F)

Cheese

$\frac{3}{4}$ cup shredded regular or low-
fat cheddar cheese (T)

Deli

6 slices bacon—2 (M), 4 (T)

FROZEN GOODS

Desserts

1 sheet puffed pastry (T)

1 pound cake (W)

1 small container (8 ounces)
frozen whipped topping (M)

1 pint vanilla ice cream (T)

1 pint almond (or other) frozen
yogurt (Th)

MONDAY

Winter Solestice

2 tablespoons fresh parsley (when chopped)
1/2 cup flour
1/2 cup cornmeal
Seasoning to taste
1/2 cup whole or low-fat milk
1*1/4* pounds sole fillets
2 tablespoons butter
2 tablespoons regular or light vegetable oil
1 tablespoon lemon juice

Breathless Baked Onions

2 large red onions
1/2 cup balsamic vinegar
4 teaspoons butter
Seasoning to taste

Dressy Green Beans

1 scallion (green onion)
2 slices bacon
1/4 pound fresh tomatoes
1 pound green beans
2 tablespoons butter
Seasoning to taste

Pumpkin Whip

1 small can (16 ounces) pumpkin
1 small container (8 ounces) frozen whipped
   topping
1 cup regular or low-fat plain yogurt
1/2 teaspoon ground cloves
1/2 teaspoon ground ginger
1/2 teaspoon ground nutmeg
2 teaspoons ground cinnamon
1 cup sugar
2 teaspoons vanilla extract
1 tablespoon grated fresh orange peel

EQUIPMENT

Blender	2 shallow bowls
Large skillet	Assorted kitchen knives
Small skillet	Measuring cups and
Medium covered	spoons
saucepan	Assorted cooking
9x9-inch glass baking	utensils
dish	Whisk

COUNTDOWN

1 Assemble the ingredients and equipment
2 Do Steps 1–4 of the *Breathless Baked Onions*
3 Do Steps 1–2 of the *Pumpkin Whip*
4 Do Step 1 of the *Winter Solestice*
5 Do Steps 1–2 of the *Dressy Green Beans*
6 Do Steps 2–3 of the *Winter Solestice*
7 Do Step 3 of the *Dressy Green Beans*
8 Do Step 4 of the *Winter Solestice*
9 Do Step 5 of the *Breathless Baked Onions*

Winter Solestice

1 Chop the parsley.

2 Combine the flour and the cornmeal in a shallow bowl and season to taste. Put the milk in a second shallow bowl. Dip the sole fillets in the milk and then dredge them in the flour mixture to coat.

3 Melt the butter in a large skillet. Arrange the fish in the skillet in a single layer and cook, turning once, until the fillets are browned and crisp, 2 to 3 minutes per side. Remove the sole and cover to keep warm.

4 Drain any fat from the skillet. Add the oil, the parsley and the lemon juice. Whisk until the mixture is hot and well blended. Spoon the sauce over the sole.

Breathless Baked Onions

1 Preheat the oven to 375°F.

2 Trim, but do not peel, the onions and cut them in half.

3 Pour the vinegar into a 9x9-inch glass baking dish. Place the onion halves, cut side down, in the dish.

4 Bake until the onions are soft when pressed, 35 to 45 minutes.

5 Scoop the onions from their skins, top them with a pat of butter and season to taste.

Dressy Green Beans

1 Trim and chop the scallion. Dice the bacon. Chop the tomatoes. Sauté the scallion and the bacon in a small skillet until the bacon is crisp, about 5 minutes. Drain both on paper towels.

2 Bring water to a boil in a medium saucepan. Trim the green beans, cut them into 1-inch pieces and cook until they are crisp-tender, 5 to 7 minutes.

3 Drain the beans. Melt the butter in the saucepan, add the scallion, the bacon, the beans and the tomatoes. Season to taste and toss to combine and heat through. Remove the saucepan from the heat, and cover to keep warm.

Pumpkin Whip

1 Place half of the pumpkin, half of the whipped topping and half of the yogurt in a blender. Add half of the ground cloves, half of the ground ginger, half of the nutmeg, half of the cinnamon, half of the sugar and half of the vanilla. Process the mixture until it is thoroughly blended and divide it between 2 parfait glasses. Repeat with the remaining ingredients. Sprinkle with the orange peel.

2 Refrigerate the whips for at least 15 minutes.

TUESDAY

Middle American Macaroni

4 slices bacon
3 small onions
12 ounces elbow macaroni
4 tablespoons butter
2 tablespoons flour
2$^{1}/_{4}$ cups whole or low-fat milk
$^{3}/_{4}$ cup shredded regular or low-fat cheddar
    cheese
$^{1}/_{4}$ teaspoon ground nutmeg
$^{1}/_{4}$ cup half-and-half
Seasoning to taste
$^{1}/_{4}$ cup plain bread crumbs
2 tablespoons grated Parmesan cheese
$^{1}/_{4}$ teaspoon cayenne pepper

Vegetable Patch Salad

1 medium head lettuce
1 medium yellow squash
1 stalk celery
1 small green bell pepper
1 small bunch radishes
$^{1}/_{2}$ pound fresh tomatoes
1 medium cucumber
4 medium mushrooms
1 ripe avocado
3 tablespoons lemon juice
4 tablespoons regular or light olive oil
1 teaspoon Dijon mustard
1 teaspoon honey
$^{1}/_{4}$ teaspoon garlic powder
Seasoning to taste

Johnny Apple Puffs

1 sheet frozen puff pastry
1 egg
1 can (21 ounces) apple pie filling
1 pint vanilla ice cream

EQUIPMENT

Medium skillet	Measuring cups and
Large saucepan	spoons
1$^{1}/_{2}$-quart casserole	Assorted cooking
Cookie sheet	utensils
Large bowl	Whisk
2 small bowls	Vegetable peeler
Colander	Pastry brush
Assorted kitchen knives	Ice cream scoop

COUNTDOWN

1 Assemble the ingredients and equipment
2 Do Step 1 of the *Johnny Apple Puffs*
3 Do Steps 1–8 of the *Middle American Macaroni*
4 Do Steps 1–2 of the *Vegetable Patch Salad*
5 Do Steps 2–5 of the *Johnny Apple Puffs*
6 Do Step 3 of the *Vegetable Patch Salad*
7 Do Step 6 of the *Johnny Apple Puffs*

Middle American Macaroni

1 Preheat the oven to 350°F. Grease a 1½-quart casserole.

2 Bring water to a boil in a large saucepan.

3 Chop the bacon. Peel and chop the onions.

4 Cook the macaroni until it is almost tender, 8 to 10 minutes.

5 Sauté the bacon and the onions in a medium skillet until the bacon is crisp, about 5 minutes. Drain both on paper towels.

6 Melt the butter in the skillet. Add the flour and cook, stirring, until well blended, about 1 minute. Gradually add the milk, stirring constantly, until the mixture comes to a light boil. Add the cheddar cheese, the nutmeg and the half-and-half. Continue cooking and stirring until the cheese is melted and the sauce is well blended. Season to taste.

7 Drain the macaroni, return it to the saucepan and toss it with the bacon and the onions. Turn the mixture into the casserole.

8 Pour the cheese sauce over the macaroni mixture. Sprinkle the top with the bread crumbs, the Parmesan cheese and the cayenne pepper. Bake until the macaroni is hot and bubbly, about 30 minutes.

Vegetable Patch Salad

1 Wash and dry the lettuce and tear it into bite-size pieces. Trim and slice the squash. Trim and slice the celery. Seed and slice the bell pepper. Trim and slice the radishes. Chop the tomatoes. Peel and slice the cucumber. Wash, pat dry, trim and slice the mushrooms. Combine the ingredients in a large bowl. Peel, pit and chop the avocado and sprinkle it with 1 tablespoon of the lemon juice.

2 In a small bowl, whisk together the oil, the remaining lemon juice, the mustard, the honey and the garlic powder. Season to taste.

3 Combine the avocado with the salad and toss with the dressing.

Johnny Apple Puffs

1 Place the sheet of puff pastry in the refrigerator to thaw.

2 Cut the thawed pastry sheet into quarters. Cut a ¼-inch strip off all 4 sides of each quarter.

3 Preheat the oven to 350°F. Lightly beat the egg and brush it over each pastry square.

4 Place the pastry strips around the edges of the squares to form a border. Place the squares on an ungreased cookie sheet and bake for 10 minutes.

5 Divide the pie filling among the pastry shells and return them to the oven. Bake until the apples are hot and bubbly, about 10 minutes.

6 Top the puffs with scoops of ice cream.

WEDNESDAY

Lemon-Caper Pork

2 eggs
1 tablespoon water
1 1/2 cups plain bread crumbs
1 1/2 pounds lean boneless pork loin
Seasoning to taste
1/4 cup flour
2 tablespoons regular or light olive oil
2 small lemons
2 tablespoons butter
3 tablespoons lemon juice
3 tablespoons capers

Peachy Keen Beans

1 small onion
1 medium can (16 ounces) sliced peaches
1 tablespoon butter
1 large can (28 ounces) baked beans
1 tablespoon corn syrup
1 tablespoon molasses

Lettuce Alone

1 large head lettuce
2 scallions (green onions)
3 tablespoons regular or light vegetable oil
2 tablespoons red wine vinegar
1/8 teaspoon paprika
1/8 teaspoon dry mustard
1/8 teaspoon sugar
1/8 teaspoon garlic powder
1 tablespoon ketchup
Seasoning to taste

Rumble Cake

1 frozen pound cake
25 vanilla wafers
3/4 cup chopped walnuts
3 tablespoons rum (or nonalcoholic Italian
    hazelnut syrup)
1/4 cup honey
3 tablespoons confectioners' sugar
8 whole walnuts

EQUIPMENT

Blender	2 shallow bowls
Large covered skillet	Assorted kitchen knives
Medium saucepan	Measuring cups and
9x9-inch glass baking	spoons
dish	Assorted cooking
Large bowl	utensils
Medium bowl	Whisk
Small bowl	Sifter

COUNTDOWN

1 Assemble the ingredients and equipment
2 Do Step 1 of the *Rumble Cake*
3 Do Steps 1–5 of the *Peachy Keen Beans*
4 Do Steps 2–5 of the *Rumble Cake*
5 Do Steps 1–3 of the *Lemon–Caper Pork*
6 Do Steps 1–2 of the *Lettuce Alone*
7 Do Steps 4–5 of the *Lemon–Caper Pork*
8 Do Step 3 of the *Lettuce Alone*

Lemon-Caper Pork

1 Beat the eggs with the water in a shallow bowl. Place the bread crumbs in a second shallow bowl.

2 Trim any excess fat from the pork and cut the meat into 8 slices. Season to taste and dust the slices with the flour. Dip the pork slices in the egg and then dredge them in the bread crumbs, patting gently to help the crumbs stick.

3 Heat the oil in a large skillet. Add the pork and cook until the slices are lightly browned, 3 to 4 minutes per side. Reduce the heat, cover and simmer until the pork is white throughout but still moist inside, about 8 minutes.

4 Remove the pork and cover to keep warm. Cut the lemons into 8 thin slices.

5 Wipe out the skillet. Melt the butter until it just begins to turn brown, about 2 minutes. Add the lemon juice and the capers and stir until the mixture is hot. Return the pork to the skillet and coat the slices with the sauce. Garnish with the lemon slices.

Peachy Keen Beans

1 Preheat the oven to 350°F.

2 Peel and mince the onion. Drain the peaches, reserving $1/3$ cup of the syrup.

3 Melt the butter in a medium saucepan and sauté the onion until it is soft, about 5 minutes.

4 Add the baked beans, the corn syrup and the molasses to the saucepan. Combine and heat through.

5 Turn the bean mixture into a 9x9-inch glass baking dish. Top with the sliced peaches. Drizzle the reserved syrup over the top and bake until the mixture is hot and bubbly, about 30 minutes.

Lettuce Alone

1 Wash and dry the lettuce, tear it into bite-size pieces and place it in a large bowl.

2 Trim and mince the scallions. In a small bowl, whisk the scallions with the oil, the vinegar, the paprika, the mustard, the sugar, the garlic powder and the ketchup. Season to taste.

3 Toss the lettuce with the dressing.

Rumble Cake

1 Set the pound cake out to thaw.

2 Place the vanilla wafers and the chopped walnuts in a blender and process until they are coarsely ground.

3 In a medium bowl, combine the wafer mixture with the rum and the honey.

4 Slice the cake into 3 horizontal layers.

5 Spread half of the mixture on the bottom layer of the cake and the remaining mixture on the second layer of the cake. Dust the top with the confectioners' sugar and arrange the whole nuts in a decorative row down the center. Set aside until you are ready to serve.

THURSDAY

Chicken La Scala

1 medium onion
1 small green bell pepper
$^1/_4$ pound fresh mushrooms
1 clove garlic
$^1/_4$ cup fresh parsley (when chopped)
Seasoning to taste
1 pound boneless, skinless chicken breasts
1 tablespoon regular or light olive oil
1 medium can (14$^1/_2$ ounces) crushed
    tomatoes with puree
2 tablespoons dry red wine (or nonalcoholic
    red wine or water)
1 teaspoon dried basil
$^1/_2$ teaspoon dried oregano

Pavarotti Pasta

8 ounces spaghetti
2 tablespoons butter
$^1/_4$ teaspoon dried marjoram
$^1/_4$ teaspoon dried thyme
$^1/_8$ teaspoon cayenne pepper
Seasoning to taste

Puccini Zucchini

4 small zucchini
1 small onion
1 teaspoon fresh parsley (when chopped)
2 tablespoons regular or light olive oil
$^1/_4$ cup seasoned bread crumbs
$^1/_4$ cup grated Parmesan cheese
1 egg
$^1/_8$ teaspoon ground nutmeg
Seasoning to taste

Pineapple Arias

1 small can (8 ounces) crushed pineapple
2 tablespoons Amaretto liqueur (or
    nonalcoholic Italian almond syrup)
1 pint almond (or other) frozen yogurt
$^1/_2$ cup marshmallow topping
$^1/_4$ cup flaked coconut

EQUIPMENT

Large skillet	Colander
Large covered saucepan	Assorted kitchen knives
Medium saucepan	Measuring cups and spoons
7x11-inch glass baking dish	Assorted cooking utensils
Medium bowl	Ice cream scoop
Small bowl	

COUNTDOWN

1 Assemble the ingredients and equipment
2 Do Steps 1–6 of the *Puccini Zucchini*
3 Do Step 1 of the *Pavarotti Pasta*
4 Do Steps 1–4 of the *Chicken La Scala*
5 Do Step 2 of the *Pavarotti Pasta*
6 Do Step 1 of the *Pineapple Arias*
7 Do Step 3 of the *Pavarotti Pasta*
8 Do Step 2 of the *Pineapple Arias*

Chicken La Scala

1 Peel and chop the onion. Seed and dice the bell pepper. Wash, pat dry, trim and slice the mushrooms. Peel and mince the garlic. Chop the parsley.

2 Season the chicken to taste. Heat the oil in a large skillet. Add the chicken and sauté until it is lightly browned, 6 to 8 minutes. Remove the chicken and reserve.

3 Add the onion to the skillet and sauté until it is soft, about 5 minutes. Add the bell pepper, the mushrooms and the garlic and sauté for 3 minutes more. Add the tomatoes, the wine, the parsley, the basil and the oregano. Season to taste.

4 Cut the chicken into 1-inch cubes and return it to the skillet, along with any juices that have collected. Reduce the heat and simmer, uncovered, stirring occasionally, until the chicken is just cooked through and the sauce is thickened, 6 to 8 minutes.

Pavarotti Pasta

1 Bring water to a boil in a large saucepan.

2 Cook the pasta until it is almost tender, 2 to 3 minutes if you are using fresh pasta and 6 to 7 minutes if you are using dried pasta.

3 Drain the pasta, return it to the saucepan and toss it with the butter, the marjoram, the thyme and the cayenne pepper. Season to taste and cover to keep warm.

Puccini Zucchini

1 Preheat the oven to 350°F.

2 Bring water to a boil in a medium saucepan. Trim the zucchini and boil them for 3 minutes.

3 Peel and mince the onion. Chop the parsley.

4 Drain the zucchini, run them under cold water and cut them in half lengthwise. Scoop out the flesh to form a trench. Chop the flesh and place it in a medium bowl.

5 Heat 1 tablespoon of the oil in the saucepan and sauté the onion until it is soft, about 5 minutes. Add the chopped zucchini flesh, the bread crumbs and the parsley. Sauté for 2 minutes. Remove the saucepan from the heat and stir in 2 tablespoons of the cheese, the egg and the nutmeg. Season to taste.

6 Stuff the mixture into the zucchini shells and place them in a 7x11-inch glass baking dish. Drizzle the shells with the remaining oil and sprinkle them with the remaining cheese. Bake until the zucchini are heated through and the cheese is crusted, about 30 minutes.

Pineapple Arias

1 Drain the pineapple and combine it in a small bowl with the Amaretto.

2 Place scoops of frozen yogurt in individual dessert dishes and spoon the pineapple mixture over the yogurt. Garnish with dollops of marshmallow topping and sprinkle with the coconut.

FRIDAY

Puget Sound Chowder

2 pounds salmon fillets
1 can (14$^1/_2$ ounces) vegetable broth
1 bottle (8 ounces) clam juice
1 cup dry white wine (or nonalcoholic white
   wine or additional clam juice)
1 medium onion
2 stalks celery
6 tablespoons butter
$^1/_4$ teaspoon dried basil
$^1/_4$ teaspoon dried thyme
$^1/_4$ teaspoon dried marjoram
1$^1/_2$ cups whole milk
1 large can (28 ounces) cut-up tomatoes
1 can (10 ounces) whole clams
4 tablespoons flour
1 tablespoon brandy (optional)
Seasoning to taste

Oyster Crackers

The Last Slaw

1 small (or half) head green cabbage
1 small red onion
1 small yellow bell pepper
3 tablespoons sugar
$^1/_2$ teaspoon salt
3 tablespoons apple cider vinegar
2 teaspoons Dijon mustard
2 teaspoons celery seeds
4 tablespoons regular or light vegetable oil
Seasoning to taste

Featherbread

1$^1/_2$ cups flour
$^1/_2$ cup granulated sugar
1 teaspoon baking soda
1 teaspoon ground cinnamon
1 teaspoon ground ginger
$^1/_2$ cup regular or light vegetable oil
$^1/_2$ cup whole or low-fat milk
$^1/_2$ cup molasses
1 egg
1 teaspoon water
$^1/_2$ cup confectioners' sugar

EQUIPMENT

Electric hand mixer	Measuring cups and
Dutch oven	spoons
Large covered skillet	Assorted cooking
2 small saucepans	utensils
9x9-inch baking pan	Whisk
2 large bowls	Vegetable grater
Assorted kitchen knives	Sifter

COUNTDOWN

1 Assemble the ingredients and equipment
2 Do Step 1 of the *Featherbread*
3 Do Steps 1–2 of *The Last Slaw*
4 Do Step 2 of the *Featherbread*
5 Do Steps 1–5 of the *Puget Sound Chowder*
6 Do Step 3 of *The Last Slaw*
7 Do Step 3 of the *Featherbread*

Puget Sound Chowder

1 Rinse and pat dry the salmon, cut it into strips and place the strips in a large skillet. Add the broth, the clam juice and the wine. Bring the liquid to a boil, reduce the heat, cover and poach until the salmon is opaque but still moist in its thickest part, about 5 minutes.

2 Peel and chop the onion. Trim and chop the celery.

3 Remove and flake the salmon, reserving the poaching liquid.

4 Melt 3 tablespoons of the butter in a Dutch oven. Add the onion and the celery and sauté until the onion is soft, about 5 minutes. Add the basil, the thyme, the marjoram, the milk, the undrained tomatoes, the undrained clams and the reserved poaching liquid. Cover and simmer for 10 minutes.

5 Melt the remaining butter in a small saucepan. Whisk in the flour until thoroughly combined. Slowly add 1/2 cup of the hot soup and whisk until smooth. Stir the mixture back into the Dutch oven, and whisk until the soup is well blended. Add the salmon to the Dutch oven. Stir in the brandy. Season to taste. Cook for 1 minute. Top each serving with a handful of oyster crackers.

The Last Slaw

1 Grate the cabbage. Peel and chop the onion. Seed and sliver the bell pepper. Add the ingredients to a large bowl.

2 In a small saucepan, heat the sugar, the salt, the vinegar, the mustard, the celery seeds and the oil until the sugar is dissolved and the mixture is well blended. Season to taste, pour the mixture over the cabbage and toss well. Refrigerate until you are ready to serve.

3 Drain the slaw before serving.

Featherbread

1 Preheat the oven to 375°F. Grease a 9x9-inch baking pan.

2 Combine the flour, the granulated sugar, the baking soda, the cinnamon, the ginger, the oil, the milk, the molasses, the egg and the water in a large bowl and beat until well blended. Pour the batter into the baking pan and bake until the top is firm to the touch and lightly golden, about 30 minutes.

3 Dust the featherbread with the confectioners' sugar.

DECEMBER
WEEK THREE

CHECK STAPLES

- ☐ Butter
- ☐ Flour
- ☐ Baking powder
- ☐ Cornstarch
- ☐ Granulated sugar
- ☐ Dark brown sugar
- ☐ Confectioners' sugar
- ☐ Unsweetened cocoa
- ☐ Multicolored sprinkles
- ☐ Long-grain white rice
- ☐ Regular or light vegetable oil
- ☐ Regular or light olive oil
- ☐ Red wine vinegar
- ☐ White wine vinegar
- ☐ Lemon juice
- ☐ Grated fresh lemon peel
- ☐ Worcestershire sauce
- ☐ Soy sauce
- ☐ Dijon mustard
- ☐ Grated Parmesan cheese
- ☐ Ground allspice
- ☐ Dried basil
- ☐ Bay leaves
- ☐ Cayenne pepper
- ☐ Ground cinnamon
- ☐ Cream of tartar
- ☐ Ground nutmeg
- ☐ Instant minced onion
- ☐ Dried mint
- ☐ Dried oregano
- ☐ Red pepper flakes
- ☐ Dried savory
- ☐ Dried tarragon
- ☐ Pepper
- ☐ Salt
- ☐ Vanilla extract

SHOPPING NOTE

● If you are shopping once a week and cannot arrange to purchase fresh seafood on the day you plan to use it, you can purchase *not previously frozen* seafood and freeze it, placing it in the refrigerator to thaw the night before you are ready to use it. Or you can purchase *still frozen* seafood and keep it frozen until the night before you are ready to use it.

MEAT & POULTRY
1 pound regular or light sweet Italian pork or turkey sausage (Th)
3 pounds chicken pieces (M)

FISH
4 flounder fillets (1$^1/_4$ pounds) (W)
1 pound medium shrimp, shelled and deveined (F)

PRODUCE
1 pound new red potatoes (W)
$^1/_2$ pound green beans (W)
2 small zucchini (Th)
2 large rutabagas (F)
$^1/_2$ pound sugar snap peas (M)
$^1/_2$ pound spinach (W)
$^1/_4$ pound mushrooms (F)
1 pound carrots—$^1/_2$ pound (M), $^1/_2$ pound (W)
1 medium carrot (Th)
6 stalks celery—2 (M), 2 (T), 2 (Th)
4 medium onions—2 (T), 2 (Th)
2 small onions—1 (W), 1 (F)
3 scallions (green onions) (Th)
1 head garlic (M, T, Th, F)
1 bunch parsley (M, W, Th)
1 medium head lettuce (Th)
1 package (16 ounces) mixed salad greens (F)
1 ripe avocado (T)
1 medium cucumber (Th)
1 medium red bell pepper (T)
1 small green bell pepper (Th)
2 green chilies (or canned) (T)

Fruit
4 large tart green apples (T)
3 medium bananas—2 (T), 1 (F)
4 kiwifruit (F)
$^1/_4$ pound seedless green grapes (Th)
$^1/_4$ pound seedless red grapes (F)
1 small pink grapefruit (Th)
2 small oranges (Th)

CANS, JARS & BOTTLES
Soup
1 can (14$^1/_2$ ounces) chicken broth (M)

3 cans (14$^1/_2$ ounces each) vegetable broth—2 (T), 1 (W)
2 cans (14$^1/_2$ ounces each) beef broth (Th)
1 can (10$^3/_4$ ounces) beef consommé (Th)

Vegetables
2 large cans (28 ounces each) cut-up tomatoes—1 (Th), 1 (F)
1 medium can (14$^1/_2$ ounces) Cajun-style stewed tomatoes (T)
1 medium can (11 ounces) whole kernel corn (T)
1 jar (6$^1/_2$ ounces) marinated artichoke hearts (Th)

Juice
$^1/_4$ cup tomato juice (W)

Condiments
2 tablespoons capers (T)

Spreads
4$^1/_2$ tablespoons apricot preserves (F)

PACKAGED GOODS
Pasta, Rice & Grains
8 ounces fine egg noodles (M)
6 ounces bow tie pasta (Th)
16 ounces small shell pasta (F)

Soup
1 envelope (1.8 ounces) dried leek soup mix (M)

Baked Goods
1 angel food loaf cake (T)
1 small loaf Italian bread (Th)

Nuts & Seeds
$^1/_4$ cup pine nuts (F)

Dessert & Baking Needs
1 package (11 ounces) pie crust mix (M)
1 small package (3 ounces) regular vanilla pudding mix (T)

4 giant chocolate chip cookies (M)
$^1/_2$ cup semisweet chocolate chips (F)
4 individual graham cracker tart shells (F)
$^1/_4$ cup flaked coconut (Th)

WINES & SPIRITS
$^1/_4$ cup dry red wine (or nonalcoholic red wine or tomato juice) (W)
1 cup dry white wine (or nonalcoholic white wine or water) (Th)
$^3/_4$ cup dry white wine (or nonalcoholic white wine or clam juice) (F)
$^1/_4$ cup dry sherry (or nonalcoholic white wine or chicken broth) (M)
2 tablespoons rum (or 2 teaspoons rum extract) (T)
2 tablespoons Grand Marnier liqueur (or nonalcoholic Italian orange syrup) (Th)

REFRIGERATED PRODUCTS
Dairy
4$^1/_2$ cups + 2 tablespoons whole or low-fat milk—4$^1/_2$ cups (M), 2 tablespoons (F)
$^1/_4$ cup half-and-half (F)
Whipped cream for garnish (M)
1 cup regular or light sour cream (M)
1$^1/_2$ cups regular or low-fat eggnog (T)
4 eggs (W)

Cheese
$^1/_4$ cup regular or low-fat small-curd cottage cheese (W)
1 container (8 ounces) regular or light soft cream cheese (F)

Juice
$^1/_4$ cup orange juice (T)

FROZEN GOODS
Desserts
1 pint lemon frozen yogurt (Th)

MONDAY

Casanova Chicken

1/2 pound carrots
1/2 pound sugar snap peas
2 stalks celery
1 clove garlic
2 tablespoons regular or light vegetable oil
3 pounds chicken pieces
1 envelope (1.8 ounces) dried leek soup mix
1 can (14 1/2 ounces) chicken broth
1/4 cup dry sherry (or nonalcoholic white wine
*   or additional chicken broth)*
2 tablespoons Dijon mustard
1 bay leaf
2 tablespoons flour
1 cup regular or light sour cream
Seasoning to taste

Don Juan Noodles

1 tablespoon fresh parsley (when chopped)
8 ounces fine egg noodles
2 tablespoons butter
1/2 teaspoon ground allspice
Seasoning to taste

Brazen Biscuits

1/2 cup whole or low-fat milk
1 teaspoon instant minced onion
1 tablespoon fresh parsley (when chopped)
1 package (11 ounces) pie crust mix
1 tablespoon baking powder

Cheeky Cocoa 'n' Cookies

5 tablespoons unsweetened cocoa
1/2 cup sugar
1/8 teaspoon salt
1/3 cup hot water
1 quart whole or low-fat milk
3/4 teaspoon vanilla extract
Whipped cream for garnish
Multicolored sprinkles
4 giant chocolate chip cookies

EQUIPMENT

Electric hand mixer	Measuring cups and
Dutch oven	spoons
Large saucepan	Assorted cooking
Medium saucepan	utensils
Cookie sheet	Pastry board
2 medium bowls	Whisk
2 small bowls	Vegetable peeler
Strainer	Biscuit cutter
Assorted kitchen knives	

COUNTDOWN

1 Assemble the ingredients and equipment
2 Do Steps 1–4 of the *Casanova Chicken*
3 Do Steps 1–5 of the *Brazen Biscuits*
4 Do Step 5 of the *Casanova Chicken*
5 Do Step 1 of the *Don Juan Noodles*
6 Do Step 6 of the *Brazen Biscuits*
7 Do Step 6 of the *Casanova Chicken*
8 Do Step 2 of the *Don Juan Noodles*
9 Do Step 7 of the *Casanova Chicken*
10 Do Step 3 of the *Don Juan Noodles*
11 Do Step 8 of the *Casanova Chicken*
12 Do Steps 1–4 of the *Cheeky Cocoa 'n' Cookies*

Casanova Chicken

1 Peel and slice the carrots. Trim and string the snap peas. Trim and slice the celery. Peel and mince the garlic.

2 Heat the oil in a Dutch oven. Add the garlic and the chicken pieces and sauté until the chicken is nicely browned on all sides, about 12 minutes.

3 In a medium bowl, combine the dried soup mix, the broth, the sherry and the mustard.

4 Drain any fat from the Dutch oven. Add the soup mixture and the bay leaf, bring the liquid to a boil, reduce the heat, cover and simmer for 20 minutes.

5 Add the vegetables to the Dutch oven and simmer for 10 minutes more.

6 With a slotted spoon, remove the chicken and the vegetables and cover to keep warm. Bring the liquid in the Dutch oven to a boil, and cook for 5 minutes.

7 In a small bowl, combine the flour and the sour cream.

8 Reduce the heat under the Dutch oven, stir in the sour cream mixture and simmer, whisking constantly, until the sauce thickens, about 3 minutes. Season to taste. Remove the bay leaf. Pour the sauce over the chicken and vegetables.

Don Juan Noodles

1 Bring water to a boil in a large saucepan. Chop the parsley.

2 Cook the noodles until they are almost tender, 3 to 5 minutes.

3 Drain the pasta and return it to the saucepan. Toss with the butter, the allspice and the parsley. Season to taste. Cover to keep warm.

Brazen Biscuits

1 Preheat the oven to 450°F.

2 In a small bowl, combine the milk and the onion and let the mixture stand for 5 minutes.

3 Chop the parsley. In a medium bowl, combine the parsley with the pie crust mix and the baking powder.

4 Flour a pastry board.

5 Make a well in the center of the dry ingredients. Add the milk and onion mixture all at once. Stir just until the dough begins to cling together, then turn it out onto the pastry board. Knead 10 or 12 times, pat the dough into a $1/2$-inch thickness and cut it with a biscuit cutter, dipping the cutter in flour between cuts.

6 Place the biscuits on an ungreased cookie sheet and bake until they are lightly golden, 10 to 12 minutes.

Cheeky Cocoa 'n' Cookies

1 In a medium saucepan, combine the cocoa, the sugar and the salt. Blend in the hot water. Bring the mixture to a boil, and cook, stirring constantly, for 2 minutes. Add the milk. Stir and heat through, but do not let it boil.

2 Remove the saucepan from the heat. Add the vanilla and beat until foamy.

3 Pour the mixture into individual mugs and top with a dollop of whipped cream and sprinkles.

4 Serve the cocoa with the cookies.

TUESDAY

Cajun Jumble

2 medium onions
1 medium red bell pepper
2 fresh green chilies (or canned)
3 cloves garlic
2 stalks celery
1 ripe avocado
1 tablespoon lemon juice
2 cans (14^1/$_2$ ounces each) vegetable broth
1^1/$_2$ cups long-grain white rice
2 tablespoons regular or light olive oil
1 medium can (14^1/$_2$ ounces) Cajun-style
    stewed tomatoes
1 medium can (11 ounces) whole kernel corn
2 tablespoons capers
2 tablespoons Worcestershire sauce
^{1}/$_8$ teaspoon cayenne pepper
Seasoning to taste

Orange Apples

4 large tart green apples
2 tablespoons butter
^{1}/$_4$ cup orange juice
^{1}/$_4$ cup sugar
1 teaspoon ground cinnamon

Easy Over Eggnog

1 angel food loaf cake
1 small package (3 ounces) regular vanilla
    pudding mix
1^1/$_2$ cups regular or low-fat eggnog
2 tablespoons rum (or 2 teaspoons rum
    extract)
2 medium bananas
1 teaspoon ground nutmeg

EQUIPMENT

Large covered skillet	Assorted kitchen knives
Medium covered skillet	Measuring cups and
Medium covered	spoons
saucepan	Assorted cooking
Medium saucepan	utensils
Small bowl	Apple corer

COUNTDOWN

1 Assemble the ingredients and equipment
2 Do Steps 1–4 of the *Cajun Jumble*
3 Do Steps 1–3 of the *Orange Apples*
4 Do Step 5 of the *Cajun Jumble*
5 Do Steps 1–3 of the *Easy Over Eggnog*

Cajun Jumble

1 Peel and chop the onions. Seed and chop the bell pepper. Seed and chop the chilies. Peel and mince the garlic. Trim and dice the celery. Peel, pit and chop the avocado and place it in a small bowl and sprinkle it with the lemon juice.

2 Bring the broth to a boil in a medium saucepan. Stir in the rice, cover and cook until all the liquid is absorbed and the rice is tender, 20 to 25 minutes.

3 Heat the oil in a large skillet. Sauté the onions until they are soft, about 5 minutes. Add the bell pepper, the chilies and the garlic, and sauté for 3 minutes. Add the tomatoes and the celery, reduce the heat, cover and simmer until the celery is soft, about 5 minutes.

4 Add the undrained corn, the capers, the Worcestershire sauce and the cayenne pepper to the skillet. Season to taste, stir to combine, remove from the heat and cover to keep warm.

5 Fluff the rice. Add it to the skillet and stir to blend. Heat through, 2 to 3 minutes. Top with the avocado.

Orange Apples

1 Peel, core and slice the apples.

2 Melt the butter in a medium skillet. Sauté the apple slices until they are crisp-tender, about 5 minutes.

3 Add the orange juice, the sugar and the cinnamon to the skillet. Bring the mixture to a boil, reduce the heat and cook until the sauce just begins to caramelize, about 5 minutes. Remove the skillet from the heat and cover to keep warm.

Easy Over Eggnog

1 Cut the angel food loaf into small cubes and distribute them among individual dessert dishes.

2 Combine the pudding mix and the eggnog in a medium saucepan. Cook, stirring constantly, until the mixture thickens and bubbles. Stir in the rum.

3 Peel and slice the bananas and add them to the cake cubes. Top the cake with the eggnog sauce. Dust with the nutmeg.

WEDNESDAY

Funky Flounder

1 small onion
4 flounder fillets (1$^1/_4$ pounds)
$^1/_2$ pound fresh spinach
$^1/_4$ cup regular or low-fat small-curd cottage
    cheese
$^1/_8$ teaspoon ground nutmeg
Seasoning to taste
$^1/_4$ cup tomato juice
$^1/_4$ cup dry red wine (or nonalcoholic red wine
    or additional tomato juice)

Triple Hitter

1 pound new red potatoes
$^1/_2$ pound carrots
$^1/_2$ pound green beans
1 tablespoon fresh parsley (when chopped)
1 can (14$^1/_2$ ounces) vegetable broth
1 tablespoon butter
Seasoning to taste

Mellow Yellow

4 eggs
4 tablespoons butter
1$^1/_4$ cups granulated sugar
1 tablespoon cornstarch
$^1/_3$ cup lemon juice
1 teaspoon grated fresh lemon peel
1 teaspoon vanilla extract
$^1/_2$ teaspoon cream of tartar
2 tablespoons flour
$^1/_4$ cup confectioners' sugar

EQUIPMENT

Electric hand mixer	Small bowl
Large saucepan	Assorted kitchen knives
Medium covered saucepan	Measuring cups and spoons
Small saucepan	Assorted cooking utensils
8x8-inch glass baking dish	Whisk
1$^1/_2$-quart soufflé dish (or casserole)	Vegetable brush
Large bowl	Vegetable peeler
Medium bowl	Sifter

COUNTDOWN

1 Assemble the ingredients and equipment
2 Do Steps 1–6 of the *Mellow Yellow*
3 Do Steps 1–5 of the *Funky Flounder*
4 Do Steps 1–3 of the *Triple Hitter*
5 Do Step 7 of the *Mellow Yellow*

Funky Flounder

1 Peel and chop the onion. Pat dry the fish.

2 Bring water to a boil in a medium saucepan. Add the spinach, cover and cook for 2 minutes.

3 Drain and chop the spinach. In a medium bowl, combine the spinach with the onion, the cottage cheese and the nutmeg. Season to taste.

4 Place a quarter of the mixture at the wide end of each fish fillet. Roll up the fillets and place them in an 8x8-inch glass baking dish, narrow end down.

5 Preheat the oven to 425°F. Pour the tomato juice and the wine over the fish and bake until the fillets are opaque throughout and flake easily with a fork, 10 to 15 minutes.

Triple Hitter

1 Scrub the potatoes and cut them into thin sticks. Peel and cut the carrots into thin sticks. Trim and string the beans and cut them in half lengthwise. Chop the parsley.

2 Place the vegetables in a large saucepan, add the broth, bring it to a boil and cook until the vegetables are crisp-tender, about 5 minutes.

3 Drain the vegetables, return them to the saucepan and toss them with the butter and the parsley. Season to taste.

Mellow Yellow

1 Preheat the oven to 350°F.

2 Separate the eggs, placing the whites in a large bowl and the yolks in a small bowl.

3 Melt the butter in a small saucepan. Whisk 1 cup of the granulated sugar and the cornstarch into the butter. Add the lemon juice and the lemon peel. Bring the mixture to a boil, stirring constantly, and cook until slightly thickened, about 2 minutes.

4 Blend in the vanilla and pour the mixture into a 1 1/2 quart soufflé dish or casserole.

5 Beat the egg whites until frothy, add the cream of tartar and beat until stiff peaks form. Slowly beat in the remaining granulated sugar and beat until the egg whites are very stiff.

6 Beat the egg yolks with the flour until they are thickened. Gently fold the egg yolk mixture into the egg white mixture and spread it over the lemon sauce. Bake until the top is set, about 15 minutes.

7 Dust the soufflé with the confectioners' sugar.

THURSDAY

Savory Sausage Soup

1 pound regular or light sweet Italian pork or
   turkey sausage
2 cloves garlic
2 medium onions
1 medium carrot
2 tablespoons fresh parsley (when chopped)
1 small green bell pepper
2 small zucchini
1 large can (28 ounces) cut-up tomatoes
2 cans (14$^1/_2$ ounces each) beef broth
1 can (10$^3/_4$ ounces) beef consommé
1 cup dry white wine (or nonalcoholic white
   wine or water)
$^1/_2$ teaspoon dried basil
$^1/_4$ teaspoon dried savory
1 bay leaf
6 ounces bow tie pasta
Seasoning to taste
$^1/_4$ cup grated Parmesan cheese

Italian Bread

Wintergreen Salad

1 medium head lettuce
2 stalks celery
1 medium cucumber
3 scallions (green onions)
1 jar (6$^1/_2$ ounces) marinated artichoke hearts
2 tablespoons white wine vinegar
$^1/_4$ teaspoon dried tarragon
$^1/_4$ teaspoon dried mint
Seasoning to taste

Mixed Feelings

1 small pink grapefruit
2 small oranges
$^1/_4$ pound seedless green grapes
2 tablespoons Grand Marnier liqueur (or
   nonalcoholic Italian orange syrup)
1 pint lemon frozen yogurt
$^1/_4$ cup confectioners' sugar
$^1/_4$ cup flaked coconut

EQUIPMENT

Dutch oven	Assorted cooking
Large bowl	utensils
Medium bowl	Whisk
Small bowl	Vegetable peeler
Assorted kitchen knives	Ice cream scoop
Measuring cups and	Sifter
spoons	

COUNTDOWN

1 Assemble the ingredients and equipment
2 Do Step 1 of the *Mixed Feelings*
3 Do Steps 1–4 of the *Savory Sausage Soup*
4 Do Step 1 of the *Wintergreen Salad*
5 Do Step 5 of the *Savory Sausage Soup*
6 Do Steps 2–3 of the *Wintergreen Salad*
7 Do Steps 6–7 of the *Savory Sausage Soup*
8 Do Step 2 of the *Mixed Feelings*

Savory Sausage Soup

1 Cut the sausage into ¹/₂-inch slices. Peel and mince the garlic. Peel and chop the onions. Peel and slice the carrot. Chop the parsley. Seed and chop the bell pepper. Trim and cut the zucchini in ¹/₂-inch slices.

2 In a Dutch oven, sauté the sausage until it is well browned outside, about 10 minutes, and drain it on a paper towel.

3 Discard all but 2 tablespoons of the drippings from the Dutch oven. Add the garlic and the onions and sauté until the onions are soft, about 5 minutes.

4 Stir in the undrained tomatoes, the broth, the consommé, the wine, the basil, the savory and the bay leaf. Return the sausage to the Dutch oven. Bring the mixture to a boil, reduce the heat, cover and simmer for 20 minutes.

5 Stir in the carrot, the parsley, the bell pepper, the zucchini and the pasta. Cover and simmer, stirring occasionally, until the pasta is almost tender, about 10 minutes.

6 Skim off and discard any fat. Discard the bay leaf. Season to taste.

7 Ladle the soup into bowls and sprinkle with the cheese. Serve with chunks of Italian bread.

Wintergreen Salad

1 Wash and dry the lettuce and tear it into bite-size pieces. Trim and slice the celery. Peel and chop the cucumber. Trim and chop the scallions. Combine the ingredients in a large bowl.

2 Drain the artichoke hearts, reserving the oil. Chop the artichokes and add them to the salad.

3 In a small bowl, whisk together the reserved artichoke oil, the vinegar, the tarragon and the mint. Season to taste and toss with the salad.

Mixed Feelings

1 Peel and section the grapefruit. Peel and section the oranges. Wash and separate the grapes. Combine the ingredients in a medium bowl and toss with the Grand Marnier. Refrigerate until you are ready to use.

2 Place scoops of frozen yogurt in individual dessert dishes. Top with the fruit mixture, dust with the confectioners' sugar and sprinkle with the coconut.

FRIDAY

Seashells

1 small onion
1 clove garlic
1 large can (28 ounces) cut-up tomatoes
2 tablespoons regular or light olive oil
$^3/_4$ cup dry white wine (or nonalcoholic white
    wine or clam juice)
$^1/_2$ cup water
1 teaspoon dried oregano
$^1/_4$ teaspoon red pepper flakes
16 ounces small shell pasta
1 pound medium shrimp, shelled and deveined
$^1/_4$ cup half-and-half
Seasoning to taste

Rude-Abagas

2 large rutabagas
2 tablespoons butter
2 tablespoons water
$1^1/_2$ tablespoons dark brown sugar
1 teaspoon soy sauce
Seasoning to taste

Cafe Salad

1 package (16 ounces) mixed salad greens
$^1/_4$ pound fresh mushrooms
$^1/_4$ cup pine nuts
3 tablespoons regular or light olive oil
2 tablespoons red wine vinegar
1 tablespoon lemon juice
$^1/_4$ teaspoon Worcestershire sauce
Seasoning to taste

Gem of a Tart

$^1/_2$ cup semisweet chocolate chips
2 tablespoons whole or low-fat milk
4 individual graham cracker tart shells
1 medium banana
1 tablespoon lemon juice
$^1/_4$ pound seedless red grapes
4 kiwifruit
1 container (8 ounces) regular or light soft
    cream cheese
$4^1/_2$ tablespoons apricot preserves

EQUIPMENT

Stockpot	Assorted kitchen knives
Large covered skillet	Measuring cups and
Large saucepan	spoons
Small saucepan	Assorted cooking
Large bowl	utensils
Medium bowl	Whisk
2 small bowls	Vegetable grater
Colander	

COUNTDOWN

1 Assemble the ingredients and equipment
2 Do Steps 1–4 of the *Gem of a Tart*
3 Do Steps 1–2 of the *Cafe Salad*
4 Do Steps 1–4 of the *Seashells*
5 Do Steps 1–2 of the *Rude-Abagas*
6 Do Steps 5–6 of the *Seashells*
7 Do Step 3 of the *Cafe Salad*

Seashells

1 Bring water to a boil in a stockpot.

2 Peel and chop the onion. Peel and chop the garlic. Drain and chop the tomatoes.

3 Heat the oil in a large saucepan. Add the onion and the garlic and sauté until the onion is soft, about 5 minutes. Add the wine and bring it to a boil. Add the tomatoes, the water, the oregano and the red pepper flakes. Return the mixture to a boil, reduce the heat and simmer for 20 minutes.

4 Cook the pasta shells in the stockpot until they are tender but still firm, 8 to 9 minutes.

5 Add the shrimp to the sauce and cook until they turn pink, about 2 minutes. Stir in the half-and-half and cook for 2 minutes more. Season to taste.

6 Drain the pasta, return it to the stockpot and toss it with the sauce.

Rude-Abagas

1 Trim and grate the rutabagas.

2 Melt the butter in a large skillet. Add the rutabagas, the water, the brown sugar and the soy sauce. Cover and cook, stirring often, until the rutabagas are crisp-tender, about 5 minutes. Season to taste.

Cafe Salad

1 Rinse and dry the salad greens. Wash, pat dry, trim and slice the mushrooms. Combine the ingredients in a large bowl and toss them with the pine nuts.

2 In a small bowl, whisk together the oil, the vinegar, the lemon juice and the Worcestershire sauce. Season to taste.

3 Toss the salad with the dressing.

Gem of a Tart

1 Melt the chocolate chips with the milk in a small saucepan. Pour the mixture into the bottom of the tart shells and refrigerate for 5 minutes.

2 Peel and slice the banana into a small bowl and drizzle the slices with the lemon juice. Wash and separate the grapes. Peel and slice the kiwifruit.

3 In a medium bowl, mix the cream cheese with $1\frac{1}{2}$ tablespoons of the apricot preserves until well blended. Spoon the mixture over the chocolate and arrange the fruit over the cream cheese.

4 Heat the remaining apricot preserves in the chocolate saucepan until just warm and drizzle it over the tarts. Refrigerate for at least 15 minutes.

DECEMBER
WEEK FOUR

CHECK STAPLES

- ☐ Butter
- ☐ Flour
- ☐ Bisquick
- ☐ Granulated sugar
- ☐ Dark brown sugar
- ☐ Confectioners' sugar
- ☐ Unsweetened cocoa
- ☐ Chocolate syrup
- ☐ Long-grain white rice
- ☐ Brown rice
- ☐ Regular or light vegetable oil
- ☐ Regular or light olive oil
- ☐ Red wine vinegar
- ☐ Raspberry vinegar
- ☐ Lemon juice
- ☐ Lime juice
- ☐ Grated fresh lemon peel
- ☐ Grated fresh orange peel
- ☐ Worcestershire sauce
- ☐ Dijon mustard
- ☐ Prepared horseradish
- ☐ Honey
- ☐ Grated Parmesan cheese
- ☐ Dried basil
- ☐ Cayenne pepper
- ☐ Dried chervil
- ☐ Ground cinnamon
- ☐ Ground coriander
- ☐ Ground cumin
- ☐ Garlic powder
- ☐ Dried oregano
- ☐ Paprika
- ☐ Red pepper flakes
- ☐ Poultry seasoning
- ☐ Dried tarragon
- ☐ Dried thyme
- ☐ Turmeric
- ☐ Pepper
- ☐ Salt
- ☐ Vanilla extract

SHOPPING NOTE

● If you are shopping once a week and cannot arrange to purchase fresh white fish on the day you plan to use it, you can purchase *not previously frozen* white fish and freeze it, placing it in the refrigerator to thaw the night before you are ready to use it. Or you can purchase *still frozen* white fish and keep it frozen until the night before you are ready to use it.

MEAT & POULTRY
4 lean lamb chops ($3/4$-inch thick) (T)
$1^1/2$ pounds lean ground beef (W)
$1^1/4$ pounds boneless, skinless chicken breasts (M)
2 pounds boneless turkey breast (Th)

FISH
$1^1/4$ pounds white fish fillets (F)

FRESH PRODUCE
Vegetables
2 pounds yams (Th)
1 pound Brussels sprouts (T)
$1/4$ pound Swiss chard (or spinach) (M)
$1/4$ pound mushrooms (Th)
1 medium carrot (M)
6 stalks celery—1 (M), 2 (T), 1 (W), 2 (Th)
1 large onion (W)
1 medium onion (F)
5 small onions—1 (M), 2 (T), 2 (Th)
1 small red onion (W)
8 scallions (green onions)—3 (M), 2 (W), 3 (F)
1 head garlic (M, T, W)
1 bunch parsley (M, T, Th, F)
1 bunch chives (M, F)
2 medium heads lettuce—1 (M), 1 (W)
1 pound tomatoes—$1/2$ pound (M), $1/2$ pound (W)
1 medium cucumber (M)
1 medium red bell pepper (F)
1 small bunch radishes (W)

Fruit
2 papayas (or small cantaloupes) (F)
2 small bananas (F)
1 package (12 ounces) cranberries (M)
$1/2$ pound seedless red grapes (T)
1 small pink grapefruit (F)

CANS, JARS & BOTTLES
Soup
2 cans ($14^1/2$ ounces each) chicken broth (M)
2 cans ($14^1/2$ ounces each) vegetable broth—1 (M), 1 (F)

Vegetables
1 large can (28 ounces) cut-up tomatoes (W)
1 medium can ($14^1/2$ ounces) cut-up tomatoes (M)
1 medium can ($14^1/2$ ounces) stewed tomatoes (F)
1 small can ($8^3/4$ ounces) whole kernel corn (M)

Oriental Foods
1 can (8 ounces) sliced water chestnuts (W)

Fruit
1 small can (8 ounces) jellied cranberry sauce (Th)

Condiments
1 small can (3.3 ounces) sliced black olives (F)

Dessert Needs
1 can (14 ounces) regular or low-fat sweetened condensed milk (T)
1 jar (3 ounces) silver sprinkles (optional) (Th)

PACKAGED GOODS
Pasta, Rice & Grains
8 ounces dried capellini (angel hair pasta) (M)
16 ounces bucatini (or any small tubular pasta) (W)

Baked Goods
3 cups fresh bread crumbs (Th)
1 package (3 ounces) ladyfingers (or angel food cake) (Th)

Nuts & Seeds
$1/4$ cup pecan pieces (W)
2 tablespoons sunflower seeds (M)

Dessert & Baking Needs
1 small package (3.4 ounces) instant vanilla pudding mix (Th)
1 small package (7 ounces) chopped candied fruit (Th)
1 small package (9 ounces) chocolate wafers (T)
1 prepared 9-inch graham cracker pie shell (W)

$1/2$ cup semisweet chocolate chips (T)

WINES & SPIRITS
$1/2$ cup dry white wine (or nonalcoholic white wine or water) (M)
$3/4$ cup dry red wine (or nonalcoholic red wine or beef broth)—$1/2$ cup (T), $1/4$ cup (W)
2 tablespoons Grand Marnier liqueur (or nonalcoholic Italian orange syrup) (M)
$1^1/2$ tablespoons sweet sherry (or nonalcoholic Italian praline syrup) (Th)

REFRIGERATED PRODUCTS
Dairy
$1^1/4$ cups whole milk (Th)
$1/4$ cup whole or low-fat milk (Th)
$2/3$ cup buttermilk (M)
$1^3/4$ cups regular or light sour cream—1 cup (W), $3/4$ cup (Th)
Whipped cream for garnish (Th)
1 egg (Th)

Cheese
1 cup regular or low-fat small-curd cottage cheese (Th)
1 container (8 ounces) regular or light soft cream cheese (W)

Juice
$1^1/2$ cups orange juice—$1/2$ cup (M), 1 cup (T)

FROZEN GOODS
Vegetables
1 package (9 ounces) green peas (W)
1 package (9 ounces) chopped spinach (Th)
1 package (9 ounces) mixed vegetables (F)

Desserts
1 pint peppermint (or other) ice cream (M)
1 container (8 ounces) frozen whipped topping (W)

MONDAY

Angel Soup

1 small onion
2 cloves garlic
1 medium carrot
1 stalk celery
$1/4$ pound Swiss chard (or spinach)
$1^1/4$ pounds boneless, skinless chicken breasts
2 tablespoons butter
$1/4$ teaspoon dried thyme
1 teaspoon sugar
2 cans ($14^1/2$ ounces each) chicken broth
1 can ($14^1/2$ ounces) vegetable broth
$1/2$ cup dry white wine (or nonalcoholic white
   wine or water)
1 medium can ($14^1/2$ ounces) cut-up tomatoes
8 ounces dried capellini (angel hair pasta)
Seasoning to taste
$1/2$ cup grated Parmesan cheese

Earthbound Salad

1 medium head lettuce
1 medium cucumber
$1/2$ pound fresh tomatoes
3 scallions (green onions)
1 small can ($8^3/4$ ounces) whole kernel corn
2 tablespoons sunflower seeds
2 cloves garlic
4 tablespoons regular or light vegetable oil
3 tablespoons red wine vinegar
1 teaspoon Worcestershire sauce
$1/2$ teaspoon dried chervil
$1/4$ teaspoon paprika
1 tablespoon sugar
Seasoning to taste

Biscuits From Heaven

$1^1/2$ tablespoons fresh parsley (when chopped)
$1^1/2$ tablespoons fresh chives (when chopped)

4 tablespoons softened butter
1 teaspoon dried basil
$1/2$ teaspoon lemon juice
$2^1/4$ cups Bisquick
$2/3$ cup buttermilk

Peppermint Halo

1 package (12 ounces) fresh cranberries
$1^1/2$ cups dark brown sugar
$1/2$ cup orange juice
2 tablespoons Grand Marnier liqueur (or
   nonalcoholic Italian orange syrup)
1 pint peppermint (or other) ice cream
2 teaspoons grated fresh orange peel

EQUIPMENT

Dutch oven	Assorted cooking
Medium saucepan	utensils
Cookie sheet	Pastry board
Large bowl	Whisk
Medium bowl	Vegetable peeler
2 small bowls	Biscuit cutter
Strainer	Ice cream scoop
Assorted kitchen knives	
Measuring cups and	
spoons	

COUNTDOWN

1 Assemble the ingredients and equipment
2 Do Steps 1–3 of the *Peppermint Halo*
3 Do Steps 1–2 of the *Earthbound Salad*
4 Do Steps 1–2 of the *Angel Soup*
5 Do Steps 1–5 of the *Biscuits From Heaven*
6 Do Steps 3–5 of the *Angel Soup*
7 Do Step 3 of the *Earthbound Salad*
8 Do Step 4 of the *Peppermint Halo*

Angel Soup

1. Peel and mince the onion. Peel and mince the garlic. Peel and thinly slice the carrot. Trim and thinly slice the celery. Rinse, dry and chop the Swiss chard. Cube the chicken.

2 Melt the butter in a Dutch oven. Add the onion and the garlic and sauté until the onion is soft, about 5 minutes. Stir in the thyme and the chicken and sauté until the chicken cubes are opaque, about 3 minutes. Add the sugar, the broths, the wine, the undrained tomatoes, the carrot and the celery. Bring the mixture to a boil, reduce the heat, cover and simmer until the vegetables are tender, about 15 minutes.

3 Break the capellini strands in half, add them to the soup and return it to a boil. Cook uncovered, stirring often, until the pasta is almost tender, 3 to 4 minutes.

4 Add the Swiss chard. Season to taste, cover, remove the Dutch oven from the heat and let it stand until the Swiss chard is heated through, about 2 minutes.

5 Sprinkle bowls of soup with the cheese.

Earthbound Salad

1 Wash and dry the lettuce and tear it into bite-size pieces. Peel and chop the cucumber. Chop the tomatoes. Trim and chop the scallions. Drain the corn. Combine the ingredients in a large bowl and toss them with the sunflower seeds.

2 Peel and mince the garlic. In a small bowl, whisk together the garlic with the oil, the vinegar, the Worcestershire sauce, the chervil, the paprika and the sugar. Season to taste.

3 Toss the salad with the dressing.

Biscuits From Heaven

1 Chop the parsley. Chop the chives. In a small bowl, combine the softened butter with the parsley, the chives, the basil and the lemon juice until the mixture is formed into a well-blended ball, and refrigerate until you are ready to use.

2 Preheat the oven to 450°F. Dust a pastry board with Bisquick.

3 In a medium bowl, combine the Bisquick and the buttermilk until a soft dough forms. Turn it out on the pastry board. Knead the dough gently 9 or 10 times and pat it out into a ½-inch thickness.

4 Cut the dough with the biscuit cutter, dipped in Bisquick between cuts.

5 Place the biscuits on an ungreased cookie sheet and bake until they are golden, 10 to 12 minutes.

Peppermint Halo

1 Carefully rinse the cranberries, discarding any that are soft or discolored, and drain well.

2 In a medium saucepan, combine the cranberries, the brown sugar and the orange juice. Bring the mixture to a boil and cook until the cranberry skins pop, 5 to 7 minutes.

3 Remove the saucepan from the heat, stir in the Grand Marnier and let the mixture stand.

4 Place a scoop of ice cream in the bottom of individual parfait glasses. Cover the ice cream with half of the cranberry mixture. Repeat with another layer of ice cream and top it with the remaining sauce. Sprinkle with the orange peel.

TUESDAY

De-Lush-Us Lamb Chops

Seasoning to taste
4 lean lamb chops ($^3/_4$-inch thick)
1 clove garlic
1 small onion
2 tablespoons fresh parsley (when chopped)
1 tablespoon butter
1 tablespoon regular or light olive oil
$^1/_2$ cup dry red wine (or nonalcoholic red wine
    or beef broth)
1 teaspoon dried thyme

Orange Rice

2 stalks celery
1 small onion
3 tablespoons butter
1 cup long-grain white rice
1 cup water
1 cup orange juice
2 teaspoons grated fresh orange peel
$^1/_8$ teaspoon dried thyme

Belgian Honeys

1 pound Brussels sprouts
$^1/_2$ pound seedless red grapes
1 clove garlic
3 tablespoons butter
3 tablespoons honey
Seasoning to taste

Chocolate Crunch Cake

1 package (9 ounces) chocolate wafers
1 cup Bisquick
$^1/_4$ cup unsweetened cocoa
1 can (14 ounces) regular or low-fat
    sweetened condensed milk
1 teaspoon vanilla extract
$^3/_4$ cup chocolate syrup
$^1/_2$ cup hot water
$^1/_2$ cup semisweet chocolate chips

EQUIPMENT

Medium skillet	Strainer
2 medium covered	Assorted kitchen knives
saucepans	Measuring cups and
8x8-inch baking pan	spoons
Large bowl	Assorted cooking
Small bowl	utensils

COUNTDOWN

1 Assemble the ingredients and equipment
2 Do Steps 1–4 of the *Chocolate Crunch Cake*
3 Do Steps 1–3 of the *Orange Rice*
4 Do Step 1 of the *De-Lush–Us Lamb Chops*
5 Do Steps 1–3 of the *Belgian Honeys*
6 Do Step 2 of the *De-Lush–Us Lamb Chops*
7 Do Steps 4–5 of the *Belgian Honeys*
8 Do Step 3 of the *De-Lush–Us Lamb Chops*
9 Do Step 4 of the *Orange Rice*

De-Lush-Us Lamb Chops

1 Preheat the broiler. Season both sides of the lamb chops to taste. Peel and mince the garlic. Peel and mince the onion. Chop the parsley.

2 Broil the chops, 3 or 4 inches from the heat, turning once, until they are done to taste (5 to 7 minutes for rare).

3 Melt the butter with the oil in a medium skillet. Sauté the garlic and the onion until the onion is soft, about 5 minutes. Add the wine and the thyme. Bring the liquid to a boil and cook until it is reduced to about 2 tablespoons, about 3 minutes. Add the parsley, season to taste and pour the sauce over the chops.

Orange Rice

1 Trim and finely chop the celery. Peel and mince the onion.

2 Melt the butter in a medium saucepan and sauté the celery and the onion until the onion is soft, about 5 minutes.

3 Add the rice, the water, the orange juice, the orange peel and the thyme. Reduce the heat, cover and simmer until all the liquid is absorbed and the rice is tender, 20 to 25 minutes.

4 Fluff the rice before serving.

Belgian Honeys

1 Bring water to a boil in a medium saucepan.

2 Trim and halve the Brussels sprouts. Wash, dry, separate and halve the grapes. Peel and mince the garlic.

3 Cook the sprouts in the boiling water until they are crisp-tender, about 5 minutes.

4 Drain the sprouts and melt the butter in the saucepan. Sauté the garlic until it is golden, 3 to 5 minutes. Blend in the honey.

5 Return the sprouts to the saucepan. Add the grapes. Toss until the sprouts and grapes are well coated and heated through. Season to taste, remove the saucepan from the heat and cover to keep warm.

Chocolate Crunch Cake

1 Preheat the oven to 375°F. Grease an 8x8-inch baking pan. Crumble the chocolate wafers.

2 In a large bowl, combine the Bisquick, the cocoa, 1 cup of the condensed milk, the vanilla and $1/4$ cup of the chocolate syrup until well mixed, and spoon the mixture into the baking pan.

3 In a small bowl, combine the remaining condensed milk, the remaining chocolate syrup and the hot water. Pour the mixture over the cake batter. Do not stir. Top with the cookie crumbs and the chocolate chips.

4 Bake until the center of the cake is set and begins to pull away from the sides of the pan, 30 to 35 minutes.

WEDNESDAY

Merry Little Pasta

1 large onion
2 cloves garlic
1 tablespoon regular or light olive oil
1 1/2 pounds lean ground beef
1 large can (28 ounces) cut-up tomatoes
1/4 cup dry red wine (or nonalcoholic red wine or beef broth)
1 teaspoon dried basil
1 teaspoon dried oregano
Seasoning to taste
16 ounces bucatini (or any small tubular pasta)
1/3 cup grated Parmesan cheese

Peas on Earth

1 package (9 ounces) frozen green peas
1 small red onion
1 can (8 ounces) sliced water chestnuts
2 tablespoons butter
1 tablespoon dark brown sugar
Seasoning to taste
1/2 teaspoon paprika

Dickens of a Salad

1 medium head lettuce
1/2 pound fresh tomatoes
1 small red bell pepper
2 scallions (green onions)
1 stalk celery
1 small bunch radishes
3 tablespoons regular or light olive oil
2 tablespoons red wine vinegar
1/2 teaspoon dried tarragon
1/4 teaspoon garlic powder
1/8 teaspoon prepared horseradish
1/8 teaspoon cayenne pepper
Seasoning to taste

Scrooge Pie

1 cup regular or light sour cream
1 container (8 ounces) regular or light soft cream cheese
1/3 cup sugar
2 teaspoons vanilla extract
1 small container (8 ounces) frozen whipped topping
1 prepared 9-inch graham cracker pie shell
1/4 cup pecan pieces
2 tablespoons grated fresh lemon peel

EQUIPMENT

Stockpot	Assorted kitchen knives
Large covered skillet	Measuring cups and
Medium skillet	spoons
2 large bowls	Assorted cooking
Small bowl	utensils
Colander	Whisk

COUNTDOWN

1 Assemble the ingredients and equipment
2 Do Step 1 of the *Peas on Earth*
3 Do Step 1 of the *Scrooge Pie*
4 Do Steps 1–4 of the *Merry Little Pasta*
5 Do Steps 1–2 of the *Dickens of a Salad*
6 Do Step 5 of the *Merry Little Pasta*
7 Do Steps 2–3 of the *Peas on Earth*
8 Do Step 6 of the *Merry Little Pasta*
9 Do Step 3 of the *Dickens of a Salad*
10 Do Step 2 of the *Scrooge Pie*

Merry Little Pasta

1 Bring water to a boil in a stockpot.

2 Peel and chop the onion. Peel and mince the garlic.

3 Heat the oil in a large skillet until hot. Add the ground beef, the onion and the garlic and sauté until the onion is soft and the beef is no longer red, about 5 minutes.

4 Add the undrained tomatoes, the wine, the basil and the oregano. Season to taste, reduce the heat, cover and simmer for 20 minutes, stirring occasionally.

5 Cook the pasta until it is almost tender, 9 to 11 minutes.

6 Drain the pasta, return it to the stockpot, toss it with the sauce and sprinkle with the cheese.

Peas on Earth

1 Set the frozen peas out to thaw.

2 Peel and chop the red onion. Drain and rinse the water chestnuts.

3 Melt the butter in a medium skillet and sauté the onion until it is soft, about 5 minutes. Add the brown sugar, the water chestnuts and the thawed peas, season to taste and sauté for 2 minutes. Sprinkle with the paprika.

Dickens of a Salad

1 Wash and dry the lettuce and tear it into bite-size pieces. Chop the tomatoes. Seed and chop the bell pepper. Trim and chop the scallions. Trim and slice the celery. Trim and slice the radishes. Combine the ingredients in a large bowl.

2 In a small bowl, whisk together the oil, the vinegar, the tarragon, the garlic powder, the horseradish and the cayenne pepper. Season to taste.

3 Toss the salad with the dressing.

Scrooge Pie

1 In a large bowl, combine the sour cream, the cream cheese, the sugar and the vanilla until well blended. Fold in the whipped topping. Pour the mixture into the prepared pie shell and refrigerate for at least 20 minutes.

2 Sprinkle the pie with the nuts and the lemon peel.

THURSDAY

Turkey Thyme

2 pounds boneless turkey breast
1 small onion
2 tablespoons butter
1 small can (8 ounces) jellied cranberry sauce
6 tablespoons raspberry vinegar
$^1/_4$ cup Dijon mustard
1 tablespoon grated fresh orange peel
$^1/_2$ teaspoon dried thyme
Seasoning to taste

I Yam What I Yam

2 pounds yams
2 tablespoons butter
$^1/_4$ cup whole or low-fat milk
$2^1/_2$ tablespoons dark brown sugar
$1^1/_2$ tablespoons sweet sherry (or nonalcoholic
    Italian praline syrup)
Seasoning to taste

All Dressed Up

1 package (9 ounces) frozen chopped spinach
$^1/_4$ pound fresh mushrooms
2 stalks celery
1 small onion
1 tablespoon fresh parsley (when minced)
1 egg
4 tablespoons butter
3 cups fresh bread crumbs
1 cup regular or low-fat small-curd cottage
    cheese
$^1/_2$ teaspoon poultry seasoning
Seasoning to taste

Sleigh-Bell Pudding

$1^1/_4$ cups whole milk
$^3/_4$ cup regular or light sour cream
1 small package (3.4 ounces) instant vanilla
    pudding mix
1 small package (7 ounces) chopped candied
    fruit
1 package (3 ounces) ladyfingers (or angel
    food cake)
Whipped cream for garnish
2 tablespoons confectioners' sugar
1 jar (3 ounces) silver sprinkles (optional)

EQUIPMENT

Electric hand mixer	Assorted kitchen knives
Large covered skillet	Measuring cups and
Large covered	spoons
saucepan	Assorted cooking
2 medium saucepans	utensils
1$^1/_2$-quart casserole	Sifter
2 medium bowls	

COUNTDOWN

1 Assemble the ingredients and equipment
2 Do Steps 1–2 of the *All Dressed Up*
3 Do Steps 1–3 of the *Turkey Thyme*
4 Do Step 1 of the *Sleigh-Bell Pudding*
5 Do Step 1 of *I Yam What I Yam*
6 Do Step 4 of the *Turkey Thyme*
7 Do Steps 3–4 of the *All Dressed Up*
8 Do Step 2 of *I Yam What I Yam*
9 Do Step 2 of the *Sleigh-Bell Pudding*

Turkey Thyme

1 Cut the turkey breast into 4 portions. Peel and finely chop the onion.

2 Melt the butter in a large skillet and sauté the onion for 3 minutes. Add the turkey portions and sauté until they are lightly browned, about 10 minutes.

3 In a medium saucepan, combine the cranberry sauce, the vinegar, the mustard, the orange peel and the thyme. Bring the mixture to a boil and cook until the sauce reduces by a third, 8 to 10 minutes.

4 Discard the onion and drippings. Add the cranberry mixture to the skillet, bring it to a boil, reduce the heat, cover and simmer until the turkey is cooked through, about 30 minutes. Season to taste.

I Yam What I Yam

1 Peel and quarter the yams and cover them with water in a large saucepan. Bring the water to a boil and cook until the yams are tender, 15 to 20 minutes.

2 Drain the yams and return them to the saucepan. Add the butter, the milk, the brown sugar and the sherry. Season to taste. Beat until the mixture is light and fluffy, about 2 minutes. Cover to keep warm.

All Dressed Up

1 Set the spinach in a medium bowl of hot water to thaw.

2 Preheat the oven to 350°F. Grease a 1½-quart casserole.

3 Wash, pat dry, trim and slice the mushrooms. Trim and dice the celery. Peel and chop the onion. Mince the parsley. Squeeze the spinach dry. Lightly beat the egg.

4 Melt the butter in a medium saucepan and sauté the mushrooms, the celery and the onion until the onion is soft, about 5 minutes. Remove the saucepan from the heat. Add the bread crumbs, the cheese, the egg, the parsley, the poultry seasoning and the spinach. Season to taste, combine the mixture, turn it into the casserole and bake until it is hot and bubbly, about 30 minutes.

Sleigh-Bell Pudding

1 In a medium bowl, beat the milk, the sour cream and the pudding mix until well blended. Fold in the chopped candied fruit. Refrigerate for at least 20 minutes.

2 Spoon the pudding into dessert dishes. Lay 2 whole ladyfingers parallel to each other over each portion of pudding. Cut the remaining ladyfingers in half and insert them between the whole ladyfingers to resemble sleigh runners. Garnish with a dollop of whipped cream. Dust with the confectioners' sugar and top with the silver sprinkles.

FRIDAY

Ghana Fishin'

1 medium red bell pepper
1 medium onion
2 tablespoons fresh chives (when chopped)
$1/4$ cup fresh parsley (when chopped)
1 small can (3.3 ounces) sliced black olives
4 tablespoons regular or light olive oil
1 teaspoon grated fresh lemon peel
1 teaspoon ground cumin
$1/4$ teaspoon ground coriander
$1/4$ teaspoon red pepper flakes
$1/2$ cup flour
Seasoning to taste
$1^{1}/_{4}$ pounds white fish fillets
$1/4$ cup lemon juice

Congo Rice

1 package (9 ounces) frozen mixed vegetables
3 scallions (green onions)
1 tablespoon regular or light vegetable oil
1 can ($14^{1}/_{2}$ ounces) vegetable broth
1 teaspoon ground cinnamon
1 teaspoon turmeric
$1/8$ teaspoon cayenne pepper
1 medium can ($14^{1}/_{2}$ ounces) stewed tomatoes
$1^{1}/_{4}$ cups brown rice

Lime Light

2 papayas (or small cantaloupes)
1 small pink grapefruit
2 small bananas
4 tablespoons lime juice
3 tablespoons confectioners' sugar

EQUIPMENT

Large skillet	Assorted kitchen knives
Medium covered skillet	Measuring cups and
Medium covered	spoons
saucepan	Assorted cooking
Medium bowl	utensils
2 small bowls	Whisk
Shallow bowl	

COUNTDOWN

1 Assemble the ingredients and equipment
2 Do Steps 1–2 of the *Congo Rice*
3 Do Steps 1–2 of the *Lime Light*
4 Do Steps 1–6 of the *Ghana Fishin'*
5 Do Step 3 of the *Congo Rice*
6 Do Steps 3–4 of the *Lime Light*

Ghana Fishin'

1 Seed and chop the bell pepper. Peel and chop the onion. Chop the chives. Chop the parsley. Drain the olives.

3 Heat 2 tablespoons of the oil in a medium skillet until hot. Add the bell pepper and the onion and sauté until the onion is softened, about 5 minutes.

4 Add the olives, the parsley, the lemon peel, the cumin, the coriander and the red pepper flakes. Cook, stirring, for 2 minutes. Cover the skillet and remove it from the heat.

2 Place the flour in a shallow bowl and season it to taste. Lightly coat the fish on both sides, shaking off any excess.

5 Heat the remaining oil in a large skillet. Arrange the fillets in a single layer and cook, turning once, until they are golden on both sides and just opaque in the center, 6 to 8 minutes.

6 Return the vegetables to the heat. Add the lemon juice and cook, stirring, until the mixture is heated through, about 2 minutes. Pour the vegetables over the fish and sprinkle with the chives.

Congo Rice

1 Set the package of frozen vegetables in a medium bowl of hot water to thaw.

2 Trim and chop the scallions. Heat the oil in a medium saucepan, and sauté the scallions until they are soft, about 3 minutes. Add the broth, the cinnamon, the turmeric, the cayenne pepper, the tomatoes and the rice. Stir well. Add the thawed vegetables. Reduce the heat, cover and simmer until all the liquid is absorbed and the rice is tender, about 35 minutes.

3 Fluff the rice before serving.

Lime Light

1 Cut the papayas in half. Scoop out the seeds, reserving 1 tablespoon. Place the papaya halves on individual dessert plates and refrigerate until you are ready to use.

2 Peel and section the grapefruit, set it on a plate and refrigerate until you are ready to use. Peel and slice the bananas into a small bowl and drizzle them with 1 teaspoon of the lime juice.

3 Combine the grapefruit and the bananas and spoon the fruit into the papaya cavities.

4 In a small bowl, whisk together the reserved papaya seeds, the remaining lime juice and the sugar and drizzle the mixture over the fruit-filled papaya halves.

INDEX